CISSP Guide to Security Essentials

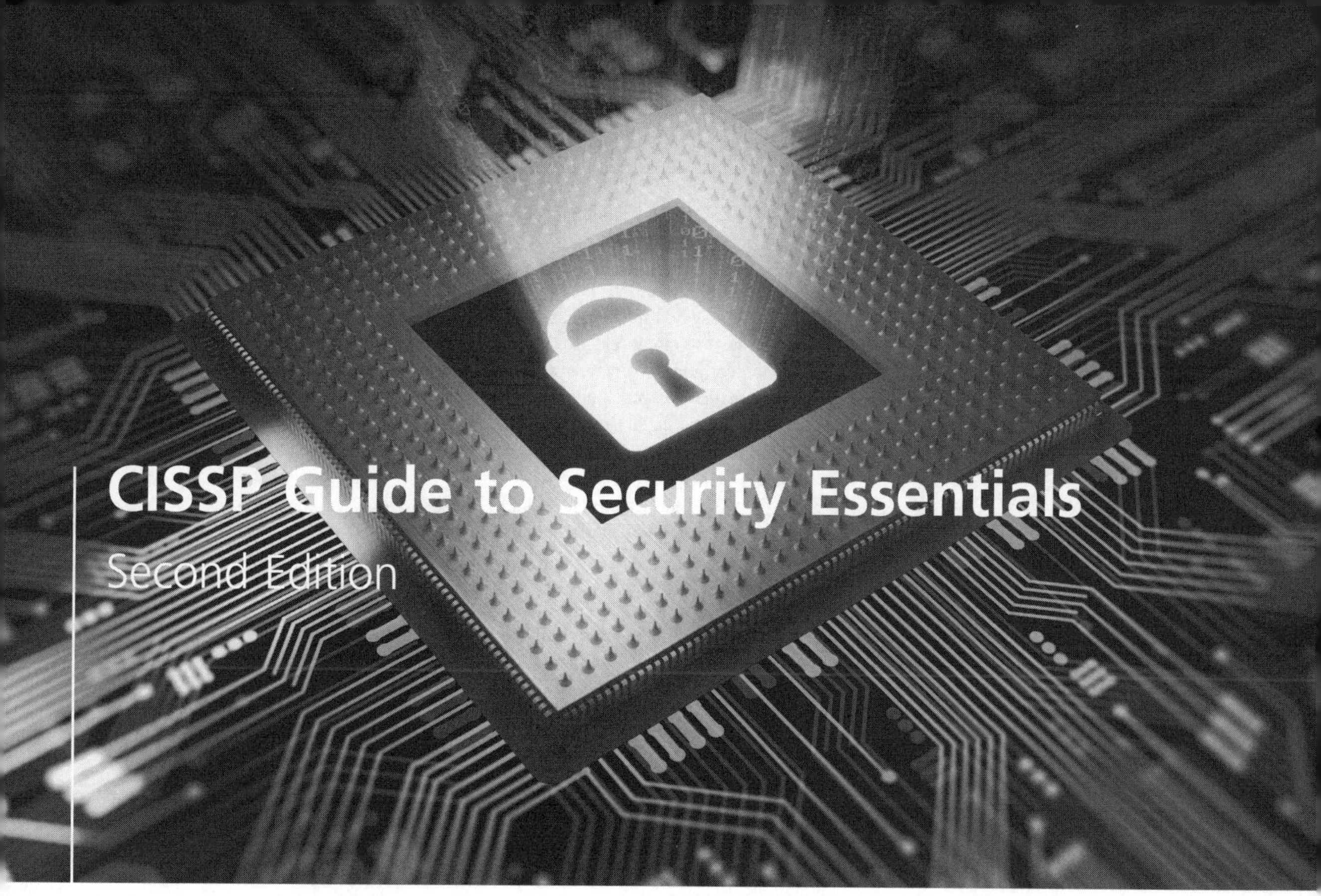

CISSP Guide to Security Essentials

Second Edition

Peter H. Gregory

Australia • Brazil • Mexico • Singapore • United Kingdom • United States

CISSP Guide to Security Essentials, Second Edition
Peter H. Gregory

SVP, GM Skills & Global Product Management: Dawn Gerrain

Product Development Manager: Leigh Hefferon

Senior Content Developer: Julia Leroux-Lindsey

Product Assistant: Scott Finger

Vice President, Marketing Services: Jennifer Ann Baker

Marketing Director: Michele McTighe

Marketing Manager: Eric La Scola

Marketing Coordinator: Will Guiliani

Senior Production Director: Wendy Troeger

Production Manager: Patty Stephan

Senior Content Project Manager: Brooke Greenhouse

Art Director: GEX Publishing Services

Cover Photo: © iStockPhoto.com/Henrik5000

Library of Congress Control Number: 2014949536

ISBN-13: 978-1-285-06042-2

ISBN-10: 1-285-06042-3

Cengage Learning
20 Channel Center Street
Boston, MA 02210
USA

Cengage Learning is a leading provider of customized learning solutions with office locations around the globe, including Singapore, the United Kingdom, Australia, Mexico, Brazil, and Japan. Locate your local office at: **www.cengage.com/global**

Cengage Learning products are represented in Canada by Nelson Education, Ltd.

To learn more about Cengage Learning, visit **www.cengage.com**

Purchase any of our products at your local college store or at our preferred online store **www.cengagebrain.com**

Printed in the United States of America
Print Number: 01 Print Year: 2014

To Rebekah and Shannon, and to the memory of my son and daughters.

Brief Table of Contents

Table of Contents

CHAPTER 5

CHAPTER 10

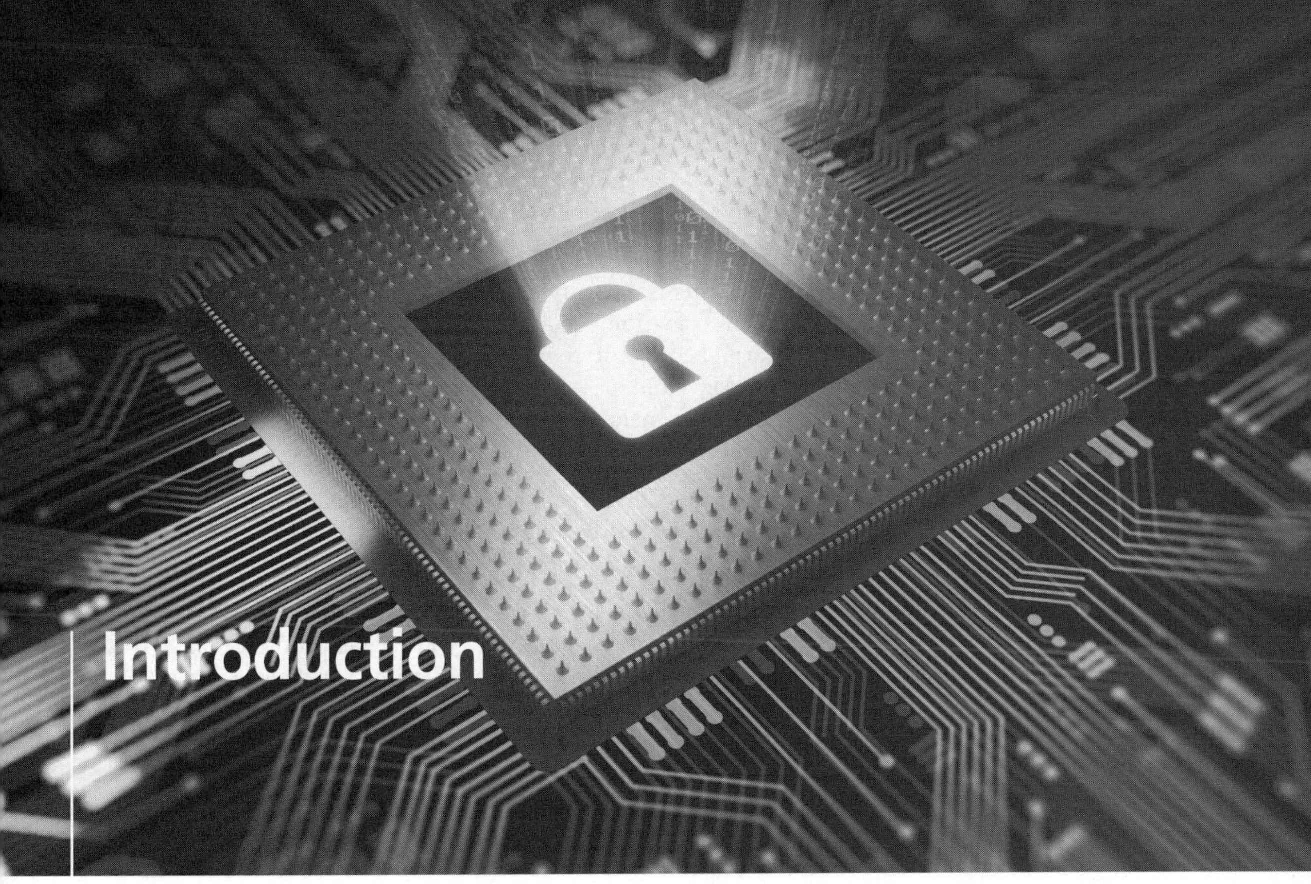

Introduction

"If the Internet were a city street, I would not travel it in daylight," laments a chief information security officer for a prestigious university.

The Internet is critical infrastructure supporting the world's commerce, industrial control systems, and the daily lives of over a billion people. Cybercrime is escalating; once the domain of hackers and script kiddies, cyber-gangs, and organized criminal organizations have developed business opportunities for extortion, embezzlement, and fraud that surpasses income from illegal sex and drug trafficking. Criminals are going for the gold, the information held in information systems that are easily accessed and compromised anonymously from the Internet.

The information security industry is unable to keep up. Cybercriminals and hackers always seem to be at least one step ahead, and new threats and vulnerabilities crop up at a rate that exceeds our ability to continue protecting our most vital information and systems. Like other sectors in IT, security planners, analysts, engineers, and operators are expected to do more with less. Cybercriminals have never had it so good.

There are not enough good security professionals to go around. As a profession, information security in all its forms is relatively new. Fifty years ago there were perhaps a dozen information security professionals, and their jobs consisted primarily of making sure the doors were locked and that keys were issued only to personnel who had an established need for access. Today, whole sectors of industries are doing virtually all of their business online, and other critical infrastructures such as public utilities are controlled online via the Internet. The rate of growth in the information security profession is falling way behind the rate of growth of critical information and infrastructures going online. This is making it all the more critical for today's and tomorrow's information security professionals to have a good understanding of the vast array of principles, practices, technologies, and tactics that are required to protect an organization's assets.

The CISSP (Certified Information Systems Security Professional) is easily the most recognized security certification in the information security industry. CISSP is also one of the most difficult certifications to earn, because it requires knowledge in almost every nook and cranny of information technology and physical security. The CISSP is a jack-of-all-trades certification that, like that of a general practitioner physician, makes us ready for nearly any threat that could come along.

The required body of knowledge for the CISSP certification is published and updated regularly. This book covers all of the material in the published body of knowledge, with each chapter clearly mapping to each of the ten categories within that body of knowledge.

With the demand for security professionals at an all-time high, whether you are a security professional in need of a reference, an IT professional with your sights on the CISSP certification, or a course instructor, *CISSP Guide to Security Essentials* has arrived just in time.

Intended Audience

This book is written for students and professionals who want to expand their knowledge of computer, network, and business security. It is not necessary that the reader specifically target CISSP certification; while this book is designed to support that objective, the student or professional who desires to learn more about security, but who does not aspire to earn the CISSP certification at this time, will benefit from this book as equally as a CISSP candidate.

CISSP Guide to Security Essentials is also ideal for someone in a self-study program. The end of each chapter has not only study questions, but also Hands-On Projects and Case Projects that you can do on your own with a computer running Windows, MacOS, or Linux.

The structure of this book is designed to correspond with the ten domains of knowledge for the CISSP certification, called the Common Body of Knowledge (CBK). While this alignment will be helpful for the CISSP candidate who wants to align her study with the CBK, this is not a detriment to other readers. This is because the CBK domains align nicely with professional practices such as access control, cryptography, physical security, and other sensibly organized categories.

This book's pedagogical features will help all readers who wish to broaden their skills and experience in computer and business security. Each chapter contains several Hands-On Projects that guide the reader through several key security activities, many of which are truly hands-on with computers and networks. Each chapter also contains Case Projects that take the reader into more advanced topics to help them apply the concepts in the chapter.

Chapter Descriptions

Here is a summary of the topics covered in each chapter of this book:

Chapter 1, "Information Security and Risk Management," begins with the fundamentals of information and business security—security and risk management—by explaining how an organization's security program needs to support the organization's goals and objectives. The chapter continues with risk management, security management and strategies, personnel security, and professional ethics.

Chapter 2, "Access Controls," discusses access control principles and architectures, and continues with descriptions of the types of attacks that are carried out against access control systems. The chapter also discusses how an organization can test its access controls to make sure they are secure.

Chapter 3, "Software Development Security," begins with a discussion of the types of operating systems and application software, application models, and technologies. The chapter continues by exploring threats to software and countermeasures to deal with them. It explores how to secure the software development life cycle—the process used for the creation and maintenance of software. The chapter discusses software environment and security controls, and concludes with a discussion of the security of databases and data warehouses.

Chapter 4, "Business Continuity and Disaster Recovery," explores the concepts and practices in business continuity planning and disaster recovery planning. The chapter provides a lengthy discourse on a practical approach to running a BCP / DRP project. Next, the chapter describes several approaches to testing BCP and DRP plans, and how such plans are maintained over time.

Chapter 5, "Cryptography," begins with an introduction to the science of cryptography, the practice of hiding data in plain sight. The chapter continues with a discussion of the applications and uses of cryptography, and on the methodologies used by cryptographic algorithms. The chapter also includes a discussion of cryptography and key management.

Chapter 6, "Legal, Regulations, Compliance, and Investigations," starts with a discussion of the different types of computer crime and the various ways that computers are involved in criminal activity. The next discussion focuses on the types and categories of laws in the U.S. and other countries, with a particular focus on computer-related laws. The chapter continues with a discussion of security incident response, investigations, and computer forensics, and concludes with a discussion of ethical issues in the workplace.

Chapter 7, "Security Operations," introduces and discusses the broad topic of putting security controls, concepts, and technologies into operation in an organization. The specific topics discussed includes records management, backup, anti-virus, remote access, administrative access, resource protection, incident management, vulnerability management, change management, and configuration management. The chapter discusses resource protection, high-availability application architectures, and attacks and countermeasures for IT operations.

Chapter 8, "Physical and Environmental Security," begins with a discussion of site access controls for the physical protection of worksites that may include IT systems. The chapter discusses secure siting, which is the process of identifying risk factors associated with the location and features of an office building. The chapter provides an overview of fire prevention and suppression, theft prevention, and building environmental controls including electric power and heating, ventilation, and air conditioning.

Chapter 9, "Security Architecture and Design," discusses security models that have been developed and are still in use from the 1970s to the present. The chapter continues with a discussion of information system evaluation models including the Common Criteria. The chapter discusses computer hardware architecture and computer software, including operating systems, tools, utilities, and applications. Security threats and countermeasures in the context of computer software are also explored.

Chapter 10, "Telecommunications and Network Security," is a broad exploration of telecommunications and network technologies. The chapter examines the TCP/IP and OSI protocol models, and continues with a dissection of the TCP/IP protocol suite. The chapter addresses TCP/IP network architecture, protocols, addressing, devices, routing, authentication, access control, tunneling, and services. The chapter concludes with a discussion of network-based threats and countermeasures.

Appendix A, "The Ten Domains of CISSP Security," provides a background on the CISSP certification, and then describes the ten domains in the CISSP Common Body of Knowledge.

Appendix B, "The (ISC)^2 Code of Ethics," contains the full text of the (ISC)^2 Code of Ethics, which every CISSP candidate is required to support and uphold. The Code of Ethics is a set of enduring principles to guide the behavior of every security professional.

Appendix C, "The CISSP Certification," describes the certification qualifications, the exam registration process, and the certification exam itself. The chapter includes tips to help the reader establish a study plan. Requirements for maintaining the CISSP certification are discussed.

Glossary lists common information security and risk management terms that are found in this book.

Features

To aid you in fully understanding computer and business security, this book includes many features designed to enhance your learning experience.

- **Maps to the CISSP Common Body of Knowledge (CBK).** The material in this text covers all of the CISSP exam objectives. Aside from Information Security and Risk Management being addressed first in the book, the sequence of the chapters follows the ten CISSP domains.
- **Common Body of Knowledge objectives included.** Each chapter begins with the precise language from the (ISC)^2 Common Body of Knowledge for the respective topic in the CISSP certification. This helps to remind the reader of the CISSP certification requirements for that particular topic.
- **Chapter Objectives.** Each chapter begins with a detailed list of the concepts to be mastered within that chapter. This list provides you with both a quick reference to the chapter's contents and a useful study aid.
- **Illustrations and Tables.** Numerous illustrations of security vulnerabilities, attacks, and defenses help you visualize security elements, theories, and concepts. In addition,

the many tables provide details and comparisons of practical and theoretical information.

- **Chapter Summaries.** Each chapter's text is followed by a summary of the concepts introduced in that chapter. These summaries provide a helpful way to review the ideas covered in each chapter.
- **Key Terms.** All of the terms in each chapter that were introduced with bold text are gathered in a Key Terms list with definitions at the end of the chapter, providing additional review and highlighting key concepts.
- **Review Questions.** The end-of-chapter assessment begins with a set of review questions that reinforce the ideas introduced in each chapter. These questions help you evaluate and apply the material you have learned. Answering these questions will ensure that you have mastered the important concepts and provide valuable practice for taking the CISSP exam.
- **Hands-On Projects.** Although it is important to understand the theory behind network security, nothing can improve upon real-world experience. To this end, each chapter provides several Hands-On Projects aimed at providing you with practical security software and hardware implementation experience. These projects can be completed on Windows 7 or Windows 8 (and, in many cases, Windows XP, MacOS, Linux). Some will use software downloaded from the Internet.
- **Case Projects.** Located at the end of each chapter are several Case Projects. In these extensive exercises, you implement the skills and knowledge gained in the chapter through real analysis, design, and implementation scenarios.
- **(ISC)^2 Code of Ethics.** The entire (ISC)^2 Code of Ethics is included at the end of this book. It is this author's opinion that the security professional's effectiveness in the workplace is a direct result of one's professional ethics and conduct.

Text and Graphic Conventions

Wherever appropriate, additional information and exercises have been added to this book to help you better understand the topic at hand. Icons throughout the text alert you to additional materials. The icons used in this textbook are described below.

The Note icon draws your attention to additional helpful material related to the subject being described.

Hands-On Projects in this book are preceded by the Hands-On icon and descriptions of the exercises that follow.

Case Project icons mark Case Projects, which are scenario-based assignments. In these extensive case examples, you are asked to implement independently what you have learned.

Instructor's Materials

The following additional materials are available when this book is used in a classroom setting. All of the supplements available with this book are provided for download at our Instructor Companion Site. Simply search for this text at *login.cengage.com.*

Electronic Instructor's Manual—The Instructor's Manual that accompanies this textbook provides additional instructional material to assist in class preparation, including suggestions for lecture topics, suggested lab activities, tips on setting up a lab for the hands-on assignments, and solutions to all end-of-chapter materials.

Cognero(R) Cengage Learning Testing Powered by Cognero is a flexible, online system that allows you to author, edit, and manage test bank content from multiple Cengage Learning solutions; create multiple test versions in an instant; and deliver tests from your LMS, your classroom or wherever you want.

PowerPoint Presentations—This book comes with a set of Microsoft PowerPoint slides for each chapter. These slides are meant to be used as a teaching aid for classroom presentations, to be made available to students on the network for chapter review, or to be printed for classroom distribution. Instructors are also at liberty to add their own slides to cover additional topics.

Practice Questions—250 sample exam questions are included.

Notes About This Edition

This is the second edition of this book. The second edition of this book was produced for three primary reasons:

- Six years will have passed since publication of the first edition. There have been changes and advances in security practices and security technologies in the intervening five years.
- (ISC)^2 completed a significant update to the CISSP Common Body of Knowledge (CBK), reflecting these same changes in security technologies and practices.
- (ISC)^2 has made fundamental changes to its CISSP exam, changing it from paper based to computer based. The locations where candidates take the CISSP exam have also changed.

Acknowledgments

First, I want to thank my wife and best friend, Rebekah. Without her patience and support, writing this book could not have been possible.

It takes a team of professionals to produce a teaching book. Those with whom I worked directly are mentioned here.

Several individuals at Cengage Learning have also been instrumental in the production of this book. First, Product Manager Nick Lombardi established the scope and direction for this book. Senior Content Developer Julia Leroux-Lindsey managed the author through the entire writing, reviewing, and production process, keeping track of the details as the author sent in chapter files, images, and other materials. Next, Senior Content Project Manager Brooke Baker kept track of the details as the author sent in chapter files, images, and other materials. Manuscript Quality Assurance tester Serge Palladino ensured that the text was free from errors. Certainly there were others: editors, compositors, graphic artists, who were also involved in this book project. Heartfelt thanks to all of you.

Special recognition goes to the book's technical reviewers. These are industry and academic subject matter experts who carefully read through the manuscript to make sure that it is both technically accurate and also well organized, with accurate and understandable descriptions and explanations. This book's technical reviewers are:

- Dr. Barbara Endicott-Popovsky, the Director for the Center of Information Assurance and Cybersecurity at the University of Washington, designated by the NSA as a Center for Academic Excellence in Information Assurance Education.
- Michael Simon, a leading expert in computer security, information assurance, and security policy development. Mike and I have also written two books together.
- John Sanderson at St. Clair College in Windsor, who provided valuable and thoughtful feedback in several important areas.
- Guy Garrett at Gulf Coast State College, whose insight challenged me to go the extra mile on several technical explanations.

Special thanks to Kirk Bailey for his keen insight over the years and for fighting the good fight.

I am honored to have had the opportunity work with this outstanding and highly professional group of individuals at Cengage Learning, together with the reviewers and others of you who never compromised on the pursuit of excellence.

About the Author

Peter H. Gregory, CISSP, CISA, CRISC, CCSK, PCI-QSA, is the author of over thirty books on information security and technology, including *CISA All-In-One Study Guide, IT Disaster Recovery Planning For Dummies, Biometrics For Dummies,* and *Solaris Security*. He has spoken at numerous security conferences, including RSA, SecureWorld Expo, InfraGard, and the West Coast Security Forum.

Peter is a Director of Strategic Services at FishNet Security, the leading provider of information security solutions that combine technology, services, support and training. He is the lead instructor and advisory board member for the University of Washington's certificate program in information security, and an advisory board member and guest lecturer for the University of Washington's certificate program in information security and risk management. He is a graduate of the FBI Citizens Academy.

In his free time he enjoys the outdoors in Washington State with his wife and family.

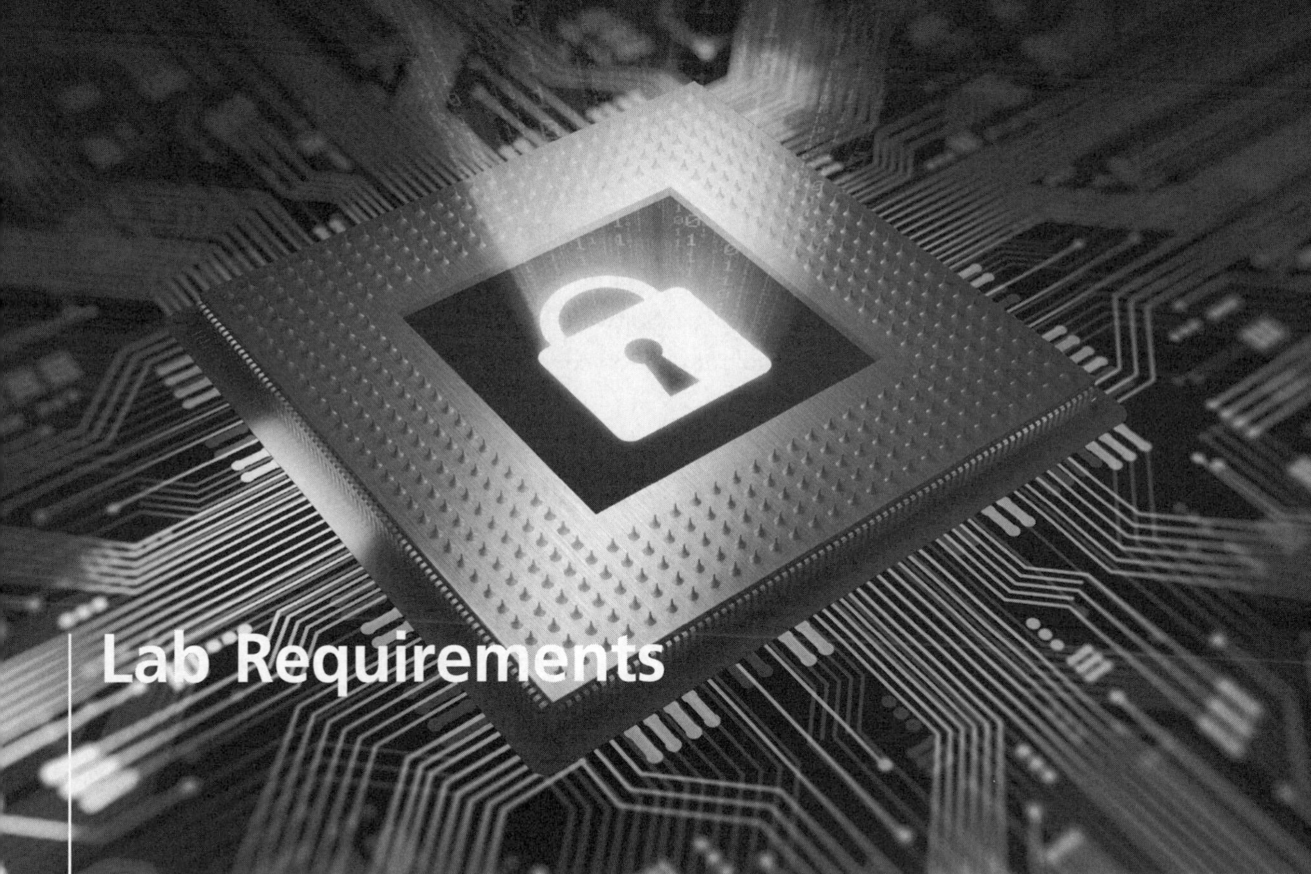

Lab Requirements

To the User

This book contains numerous hands-on lab exercises, many of which require a personal computer and, occasionally, specialized software.

Information and business security is not just about the technology; it's also about people, processes, and the physical facility in which all reside. For this reason, some of the labs do not involve the exploration of some aspect of computers or networks, but instead are concerned with business requirements, analysis, or critical evaluation of information. But even in these non-technical labs, a computer with word processing, spreadsheet, or illustration software will be useful for collecting and presenting information.

Hardware and Software Requirements

These are all of the hardware and software requirements needed to perform the end-of-chapter Hands-On Projects:

- Windows 7 or Windows 8 (in some projects, Windows XP, MacOS, or a current Linux distribution are sufficient)
- An Internet connection and Web browser (e.g., Firefox or Internet Explorer)
- Anti-virus software

Specialized Requirements

The need for specialized hardware or software is kept to a minimum. However, the following chapters do require specialized hardware or software:

- Chapter 2: Zone Labs' Zone Alarm firewall, or Comodo Firewall
- Chapter 3: Secunia Personal Software Inspector (PSI), IBM AppScan
- Chapter 10: Notebook or desktop computer with Wi-Fi NIC compatible with the Vistumbler tool

Free Downloadable Software Is Required in the Following Chapters

Chapter 2:

- Zone Labs' Zone Alarm firewall or Comodo Firewall
- WinZip version 9 or newer

Chapter 3:

- Secunia Personal Software Inspector (PSI)
- Microsoft Threat Analysis & Modeling tool

Chapter 5:

- TrueCrypt
- GnuPG
- OpenStego
- WinZip version 9 or newer

Chapter 9:

- Microsoft Process Explorer
- NMAP

Chapter 10:

- Wireshark
- NMAP
- Vistumbler

chapter 1

Information Security and Risk Management

Topics in This Chapter:

- How Security Supports Organizational Mission, Goals, and Objectives
- Risk Management
- Security Management
- Personnel Security

The *International Information Systems Security Certification Consortium* (ISC)[2] *Common Body of Knowledge* (CBK) defines the key areas of knowledge for Information Security Governance and Risk Management in this way:

The Information Security Governance and Risk Management domain entails the identification of an organization's information assets and the development, documentation, implementation and updating of policies, standards, procedures and guidelines that ensure confidentiality, integrity, and availability. Management tools such as data classification, risk assessment, and risk analysis are used to identify the threats, classify assets, and to rate their vulnerabilities so that effective security measures and controls can be implemented.

The candidate is expected to understand the planning, organization, roles and responsibilities of individuals in identifying and securing an organization's information assets; the development and use of policies stating management's views and position on particular topics and the use of guidelines, standards, and procedures to support the policies; security training to make employees aware of the importance of information security, its significance, and the specific security-related requirements relative to their position; the importance of confidentiality, proprietary and private information; third-party management and service level agreements related to information security; employment agreements; employee hiring and termination practices; and risk management practices and tools to identify, rate, and reduce the risk to specific resources.

Key areas of knowledge:

- *Understand and align security function to goals, mission, and objectives of the organization*
- *Understand and apply security governance*
- *Understand and apply concepts of confidentiality, integrity, and availability*
- *Develop and implement security policy*
- *Manage the information life cycle (e.g., classification, categorization, and ownership)*
- *Manage third-party governance (e.g., on-site assessment, document exchange and review, process/policy review)*
- *Understand and apply risk management concepts*
- *Manage personnel security*
- *Develop and manage security education, training, and awareness*
- *Manage the security function*

Even though this domain is positioned as number 3 in the Certified Information Systems Security Professional (CISSP) common body of knowledge, it is placed first in this book because all security activities should take place as a result of security and risk management processes.

Organizational Purpose

In order to protect an organization's assets, it is first necessary to understand several basic characteristics of the organization, including its goals, mission, and objectives. All of these are statements that define what the organization desires to achieve and how it will proceed to achieve them. These three terms are described in more detail as follows:

Mission

The mission of an organization is a statement of its ongoing purpose and reason for existence. An organization usually publishes its mission statement, so that its stakeholders, including employees, customers, suppliers, shareholders, and owners, share a common understanding of the organization's stated purpose. Some example mission statements:

> *"Support and provide members and constituents with credentials, resources, and leadership to secure information and deliver value to society."*—(ISC)²

> *"Global cryptologic dominance through responsive presence and network advantage."*—United States National Security Agency

> *"Organize the world's information and make it universally accessible and useful."*—Google

> *"Facebook's mission is to give people the power to share and make the world more open and connected."*—Facebook

As security professionals, we need to be aware of our organization's mission, because it will, in part, influence how we will approach the need to protect the organization's assets.

Objectives

Objectives clearly define the results an organization and its managers want to achieve in a specific time frame. Objectives reflect the broader purposes given by the mission statement and provide specific, observable, and measurable outcomes. Stakeholders periodically review the organization's results by comparing them to the objectives. This process determines the success of the organization and its management. Objectives state strategic priorities. When these are distilled into specific, achievable steps, they become goals.

Sample organization objectives include:

> *"Become the world's leading business human capital management company."*

> *"Reduce delayed flight departures to less than 5% of all scheduled flights."*

> *"Achieve the lowest personnel turnover in field sales."*

Security personnel need to understand and use the organization's objectives to guide their plans. Security often impedes activities needed to achieve objectives. Achieving the proper balance between security and operations requires evaluating threats through the lens of risk. The optimum solution allows employees to reach goals and achieve the organization's objectives with a minimum amount of risk to confidential data.

Goals

While objectives describe desired outcomes for an organization, goals specify specific accomplishments that will enable the organization to meet its objectives.

Some sample organization goals are:

> *"Obtain ISO 27001 certification by the end of third quarter."*

> *"Reduce development costs by twenty percent in the next fiscal year."*

> *"Complete the integration of CRM and ERP systems by the end of November."*

Security Support of Mission, Objectives, and Goals

Security professionals support an organization's mission, objectives, and goals by developing processes, practices, and procedures for protecting assets. They assess threats and develop mitigation steps in the context of probability, or risk, that a potential threat can occur. Effective security policy requires including this important consideration in every significant organizational decision. *Forbes* cited a PricewaterhouseCoopers survey showing a significant increase in employment of chief security officers. The report indicated that 41 percent of companies employed a CSO compared to 27 percent one year earlier. Employment of chief information security officers rose from 29 to 44 percent (Greenberg, 2008). Security programs fail without executive support, and the presence of security professionals in the organization's highest management levels reflects the growing importance of this field.

This is discussed in greater detail later in this chapter in the Security Management section.

Risk Management

Risk management is the process of minimizing potential losses. Even though a potential for loss always exists, many can be minimized or avoided. In the event a loss occurs, risk management practices determine how to reduce the costs. Since the potential for loss always exists, the key is to determine the probability or level of risk from a potential threat, scenario, or activity and determine its acceptability. Risk assessment techniques determine the level of risk and determine if the level of risk exceeds an organization's risk tolerance. In that case, the next step requires the development of a strategy to ameliorate specific risks in order to achieve an acceptable level of overall risk to the organization. In the vernacular this means: find the level of risk (associated with a given activity or asset) and improve if needed.

The National Institute of Standards and Technology (NIST) defines four risk management processes—framing, assessing, monitoring, and responding—in Special Publication 800-39. NIST develops security standards for U.S. government agencies, and these publications often assist private-sector organizations with risk management planning.

Risk Management Principles

Risk Assessment

Risk assessments are activities that are carried out to discover, describe, analyze, and evaluate risks. Risk assessments may be qualitative, quantitative, or a combination of these.

Internal audit is related to risk assessment; internal audit is discussed in a separate section in this chapter.

Qualitative Risk Assessment A qualitative risk assessment occurs with a predefined scope of **assets** or activities. Assets can, for example, consist of software applications, information systems, business equipment, business processes, or buildings. Activities may consist of actions or tasks carried out by an individual, group, or department.

A qualitative risk assessment collects descriptive information, including information that cannot be reduced to measurable values. It will typically identify a number of characteristics about an asset or activity, including:

- *Classification*. Assets may be classified according to risk level, business function, or the sensitivity or criticality of data stored or processed by an asset.
- ***Vulnerabilities***. These are weaknesses in design, configuration, documentation, procedure, or implementation.
- ***Threats***. These are potential activities that would, if they occurred, exploit specific vulnerabilities and result in a security incident.
- *Threat probability*. An expression of the likelihood that a specific threat will be carried out, usually expressed in a Low-Medium-High or simple numeric (1–5 or 1–10) scale. In a qualitative risk assessment, this is not a numeric probability but an arbitrary ranking of probability, as a way of distinguishing low probability from high probability.
- *Impact*. An expression of the influence upon the organization if a threat was carried out.
- ***Countermeasures***. These are actual or proposed measures that reduce the risk associated with vulnerabilities or threats.

Here is an example. A security manager is performing a qualitative risk assessment on assets in an IT environment. For each asset, the manager builds a chart that lists each threat, along with the probability of realization. The chart might resemble the list in Table 1-1.

This is an oversimplified example, but sometimes qualitative risk analysis won't be much more complicated than this—although a real risk analysis should list many more threats and countermeasures.

Quantitative Risk Assessment Although qualitative criteria do provide guidance for assessing and evaluating risks, quantitative assessments treat these conditions as discrete mathematical valuations. Often quantitative risks produce stronger arguments for security policies and encourage leaders to support aggressive implementation of security controls. A quantitative risk assessment can be thought of as an extension of a qualitative risk assessment.

Threat	Impact	Probability	Countermeasure	Probability with Countermeasure
Flooding	H	L	Water alarms	L
Theft	H	L	Key card, video surveillance, guards	L
Earthquake	M	M	Lateral rack bracing; attach all assets to racks	L
Logical intrusion	H	M	Network-based intrusion detection system; host-based intrusion detection system	L

Table 1-1 Risk assessment chart

A quantitative risk assessment will include the elements of a qualitative risk assessment but will contain additional items, including:

- *Asset value*. Usually this is a dollar figure that may represent the replacement cost of an asset, but it could also represent income derived through the use of the asset.
- *Exposure factor (EF)*. The proportion of an asset's value that is likely to be lost through a particular threat, usually expressed as a percentage. Another way to think about exposure factor is to consider the *impact* of a specific threat on an asset.
- *Single loss expectancy (SLE)*. This is the cost of a single loss through the single event realization of a particular threat. This is a result of the calculation:

$$\text{SLE} = \text{asset value (\$)} \times \text{exposure factor (\%)}$$

- *Annualized rate of occurrence (ARO)*. This is the probability that a loss will occur in a year's time. This is usually expressed as a percentage, which can be greater than 100% if it is believed that a loss can occur more than once per year.
- *Annual loss expectancy (ALE)*. This is the yearly estimate of loss of an asset, calculated as follows:

$$\text{ALE} = \text{ARO} \times \text{SLE}$$

Let's look at an example: an organization asset, an executive's laptop computer that is worth $2,000. The asset value is $2,000.

Now we will calculate the exposure factor (EF), which is the proportion of the laptop's value that is lost through a particular threat. The threat of theft will, of course, result in the entire laptop's value to be lost. For theft, EF = 100%. For sake of example, let's add another threat, that of damage, if the executive drops the laptop and breaks the screen. For that threat, the EF = 50% (presuming a $1,000 repair bill to replace the LCD screen).

For theft, the single loss expectancy (SLE) is $2,000 × 100% = $2,000. For damage, the SLE is $2,000 × 50% = $1,000.

Now we need to calculate how often either of these scenarios might occur in a single year. For theft, let us presume that there is a 10% probability that this executive's laptop will be stolen. Thus, the ARO = 10%. This particular executive is really clumsy and drops his laptop computer a lot, so the ARO for the threat of accidental damage is 25%.

The annual loss expectancy (ALE) for theft is 10% × $2,000 = $200.

The ALE for accidental damage is 25% × $1,000 = $250.

This all means that the organization may lose $450 ($200 for theft and $250 for damage) each year in support of the executive's laptop computer. Knowing this will help managers make more intelligent spending decisions for any protective measures that they feel will reduce the probability or impact of these and other threats. An example of such a measure is a remote wipe capability for laptop computers and smartphones.

Quantifying Countermeasures **Annual loss expectancy** (ALE) is the cost that the organization is likely to bear through the loss or compromise of the asset. Because ALE is expressed in dollars (or other local currency), the organization can now make decisions

regarding specific investments in countermeasures that are designed to reduce the risk. The risk analysis can be extended to include the impact of countermeasures on the overall risk equation:

- *Costs of countermeasures*. Each countermeasure has a specific cost associated with it. This may be the cost of additional protective equipment, software, or labor costs.
- *Changes in exposure factor*. A specific countermeasure may have an impact on a specific threat. For example, the use of an FM-200-based fire extinguishment system will mean that a fire in a business location will cause less damage than a sprinkler-based extinguishment system, but it is more expensive to reload.
- *Changes in single loss expectancy*. Specific countermeasures may influence the probability that a loss will occur. For instance, the introduction of an advanced malware protection appliance will reduce the frequency of successful malware attacks.

Geographic Considerations Organizations can take quantitative risk analysis a step or two further by calculating SLE, ALE, and ARO values in specific geographic locations. This is useful in organizations with similar assets located in different locations where the probability of loss or the replacement cost of these assets varies enough to be identified.

Specific Risk Assessment Methodologies The risk assessment steps described in this section are purposely simplistic, with the intention of illustrating the concepts of identifying the value of assets and by using formulas to arrive at a quantitative figure that represents the probable loss or compromise of assets in a year's time. For some organizations, this simple approach may be sufficient. On the other hand, there are several formal approaches to risk assessment that may be suitable for larger or more complex efforts. Among these approaches are:

- *OCTAVE (Operationally Critical Threat, Asset, and Vulnerability Evaluation)*. Developed by Carnegie Mellon University's Software Engineering Institute (SEI), OCTAVE is an approach where analysts identify assets and their criticality, identify vulnerabilities and threats, evaluate risks, and create a protection strategy to reduce risk.
- *FRAP (Facilitated Risk Analysis Process)*. This is a qualitative risk analysis methodology that can be used to prescreen a subject of analysis as a means to determine whether a full-blown quantitative risk analysis is needed.
- *Spanning Tree Analysis*. This can be thought of as a visual method for identifying categories of risks, as well as specific risks, using the metaphor of a tree and its branches. This approach would be similar to a Mind Map for identifying categories and specific threats and/or vulnerabilities.
- NIST 800-30, *Risk Management Guide for Information Technology Systems*. This document describes a formal approach to risk assessment that includes threat and vulnerability identification, control analysis, impact analysis, and a matrix depiction of risk determination and control recommendations.

Risk Treatment

When a qualitative or quantitative risk assessment is performed, an organization's management can begin the process of determining what steps, if any, can be taken to manage the risks identified in the risk assessment. The four general approaches to risk treatment are:

- Risk acceptance
- Risk avoidance
- Risk mitigation
- Risk transfer

It is important to remember that the objective of risk treatment is typically not to eliminate risk—often risk cannot be completely eliminated, but only managed.

Risk Avoidance The associated activity that introduces the risk is discontinued. For instance, an organization performs a risk analysis of an Internet-based shopping cart application, and then decides to abandon the use of the application altogether. This is **risk avoidance.**

Risk Mitigation This involves the use of countermeasures to reduce the risks initially identified in the risk analysis. Examples of **risk reduction** in information systems include firewalls, intrusion detection systems, access reviews, and DMZ networks.

Risk Acceptance In a typical risk assessment, there will be many identified risks, typically ranked as high, medium, and low risk. In an organization with scarce resources, management may choose to forego mitigation of all of the risks ranked low, in other words leaving things as they are and accepting the stated risks. This is known as **risk acceptance.** Occasionally, medium and high risks will also be accepted, although such a decision usually requires more thoughtful consideration as well as formal management approval.

Risk Transfer **Risk transfer** typically involves the use of insurance as a means for mitigating risk. For instance, a risk analysis on the use of laptop computers may identify theft as one risk. While the organization may mitigate the risk through the use of cable locks, it may transfer part of the risk to an insurance company. Note that risk transfer usually involves a cost (insurance premiums) that should be considered in a quantitative risk analysis.

Residual Risk In any particular risk situation, generally only some of the risk can be avoided, reduced, or transferred. There is always some remaining risk, called **residual risk.** Typically this risk must be accepted, unless management can enact another round of analysis and a fresh set of countermeasures to avoid, reduce, or transfer the risk. But even then, there will typically be some "leftover" risk, called *residual risk*.

Security Management Concepts

As security moved from a task to a standalone professional discipline, practitioners developed a de facto framework of foundational concepts. These include:

- Security controls
- CIA Triad
- Defense in depth
- Single points of failure
- Fail open, fail closed, fail soft
- Privacy

The ISO 27001 standard, "Information Technology—Security Techniques—Information Security Management Systems—Requirements," is a respected standard for information security management. Originally developed as British Standard 7799, the standard was adopted by the International Standards Organization (ISO) in 2000. ISO 27001 was later updated in 2005. ISO 27001 is a top-down process approach to security management that requires continuous improvement in an organization's security management system.

Security Controls

Security controls are the measures that are taken to reduce risks through the origination and enforcement of **security policies**. The types of controls used are detective, deterrent, preventive, corrective, recovery, and compensating. These controls are discussed in detail in Chapter 3, "Software Development Security."

The CIA Triad

The core principles of information security are confidentiality, integrity, and availability, often coined as **CIA**. All other concepts and activities in information security are based on these principles. The CIA Triad is depicted in Figure 1-1.

Confidentiality The principle of confidentiality asserts that only properly authorized parties can access information and functions.

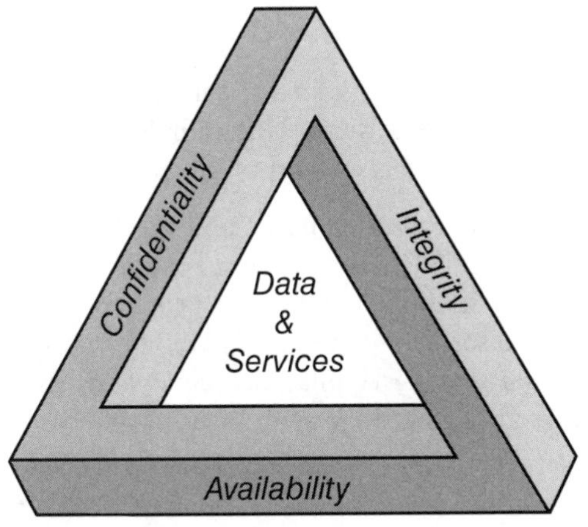

Figure 1-1 The CIA Triad

Mobile devices can access information and entertainment for someone at any time or place. However, the freedom of mobility threatens the freedom to keep some aspects of life private. Government agencies and private-sector companies like Google and Facebook collect the data people send across the Internet. These prying eyes place the idea of confidentiality at risk, because individuals cannot control the use of their information or who can look at it.

Individuals expect that their confidential information will not be disclosed to unauthorized parties and that it will be properly protected. However, we have come to expect that some organizations will not handle information properly, resulting in an unauthorized disclosure that, in its worst case, could result in an attempted identity theft or financial fraud carried out against the persons whose information was compromised. The Target stores breach of 2013 is an example of a widespread data compromise.

Integrity The principle of integrity asserts that information and functions can be added, altered, or removed only by authorized persons and means.

The general expectation of information systems is that information will be properly and accurately introduced into a system, and throughout its lifetime the information will remain accurate. While the principle of confidentiality states that only authorized parties will be able to view information, the principle of integrity states that only authorized parties will be able to modify information. Integrity is achieved through role-based access control, which is the generic name for a mechanism that defines and limits the actions individuals may perform. In the context of information stored in a database, which consists of tables, rows, and fields, the concept of integrity will govern which individuals are able to modify which tables, rows, and fields in the database.

In data security, the need for integrity encompasses software, systems, networks, and the people who design, build, and operate them. Software must be correctly developed, configured, and maintained and must operate properly, particularly when a program is accessing and modifying data. Systems must be properly configured so that the data that resides on them is managed and updated correctly. The people who design, build, and operate software and systems must be properly trained on the technologies that they are using, and they must also adhere to a code of professional ethics that guides their behavior and decision-making.

Availability The principle of availability asserts that systems, functions, and data must be available when an authorized user needs to access them. Different levels of availability exist based upon predefined parameters regarding levels and types of service.

Availability is multifaceted and involves many separate safeguards and mechanisms to ensure that systems and data are available when needed. These safeguards range from preventing damage through the use of firewalls, anti-virus software, and surge protectors to redundant architectures used for business continuity and disaster recovery. Availability requires planning and includes change and configuration management. Availability covers nearly all of the aspects of data security that directly or indirectly protect a system from harm.

Defense in Depth

The term **defense in depth** implies a *layered defense* consisting of two or more protective methods that protect some asset. According to the National Security Agency, defense in

depth defines a process for balancing protection capability, cost, performance, and operations considerations (National Security Agency, 2013). Some of the characteristics of defense in depth are:

- *Heterogeneity*. A good defense in depth mechanism may contain different types of protective mechanisms. For example, two layers of firewalls of different brands.
- *Holistic or comprehensive protection*. Each layer of the defense fully protects an asset against the type of threat that the defense is designed to block. For example, anti-virus on an e-mail server and also on end-user workstations.

The classic example of a good defense in depth is the medieval castle's defenses that include a drawbridge, a moat, a moat monster, archers, soldiers to pour boiling oil, and so on. These defenses are all different from one another but are all designed to protect the castle (and its assets) from attack from outsiders. Each defense operates on its own and does not require others for it to properly function.

The objective of defense in depth is to reduce the probability that a threat can act upon an asset. This occurs in three ways:

- *Single vulnerability*. If one of the components of a defense in depth had an exploitable vulnerability, chances are that another layer in the defense will not have the same vulnerability.
- *Single malfunction*. If one of the components of a defense in depth malfunctions, chances are that another layer in the defense will not malfunction.
- *Fail open*. If one of the components in a defense in depth fails open, the other component(s) will continue to operate and protect the asset.

Single Points of Failure

A **single point of failure** is the characteristic of an individual component in a system if the failure of the component will result in the failure of the entire system.

Single points of failure are generally discussed only in a system that is designed for resilience and that contains redundant components. A single point of failure in such a system would be any portion of the system where redundancy does not exist.

For example, the firewall in Figure 1-2 would be a single point of failure. If the firewall fails, the system will be unreachable. The firewall is a single point whose failure will cause the failure of the entire system's objectives.

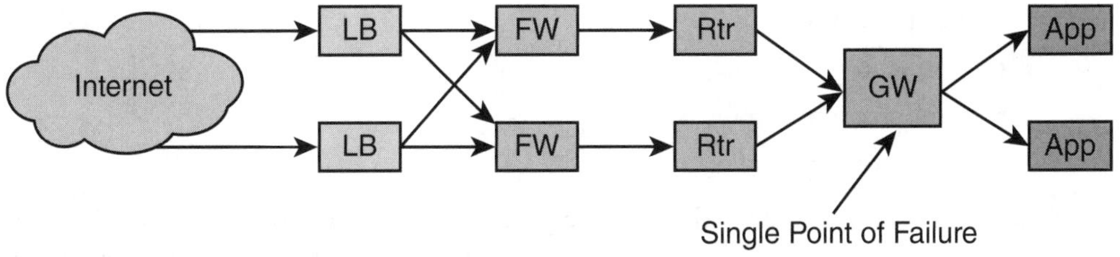

Figure 1-2 Single point of failure in an otherwise resilient environment

Fail Open, Fail Closed, Fail Soft

The concepts of *fail open*, *fail closed*, and *fail soft* are related to what happens to the protection in the event of a failure of a security control.

When a security control fails, generally one of two things happens: either the control blocks all access, or it permits all access. If the control fails and it blocks all access, it is said to **fail closed**. Another term for fail closed is **fail safe.**

If the control fails and permits all access, it **fails open**.

A system can take action during an adverse situation such as a hardware failure. **Fail soft** is the process of shutting down nonessential components on a system, thereby freeing up resources so that critical components can continue operating.

Generally speaking it is more desirable for a control to fail closed than to fail open. This, however, is dependent upon the objective and design of the entire system.

An example of undesirable fail open is a doorway controlled by a key card access system that can be bypassed if the key card system fails. A desirable fail open would be the automatic opening of security doors to facilitate personnel exiting in case of fire.

Most security controls fail closed. For example, if a key card system fails, personnel cannot enter or move about the premises. If an application server is unable to access an LDAP authentication server, then no users can log on to the application.

Privacy

The Merriam-Webster dictionary defines **privacy** as "freedom from unauthorized intrusion." Wiktionary defines privacy as "the state of not being seen by others." The practice of privacy in business refers to the protection of individuals' private information so that it is used only for intended and agreed-upon purposes, as well as being protected from unauthorized disclosure.

Personally Identifiable Information

Personally identifiable information (PII) refers to the items that comprise a person's identity, usually including:

- Full name
- National identification number (in the United States, social security number)
- Telephone number
- Driver's license number
- Passport number
- Residential address
- Bank account numbers
- Credit card numbers

In many locales, organizations are required to protect many of, or combinations of, these items, and sometimes others, from unauthorized disclosure. Organizations are also usually required to disclose all uses of private information, as well as the parties to whom they send this information. Most often these requirements are in the form of laws and regulations

intended to curb the proliferation of this information to others. The objective of these laws and regulations is the prevention of identity theft, fraud, and harassment by those who might obtain a person's PII.

Security Management

Security management is primarily concerned with strategic-level activities that influence the operation of systems and the behavior of employees. Security management involves several key activities, including:

- Executive oversight
- Governance
- Policy, guidelines, standards, and procedures
- Roles and responsibilities
- Service level agreements
- Secure outsourcing
- Data classification and protection
- Certification and accreditation
- Internal audit

Security Executive Oversight

The support and oversight by executives of security-related activities is vital to the viability of a security program in an organization. Several activities are related to this oversight, including:

- *Support of policies.* Executive support is needed to ensure that security policies and other policies are taken seriously by all members of the organization. Support should come in the form of communication (memos stating that adherence to policy is a required condition of employment) and leadership by example.
- *Allocation of resources.* Executives control the allocation of resources in an organization, primarily through budgeting and staffing levels. In order for a security program to be effective, executives must allocate sufficient resources to security.
- *Support of risk management.* One of the primary activities in a security management function is the performance of risk assessments, which result in the treatment of identified risks. Executives need to formally accept the disposition of risks as documented in risk assessments whether risks are accepted, transferred, mitigated, or avoided.

Security Governance

The IT Governance Institute in its *Board Briefing on IT Governance, 2nd Edition*, defines security **governance** this way:

> *"Security governance is the set of responsibilities and practices exercised by the board and executive management with the goal of providing strategic*

> *direction, ensuring that objectives are achieved, ascertaining that risks are managed appropriately, and verifying that the enterprise's resources are used responsibly."*

In other words, strategy, objectives, and risks are developed and executed in a top-down manner. In a governance model, executive management is in control of the activities intended to protect organization assets from known threats. Usually this translates into a series of activities that include:

- *Steering committee oversight*. A group of executives are regularly briefed on activities related to security and risk management. Discussions about incidents and events take place, changes to policies are made, and decisions and opinions are solicited.
- *Resource allocation and prioritization*. Executives allocate resources to security-related activities in order that required activities may be carried out.
- *Status reporting*. Information about events, trends, issues, and other security-related matters are collected and sent to upper management through status reports that provide feedback on decisions, strategic direction, and overall effectiveness of the security program.
- *Decisions*. Decisions made at the steering committee level (and at lower levels) are sent downwards to appropriate levels to be carried out by managers and staff members.

Security Policies, Requirements, Guidelines, Standards, and Procedures

Organizations establish documented processes for managing their security profiles. Taking a formal approach increases costs, generally substantiated by regulatory compliance or reduced civil liability. Security programs consist of policies, requirements, guidelines, standards, and procedures that address human and systems behavior. They define acceptable standards and usage and detail consequences for violations. Formal processes provide the organization with a consistent set of standards and methods for handling individuals and incidents. They also detail the frequency of audits and periodic policy reviews.

Policies, requirements, guidelines, standards, and procedures are a hierarchy, where policies are very general statements of *what* should be done. Requirements, guidelines, standards, and procedures are much more specific and describe *how* policies should be carried out. Because of this, a well-written set of policies will not need to be changed very often, while requirements, guidelines, standards, and procedures may need to be changed more frequently.

Policies Security **policies** describe constraints of behavior for an organization's personnel as well as the acceptable use of its information systems, data, and other mechanisms. Put another way, security policy specifies the activities that are required, limited, or forbidden in an organization.

An example policy is, *Information systems should be configured to require compliant security practices in the selection and use of passwords.*

Policy Standards The international standard, ISO 27002:2013, *Information technology—Security techniques—Code of practice for information security management*, is a well-known

framework on which an organization can build its security policy. The sections in the standard are:

- Information security policies
- Organization of information security
- Human resources security
- Asset management
- Access control
- Cryptography
- Physical and environmental security
- Operations security
- Communications security
- Systems acquisition, development, and maintenance
- Supplier relationships
- Information security incident management
- Information security aspects of business continuity management
- Compliance; with legal requirements, such as policies, and with external requirements, such as laws

The SANS organization has a well-known security policy model in the *SANS Security Policy Project* found at http://www.sans.org/security-resources/policies/. Here the reader can find articles on policies, standards, guidelines, example policies, and white papers on the development of security policy.

Policy Effectiveness An organization that enacts policies should take steps to ensure that its policies are effective. Policy effectiveness requires a top-down approach. To be effective, a security policy must be:

- Approved by senior management
- Communicated to employees
- Periodically reviewed
- Assessed for effectiveness

Security policy must reflect and support the mission, objectives, and goals of an organization. If the organization is risk-averse, then its security policy should support risk aversion. If the organization has a greater appetite for risk, then its security policy should reflect this also.

Requirements The term **requirements** usually refers to characteristics of an information system or business process. Typically, a set of requirements will be created when a new information system is being developed or purchased. The requirements will help the organization make suitable selection, design, or configuration decisions.

Requirements should reflect security policy; if security policy says, "a system shall be configured to prevent unauthorized access," then a corresponding requirement would specify how this is accomplished. In this instance the requirement might state that users must lock out their systems when they leave the work area and also specify that system configurations automatically lock out after two minutes of inactivity. Notice how the requirement fulfills the policy with specific actions addressing human behavior and systems configuration, which compensates for human failure. The goal of security requirements is to constrain a system or process so that, when implemented, it complies with the organization's security policy.

Another example of a requirement is, *Information systems must enforce password quality standards and must be able to reference a central authentication service, either LDAP or Active Directory.*

Guidelines Whereas security policy defines *what* should be done (or not done), **guidelines** provide information on *how* policy can be implemented. Generally, guidelines are suggestions or ideas on how specific policies may be implemented. Which approach (including a blended approach) is adopted is up to the organization.

For example, if a security policy states that *personnel access to business facilities shall be controlled*, guidelines can suggest that key card systems with PIN pads be used at building entrances and within sensitive areas inside buildings.

An example guideline is, *Users should choose a password that is easy for the user to remember, but hard for others to guess. The types of passwords that should be avoided include: employee, spouse, or pet names, significant anniversaries, common words such as "password," words related to work functions, and other easily guessed words.*

Standards **Standards** are statements that specify *what* shall be used to support security policies and guidelines. Typically, standards will comprise the following:

- *Product standards*. These are specific names of products that shall be used to support a policy.
- *Process standards*. These may cite process templates, names, or methodologies.
- *Technology standards*. This includes the use of technology standards such as TCP/IP or OSPF, computer languages, and so on.
- *Reference configurations*. These include server build specs, router configurations, software configurations, hardening specifications, and so on.
- *Reference architectures*. These include schematics for building networks, specifications for integrating applications, and so on.

It is expected that standards will change far more frequently than policies and guidelines.

An example standard is: *Minimum password length is 8 characters. Passwords must consist of lower case, upper case, and numeric characters. Passwords shall expire after no more than 90 days. Accounts must automatically lock if a user has entered an incorrect password more than three times in ten minutes; accounts must be unlocked by an access administrator, or may be automatically unlocked one hour after the last logon attempt. Users may not use any of the previous 10 passwords used.*

Procedures **Procedures** are the instructions that specify *how* tasks are to be performed. True to the hierarchical form, procedures must support policies, guidelines, and standards.

The purpose of a procedure is to ensure the consistent and methodical completion of repetitive tasks. Consistency builds quality and reduces incidents, which allows the organization to operate more efficiently and at greater levels of service.

Security Roles and Responsibilities

Management should define security roles and responsibilities in the organization. This includes not only the roles and responsibilities of dedicated security personnel, but of all employees in the organization. Roles and responsibilities should be formally defined in two places:

- *Security policy*. General and specific expectations of security staff and other employees should be defined in the organization's security policy.
- *Job descriptions*. Individual job descriptions of security staff and other employees should define specific security-related roles and responsibilities.

The roles and responsibilities that need to be defined include:

- *Ownership of assets*. Individual assets and groups of assets need to have designated owners who are responsible for their operation and protection.
- *Access to assets*. The owners of assets should be designated as the persons who decide who may access or use those assets. A higher level of management may be responsible for approving nonstandard access to assets.
- *Use of assets*. All employees should be explicitly designated as responsible for their individual use of assets.
- *Managers*. Managers should be designated as being responsible for the behavior of employees under their control.

Service Level Agreements

A **service level agreement** (**SLA**) is a formally defined level of service provided by an organization. Within the context of security management, SLAs may be defined for many activities, including:

- *Security incident response*. A security team may be required to mobilize within a stated period of time when a security incident has been called.
- *Security alert delivery*. Security alerts, which may be bulletins of threats or vulnerabilities, may need to be delivered to recipients within a stated period of time.
- *Security investigation*. A security investigator may be required to respond to a call for assistance within a stated period of time.
- *Policy and procedure review*. A security team may be required to periodically review policies, procedures, and other documents at regular intervals.

SLAs can be defined for other tactical activities performed by security management and staff.

Secure Outsourcing

Outsourcing is the subcontracting of a business process to a third-party company. Organizations outsource many different functions for a variety of reasons, including:

- Redirecting energy to the organization's core competencies
- Controlling the efficient use of capital and other resources

There are some risks associated with the outsourcing of business processes to third parties, including:

- *Control of confidential information*. An organization will need to equip the third-party provider with the information required to perform its functions properly. Because this information is now out of its direct control, protection of that information is now entirely dependent upon the outsourcer's actions.
- *Loss of control*. Organizations that outsource functions to third parties give up a measure of control to that organization.
- *Accountability*. While the organization has outsourced functions to a third party and is at the complete mercy of the third party's integrity, the organization is still completely accountable for the actions performed by the vendor.

Organizations with a large number of outsourcing relationships may need to develop an outsourcing classification scheme that categorizes each supplier according to one or more criteria, including:

- Sensitivity of the data it processes for the organization
- Volume of data it processes for the organization
- Criticality of the business process(es) supported in the organization

These classifications will help the organization determine what measures are necessary to confirm that each supplier is performing its activities correctly and that it is adequately protecting the organization's information.

Additional terms related to the practice of outsourcing include:

- ***Insourcing***. The use of internal staff to perform a business function.
- ***Offshoring***. The use of internal or external staff in another country.
- ***Onshoring***. The use of internal or external staff within a country.

Note that outsourcing and insourcing are related to whether an organization uses its own staff to perform business functions, while the terms offshoring and onshoring are related to the location of insourced or outsourced personnel.

Data Classification and Protection

Organizations store, transmit, and manage a wide variety of types of information, ranging from personnel and payroll records to computer source code to content on public-facing web sites. Information security professionals who are responsible for protecting this information need to decide what measures are required to protect the data. Data of widely varying levels of sensitivity exists in many forms; while it is possible to develop criteria for protecting every set of data in the organization, this approach scales poorly.

Data classification is the undertaking of developing levels of sensitivity for information, and assigning those levels for the purpose of establishing appropriate modes of protection for those data sets. This orderly system of assigning classification levels is preferable to a chaotic environment where information is protected in an ad hoc style.

A formal data classification program consists of several parts, which are:

- Sensitivity levels

- Marking procedures
- Access procedures
- Handling procedures
- Destruction procedures

Sensitivity Levels In a data classification program, a set of **sensitivity levels** is established, which reflects the nature of data that is used in the organization. Such a set of sensitivity levels could be, for example:

- Top Secret
- Secret
- Confidential
- Restricted
- Official
- Unclassified
- Public

Most organizations don't have more than four or five levels, since each level generally will have its own sets of marking and handling procedures. The more levels there are, the more complicated the classification program will be. Pragmatically, establishing too many levels will introduce unnecessary complications, increasing the likelihood of errors, while providing only marginally more security than a simpler program. A data classification program that is too complex may be ignored altogether if personnel are unsure of how to carry it out or the requirement is too onerous.

Because information classification and handling is largely a human-driven and -operated process, it is preferable to use a simpler scheme of classification levels that will encourage compliance and reduce ambiguity and errors.

Information Labeling **Labeling**, or **marking**, is the process of affixing a word, symbol, or phrase on a set of data. The purpose of labeling is to make other readers aware of the level of classification on a set of data. When others are aware of the classification level of a particular set of data, they are more apt to be aware of the classification level and handle the data properly.

Using the example of the four levels of classification above, here are some sample labels that can be affixed to human-readable documents, shown in Table 1-2.

Marking is not as simple as it may first appear. While it can be relatively simple to mark a document or report with a header or footer containing a classification word or phrase, or affix a classification label on a backup tape, effectively labeling stored or transmitted data is not so clear-cut. Other situations include:

- *On-screen labeling*. Software programs that display classified information can include on-screen labeling.

Level	Label
Top Secret	"COMPANY Top Secret" in at least 48 pt type on cover page. "COMPANY Top Secret: for registered personnel only" in at least 24 pt type on every page.
Secret	"COMPANY Secret: for authorized personnel only with a business need-to-know" in at least 20 pt type on every page.
Confidential	"COMPANY Confidential: for employees and customers only" in at least 14 pt type on every page.
Public	"COMPANY Approved for Public Use" on every page.

Table 1-2 Sample classification labels

- *Data transmission.* Devices that transmit classified information can have labels affixed to them; further, administrative interfaces (used by network or systems engineers) can have a label displayed at login time. Cabling used to transmit classified information can be labeled or color-coded.

Handling Once information is introduced into an organization, it needs to be appropriately categorized and properly handled in every type of situation. Handling guidelines need to be developed for each level of classification, for each possible type of activity, including these listed here and possibly several more:

- *Computer storage.* Classification guidelines can include which systems (or classes of systems) are permitted to store the data and under what specific conditions.
- *Computer access control.* Classification guidelines may include business rules about which personnel (individuals, groups, departments, roles, security clearance level, etc.) may access classified information.
- *Backup tape and other portable media.* Classification guidelines will determine when and how data at different classification levels may be written to various types of portable media. For instance, data at the highest levels of secrecy might be forbidden from most or all portable media, and at other levels, encryption may be required.
- *Network transmission.* Classification guidelines should specify if and how data at various classification levels may be transmitted over networks. Of course there are different types of networks (internal, external, and perhaps physically separate high-secrecy networks), so this guideline alone will probably be multidimensional.
- *E-mail transmission.* Classification guidelines may determine which classification levels permit e-mail to be used to transmit classified information to another person. Like network transmission, e-mail transmission will probably contain conditions such as encryption, internal versus external recipients, and so on.
- *Facsimile.* Classification guidelines should address whether information at different classification levels can be faxed and, if so, what conditions should be imposed, such as confirming that the sender's and recipient's fax machines will be attended throughout the transmission.
- *Printing.* Classification guidelines should address the conditions under which information at various classification levels may be printed.

- *Mailing/shipping/courier*. Classification guidelines need to address whether and how classified information may be mailed or shipped. Possible conditions include lockbox, registered, insured, and double-sealed packages.
- *Carrying*. Classification guidelines need to include guidance on the safeguards that individuals need to take when carrying classified information.
- *Hard copy storage*. Classification guidelines should address how hard copies of classified information must be stored. Some levels may require double-locking (stored in a locked desk or cabinet in a locked office, for instance).

Destruction **Classification** guidelines need to include information on the proper disposal of classified information. **Destruction** procedures—steps to ensure that information is discarded in a way that renders it non-retrievable—need to include every type of media and likely context.

For example, media destruction procedures should include proper disposal of hard copy documents. In the workplace there are sure to be shredders or secure document disposal bins, but what about staff members who work primarily in home offices? And how does someone on extended travel safely dispose of a classified document?

Certification and Accreditation

Certification and accreditation are the activities associated with the evaluation of a system against a set of standards or policies. These activities are carried out as part of a formal approval process for initiating or continuing the use of a system.

- **Certification** is the process of evaluating a system against a set of formal standards, policies, or specifications.
- **Accreditation** is the formal approval for the use of a certified system, for a defined period of time (and possibly other conditions).

Internal Audit

In the context of information security, **internal audit** is the activity of self-evaluation of security controls and policies to measure their effectiveness.

In order to be effective, the internal audit function must be objective and independent. This means that the staff members performing internal audit activities should not be a part of the department or division that they are examining. Instead, internal audit should report to a dissociated part of the organization such as Legal.

Internal audit should follow a formal methodology that will further the objectivity and quality of the examination of security controls. Two of the most widely recognized methodologies are:

- Standards and practices of internal auditing from The Institute of Internal Auditors, available at www.theiia.org
- *IT Audit and Assurance Standards, Tools, and Techniques* from the Information Systems Audit and Control Association (ISACA), available at www.isaca.org /standards

Security Strategies

Management is responsible for developing the ongoing strategy for security management. The development and changes to the security strategy will be based upon several factors, including the organization's mission, objectives, and goals; the organization's risk tolerance; applicable security and privacy regulations; security requirements from customers, partners, and suppliers; and the results of past events, including:

- *Incidents.* If any security incidents have occurred, the facts uncovered in the handling of the incident, as well as its root cause, may prompt management to make changes.
- *Performance of SLAs.* If the performance of SLAs is below expectations, management may make changes to improve this.
- *Certification and accreditation.* The outcomes of recent certifications and accreditations may provide cause for strategic changes.
- *Internal audit.* The results of internal audits may prompt management to make changes to audited processes or to the audit process itself.

Strategic changes should be made in consultation with executive management and through the governance function described earlier in this section.

Personnel Security

Organizations are becoming more dependent upon information systems in support of key business processes, and more personnel have access to vast stores of organizational data. The risk of security incidents caused by employees' innocent mistakes as well as deliberate malicious acts cannot be eliminated: personnel require access to information to carry out their duties. Organizations need to protect themselves through effective hiring and personnel management practices that include:

- Prescreening employee backgrounds including checks for arrests, convictions, bankruptcy, and verification of employment and educational credentials
- Requiring workers to sign various agreements aimed at protecting the organization's assets
- Training and testing workers so that they are aware of the organization's security policies and practices
- Enacting common practices to reduce behavioral risk
- Performing effective employment terminations

These topics are addressed in this section.

Hiring Practices and Procedures

The near-universal practice among organizations is the use of written agreements that employers and employees sign at various stages of the employment relationship.

Non-Disclosure Agreement As soon as an employer and an employment candidate are discussing the candidate's potential employment in the organization, the employer may require the candidate to sign a **non-disclosure agreement** (NDA). This agreement will require that the candidate not discuss any nonpublic details about the organization with any other party.

The advantage of the preemployment NDA is that the employer will have some written assurance that the candidate will not share any information shared during interviews. While an employment agreement will certainly have a non-disclosure clause in it, a separate preemployment NDA provides some protection from disclosure by those individuals whom the organization does not hire but may share sensitive information with during the interview process.

Background Verification As the preemployment relationship advances, an employer that is considering making an offer of employment to a candidate will, in most jurisdictions, be required to obtain a signed consent to obtain background information from the candidate. In this simple form, the candidate is providing basic identifying information (e.g., full name, aliases, date of birth, country of citizenship, social/insurance number), together with a written consent for the employer to obtain background information.

The consent form may also contain a clause that states that the employer may refuse employment, terminate employment, and even turn the candidate over to law enforcement authorities if the candidate provides false or misleading information or is found to have an undesirable background.

The employer may also use information obtained from the employment application form to confirm certain aspects of a candidate's background.

There is increased reliance on the use of electronically stored and delivered information. Thus, there is a higher potential consequence of hiring an employee with a criminal background. An organization that is considering hiring a candidate should complete a **background verification** to validate the truthfulness of the candidate's claims and to investigate the candidate's potential criminal background. The following checks may be included in a background verification:

- Confirmation of citizenship, identity, and the candidate's legal right to employment
- Confirmation of employment history
- Confirmation of education background
- Confirmation of professional certifications and licenses
- Investigation of potential criminal history
- Investigation of credit history, important for positions involving financial management responsibility
- Investigation of potential ties with terrorist or criminal organizations
- Check of professional references

Some organizations also attempt to gather information about a prospective employee's character. Organizations that do this may perform online searches to see what information about the candidate is freely available online. Employers may also search social networking sites such as Facebook, LinkedIn, and Twitter.

Offer Letter An organization intent upon hiring a candidate will next issue an offer of employment, or **offer letter**, which usually contains:

- Position title and description
- Start date
- Compensation
- Name of manager

The offer letter should tie together the other elements of the hiring process, including non-disclosure, background check, non-compete, and the requirement that the candidate always abide by security policy and other policies.

Non-Compete Agreement In some locales, an organization can also restrict an employee's ability to change employers to work for a competitor. Organizations intent on enforcing non-compete are concerned with the protection of their intellectual property and other insider information. A **non-compete agreement** is a legal agreement that specifies terms and conditions related to the possibility of an employee accepting employment with a competing organization in the future.

Intellectual Property Agreement An **intellectual property agreement** guarantees that the organization owns all intellectual property (IP) that may be created by an employee. Often this includes IP that an employee may create while working on his or her own time using his or her own resources.

Employment Agreement Sometimes an organization and a new employee will sign an **employment agreement** that defines terms and conditions of the employment relationship. Where labor unions are sometimes used to manage employer-employee relationships, employment agreements often represent an entire segment of the organization's workforce.

Employee Handbook Many organizations have an **employee handbook**, a formal document that describes the terms and conditions of employment, including but not limited to:

- Working hours and locations
- Expected behavior
- Compensation and benefits
- Paid and unpaid leave
- Policies, including security policy
- Acceptable use of organization assets, including workstations and other information systems

In many situations, employees are required to sign the employee handbook, which provides a written attestation that the employee understands all of the terms and conditions of employment and of the organization's principal policies.

Formal Job Descriptions Many organizations have developed formal **job descriptions**, which are formal documents that typically include:

- Job title

- Pay range
- Description of duties
- Description of responsibilities
- Required experience

Often, organizations include adherence to policies in the list of responsibilities. This further strengthens the organization's message that all policies, including security policies, are taken seriously.

Termination

Various circumstances lead to a separation of employment, which are either employee-initiated or employer-initiated. Regardless of the cause, organizations need to perform certain critical tasks upon **termination** of an employee, including:

- Terminate access to all information systems and networks
- Change administrative passwords that may be known to the employee
- Recover all organization-owned assets
- Have incoming e-mail for the terminated employee routed to a designated person or group

Some termination situations call for an urgent revocation of access by the terminated employee, to prevent the former employee from accessing information systems for the purpose of causing harm to the organization. At times the organization will need to take additional steps, including:

- A review of all recent activities related to the terminated employee
- Code reviews of software source code that the terminated employee had access to
- Change control and configuration management reviews of systems under the control of the terminated employee

These reviews may be needed, on the chance that the employee sensed the termination was imminent and had reason to damage information systems.

Work Practices

Several practices, when put into place, will reduce behavioral-based risk in an organization.

These practices are:

- Separation of duties
- Job rotation
- Mandatory vacations

Separation of Duties The principle of **separation of duties** (sometimes known as *segregation of duties*) states that important tasks should require more than one person to complete. A group of two or more employees are less likely to carry out an unauthorized task. Examples of tasks that should employ separation of duties include:

- Payment requests
- Requests for privileged access

In these examples, no single individual should be able to perform these duties. Instead, strictly controlled processes should be established that require at least two individuals (and not just *any* two, but two designated persons or roles not in a hierarchical reporting relationship with each other) to perform these functions.

Job Rotation Personnel in sensitive roles may, after extended intervals, be tempted to collusion for personal gain and other unauthorized activities. When employers occasionally rotate personnel through various roles, especially when unannounced, employees are less likely to perform these "extra" activities. This practice is known as **job rotation**. Enacting this can be difficult in smaller organizations that have only single individuals in various roles.

Mandatory Vacations While it is laudable that some employees are so loyal to their employers that they wish to never leave their posts, mandatory vacations provide something akin to short-term job rotation that sometimes enables an organization to spot irregularities that may be a sign of unauthorized activities. When mandatory vacations are institutionalized, employees are less likely to carry out prohibited activities that could be detected during their absence.

Security Education, Training, and Awareness

In order to adequately protect their assets, organizations need their employees to exercise due diligence and be keen to irregularities that could be signs of trouble. But because "security common sense" is not yet common (and because organizations' security policies vary from one another), organizations need to take time to teach their employees the "dos and don'ts" of information security. This formal education is known as **security awareness training** and needs to be strategic, formal, and presented in a variety of ways, including:

- *Security content in new-hire paperwork*. This includes the employee handbook and documents that a new employee is required to sign upon hire. This is covered earlier in this chapter in the Hiring Practices and Procedures section.
- *Security content in day-one orientation*. New employees need to be made aware of key security policies on their first day of employment.
- *Security training*. Soon after starting employment, new employees should be enrolled in more comprehensive security awareness training, which may take the form of classroom or web-based training.
- *Specialized training*. Employees in some job categories may be required to attend additional specialized training, including:
  - Secure programming for software developers
  - Fraud prevention for finance department employees
  - Network and system protection for network and system engineers
- *Other messaging*. In addition to training, messages of other forms need to be periodically made available to employees, including:
  - E-mail
  - Posters and flyers
  - Promotions

  - Voice mails
  - Incentive programs
- *Testing*. In addition to providing educational material on security and asset protection, many employers also test employees to assess their knowledge. Employees may even be required to attain a minimum test score or be required to repeat security training.

Chapter Summary

- An organization's security program should support the organization's mission, objectives, and goals.
- *Risk management* is the process of determining the acceptable level of risk and the use of risk assessment and mitigation to reduce risk to an acceptable level.
- The core principles of information security are *confidentiality*, *integrity*, and *availability*.
- *Defense in depth* is a technique of using a layered defense to protect an asset.
- A *single point of failure* is the characteristic of a component in a system if the failure of the component will result in the failure of the system.
- *Fail open* is the characteristic of a control to permit all accesses when the control fails.
- *Fail closed* is the characteristic of a control to block all access when the control fails.
- *Privacy* is related to the protection of private information associated with private citizens.
- Executive oversight is needed for the support of policies, allocation of resources, and support of risk.
- *Security governance* is the set of responsibilities and practices related to the development of strategic direction and risk management.
- *Security policies* specify the required characteristics of information systems and the required conduct of employees.
- *Security requirements* specify required characteristics of information systems and processes and are usually used during systems development and acquisitions.
- *Guidelines* are statements that specify how security requirements may be carried out.
- *Standards* specify the types of systems, tools, technologies, configurations, and architectures used in an organization.
- *Procedures* are the step-by-step instructions used to perform tasks.
- Security-related roles and responsibilities are defined in security policies and job descriptions.
- Security roles and responsibilities define the ownership, access, and use of assets, and the general responsibilities of managers and employees.
- *Service level agreements (SLAs)* are formal statements that specify levels of service provided by a service organization.
- An organization that *outsources* information systems or business processes needs to ensure that its intellectual property, service levels, and operational integrity are adequately protected.

- A *data classification* and protection policy defines levels of sensitivity for business information, as well as handling procedures for each level of sensitivity.
- *Certification* is the process of evaluating a system against a set of evaluation criteria.
- *Accreditation* is the act of permitting the use of a certified system.
- *Internal audit* is the activity of evaluating security controls and policies to measure their effectiveness.
- Management is responsible for the development of security strategies, in order to maintain and improve security-related activities in the organization.
- An organization's hiring process should include the use of non-disclosure, employment, non-compete, intellectual property, and acceptable use agreements, as well as background checks.
- An *employee handbook* should highlight all terms and conditions of employment.
- Job descriptions should explain all responsibilities and requirements for each position in the organization.
- Upon termination of employment, the organization should retrieve all assets issued to the terminated employee and immediately rescind the employee's access to all information systems.
- Sound work practices include separation of duties, job rotation, and mandatory vacations.
- A security education, training, and awareness program should keep employees regularly informed of their expectations.

Key Terms

Accreditation The process of formally approving the use of a system.

Annual loss expectancy (ALE) The yearly estimate of loss of an asset, calculated as ALE = ARO × SLE.

Annualized rate of occurrence (ARO) The probability that a loss will occur in a year's time.

Asset An object of value to the organization. An asset may be a physical object such as a computer, or it can be information.

Availability The concept that asserts that information systems can be accessed and used when needed.

Background verification The process of verifying an employment candidate's employment, education, criminal, and credit history.

Certification The process of evaluating a system against a specific criterion or specification.

CIA Confidentiality, integrity, and availability.

Classification See *data classification.*

Confidentiality The concept of information and functions being protected from unauthorized access and disclosure.

Countermeasure A control or means to reduce the impact of a threat or the probability of its occurrence.

Data classification The process of assigning sensitivity levels to documents and data files in order to assure their safekeeping and proper handling.

Defense in depth A strategy for protecting assets that relies upon several layers of protection. If one layer fails, other layers will still provide some protection.

Destruction The process of discarding information in a way that renders it non-retrievable.

Employee handbook A formal document that defines terms and conditions of employment.

Employment agreement A legal agreement that specifies terms and conditions of employment for an individual employee.

Exposure factor (EF) The proportion of an asset's value that is likely to be lost through the realization of a particular threat.

Fail closed The characteristic of a security control—upon failure, it will deny all access.

Fail open The characteristic of a security control—upon failure, it will permit all access.

Fail safe See *fail closed.*

Fail soft The process of shutting down nonessential components on a system, thereby freeing up resources so that critical components can continue operating.

Governance The entire scope of activities related to the management of policies, procedures, and standards.

Guideline Information that describes how a policy may be implemented.

Insourcing The practice of using internal staff to perform a business function.

Integrity The concept of asserting that information may be changed only by authorized persons and means.

Intellectual property agreement A legal agreement between an employee and an organization that defines ownership of intellectual property (IP) that the employee may develop during employment.

Internal audit The activity of self-evaluation of controls and policies to measure their effectiveness.

Job description A formal document that defines a particular job title, responsibilities, duties, and required experience.

Job rotation The practice of rotating personnel through a variety of roles in order to reduce the risk of unauthorized activities.

Labeling The process of affixing a sensitivity identifier to a document or data file.

Marking See *labeling.*

Non-compete agreement A legal agreement that stipulates terms and conditions regarding whether the employee may accept employment with a competing organization in the future.

Non-disclosure agreement (NDA) A legal agreement that requires one or both parties to maintain confidentiality.

Offer letter A formal letter from an organization to an employment candidate that offers employment under a basic set of terms.

Offshoring The use of internal or external staff in another country.

Onshoring The use of internal or external staff within a country.

Outsourcing A business arrangement where an organization contracts out a business process, which was previously performed internally, to another organization.

Personally identifiable information (PII) Items associated with an individual such as name, passport number, driver's license number, and social security number.

Policy An official statement that establishes plans, boundaries, and constraints on the behavior of information systems and employees.

Privacy The protection of sensitive information associated with individuals.

Procedure Step-by-step instructions for performing a task.

Requirements Statements of necessary characteristics of an information system.

Residual risk The risk that remains after countermeasures are applied.

Risk acceptance A form of risk treatment where an identified risk is accepted as is.

Risk assessment The process of examining a system or process to identify potential risks.

Risk avoidance A form of risk treatment where the activity associated with an identified risk is discontinued, thereby avoiding the risk.

Risk management The strategic activities related to the identification of risks through risk assessment and the subsequent treatment of identified risks.

Risk mitigation See *risk reduction.*

Risk reduction A form of risk treatment where an identified risk is reduced through countermeasures.

Risk transfer A form of risk treatment where an identified risk is transferred to another party, typically through an insurance policy.

Security awareness training A formal education program that teaches security principles and expected behavior to employees.

Security management Activities related to the development and implementation of security policies and controls.

Security policy A branch of organizational policy that defines security-related controls and behaviors.

Sensitivity level A category of information sensitivity in an information classification scheme.

Separation of duties The work practice where important tasks are structured to be carried out by two or more persons.

Service level agreement (SLA) Formal statement that specifies level of service provided by a service organization.

Single loss expectancy (SLE) The cost of a single loss through the realization of a particular threat. This is a result of the calculation SLE = asset value × exposure factor (EF).

Single point of failure A component in a system that lacks a redundant or backup counterpart; the failure of the component will cause the failure of the entire system.

Standard A statement that specifies the brand, model, protocol, technology, or configuration of a system.

Termination The cessation of employment for an employee.

Threat A potential activity that would, if it occurred, exploit a vulnerability in a system.

Vulnerability A weakness in a system that may permit the realization of a threat.

Review Questions

1. An organization that needs to understand vulnerabilities and threats needs to perform a:
   a. Penetration test
   b. Business impact analysis
   c. Qualitative risk assessment
   d. Quantitative risk assessment
2. A risk manager has performed a risk analysis on a server that is worth \$120,000. The risk manager has determined that the single loss expectancy is \$100,000. The exposure factor is:
   a. 83%
   b. 1.2
   c. 80%
   d. 120%
3. A risk manager has performed a risk analysis on a server that is worth \$120,000. The single loss expectancy (SLE) is \$100,000, and the annual loss expectancy (ALE) is \$8,000. The annual rate of occurrence (ARO) is:
   a. 12.5
   b. 92%
   c. 8
   d. 8%
4. A risk manager needs to implement countermeasures on a critical server. What factors should be considered when analyzing different solutions?
   a. Original annualized loss expectancy (ALE)
   b. Annualized loss expectancy (ALE) that results from the implementation of the countermeasure
   c. Original exposure factor (EF)
   d. Original single loss expectancy (SLE)
5. The general approaches to risk treatment are:
   a. Risk acceptance, risk avoidance, and risk reduction
   b. Risk acceptance, risk reduction, and risk transfer
   c. Risk acceptance, risk avoidance, risk reduction, and risk transfer
   d. Risk analysis, risk acceptance, risk reduction, and risk transfer

6. CIA refers to:
    a. Confidence, integrity, and audit of information and systems
    b. Confidentiality, integrity, and assessment of information and systems
    c. Confidentiality, integrity, and availability of information and systems
    d. Cryptography, integrity, and audit of information and systems
7. A recent failure in a firewall resulted in all incoming packets being blocked. This type of failure is known as:
    a. Fail open
    b. Access failure
    c. Circuit closed
    d. Fail closed
8. The definition of PII:
    a. Is name, date of birth, and home address
    b. Is name, date of birth, home address, and home telephone number
    c. Is name, date of birth, and social insurance number
    d. Varies by jurisdiction and regulation
9. The statement, "All financial transactions are to be encrypted using 3DES" is an example of a:
    a. Procedure
    b. Guideline
    c. Standard
    d. Policy
10. The purpose of information classification is:
    a. To establish procedures for safely disposing of information
    b. To establish procedures for the protection of information
    c. To establish procedures for information labeling
    d. To establish sensitivity levels for information
11. An organization is concerned that its employees will intentionally reveal its secrets to other parties. The organization should implement:
    a. Document marking
    b. Non-disclosure agreements
    c. Logon banners
    d. Security awareness training

12. The purpose of a background verification is to:
    a. Obtain independent verification of claims on an employment application
    b. Determine if the applicant should be hired
    c. Determine if the applicant is suitable for the job description
    d. Determine the applicant's honesty
13. When an employee is terminated from employment, the employee's access to computers should be terminated:
    a. At the next monthly audit
    b. At the next quarterly audit
    c. Within seven days
    d. Within one day
14. Security awareness training should be:
    a. Mandatory for information workers only
    b. Optional
    c. Provided at the time of hire and annually thereafter
    d. Provided at the time of hire
15. Management in an organization regularly reassigns employees to different functions. This practice is known as:
    a. Job rotation
    b. Reassignment
    c. Separation of duties
    d. Due diligence

Hands-On Projects

Project 1-1: Defense in Depth Network Design

In this project you will design a new network infrastructure for a five-hundred-employee law firm. The design of the network should incorporate several elements that demonstrate a defense in depth architecture.

The design of the network should incorporate protection against the following threats:

- Malicious software
- Phishing
- Spam
- Leakage of intellectual property

- Non-company-owned devices on the internal network ("bring your own device," or BYOD)
- Rogue access points

For each type of threat, indicate the controls or features in the architecture that reduce or eliminate the threat.

This project is not so much about network technology as it is about the concept of defense in depth. Do not worry about whether you have incorporated the latest or the most precisely correct technologies in your design.

Project 1-2: Data Sensitivity Procedures

In this project you will develop data sensitivity procedures.

1. Develop a matrix with three columns, one for each of three levels of increasing sensitivity. Choose easily understood titles for each level.
2. The rows of the matrix should consist of various data-handling activities including:
   - E-mail
   - Fax
   - Courier
   - Laptop computer
   - Hard copy
3. The cells of the matrix should specify whether the activity is permitted (for instance, if the most sensitive documents are permitted to be faxed) and, if so, under what conditions.
4. Opine on the matter of the number of sensitivity levels: how few or how many are needed, and how realistic is it to expect employees in an organization to be able to understand the classification levels and the procedures for protecting information at each level.

Project 1-3: Security Awareness Training

In this project you will develop an outline for a security awareness training plan for a thousand-employee company. You are to determine:

1. What training new employees should receive upon hire.
2. What written materials should be issued to new employees.
3. What materials should be available on an intranet site.
4. What types of security awareness messages should be issued to employees.

5. What specialized training should be available to IT personnel.
6. What recordkeeping for training should take place.

Case Projects

Case Project 1-1: Qualitative Risk Assessment

As a consultant with the Risk Analysis Consulting Co., you have been asked to perform a qualitative risk assessment for the TRC Chemical Company.

TRC Chemical has a large outside sales force, numbering in the hundreds. Most of these employees use their own home computers (70% laptops, 30% desktops) to conduct TRC Chemical business. You have been asked to assess the risks associated with the use of home computers versus company-owned and -managed computers.

Case Project 1-2: Quantitative Risk Assessment

As a consultant with the Risk Analysis Consulting Co., you have completed a qualitative risk assessment regarding the risks associated with using non-company-owned computers to conduct company business. Your customer, TRC Chemical, is pleased with the results of the qualitative risk assessment and wants to see hard numbers to see whether it can justify the capital and expense burden of equipping the sales force with company-owned computers, based upon risk mitigation alone.

In your risk assessment, make best estimates on the value of information and costs associated with purchasing and supporting company-owned computers.

Case Project 1-3: Segregation of Duties Matrix

As a consultant with the Risk Analysis Consulting Co., you have been asked to help the BBX Internet Stock Trading Company develop a viable segregation of duties for the management of its online software and supporting infrastructure.

The activities that BBX is concerned with include:

- Request and assignment of privileged access at the network, operating system, database, and application layers
- Setup of new customers
- Changes to audit alert settings

For each of the activities listed above, develop a segregation of duties matrix where different parts of each process are performed by different individuals. Things to consider:

- Separate the activity of requesting an action from performing the action.
- Add an activity of confirming correct completion of the action.
- Include any recordkeeping for the action so that an auditor can examine the action after the fact to see if the action was appropriately carried out.

Topics in This Chapter:

- Identification and Authentication
- Centralized Access Control
- Decentralized Access Control
- Access Provisioning Life Cycle
- Access Control Attacks
- Testing Access Controls

Access control is the general term in information technology that encompasses the various methods used to control who (and what) is permitted to access specific information and perform specific functions.

The $(ISC)^2$ *Common Body of Knowledge* (CBK) defines the key areas of knowledge for access controls in this way:

Access control covers mechanisms by which a system grants or revokes the right to access data or perform an action on an information system.

Access Control systems include:

- *File permissions, such as "create," "read," "edit," or "delete" on a file server.*
- *Program permissions, such as the right to execute a program on an application server.*
- *Data rights, such as the right to retrieve or update information in a database.*

CISSP candidates should fully understand access control concepts, methodologies and their implementation within centralized and decentralized environments across an organization's computing environment.

Key areas of knowledge:

- *Control access by applying concepts/methodologies/techniques*
- *Understand access control attacks*
- *Assess effectiveness of access controls*
- *Identify and access provisioning lifecycle (e.g., provisioning, review, revocation)*

Controlling Access to Information and Functions

Computer systems, databases, and storage and retrieval systems contain information that has some monetary or intrinsic value. For this reason, the organization will take steps to control access to the information that it has collected and stored.

Access controls are used to control access to information and functions. In simplistic terms, the steps undertaken are something like this:

1. *Authentication*: Reliably identify the subject (e.g., the person, program, or system);
2. Find out what object (e.g., information or function) the subject wishes to access;
3. *Authorization*: Determine whether the subject is allowed to access the object;
4. *Access*: Permit (or deny) the subject's access to the object;
5. *Accounting*: Log the access that was requested.

The actual practice of access control is far more complex than these five steps. This is due primarily to the high-speed, automated, complex, and distributed nature of information systems. Even in simple environments, information often exists in many forms and locations, and yet these systems must somehow interact and quickly retrieve and render the desired information, without violating any access rules that are in place. These same systems must also be able to quickly distinguish "friendly" accesses from hostile and unfriendly attempts to access—or even alter—this same information.

The success of an access control system is completely dependent upon the effectiveness of the business processes that support it. User access provisioning, review, and revocation are key activities that ensure only authorized persons may have access to information and functions.

The remainder of this chapter examines these topics in detail.

Identification and Authentication

Whenever a person, a program, or another computer wants to contact an information system for the purpose of adding information, retrieving information, or performing some function, the information system being contacted first wants to identify the subject that is making the contact. There are two primary reasons that the contacted information system does this:

- So that the contacted information system can associate any accesses or transactions with the identity of the requesting person or system. Systems and applications usually have transaction logs or audit logs that list the events that took place, and such logs almost always associate events with the subjects that performed them.
- So that the contacted information system can verify that the requested activity is permitted.

The two principal terms that need to be defined are *identification* and *authentication.*

- **Identification** is the unproven assertion of an identity.
- **Authentication** is the assertion of an identity that is confirmed through some means such as a **password** (a secret word or phrase) or access **token**.

Information systems often use *levels* of identification and authentication when interacting with users. Here is an example: a web site distinguishes new visitors from returning visitors through the use of cookies. The web site prompts the user for a password before the user is permitted to view sensitive information such as an account profile or an order history. The web site may prompt the user *again* before approving a transaction such as a purchase, to ensure that the user performing the transaction is the same person who provided a userid and password earlier.

Authentication Methods While most information systems authenticate users through a userid and password, there are other methods in wide use. Conceptually, information systems authenticate users by challenging the user in one or more of three ways:

- What the user *knows*. Known as knowledge-based authentication, this method requires the user to input information that the user has committed to memory or has written down. Typically this consists of a userid and password or a userid and **personal identification number (PIN)**. The weakness with this type of authentication is that the information that the user knows can be guessed by others, or it may be written down and subsequently discovered by other persons. The advantage of this type of authentication is that it is usually inexpensive and easy to implement.
- What the user *has*. Known as possession-based authentication, this form of authentication relies on something that the user has in his or her possession. This type of authentication, when combined with one of the other methods, is often called **two-factor authentication** or **strong authentication** because it relies on two factors: what the user *knows* and what the user *has*. Examples of two-factor authentication include

smart card, token, and **USB key** (described in more detail later in this section). In order to log in to an information system, the user must know information such as a userid and password, and the user must also have the physical object (the token, USB key, or smart card) in his or her possession and use it properly. The disadvantage of this type of authentication is that it's more costly to implement, and users sometimes damage or lose their devices. Sometimes, users store their authentication devices with their notebook computers, and when the notebook computer is stolen, the authentication device is stolen along with it. The advantage of strong authentication is that the information system is much more difficult to break into without possession of the authentication device.

- What the user *is*. Known as entity-based authentication, this type of authentication involves some form of **biometric** device, used to measure a characteristic of the user's body such as a fingerprint, hand scan, signature, iris scan, facial scan, voice, and so on. The intention of biometrics is to ensure that only the designated person will be able to access an information system, even if a user's userid and password have been compromised.

Strong authentication and biometrics are described in more detail later in this chapter.

How Information Systems Authenticate Users Most information systems authenticate users by requesting their userid and password. This is usually done through an interactive dialog that the information system presents to the user on a screen. The user types in his or her userid in the spaces provided, like the login dialog shown in Figure 2-1.

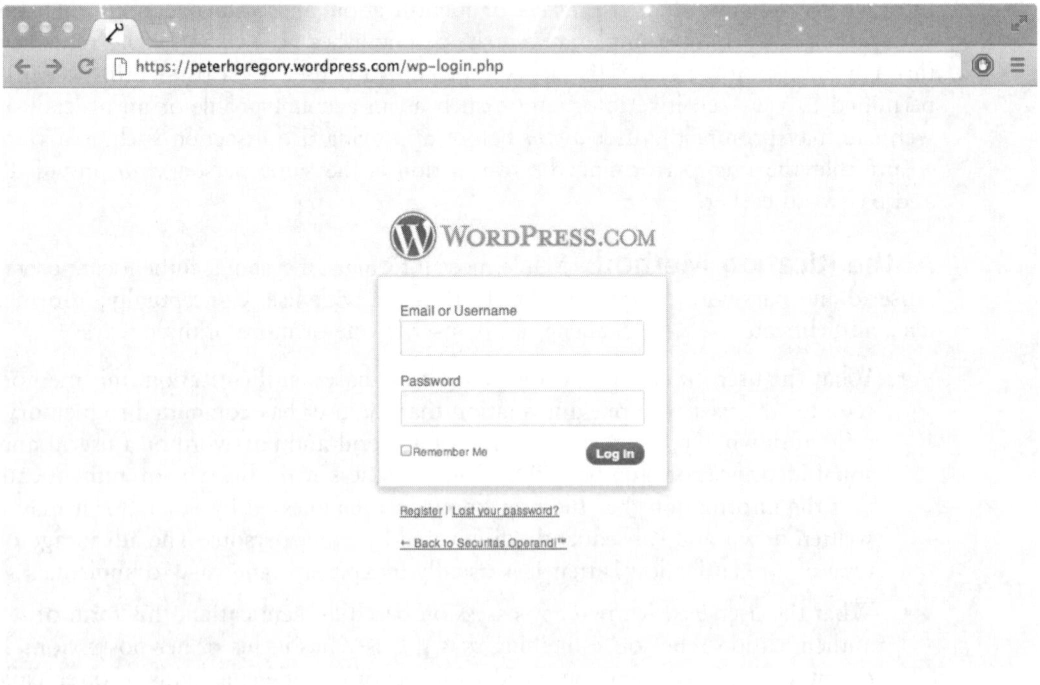

Figure 2-1 User login screen

Source: WordPress.com

After the user presents his or her credentials, the system verifies the userid and password by looking up the information in one of several ways, including:

- Looking up the userid and password in a stored file or database table
- Making a request to an authentication service that may be present on the same system, or to a centralized authentication service elsewhere

If the userid and password match, then the system permits the user to perform whatever permitted functions have been configured for that user. If the userid and password do not match, the system will display a message that tells the user that the userid or password is incorrect.

How a User Should Treat Userids and Passwords A user's userid may be known to other persons. For instance, in an e-mail system, a user's userid may be their e-mail address. In many cases, userids must be known so that user interaction may take place.

While userids are usually well known, users are always required to keep their passwords secret. When a user keeps the password a secret, other users are unable to use that user's account without first guessing the password. This and other issues related to authentication are discussed later in this chapter.

How a System Stores Userids and Passwords Because passwords are supposed to be secret, they must be stored with a greater degree of protection than other information. Generally, a password is stored in an **encrypted** (a reversible process of scrambling the data to make it unreadable) or **hashed** (a process similar to encryption that is irreversible) form, so that someone (such as a database administrator) who has access to the information where passwords are stored will not be able to see users' passwords. The preferred method for storing passwords is hashing, a method for storing information that makes it impossible for anyone to know the password.

Hashing is a cryptographic algorithm where the bits in the password are subjected to a mathematical algorithm that transforms the cleartext password into a hash value. The system stores only the ciphertext. Then, when a user logs into the system, the system hashes the password that the user typed in and compares it to the stored hash. If the two hashes are equal, then we know that the user typed in the password correctly. If the two hashes are not equal, then the user typed in the wrong password.

In order to resist compromise, a "salt" is usually added to the password during the hashing operation. This makes it more difficult for an intruder (e.g., someone who is able to steal a system's userids and hashed passwords) to determine users' passwords through an attack on the hashing algorithm. For more information, see the Cryptanalysis section in Chapter 5, "Cryptography."

Possession-Based Authentication **Possession-based authentication** involves the use of a hardware device or nontransferrable digital certificate that is required to complete the authentication process. Often known as *token authentication*, the advantage of possession-based authentication is its improved resistance to compromise over knowledge-based authentication, which is more easily compromised through someone else obtaining a userid and password. It is not so simple to obtain another person's hardware token, especially over great distance.

Possession-based authentication is sometimes referred to as two-factor authentication, but this is not necessarily true. Two-factor authentication is discussed later in this chapter in the Multi-Factor Authentication section.

There are several types of possession-based authentication, including:

- ***Digital certificate***. A user's workstation or USB key contains a digital certificate that must be present for the user to log in. The certificate can be constructed with elements that identify both the user and the workstation, so that the certificate cannot function in any other workstation. Like other types of two-factor authentication, the user is also required to furnish a userid and password.
- *Smart card*. A credit card-sized plastic card that contains a microchip that stores a digital certificate or other identifying information.
- *Password token*. A small fob device that displays a passcode that changes periodically, usually every minute. When the user logs on, he must supply a userid, password, and the passcode that is present on the token.
- *USB token*. A small USB key contains a digital certificate or other information. The token must be inserted into a USB port on the workstation to permit the user to log on. The user is still required to furnish a userid and password.
- *Software token*. A software program running on a device such as a smartphone or mobile device simulates the behavior of a password token. When a user logs on, he or she invokes the software token program and provides the passcode displayed to the system.
- *Text message to registered device*. A user logs on to a system, providing a userid and password. The system then sends a text message to a preregistered mobile device, which the user then provides to the system to complete authentication.

The distinct advantage of possession-based authentication is the additional difficulty presented to an intruder who wishes to enter a system through the "front door." There are also some disadvantages of possession-based authentication that organizations need to consider, including:

- *Implementation cost*. The costs associated with implementing possession-based authentication may be greater than userid-and-password solutions. Additional costs include:
  - Tokens, smart cards, or other hardware
  - Hardware to support the two-factor hardware (e.g., smart card readers)
  - Software license fees
  - Time and effort to provision and train each user
- *Increased support cost*. Until they are accustomed to their operation, users will call with questions when they have difficulty logging in.
- *Lost and damaged devices*. Hardware and USB tokens may be lost or damaged and will need to be replaced. This will be logistically more challenging when users are located in remote places.

These costs all need to be factored in so that an organization that is considering possession-based authentication will have more realistic expectations and a higher satisfaction rate for management and users.

Biometric Authentication Organizations that are not satisfied with the additional security afforded by knowledge- or possession-based authentication may consider biometric authentication, which is often called entity-based authentication or *biometrics*. Biometrics, which are also considered a form of two-factor or strong authentication, measure a physical or physiological characteristic of the end user in order to identify whether the person requesting entry to an information system or facility is who he or she claims to be.

There are several forms of biometrics, including:

- *Fingerprint reader*. Reads a user's fingerprint.
- *Palm scan*. Reads the geometry of a user's entire hand, primarily the angle and length of the fingers.
- *Iris scan*. Reads the image of a user's iris.
- *Facial scan*. Reads key geometric dimensions of a user's face, primarily the position of facial bones.
- *Handwriting (signature) scan*. There are several forms of handwriting biometrics, including a) recognition of the signature image, b) measurement of the pen motions used to write a signature, and c) measurement of the pressure of a stylus on a writing pad when a user writes his or her signature.
- *Retina scan*. Reads the image of a user's retina.
- *Voice recognition*. Measurement of a user's voice patterns.

The single greatest advantage of biometrics is that while an intruder can obtain a user's userid and password, and even an authentication device, it is exceedingly difficult for an intruder to obtain or impersonate a physical or physiological characteristic of any particular user.

Still, there are some disadvantages and challenges associated with the use of biometrics, including:

- *Costs for implementation and maintenance*. Biometric systems are often complex and have capital costs, implementation costs, and ongoing costs associated with them. These need to be taken into account to ensure that the organization is not spending $100,000 to protect a $10,000 asset.
- *Gradual changes in users' characteristics*. No matter what biometric methods are used, it's an accepted fact that the measured characteristics change slowly over time. For instance, a person's signature and voice gradually change over time, as do iris scans.
- *Sudden changes in users' characteristics*. A user's voice may change quickly if they are suffering from an upper respiratory infection or yelled too much at last night's soccer game. A home hobby project such as sanding may scuff up a user's hands enough to confuse a fingerprint reader.
- *False readings*. This is explained below.

Biometric systems are known to sometimes reject valid users and sometimes accept invalid users. The formal terms for these are:

- ***False Reject Rate (FRR)***. This is how often a biometric system will reject a valid user.
- ***False Accept Rate (FAR)***. This is how often a biometric system will accept an invalid user.

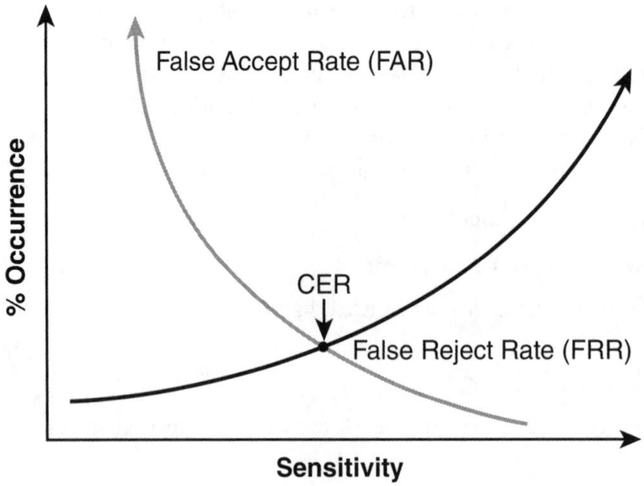

Figure 2-2 Biometric crossover error rate

- *Crossover Error Rate (CER)*. This is the point where the False Reject Rate and the False Accept Rate are equal. The smaller the CER, the more accurate and reliable the biometric system will be.

The relationships of FRR, FAR, CER, and sensitivity are illustrated in Figure 2-2.

When tuning a biometric system, the error rate must be as low as possible in order to ensure reliability and usability. If the error rate is too high, users of the system will complain and attempt to bypass or manipulate the system.

Multi-Factor Authentication **Multi-factor authentication** involves the use of two or more authentication methods (knowledge-based, possession-based, or entity-based, which are described earlier in this section). It is considerably more difficult for an intruder to break into an environment's authentication when multi-factor authentication is used. This is because the intruder, in addition to knowing a userid and password, must also have in his or her possession the hardware device or body part that is also required for a user to successfully authenticate.

Other common terms for multi-factor authentication are **two-factor authentication** and **strong authentication.**

Here is a physical world analogy: personnel are required to key in a six-digit key code to enter a building. This is functionally similar to entering a userid and password in an information system. But if personnel were also required to insert a smart card to enter the building, this would be similar to a two-factor authentication for an information system. While an intruder may be able to obtain an employee's key code, the intruder would have to also obtain the employee's smart card in order to successfully enter the facility.

The preceding analogy simplifies access controls somewhat. The example does not, for instance, discuss whether an intruder can gain access to the facility by breaking in and bypassing the entry controls altogether. These are also valid concerns for information systems, where intruders can attempt to bypass security controls and use other means to gain illicit entry. This is discussed in more detail later in this chapter in the Access Control Attacks section.

Authentication Issues Authentication systems request identifying information from users in order to permit access to legitimate users and deny access to invalid users. Authentication systems don't always work right, and users don't always operate them correctly. In short, things can and do go wrong. Some of the significant issues include:

- *Password quality*. Each organization needs to establish standards for password quality. Passwords need to be complex enough to prevent brute force password attacks, but not so complex that users resort to writing down passwords and leave them where they are easily discovered.
- *Forgotten credentials*. Users sometimes forget their userids and passwords. There needs to be some way for users to recover or reset these items so that they can access the systems they need.
- *Compromised credentials*. Organizations need a way to know when a user's credentials have been compromised (that is, exposed to any third party, which greatly increases the risk of unauthorized entry) and be able to quickly reset credentials or temporarily restrict compromised users' access to systems.
- *Staff terminations*. Regardless of the circumstances related to a user's termination from an organization, those users' credentials must be quickly rescinded so that the user may no longer access systems and information.

These and other issues present themselves in every environment where authentication is required to access information.

Access Control Technologies and Methods

Several technologies and methods are in more-or-less common use for authenticating users to systems and applications. Authentication is such a common feature in information systems that virtually no one tries to invent a technology any more, but instead supports one or more of the standard technologies and methods that are already available. Those that are discussed in this chapter are:

- Single Sign-On
- Reduced Sign-On
- LDAP
- Active Directory
- RADIUS
- Diameter
- TACACS
- Kerberos

Single Sign-On **Single sign-on**, or SSO, is an access control method whereby a user can authenticate once and be able to access many different information systems without having to reauthenticate into each one separately.

In SSO, applications and systems are logically connected to a centralized authentication service that controls user authentication. When a user first logs in to an application, the user will be required to provide a userid and password or multi-factor credentials. The application—and the centralized service—will recognize the user as being logged in. Later, when the user wishes to access a different application or system, the user's logged-in state will be recognized and directly admitted to the next application.

The advantage of SSO is the convenience of eliminating many redundant logins for busy end users, and the centralized management of access for many applications and systems. A distinct disadvantage of SSO is that a user's compromised login credentials means that an intruder will have access to all of the applications and systems that the user also has access to.

Reduced Sign-On SSO is similar to **reduced sign-on**, an authentication method where many applications and systems in an organization will utilize a centralized user management service such as LDAP or Active Directory. However, applications and the centralized service will not manage the logged-in state, which means that users will have to log in to each application and system using their single userid and password.

LDAP Lightweight Directory Access Protocol, commonly known as **LDAP** (and pronounced "el-dap"), is an open standard that is defined in **RFC** 4510 (RFCs, or "Request for Comments," are the documents that describe the Internet's technical and procedural standards).

LDAP is a TCP/IP-based communications protocol that is used for various directory purposes, including authentication. LDAP is also a data storage model that provides specific methods for storing directory-type information. Because it is an open standard, LDAP is very popular and is the basis for a number of commercial products, including Microsoft **Active Directory**. Other commercial LDAP server products include:

- Apache Directory Server
- Apple Open Directory
- Fedora Directory Server
- IBM Tivoli Directory Server
- Novell eDirectory
- OpenDS
- OpenLDAP
- Oracle Directory Server Enterprise Edition
- Oracle Internet Directory
- Penrose
- SIDVault

Active Directory Microsoft Active Directory is a commercial implementation of LDAP. "AD," as it is commonly called, is built into Microsoft server operating systems and is tightly coupled with Microsoft's workstation and domain authentication and also Exchange e-mail.

RADIUS The Remote Authentication Dial In User Service, or **RADIUS**, is a UDP-based authentication protocol that traces its origins to dial-up remote access. Another popular use for RADIUS is centralized control of authentication for network devices such as routers.

RADIUS is described in RFCs 2865 and 2866.

Like LDAP, there are many open source and commercial implementations of RADIUS servers available.

Diameter Diameter is an authentication protocol similar to RADIUS. The name is a pun on RADIUS (in geometry, a circle's diameter is twice the radius) and provides an upgrade path for RADIUS. Diameter has several advantages over RADIUS, including:

- Diameter uses the more reliable TCP protocol instead of UDP.
- A Diameter session can be encrypted with SSL (TLS).

RADIUS and Diameter are not forwards or backwards compatible.

Diameter is described in RFC 3588.

TACACS Terminal Access Controller Access-Control System (TACACS, pronounced "tack-acks") is a remote access authentication protocol that permits a device to communicate to a central authentication server to determine whether a user should be permitted to log on to the device. TACACS is defined in RFC 1492.

TACACS has been largely replaced by TACACS+ and RADIUS. An RFC draft has been developed for TACACS+.

Kerberos Kerberos is a standard protocol that provides for mutual authentication (an end user and a Kerberos server authenticate each other) over a nonsecure network. There are several components in a Kerberos environment:

- *Client*. The workstation (usually) that desires to access systems or services
- *AS (authentication server)*. A centralized system to which a user initially authenticates
- *TGS (ticket granting server)*. A centralized system that issues tickets
- *SS (service server)*. A server that provides some useful service
- *TGT (ticket granting ticket)*. A token that permits access to an SS
- *ST (service ticket)*. An encrypted key

When a user wishes to log on to the network and access a service or application, the following steps are performed:

1. The client authenticates to the AS. This creates a user session that will expire, typically in eight hours.
2. The AS sends a TGT back to the client system.
3. The client sends the TGT to the TGS to get authenticated.
4. The TGS creates an encrypted key with an expiration time and sends it to the client.
5. The client sends the ST to an SS that the user wishes to access.
6. The SS confirms that the ST is still valid (by checking the expiration time). If the ST is valid, communication is established between the client and the server (SS).

The components that participate in Kerberos authentication are shown in Figure 2-3.

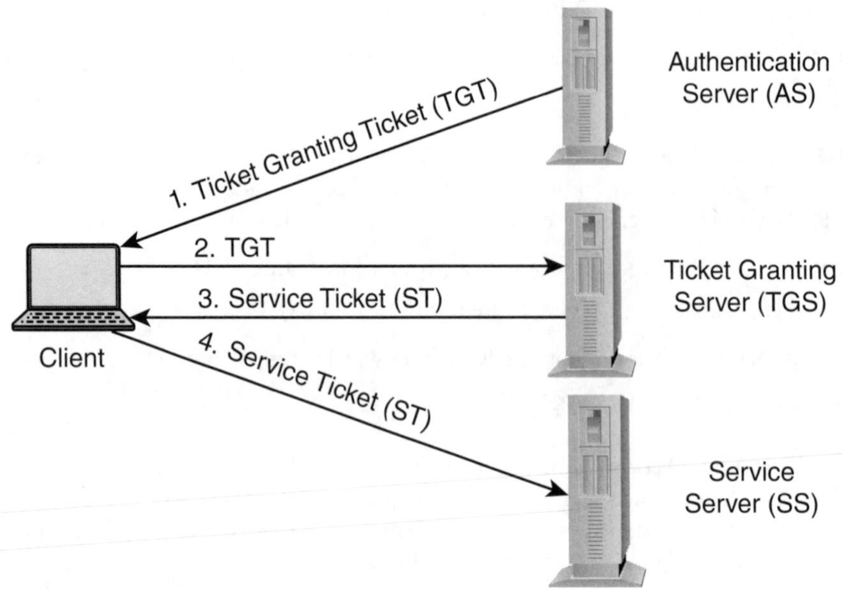

Figure 2-3 Kerberos authentication components

Access Control Attacks

Several methods can be used to attack a system's access control mechanism as a means for gaining access to the system. Usually the motivation for such an attack is to steal information, alter information, or gain access to functions. Persons who desire to launch an attack usually do not possess a working userid and password, so they must resort to an attack in order to access the desired information or function. The types of attacks include:

- Buffer overflow
- Script injection
- Data remanence
- Denial of service
- Dumpster diving
- Eavesdropping
- Emanations
- Spoofing and masquerading
- Social engineering
- Phishing, spear phishing, and whaling
- Pharming
- Password guessing
- Password cracking

- Rainbow tables
- Malicious code

Each of these attack methods is described in more detail in the remainder of this section.

Buffer Overflow

A **buffer overflow** attack is an attempt to cause a malfunction of an application by sending more data to a program than it was designed to handle properly, causing the program to malfunction or abort. If a program does not properly check input data, a too-long input string can fill the input buffer and overwrite other memory locations in the program.

Sometimes it is possible to insert specially crafted computer instructions into an input string that the program will begin to execute. This can cause the program to begin executing instructions of the attacker's choosing, which can result in a potentially devastating malfunction or security breach.

Buffer overflows are easily prevented by having all programs properly set up input variables and by limiting their bounds when they accept input. But much software was written in an era prior to buffer overflow being a serious threat, and much of this older software is still in circulation today.

Script Injection

A **script injection** attack (also known as *code injection*) is similar to a buffer overflow attack. Script injection occurs when software programs do not parse input data for script commands, and they inadvertently execute the script commands in subsequent processing steps.

A common form of script injection is known as **SQL injection**, whereby specially crafted SQL statements can be inserted into an input field, causing the database server on the back end to execute the injected SQL statements. This is aptly illustrated in a comic in Figure 2-4.

Like buffer overflow, script injection is an easily prevented attack, and yet there is much online software that does not properly detect and block attempts at script injection.

Figure 2-4 An SQL injection illustration

Image courtesy xkcd.com

Data Remanence

Data remanence refers to data that remains on a storage device, often unintentionally. Data can remain on a device even after a user "removes" the data. This data can fall into the hands of others, sometimes to the detriment of the original owner of the data.

A typical scenario is a company or individual who sells their computer to another party, who then discovers the prior owner's data still on the hard drive.

Some examples of data remanence include:

- *Deleted hard drive files*. Deleting files does not actually remove them, but only "dereferences" them. Tools are available to easily recover these files, often in their entirety. The contents of these "deleted" files may provide valuable clues to an attacker.
- *Data on slack space*. Slack space is the space on a hard drive between the end of the file and the end of the disk sector used by the file.
- *Erased hard drive files*. Even if tools are used to erase files, it may still be possible to recover them. This is particularly true on solid-state drives (SSDs), where file erasure is not as straightforward as on magnetic-based hard disk drives (HDDs).
- *Formatted hard drive*. Formatting a hard drive does not erase old data files. Tools are available to easily recover many files on a formatted hard drive.
- *Discarded CDs, memory cards, floppy discs, and backup tapes*. Important data can be present on other types of discarded media such as those listed here.

Denial of Service

An attack that disables a service or makes it unreachable to its users is a **denial-of-service (DoS)** attack. There are two primary ways of carrying out a DoS attack:

- Sending a flood of messages to a service that is so heavy that legitimate use of the service is all but impossible. This is usually achieved by sending a high volume of messages over a prolonged period of time. This type of attack can sometimes result in malfunctions of an application's operating system.
- Sending specially crafted messages that cause the application or service to malfunction or abort, making it unavailable for legitimate users.

A **distributed denial-of-service (DDoS)** attack is an attack launched from many places at once. The objective of a DDoS attack is to incapacitate a system or service in a way that is more difficult to block than an attack originating from a single location. A DoS attack that originates from a single system is easy to block by configuring a router to drop packets from the attacking system. However, a DDoS attack can simultaneously originate from thousands of systems, making it virtually impossible to block by any normal means.

Dumpster Diving

Some organizations are not careful about the printed matter that they discard. They throw documents containing sensitive information into recycling or trash bins. Someone who attempts to find discarded documents in the trash is **dumpster diving**.

In many jurisdictions, it is not illegal to rummage through someone else's garbage. Illegal or not, it is not a good practice to discard sensitive information into recycling or trash bins. Instead, documents with sensitive information should be shredded.

Eavesdropping

Eavesdropping takes many forms, but the effect is the same: people who desire sensitive information will attempt to obtain it by observing communications. Forms that eavesdropping takes include:

- *Network sniffing.* An intruder (who could be an employee or an outsider who has gained access to an internal system by some malicious means) can start a network **sniffing** program on a computer that will enable the capture and storage of all network traffic. Depending upon the architecture and technologies used in the network, an intruder can capture quite a lot of network traffic and possibly harvest some sensitive information that could be contained in e-mails, web browsing sessions, file transfers, and so on. Some older protocols such as Telnet and FTP do not encrypt userids and passwords as they traverse the network, which makes them especially vulnerable to sniffing.
- *Wireless network sniffing.* Many public WiFi hotspots employ no encryption, which means that all WiFi network traffic is being transmitted "in the clear," making it easy for an eavesdropper to capture and record for later analysis and use. A growing segment of the workforce is mobile, and workers often "hang out" at cafés and other venues with WiFi connectivity, much of which is unprotected.
- *Key logging.* An attacker can trick a user into installing software that records the user's keystrokes and sends them back to the attacker. Or, an attacker with physical access to a system may be able to install a hardware key logger (often a device that plugs into the keyboard cord). In either case, such an attack can result in an attacker obtaining login credentials and other sensitive information.
- *Shoulder surfing.* Someone who uses a laptop computer in a public location such as a restaurant, café, airport, train, or airplane is potentially exposing sensitive information on the screen to anyone who can see it. It is also easy to observe someone's typing, especially when they are typing in a password. If the user is using a complex password, they might be typing it more slowly, which can make it even easier for an observer to view.
- *Mobile calls and conversations in public places.* Some people have a naturally loud voice, making it easy for anyone nearby to overhear a conversation that may be sensitive in nature. Someone who wants to learn more about a big company just needs to hang out at a nearby coffee shop or restaurant to overhear conversations by people who are unaware that outsiders may be listening.

Emanations

Computer and network hardware devices employ high-speed electronics that can emanate electromagnetic radiation (EMR). Sometimes these **emanations** contain data that can be sensitive in nature. Three examples of EMR emanations are:

- *Network cabling.* Faulty or improperly terminated network cabling, particularly the coaxial type of cabling, can sometimes act like an antenna, broadcasting whatever data is being transmitted over the network.

- *Computer monitors*. The older CRT-type monitors can emit EMR containing information about what is being displayed on the monitor.
- *Processor chips*. A computer's central processing unit (CPU) can emanate EMR that may give an observer information about the data that the computer is processing. Recent research suggests that CPUs may even emit high-frequency sound that can also reveal much about the computer's processing.

TEMPEST is a code name for a U.S. military project dedicated to the study of **compromising emanations** (CE). The U.S. Army, the NSA, and agencies in other NATO countries have laboratories and certifications that are used to test systems to ensure that they do not emit compromising emanations that could result in the compromise of military secrets.

The process of intercepting emanations is considered an advanced form of eavesdropping.

Spoofing and Masquerading

An attack can be successful if the attacker pretends to be someone (or some*thing*) they are not. Weaknesses in the TCP/IP protocol make it fairly easy for a system to create messages that claim to be originating from any IP address. This **spoofing** can fool the target system into thinking that the messages are originating from a trusted system instead of from an untrusted system.

Network routers can be configured to repel some of these attacks by rejecting incoming messages that claim to be originating from inside the trusted network. Firewalls also help to mitigate this threat.

Because TCP/IP permits the creation of messages that claim to be originating from any IP address, systems should not authenticate incoming messages based only on their IP address. Instead, systems should use additional means for authenticating incoming messages to make sure that they are genuine.

Spoofing can take many other forms besides that of falsifying source IP addresses. An intruder can attempt to break in to a web application by stealing cookies from legitimate users. Stealing cookies is not particularly easy, but there have been vulnerabilities in web browsers that make end user workstations vulnerable to cookie theft. It's also quite easy to spoof the "from" address of an e-mail message, to give the appearance of having originated in a specific organization. This type of attack has aspects of social engineering, another type of attack discussed below.

Social Engineering

Many intruders are skilled at **social engineering**, a deceptive method of communicating with others by pretending to be fellow employees or business partners in need of some help. Because of humans' natural desire to help others (either for the intrinsic value of helping or from the good feeling that comes from helping another person in need), employees can sometimes easily be convinced that the stranger who is attempting to gather intelligence is actually a fellow colleague who needs assistance.

Social engineering can rely on other motivations besides helping people. Promises of money, favor, or just a look at an attractive person can be enough to trick someone into providing information or assistance to an intruder.

A social engineer may opt to make several contacts into an organization and get small bits of information from each person. One such social engineering scenario can go something like this:

1. The social engineer calls an IT employee, claiming to be another employee on travel, and asks for the URL for the VPN (remote access) server or external employee portal.
2. The social engineer calls another employee and asks for the e-mail address of a targeted employee. The intruder assumes that the part of the e-mail address preceding the '@' is the user's userid.
3. The social engineer calls another employee and asks for the targeted employee's cube number; he claims to have forgotten his cube number, and because he's on travel, he can't just get up and look.
4. The social engineer calls another employee and asks for the phone number for the IT helpdesk.
5. The social engineer calls the helpdesk, claiming to be the targeted employee (from step #2). He correctly identifies himself by providing his cube number. The social engineer claims to have forgotten his password and requests a password reset. He claims to be the targeted employee out on business travel in urgent need of information on a file server, and therefore cannot go through a typical password reset. He needs to have the new password so that he can log in to the VPN or external portal. Wanting to be the hero who helped, the helpdesk person willingly complies and provides the password. If he's particularly brazen, the social engineer might even verify the userid.

Assuming that the company does not use multi-factor authentication for their VPN, the information that the social engineer/intruder obtained from five people in a short space of time was enough for him to log on to the company VPN and then go anywhere inside the network where the real employee was allowed to go. The intruder could read and send e-mail messages on behalf of the targeted person and access file servers to harvest vast amounts of sensitive information.

Another form of social engineering involves incoming e-mail and is described in the next section.

Phishing

A spammer's frequent ruse is a **phishing** attack, which is the creation of forged e-mails that appear to have originated from a financial institution or other high-value organization. The forged e-mail will contain instructions that direct the recipient to click on a link and provide information on a form. The victim is led to believe that he or she is helping the institution by verifying sensitive credentials, when in reality the person is handing those credentials over to a criminal. Figure 2-5 shows a typical spam e-mail that attempts to lure users to a phishing site.

Spear phishing is a form of phishing where the attacker targets specific users or groups of users in phishing scams. **Whaling** is another form of phishing where attackers target top executives in an organization and attempt to lure them to fake web sites (or embed attachments with malicious code) to harvest sensitive information.

From: Internal Revenue Service (info@irs.gov)
To: user@some.domain.com
Date: Friday, December 7, 2013 2:30:53 AM
Subject: IRS Notification Tax refund

Tax Notification

Internal Revenue Service (IRS)
United States Department of the Treasury

Date: 11/24/2013

After the last annual calculations of your fiscal activity we have determined that you are eligible to receive a tax refund of **$1,734.80.**

Please submit the tax refund request and allow us 6–9 days in order to process it.

A refund can be delayed for a variety of reasons. For example submitting invalid records or applying after the deadline.

To access the form for your tax refund, Click here.

Regards,
Internal Revenue Service

Document Reference: (92054568).

Figure 2-5 Spam message that lures unsuspecting users to a phishing site

Pharming

In a **pharming** attack, an attacker directs traffic destined for a specific web site to an imposter site, usually for the purpose of harvesting logon credentials from unsuspecting users. The attack is directed at a DNS server, by exploiting one of several known vulnerabilities that permit the attacker to "poison" the DNS server with data that directs users to the imposter site. The attacker can also attack users' systems by planting a fraudulent entry in the system's *hosts* file.

Password Guessing

A common form of attack against an information system is an attempt to guess someone's legitimate logon credentials through a technique called **password guessing**. An intruder knows that easy entry to an information system is often no more difficult than the right combination of userid and password. There are a number of methods that an intruder may use, including:

- *Guessing*. The intruder may use a dictionary attack, where the most common passwords are tried, to see if the intruder can get lucky and gain entry into a target system. If the intruder is attempting to gain entry using a specific person's userid, the intruder can try and find out personal information about that person such as birth date, pet's name, and partner's name, and try combinations of these to gain entry to a system.
- *Brute force*. In a brute force attack, an intruder will try many passwords in hopes that one of them will work. A brute force attack typically consists of sequential guesses at a password until the correct value is found. This type of attack can take a long time, since there can be millions of possible passwords for a given user account.

Information systems now typically lock a user account after several unsuccessful attempts have been made to log in. This type of control helps to hinder password-guessing attacks by severely limiting the number of guesses that an intruder may use before the user account is locked.

Password Cracking

If an intruder is able to access the hashed passwords on a system, then the intruder may resort to **password cracking** to obtain those passwords. The intruder who is able to obtain hashed or encrypted passwords must then programmatically hash or encrypt every possible combination of characters until the hashed value from his guessed password matches the hashed passwords he obtained.

An advantage (from the intruder's point of view) of this type of attack is that the intruder can perform this password cracking on his own system. And while password cracking is resource intensive, it requires no resources on the target system and hence should not raise any alarms (associated with resource consumption) on the target system. When the intruder has successfully cracked a password, he or she can then easily use it to log on to the target system without any incorrect guesses that would otherwise result in a locked account.

A technique known as "salting" a hashed password makes password cracking more difficult.

Tools that are used for password cracking include *crack*, *L0phtcrack*, and *John the Ripper*. These tools are free and reliable.

Rainbow Tables

Intruders increasingly are relying upon rainbow tables for obtaining passwords. A **rainbow table** is a database containing every possible hash and its corresponding password.

Once considered large in size, a rainbow table fits on larger laptop hard drives. Equipped with a rainbow table, an intruder who has obtained a system's password hashes can almost instantaneously obtain passwords.

Rainbow tables enable an intruder to determine a system's passwords far more quickly than brute force tools such as crack and John the Ripper. However, the practice of "salting" hashes is an effective defense against rainbow table attacks.

Malicious Code

Malicious code—also known as **malware**—started with Creeper, Elk Cloner, and ©Brain and has taken on a life of its own in the years since. More often, malicious code is designed to exploit vulnerabilities in information system software, not for its own sake, but to achieve some objective such as stealing information or installing bot software that is used to remotely control the system later on.

There are several different forms of malicious code in circulation, including:

- *Viruses*. The original malware—viruses embed themselves in a DOS or Windows system .exe file and hide there until the user runs the .exe file, activating the virus code. Once active, the virus can attach itself to other .exe files and perform other interesting and harmful tricks on an end user's system.
- *Worms*. A worm does not embed itself in an executable file but instead exists as one or more separate, independent programs. Many worms can replicate automatically without human intervention, which has led to some worms infecting hundreds of thousands of systems within minutes of release.
- *Trojan horses. Click here for your income tax refund.* That is a common ploy that is used by virus writers to trick unsuspecting victims into running their malicious programs.

In the 1980s when viruses first became active, they most often circulated via floppy diskettes when users exchanged information with each other. In the 1990s, e-mail became the new preferred mode of travel, and some malicious code known as mass-mailing worms actively exploited e-mail programs to propagate themselves to all recipients in users' address books. Phishing attacks, malicious web sites, and watering hole attacks are now prevalent means for propagating malicious code.

While malicious code still propagates via executable files and e-mail, a lot of malicious code is transported via web browsers. Vulnerabilities in web browser programs and end user operating systems have given rise to a wave of web sites with built-in malicious code that is downloaded to unsuspecting victims who visit those sites. These are known as **watering hole attacks**, so named from a habit of some animal predators that simply wait at a watering hole for their prey to show up.

Malicious code is developed to spread via image files, Flash movies, PDF files, Zip archives, macros in documents and spreadsheets, instant messaging programs, and mobile devices. It seems as though every new type of device or communication technology is soon desecrated by malicious code that either exploits weaknesses in those technologies or simply uses them to move around.

Access Control Processes

In this section I discuss the business processes that support access control management activities.

An organization with excellent access control technologies must also have effective processes governing the use of those technologies. Organizations lacking effective access management processes soon find themselves in a situation where they have lost control of access to their systems.

The business processes discussed in this section include:

- Access requests and provisioning
- Internal transfer
- Termination
- Periodic access review
- Internal and external audit

Access Requests and Provisioning

Organizations of any size need to have a formal access request process. The purpose of this process is to document each request for access to information and other resources, including the reason for the access, as well as approvals and other details. The typical steps in a mature access request process are:

- *Request.* Here, the requestor specifies the subject(s) (persons or systems) and the objects (files, programs, networks, work locations, or other controlled resources) that the subject needs to access. Usually the reason for the access is also included. If the access is required only for a specific period of time, the start and end dates and times are included in the request.
- *Review.* The request is examined by one or more persons, to better understand the request and its purpose. Sometimes a reviewer will need to ask further questions of the requestor to better understand the nature and purpose of the request. A review might also include a "segregation of duties" check, to make sure that the new request does not result in a user having a combination of privileges that could permit the user to defraud the organization. Usually the discovery of a segregation of duties conflict will require additional approvals, or the access request must be withdrawn.
- *Approval.* The request is approved by one or more approvers. Depending upon the identity of the subject and the nature of the object, different approvers may be needed.
- *Provisioning.* When the request has been approved, the subject's access is provisioned. Access provisioning may be performed automatically, or it may be assigned to an individual who will perform the provisioning. Usually there are additional details recorded, such as the date and time of the provisioning, who performed the provisioning, and any details about the provisioning such as a userid and when it was given to the subject.

Usually the access request and provisioning processes are managed by an automated workflow system that is configured to select the appropriate approvers and provisioning personnel. Such a system might also perform automated provisioning.

Personnel Internal Transfers

When an employee moves from his or her current position into a different position, sometimes the result is that the employee will require additional access privileges to perform the new job. In such cases, the employee's access privileges for the former position will be removed. However, there are often circumstances that prohibit this removal right away: the employee may be completing work in the old position that requires continuation of access, there may be a trainee who needs assistance, or the old position may be unfilled, meaning the employee is performing both old and new duties. In any of these cases, organizations often forget to remove the employee's old privileges, resulting in the **accumulation of privileges** over time.

Personnel Termination

When an employee leaves the organization, the former employee's access privileges need to be revoked. Sometimes, organizations do not remove former employees' access soon enough, or they may forget to remove all of a former employee's privileges. This is a serious threat and, in some regulatory environments, organizations are subject to fines of up to $1 million per day if they are unable to remove terminated user accounts quickly.

Periodic Access Review

Even in organizations with effective automatic controls (and even more vital in organizations without them), access rights and records should be reviewed periodically.

These reviews may include several different types of tests, including:

- Verifying that terminations were processed on time.
- Verifying that individual users still require the access rights they have (this is called an **access rights recertification**).
- Looking for accounts that have been unused for an extended period of time (90 days is typical).
- Looking for combinations of access rights that would represent violations of *segregation of duties* rules.
- Looking for access rights that would exceed least privilege.

Internal and External Audit

Access management is such a vital activity that it is often the subject of audits, whether carried out by external auditors or by auditors within the organization. Usually, auditors will focus on a number of approaches, including:

- Examining records in information systems to see what access rights have been granted to users, and then examining access control request and approval records to see whether those granted access rights were properly requested and approved.
- Examining access request and approval records to see what access rights were approved, and then examining information systems to see whether those access rights were properly provisioned.
- Examining business records from Human Resources for employee terminations, and then examining information systems to see whether those access rights were terminated, and if those terminations were processed timely.

- Examining business records from Human Resources for employee transfers, and then examining information systems to see whether access rights in employees' old roles were terminated timely; or, in cases where old role access rights were extended, whether there is adequate documentation showing justification and approval.
- Examining access request and approval records to see whether requests, approvals, and provisioning were performed according to established policies and procedures.

While this may appear to be a lot of scrutiny for a single business process, it is important to understand that sloppiness in access control processes can have disastrous consequences. An organization whose internal or external auditors have found significant deficiencies should accept these findings and make improvements in processes and technologies as needed.

Access Control Concepts

Many terms and models are used to describe and classify access control. This section contains principles, types, and categories of controls.

Principles of Access Control

We need to step back and take a look at the big picture with regards to access control and authentication. The issue at stake is, *who and what are permitted access to which systems, data, and functions?* This is not so much a question about technology, but policy. Deciding which persons and systems (subjects) have access to what systems, data, and functions (objects) should be a business policy. Then the technology should be designed, configured, and operated to support that policy. Likewise, business processes must also align with policy—not the other way around.

Two important principles of access control are *separation of duties* and *least privilege.*

Separation of Duties The principle of **separation of duties** (which is sometimes known as *segregation of duties*) states that no single individual should have so many privileges that the individual is able to complete important technical or business functions on his or her own.

When a single individual is able to perform some important business functions, there is a potential for fraud or abuse. These functions should be divided into individual tasks that should be performed by separate individuals or groups.

Some examples of functions that should be divided into two or more roles are:

- *Creation of computer user accounts.* The functions of requesting a computer account, approval, and creation of a computer account should be performed by separate persons. The separation of duties in this example will reduce the chances of the creation of inappropriate user accounts. There should be additional approvals required for privileged or administrative accounts such as those used by system administrators or database administrators.
- *Financial payments.* In an accounting department, the functions of creating a new payee, requesting a payment, and making a payment should be done by separate

individuals. The separation of duties in this case will reduce the likelihood of fraudulent payments perpetrated by an individual employee.

- *Software changes*. Any change to software code should be formally requested by one individual, performed by another person, verified through a code review by another person, and tested by yet another person. The separation of duties here will reduce the chances of unauthorized code being released.

Least Privilege The principle of **least privilege** states that individuals should have access to *only* the systems, data, and functions that they *require* to perform their stated duties.

Least Privilege and Server Applications Least privilege does not apply just to people. Applications and service processes on a system should never be configured to run at root or administrative level, but instead at the lowest privilege possible. The primary reason for this is that an application malfunction or misconfiguration could harm the entire system if the application runs as root or administrator. But if an application is configured to run as a non-privileged user, then the application cannot harm the operating system or other users on the system. And if an attacker is able to compromise an application that runs with administrative privileges, then the attacker may be able to modify the underlying operating system.

User Permissions on File Servers and Applications Probably the most useful context to view least privilege is a workplace file server. Typically a file server is used to share files and directories among and between groups of users. It may be tempting to give all users access to all directories—this approach would incur almost zero overhead on system administrators—but this would be a blatant violation of least privilege.

Another approach to use is to give users access to nothing on the file server, and then add whatever specific accesses they may require. This would support the concept of least privilege, although this approach would incur a lot of support overhead, since every time a user needed access to some other file or directory, they would have to ask someone to permit this access. Yet another approach is the application of role-based access, which is discussed below.

Least Privilege on Workstations Another situation where least privilege is vitally important is end user workstations. Many versions of Microsoft Windows are configured for ordinary users to run with administrative privileges. This can result in great harm to the operating system if the user makes an error or downloads and activates malware. The impact of user errors and malware is much more limited if the user is not running as an administrator.

Role-based access is a practice that enables more effective management of user access. Instead of granting individual users access to objects, users are assigned to one or more appropriate *roles*, which are given permissions accordingly.

For example, a financial system has roles such as *accounts payable clerk*, *accounts receivable clerk*, and *payroll clerk*. These roles are assigned all of the appropriate permissions needed for persons in those roles. Then, individual users are assigned to these roles, which effectively gives them access to things they need.

The power of role-based access lies in the simplicity of assigning permissions to people. Instead of having to figure out all of the details that an individual needs, the individual is assigned a role, whose access details are already set up. And, if some change is needed in a role's access, those access permissions for the role are changed, which automatically applies to all persons with that role.

Non-repudiation is a concept that is related to access control. Non-repudiation is discussed fully in Chapter 5, "Cryptography."

Types of Controls

From a "big picture" perspective, controls that govern access and operation of information systems are classified into three types: technical, physical, and administrative. A **control** is an activity, process, or apparatus that ensures the confidentiality, integrity, or availability of an asset. Each is explained here.

Technical Controls **Technical controls**, which are sometimes called **logical controls**, are the programs and mechanisms on information systems that control system behavior and user access. Some examples of technical controls are:

- *Authentication.* Information systems utilize authentication to control which users are permitted to access data or functions.
- *Access control list (ACL).* These control user or system access to files, networks, applications, or systems.
- *Firewall.* This is a network-level device placed at a network boundary that blocks unwanted network traffic.
- *Remote access.* Used to facilitate access to a system or application from a remote location.
- *Anti-virus and anti-spyware.* This software is used to detect and block malicious and unwanted software from being installed on a system.
- ***Encryption.*** The practice of scrambling information so that it can only be read by authorized parties.
- *Configuration management.* A software application that is used to monitor and manage the configuration of systems and/or applications in an environment.

Physical Controls **Physical controls** are used to manage physical access to work areas containing information systems such as application servers and network devices. Some examples of physical controls include:

- *Video surveillance.* A detective control used to observe the movements of people and equipment in various places.
- *Key card access control.* A preventive control that limits which personnel are permitted to access a building and/or various areas or zones within the building. It is also a detective control, as most key card systems also record all attempted (whether successful or unsuccessful) entries.
- *"No Trespassing" signs.* A deterrent control that notifies persons that unauthorized persons should not enter a facility.

- *"Video Surveillance in Use" signs*. A deterrent control that notifies persons that activities in some work locations are viewed and possibly also recorded.
- *Fencing*. A preventive control that restricts peoples' movements.

Administrative Controls **Administrative controls** represent a broad set of actions, policies, procedures, and standards put in place in an organization to govern the actions of people and information systems. Some examples of administrative controls include:

- *Policies*. These are the high-level statements made and communicated by the organization's management that say, in effect, *this is how we are going to run this organization*. Some of the policies that would be in place include:
  - Security policies
  - Acceptable use policies
- *Processes and procedures*. Critical business activities that are documented and managed include user access administration, change control, configuration management, new employee hiring, vulnerability management, and service continuity management.
- *Standards*. These are the formal statements that specify what suppliers, makes and models of products, system configurations, and so on will be used in an organization. Standards state, *this is* how *we will do things in this organization.*

Categories of Controls

Another way to classify controls, the six categories of controls that are used to protect information are:

- Detective
- Deterrent
- Preventive
- Corrective
- Recovery
- Compensating

Associating activities with one of these six categories of controls is not always an exact science. Some controls can be both preventive and deterrent, for instance.

Detective Controls **Detective controls** are mechanisms that record events that occur. Detective controls are entirely *passive*—they *detect*, but do nothing else. They do not prevent unwanted events from occurring, although personnel may be aware of them, potentially making them deterrent as well.

Examples of detective controls include:

- *Video surveillance*. Cameras can be placed in key locations such as building entrances and locations where high-value activities take place such as bank vaults, gold refineries, and data processing centers. When connected to recording equipment, whatever happens within the view of surveillance cameras is recorded and archived for a period of time ranging from a few days to several years.

- *Access logs.* Information systems usually record events such as users logging in. Systems also usually record unsuccessful logins, which can be a sign of attempted intrusions by unauthorized parties who are trying to guess a user's password.
- *Transaction logs.* In addition to recording logins, information systems often record actions performed by users. These can range from making adjustments in a financial ledger to creating new user accounts. An action that is captured in a transaction log can also include when a user merely accesses information, such as a customer profile that includes sensitive information such as health or financial details.
- *Intrusion detection systems (IDS).* An IDS monitors activities and is designed to recognize unwanted activities that may be signs of an intrusion. There are two types of IDS: network-based IDS (NIDS) and host-based IDS (HIDS). NIDS systems monitor network traffic and generate alerts when unwanted or unusual network traffic is seen. HIDS are usually software programs that run on servers and monitor network traffic going to and from the server, as well as other activities on the server.

Detective controls are only effective if the controls are monitored. This is because detective controls only *record* activities; they do not *prevent* unwanted activities.

There are situations where implementing a preventive control is not feasible. In such a situation, a detective control should be implemented, so that it will be possible to at least record unwanted accesses.

Deterrent Controls **Deterrent controls** are designed to be highly visible and give persons the impression that any unauthorized activities will be stopped or detected and/or persons apprehended. Deterrent controls are designed to dissuade an individual from attempting to trespass, steal, destroy, or cause any other unwanted event.

Deterrent controls may consist of signs that alert persons of controls (which may or may not actually exist), or of detective or preventive controls that are deliberately made visible to onlookers.

Some examples of deterrent controls include:

- *Signs.* From "No Trespassing" to "These premises are under video surveillance" to "Beware of guard dogs," signs send a clear message to a would-be troublemaker that he or she is likely to be caught or their activities hindered in some manner.
- *Guards.* The presence of security personnel can be an effective deterrent, particularly if they are armed.
- *Guard dogs.* Often used to protect facilities from intruders.
- *Visible surveillance cameras and monitors.* Cameras and monitors that are placed out in the open say, "We are watching you and we may also be recording you."
- *Barbed wire and razor wire.* Those sharp edges often dissuade even a physically fit person from wanting to scale a fence, because of the fear of injury.

Controls that are labeled as deterrent are usually also preventive or detective, as deterrent controls often perform real actions. But an example of a *purely* deterrent control would be a sign that warns of guard dogs when no guard dogs actually exist.

Preventive Controls **Preventive controls** are designed to prevent unwanted activities. These controls are usually preferred over detective controls, since they are designed to actually prevent unwanted events from occurring in the first place. A prevented event is far easier to deal with than a detected event.

Preventive controls may prevent all persons from performing an activity, or they may prevent only unauthorized persons from performing unwanted actions. In a pure sense, a preventive control may absolutely prevent unwanted activity, or it may make the activity much more difficult or time-consuming to perform. A few types of preventive controls include:

- *Firewalls*. These devices block unwanted network traffic by examining each incoming packet and making a block-or-pass decision, based upon a set of rules that are configured by a network administrator.
- *Anti-virus software*. Programs on a PC or server that are designed to watch for specific known viruses and other malware, and block the entry of these unwanted programs. Anti-virus programs recognize viruses through the use of "signatures," where the virus is recognized and blocked. Anti-virus programs also utilize a mechanism known as *heuristics*, where the anti-virus program detects a virus through its behavior.
- *Anti-spyware software*. Similar to anti-virus software, anti-spyware blocks spyware and other unwanted programs through signatures and heuristics.
- *Encryption*. Files, directories, entire volumes, and backup tapes can be encrypted to protect sensitive information from disclosure to unauthorized parties.
- *Intrusion prevention system (IPS)*. These devices listen to network traffic, watching for specific patterns and anomalies, and then block traffic directly or by instructing a network device such as a switch or firewall to block specific traffic. Like anti-virus software, IPSes watch for traffic that matches specific signatures and also make blocking decisions by observing behavior using a mechanism known as heuristics.
- *Data loss prevention (DLP) system*. These systems listen to network traffic, watching for specific types of sensitive or valuable data, and then block traffic directly or by instructing another device or system to block the activity. DLP systems watch for traffic containing specific patterns such as credit card numbers, bank account numbers, and intellectual property such as source code.
- *Fencing*. Physical fences prevent unwanted persons from trespassing on a protected facility.
- *Bollards*. These are the heavy rigid posts that prevent motor vehicles from entering a protected area. Figure 2-6 shows bollards protecting the entrance of an office building.

Corrective Controls **Corrective controls** are activities that are carried out after a security event has occurred. Generally, corrective controls are those activities that are undertaken in order to prevent the recurrence of an unwanted event.

Here is an example. A recently terminated employee who was unhappy about his unemployment decided to sabotage his former employer's information systems. He was able to log on to these systems remotely because his logon credentials had not yet been revoked. The organization discovered this and made some improvements in the termination process in order to ensure that terminated employees' logon credentials are immediately removed. These process improvements are the corrective actions in this case.

Figure 2-6 Bollards control motor vehicle traffic and block entry to protected areas

Courtesy of Rebecca Steele

Recovery Controls Like corrective controls, **recovery controls** take place after an incident has occurred. Recovery controls are activities that enable the restoration to normal operations after some event. In the example above, any repairs necessary after the terminated employee logged onto systems would be considered recovery controls.

An example of a recovery control is the restoration of system files after a virus infection that corrupted critical system data.

Compensating Controls Sometimes a system may lack certain capabilities, which makes it difficult or impossible to enact specific controls. In order to compensate for the missing or deficient control, another control can be introduced to manage the risk. Such a substitute control is called a **compensating control**, because it compensates for the lack, or failure, of another control. For example, an organization that lacks automated access termination controls may perform a monthly review of terminated employee access to ensure that all user account terminations were done properly.

Using a Defense in Depth Controls Strategy

To reduce the risk of unauthorized access, it is recommended that several controls be put into place to protect an asset, particularly any asset with significant value. The existence of several layers of controls may reduce the likelihood that an asset will be compromised, more than if there was only one control protecting the asset. The practice of using layers of controls to protect an asset is known as defense in depth.

The advantage of a defense in depth strategy is that a malfunction, defect, or compromise of a single control does not completely compromise the protection of the asset. The other controls that are still in place contribute to the protection of the asset.

In order to be most effective, a defense in depth strategy should employ various types of controls, perhaps from two or more vendors. This will result in the greatest protection from compromise. For example, if a database is protected by several layers of firewalls of the same type, a failure or compromise in one layer may render all layers vulnerable to compromise.

Example 1: Protected Application A financial institution wishes to protect its online customer financial data from unauthorized access while still providing access to authorized customers. The financial data is protected through an architecture that provides for several layers of controls in order to provide the greatest possible protection. The security features of this architecture could include the following:

- Authentication that requires a user name, strong password, and account number
- Entire user session protected with 128-bit SSL (TLS) encryption
- Access permitted only from previously registered workstations
- Session timeout that requires reauthentication by the user
- High-value transactions that require reauthentication by the user
- Removal of all unnecessary services on all servers in the environment
- Up-to-date security patches on all servers
- Up-to-date anti-virus software on all servers
- Intrusion prevention systems in one or more places in the application environment
- Data leakage prevention systems to prevent unauthorized movement of customer data
- Three-layer application architecture with web servers on the front end, application servers in the middle tier, and database servers in the third tier
- Different brands of firewalls at the first, second, and third tiers of the environment
- Two-factor authentication required for all administrative access to devices, servers, operating systems, and databases
- Application servers permit connections only from front-end web servers. Database servers permit connections only from application servers
- Encryption of sensitive data on databases

While this may sound like a long list of controls, many organizations will employ these and many more.

It may be evident to the reader that the controls in this example protect the sensitive data from more than one type of threat. It is necessary to understand all types of threats and vulnerabilities and to implement controls to address each one.

Example 2: Protected Facility The research and development division of a large manufacturing company wishes to protect its research and development facilities from unwanted access. The company operates in a highly competitive market that has experienced espionage incidents by competitors and foreign government agents. The organization employs several methods to prevent and detect access by unauthorized persons, including:

- Security cameras connected to a manned surveillance center
- Fences with barbed wire
- Guard dogs and security guards patrolling the grounds
- Checkpoint that challenges all incoming vehicles
- Bollards that prevent vehicles from entering restricted areas
- Entry doors require key card and biometric hand scan
- Special coating on windows that prevents eavesdropping on conversations
- Zones of security within the facility that restrict different classes of employees to different areas in the facility
- Security guards within the facility

Like the preceding example, an organization like this probably employs additional means for protecting the facility.

Testing Access Controls

Because access controls are so vital to the confidentiality, integrity, and availability of information, they should be tested in order to be sure that they are working properly and free of defects. The two types of testing that can be performed on a system are vulnerability scanning and penetration testing. The purpose of these two types of testing is to discover vulnerabilities that could be exploited by an attacker to gain unauthorized access to a system.

In addition to testing, access controls on live systems typically create audit log entries to record significant events.

Vulnerability Scanning

Vulnerability scanning is used to discover defects in operating systems, related subsystems such as database servers or web servers, and applications. There are tools specifically made for vulnerability scanning that identify open ports and exploitable weaknesses. Vulnerability scanning consists of transmitting TCP/IP packets to the target system in attempts to communicate with various common (and not-so-common) services, in order to discover which services are operating on the target system.

Vulnerability scanning tools in common use include:

- Nessus
- Metasploit
- Nikto
- GFI LANguard

- Superscan
- Retina
- ISS Scanner
- Qualysguard
- Microsoft Baseline Security Analyzer

These and other tools can find vulnerabilities of many varieties, including:

- Missing patches
- Old versions of services
- Misconfigured services

Many of these and other vulnerabilities are easily exploited by intruders who wish to gain access to vulnerable systems, particularly for systems that are accessible over the Internet.

Penetration Testing

Penetration testing, often coined "pen testing," is a procedure that is used to discover and exploit defects at the operating system or server level. Penetration testing is a step beyond vulnerability scanning: in penetration testing, potential weaknesses are exploited in order to prove their existence.

Penetration testing usually begins with vulnerability scanning, followed by the use of additional tools to manually search for and exploit vulnerabilities.

Application Vulnerability Testing

The proliferation of web-based applications has naturally led to a vast number of these applications containing vulnerabilities that intruders can exploit for various nefarious purposes, including stealing or damaging information. High-value applications such as online banking are naturally those that are targeted intensely by intruders. Some tools that are available to identify vulnerabilities include:

- IBM AppScan
- HP WebInspect
- Acunetix WVS
- Burp Suite
- Zaproxy
- Paros
- Skipfish
- Nessus

Vulnerabilities that can be found with help from these **application vulnerability testing** tools include:

- Injection
- Cross-Site Scripting (XSS)
- Broken Authentication and Session Management

- Insecure Direct Object References
- Cross-Site Request Forgery (CSRF)
- Security Misconfiguration
- Insecure Cryptographic Storage
- Failure to Restrict URL Access
- Insufficient Transport Layer Protection
- Unvalidated Redirects and Forwards

(Source: Open Web Access Security Project: owasp.org)

These vulnerabilities usually exist as a result of improper web application design or coding. Increasingly, organizations use application vulnerability scanning tools to discover vulnerabilities in their own web applications so that they can fix those vulnerabilities before intruders can discover them.

Application vulnerability testing also falls into two tiers: vulnerability scanning and penetration testing. Scans are run to find easily identified vulnerabilities, and additional tools and techniques are used to discover additional vulnerabilities and exploit them.

Audit Log Analysis

Access controls on information systems should create audit logs that should be regularly examined; this activity is called **audit log analysis**. Several types of problems can occur on a system that might otherwise go unnoticed, including:

- *Intruder reconnaissance*. Prior to attempting to break into a target system, intruders will conduct reconnaissance to learn more about the makeup and defenses of the target system. Often, these activities are recorded in network, system, and application logs.
- *Attempted break-ins*. Often, systems will log all successful and unsuccessful login attempts. A significant number of unsuccessful login attempts may be an indication that an intruder is attempting to break in to a user account.
- *System malfunctions*. System error logs may include entries that could be a sign of tampering or attempted break-ins.
- *Account abuse*. Close examinations of user logs can sometimes identify account abuse, including credential sharing, where a user shares his or her credentials with others, resulting in concurrent logins.

Because they contain important data about system accesses and events, audit logs themselves can be the target of an attack, primarily as a means for an intruder or insider to gather intelligence about a system and to erase his or her tracks. For this reason it is recommended that one or more of the following measures be taken to protect audit logs:

- Write audit logs onto a write-once medium such as optical storage
- Write audit logs onto a central, highly protected server that administrators cannot access
- Extend intrusion detection capability to systems that store audit logs
- Employ measures to prevent a denial-of-service attack that attempts to exceed the storage capacity of audit log media

Chapter Summary

- Identification is the assertion of a subject's identity without confirmation.
- Authentication is used to identify a subject with confirmation, such as a password, token, or biometric.
- Authentication can be based upon something the user *knows* (knowledge-based), something the user *has* (possession-based), or something the user *is* (entity-based).
- Multi-factor authentication is authentication that relies on two or more factors: knowledge-based, possession-based, or entity-based. Two-factor authentication uses any two of these.
- Biometric authentication involves measuring some physiological characteristic of the subject such as fingerprint, hand shape, iris pattern, speech, or handwriting.
- Commonly used standards for authentication include LDAP, RADIUS, Diameter, TACACS, and Kerberos.
- Single Sign-On (SSO) is a means of authenticating a user once to an environment and utilizing that authentication to permit the user access to all applications in the environment without having to authenticate to each one separately.
- Information systems are often attacked as a means of bypassing access controls and gaining control of a system. Methods of attack include buffer overflow, script injection, malicious code, denial of service, eavesdropping, spoofing, social engineering, phishing, and password attacks.
- Malicious code is used to attempt to interfere with or gain control of a system. The types of malicious code are viruses, worms, and Trojan horses.
- Access management processes include access requests and approvals, internal transfers, terminations, periodic reviews, and audits.
- The concept of *separation of duties* is used to ensure that no single individual has both request and approval duties in a business process.
- The concept of *least privilege* means that any user should have only the access privileges required to carry out his or her responsibilities.
- The types of controls used to protect a system or process are *technical*, *physical*, and *administrative*.
- The categories of controls are *detective*, *deterrent*, *preventive*, *corrective*, *recovery*, and *compensating*.
- The concept of *defense in depth* states that several layers of controls should be used to protect an asset. Then if any single control fails, other controls will still provide some protection.
- Access controls should be tested to ensure that they function properly. The types of tests available include *vulnerability scanning* and *penetration testing*.
- Audit logs should be in place to record events, including intruder reconnaissance, attempted break-ins, system malfunctions, and abuse. Audit logs themselves should be protected to prevent tampering.

Key Terms

Access rights recertification The process of reviewing users' access rights to determine if each user still requires specific access rights.

Accumulation of privileges The process of gaining more access privileges over a long period of time, most often by personnel who transfer from role to role in an organization.

Active Directory A Microsoft implementation of LDAP.

Administrative controls The policies, procedures, and standards put in place in an organization to govern the actions of people and information systems.

Application vulnerability testing A means of testing an application to identify any vulnerabilities.

Audit log analysis An activity used to detect unwanted events that are recorded in an audit log.

Authentication The act of proving one's identity to an information system by providing two or more pieces of information, such as a userid and a password, in order to gain access to information and functions.

Biometrics A means for measuring a physiological characteristic of a person as a means for positively identifying him or her.

Buffer overflow An attack on a system by means of providing excessive amounts of data in an input field.

Compensating control A control that compensates for the absence or ineffectiveness of another control.

Compromising emanations (CE) Emanations of electromagnetic radiation (EMR) that disclose sensitive information.

Control An activity, process, or apparatus that ensures the confidentiality, integrity, or availability of an asset.

Corrective control An activity that occurs after a security event has occurred in order to prevent its reoccurrence.

Crossover Error Rate (CER) The point where False Reject Rate and False Accept Rate are equal.

Data remanence The unintentional data that remains on a storage device or medium.

Denial of service (DoS) An attack where data is sent to a target system in an attempt to cause the target system to malfunction.

Detective control A control that is used to detect specific types of activity.

Deterrent control A control used to deter unwanted activity.

Diameter An authentication, authorization, and accounting protocol that is a replacement for RADIUS.

Digital certificate An electronic document that utilizes a digital signature and an identity, used to reliably identify a person or system.

Distributed denial of service (DDoS) A denial-of-service attack that originates from many systems. See also *Denial of service*.

Dumpster diving An attack where an attacker rummages through refuse bins ("Dumpsters") in an attempt to discover sensitive discarded information.

Eavesdropping An attack where an attacker attempts to intercept communications.

Emanations Typically RF emissions from a computer or conductor that permits eavesdroppers to eavesdrop on computer activity.

Encryption A means of scrambling information to make it unreadable except by parties who possess a key.

False Accept Rate (FAR) How often a biometric system accepts an invalid user.

False Reject Rate (FRR) How often a biometric system rejects valid users.

Hash A computational transformation that receives a variable-sized data input and returns a unique fixed-length string. Hashing is considered irreversible; it is not possible to obtain an original plaintext from a known hash.

Identification The act of claiming identity to an information system.

Kerberos An authentication service that utilizes a centralized authentication server.

LDAP Lightweight Directory Access Protocol, a centralized directory service often used for access management and authentication.

Least privilege The access control principle that states that individuals should have only the accesses required to perform their official duties.

Logical controls See *technical controls*.

Malicious code Computer instructions that are intended to disrupt or control a target system.

Malware See *malicious code*.

Multi-factor authentication Authentication that involves the use of two or more authentication methods (knowledge-based, possession-based, or entity-based).

Password A secret word or phrase entered by a user to authenticate to a system.

Password cracking An attack where the attacker uses tools to methodically guess passwords in order to gain access to a system.

Password guessing An attack where the attacker guesses likely passwords in an attempt to gain access to a system.

Penetration testing An activity used to identify and exploit vulnerabilities on a target system, subsystem, or application.

Personal identification number (PIN) A numeric password. See also *password*.

Pharming An attack where the attacker poisons *DNS* or *hosts* information to redirect communications intended for a legitimate system instead to an imposter system, as a means for harvesting sensitive information.

Phishing Fraudulent e-mail messages that attempt to lure an unsuspecting user to provide private information via a fraudulent web site (usually) or in an e-mail reply (less often).

Physical controls Mechanisms that control or monitor physical access and environmental systems.

Possession-based authentication Authentication that involves the use of a hardware device or non-transferrable digital certificate that is required to complete the process.

Preventive control A control that blocks unauthorized or undesired activity.

RADIUS Remote Authentication Dial In User Service, a remote access authentication protocol.

Rainbow table A table of hashes, usually for the purpose of cracking passwords.

Recovery control A control that is used to restore conditions to normal.

Reduced sign-on A type of authentication where users have a limited set of userids and passwords that are used to access systems and applications.

RFC Request for Comments; the formalized documents that describe the Internet's technical and procedural standards.

Script injection An attack on a system where script language accompanies input data in an attempt to execute the script on the target system.

Separation of duties The work practice where high-risk tasks are structured to be carried out by two or more persons.

Single sign-on An access control method where users can authenticate once and be able to access other systems and applications without being required to reauthenticate to each one.

Smart card A credit card-sized memory device used for authentication.

Sniffing The act of eavesdropping on a network by capturing traffic.

Social engineering An attack on an organization where the attacker is attempting to gain secrets from staff members, usually for gaining unauthorized access to the organization's systems.

Spear phishing A specially targeted phishing attack. See also *phishing*.

Spoofing An attack where the attacker forges the origin of a message as an attempt to disrupt or control a system.

SQL injection An attack where SQL statements are injected into an input stream in the hopes that the SQL commands will be executed by the application's database server.

Strong authentication A means of authenticating to a system using a means stronger than userid and password, such as a hardware token, smart card, or biometric. Also known as *two-factor authentication*.

Technical controls Programs and mechanisms that control user access system behavior.

TEMPEST The code name for a U.S. military project dedicated to the study of compromising emanations (CE).

Terminal Access Controller Access-Control System (TACACS) A remote authentication protocol used to authenticate user access to a computer or network-based resource. Superseded by TACACS+ and RADIUS.

Token A hardware device used for authentication.

Two-factor authentication See *strong authentication*.

USB key A device, plugged into a computer's USB port, usually containing a digital certificate and used for strong authentication.

Vulnerability scanning An activity where tools are used to identify vulnerabilities on a target system or application.

Watering hole attack An attack where a web site is implanted with malicious code, which is used to infect the computers used by visitors to the site.

Whaling A specially targeted phishing attack that targets executives in an organization.

Review Questions

1. The process of obtaining a subject's proven identity is known as:
   a. Enrollment
   b. Identification
   c. Authentication
   d. Authorization
2. Which of the following is the best example of multi-factor authentication?
   a. Biometric
   b. None of these
   c. What the user knows
   d. Token
3. The only time that a user may share his or her password with another user is:
   a. When the other user requires higher access privileges
   b. During a disaster
   c. Only temporarily until the other user is issued a userid and password
   d. It is never appropriate for a user to share their password
4. The term *False Reject Rate* refers to:
   a. How often a biometric system will reject an invalid user
   b. How often a biometric system will accept an invalid user
   c. How often a biometric system will reject a valid user
   d. How often a biometric system will accept a valid user
5. *Password quality* refers to:
   a. Password encryption
   b. Password expiration
   c. Password complexity
   d. All of the above

6. Every month, the human resources department issues a list of employees terminated in the previous month. The security manager should:
   a. Use the list to conduct an audit of computer accounts to make sure the terminated employees' accounts have been terminated
   b. Make sure that computer accounts are terminated as soon as possible after the issuance of the list of terminated employees
   c. Request that the human resource department notify account managers of terminations daily instead of monthly
   d. Request that the list of terminated employees be encrypted for security reasons
7. The principal security weakness with RADIUS is:
   a. Traffic is not encrypted
   b. Passwords do not expire
   c. It uses the TCP protocol
   d. RADIUS sessions are connectionless
8. The use of LDAP as a single source for authentication data helps an organization to achieve:
   a. Fewer password resets
   b. Effective password management
   c. Single sign-on
   d. Reduced sign-on
9. An auditor has produced a findings report that cites the lack of separation of duties as a significant problem. Management should consider:
   a. Separating development and production environments
   b. Outsourcing the indicated process
   c. Stop outsourcing the indicated process
   d. Examining the indicated process and reassigning duties among a greater number of individuals
10. All of the following controls are preventive controls EXCEPT:
    a. Fencing
    b. Surveillance cameras
    c. Firewalls
    d. Bollards
11. An attack on a server that originates from many sources is known as a:
    a. DDoS
    b. DoS
    c. Botnet
    d. Teardrop

12. The most effective way to protect audit log data is to:
    a. Write audit log data to tape
    b. Write-protect audit log data
    c. Write audit log data to write-once media
    d. Write audit log data to optical storage
13. The purpose of a defense in depth strategy is:
    a. To make protected assets difficult to find
    b. To ensure that protected assets are reachable
    c. To protect assets from unauthorized access
    d. To protect assets using a variety of controls
14. Anti-malware is a form of:
    a. Preventive control
    b. Detective control
    c. Corrective control
    d. Recovery control
15. The most effective way to prevent password cracking is:
    a. Make the password hash files inaccessible
    b. Remove password cracking tools from the target system
    c. Protect passwords using strong encryption
    d. Remove the target system from the network

Hands-On Projects

Project 2-1: Levels of Authentication

Required for this project:

- Windows, Apple Mac OS X, Linux, or Unix with a web browser

In this project you will explore the levels of identification and authentication used by the online merchant web site Amazon.com. Many web sites use several levels of identification and authentication that correspond to various activities and functions that a user might perform on the web site.

1. If you do not have an online account with Amazon.com, set one up now. Log in, then log off.
2. Remove any cookies associated with Amazon.com. In Firefox for Windows, go to Tools > Options > Privacy > Cookies, then search for and remove amazon.com cookies. For Firefox on a MAC, it's slightly different. You have to click Firefox, then Preferences, then click Privacy, then if necessary, click Use custom settings for history, then you will see the Show Cookies button. In IE, go to Tools > Internet Options > Privacy > Sites.

In Safari for Windows, go to Edit > Preferences > Security > Show Cookies. For Safari on a MAC, you have to click the Safari button, then Preferences, then click the Privacy tab, then Details button. Note: Browser design over time may mean that the method used to view cookies may have changed.

3. Go to the Amazon.com web site and note how it identifies you. Since you have removed your cookies, you should appear as an anonymous user or first-time visitor to Amazon.com, similar to Figure 2-7.
4. Log in to the Amazon.com web site, and then log out. This will reestablish your userid cookie with the web site.
5. Visit Amazon.com again. This time, Amazon should recognize you and display a "Welcome back" message, similar to what is shown in Figure 2-8.
6. Sometime in the future (maybe in a few hours or days), visit Amazon.com again, using the same computer and browser. The site should still recognize you. This time, visit your account settings page or order merchandise. Even though the web site recognizes you, it may ask you to reenter your password, proving your identity through authentication, before showing you potentially sensitive information.
7. You will have viewed three different levels of authentication: an anonymous/unknown user, a weakly identified user (through your userid cookie), and a more strongly identified user (through userid and password authentication).

What mechanisms were used to identify you in this project?

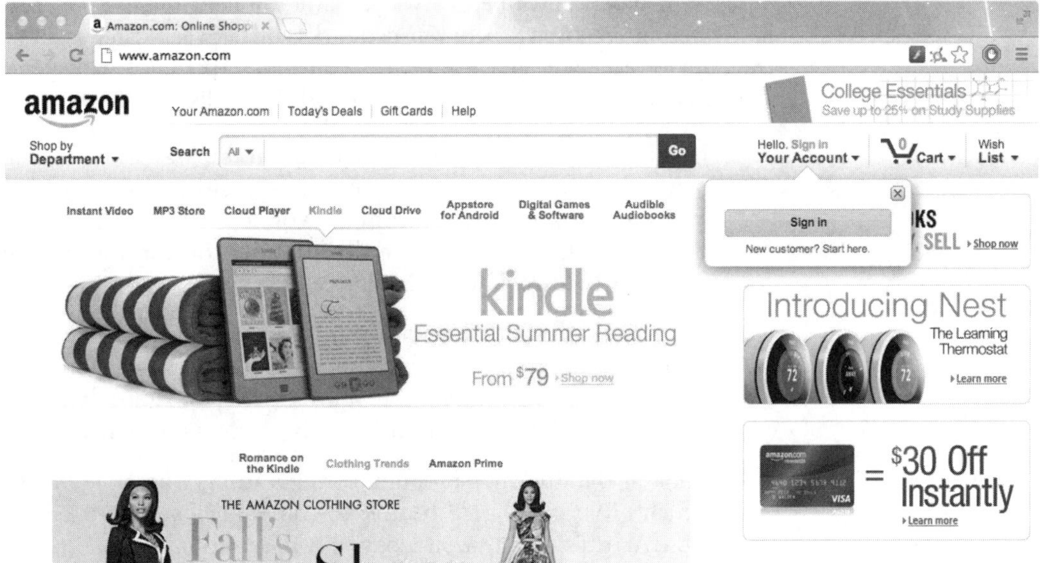

Figure 2-7 Application session, user is logged out

Source: Amazon.com

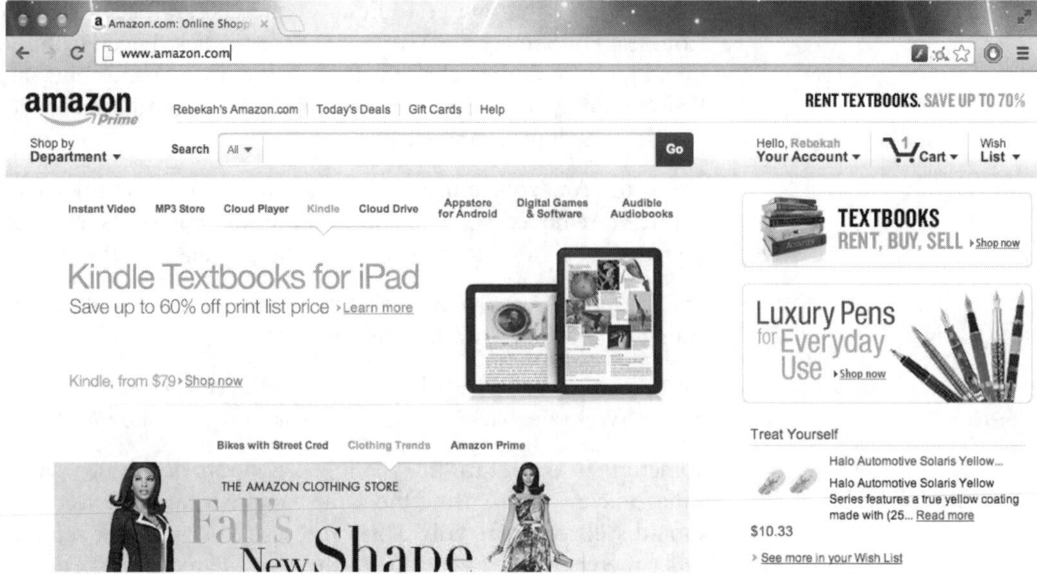

Figure 2-8 Application session, user is logged in

Source: Amazon.com

Project 2-2: Personal Firewalls

Required for this project:

- Windows 2000, XP, Vista, 7, or 8; Apple Mac OS X

In this project you will install and experiment with firewall software. Firewalls are used to block unwanted network traffic by controlling the type of traffic that is permitted to pass between networks, or between a network and a system. This project will give you some hands-on experience with personal firewall software and insight into how network firewalls function.

1. If you are using Windows, download and install ZoneAlarm (www.zonelabs.com and look for the free version) or Comodo (www.personalfirewall.comodo.com). If you are using a Mac, the OS X operating systems have firewalls built-in; you can find information on using the firewall on the Apple web site.

2. Observe the firewall in action. ZoneAlarm detects when a program is trying to communicate over the network and will ask you if the program should be permitted to. Figure 2-9 shows ZoneAlarm asking whether SSLDigger should be able to access the Internet.

3. Look at the firewall's program configuration, where the firewall knows which programs should be able to communicate. Figure 2-10 shows ZoneAlarm's Application Control configuration.

4. Look at the firewall log to see what network traffic the firewall is permitting and blocking. Figure 2-11 shows ZoneAlarm's firewall log.

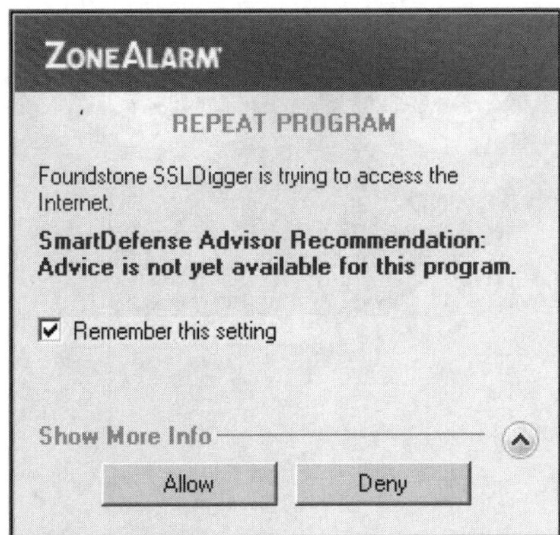

Figure 2-9 ZoneAlarm asks whether SSLDigger may communicate

Source: ZoneAlarm

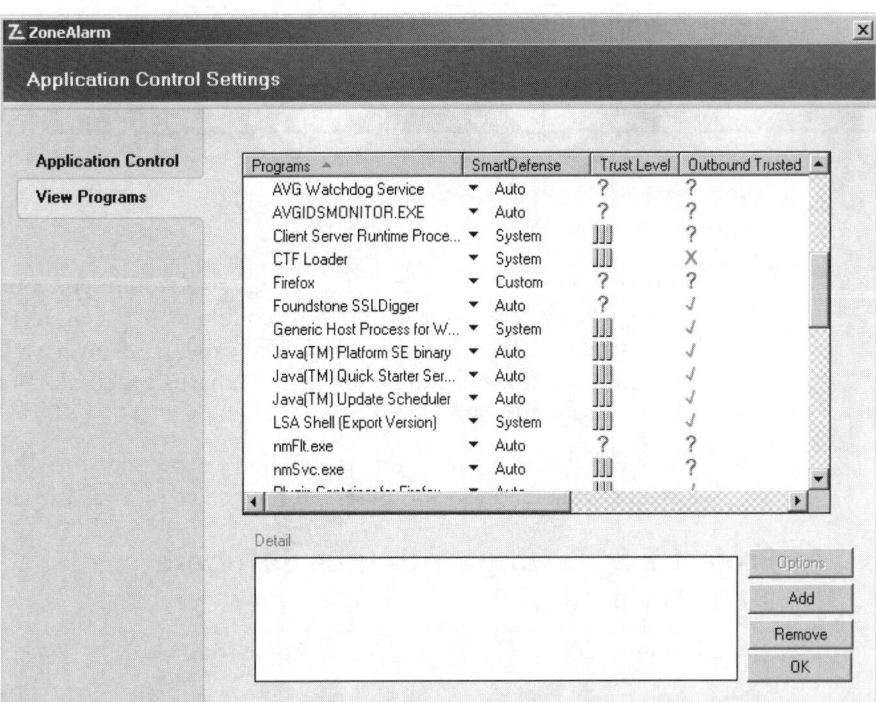

Figure 2-10 ZoneAlarm application control settings

Source: ZoneAlarm

5. Test the firewall by attempting to communicate with your computer from an external source. You can try to ping the computer from an external system. Or, use one of the readily available Internet firewall test sites to see if your computer is reachable from the site.

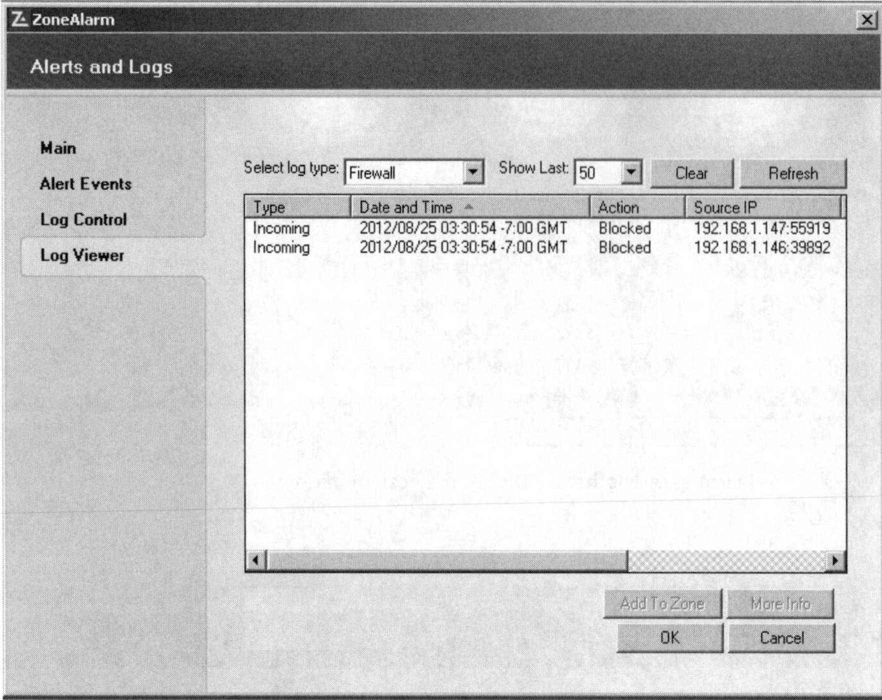

Figure 2-11 ZoneAlarm firewall log

Source: ZoneAlarm

Some sites to try: security.symantec.com, www.auditmypc.com, or www.hackerwatch.org/probe/. If your computer is not protected by a hardware firewall (many newer DSL and cable modems have firewalls built-in), your firewall should log activity that is generated by the site you used to scan your system.

6. You have viewed a firewall in action: you've responded to alerts, made configuration changes, and observed the effects of a security scan.

Project 2-3: Testing Anti-Virus Software

Required for this project:

- Windows 2000, XP, Vista, 7, or 8; Apple Mac OS X

In this project you will test your anti-virus software to see if it really works, without exposing you to the risks associated with real malware. Unless you partake in high-risk activities that regularly expose you to active malware, you may never have seen your anti-virus software actually catch a virus. So, then, how can you tell whether it actually works?

1. Check your anti-virus program's status and make sure that its real-time detection is functioning. Usually you can do this by double-clicking on the anti-virus program in your Windows system tray.

2. Go to the virus test web site, www.eicar.org. EICAR is the European Institute for Computer Antivirus Research. Click on the Anti-Malware Test File link (alternately, go to http://eicar.org/anti_virus_test_file.htm).
3. Carefully read the instructions on the next page, "The Anti-Virus or Anti-Malware test file." On this page you can download any of several forms of the EICAR test file.
4. Try downloading each form of the EICAR test file and note how your anti-virus software responds. Your anti-virus software should immediately pop up a window similar to the following when you try to download and save the *eicar.com* or *eicar.com.txt* file. An example virus detection pop-up window is shown in Figure 2-12.
5. Try downloading the *eicar_com.zip* file. In this download, the *eicar.txt* file is in a compressed Zip archive. Did your anti-virus program recognize the EICAR test file?
6. Try downloading the *eicarcom2.zip* file. This download file consists of the EICAR test file in a compressed Zip archive that is within another compressed Zip archive. If your anti-virus software is *really* good, it will have detected the EICAR test file here too.

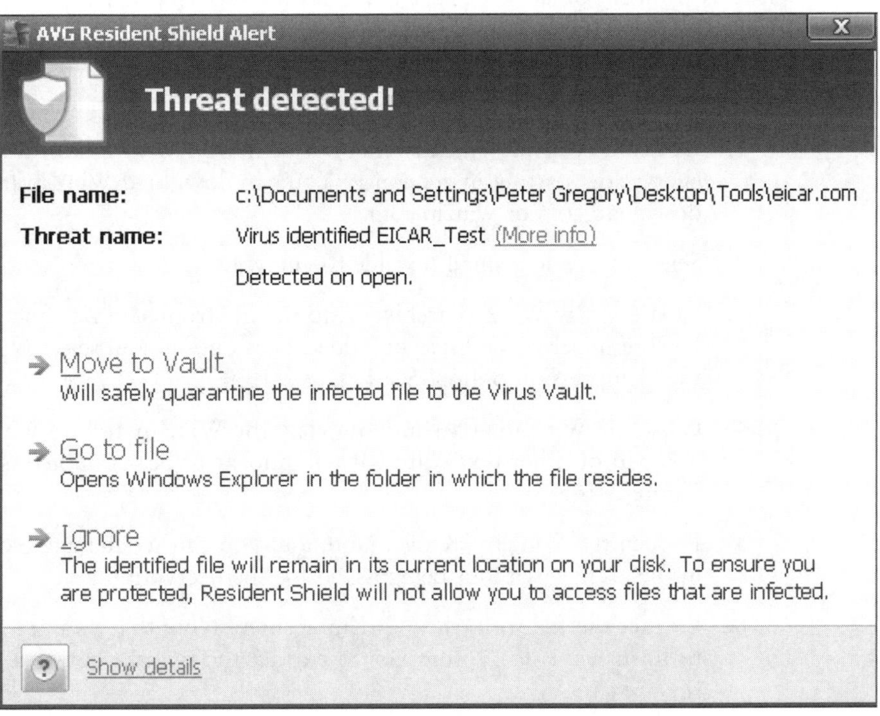

Figure 2-12 Anti-virus software pop-up window

Source: AVG Resident Shield

7. If your anti-virus software did not detect the EICAR test file in any of these cases, then you should suspect that your anti-virus software real-time virus detection is not working. Take another look at your anti-virus software configuration. Contact the anti-virus software vendor if you are still having problems.

8. If your anti-virus software did not detect the EICAR test file, another thing to try is to scan your hard drive with your anti-virus program. If the scan does detect the EICAR test file, then you may conclude that your real-time detection is not working, but scanning is still functioning.

It may be difficult to download the EICAR file on networks with firewalls or other devices designed to block downloading malware.

Project 2-4: Protect Data with Encryption

Required for this project:

- Windows 2000, XP, Vista, 7, or 8; Apple Mac OS X

In this project you will encrypt text files and see how encryption can protect files from unauthorized disclosure. Encryption is one common way that data can be protected from unauthorized access from unauthorized persons.

1. Obtain a copy of WinZip version 9 or newer. WinZip introduced AES encryption starting in version 9. You can download WinZip from download.com or winzip.com.

2. Select or create a small text file to encrypt.

3. Create a new WinZip archive. Add the file from step 2 to the archive. Be sure to select the Encrypt Added Files option, and select None for the Compression option. See Figure 2-13.

4. Close the WinZip archive. Now view the WinZip archive with notepad or other text editor. It will appear to be scrambled, similar to Figure 2-14.

5. Reopen the WinZip archive. Note that you can see the name of the file in the archive without being asked for the decryption key.

6. Extract the file from the WinZip archive. Note that you are required to furnish the decryption key to extract the file; the contents of the file are safe.

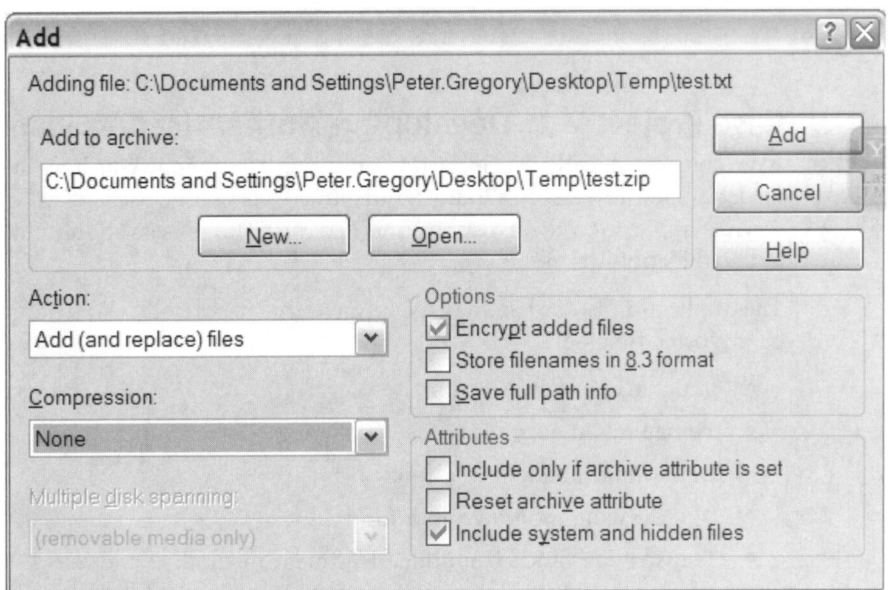

Figure 2-13 Using WinZip to encrypt a file

Source: WinZip

test.zip - Notepad

File Edit Format View Help

Figure 2-14 WinZip and AES encryption protect a file from unauthorized persons

Source: WinZip

If you are using a Mac, you can get similar results from the command line with the command `zip -ejr [name] [path to folder]`, where [name] is the Zip archive you wish to create, and [path to folder] is the complete name of the folder you wish to encrypt. Mac OS will prompt you for the password.

On Windows computers, the 7Zip program may be used instead of WinZip. The principles of operation are the same, and the user interfaces are similar. 7Zip is available at http://7-zip.org/.

Case Projects

Case Project 2-1: Develop an Authentication Plan

As a consultant with the Security Consulting Company, you have been hired to determine how users should be identified and authenticated to a financial services application. You also need to determine how users should first register to use the application.

The application is used to manage an investment portfolio. Functions that can be performed include:

- Initial account registration
- Managing an account profile, including contact information
- Depositing money into a fund
- Withdrawing money from a fund
- Transferring funds from one investment method to another

Develop use cases for each of the above functions, and specify how users should identify themselves to the application for each use case.

Case Project 2-2: Observe a Defense in Depth Environment

Identify a work facility or an IT environment that you can visit. Study the environment; what assets are being protected? What controls can you find that are used to protect assets? Write down all of the controls that you can find and describe how they protect assets.

If possible, have an employee give you a tour of the environment. What additional controls can be found?

When you list the controls that you find, identify their type: detective, preventive, deterrent, compensating, recovery, or corrective.

Identify any additional controls that could be implemented to further protect assets.

Case Project 2-3: Learn about Script Injection Vulnerabilities

Search for a script injection demo on the Internet. Search on one of the following terms:

- SQL injection demo
- Script injection demo

Find a site that shows an actual SQL or script injection exploit on a demo web site. Observe the exploitation in action. How did the script injection work? If an actual attack was launched against a vulnerable site, what are the possible consequences? What safeguards can be taken to protect an application from such attacks?

Case Project 2-4: Develop a User Access Request Process

As a consultant with the Security Consulting Company, you have been hired to develop a user access request process for a client organization that does not have a process today. You have been asked to develop:

- A user access request form
- A procedure for routing the request to appropriate approvers
- A procedure for user account administrators to follow when they receive an approved access request
- A method for saving requests, approvals, and provisioning records

Describe scenarios that would require "exception processing" in this process. Describe how a larger organization might need to modify this process. Discuss how auditors would audit this process.

chapter 3

Software Development Security

Topics in This Chapter:

- Operating Systems
- Types of Applications
- Application Models and Technologies
- Application Threats and Countermeasures
- Security in the Software Development Life Cycle
- Application Security Controls
- Databases and Data Warehouses

The (ISC)[2] *Common Body of Knowledge* (CBK) defines the key areas of knowledge for software development security in this way:

Software Development Security domain refers to the controls that are included within systems and applications software and the steps used in their development (e.g., SDLC).

Software refers to system software (operating systems) and application programs such as agents, applets, software, databases, data warehouses, and knowledge-based systems. These applications may be used in distributed or centralized environments.

The candidate should fully understand the security and controls of the systems development process, system life cycle, application controls, change controls, data warehousing, data mining, knowledge-based systems, program interfaces, and concepts used to ensure data and application integrity, security, and availability.

Key areas of knowledge:

- *Understand and apply security in the software development life cycle*
- *Understand the environment and security controls*
- *Assess the effectiveness of software security*

Operating Systems

Operating systems are the software programs that manage a computer's hardware resources and facilitate the running of software applications and utilities. Examples of modern operating systems are Linux, Apple OS X, Microsoft Windows, Android, and Apple iOS.

Operating System Components

The central component of an operating system (OS) is the **kernel**. The main functions of the kernel include:

- *Process management.* Processes are the individual programs that are running on a computer system. The kernel controls the start, execution, and completion of processes. The kernel enforces process isolation, so that processes are not able to access each other's resources such as system memory. The kernel also facilitates a process's access to files and other resources.
- *Memory management.* The kernel manages the allocation, release, and reuse of a computer's memory by individual processes.
- *Hardware resource management.* The kernel manages the use of hardware resources to ensure that processes that require access to hardware are able to do so. The kernel makes sure that processes that require access to the same hardware (e.g., the network adaptor, facilitating network communications) can do so without conflicts.

The second primary component of an operating system is its *device drivers*. These consist of software code that helps the kernel understand how it needs to communicate with various types of hardware present in the computer system. This kernel–device drivers architecture allows a kernel to include only generic communications to devices, while device drivers translate those generic communications into specific commands that the computer's hardware components will understand.

The third component of the operating system is its *tools*. These are standalone programs that are delivered with the operating system that are used to manage the operating system's configuration, file systems, and devices. For the most part, an operating system's tools are no different than applications, which are discussed later in this chapter.

Operating System Security Functions

Operating systems carry out several security functions on a system, including these:

- *Authentication*. The operating system performs the task of authenticating users to the system. For example, when users log in to a computer by providing a userid and password, the operating system examines its configuration for authentication and then verifies the login credentials provided by the user. If the login credentials are correct (whether verified locally or through a network-based service), the user is permitted to establish a session on the system.
- *Resource access*. The operating system controls each process's access to resources on the computer, so that processes are able to access and share resources without conflicts taking place.
- ***Access control***. The operating system controls each user's and process's access to resources on the system. Whenever a user or process makes a request to access a resource, the operating system first examines any access control restrictions for the resource before providing access.
- *Communication*. The operating system facilitates all communication between running processes and whatever it is that those processes wish to communicate with. This includes network-based communications via Ethernet, WiFi, or Bluetooth to external devices or systems, communications to printers and other peripherals, and communications to end users through the computer's display, keyboard, and mouse.
- *Event logging*. The operating system automatically records system events to one or more system logs or event logs, which are usually files or databases on the system. The types of events logged typically include user logins, hardware errors, and system configuration changes.

Threats to Operating Systems

Because operating systems are used to control all of the activity on a computer system, they are frequent targets of attack. Often, the compromise of an operating system can lead to the compromise of any other program on the system, as well as any resource present on the system such as databases and files.

Threats to operating systems, and countermeasures that can curb these threats, are detailed later in this chapter in the Threats in the Software Environment section.

Applications

Applications are computer programs that perform user-initiated tasks such as word processing, e-mail, or web searches. They may be as complicated as a corporate financial management system or an enterprise resource planning (ERP) system, or as simple as a bank loan calculator. Applications perform a set of instructions: they may accept input data, perform calculations, and create output data. *How* they do these things varies widely, depending upon the purpose of the application and the technologies used to build and operate it.

In this section, the following types of applications will be discussed:

- Agents
- Applets
- Client-server
- Distributed
- Web applications

Agents

Agents are small, standalone programs that are part of a larger application. Agents carry out specific functions, such as remote status collection or remote system management.

Agents generally run autonomously and without any human interaction. On a Windows system, an agent often runs as a service, and on Unix an agent is usually a background process started by system startup scripts or as scheduled tasks. Another term for agent is *daemon.*

Some examples of agents include:

- *Anti-virus.* You could consider the anti-virus program on a workstation or server as an agent in an enterprise environment that includes a central management console.
- ***Patch management.*** An agent on each server periodically queries the OS on the existence of software patches and will install patches when commanded to do so from the central patch management server.
- ***Configuration management.*** A central server tracks and manages the OS configuration of each server and workstation by communicating to agents on those managed systems. Agents will collect configuration information and pass it back to central servers; agents will also perform configuration changes upon command.

Applets

An **applet** is a software program that runs within the context of another program. Unable to run on its own, an applet performs a narrow function.

Unlike a subroutine, which is a part of a running program, an applet is a separate object. Probably the most common use of applets is within web browsers.

Examples of web browser applets include media players such as Flash and Shockwave players, Java applets, and content viewers such as Adobe Reader. Figure 3-1 shows a Java applet running in a web browser window.

Client-Server Applications

The software components in **client-server applications** are not centralized but instead are located in two places: clients and servers. Client and server components communicate with each other via network connections. Specific characteristics of clients and servers are explained here.

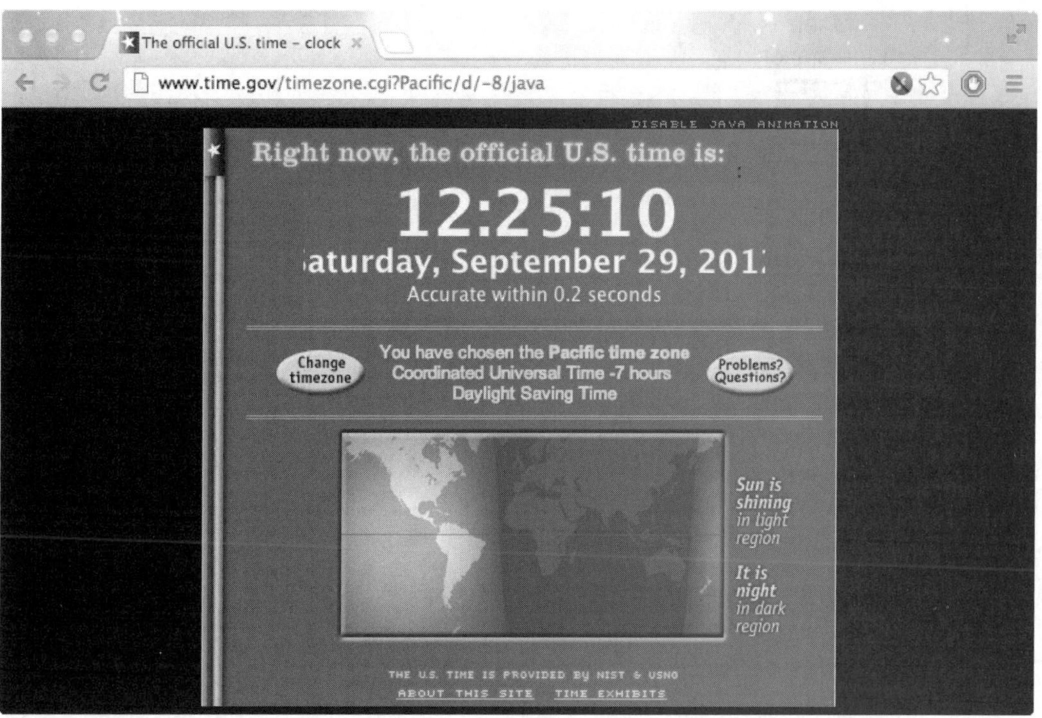

Figure 3-1 Java applet running in a browser window

Source: www.time.gov

- *Client characteristics*. Client software is the part of the application typically used by humans, and it primarily contains user interface logic that displays instructions and data, accepts input data from a keyboard or other device, and accepts instructions or directives from users. Client software is dominantly built upon personal workstations running Windows, UNIX, Mac OS, or Linux operating systems. Mobile devices also have operating systems scaled and configured for use with wireless connections, including Apple's iOS and Google's Android system.
- *Server characteristics*. In typical client-server applications, the server component runs business logic and provides a centralized platform for access to services, processes, and data. For example, with a customer relationship management software package, the server responds to a client's database queries and returns the information. Server components typically do not have direct user interface logic but instead run as daemons or services. Servers run a more robust class of operating system, a network operating system, which must be updated and protected from attacks. Like client operating systems, the server class of this software remains a highly attractive target for intruders since it is the gateway to the organization's data.

Client-server architectures were developed to meet the higher-processing demands of increasingly sophisticated graphical user interfaces by moving the display and input logic from a central system to the end user workstation. Database and other back-end functions remained on central servers. Clients and servers often communicated with each other over TCP/IP

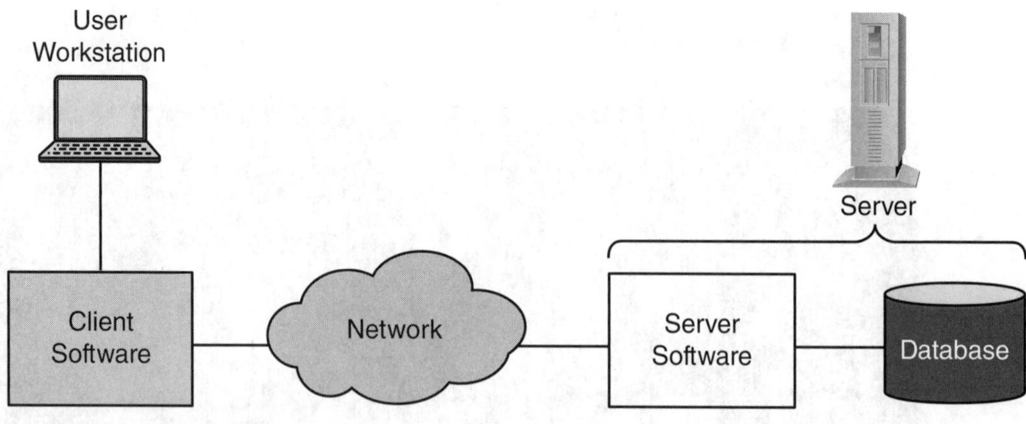

Figure 3-2 Typical client-server architecture

using protocols such as **ODBC (Open Database Connectivity)**, **CORBA (Common Object Request Broker Architecture)**, and **SQL*Net**. Figure 3-2 depicts a typical client-server architecture.

Client-server networks addressed inefficiencies created by peer-to-peer configurations. Although servers and client machines often share many of the same hardware components, including processors, memory, and hard drives, servers have space for larger quantities of storage and multiple processors. They are designed for redundancy and protect the entire network from a single point of failure.

Current client-server architectures leverage **virtualization** software and storage area networks. Virtualization software offers improved system utilization using a hypervisor to control access to the server's underlying hardware. Operating systems hand off these responsibilities to the hypervisor, allowing a single physical server to simultaneously host multiple operating systems. Virtualization software including VMware and Microsoft's Hyper-V gives organizations the ability to reduce the overall server footprint. This curtails equipment costs and also reduces energy costs.

Storage area networking devices offload the responsibility for recording, serving, and storing data away from individual servers. Storage area networks (SANs) are highly redundant systems often manufactured with high-quality components to reduce the possibility of failure. Servers and SANs are connected through distribution layer switches to offer another layer of redundancy, this time in the connectivity between the devices. If a server fails or needs maintenance, its virtual machines can move to another server as long as the new server connects to the SAN so it can answer the client calls for information.

More recent trends shift data storage out of locally controlled networks and into a cloud architecture. Clients access cloud-based applications using TCP/IP Ethernet connections. In some cases, a third-party provider supplies the data center equipment and support personnel, with additional services coming from an Internet service provider. Communications can be secured through the use of encrypted tunnels. This new model also suffers from risks associated with lack of local control and availability concerns resulting from inadequate pipeline throughput.

At first, client-server systems did not always scale well. With throughput speeds limited to 10/100 Mbps, bottlenecks occurred during peak usage periods. Although fiber channel connectivity provided significantly better throughput rates, the cost was often too high for many small to mid-size (under five hundred employees) organizations. Improvements in connectivity, including gigabit and 10-gigabit speeds, eliminated most of these concerns. Before virtualization software and affordable storage area network platforms, servers often outgrew their storage capacities. Heavy transactional use also created drive contention on the servers, resulting in reduced performance levels. Software improved as well. Instead of proprietary interfaces, many server-based applications provide application-layer access using common web browsers. These interfaces make transitioning to cloud-based storage platforms easier, since the process becomes nearly seamless from the user's perspective.

Distributed Applications

Distributed applications have software components running on several separate systems in a wide variety of architecture including two-tier, three-tier, and multi-tier. Usually, distributed systems are designed in a way to physically or logically separate different functions in the application. There are many possible reasons for this separation, including scalability, performance, geographical, and security.

Often, distributed applications consist of separate components that come from different origins. For instance, an application may be written in Java and designed to run on a specific run-time environment, and use a database management system from another company that, for performance and other reasons, will reside on separate systems. More complex systems may have additional components that, for different reasons, may reside on separate platforms. Figure 3-3 shows a typical distributed application environment.

As previously stated, the software components in a distributed application may be separated for performance reasons. There may be a large user base, and it may make better economic sense to build the application on several smaller servers instead of one large server. Components may also be separated for legal reasons, when different components are provided by different organizations.

Distributed applications are often designed to reduce security risk. For example, an application that is used to manage sensitive information, or one that is accessed over the Internet, may be designed with multiple tiers in order to reduce the risk of unauthorized disclosure of information. For instance, a **two-tier application** may have a business logic front end and a database back end, and a **three-tier application** typically consists of a user interface front end, a middle tier containing business logic, and a database management system back end.

A significant issue with distributed applications is version control and standardization. Managing and tracking the versions of software throughout the tiers of the distributed application and making sure that components continue interoperating properly is a challenge, particularly when various components are updated periodically. The near-constant state of change requires coordination and regression testing to keep the distributed application working properly.

Thin Client Web Applications

In the late 1990s, the near-ubiquity of web browsers and advances in browser-related technologies created the next opportunity for client-server and distributed applications:

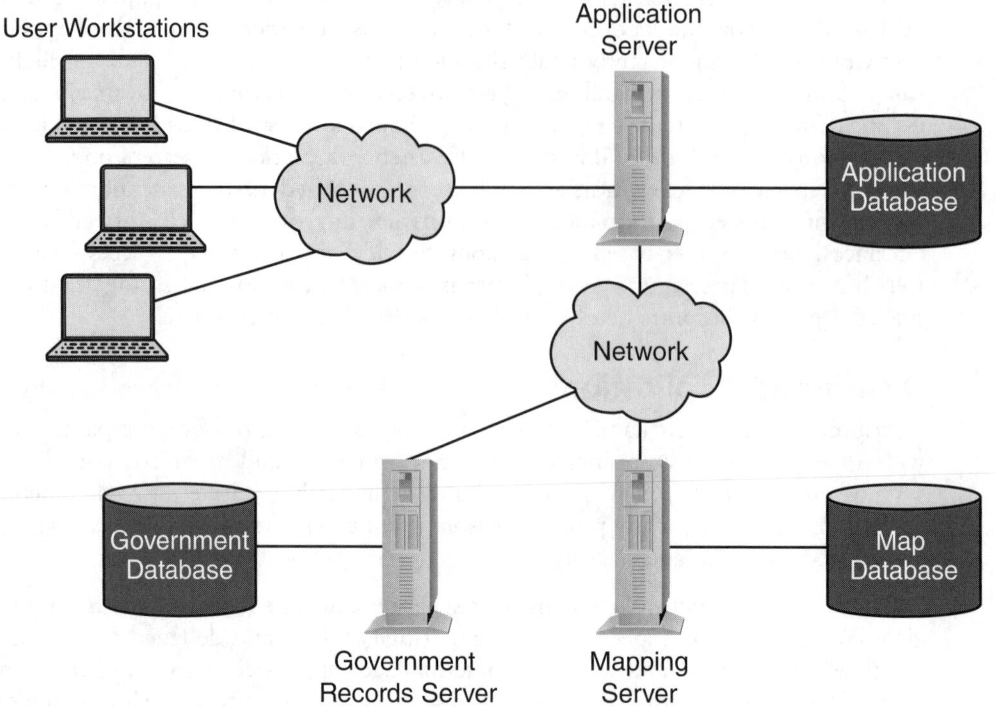

Figure 3-3 Typical distributed application architecture

web applications, a type of **thin client application**. Web applications provide several significant advances over client-server applications, including:

- *Thinner clients*. End user workstations need only a lightweight OS and a web browser. The browser becomes the client software, which works with all of the enterprise's centralized web applications.
- *Better network performance*. Business logic resides on the server, and only display logic resides on the workstation, significantly reducing demands on the network. This enables more users to use the application without incurring meltdowns on the network.
- *Lower cost of ownership*. The organization only needs to make sure that workstations have a reasonably current version of a web browser, and perhaps additional software components such as Java and Adobe Flash Player. The administrative overhead related to maintaining versions of client software components for all of the organization's client-server applications is greatly reduced.
- *More terminal types supported*. Because the client side of the application standardizes on HTML, several browser and terminal types are supported. Users are no longer locked into a hardware or OS platform but can access applications using a variety of terminal types including Windows, UNIX, Mac workstations, and also mobile devices such as smartphones and tablet computers.

- *Any user can access the application.* Because a web application requires only a browser as a client, any user anywhere in the world can potentially access the application without having to install special client software.

Web applications significantly reduce the number of software programs that must be installed and maintained in end user workstations. This in turn has curbed the increase in hardware resources required for many workstations.

There are a few disadvantages to the use of web applications, namely:

- *Complete reliance on network connectivity.* Web applications cannot work without a working connection between the client and server.
- *Browser compatibility.* Some web applications are written for specific browsers such as Microsoft Internet Explorer and do not function correctly with other browsers such as Chrome, Firefox, and Safari.
- ***Browser plug-in compatibility.*** Web-based business applications may require different, conflicting versions of browsers and plug-ins to work properly. For example, a payroll application may require IE 9 and Java 29, whereas a financial application may require IE 10 and Java 32. Both cannot exist on a workstation simultaneously.
- ***Attacks.*** Browsers are a **monoculture** and are the target of sophisticated attacks.

Software Models and Technologies

Computer systems and application programming languages are generally built upon models that give the language some form and structure. Four models that have been the most popular are control flow, structured, object-oriented, and knowledge-based.

Control Flow Languages

The earliest computer languages, known as **control flow**, were sequential in nature—that is, they executed statements one after the other. Most languages used some variation of an "if-then" construct as well as a "goto" construct to alter the sequence of instructions.

The disadvantage of control flow is the difficulty in verifying a program's integrity. Excessive use of "goto" statements turned linear logic into "spaghetti" code that is difficult to analyze and understand. The "goto" statement was demonized, and structured languages won favor.

Structured Languages

Programming languages with procedural structure were developed to overcome the deficiencies of control flow applications with their "goto" statements. **Structured languages** used *subroutines* or *functions* and relied less on *goto* (some structured languages do not have *goto* at all).

Structured languages tend to be structured in "blocks" of code that are bracketed by keywords such as `if…fi`, `BEGIN…END`, `{…}`, `if…then…else…endif`, and so on. The flow of logic in structured languages tends to be hierarchical rather than linear, which tends to make analysis and verification somewhat easier. Programming languages continued to evolve, and the next level of maturity was object-oriented programming.

Object-Oriented Systems

Object-oriented (OO) systems were developed to face the growing problem of programmer inefficiency by providing an environment in which objects (pieces of software) could be easily reused. Object oriented is more than just hierarchical programming—it provides a framework for easily building large, complex systems that have reusable code written in different languages and which reside in a distributed environment.

Object-Oriented Programming **Object-oriented programming** (OOP) originated in the 1960s with the computer languages Simula and Smalltalk. Then, as now, object-oriented (commonly known as OO, and pronounced *oh-oh*) programming is a completely different approach to computer languages than the structured languages in use such as BASIC, C, and Pascal. Object-oriented programming has a particular vocabulary that is used to describe how components are named and assembled into programs. These terms are:

- Class
- Object
- Method
- Encapsulation
- Inheritance
- Polymorphism

Class A **class** defines the characteristics of an *object*, including its characteristics such as attributes, properties, and fields, plus the *methods* it can perform.

Object An **object** is a particular *instance* of a *class*. The class *superhero* defines all superheroes and lists their characteristics. The object *Superman* is one particular superhero. The object *Superman* is an instance of the class *superhero*.

Method A **method** defines the abilities that an object can perform. It may contain instructions, as well as input variables and output variables. A method is similar to a *function* or *subroutine* in structured programming. It consists of some instructions or calculations, and communicates using *message passing*. The method *fly()* is one of Superman's *methods*. In a gaming program featuring Superman, the *fly()* method would be used to allow the player to lift the character off the ground.

Encapsulation **Encapsulation** refers to the implementation details in a method that are concealed. For example, the code for Superman's *fly()* method contains several other methods like *propulsion()* and *steering()* that other objects do not need to be concerned about.

Inheritance The term **inheritance** refers to the characteristics of a subclass that inherit attributes from their parent classes. And in turn, subclasses can introduce their own attributes that are passed to *their* subclasses.

Polymorphism The characteristic of **polymorphism** allows *objects* of different types to respond to *method* calls differently, depending upon their *type*. For instance, a call to a *computeTax()* method will result in different behavior depending upon the country (*type*) where the transaction takes place (there are not only different tax rates, but different taxable goods, and some people are taxed at different rates).

Distributed Object-Oriented Systems Distributed systems may be built upon object-oriented (OO) frameworks. These systems may be programmed with OO languages such as Java or C++. Modules on different systems that need to communicate with each other will typically use an Object Request Broker (ORB), a service that is used to locate an object on another system across networks. Common ORBs in use include CORBA (Common Object Request Broker Architecture), .Net Remoting, EJB (Enterprise Java Beans), DCOM (Distributed Common Object Model), or JRMI (Java Remote Method Invocation).

Knowledge-Based Systems

Knowledge-based systems are applications that are used to make predictions or decisions based upon input data. They include feedback mechanisms that enable them to learn and refine their guidance, improving their accuracy over time. The objective of knowledge-based systems is the ability for a system to possess some of the qualities of human reasoning. It is for this reason that knowledge-based systems are often termed *artificial intelligence.*

Examples of knowledge-based applications include weather forecasting, statistical data modeling, and decision makers for mortgage and credit applications.

Neural Networks **Neural networks** are so-named because they are modeled after biological reasoning processes that humans possess. A neural network (NN) consists of interconnected artificial neurons that store pieces of information about a particular problem. Neural networks are given many cases of situations and outcomes; the more events the neural network is given, the more accurately it will be able to predict future outcomes. This is done primarily through the NN being able to assign weights to different inputs. For instance, a hurricane-forecasting neural network that is used to make landfall predictions will heavily weigh the storm's location, wind speed, and ocean temperature but place less weight on the phase of the moon and little or no weight on the day of the week.

Expert Systems **Expert systems** accumulate knowledge on a particular subject, including conditions and outcomes. The more samples that the expert system is able to obtain, the greater is its ability to predict future outcomes.

An expert system contains a *knowledge base* that is the total accumulated knowledge and outcomes of past events that have been entered into the expert system. The expert system also includes an *inference engine* that analyzes information in the knowledge base in order to arrive at a decision or solution to a new problem.

Threats in the Software Environment

Because software applications are so often used to manage things of value, they may be subject to attack by those who wish to steal those assets and take them for their own. But value is not the only reason that applications are attacked; other reasons that applications are attacked include:

- *Industrial espionage.* Organizations with valuable secrets are often targeted by those who wish to steal those secrets for their own gain.
- *Vandalism and disruption.* Individuals and groups who, for a wide variety of reasons, wish to vandalize and harm the operations of specifically or randomly targeted organizations.
- *Denial of service.* A more targeted attack where the attackers' objective is to impair or completely disable the target system.
- *Political/religious.* Attacks perpetrated for political or religious motives at a national or international scale. The individuals who perpetrate these attacks are also known as **hacktivists**.

Software Attack Approaches

There are several approaches used by adversaries when they attack software applications. These include:

- *Authentication bypass.* Here, an attacker is attempting to access a system's resource without having to supply authentication credentials.
- ***Privilege escalation.*** Adversaries who have accessed a system attack the system in attempts to gain higher levels of privileges, which may give them access to more information or allow them to control the system.
- *Denial of service.* Adversaries will attempt to incapacitate a system either by flooding it with messages or by sending specially crafted messages in hopes that the target system will malfunction.

Regardless of the approach, attackers are generally attempting to compromise a system so that they can either steal data, alter data, or render the system unusable for others.

The threats to software applications discussed in this section involve several attack methods, including:

- Buffer overflow
- Malicious software
- Input attacks
- Logic bombs
- Object reuse
- Mobile code
- Social engineering
- Back door
- These threats are discussed in detail below.

Buffer Overflow

Software applications usually function by soliciting and accepting input from a user (or another application) through an interface. An attacker can attempt to disrupt the function of a software application by providing more data to the application than it was designed to handle. A *buffer overflow* attack occurs when someone attempts to disrupt a program's operation in this manner.

In a buffer overflow attack, the excess input data overflows the program's input buffer and overwrites another part of the program's memory space. Depending upon the hardware and software architecture of the attacked program, this can lead to corruption of other variables in the program (which could lead to an unexpected change in the program's behavior), or the overflow could overwrite instructions in the software. A well-formed attack can plant specific instructions in the input buffer (that will be known to overflow the instruction space in the attacked program) that will result in a distinct change in the program's behavior that was not intended or anticipated by its designers.

Types of Buffer Overflow Attacks There are several specific types of buffer overflow attacks, discussed here.

Stack Buffer Overflow In this type of attack, the program writes more data to a buffer located on the stack than was allocated for it. This causes the corruption of other data in the stack, which results in the program's malfunction.

If familiar with the program that he or she is attacking, the attacker can attempt to place specific data in the overflowed portion of the stack in order to cause a specific type of malfunction to occur. The particular malfunction that is desired will depend upon the motives of the attacker.

NOP Sled Attack The **NOP sled** attack is a specific stack overflow attack where the attacker overflows the stack with harmless NOP (no-operation) instructions. The point of the NOP sled attack is to improve the chances that the attacker will be able to find an attack point. By flooding the stack with lots of NOPs, the program will encounter and "slide down" the NOPs until it reaches the pointer that the attacker placed in the buffer. The program will then jump to the memory location referenced by the pointer, resulting in whatever behavior the attacker intended.

When an attacker is attempting a buffer overflow attack, he or she cannot see the attacked program's memory space; instead, the attacker must guess its structure. The NOP sled attack helps to improve the attacker's guesswork at how to exploit the target program.

Heap Overflow The heap is the dynamically allocated memory space created by a program for storage of variables. Usually a **heap overflow** attack will result in the corruption of other variables that are already on the heap. A heap overflow attack will result in corrupted data that may change the actual behavior of the program or simply alter data used by the program, which could affect other users or stored data.

Jump-to-Register Attack The **jump-to-register** attack is another approach to buffer overflows. In this attack, the return pointer is overwritten with a value that will cause the program to jump to a known pointer stored in a register that points to the input buffer.

Historic Buffer Overflow Attacks Several wide-scale buffer overflow attacks have been perpetrated through the Internet, and some have caused significant damage totaling hundreds of millions to billions of U.S. dollars. Notable buffer overflow attacks are described here.

- *Morris worm*. Created by Robert Tappan Morris in 1988, the Morris worm exploited a buffer overflow vulnerability in the "finger" program on UNIX systems. It also exploited several other vulnerabilities including default passwords and the excessive use of trusted relationship between computers. The Morris worm did no real damage other than make thousands of computer systems unavailable for use until the worm could be eradicated.

- *Ping of Death*. The ping of death (POD) is a buffer overflow attack wherein the attacker sends a "ping" (literally, an ICMP echo request) packet with a very large payload to a target system. A ping is usually 64 bytes in length, whereas a ping of death packet is as large as or larger than the maximum IP packet size, which is 65,535 bytes. The target is often unable to properly process the incoming packet, resulting in a buffer overflow that causes the system's TCP/IP stack to malfunction. The ping of death attack is also a denial-of-service attack because it renders the target system unusable by its users.
- *Code Red*. Released in July 2001, this computer worm attacked a buffer overflow vulnerability in Microsoft's IIS web server, for which a patch had been available for about a month.
- *SQL Slammer*. This worm exploited a buffer overflow in Microsoft SQL Server and Data Engine (MSDE) database products in January 2003. Slammer had a network-scanning propagation mechanism that allowed it to infect most of its 75,000 victim servers within minutes of release. A patch to mitigate the buffer overflow vulnerability had been available for six months, but few organizations had installed the patch.
- *Blaster*. This worm exploited a buffer overflow in the DCOM RPC service on Windows systems. A patch for the vulnerability was issued in July 2003, but few organizations had installed it by the time this worm appeared on August 11, 2003.
- *Sasser*. Released in April 2004, the Sasser worm exploited a buffer overflow in the LSASS (Local Security Authority Subsystem Service) in Windows 2000 and Windows XP. A patch had been available for only seventeen days.
- *Conficker*. This worm exploited vulnerabilities in Windows and attacked administrator passwords on target systems. It has several advanced techniques for evading detection and resisting removal.

Buffer Overflow Countermeasures Several tactical and strategic countermeasures are available to reduce or eliminate the risk of buffer overflow attacks. Buffer overflow countermeasures are used to either remove buffer overflow capabilities or detect and block buffer overflow activity.

- *Choose a safe language*. Programming languages like C and C++ do not automatically check input buffer lengths or perform other boundary checking. For instance, the strcpy () function that is used to copy strings performs no boundary checking and will merrily copy data right over other variables. Java, .NET, and many other languages have built-in boundary checking that—in most cases—prevents buffer overflows. Newer versions of C and C++ compilers introduce boundary checking as added protection.
- *Use of safe libraries*. Whether C or C++, or a "safer" programming language is used, libraries with functions for inputting and processing data will significantly reduce the risk of events like buffer overflows.
- *Executable space protection*. Attackers use buffer overflows to insert code into the memory of a program. **Executable space protection**, a feature of some operating

systems, forces programs to abort if they attempt to execute code in the stack or the heap. Some CPUs support executable space protection in hardware.

- *Stack smashing protection.* This refers to techniques used to detect changes in the stack. Typically a "canary value" is placed between a buffer and the stack. The canary value is so-called after the use of canaries in underground mines as an indicator of deteriorating air quality. In stack smashing protection, the canary value is set to a known, random value, and after a function call is returned, the canary value is checked again. If the stack has been smashed by a buffer overflow, the canary value will have changed, and the program can take evasive action. If the canary value is unchanged, then the program has probably not been tampered with—at least not in this way.

- *Application firewalls.* Firewalls that perform deep packet inspection (DPI) examine the payload of each packet entering a system. An **application firewall** recognizes the patterns used in buffer overflow, script injection, and other attacks and will block those packets, effectively preventing most attacks.

Malicious Software

Malicious software, also known as malicious code or malware, is a class of software that comes in many forms and performs a variety of damaging actions. The purposes of malware include:

- *Propagation.* Sometimes the ability for malware to propagate—that is, to spread from system to system—is the only purpose for particular malware programs.
- *Damage and destruction of information.* Malware can alter or delete files on target systems.
- *Steal information.* Malware can locate and steal valuable information such as e-mail addresses, userids and passwords, bank account numbers, and credit card numbers. Malware can harvest and transmit this information back to the malware's owner or operator.
- *Usage monitoring.* Malware can implant the means to record subsequent communications, keystrokes, and mouse clicks, and send this data back to the malware's owner-operator.
- *Denial of service.* Malware can consume some or all available resources on a target system, or cause a target system to malfunction; in either case, rendering it essentially useless for its intended use.
- *Remote control.* Malware can implant a bot onto a target system that allows an attacker to remotely control the system. Large collections of bots are called *bot armies*, and the people who build and control bot armies are known as *bot herders* or *botnet operators*.

Components of Malicious Software There are typically three different components present in malware that make it work. These components are:

- *Exploit.* The exploit is code that is designed to take advantage of a vulnerability in a software program such as a browser, word processing program, or spreadsheet program. The exploit code exploits the vulnerability, which allows the malware to begin to execute its own instructions.

- *Dropper*. This is the component that installs the actual malware on the target machine.
- *Malware*. This is the component that performs whatever function is intended by its operator: stealing data, destroying data, sniffing the network, or perhaps just looking for more target systems to infect.

Sometimes malware will contain all of these components in a single package, but sometimes these components are separate. Malware considered more sophisticated will contain multiple types of exploit code, dropper code, and multipurpose malware. Further, some types of malware do not contain all three components; for instance, a **Trojan horse** might not contain an exploit, since some other means (usually, tricking a user) is used to execute the malware.

Types of Malicious Software Malware has been developed into many forms that are described in this section. It can be said that malware has undergone the same types of innovation that software has undergone. New methods of development and propagation have been developed that give malware new ways of spreading from system to system, and also new ways of evading system and network defenses.

- Viruses
- Worms
- Trojan horses
- Rootkits
- Bots
- Remote access Trojans
- Spam
- Pharming
- Spyware and adware

Viruses **Viruses** are the original malware on Intel x86 processor systems popularized by Microsoft DOS and Windows since the 1980s. Viruses are computer code fragments that attach themselves to a legitimate program file on a computer. The virus can only run when the legitimate program is run.

By definition, viruses generally require human intervention to propagate. A user must run a program in order to make the virus spread.

Viruses used to propagate through file sharing (when users would trade information or programs via floppy disks), but more often they travel through e-mail and web traffic.

Several types of viruses are discussed here.

- *Master boot record (MBR) viruses*. One of the earliest methods of virus propagation, MBR viruses attach themselves to the master boot record of a floppy disk. If the system is booted when the floppy disk is present in the system, the virus will be activated on the system. When other floppy disks are inserted after activation, the virus may be copied onto those floppy disks also. When floppy disks were the primary means for transferring data from computer to computer, this was a common way for viruses to propagate from computer to computer.

- *File infector viruses*. These are the viruses that attach themselves to executable programs (.EXE and .COM files) and are activated each time the executable program is run.
- *Macro viruses*. In the early 1990s, Microsoft and other companies developed the concept of macros that could be embedded into document and spreadsheet files. Writers of viruses and other malicious code quickly realized that these new capabilities could be used to propagate malware. When a user opens a document that contains a macro, the macro is executed. The embedded macro may be written in a script language such as Visual Basic or Visual C++. The macro may contain any legitimate instructions that may vastly exceed anything that the user would want. *Melissa* and *I Love You* were macro viruses that propagated through documents that contained macro instructions to mail copies of themselves to everyone in a user's local e-mail address book. These macro viruses spread quickly through the Internet and caused considerable damage primarily through clogging e-mail servers with thousands of virus-caused messages.

Viruses employ several methods to avoid detection by anti-virus programs. The methods in use include:

- *Multipartite viruses*. These use more than one means for propagating from one system to another. For example, Ghostball infected both executable .COM program files as well as floppy disk boot sectors.
- *Stealth viruses*. A stealth virus uses some means to hide itself from detection from the operating system.
- *Polymorphic viruses*. Viruses are easily stopped when anti-virus programs recognize the virus through its signature. Virus creators have introduced polymorphic viruses that change themselves as they move from system to system in order to avoid detection. However, engineers in the anti-virus companies are able to solve the puzzle of polymorphic viruses and create a signature for them.
- *Encrypted viruses*. In another method to avoid detection, viruses will encrypt most of their code, using a different encryption key on each system they infect, which makes most of the body of the virus different on each detected system. However, a part of the virus—the decryption code—must remain the same; it is this portion of the virus that the anti-virus software must be able to identify in order to stop the virus.

Worms Generally speaking, **worms** are like viruses, but they usually require little human intervention to spread. Instead, they have their own means of propagation built in.

Two common types of worms that are found today include:

- *Mass-mailing worms*. Mass-mailing worms propagate via e-mail. Generally, when a mass-mailing worm arrives in a user's inbox, the worm is activated when the recipient opens the message. The worm's malicious code could reside within the HTML code in the message, or in an attached file.
- *Port-scanning worms*. A port-scanning worm is able to propagate with no human intervention at all. A port-scanning worm scans the network for other systems that may be vulnerable and attempts to spread to those neighboring systems. If it's able to infect a new system, it will install itself and begin the scanning to look for new victims.

Several infamous worms utilized port scanning to identify new targets that they would attack with specific buffer overflow attacks. The Morris worm, Blaster, SASSER, Code Red, and Slammer are described in the Buffer Overflow section earlier in this chapter. Figure 3-4 shows the rapidity with which the Code Red and Nimda worms spread through the Internet in 2001.

Trojan Horses Like the ancient Greek legend, a computer-based Trojan horse is a lie. A Trojan horse claims to be one thing, but is instead something else—something with more malicious intent.

For example, a user may receive an e-mail message that says, "Take a look at this great new computer game," or, "Have a look at these pictures of <some popular model or celebrity>." Unsuspecting users willingly execute these programs without a second thought.

The user who runs a Trojan horse program may or may not see some visual resemblance of what the program claims to be. However, the Trojan horse is also performing some additional (and probably malicious) action. It might be corrupting or destroying files, stealing data, or sending e-mails to your friends.

Rootkits **Rootkits** are malware programs that are designed to avoid detection by being nearly or absolutely invisible to the operating system. Rootkits achieve this by altering the OS itself so that their presence is nearly impossible to detect.

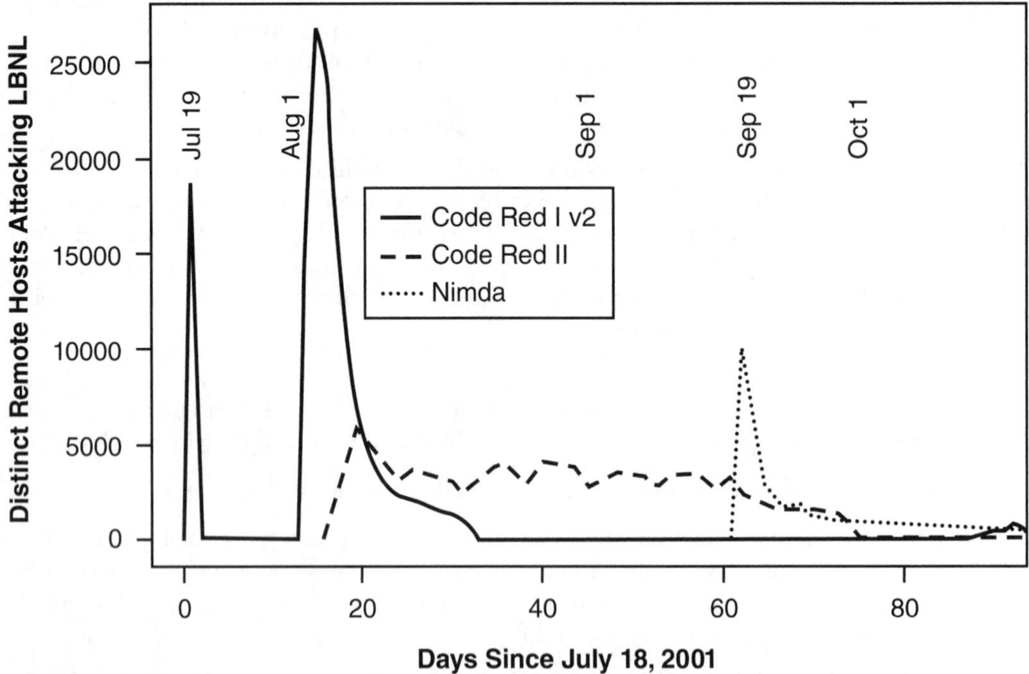

Figure 3-4 Code Red and Nimda spread quickly through the Internet

Diagram with permission from "How to 0wn the Internet In Your Spare Time," S. Staniford, V. Paxson, and N. Weaver, Proc. USENIX Security Symposium 2002

Methods used by rootkits to avoid detection include:

- *Process hiding*. Rootkits can hide their own process(es) from users by altering the tools that are used to list processes on a system. By manipulating process-listing tools into "looking the other way," rootkits can hide themselves from most users.
- *File hiding*. Rootkits can hide files as a way of avoiding detection. However, legitimate programs also sometimes hide files, so this alone is not a dependable way of identifying a rootkit.
- *Registry hiding*. Rootkits can hide registry entries in an attempt to function without being detected. However, some legitimate programs also hide registry entries, so this alone is not a sure-fire way to identify a rootkit.
- *Running as a hypervisor*. A rootkit can hide from the OS by running as a hypervisor, where the OS runs as a guest system.

Like anti-virus technology, anti-rootkit technology will become engaged in a cat-and-mouse struggle with rootkit developers in what could be a long-term conflict.

Bots Short for "robots," **bots** are sometimes a part of the malicious payload found in malware. Bots enable a "bot herder" (the owner of the bot program) to remotely control the infected computer for a variety of purposes including:

- *Relaying spam*. Spammers and bot herders can cooperate to use bots as systems to relay spam in order to evade blacklisting (a technique that spam blockers use to block spam by blocking all e-mail from specific IP addresses).
- *Hosting phishing sites*. Phishing scams can use systems owned by bots to host the sites where victims are solicited for sensitive information. By moving the sites quickly from bot-system to bot-system, phishers can evade detection and shutdown.
- *Denial-of-service attacks*. Bot herders can launch denial-of-service (DoS) attacks from bot-controlled systems by instructing those systems to launch thousands of network messages per second to a target system. A bot herder can launch a distributed denial-of-service (DDoS) attack by directing hundreds, thousands, or tens of thousands of bot-systems to attack the same target simultaneously.

Remote Access Trojans (RATs) This is a type of malware that permits an attacker to remotely control a victim machine, either manually or automatically. A target system with a RAT may be a part of a targeted attack on an organization, where the intruder wishes to conduct reconnaissance on the target organization.

Spam In a nutshell, **spam** is unwanted e-mail. It accounts for well over 90 percent of all e-mail on the Internet. But more than that, spam is unsolicited "junk mail" that takes many forms, including:

- *Unsolicited commercial e-mail (UCE)*. There are e-mails that are trying to sell every sort of goods and services ranging from porn to prescription drugs to get-rich-quick schemes. Although UCE is also used to market even legitimate goods and services, users often frown on this type of advertising and frown at companies that advertise in this way.

- ***Phishing***. These two-part attacks consist of legitimate-looking e-mail messages from large and well-known organizations (often financial institutions) that use some means to trick a user into visiting a web site. This web site will resemble a legitimate site and ask for login or other credentials or information such as credit card numbers, social security numbers, or other information that will be used to defraud the user. The most common phishing scams purport to come from banks that ask users to log in and confirm account numbers or credit card numbers.
- ***Spear phishing***. These are phishing attacks that specifically attack companies or even specific groups of people in companies. These attacks will contain victim-specific messaging in an attempt to fool victims into running malware or clicking on links.
- ***Whaling***. These are phishing attacks that specifically attack wealthy individuals and executives in targeted organizations. One could consider this a specialized form of spear phishing.
- *Malware*. Spam is often used to directly deliver malware to users' computers, but it is also often used to lure people to web sites that contain malicious code in the form of viruses, worms, or bots.

Pharming In a pharming attack, an attacker directs all traffic destined for a particular web site towards an imposter web site. The attack diverts traffic by "poisoning" the organization's DNS servers or by changing the **hosts file** on individual users' systems.

For instance, an attacker may wish to defraud users by stealing their online banking credentials for the well-known (and fictitious) Spendthrift Savings and Loan (ssloan.com). The attacker will set up a phony site that looks just like the real ssloan.com site. Then, the attacker will attack organizations' DNS servers in an attempt to poison their cache files. The attacker might also craft some malware that will insert a phony record into users' hosts file on their workstations.

Both attack methods will result in users' browsers going to the *fake* ssloan.com web site instead of the legitimate one. Users who do not notice this will enter their ssloan.com credentials, which the attacker can later use to log in to the *real* ssloan.com to steal users' funds.

Figure 3-5 shows how a typical pharming attack works.

Spyware and Adware **Spyware** and **adware** encompass a wide variety of means that have been developed to track the behavior of users' Internet usage patterns. While not strictly malicious, many find the techniques and motives used by spyware and adware to be suspicious and an invasion of their privacy. Spyware and adware take on many forms, including:

- *Tracking cookies*. Many web site operators will track users' individual visits to web sites through the use of tracking cookies that may accompany banner ads. There are a few, very large banner ad placement companies, and their use of cookies can range from legitimate to downright abusive.
- *Web beacons*. Sometimes known as "web bugs," web beacons are tiny 1×1 pixel images that are embedded in web pages or HTML-rendered e-mails as a means for tracking users' Internet usage. An alternative to cookies, web beacons are far more difficult to detect and block but can have the same degree of tracking ability as cookies.

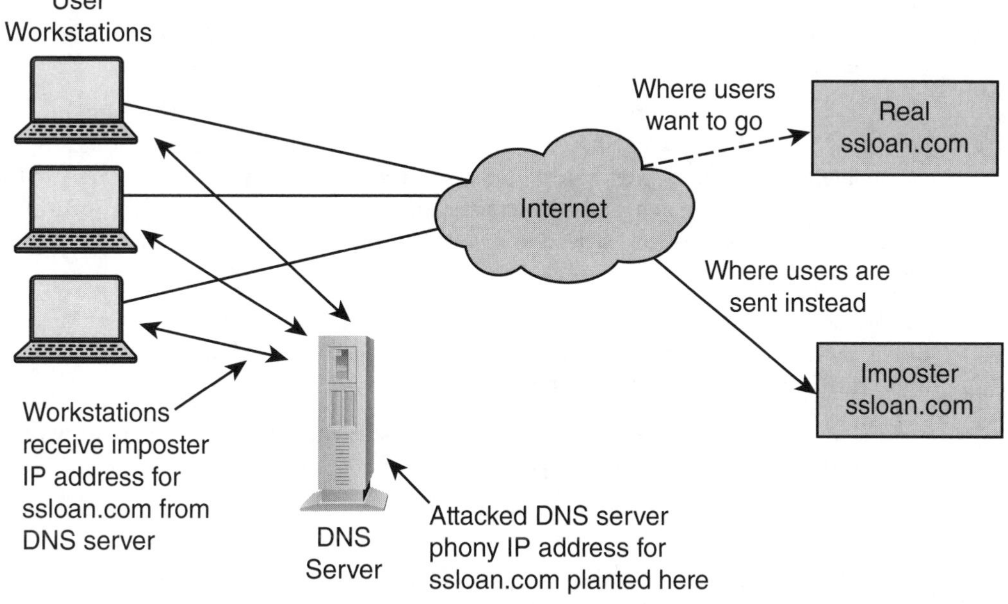

Figure 3-5 Pharming attack redirects users to a phony application server

Redrawn diagram with permission from S. Staniford, V. Paxon, and N. Weaver, "How to 0wn the Internet In Your Spare Time," Proc. USENIX Security Symposium 2002

- *Browser helper objects (BHOs)*. Sometimes they take the form of helpful toolbars, but at other times they are completely invisible and "stealthy." BHOs can be used to track use of users' web browsers. I should be quick to point out that not all BHOs are malicious—many serve a useful and legitimate purpose.
- *Key loggers*. Arguably the most invasive form of spyware, a **key logger** actually records a user's keystrokes (and, often, mouse movements and clicks) and transmits that data back to a central location.

Malicious Software Countermeasures Several measures are needed to block the ability for malware to enter and run on a system. These countermeasures include:

- Anti-virus
- Anti-rootkits
- Anti-spyware
- Anti-spam
- Firewalls
- Decreased privilege levels
- Application whitelisting
- Process profiling
- Penetration testing
- Hardening

Anti-Virus **Anti-virus** programs run on a system and employ various means to detect the possible entry of malware and have the ability to block its entry. Anti-virus software can often remove or incapacitate malware if it is already present on a system.

Anti-virus software uses two primary means for detecting malware: signature-based and heuristics-based. In signature-based detection, the anti-virus program periodically downloads an updated list of virus "signatures"—usually fragments of actual malware—that anti-virus software can use to match and confirm the presence of malware. In heuristics-based detection, the anti-virus software detects malware's presence through its anomalous behavior on the system.

Anti-virus programs are found in many places in an organization as part of a defense in depth architecture to prevent the unwanted consequences of malware. The places where anti-virus software can be found include:

- *End user workstations*. In the beginning this is the only place where anti-virus software was used. Today this is considered the last defense.
- *E-mail servers*. Because so much malware spreads through e-mail, e-mail servers are a natural choice.
- *File servers*. Because malware can hide in documents and program files, anti-virus software is often utilized on file servers.
- *Web proxy servers*. Many organizations funnel all web traffic (that is, the inbound and outbound traffic that results from employees' visiting web sites) through proxy servers. This can help the organization control web usage by blocking access to unwanted (porn, gambling, hate-related, illegal, and so on) web sites and also block malware.
- *Security appliances*. The drive to simplicity and lower TCO has given rise to a generation of all-in-one security appliances that perform several functions including firewall, web content filter, spam filter, and anti-virus.

It should be noted that anti-virus software is widely recognized to be ineffective at stopping advanced malware. Other means, such as decreasing privilege levels, process profiling, and application whitelisting, are necessary to stop advanced malware.

Anti-Rootkit Software **Anti-rootkit software** uses techniques to find hidden processes, hidden registry entries, unexpected kernel hooks, and hidden files in order to find rootkits that may be present on a system. Anti-rootkit software programs use various means to find these hidden objects in a system, generally through the use of directly examining the running operating system instead of using tools that the rootkit may have been able to manipulate.

Anti-Spyware Software Software to block spyware and adware is similar to anti-virus software: it monitors incoming files and examines them against a collection of signatures, and blocks those files that match known signatures.

Like anti-virus software, **anti-spyware** can scan a hard drive to identify spyware, adware, and other unwanted programs, and remove them as directed by the user.

It used to be necessary to use separate, unbundled anti-spyware programs, but increasingly anti-spyware accompanies many of the popular anti-virus programs. In the long run, separate anti-spyware may disappear from the market altogether, the feature reduced to an option in anti-virus programs, whether or not to detect and block spyware.

Anti-Spam Software Spam blockers effectively eliminate most of the spam coming into an organization, blocking the majority of the unwanted e-mail that carries malware, phishing scams, fraudulent advertising, and porn.

Spam filters examine all incoming e-mail messages and perform a content analysis in order to arrive at a "score" for each message. Messages whose score exceeds a threshold are diverted to a quarantine or deleted. Messages whose score does not exceed the threshold are delivered to the end user's inbox.

Blocking spam is an inexact science because spammers are always finding new ways to get through, and the spam filters seem to be in a game of endless catch-up. Still, the better spam blockers eliminate 95–98 percent of incoming spam, while inadvertently flagging legitimate e-mails as spam less than 1 percent of the time.

There are four common spam-blocking architectures in use, including:

- *Client-based.* In this architecture the spam-blocking software resides on the end user workstation. This method has fallen out of favor because of the administrative overhead required to keep yet another defensive software program operating on client workstations. Another disadvantage of this model is the failure to eliminate spam from the network and e-mail servers, since it has to be delivered to the end user before it is detected and removed.
- *E-mail server-based.* Here, the spam-blocking software is installed on the e-mail server. The advantage to this method is that the spam-blocking software is centralized, and spam is not delivered to end users.
- *Appliance-based.* A spam-blocking appliance sits in front of corporate e-mail servers, blocking all incoming spam and delivering only the legitimate e-mail to the mail server. The advantage of this architecture is that the e-mail server is relieved of the burden of receiving all of the legitimate e-mail plus the spam.
- *Spam-blocking service.* In this model, incoming e-mail is delivered to an off-site spam-blocking service provider that filters out the spam and delivers only legitimate e-mail to corporate e-mail servers. The advantage of this model is that spam no longer consumes network bandwidth on organizations' Internet connections.

Most organizations opt to allow users to be able to access their own quarantines. This gives end users the ability to recover any incoming e-mails that were incorrectly marked as spam.

Firewalls **Firewalls** are the time-tested and still-preferred means for blocking unwanted network traffic from crossing a network boundary. Firewalls are typically used as perimeter devices, protecting organizations from unwanted traffic that originates from the Internet.

Firewalls examine each inbound packet and compare the source and destination addresses and port numbers against a list of permitted and blocked addresses. The list of permitted and blocked addresses on a firewall is called the list of *firewall rules*.

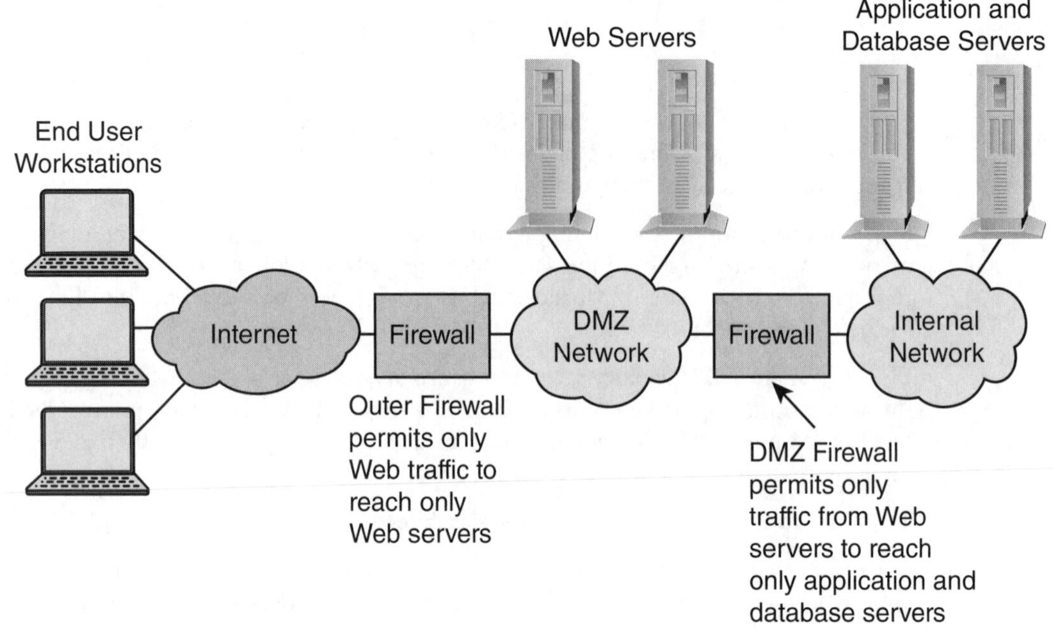

Figure 3-6 Typical DMZ network architecture protected by firewalls

Firewalls are also used to segregate various networks within organizations. Examples of such uses include:

- *Isolation of labs*. In organizations where employees are developing and experimenting with software and systems in a lab, often a firewall will be used to isolate the lab from the rest of the enterprise. A firewall in this case will protect the enterprise from the lab—as well as protect the lab from the enterprise.
- *Isolation of production service networks*. Organizations that are network-based service providers often segregate their production networks from their corporate networks. This prevents ordinary corporate users from being able to directly access production systems.
- ***Demilitarized zones (DMZ)***. Online applications that store or process sensitive information often require firewalls to separate front-end systems from back-end systems, so that back-end systems like database management servers cannot be directly accessed from the Internet. Firewall rules separating tier-one and tier-two systems provide an additional layer of defense by permitting only front-end applications servers to directly contact back-end database servers. Figure 3-6 shows a typical DMZ architecture with firewalls isolating each layer.
- *End user workstations*. Most end user workstations are laptop computers that are often taken outside the confines of the enterprise network and connected directly to the Internet, away from the protection of organizations' central firewalls. This necessitates the use of so-called *personal firewalls* that are used to block unwanted traffic. Personal firewalls are software programs that operate on workstations and, like

physical network firewalls, examine each incoming network packet and make a pass-or-drop decision based upon a preconfigured set of rules.

Decreased Privilege Levels When malware successfully breaks into a system and is executed by the user, the malware usually is executing with the same privilege level as the user. This is a serious problem for most organizations, since the default privilege level for most end user workstations is set to "administrative." In other words, when the end user has administrative-level privileges on a system and the user has activated malicious code, then the malicious code is able to execute with administrative privileges and do whatever it wants on the system, including any of the following:

- Change system configurations
- Alter or remove system programs
- Disable anti-virus, anti-spyware, firewall, and security update software
- Access, change, or remove any file on the system

For this reason, many organizations are moving towards a model where end users do not have administrative privileges on their workstations, but instead operate at an "end user" privilege level. Because users at end user privilege level are not able to make most changes to the operating system, any malicious code that the user unintentionally brings in will likewise be unable to make changes to the operating system. The risk of harm to the end user and to the enterprise as a whole is reduced considerably.

A side benefit of reducing user privileges to end user level is a decreased number of tech support calls to repair user-generated incidents, when often inexperienced end users muddle up operating system configurations.

Application Whitelisting Another approach to the malware problem is the use of application whitelisting. Here, a mechanism on a user's workstation controls whether any program is permitted to run. If the program is on the application whitelist, it will be able to run. Naturally, malware will not be present in the whitelist, so it will not be able to run.

Application whitelisting is also used to control the practice of end users downloading and installing software on their workstations.

Process Profiling Yet another approach to malware is the observation of running processes. An agent on a server or workstation can observe each running process and block further execution of that process if it enters a new, unknown state that may represent its compromise by malware.

Penetration Testing Rather than simply relying upon security configuration settings, an organization should also test the settings by using tools to simulate a hacker's attempt to find weaknesses in a system. Such tests are known as *penetration tests*, often known as "pen tests." Pen tests send network packets to a target system in an attempt to discover the network-based services that are present and active on a system, and whether any of those services have any exploitable vulnerabilities. If any vulnerabilities are present, they'll be noted along with their severity in a report or other output created by the pen testing tool.

The object of penetration testing is to discover and fix vulnerabilities before a hacker is able to discover and exploit them. It's typically a race against time to fix serious vulnerabilities before hackers discover them, particularly on high-value sites.

Hardening Server operating systems are very complex and often are preconfigured for a wide variety of tasks. This often means that many of the programs and features that are available are activated by default. The result is a server with its necessary feature(s) activated, plus many additional unnecessary features also activated and ready to accept input from any friendly or unfriendly party.

If any vulnerability is discovered in any of these unnecessary features, an attacker may be able to exploit one or more of these vulnerabilities and break in to the server. Certainly this type of situation is one that should be avoided. The practice of **hardening** is used to identify and remove these vulnerabilities.

Situations like this have led to the publication of "server hardening" guidelines that, when followed, result in a server that is "lean and mean," with far fewer potential vulnerabilities. The common principles behind server hardening include these concepts:

- *Deactivate or remove unnecessary services*. Every software component that is not required for a server to fulfill its purpose should be either deactivated (good) or removed altogether (better).
- *Robust network configuration*. Servers' TCP/IP configuration should be set to recommended values to make the server more able to repel **network-stack attacks**, which are attacks against network drivers on a target system.
- *Robust software configuration*. Any required software programs on the server should be configured to be as secure as possible. Server programs should be configured to run with the lowest possible privilege levels—following the principle of *least privilege*.
- *Administrator account hardening*. Administrator account names should be changed, and passwords set to highly complex and not easily broken values. All unused administrator accounts should be locked or removed.
- *Security patches*. Servers, particularly those that are exposed to the Internet, should have up-to-date security patches installed regularly.

Server hardening guides are available from operating system vendors (Microsoft, Sun Microsystems, Red Hat, etc.) as well as from security organizations like the U.S. National Institute for Standards and Technology (NIST), the Center for Internet Security (CIS), the U.S. Computer Emergency Response Team (US-CERT), and the SANS Institute. Organizations often use one or more of the server hardening guides or build one of their own, borrowing guidance from one or more of these guides or others.

Input Attacks

Applications and tools often request input from users as well as from other programs. A common method of attacking an application is to provide data that causes unexpected behavior in the application.

Input attacks—sometimes called malformed input attacks or **injection attacks**—are designed to exploit weaknesses in the application by causing unexpected behavior, including:

- *Elevation of privileges*. The attacker will input specially coded data in an attempt to cause a malfunction that will result in the attacker having a higher level of access or privilege in the application.
- *Execution of arbitrary code*. The attacker may wish to run specific commands on the target system.
- *Malfunction*. The attacker may wish to cause the application to malfunction and be in a disabled state for legitimate users.

- *Abort*. The attacker may wish to cause the application to completely abort and thus be unavailable for any legitimate use.

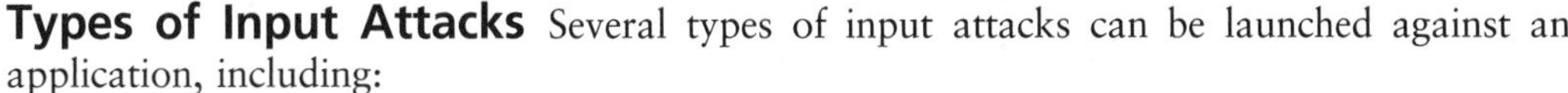

Types of Input Attacks Several types of input attacks can be launched against an application, including:

- *Buffer overflow*. This is discussed in detail earlier in this chapter.
- *Integer overflow*. An attack where the attacker attempts to cause an application to perform an integer operation that will create a numeric value larger than can be represented in the available storage.
- *SQL injection*. In this type of attack, the attacker inserts specially coded and delimited SQL statements into an input field in the hopes that the injected SQL will be executed on the back-end database. This type of attack is possible in applications that dynamically build SQL statements.
- *Script injection*. Similar to SQL injection, an attacker inserts script language into an input field in the hopes that the scripting language will be executed.
- ***Cross-site scripting (XSS)***. An attack where an attacker can inject a malicious script into HTML content in order to steal session cookies and other sensitive information.
- ***Cross-site request forgery (CSRF)***. This is an attack where malicious HTML is inserted into a web page or e-mail that, when clicked, causes an action to occur on an unrelated site where the user may have an active session.

Input Attack Countermeasures Measures that can be used to prevent input attacks include:

- *Effective input field filtering*. Input fields should be filtered to remove all characters that might be a part of an input attack. Which characters are removed will depend upon the types of software used by the application. For numeric fields, reasonableness checks should be performed to prevent overflow attacks.
- *Application firewall*. Network firewalls inspect only the source and destination addresses and the port numbers, but not the contents of network packets. Application firewalls (also known as *web application firewalls*) examine the contents of packets and block packets containing input attack code and other unwanted data.
- *Application vulnerability scanning*. Organizations that develop their own applications for online use should scan those applications for input attack vulnerabilities, in order to identify vulnerabilities prior to their being discovered and exploited by outsiders. Application vulnerability scanning is discussed in more detail later in this chapter in the Security in the Software Development Life Cycle section.

- *Developer training*. Software developers should be trained in secure application development techniques. This is discussed in more detail later in this chapter in the Security in the Software Development Life Cycle section.

Object Reuse

Many system resources are shared in multiprocessing systems. This includes memory, databases, file systems, and paging space. When one process utilizes a resource, the process may write some information to the resource temporarily.

Operating systems generally zero out or overwrite memory used by a previous process before allocating it to another process. But a flaw in the design of an OS may make it possible for a process to discover the residual data left by a process that previously occupied a particular part of memory. This flaw is known as **object reuse**.

Similarly, processes may create temporary files in a file system or records in a database that are not intended for use by other processes. However, design flaws or malfunctions may make it possible for a process (or malicious code) to discover and use this residual information.

Object Reuse Countermeasures Several measures should be taken to prevent object reuse vulnerabilities. Among these measures are:

- *Application isolation*. Applications should be isolated to individual systems. In this way, applications are less likely to encounter residual information left by other applications.
- *Server virtualization*. Often it is not feasible to isolate applications to one-per-machine. However, virtualization technology may make it more cost-effective to isolate applications by running them on virtual machines.
- *Developer training*. Software developers can be shown how to write secure software that does not leave residual code that can be used by other processes.

Mobile Code

Also known as executable code, active content, and downloadable content, **mobile code** can be downloaded or transferred from one system for execution on another system. Examples of mobile code include:

- *Active web site content*. This includes ActiveX, Java, JavaScript, Flash, Adobe Acrobat, Shockwave, and so on. This content originates on a web server and executes on a user's workstation. Depending upon the technology associated with the downloaded content, this mobile code may have restricted access to the end user's system or may have partial or full control over it.
- *Downloaded software*. This includes software of every kind from legitimate (and not-so-legitimate) sites. Some of this software may be purely benign, but others can be Trojan horse programs and worse. Some are outright malware, with or without a disguise.

Mobile Code Countermeasures Measures to protect systems from unwanted mobile code include the following:

- *Anti-malware*. This includes anti-virus, anti-spyware, and so on. These protective programs should be in place, properly configured, and up to date.

- *Reduced user privileges*. End users should not be permitted to install or execute mobile code on their workstations, except in explicitly permitted situations such as company-produced mobile code.
- *Mobile code access controls*. Access controls should be in place to prevent unauthorized persons from downloading any mobile code that they are not permitted to access or use.
- *Application whitelisting*. This is a control used to permit only approved programs to run on a system.
- *Secure workstation configuration*. Workstations should be configured to restrict mobile code except in cases where specific mobile code is permitted. This may involve centralized workstation configuration that cannot be defeated or circumvented by end users.

Social Engineering

A social engineering attack is an attack on the *personnel* in an organization. Usually the purpose of a social engineering attack is to gain secrets from individuals that can later be used to gain unauthorized access to the organization's systems. The social engineer uses a technique known as **pretexting** in an effort to pretend to be someone else.

Social engineering owes its success to basic human nature: people are willing to help others in need and "be the hero." Social engineers prey on this weakness in feigned requests for assistance.

Social Engineering Countermeasures The best countermeasure against social engineering is education: people in the organization, particularly those with administrative privileges (system administrators, network administrators, database administrators, and so on), need to be educated on the proper procedures for providing company sensitive information to others. For instance, all calls to staff members about IT access should be referred to the IT helpdesk, calls about legal contracts should be referred to the legal department, and so on.

IT helpdesk personnel (and those in other parts of the organization who take calls from employees) should have precise instructions on identifying other staff members and on what information is permissible to provide (and what is not).

Back Door

A **back door** is a mechanism that is deliberately planted in a system by an application developer that allows the developer or other person to circumvent security. Back doors may be present in an application for several reasons, including:

- *To facilitate testing during application development*. For instance, back doors can be activated by entering specific values that will cause the program to enter an interactive debug mode.
- *To facilitate production access*. For example, a back door is created so that a developer can access an application while it is in production. This would be considered an inappropriate use of a back door (as if there were any legitimate use), since developers should never have access to a production application or production data.
- *To facilitate a break-in*. Sometimes back doors are inserted into an application to permit an unauthorized party to access application functions or data that the party should not have access to. This is clearly inappropriate. This use resembles a logic bomb, which is discussed in the next section.

Back Door Countermeasures Back doors can be difficult to find, particularly if they are inserted for disreputable purposes. Routine functional testing and QA testing may not reveal back doors, whatever their purpose. Instead, other means are required to find them, including:

- *Code reviews*. When one developer makes changes to a software application, one or more other developers should examine the software to identify and approve of all changes. This should prevent both the "legitimate" back doors as well as illegitimate ones.
- *Source code control*. A formal source code management system should be used that will identify and record all changes made to the code. Such capabilities should make it easier for someone to see all changes in the code, making it more difficult for someone to plant an illegitimate back door.
- *Source code scanning*. Tools that are used to scan static source code for security vulnerabilities should be able to find back doors (or at least flag the unusual logic associated with a back door).
- ***Data loss prevention (DLP)***. A data loss prevention system may be able to detect (and perhaps block) unauthorized data transmissions that could be related to a back door.
- *Third-party code reviews and assessments*. Occasionally, outside personnel should be contracted to examine static and running code in order to identify any vulnerabilities and undesired features such as back doors. A third-party organization will be more motivated to find anomalies in software than its own developers.

Logic Bomb

Logic bombs, sometimes known as **time bombs**, are instructions deliberately placed in application code that perform some hostile action when a predetermined condition is met. Typically a logic bomb consists of code that performs some damaging action on a date in the distant future. Most often, a developer will plant a logic bomb in an application if he believes he will be terminated from employment. The logic bomb will activate at some later date, and the terminated programmer will feel that he got his un-just revenge.

Logic Bomb Countermeasures Logic bombs and back doors are very similar: both involve unwanted code in an application. The countermeasures for logic bombs are the same as for back doors: code reviews, source code control, source code scanning, and third-party assessments. See the previous section on back door countermeasures for additional details.

Security in the Software Development Life Cycle

The **software development life cycle** (SDLC) is the collection of processes and procedures used to develop and maintain software applications. Applications can be far more secure if the SDLC includes the right security-related activities in the right places. The details discussed in this section are:

- Security in the conceptual stage
- Security application requirements and specifications
- Security in application design
- Threat risk modeling

- Security in application coding
- Security in testing

NIST 800-64, *Security Considerations in the System Development Life Cycle*, is a high quality standard that was developed by the U.S. National Institute of Standards and Technology. Security and development professionals are urged to incorporate recommendations found in this work into their organizations' software development processes.

Security in the Conceptual Stage

Changes to applications (as well as the creation of new applications) begin with conceptual ideas. Even at the idea stage, some notions of security need to be taken into account. Example mentions of security might include:

- *Sensitive information*. What sensitive information will be present in the application? Should the information be protected?
- *Information flows*. How will sensitive data be transmitted into the application? How will sensitive data be transmitted out of the application? Are any of these information flows with outside organizations?
- *User access*. Who are the application's users, and how will they access the application?
- *Administrative access*. What personnel will be required to access the application and its supporting infrastructure? How will these accesses take place?
- *Third-party access*. Will any third-party personnel be required to access the application? How will this access be controlled?
- *Regulatory requirements*. Are there any regulatory requirements that must be met in this application? Examples include PCI DSS, HIPAA, GLBA, FERC, NERC, Sarbanes Oxley, Canada's PIPEDA (Personal Information Protection and Electronic Documents Act), and the European Privacy Directive 95/46/EC.
- *Use of services infrastructure*. Will the application utilize any enterprise-wide services such as authentication, single sign-on, configuration management, or access to centrally managed storage on a SAN (Storage Area Network) or NAS (Network Attached Storage)?
- *Application dependencies*. What other applications will depend upon this application? Which other applications does this application depend upon?

An organization with a mature development life cycle may wish to develop worksheets for conceptual-stage activities that will help facilitate the identification of security-related issues that need to be addressed early in the development of the application.

Security Application Requirements and Specifications

After the application has been conceptualized, one or more persons will be charged with the development of functional requirements and specifications. Requirements and specifications are detailed statements that describe the behavioral characteristics of the application.

Requirements and specifications can become quite voluminous. Even for a modest project, an application can have hundreds of requirements and specifications that easily exceed one hundred pages in length!

To give you an idea of how detailed the requirements and specifications should be: a developer should be able to develop the entire application, all the way down to individual input forms and fields, and produce absolutely correct operating code without ever having to speak to another person about it. Not that a developer *should* develop this way, but only to say that a developer *could*, because the requirements and specs should be *that detailed*.

Requirements and specifications should provide detailed descriptions of every form, every field, every calculation, and every page, column, heading, and subtotal in every report. Every inbound and outbound flow should be described in exhaustive detail, and every behavioral characteristic in the application should be described in enough detail so that the developer can develop everything.

Further, the requirements should be able to form the kernel of a completely detailed test plan, so that every function of the application can be tested and verified, without the need for any additional functional information about the application.

Characteristics that should be included in requirements and specifications include:

- User and administrative roles
- Access control mechanisms and settings
- Audit logging
- Configuration management
- Workflow
- Look and feel
- Use cases
- Reports
- Interfaces to other internal and external systems

Security in Application Design

When the application's detailed functions and specifications have been completed, the application itself can be designed. The design elements that can be completed in the application design include all database schema, input and output records and fields, workflows, use cases, user roles, administrative roles, audit logs, connections to management systems and services, and other points of integration with other applications, systems, and services. These elements and concepts are described in detail in this section.

When the application's functional specifications and requirements have been developed, creation of the application's design should be straightforward. Still, the designers may discover ambiguities and may need to consult with the persons who developed the functional specs and requirements to eliminate the ambiguities, allowing the designer to complete the design.

The design should be reviewed by those who developed the functional specifications and requirements, to ensure that the design properly reflects the application's specs and requirements. The application's developers should also be present in the review, since they are the personnel who will soon be building the application.

The resulting application design should accurately depict the application's specifications and requirements and be smoothly and harmoniously integrated into the overall technology environment.

Threat Risk Modeling

Building an application according to sound requirements, specifications, and design and testing against those same bodies is not enough to know whether the application will be vulnerable to known threats. **Threat risk modeling** should be performed, to identify those threats that may require controls or other countermeasures as a part of the application's design.

The proper time to perform threat risk modeling is after the application has been designed, but before the application coding begins. Threat risk modeling can be thought of as a security test of the design, like a stress test, that is conducted before the application is built. This is similar to the kinds of computer model stress testing that are performed on large engineering structures such as dams and bridges. Assuredly those kinds of structures are thoroughly tested for physical strength before a shovelful of cement is poured or a pound of steel is erected. Similarly, applications should be stress tested with threat risk analysis before anything is built.

Suggested tools for threat modeling:

- Microsoft SDL Threat Modeling Tool
- Minaccia
- ThreatMind
- Trike

Security in Application Coding

When all requirements, specifications, design, risk threat modeling, and review of all of these works have been completed, application coding may begin. To many, this may seem an arduous and burdensome process, but nowhere in the software development life cycle is it more cost effective to ensure that an application is secure than in the specifications and design phase.

Remember the "1-10-100 Rule." It costs ten times as much to secure an application after it has been developed, and one hundred times as much to secure an application after it has been implemented. Clearly, the best way to secure an application is in its design.

Common Vulnerabilities to Avoid Applications should be coded defensively to ensure that they are free of vulnerabilities. The most common vulnerabilities in web-based applications, according to OWASP (Open Web Application Security Project—a nonprofit organization dedicated to the secure development of web applications) are:

- *Injection flaws*. The application should reject all script injections, for example SQL statements or JavaScript.
- *Broken authentication and session management*. Application users should not be able to manipulate authentication and session management in order to bypass security controls.
- *Cross-site scripting flaws*. Applications should parse all input data and strip out delimiters and other data that could be a part of a scripting attack.
- *Insecure direct object references*. Applications do not always verify whether the user is authorized to access an object.
- *Security misconfiguration*. Security settings may not be set correctly, thereby making an attack possible.

- *Sensitive data exposure*. Applications may not properly protect sensitive data from exposure to persons without authorization to access it.
- *Missing function-level access control*. Applications may not confirm whether a person is permitted to access a function in an application. Hiding a URL for persons in a specific role may not actually prevent someone from executing the function.
- *Cross-site request forgery*. An attacker creates a forged HTTP request and tricks a user into submitting the request. If the user is logged in, the attack may succeed.
- *Use of components with known vulnerabilities*. An application may have components in its environment that are vulnerable to attack.
- *Unvalidated redirects and forwards*. Applications may not validate URLs in redirects and forwards, resulting in users being sent to malicious sites.

Previously published lists of vulnerabilities from OWASP include:

Use Safe Libraries One great way to avoid many common vulnerabilities (such as script injection and buffer overflow) is to use source code libraries that have been thoroughly tested against these vulnerabilities. Objects and functions in these libraries should be used to parse all input strings, for example.

Security in Testing

After the application has been developed, it must be tested to ensure that it was coded properly and is free from errors. A proper software development project has a comprehensive set of functional specifications and requirements, which become a part of the application's test plan.

All functional aspects of the application need to be tested. This includes all fields, workflows, use cases, reports—everything. Detailed testing should be organized and planned, and all test results archived.

The entire application environment needs to be tested with security testing tools to ensure that the application is free from security defects. Applications that are web-based should be tested with scanning tools that are designed to identify common and not-so-common web application vulnerabilities. The two leading tools made for this purpose are WebInspect from HP and AppScan from IBM. Figure 3-7 shows a screenshot of AppScan.

Protecting the SDLC Itself

In addition to the measures described above that result in more secure software, other steps should be taken to protect the SDLC process itself. These measures include:

- *Source code access control*. Only authorized developers should have access to all application source code. Fewer still should have permission to make changes to application source code. The organization should be able to retrieve older versions of source code in case it has been tampered with.
- *Protection of software development tools*. All tools and libraries used to develop software should be protected from unauthorized access and modification. This will help reduce the possibility of vulnerabilities being introduced into an application through tampering with its development tools.

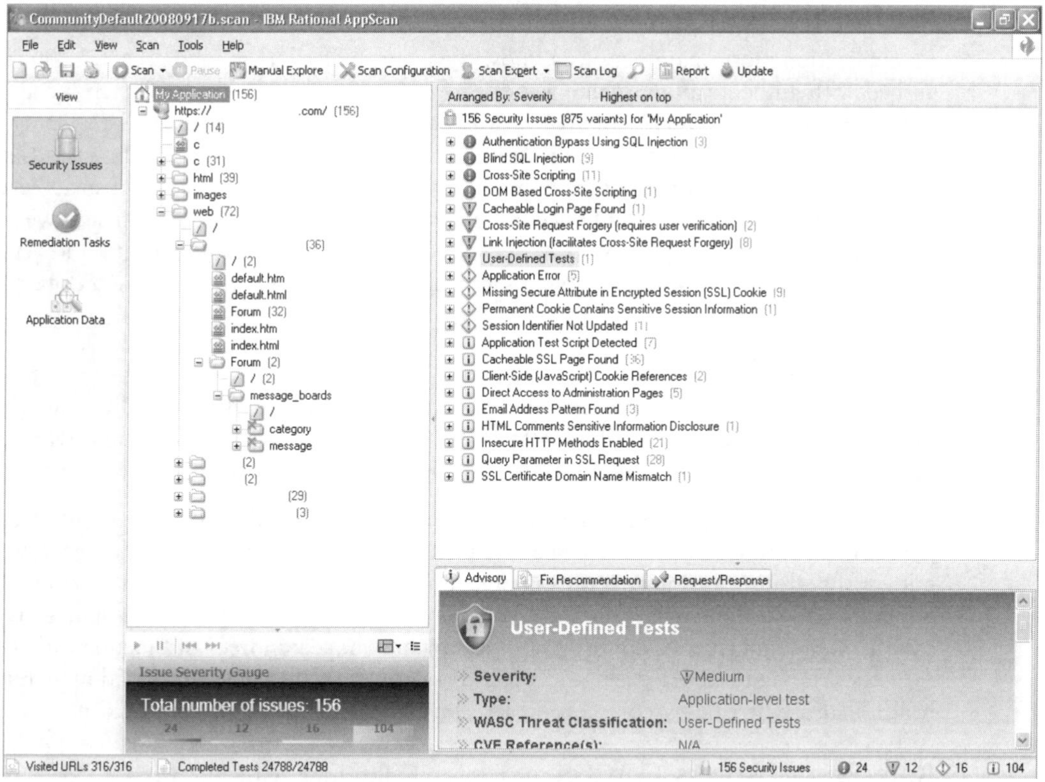

Figure 3-7 IBM's AppScan is used to identify web application vulnerabilities

Source: IBM/Watchfire

- *Protection of software development systems.* Systems used in the development of applications, ranging from developer workstations to source code repositories, should be protected with the same rigor as application servers. As application servers become more hardened, software development systems will otherwise become the next "soft target."

Application Environment and Security Controls

Applications typically require their own security controls, in order to manage and measure activities and events performed by the application. These security controls are required in order to control and verify the integrity of the application, often a necessary task in environments where applications control critical business processes that must be audited from time to time. Without these controls it would be impossible to be able to verify that the applications are operating properly.

The controls that are required by applications are:

- Authentication
- Authorization
- Audit logging

Authentication

An application must unambiguously know the identity of all users who access it. This is accomplished with authentication, where a user proves his or her identity to a system or application, usually by providing a userid and password. The application's designers will decide whether the application should perform authentication on its own (which includes storing userids and passwords in the application's database) or whether the application should instead leverage an enterprise-wide authentication service that may be implemented with LDAP (Lightweight Directory Access Protocol) or Microsoft Active Directory. Centralized authentication lowers the cost of user access administration, and end users will have fewer userids and passwords to remember.

Authorization

One of the two purposes of access control is to determine whether the individual who wishes to access the application is allowed to. The second purpose is to determine what data and functions the person is permitted to do. This is known as authorization.

Authorization is the concept of giving users access to data and functions. An application controls access typically by reading some sort of a *profile* that states which functions a user is permitted to perform. This may seem simple enough, were it not for the fact that some enterprise applications (like a financial management application, customer relationship management application, or a manufacturing control application) could have hundreds of functions and thousands of users. Managing those users and functions could require considerable administrative overhead. That is why role-based access control was invented. This is described in the next section.

Role-Based Access Control In larger applications with hundreds or even thousands of assignable functions and thousands of users, managing, tracking, and auditing these function assignments could become a logistical nightmare. It's for this reason that **role-based access control** is used by many applications. Role-based access control, often known as RBAC, simplifies access control in large applications.

In an RBAC-enabled system, analysts and administrators develop a set of *roles*, which are typically tied to organization job descriptions. Permissions for each of the functions are assigned to each role, which represents the typical worker with the job description that corresponds to the role. Then, each user of the system is assigned to the *role*, which automatically gives the user the permissions that are set up for the role.

Audit Log

An **audit log** is a listing of all of the significant events that occur in an application environment. The purpose of an audit log is to provide a running record or diary of all events that take place in an application: when the events occurred, who performed the events, and details about events such as the details about changed data.

Applications must separately record all significant events and transactions in an audit log. A separate audit log provides a linear (time-based) sequence of events that take place throughout the application's use.

A precise list of the events and transactions that should be recorded is determined in the requirements and functional specifications stage in the software development life cycle (SDLC). The SDLC is examined in greater detail earlier in this chapter.

Audit Log Contents At a minimum, the following information must be present in each audit log entry:

- *Date and time*. The exact time of the event. The time zone should be unambiguous.
- *User*. The userid or name of the user associated with the event.
- *User's location*. This may be a terminal ID, IP address, or other identifying information to show where the user was likely located when the event occurred.
- *Event name*. The name of the event (such as "Update salary").
- *Relevant data*. If a user changed a value in a database, the audit log should show the old and new values. If a new record is entered, its original data should be included. However, some regulations such as the Payment Card Industry Data Security Standard (PCI DSS) prohibit the practice of including credit card numbers in audit logs. This is but one example of the occasional conflict between audit log integrity and privacy.

Audit Log Protection Audit logs must be protected against alteration, destruction, and tampering. Characteristics of audit logs should include:

- *Free from alteration*. No individual should be able to alter any information in an audit log. Ideally an audit log should be written to write-once media.
- *Free from erasure*. The audit log should not be able to be erased.
- *Free from unauthorized initialization*. Only authorized individuals or mechanisms should be able to initialize an audit log. Audit log initialization should itself be an audit event.

Databases and Data Warehouses

Databases are often used to store business data on information systems. While end users may store small pieces of data in documents, spreadsheets, and presentation files, most applications store their information in database management systems (DBMSs) like Microsoft SQL Server, Oracle, IBM DB2, and MySQL.

Database Concepts and Design

This section describes various architectures used by database management systems. A **database** is an ordered collection of data that exists for a common purpose. For instance, an organization may build a database of its employees in order to store information about employees including contact information, compensation, benefits, continuing education, and disciplinary action.

A **data warehouse** is a type of database that is used for decision support and research purposes. It is easy to think about a data warehouse as a functional copy of a live database that is used for analysis of historic data. For example, an online retailer may build a data warehouse that consists of all of its customer transactions. Analysts can use various tools to access and analyze historic transactions in order to identify trends that may help the organization to improve its business in the future. Business intelligence tools can help an analyst to easily identify trends and conditions that may otherwise be unapparent.

Transactions are used to update data within a database. For instance, an online banking application utilizes transactions to record deposits, withdrawals, and other activities in customer bank accounts.

Database Architectures **Database management systems** (DBMSs) have a design that governs how data will be organized. Generally, a given make and model of database will be built around one particular model. If you prefer that your data be stored using a different model, then you will need to find yourself a different database product.

The common architectures used by DBMSs are:

- Relational
- Hierarchical
- Network
- Object oriented
- Distributed
- NoSQL

Relational Databases Fields and records in **relational databases** are designed to be related to other fields and records. A relational database is two-dimensional, having *rows* and *columns* (sometimes known as fields). The structure of a relational database is defined by its *schema*, which is essentially a lengthy keywords-delimited text file called Data Definition Language (DDL) that define tables, rows, columns, keys, and indices. Tools called *data modelers* are used to create a relational database schema.

The power of relational databases comes from relationships, which are used to identify related records. For instance, a field in a *sales* table can be used to store a *salesman* number, a *foreign key* that points to the *primary key* on a salesman table elsewhere in the database. Other tables can also have a salesman field that will also point back to the salesman table.

Large applications can have databases that contain hundreds of tables, all linked together through these relationships.

Object-Oriented Databases In an **object-oriented database** (**OODB**), data is organized and stored as objects. Like OO programming languages, these objects can be organized with classes, inheritance, and encapsulation. The operations that can be performed with OODB database objects are stored in the objects themselves.

Distributed Databases **Distributed databases** are so-called because of their physical nature more than by whether they are relational, hierarchical, or object oriented. Distributed databases may be on one system, on two or more systems in a single location, or in several geographic locations.

Hierarchical Databases In a **hierarchical database**, data is organized in a tree structure. Each field or record has only a single parent field or record, but can have zero, one, or many child fields or records. An example of a hierarchical data model is the Internet's

Domain Name Service (DNS) model. The hierarchical database model is considered legacy, because this model has not been used by database producers in many years.

Network Databases **Network databases** are an extension of hierarchical databases, in which records can be "networked" to other records elsewhere in the database than through the hierarchy itself. Like hierarchical databases, network databases are considered legacy.

NoSQL Databases **NoSQL databases** provide structure by means other than tabular relations found in relational databases. There are several types of NoSQL database management systems, including:

- *Graph*. Based on graph theory, nodes in a graph database contain direct pointers to related elements. No index lookups are used.
- *Document Store*. Intended for document-oriented information, where documents may be retrieved based on their key, tags, and metadata.
- *Key-Value*. These use associative arrays for data storage of (key, value) pairs.

Database Transactions The real power in databases comes from the ability for software applications to perform transactions. By this I mean that the database management system (DBMS) becomes the engine for storing, changing, and retrieving data, relieving the software developer from the details of file manipulation. In the vernacular, the programmer can write simple language to instruct the database, "get record number 1234 from the *salesman* table and change the *salary* value to 3000," or, "create a new record in the products table with the following data in the fields..."

SQL is the common language used in software applications to communicate these transactions to relational databases. SQL is a standard data manipulation language supported by nearly all modern programming languages, which usually provide some easy means for constructing SQL statements to manipulate data in the relational database management system (RDBMS).

Relational databases also have a notion of "transactional integrity" in which a complex transaction will never be partially completed under any circumstance. This is achieved by delimiting a series of transaction statements with the terms, "Begin work" and "Commit." For example:

```
BEGIN WORK
INSERT INTO salestable (number, name, phone) VALUES
('551', 'Scott Brewer', '206-555-1212');
UPDATE commission SET rate= '440' WHERE
salesman='551';
COMMIT;
END WORK
```

In this example, the developer can be confident that the two commands (*insert* and *update*) will *both* be performed, or *neither* will be performed. Regardless of any error or malfunction that can occur, a situation where only one of these two commands has completed will not happen.

Database Security Controls

Databases have security controls that determine who can access a database, as well as which data a user or role is permitted to view or change. Two primary ways of controlling access in a database are **access controls** and **views**.

Access Controls Databases embody the concept of a userid and password that must be provided before any person can access the database. But since most users don't access a database directly, often user authentication is done at the application layer, and then the application accesses the database directly, on behalf of the user.

RDBMSs use Data Control Language (DCL) to define which users are able to view and manipulate which tables, records, and fields in a database. The DCL serves as a way to configure a database's access controls—the mechanisms used to control how objects (in this case, data or stored procedures) may be accessed by users. A sample DCL statement reads:

```
GRANT SELECT ON salestable TO user1, user2, user3.
```

Views A view is a virtual table that can be created in a relational database. A view does not take up additional data storage. Views can be used to control access to data in two ways:

- *Access controls on views.* Users who need to be able to view certain information can be given permission to access the view only, but not the underlying tables.
- *Include only the viewable fields.* If users should be able to see some fields but not others, a view can be created that includes only the fields that they are permitted to see.

Chapter Summary

- Applications are computer programs that perform useful work for people. The common types of application programs are agents, applets, client-server, distributed, and web applications.
- Application languages are based upon design models. Four such models in common use are control flow, structured, object-oriented, and knowledge-based.
- Application software faces a large number of threats, including buffer overflow, malicious software, input attacks, logic bombs, object reuse, mobile code, social engineering, and back doors. The types of malicious code include viruses, worms, Trojan horses, remote access Trojans (RATs), spyware and adware, pharming, and rootkits.
- Countermeasures against the threats to application software include using safe programming languages and libraries, firewalls, anti-malware tools (anti-virus, anti-spyware, anti-rootkit, etc.), decreasing application privilege levels, application scanning, penetration testing, application firewalls, data leakage prevention, source code reviews, developer training, and system hardening.
- Social engineering is an attack on personnel in an attempt to trick them into giving up secret information.

- The software development life cycle (SDLC) is the collection of processes and procedures used to design, build, and maintain software. Security needs to be a part of every of stage of the SDLC to ensure that the application that is being built and maintained has security incorporated into the design instead of added on at the end of the project. Also, all project information including requirements, design, test plans and results, and source code need to be protected against unauthorized access and use.
- Security controls are required to control and verify the integrity of the application. The controls that are needed include authentication, authorization, and audit logging.
- The types of databases are hierarchical, network, relational, object oriented, distributed, and NoSQL. Database transactions are the actions performed on databases when data is added or changed. Databases have access controls that control the actions that users may perform and who may perform them.

Key Terms

Access control Any means used to control which subjects are permitted to access objects.

Adware Cookies, web beacons, and other means used to track individual Internet users and build behavior profiles for them.

Agent Small, standalone programs that perform some task for a larger application environment.

Anti-rootkit software Software that uses techniques to find hidden processes, hidden registry entries, unexpected kernel hooks, and hidden files in order to find rootkits that may be present on a system.

Anti-spyware software Software that is designed to detect and remove spyware.

Anti-virus software Software that is used to detect and remove viruses and other malicious code from a system.

Applet A small program that runs within the context of another program.

Application firewall A firewall that examines the contents of incoming messages in order to detect and block attempted attacks on an application.

Application whitelisting A means of controlling what software programs are permitted to run on a system, thereby preventing the execution of malware and unauthorized software.

Audit log The record of events that occur in an application environment.

Authorization The process of permitting a user to perform some specific function or access some specific data.

Back door A feature in a program that allows access that bypasses security.

Bot Malicious software that allows someone to remotely control someone else's computer for illicit purposes.

Class The defining characteristics of an object.

Client-server application An application in which user interface logic resides on a client system and data storage and retrieval logic resides on a server.

Configuration management The process of recording configuration changes that are made in an environment.

Control flow A computer language methodology where instructions are followed sequentially until a "goto" type statement is encountered, in which case the control is transferred to the location specified by the goto statement.

CORBA (Common Object Request Broker Architecture) A standard used to facilitate communications between systems.

Cross-site request forgery (XSRF) This is an attack where malicious HTML is inserted into a web page or e-mail that, when clicked, causes an action to occur on an unrelated site where the user may have an active session.

Cross-site scripting (XSS) An attack where an attacker can inject a malicious script into HTML content in order to steal session cookies and other sensitive information.

Database An ordered collection of data that exists for a common purpose.

Database management system (DBMS) A set of software programs used to manage large organized collections of data called databases.

Data loss prevention (DLP) A system used to detect and block unauthorized data transmissions on a network.

Data warehouse A database management system that is designed and built to store archival data for decision support and research purposes.

Demilitarized zone (DMZ) A means of protecting application servers and the remainder of an enterprise network by placing them on a separate firewalled network.

Distributed application An application in which its components reside on many systems.

Distributed database A database that is logically or physically distributed among several systems.

Elevation of privileges An attack where an attacker is able to perform some manipulation in order to raise his or her privileges, enabling the attacker to perform unauthorized functions.

Encapsulation A design attribute that permits the hiding of internal details about an object in an OO system.

Executable space protection An operating system or CPU feature that prevents programs from executing code in the stack or heap.

Expert system A software system that accumulates knowledge on a particular subject and is able to predict outcomes based upon historical knowledge.

Firewall A hardware device or software program that controls the passage of traffic at a network boundary according to a predefined set of rules.

Hacktivist A person who attacks information systems for political or religious motives.

Hardening The process of configuring a system to make it more robust and resistant to attack.

Heap overflow An attack that attempts to corrupt a program's heap (the dynamically allocated memory space created by a program for storage of variables).

Hierarchical database A database model that is built on a tree structure.

Hosts file A file on a workstation or server that associates host names and IP addresses.

Inheritance The characteristics of a subclass that inherits attributes from its parent class.

Injection attack An attack on a system where some scripting or procedural language is inserted into a data stream with the intention that the scripting will be performed.

Input attack Any attack on a system where specially coded data is provided in an input field with the intention of causing a malfunction or failure of the system.

Jump-to-register A type of buffer overflow attack where a function's return pointer is overwritten, in order to alter the behavior of a program.

Kernel The part of an operating system that actively manages processes and access to resources.

Key logger A hardware or software component that records keystrokes on a computer.

Knowledge-based system A system that is used to make predictions or decisions based upon input data.

Logic bomb Computer code placed in a system that is intended to perform some harmful event when certain conditions are met—usually a specific day or time in the future.

Method A function or calculation that an object is capable of performing.

Mobile code Computer code that is downloaded or transferred from one system for execution on another system.

Monoculture A set of systems that runs the same version of software.

Network database A database model based upon the hierarchical model, but with the ability for records to be related to other records in the database.

Network-stack attack An attack against network components of a target system.

Neural network A software system that simulates the human reasoning process and is able to make predictions and decisions based on prior results.

NOP sled A type of stack overflow attack where the attacker floods the stack with NOP (no-operation) instructions in an attempt to take control of the program.

NoSQL Any of several database models that use non-tabular means for organizing data.

Object An instance of an OO class.

Object orientation (OO) A methodology for organizing information and software programs that supports objects, methods, and object reuse.

Object-oriented database (OODB) A database that is organized and stored as objects.

Object-oriented programming (OOP) A programming language methodology that consists of code contained in reusable objects.

Object reuse An attack on a system where one user or program is able to read residual information belonging to some other process, as a means for exploiting the other process through a weakness that can be discovered in the residual data.

Open Database Connectivity (ODBC) A TCP/IP-based client-server communications protocol used to facilitate database transactions over a network.

Patch management The process of managing the installation of patches on target systems.

Phishing Fraudulent e-mail messages that attempt to lure an unsuspecting user to provide private information via a fraudulent web site (usually) or in an e-mail reply (less often).

Polymorphism The ability for an object to respond to a call differently, depending upon the object's type.

Pretexting An act of deception intended to persuade a targeted individual to provide information under false pretenses.

Privilege escalation An attack in which the attacker attempts to cause a system malfunction that will result in the attacker gaining additional system privileges.

Relational database A database model based upon tables of data and the relationships between them.

Remote access Trojan (RAT) A type of malware that permits an attacker to remotely control a victim system.

Role-based access control (RBAC) An access control method where access permissions are granted to roles, and users are assigned to those roles.

Rootkit Malicious code that is designed to avoid detection by hiding itself by some means.

Software development life cycle (SDLC) The overall process used to design, create, and maintain software over its lifetime.

Spam Unwanted e-mail that usually contains unsolicited commercial advertisements, pornography, or attempts to lure recipients into opening malicious attachments or visiting malicious web sites.

Spear phishing A specially targeted phishing attack. See also *phishing*.

Spyware Usually unwanted and sometimes malicious software that is used to harvest Internet usage information from a user's workstation.

SQL*Net A TCP/IP-based client-server communications protocol used to facilitate database transactions over a network.

Structured language A hierarchical computer language methodology that consists of main programs and called subroutines or functions.

Thin client application A client application that relies on other (usually central) computers to perform most functions.

Threat risk modeling A process where threats in an environment are identified and ranked, and mitigating controls introduced to counter the identified threats. Also known as *threat modeling*.

Three-tier application An application that consists of three logically separate layers, usually a user interface front end, business logic middle tier, and database management third tier.

Time bomb See *logic bomb*.

Transaction An event where data is updated within a database.

Trojan horse Malicious computer code that claims to perform some benign function while actually performing some additional, malicious function.

Two-tier application An application that consists of two logically separate layers, usually a user interface and business logic front end and a data management back end.

View A virtual table in a relational database.

Virus Malicious code that attaches to a file, document, or master boot record (MBR).

Virtualization The use of specialized software to facilitate the existence of two or more logically separate running operating systems (virtual machines) on a single physical system.

Web application An application that utilizes a web browser as the client software.

Whaling A specially targeted phishing attack that targets executives in an organization.

Worm Malicious code that has the ability to self-propagate and spread rapidly from system to system.

Review Questions

1. A media player that is running within a web browser is known as a(n):
   a. Agent
   b. Mashup
   c. Applet
   d. Script
2. The chief advantage of web-based applications is:
   a. Client-side software updates are unnecessary
   b. Built-in SSL encryption
   c. Ease of use
   d. Better security
3. Enterprise Java Beans, Distributed Common Object Model, and Java Remote Method Invocation are examples of:
   a. Object request brokers
   b. Object-oriented frameworks
   c. Object-oriented languages
   d. Distributed systems
4. An attacker is experimenting with an application by inserting long strings of machine language code in the application's input fields. The attacker is attempting:
   a. A denial-of-service attack
   b. A buffer overflow attack
   c. A stack smashing attack
   d. Any of the above
5. A risk manager requires that his organization implement a control to prevent application attacks. The best solution is to use:
   a. Multi-tier architecture
   b. Code reviews
   c. An application vulnerability scanner
   d. An application firewall

6. An astute security engineer has discovered that a perpetrator has installed a device that is eavesdropping on wireless network communications. The technique used is:
   a. Emanations
   b. A side channel attack
   c. A covert channel
   d. Steganography
7. Rootkits can be difficult to discover because:
   a. They subvert the operating system
   b. They install themselves in master boot records (MBRs)
   c. They install themselves in flash memory
   d. They use hidden processes
8. The purpose of a botnet is:
   a. To launch denial-of-service attacks
   b. To relay spam, host phishing sites, or launch denial-of-service attacks
   c. To remotely control zombie computers
   d. To build a massively parallel system
9. An IT manager is considering an anti-spam solution. Because one of the primary concerns is e-mail server performance, which solution can be eliminated from consideration?
   a. Appliance
   b. Outsourced
   c. Server-based
   d. Client-based
10. Web beacons are an effective site usage tracker because:
   a. They use hidden form variables
   b. Browsers cannot detect them
   c. Browsers do not block them
   d. They are encrypted
11. The most effective countermeasure for malware is:
   a. Rootkit detection
   b. Decreasing user privilege levels
   c. Anti-virus
   d. Firewalls
12. The primary purpose for decreasing user privilege levels is:
   a. To reduce support costs
   b. To limit the effects of malware
   c. To improve system performance
   d. All of the above

13. Which of the following is NOT normally used in system hardening?
    a. Changing TCP/IP parameters
    b. Removing unnecessary services
    c. Removing unnecessary NICs
    d. Renaming administrator userids

14. The purpose of input field filtering is:
    a. To prevent input injection attacks
    b. To detect application scanning
    c. To prevent SQL injection attacks
    d. To detect unsafe code

15. The best time to develop application test plans is:
    a. During requirements and specifications development
    b. During application design
    c. During application testing
    d. During application coding

Hands-On Projects

Project 3-1: Vulnerability Scanning

Required for this project:

- Windows Vista, 7, or 8

In this project, you will perform vulnerability scanning. Various tools are available to scan a Windows computer to identify unsecure configurations and/or determine which patches are missing. Microsoft has published an interface that is used to determine which patches are installed on a system, and also which patches are available. The Secunia Personal Software Inspector (PSI) tool is used to scan a system and identify which patches are missing.

1. Download PSI from Secunia at https://psi.secunia.com/.
2. Install PSI on your system and start the tool. It may appear only as a Systray icon, in which case you need to double-click the Systray icon to pull up the user interface.
3. Click **Scan**.
4. On the Scan window, click **Scan Now**. PSI will begin scanning the system for patches. See Figure 3-8.

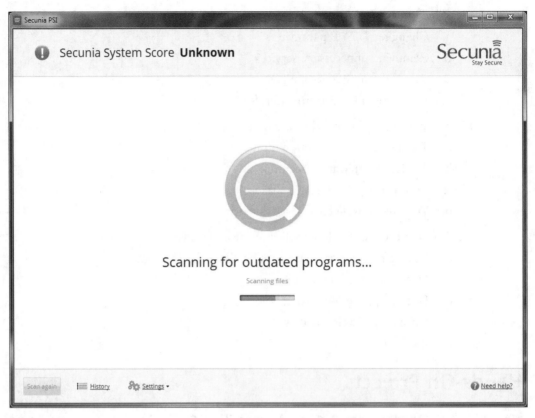

Figure 3-8 Secunia Personal Software Inspector tool scanning for vulnerabilities
Source: Secunia Personal Inspector

5. Which Microsoft patches have been identified that need to be installed?
6. What other vulnerabilities has the tool identified?

The Microsoft Baseline Security Analyzer (MBSA) may also be used for this project.

Project 3-2: Threat Risk Modeling

Required for this project:

- Windows Vista, 7, or 8

In this project you will download and work with Microsoft's Threat Analysis & Modeling tool. Threat risk modeling is used to identify threats to an application's design before it is built. You may wish to use your knowledge about an existing application to enter information.

1. Download the Microsoft Threat Analysis & Modeling tool from this site: http://msdn.microsoft.com. Search on *Microsoft Threat Analysis & Modeling* to find the download link. You will need to download the Getting Started Guide to learn how to use the tool.
2. Install and start the tool.
3. Select **New Model.**
4. Create a simple application diagram, such as the diagram shown in Figure 3-9.
5. Why does the trust boundary in Figure 3-9 not include the browser?

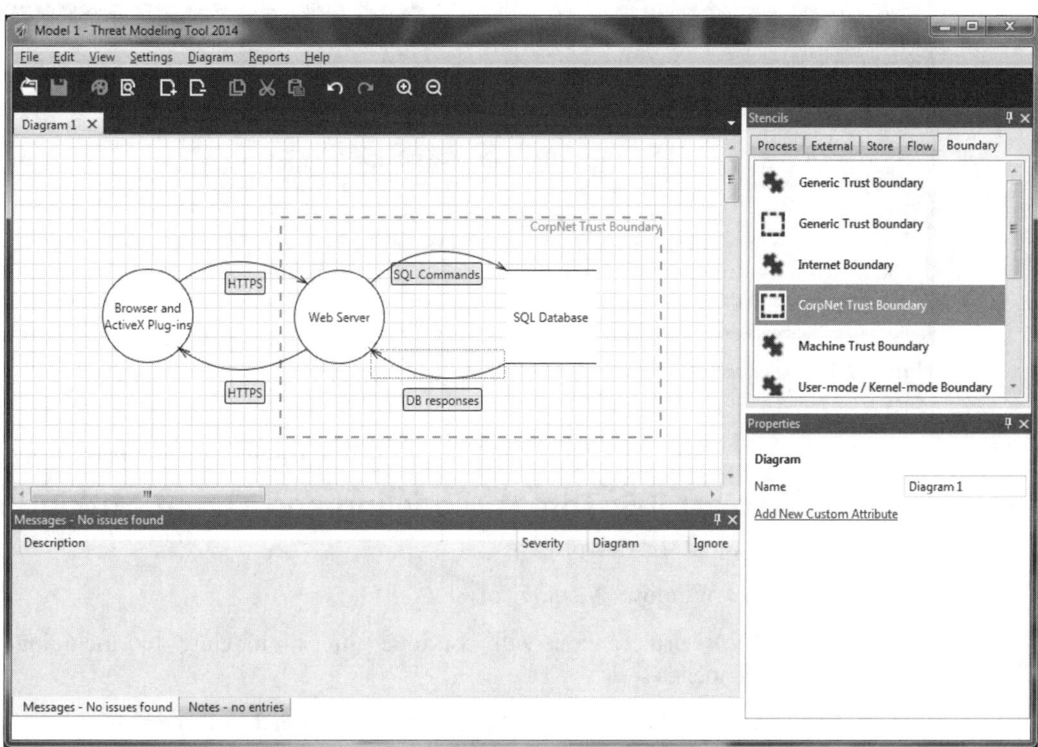

Figure 3-9 Microsoft's Threat Analysis & Modeling Tool

Source: Microsoft

6. Click View, then Analysis View. What is the nature of the threats displayed in the Threat Information table? See Figure 3-10.

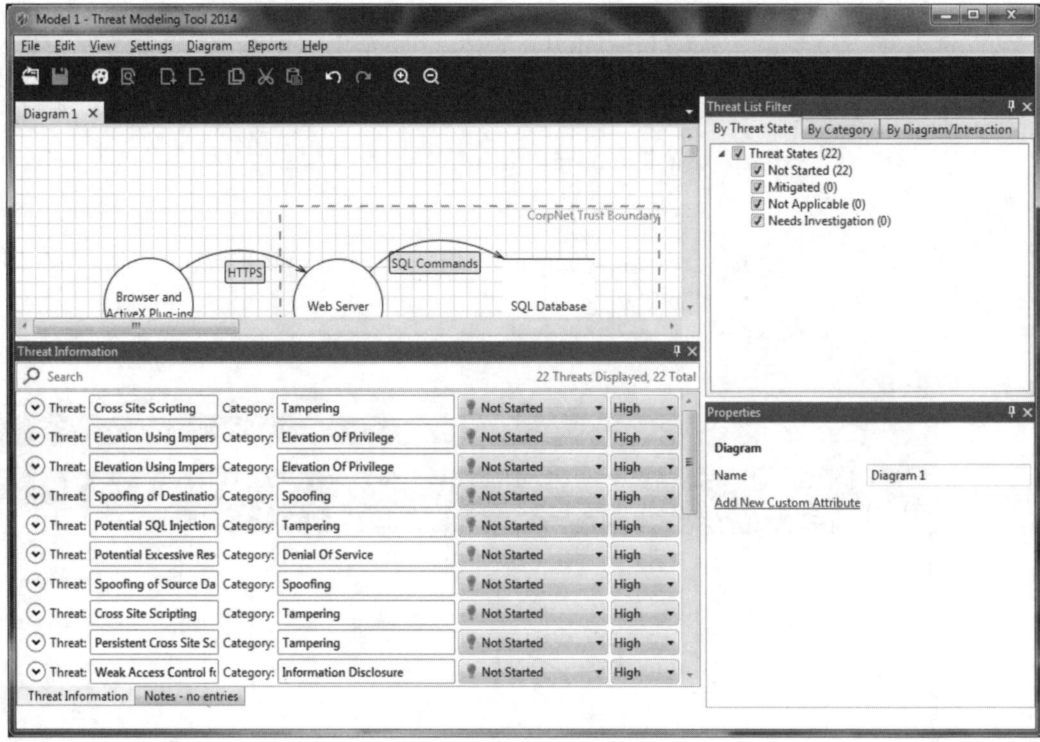

Figure 3-10 Analysis View lists potential threats to an application

Source: Microsoft

7. Save your model and leave the tool running for the next project.

Project 3-3: Threat Modeling and Threat Mitigation

Required for this project:

- Windows Vista, 7, or 8

In this project you will continue threat modeling by including external dependencies.

This project utilizes the threat model developed in Project 3-2.

1. Start the Microsoft Threat Analysis & Modeling Tool. Open the model created in Project 3-2.

2. Open one of the threats in the model by clicking on the arrow icon to the left of the word Threat. See Figure 3-11.

3. The tool describes the nature of the threat in the Description field. In the Justification for threat state change field, you can enter information describing the task performed that mitigates the threat. The state of the threat can be changed from Not Started to Mitigated, as shown in Figure 3-11.

4. How can a developer or security analyst use the threat description and mitigation fields in a real software development organization?

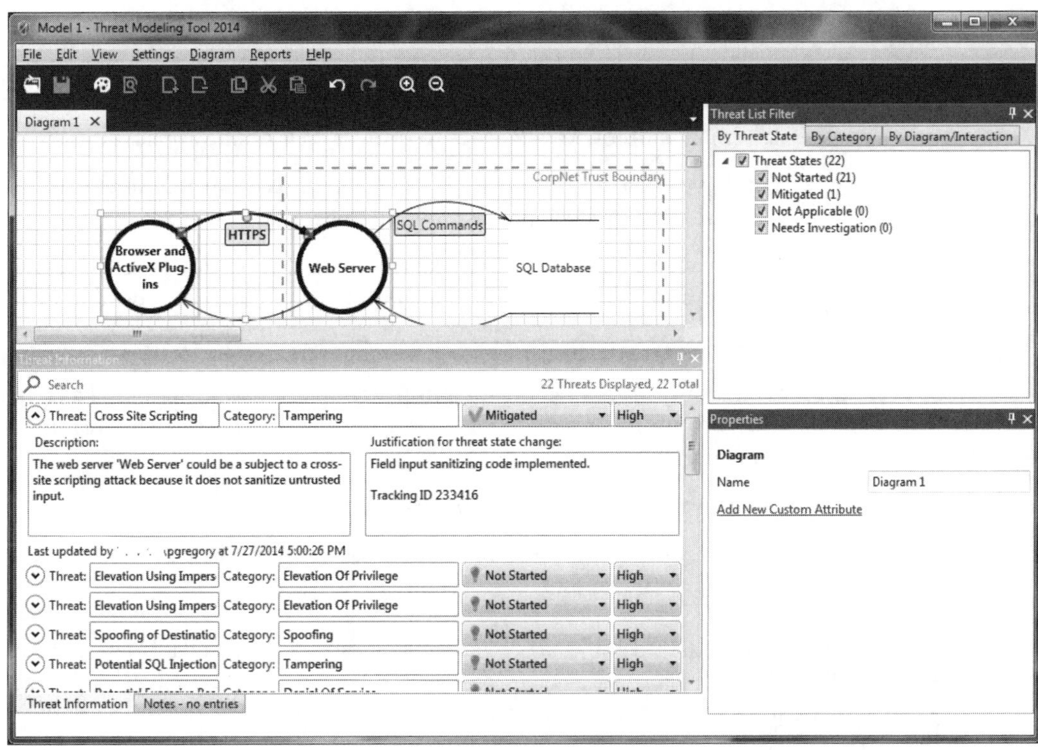

Figure 3-11 Description of individual threat and its mitigation status

Source: Microsoft

Case Projects

Case Project 3-1: Web Application Vulnerability Scanning

Required for this project:

- Windows Vista, 7, or 8

1. Download an evaluation copy of IBM AppScan from this web site: http://www-01.ibm.com/software/awdtools/appscan/
2. Identify a web site that you have permission to scan (note that the trial version of AppScan may only permit scans of certain sites; information may be available on the download page). Scan the site with AppScan. What vulnerabilities were identified? Were there any false positive findings?

If you would like more freedom than is offered with the evaluation version of AppScan, it is suggested that you search for "free web application penetration testing tools" and select another tool that meets your needs.

Case Project 3-2: Develop an Application Security Test Plan

As a consultant with the Security Consulting Company, you have been hired to develop a plan for ABC Plastics to protect their online applications.

You have been asked to examine and make recommendations in ABC Plastics' software development process. What changes will you make?

You have also been asked to make recommendations for tools that can be used to measure application security. Which tool(s) will you recommend and why?

Case Project 3-3: Observe Script Injection in Action

How many web sites adequately filter out script injection? Take the sample code below and insert it into form fields on various web sites and see what happens.

```
<script>alert("hello")</script>
```

When a web application does not filter scripting language, is there a security risk? Why or why not?

This activity may be unlawful in some locales. Students or instructors should first determine whether this activity is permitted, and under what circumstances.

Case Project 3-4: Pharming Attack Countermeasures

As a consultant with the Security Consulting Company, you have been hired to perform an assessment on the risk of a pharming attack.

Congo River Adventures purchases its supplies through several online merchants. Congo River Adventures' web site advertises which merchants they use, as a way of showing that their services are superior to their competitors. However, Congo River Adventures is now concerned that a hacker could launch a pharming attack against them and divert its employees to imposter supplier web sites. What approach will you take in order to understand and mitigate any risk?

Case Project 3-5: Web Application Security Architecture

As a consultant with the Security Consulting Company, you have been hired to develop a secure application architecture for ABC Plastics' online web application.

Some of the questions that officials at ABC Plastics are asking include:

- Should the database server and the web server be on the same system?
- How many firewalls should protect the application?
- What forms of access controls should be used to protect the application and its database?

chapter 4

Business Continuity and Disaster Recovery Planning

Topics in This Chapter:

- Running a Business Continuity and Disaster Recovery Planning Project
- Developing Business Continuity and Disaster Recovery Plans
- Testing Business Continuity and Disaster Recovery Plans
- Training Users
- The Business Continuity and Disaster Recovery Planning Life Cycle

The (ISC)^2 *Common Body of Knowledge* (CBK) defines the key areas of knowledge for business continuity and disaster recovery planning in this way:

The Business Continuity Planning (BCP) and Disaster Recovery Planning (DRP) domain addresses the preservation of the business in the face of major disruptions to normal business operations. BCP and DRP involve the preparation, testing and updating of specific actions to protect critical business processes from the effect of major system and network failures.

Key areas of knowledge include:

- *Understand business continuity requirements*
- *Conduct Business Impact Analysis*
- *Develop recovery strategy*
- *Understand the disaster recovery process*
- *Exercise, assess and maintain the plan (e.g. version control, distribution)*

Business Continuity and Disaster Recovery Planning Basics

A disaster is a natural or man-caused event that impairs the ability for organizations to continue operating. **Business continuity planning** (BCP) is the set of activities required to ensure the continuation of critical business processes when a disaster occurs. **Disaster recovery planning** (DRP) is the set of activities concerned with the assessment, salvage, repair, and restoration of damaged facilities and assets that support critical business processes. BCP and DRP work together to ensure effective response and continuity of operations before, during, and after a disaster.

What Is a Disaster?

A **disaster** is any natural or man-made event that disrupts the operations of a business in such a significant way that a considerable and coordinated effort is required to continue business operations and achieve a recovery.

Two main categories of disasters can strike an organization: natural disasters and man-made disasters.

Natural Disasters **Natural disasters** comprise a wide range of natural events that cause damage over often wide areas. These natural events can be more severe versions of ordinary events, or less common events. The types of natural disasters are:

- *Geological*. These events include earthquakes, volcanoes, lahars, tsunamis, landslides, and sinkholes.
- *Meteorological*. Events in this category include hurricanes, tornados, windstorms, hail, ice storms, snow storms, rainstorms, and lightning.
- *Health*. This category includes widespread illnesses, quarantines, and pandemics.
- *Other*. These include avalanches, fires, floods, meteors and meteorites, and solar storms.

The events described above vary widely in predictability. Many types of storms can be predicted hours or days in advance, giving people a few hours' warning for evacuation or last-minute preparation. On the other hand, earthquakes are only statistically predictable, meaning that geographic areas are generally classified as being low, medium, or high risk for earthquakes, but the precise or even approximate time of an upcoming earthquake generally is unknown.

Some natural events cause damage over a wide geographic area, while others are very limited. Hurricanes and earthquakes can damage buildings and roads over hundreds of square miles, while tornadoes and hail can affect just a few square miles—or less.

Man-Made Disasters **Man-made disasters** are caused—or exacerbated—by the action (or inaction) of people or organizations. The types of man-caused disasters are:

- *Labor*. The types of events here include strikes, walkouts, and slowdowns that disrupt services and supplies.
- *Social-political*. These include war, terrorism, sabotage, vandalism, civil unrest, protests, demonstrations, cyber attacks, and blockades.
- *Materials*. These include fires and hazardous materials spills.
- *Utilities*. These events include power failures, communications outages, water supply shortages, fuel shortages, and radioactive fallout from power plant accidents.

How Disasters Affect Businesses Disasters can affect businesses in a number of different ways, and this depends both on the nature of the disaster as well as the nature of the business. There are several ways in which a disaster impacts a business.

Direct Damage Some disasters will directly affect business facilities and equipment, making them temporarily unusable or unreachable. For example, a severe windstorm or tornado can damage a part of a building that can be repaired, and/or render business equipment unusable until building repairs have been completed.

Disasters can also permanently damage buildings and equipment, to the extent that they cannot be repaired but instead must be replaced.

Casualties Disasters often frighten, injure, and even kill people, including people who work in organizations, as well as customer and supplier organizations. The loss of manpower may directly affect an organization's ability to produce goods and services.

Even if an organization's employees are not injured themselves, if there are affected family members, those employees are likely going to consider caring for their family members a higher priority than reporting for work, even during a business emergency such as a disaster.

Transportation Disasters are well known for disrupting transportation systems. Earthquakes, floods, landslides, and other events can damage freeways, bridges, and roads. This sort of damage can have several effects on businesses, including:

- *Supply disruption*. When transportation infrastructure is damaged, shipments of supplies are delayed, which could have a dampening effect on a business's ability to produce goods and services. If a business produces goods that are shipped to customers, then this too will affect the business.

- *Customer disruption.* Damaged transportation will prevent customers from being able to reach businesses. Even if businesses themselves are not damaged, a disaster can have devastating consequences on businesses that depend upon visits by retail or wholesale customers.
- *Employee disruption.* Damaged transportation systems can prevent employees from being able to report for work. Again, even if the business is not directly affected by the disaster, if employees are unable to reach the business then the business's ability to deliver goods or services will be affected.

Figure 4-1 shows a roadway made impassable by an earthquake.

Communications Disasters also commonly affect communications infrastructure. Earthquakes, floods, landslides, and other events can damage communications cables, towers, switching centers, and other facilities. Disasters can directly damage communications cables, antennas, switch centers, and other communications facilities, and damage to transportation facilities (described in the preceding section) can keep communications workers away from their jobs, which will have a dampening effect on communications as well.

Utilities Disasters frequently affect utilities. Storms and other natural events are especially hard on electric utilities, since most electric systems are built aboveground and are exposed

Figure 4-1 Roadway and buildings damaged in an earthquake

Courtesy US Geological Survey. Department of the Interior/USGS to the weather. Water and natural gas systems are also negatively affected by disasters, even though many of those facilities are underground.

How BCP and DRP Support Data Security

Recall that the pillars of security are confidentiality, integrity, and availability. Business continuity and disaster recovery planning are concerned with the *availability* of information and information services, particularly when faced with events that threaten to make data and services unavailable for long periods of time.

Business continuity and disaster recovery plans do need to take *integrity* and *confidentiality* into account. Even in a disaster situation, disaster procedures need to ensure that data confidentiality and integrity are preserved. Indeed, data integrity is the key issue in business continuity and disaster recovery planning, since restoring the wrong data places the organization in no better a position.

BCP and DRP Differences and Similarities

In larger organizations, BCP and DRP have traditionally been treated as separate, although similar, activities that are both concerned with the survival of an organization in a disaster scenario. In smaller organizations BCP and DRP were simply considered a single activity, called either BCP or DRP. In many smaller organizations, there is no BCP or DRP at all.

BCP has been concerned with the activities required to ensure the continuation of critical business processes in an organization. This may involve the use of alternate personnel, equipment, and facilities—whatever it takes to keep critical processes operating.

DRP has been concerned with the assessment, salvage, repair, and eventual restoration of damaged facilities and systems.

A good analogy to illustrate the differences and similarities is the breakdown of a delivery truck. BCP can be thought of as a temporary replacement rental truck that is used to continue deliveries, while DRP is the repair of the original delivery truck.

Another common distinction used to compare BCP and DRP efforts is this: DRP is often considered an effort to recover IT system and applications, whereas BCP is regarded as the effort to recover business processes that may or may not be directly dependent on IT systems.

Other terms are used in these contexts, including:

- ***IT Service continuity***—the ITIL (IT Infrastructure Library) term that ensures the continuity of IT-provided services and systems.
- *Business Continuity and Disaster Recovery Planning (BCDR)*—the combined thought of the once-separate BCP and DRP.

Industry Standards

Several standards and regulations on disaster recovery and business continuity planning have been established, including those listed here.

- *ISO27001—Requirements for Information Security Management Systems*. This new international standard on information security management systems that addresses business continuity management is presented in section A.14.

- *ISO 27002—Code of Practice for Information Security Management*. This well-known international standard on information technology security practices, presented in section 14, addresses business continuity management.
- *ISO 22301—Business Continuity Management Systems*. This new international standard specifies requirements for creation and maintenance of business continuity and disaster recovery plans.
- *NIST 800-34—Contingency Planning Guide for Information Technology Systems*. The U.S. National Institute for Standards and Technology published this seven-step process for BCP and DRP projects.
- *NFPA 1600*. This is the Standard on Disaster/Emergency Management and Business Continuity Programs that was developed by the U.S. National Fire Protection Association.
- *NFPA 1620*. The Recommended Practice for Pre-Incident Planning, a standard that guides organizations in their development of disaster recovery plans.
- *HIPAA*. The U.S. Health Insurance Portability and Accountability Act includes the "Security Rule" that requires several measures be taken to protect patient health information in electronic form. HIPAA requires that organizations that manage electronic health information have a documented and regularly tested disaster recovery plan.
- *BS 25999—Business Continuity Management Code of Practice*, developed by the British Standards Institute (BSI). Part 1 of this standard describes principles, processes, and the vocabulary of business continuity management. Part 2 of the standard, which discusses requirements for implementing and operating a business continuity program, has been superseded by ISO 22301.

Benefits of BC and DR Planning

Besides the increased likelihood of surviving a disaster, there are several other benefits that an organization will enjoy through having undertaken a business continuity and disaster recovery planning project.

- *Reduced risk*. After having undergone risk and threat analysis and mitigation, risks that may jeopardize the organization's ongoing operations will be identified and potentially reduced.
- *Process improvements*. Business processes are going to receive very close scrutiny throughout the project. Project staffers will recognize opportunities for process improvements in both the Business Impact Analysis (BIA) phase as well as when contingency plans are developed.
- *Improved organizational maturity*. A BCP/DRP project, with its intense scrutiny on processes, will likely persuade an organization to improve its process maturity.
- *Improved availability and reliability*. One of the objectives of business continuity and disaster recovery is the improved resilience of processes and systems. This will result in improved availability and reliability of business processes and the IT systems that support them. This is directly related to the measured concept of availability, where a system is measured (or promised) to be available 99 percent of the time, or 99.9 percent, 99.99 percent, or better.

- *Marketplace advantage*. An organization that has been able to reduce risks, improve processes, and enhance availability and reliability is going to have a stronger market position. This is applicable to organizations that produce goods and services considered critical or essential.

The Role of Prevention

The surprising and unexpected consequences of a disaster can have a devastating effect on an organization.

The point of BCP and DRP is not prevention of the disaster itself, but prevention of what is otherwise unpreparedness on the part of the organization. The purpose of BCP and DRP is the development of the processes, procedures, and standby assets to be placed into action when a disaster strikes.

The steps in a BCP/DRP project will identify the criticality of specific business processes and systems, which leads to investments in standby or backup capabilities that are used when a disaster strikes. The steps in running a BCP/DRP project are discussed in the next section.

Competitive Advantage

For many organizations in private industry, having a BCP and DRP program can be touted as a competitive advantage. Customers may place value on the ability for a supplier or service provider to provide goods and services even if a disaster were to occur. This is especially true of online services such as cloud-based storage and e-mail services.

The BCP and DRP Life Cycle

The entire set of activities related to the analysis, development, and testing of business continuity and disaster recovery plans can be thought of as a life cycle process. This section describes the principal elements of the BCP and DRP life cycle.

Running a BCP/DRP Project

The development of business continuity and disaster recovery plans is a significant undertaking that can consume dozens of personnel hours in the smallest businesses to thousands of personnel hours in large organizations. Any activity of this magnitude requires formal planning, budget, and support.

A business continuity and disaster recovery planning project has several distinct activities and phases. A common methodology has emerged that most organizations follow; this methodology is described in this chapter.

Pre-Project Activities

Prior to the actual start of the project, several key actions should be completed, including:

- Obtaining executive support
- Formally defining the scope of the project

- Choosing project team members
- Developing a project plan
- Developing a project charter

These steps are described in more detail in the remainder of this section.

Those readers familiar with formal project management methodology will recognize that the pre-project activities in this section apply to business projects in general. They are included here because a BCP/DRP project is unique among projects in that the deliverable does not measurably change the business at the outset, since the only deliverable may be process documentation that may never be performed if a disaster does not occur. Because of that, often BCP/DRP projects receive insufficient support.

Obtaining Executive Support Business continuity and disaster planning requires significant investments in time and financial resources to successfully develop, implement, and test a workable plan. For this reason, an organization's executive team must provide support throughout the project's life cycle. Diverting resources from everyday processes and responsibilities will have a short-term negative impact on key business activities, enough that managers will be tempted to pull staff off of the project, delaying its completion. Executive sponsorship should be exceedingly clear and unambiguous regarding:

- The scope of the project
- The priority of the project
- The budget for the project
- The appropriate staffing levels for the project
- The expected completion date for the project
- Any rewards that will be given upon the completion of the project
- The year-to-year support for the maintenance of the plan

Defining the Project Scope The scope of the BCP/DRP project is one of the most important decisions that will be made. It defines what part(s) of the organization are included in the project, and what parts are excluded from the project.

The decision about the scope of the project needs to be an informed and intentional decision. The scope of the project needs to be wide enough to include all of the known-critical parts of the organization (without which the organization would struggle mightily to survive, should a disaster occur).

The scope of the project should not include parts of the organization that are outside the control of the executive sponsors. The reason for this is two-fold: first, those outside parts of the organization may feel suspicious about the BCP/DRP project, in that it might be an attempt to gain control over that part of the organization; second, the executive(s) who sponsor and support the project cannot commit resources to the project that are outside of their span of control. In other words, one part of an organization cannot impose a BC/DR plan upon another part of the organization without their consent, participation, and executive support. The optimal condition occurs when the organization's president or its board of directors chooses to sponsor the effort.

Another factor that needs to be considered is the size of the BCP/DRP project. In a very large organization with multiple locations and/or business units, managing such a large project may be too cumbersome. Perhaps it would be better to scale down a project to include just certain locations and/or business units. Separate BCP/DRP projects in other locations or business units can be carried out by separate project teams at the same time, or at a later time. Another option is managing the effort as a portfolio of smaller projects, instead of as one comprehensive endeavor. For organizations that take this approach, executive management should establish an overall set of objectives or guiding principles, so that all of those separate BCP/DRP projects will be cohesive.

Choosing Project Team Members Once the executive sponsors define the desired outcomes and project scope, they must select a project manager and team to complete the work. Considering the importance of BCP/DRP, the project manager should have experience with large-scale, cross-functional efforts. The next position is equally vital—administrative support. This individual or individuals manage the documentation and process workflows and produce reports for management related to the project's progress. Although it may be tempting to continue selecting team members from senior staff and management levels, it is wiser to focus more attention on subject matter experts in every area impacted by the plan. The SME contingent can often reduce the time needed to define key applications, equipment, processes, and data required to create a successful recovery. Many of these individuals also comprise the emergency response team (ERT), so obtaining their input during the planning stage increases buy-in at all organizational levels. Although departmental managers may resist tapping key personnel for anything other than day-to-day operations, coordinating the project timeline with these frontline managers can improve support and provide the expertise required for the development and testing of a successful plan.

Another challenge occurs when combining individuals from various departments. Cross-functional teams support a holistic approach to restoring organizational health. In an emergency situation, some departments receive higher priority in terms of resource allocation and restoration of key processes. A thorough analysis demands evaluating each department in the context of a disaster, and each should have a specific liaison to the project team. After selecting the team, the project manager should hold meetings with managers to explain the process, timelines, and objectives. Executive sponsors should attend these meetings but should not lead them. The point is to reinforce the project's importance but allow the project manager to exert the leader's role.

Developing a Project Plan Every journey should begin with a plan. An organization's BCP/DRP project should have a detailed plan that identifies the milestones and the work: when will the milestones take place, and who will do the work to accomplish them.

The Project Management Institute includes the following requirements for developing a project plan: collect requirements, define scope, create work breakdown structures; define and sequence activities and estimate required resources and durations for their use; develop a schedule, estimate costs, and define communications and change processes. Communications processes include the creation, collection, distribution, and version control of all documents related to the project. Clearly defining the communications process constructs a preflight checklist of activities needed to technically support this aspect of the plan.

Except in the smallest organizations, the project should have an experienced project manager who knows how to develop project plans, conduct project meetings, communicate clearly, manage the people who are performing the tasks on the plan, make schedule changes, and make necessary changes to the plan that will arise throughout the project.

Ideally, the project manager will have been involved in a BCP or DRP project in the past so that he or she is familiar with these types of projects and the common issues that arise in these projects.

In a large BCP/DRP project, it is best to develop the plan in stages. Until the Business Impact Analysis is completed, for example, it will be difficult to estimate the amount of work required to develop contingency plans. This is because no one on the project team will know for certain which contingency plans will need to be developed, or what resources will be required to develop them. It is suggested that a large BCP/DRP project be split into three phases:

- Phase I: Business Impact Analysis
- Phase II: Develop Contingency Plans
- Phase III: Test Contingency Plans

One of the last milestones for Phase I should be the development of a detailed project plan for Phase II. Similarly, one of the last milestones for Phase II should be the development of a detailed project plan for Phase III.

Developing a Project Charter A charter formally structures the requirements and desired outcomes and initiates the project. All of the main items of preparation that take place prior to the actual start of the project should be documented in a project charter document. The charter document should contain all of the items being discussed in this section, and a few more:

- Purpose of the BCP/DRP project, including a business case for its inception
- Executive sponsorship and definition of stakeholders and their interests
- Scope
- Budget
- Principal team members
- Milestones

The charter document should be drafted, reviewed, and signed by the executive sponsors and principal team members. Doing so will accomplish two things: the project will be well defined, and all of the key participants in the project will be committing to its success.

Business Impact Analysis

A **Business Impact Analysis (BIA)** is essentially a catalog of all of an organization's important business processes that includes information about the criticality of each. The steps required to perform the BIA are:

- Survey business processes
- Perform risk analysis and threat assessment

- Determine Maximum Tolerable Downtime (MTD)
- Establish key recovery targets

These steps are described in the remainder of this section.

Survey In-Scope Business Processes The first and very necessary step in a BIA is a survey of all of the important business processes that are within the scope of the overall project. The survey itself need not be complicated, but it may be very labor-intensive and time-consuming in a larger organization with many important business processes.

The objective of the survey is the capture of several characteristics of each important business process and what each process contributes to the organization's mission or purpose. These characteristics will enable team members to complete subsequent steps of the BIA.

The project team will need to decide what constitutes "important" in determining which processes are important enough to be considered in the BIA, and which are not sufficiently important. Generally, processes related to revenue generation and communication with customers and employees receive the most attention.

Information Collection It is important for the collection of business process information to be as uniform as possible. I suggest that the project team develop an "intake form" that can be used to capture process information. When multiple staff members are performing process surveys, an intake form helps the survey process to be more consistent than if each staff member used his or her own "style" to get the same information. A sample intake form is shown in Table 4-1.

Staff members who are conducting interviews can bring along a notebook computer and type in the information given to them, or they can handwrite information on pads of paper and type it in later. Interviews of this type are best recorded for accuracy.

Each process needs to have its own form. In a department with many processes, a single interview can result in many completed forms.

Information Consolidation As information is collected on each process, the information should be electronically transferred from individual intake forms onto a spreadsheet or database.

It is suggested that the spreadsheet be set up as follows:

- Columns in the spreadsheet will correspond to fields in the intake form.
- Rows in the spreadsheet will correspond to individual intake forms.

The purpose of putting all of the information into a spreadsheet is that it gives analysts an opportunity to view all of the processes in a single view.

As the BIA work advances, the project manager (or other individual) should keep the process spreadsheet up to date. It will be used in later stages of the BIA.

Threat and Risk Analysis Once all processes have been identified, and basic information about each process captured on the input forms described in the previous section, a

Process Name	(name of the process)
Date	(date of the interview)
Interviewer	(name of the person conducting the interview)
Interviewee	(name of the person being interviewed)
Interviewee Contact	(e-mail, phone, location, etc.)
Department	(interviewee's department)
Process Owner Name	(department manager or other responsible party who is accountable for the performance of the process)
Process Purpose	(why the process is performed)
Process Inputs	(data, people, supplies, or other things that the process uses)
Process Outputs	(data, products, or other outcomes from running the process)
Supplier Dependencies	(names of suppliers that are essential to the ongoing operation of the process)
Personnel Dependencies	(names of staff members who are essential to the ongoing operation of the process)
Asset Dependencies	(list of assets that are essential to the ongoing operation of the process)
Information System Dependencies	(list of IT applications that are essential to the ongoing operation of the process)
Communications Dependencies	(list of communications facilities [phone, FAX, Internet, etc.] that are essential to the ongoing operation of the process)
Facilities Dependencies	(list of facilities that are essential to the ongoing operation of the process)
Other Internal Dependencies	(other internal dependencies not listed above that are essential to the ongoing operation of the process)
Other External Dependencies	(other external dependencies not listed above that are essential to the ongoing operation of the process)

Table 4-1 Sample BIA process intake form

threat risk analysis needs to be performed on each process. To support the business case for the business continuity plan, risks associated with short- and long-term operational downtime must be quantified in financial terms. Stakeholders should know the daily costs associated with downtime.

Depending upon the skills of the project team members and the needs of the project, the threat-risk analysis can be performed as a single task or broken up into a risk analysis and a threat analysis. The remainder of this section will assume that the two will be done separately.

The purpose for threat and risk analyses is to identify threats and risks that can jeopardize critical business processes—not just from a disaster recovery perspective but from *any* perspective. The ultimate objective of business continuity planning and disaster recovery planning is not just recovering from disasters but also preventing and avoiding disaster-related and other events from threatening the continuity of critical business processes. Resilience of business processes is the ultimate objective of business continuity planning: knowledge of threats and risks to business processes is an essential ingredient in the overall process of achieving this resilience.

Threat Analysis A **threat analysis**, sometimes known as threat modeling, is the process of identifying factors that may jeopardize the ongoing performance of a business process or system.

A single threat analysis can be performed for the entire business (or at least the portion of the organization that is in scope for the BCP/DRP project), or individual threat analyses can be performed on each process. Either way, the procedure for performing a threat analysis is pretty much the same:

1. Identify every threat that can reasonably materialize and adversely affect the process.
2. Identify the probability that the threat can actually occur.
3. Identify mitigating actions that can be taken to reduce the probability and/or impact of identified threats.

Risk Analysis A **risk analysis** is the process of identifying risks and weaknesses in a process or system.

A risk analysis can be performed on each process, group of processes, or the entire organization, depending upon the nature of the business and the needs of the BCP/DRP project. The procedure for performing a risk analysis is:

1. Identify every risk that has a reasonable chance of materializing and adversely affecting a process.
2. Estimate the probability that the risk can materialize into an event that can adversely affect a process.
3. Identify mitigating actions that can be taken to reduce significant risks.

An organization that periodically conducts risk and threat analyses may be able to appropriate most or all of an existing general-purpose risk and threat analysis instead of performing one separately for a BCP/DRP project. There is nothing inherently unique about a risk assessment in support of a BCP/DRP project that would require that a separate one be performed. Risk and threat analysis are covered in more detail in Chapter 1, "Information Security and Risk Management."

Determine Maximum Tolerable Downtime (MTD) Once every business process has been identified and placed on the big spreadsheet, an important metric must be assigned to it: **Maximum Tolerable Downtime** (MTD). This is defined as the period of time after which the organization would suffer considerable pain were the process unavailable. In some types of organizations, this would represent a threat to an organization's ongoing viability (or the viability of a portion of the organization).

The units of measurement for MTD may be minutes, hours, days, or longer, depending upon the nature of the organization's business activities and business model.

Determining MTD is a process all by itself that will probably undergo several iterations. It is suggested that the project team take a first pass at educated-guess MTD values for each process, and then have the sponsoring executives review, update, and approve the MTD figures established for each process.

While the project team may establish some other means for documenting the MTD for each process, it is suggested that a column be added to the process worksheet and the MTD value for each process placed there.

Even then, it's likely that at least some MTD values will be changed again, later on in the project. Still, it is important to have a good set of educated-guess figures before moving on to the next phase of the project.

Develop Statements of Impact For each process, a **statement of impact** needs to be developed that describes the impact on the organization if a process is incapacitated. Examples might include *inability to process payments*, *inability to produce invoices*, or *inability to support customers*. This information will be needed later in the project.

Recording Other Key Metrics The project team or the sponsoring executives may wish to record other metrics for each process in scope. Some possible metrics that could be used include:

- Cost to operate the process
- Cost of process downtime
- Revenue or profit derived from the process

These metrics lay the foundation for a subsequent project phase, known as the **criticality analysis.**

Develop Current Continuity and Recovery Capabilities Many organizations aren't starting with a completely clean slate: there are some BCP or DRP capabilities or plans in place already. These capabilities need to be taken into account. For each process there will be three outcomes:

- *Adequate.* The current BCP/DRP capability exists and is still adequate.
- *Inadequate.* The current BCP/DRP capability exists but no longer meets the needs of the business. Current capabilities are either defective (implemented incorrectly) or provide recovery at a lesser level of capability.
- *Nonexistent.* No BCP/DRP capability exists.

Developing Key Recovery Targets When MTD and other figures have been established, the next step in the process is to determine key recovery targets. These targets will directly determine any improvements that must take place in processes and supporting IT systems so that the targets are achievable. The four targets are:

- Recovery Time Objective (RTO)
- Recovery Point Objective (RPO)
- Recovery Consistency Objective (RCO)
- Recovery Capacity Objective (RCapO)

Recovery Time Objective (RTO) **Recovery Time Objective** (RTO) is the maximum period of time that a business process or IT system will be unavailable during a disaster. RTO is expressed in units of time and can be minutes, hours, days, or longer, depending upon the needs of the organization.

The project team needs to establish an RTO for every process that is in scope for the project. The MTD target should be a guide to the RTO value.

When setting RTO targets for processes, project teams need to realize that low values for RTOs are more expensive to achieve than higher values. This is true whether the target is being expressed for a manual business process or an IT system. While every IT application, system, and organization is different, Table 4-2 gives an approximation of the types of technologies and capabilities that are needed for different ranges of RTO.

In addition to additional equipment and potentially expensive software for clustering and replication, shorter RTOs also require more staff and facilities to support the more aggressive targets.

Project team members and executives need to quantify and compare the value of a business process to the potential cost of upgrading a system to meet a more aggressive RTO. Often, DRP/BCP project teams scale back their RTOs once they discover how expensive their targets really are. One acceptable approach is a multiyear investment in the necessary software and equipment to reach RTO targets.

Recovery Point Objective (RPO) The **Recovery Point Objective** (RPO), expressed in units of time, is the maximum acceptable amount of data loss or work loss for a given process. One pragmatic way of understanding RPO is to ask, how much rekeying will be required once a system or application has been recovered and is back up and running? Here is an example:

The database management system supporting an IT application exports data to a flat file every two hours. The RTO for the application is twenty-four hours, which means that within twenty-four hours of a disaster, the application will be available again. When the application

RTO	Technology Required
8–14 days	New equipment, data recovery from backup
4–7 days	Cold systems, data recovery from backup
2–3 days	Warm systems, data recovery from backup
12–24 hours	Warm systems, data recovery from high-speed backup media
6–12 hours	Hot systems, data recovery from high-speed backup media
3–6 hours	Hot systems, data replication
1–3 hours	Clustering, data replication
<1 hour	Clustering, near-real-time data replication

Table 4-2 Capabilities required to support various RTOs

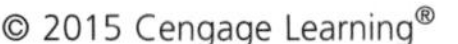

is recovered, the IT department will recover data from backups and from the flat file exports. The RPO for the application is two hours because the maximum data loss in this example is two hours.

Recovery Consistency Objective (RCO) The **Recovery Consistency Objective** (**RCO**) is a measure of the integrity and consistency of data in an emergency operations system as compared to the original data in production systems. The calculation for RCO for each environment is:

RCO = 1 − (number of inconsistent entities) / (number of entities)

In complex environments, the cost of attaining a 100 percent RCO target may be cost prohibitive.

Recovery Capacity Objective (RCapO) The **Recovery Capacity Objective** (**RCapO**) is a measure of processing capacity for a business process during a disaster. For example, the main processing site for an e-commerce system may be able to process twenty thousand transactions per hour, whereas the recovery processing site may be able to process only five thousand transactions per hour. A decision to equip a recovery process or system with less capacity than a primary process should be a part of the overall strategy for allocating resources to business recovery systems.

When the MTD, RPO, RTO, RCO, and RCapO targets have been established for each process, all of the processes can be compared to each other based upon these criteria. The point of the criticality analysis is to identify which processes in the organization are the most critical, based upon the objective measures that have been identified thus far in the Business Impact Analysis. Here are several ways in which processes can be compared:

- *Ranked by MTD*. Those processes with the lowest MTD values may be the most time-sensitive in the organization.
- *Ranked by RTO*. Processes with low RTO values are probably also time-sensitive.
- *Ranked by RPO*. Processes with low RPO values are probably time-sensitive and also high-value or labor-intensive.
- *Ranked by RCO*. Processes with high RCO values may be high-value processes, or processes that by their nature require high data integrity.
- *Ranked by RCapO*. Processes with high RCapO values may be high-value processes, or processes that are resource-intensive.
- *Ranked by revenue per hour/day/month*. Processes with high revenue rates are probably among the most valuable in the organization.
- *Ranked by profit per hour/day/month*. Processes with high profit margins may be considered among the most valuable in the organization.
- *Ranked by cost per hour/day/month*. Processes with a high cost may be the most valuable in the organization.
- *Ranked by customer visibility*. A company that relies on its customer service image may consider customer-facing services and systems at a higher criticality than others.

Establishing Ranking Criteria The project team, together with sponsoring executives, will need to establish process-ranking criteria that are appropriate for the organization. Knowing which processes and systems are the most critical may be a simple case of ranking them by one of the already-identified figures such as MTD or RTO, or it may be a little more complicated. In the end, the ranking criteria need to meet the needs of the business, and not the other way around.

Complete the Criticality Analysis Once the ranking criteria are chosen, they are applied against the entire list of processes in the Business Impact Assessment. The result will be the final rank-ordered list of processes and systems in the organization. At the top of the list will be those processes and systems that are most vital to the organization's ongoing viability.

Improving System and Process Resilience

The results of the BIA provide the team with the most critical processes and systems in the organization and how quickly each needs to be recovered.

From a strict security perspective, the rank-ordered result of the BIA also provides security personnel with a valuable list of which processes and systems may require the most protection.

Identifying Risk Factors The Threat and Risk Analysis section earlier in this chapter describes the important steps of identifying threats and risks associated with business processes. Now it is time to examine the results of those analyses, particularly for the most critical processes and systems in the organization.

The threat and risk analysis suggests one or more mitigating controls that will reduce the probability, frequency, or impact of a threat or risk. Further analysis is needed to determine whether the mitigating controls are *feasible*. These mitigating controls need to be analyzed to determine:

- Whether the mitigating control will reduce risk at a reasonable cost (*it's probably not reasonable to spend $100,000 to protect a $10,000 asset, unless there is considerable intangible value also connected to the asset, such as the organization's reputation*)
- Whether the mitigating control can be reasonably implemented and operated in a production system or process environment
- Whether mitigating controls from several systems can be consolidated into a simpler control that protects against multiple threats/risks or can protect multiple systems or processes
- Whether the mitigating control represents a best practice or a common practice

Developing Business Continuity and Disaster Recovery Plans

After the BIA, criticality analysis, and recovery targets have been established and approved by executive management, response and recovery plans can be developed and tested. This section discusses the steps required in these plans, which for most organizations include:

- Selecting recovery team members
- Emergency response
- Damage assessment and salvage

- Notification
- Personnel safety
- Communications
- Public utilities and infrastructure
- Logistics and supplies
- Fire protection
- Business resumption planning
- Restoration and recovery

Selecting Recovery Team Members When a disaster occurs, trained individuals need to respond. Disaster response team members need to be familiar with recovery and contingency procedures and be available to carry them out.

The first tendency is to choose the individuals who have the most expertise and experience with the processes and systems being recovered. While this is a logical choice, those persons may not be available for one of several possible reasons:

- *Unable to respond.* A recovery team member cannot respond for one of several possible reasons:
  - Transportation outages prevent travel
  - Team member injured in the disaster
  - Team member deceased
- *Unwilling to respond.* A recovery team member is not willing to respond for one of these reasons:
  - Team member caring for injured relatives
  - Team member unwilling to leave residence

When choosing recovery team members, many alternates need to be identified to ensure that enough qualified and/or trained personnel will be on hand to carry out the recovery.

In addition to choosing the staff members with the most direct experience, other factors should be taken into account when choosing recovery team members:

- *Location.* Members live near the recovery site.
- *Experience.* While they may not have experience on particular systems or teams, staff members who have general experience with systems or processes would be good alternates.
- *Health.* Staff members who are in better health and physical condition will tend to be more available to respond during a disaster.
- *Family.* One can argue that a staff member who is single will be more apt to be available in a disaster than one who has family members to care for.
- *Own transportation.* Staff members who own their own vehicles (and not just automobiles, but whatever is necessary and available) will be more likely to respond than those who rely upon mass transit that may be interrupted in a disaster.

Different types of disasters have different effects on a region. For this reason it may be wise to identify two or three times the number of staff members for a recovery team than are actually required in a disaster. This way, the required minimum level of staff is more likely to actually show up.

Emergency Response The emergency response plan is an organization's "first responders" plan that carries out a number of key tasks, including:

- *Personnel safety*. When workers are on-site when a disaster strikes, emergency response personnel make sure that workers are safe. Depending upon the situation, this could include administering first aid, searching for all personnel, and so on.
- *Evacuation*. Emergency response personnel should have established building, plant, and premises evacuation procedures so that all personnel can be cleared from a facility that could be damaged or present any hazard to workers.
- *Asset protection*. After ensuring the safety of personnel, the emergency response team should ensure that company assets continue to be protected after the disaster. This could include buildings, vehicles, and equipment. Mechanisms that secure these assets could be damaged or inoperative during a disaster.
- *Damage assessment*. The emergency response team needs to be able to perform a damage assessment. This could involve outside structural engineers to assess potential damage to buildings and equipment.
- *Emergency notification*. The emergency response team needs to be able to notify each other as well as initiate any emergency "call tree" or other means for communicating with staff in the organization.

Many of the tasks in this section will transition to longer-term and more formal response that is described in the remaining sections below.

A disaster response plan should always emphasize the highest priority on the safety of all personnel.

Damage Assessment and Salvage Formal assessment of all significant assets needs to take place in order to determine which assets are still usable and which are not.

For the most part, damage assessment needs to be performed by personnel who are familiar with the equipment being examined. Sure, it's easy for even a layperson to tell if some equipment is damaged and not immediately useful, but skilled personnel are needed to determine whether any latent (not obvious) damage has occurred.

Similarly, some equipment can be salvaged. Depending upon the equipment, perhaps it can be dismantled and its still-working components can be used as spares elsewhere. Or, equipment known to be damaged beyond repair can be moved away from the work area so that replacement equipment can be installed.

Notification When a disaster occurs, affected parties need to know the condition of the organization. The parties involved may include:

- *Employees*. The organization's workers need to know whether they should report to work and, if so, when and where, and what they should do upon arrival.

- *Suppliers*. The organization's suppliers need to know whether they should continue delivering supplies to the organization, or if quantities, delivery schedules, or locations should be changed.
- *Customers*. Customers and patrons will need to know whether the organization is operating at normal or reduced capacity, operating hours, and locations.
- *Regulators*. In many industries, regulators must be notified of any disaster situations.
- *Authorities*. Law enforcement and public safety organizations may need to be informed of an organization's "ready for business" status during and after a disaster.
- *Shareholders*. The organization's stockholders and shareholders may need to be notified of a disaster.

The nature of the organization, and of the disaster itself, will help to determine how all of these parties should be notified (and it may very well be a different method for each group). Some of the possibilities for notification include:

- *Telephone*. This could be through call trees or automatic outbound calling.
- *Web site*. A temporary announcement could be placed on the organization's web site. For employees, messages on the Intranet can be used to inform employees of the disaster.
- *Signage*. An organization may need to post signs to inform visitors of the status of the organization's operations.
- *Media*. Newspaper and television stations may need to be notified, as an efficient means for notifying the public.

An emergency communications plan needs to be developed to accommodate some or all of the notification and communications needs described here.

Because of the unpredictable nature of disasters, multiple alternative means of communication should be developed and tested. For instance, telecommunications are impacted in several disaster scenarios. Emergency communication that does not rely upon telecommunications carriers (both voice and data) may be considered.

Personnel Safety The safety of all workers should be the highest priority in any disaster response scenario. Emergency response plans should put worker safety first, and ahead of all other concerns. Organizations (such as retail locations) with visitors should put visitor safety on par with worker safety, although the procedures for protecting visitors may vary somewhat from workers.

Emergency response plans should include several personnel safety measures, including:

- *Emergency evacuation*. Procedures should be developed and regularly tested to evacuate personnel and visitors from a work facility. These procedures may involve the use of several trained safety personnel—workers who are trained to make sure that personnel in work areas are able to locate and use exits.
- *Medical aid*. First aid supplies should be on hand to treat injured workers and visitors.
- *Emergency supplies*. Work facilities should have a supply of emergency drinking water, food rations, blankets, and so on if a disaster results in workers being "stranded" at work locations. Supplies may also be needed for emergency response personnel should they need to remain in a work facility for several days.

Communications During a disaster, communications are both more important and more difficult. Communications are more difficult because some communications facilities may be damaged or unavailable, and some team members will be unavailable. During a disaster, it's just going to be harder to find other team members to coordinate activities.

Communications are more important during a disaster because disaster operations are, by nature, less predictable than everyday operations. This requires people to be in closer contact with one another until they are familiar with disaster operations that are taking place. In other words, during a disaster people need to communicate more until they understand what's going on.

Because some communications networks may be impaired (or just congested) during a disaster, more than one means for voice and data communications are needed to improve the likelihood that at least one will actually work. Some considerations when selecting alternate communications include:

- *Avoid common infrastructure*. Alternate communications should avoid carriers that share the same local or regional wiring plants. If the backbone fiber rings that many providers use are damaged, then chances are all of the providers' networks will not be working.
- *Diversify mobile services*. Recovery and response teams should diversify their mobile network providers. Most regions in North America have at least three mobility networks. If different team members use different networks, then an outage by one of the networks will not render the team's communication incapacitated.
- *Consider two-way radios*. Short-distance two-way radios may be a viable alternative to cellular communications if mobility infrastructure is congested or damaged.
- *Consider satellite phones*. In a severe disaster situation, all terrestrial-based communications systems (landline, mobile) may be damaged or impaired. While more expensive, satellite phones are more likely to work during a disaster since they do not depend on local communications infrastructure.
- *Consider amateur radio*. In a significant disaster, amateur radio may be the only way to communicate important information with the outside world.

Public Utilities and Infrastructure A disaster may temporarily impair or interrupt the delivery of public utility services such as electricity, natural gas, water, and steam. In a severe disaster, one or more of these utilities may be unavailable for many days. Organizations located in a disaster-stricken area will need to develop contingency plans for going without various utilities for a time.

Electricity Short interruptions in electric power are not uncommon in most areas. The impact of a power outage on an organization has a lot to do with its reliance on a continuous supply of electricity. Because most organizations have some reliance on information systems, a growing number of organizations have one or two phase contingency plans for generating their own electric power during an outage. These plans usually include:

- *Surge protectors*. Computer equipment is intolerant of noisy electric power. Usually deployed in point-of-use situations such as workstations and printers, a good surge protector will protect equipment from surges, spikes, and other noise.

- *Line conditioners.* These are essentially surge protectors, but for an entire building, as opposed to a surge protector that protects a small number of devices.
- ***Uninterruptible Power Supply (UPS).*** Computer equipment has no tolerance for interruptions in electric power. A UPS system provides continuous electric power through the use of storage batteries. Depending upon the needs of an organization, a UPS can provide electric power for as little as several minutes and as long as several hours.
- ***Electric generator.*** Powered by diesel fuel, gasoline, or natural gas, an electric generator can provide electricity for as little as a few hours and as long as many days. **Generators** can also be refueled, extending the time that they can provide electric power. Generators usually take several seconds to a minute or longer to start to provide electric power, so generators are usually used in coordination with UPSs to provide a long-term, steady supply of electricity to a facility that has a high reliance on electricity.

Water Earthquakes, landslides, and other events can damage water mains, interrupting water supplies to businesses. In severe disasters, emergency water supplies are often brought in by truck or even airplane.

The first concern for a supply of water is emergency drinking water for personnel. Organizations can maintain a supply of emergency drinking water in bottles or tanks. However, since water is also used for sanitation and fire suppression, in most locations, government authorities (usually a fire marshal or health inspector) will not permit an organization to continue operations in a building that has no reliable water supply.

Natural Gas Earthquakes and other disasters can damage natural gas lines resulting in service interruptions. Natural gas is used for heating, cooling, cooking, and other functions.

Several factors make it impractical to employ an emergency or alternative gaseous fuel supply, and few organizations do so. Contingency and response plans need to include steps to be taken if the natural gas supply is interrupted for long periods of time.

Wastewater Treatment In most areas, organizations rely upon centralized sanitary sewage treatment systems for wastewater treatment. If a disaster has damaged wastewater treatment plants or major piping systems, an organization may have to stop utilizing incoming water; health authorities may require the evacuation of the facility.

Steam Also known as *district heating*, steam heat services in cities provide heat for buildings. A disaster can cause interruptions in steam heat for hours to days. Organizations heated with steam heat need to develop contingency plans for events that may cause interruptions in heating service.

Logistics and Supplies Emergency response procedures require considerable advance planning to ensure that essential supplies and staff needed for evacuations, assessments, salvage, and recovery are at hand or readily available. Supplies that may be needed include:

- *Food and drinking water.* Emergency response teams that may need to remain for several days at a work facility will need food and drinking water for sustenance. Blankets and sleeping cots may also be needed if there is no nearby lodging available.

- *Sanitation.* Toilets, showers, and so on.
- *Tools.* Whatever tools are needed for salvage and repairs of buildings and business equipment.
- *Spare parts.* Parts and whatever is needed to repair buildings and business equipment. When a disaster occurs, transportation may be hampered and needed parts will be in short supply and difficult and costly to obtain.
- *Waste bins.* Receptacles for damaged goods as well as waste generated during salvage and repair operations.
- *Information.* This may include directories, procedures, schematics, specifications, and so on.
- *Communications.* Whatever equipment and supplies are required for emergency communications. Consider including writing pads and pens/pencils.

The specific nature of an organization will add color and depth to the logistics and supplies needed for adequate emergency response.

Fire Protection Fire prevention capabilities are required in virtually every locale in the world. Required systems in business locations include one or more of the following:

- Fire extinguishers
- Smoke detectors
- Automatic sprinkler systems
- Fire alarm systems
- Evacuation aids

Business Resumption Planning When a disaster strikes, one of the most vital activities to be undertaken is the resumption of critical business processes. Whether or not they are supported by IT applications, business processes are the vital activities in organizations. The whole point of business continuity planning is to figure out how to keep the most vital processes operating, even when a disaster strikes.

Of course, where a business process relies upon an IT application to function, then that IT application needs to have its own recovery capability to meet the needs of the process(es) it supports.

The Business Impact Analysis (BIA) should explore each process thoroughly enough to determine where the critical activities are in each process. It is then up to BCP team members to develop a contingency plan for each critical process that will enable it to meet the RPO and RTO targets that were established during the BIA.

Depending upon the nature of the business process, one or more of these considerations may be required during the development of contingency plans:

- *Alternate location.* Depending upon the nature of the process and the business, alternate locations for critical processes may need to be identified before a disaster takes place. The alternate location may need to be stocked with supplies, procedures, and records so that the process can be quickly resumed.

- *Alternate personnel*. If the alternate location is some distance away from the primary location, it may be more reasonable for alternate personnel to perform duties there. The source of these alternate personnel might be a temp agency or employees in another work location.
- *Communications*. Personnel operating out of another location will probably need communications capabilities—voice, data, or both—in order to support the critical processes performed there.
- *Standby assets and equipment*. Equipment and machinery required to support the process need to be acquired quickly, to meet the recovery targets.
- *Access to procedures*. Personnel in the alternate location need access to work procedures so that they know how to perform their duties.
- *Access to records*. Personnel may need to have access to business records in order to perform their duties.

Restoration and Recovery The point of business continuity planning and disaster recovery planning is restoring operations after a disaster. The organization's emergency response will be multifaceted in order to manage all aspects of a disaster, including personnel safety, damage assessment, and the recovery of facilities and assets to once again support business operations. This section is concerned with the restoration of business operations in a work facility.

When a disaster first strikes, emergency response is concerned primarily with personnel safety and evacuation, followed by damage assessment and salvage. Once the extent of the damage to facilities and equipment is known, efforts to restore business operations can begin.

Depending upon the extent of damage, restoration may consist of minor repair, major repairs, or (in extreme situations) a complete replacement of facilities and assets. Any staff or assets that remain in the facility may need to relocate during repair or rebuilding operations—business continuity plans need to allow for this possibility.

Remember that restoration and recovery operations are completely separate from business continuity efforts that focus on the continued delivery of services.

When repairs have been completed, business operations need to be transitioned back into the repaired and recovered facility. This may require interruptions in service as personnel and equipment are relocated from a temporary work location. This relocation will need to be scheduled and announced so that any interruptions in service can be anticipated and planned around.

Improving System Resilience and Recovery

During the Business Impact Analysis (BIA), several important recovery targets were established: Recovery Time Objective (RTO), Recovery Point Objective (RPO), Recovery Capacity Objective (RCapO), and Recovery Consistency Objective (RCO). For each IT system, an analysis needs to be made to determine whether the system is currently able to meet those objectives or whether changes in architecture are required. If improvements in RPO, RTO,

RCapO, or RCO are needed, one or more of the following architectures and technologies may be needed:

- Off-site media storage
- Server clusters
- Data replication

Off-Site Media Storage Backups of critical data should be performed frequently. The rule-of-thumb starting point for a backup strategy is a full backup once per week and an incremental backup daily, with periodic testing to ensure that backups are working properly and that data can actually be recovered from backup media. Actual business and recovery needs will determine whether full and incremental backups need to be performed more or less frequently than this.

Backup media should be stored off-site in a secure facility. The means of transport to and from the off-site facility should itself be secure. Detailed and accurate records of all media moved to and from the off-site storage facility should be available. The off-site media storage facility should be audited for adequacy and integrity of security and recordkeeping controls and should be free of security incidents.

Server Clusters In cases where RCO value is high and RPO and RTO values are less than one hour, there probably will not be sufficient time for staff members to build and ready backup servers. Server **clusters** should be considered for applications with high-availability needs, even in the event of a severe disaster that makes a primary server unavailable for any reason.

Clusters permit an application to operate on two or more servers. In a cluster, one server can be taken offline without interrupting the application. A **failover** occurs when production workload is transferred from one server to another server in a cluster.

Two types of cluster configurations are:

- *Active-Active*. In an active-active cluster, all servers in the cluster are providing service.
- *Active-Passive*. In an active-passive cluster, one or more *active* servers in a cluster are providing service, while one or more *passive* servers are in standby mode, ready to provide service if needed.

Virtualization software achieves the same goals with fewer physical servers and shared storage using a storage area network. Virtualization tools allow administrators to seamlessly transfer virtualized servers from one server to another. This can shorten the time required to restore IT operations as long as the storage has been properly backed up and can be restored using a replacement for a damaged or destroyed SAN or transferred to an off-site cold/hot site with similar equipment.

A **geographic cluster**, or geo-cluster, is a cluster in which the cluster members are located hundreds or thousands of miles apart and communicate via WAN connections. Geo-clusters may be needed for applications with very low RPO and RTO targets and high RCapO and RCO targets.

Another advantage of server clusters is that unexpected software or hardware failures or even patching and upgrades result in little or no downtime, as other cluster members can take over application workload with little or no administrative intervention.

Data Replication **Data replication** refers to any mechanism that copies data in real-time or near-real-time from one storage system to another. The storage systems can be located in the same room or thousands of miles apart.

Data replication can be performed in several ways, including:

- *Application.* The application can be programmed to store information on two different databases that can be located near each other or great distances apart. This method is not often used, since changes in remote storage may require changes to the application logic.
- *Database Management System (DBMS).* Database management systems can be configured to replicate database transactions to a remote database. This is a common replication solution that has been in use since the 1990s.
- *Operating system.* The operating system can force disk transactions to be sent to two different storage systems. When used, this is usually a part of a clustering solution.
- *Storage hardware.* The RAID, SAN, or NAS hardware platform can itself replicate disk transactions to a counterpart hardware platform in the same location or in a different location.

The advantage to data replication is that application data can be "ready" on a backup storage system in near-real-time, even in a location that is far away from the main production facility. This provides very good RPO targets for applications that tolerate very little data loss even in a disaster.

Training Staff on Business Continuity and Disaster Recovery Procedures

Organizations that invest time and resources in the development of a business continuity and disaster recovery plan need to remember that the ultimate success of a BCP and DRP plan is only as good as its employees are able to carry it out. Training on disaster response and recovery procedures is an essential and necessary part of a complete BCP and DRP project.

Training can take many forms, including:

- *Participation in testing.* Staff members will become more familiar with emergency response and disaster recovery procedures when they participate in the various types of tests that should be regularly performed. Testing is discussed in detail in the next section.
- *Formal training sessions.* Training on emergency response and disaster recovery procedures in classroom or web-based training settings will help staff members better understand how these procedures are supposed to be carried out. This type of training is especially important when new DRP/BCP plans and procedures have been developed.

Testing Business Continuity and Disaster Recovery Plans

When BCP and DRP plans have been developed, they need to be tested. The five types of testing that are available include:

- Document review
- Walkthrough
- Simulation
- Parallel test
- Cutover test

Testing is also a part of plan maintenance, which is discussed in the next section.

Document Review

In this first step of testing, **document review**, emergency response and recovery procedure documents are circulated to subject matter experts in the organization for review and comment. Those who review the documents may or may not be on response teams, and reviewers could even include outside experts.

Walkthrough

A **walkthrough** test, sometimes known as a **tabletop exercise**, is similar to document review, but it's performed by groups instead of individuals. A facilitator will step the group through a recovery or response procedure, evoking discussion and questions along the way. Group discussion helps to identify issues that individuals might not consider.

Several hours of uninterrupted time needs to be scheduled for a walkthrough so that the review team can get all the way through procedure documents. The continuity of thought helps to improve the quality of the walkthrough.

Simulation

A **simulation** is similar to a walkthrough, but with an added twist: the walkthrough is performed as though a real disaster was taking place. Usually scheduled to take place over an entire workday, a simulation begins with a facilitator reading some announcements describing a disaster that is unfolding in real-time. Over the course of the day, the facilitator will read additional announcements, simulating a real disaster and the news that trickles in over time.

A simulation helps the team to better imagine that a disaster is taking place *right now*, and it helps them to step through emergency response procedures with realism that is not present in a walkthrough.

A well-run simulation usually takes considerable advance planning in order to make it realistic and valuable.

Parallel Test

A **parallel test** is an actual test of recovery procedures and systems. As the name implies, regular business operations continue operating, and recovery processes and systems are initiated *as though* a disaster were taking place.

The advantage of a parallel test is the actual use of disaster recovery and/or emergency response procedures. Because the recovery processes and systems are run in parallel to production processes and systems, a failure of a test does not threaten actual business operations.

It is important to perform very detailed recordkeeping during a parallel test, and then to compare the results of the parallel test with actual business operations, to see if the recovery procedures and systems are operating correctly.

Cutover Test

A **cutover test** is the ultimate test of emergency response and disaster recovery procedures. In a cutover test, actual production systems and/or processes are shut down and those functions are supported entirely by DR procedures and systems.

The failure of the DR system places actual business processes at risk. If the disaster recovery processes or systems do not function correctly, actual business processes will be interrupted until the DR systems are fixed or the business resumed on normal production systems.

A successful test gives confidence that the DR system can actually support the business. This may include not only the correct processing of business processes but also the fact that DR systems are able to handle production levels of work.

Maintaining Business Continuity and Disaster Recovery Plans

DRP and BCP plans are like software: after their initial versions have been designed, built, and tested, they will enter a "maintenance mode" where they will be periodically updated over a period of several years. DRP and BCP have a life cycle that is very similar to the software development life cycle.

Some of the events that necessitate review and modification of DRP and BCP procedures include:

- Changes in business processes and procedures
- Changes to IT systems and applications
- Changes in IT architecture
- Additions to IT applications
- Changes in service providers
- Changes in organizational structure
- Changes in regulations and industry standards

Personnel who are responsible for maintaining BCP and DRP processes and procedures should be kept "in the loop" whenever changes in IT systems, business processes, or suppliers are considered. Asking the question, "Does this change also require an update to BCP or DRP?" greatly enhances the chances that the IT portions of BCP and DRP plans are current. This will help to avoid situations where disaster response procedures suddenly become outdated and ineffective. Organizations that employ formal projects to make changes to systems and processes should include BCP and DRP personnel in those projects to ensure that changes will not threaten the organization's ability to recover systems and processes in the event of a disaster.

Chapter Summary

- A disaster is a natural or man-caused event that damages property and assets, injures or kills people, and impairs the ability for organizations to continue operating.
- Disasters affect businesses by directly damaging business assets; disasters often damage transportation and public utilities, which indirectly affects businesses.
- Natural disasters include earthquakes, volcanoes, tsunamis, landslides, hurricanes, tornadoes, windstorms, ice storms, snow storms, lightning, avalanches, fires, and floods.
- Man-made disasters include strikes and other work slowdowns, war, terrorism, sabotage, vandalism, civil unrest, cyber attacks, blockades, chemical spills, power failures, communications outages, water supply shortages, fuel shortages, and radioactive fallout.
- Disasters affect businesses by interrupting the supply of necessary materials, personnel, services, and other factors necessary for continued business operations.
- BCP and DRP support security by protecting the *availability* of information and services even during a disaster.
- Industry standards related to BCP and DRP include ISO 22301, BS 25999, NIST 800-34, NFPA 1600/1620, and HIPAA.
- The benefits of business continuity and disaster recovery planning are reduced risk, improved processes, elevated organizational maturity, improved availability and reliability, and marketplace advantage.
- Steps taken at the onset of a BCP/DRP project include gaining executive support, defining scope, choosing team members, and developing a project plan.
- The first main step in a BCP/DRP project is the development of a Business Impact Analysis (BIA), which documents the effects on the organization of the failure of each important business process. The steps to creating a BIA are surveying business processes, performing a risk analysis, determining Maximum Tolerable Downtime, and establishing key recovery milestones.
- Maximum Tolerable Downtime (MTD) is the period of time after which the organization would suffer considerable pain were the process unavailable.
- Recovery Time Objective (RTO) is the maximum period of time that a business process or IT system will be unavailable during a disaster.
- Recovery Point Objective (RPO) is the maximum acceptable amount of data loss or work loss for a given process.
- Recovery Consistency Objective (RCO), expressed as a percentage, is the minimum required consistency of complex data sets.

- Recovery Capacity Objective (RCapO), expressed as a percentage, represents the capacity of a recovery system compared to the primary system.
- Criticality analysis is the process of ranking business processes in order of criticality to the organization. The processes listed first would be considered the most critical, while those further down the list would be less critical.
- Recovery team selection needs to take into account not only the expertise that each team member has in a particular functional area, but also the likelihood that he or she will actually be able to respond in a disaster.
- The initial stages of emergency response are primarily concerned with personnel safety, evacuation, and initial damage assessment.
- Damage assessment and salvage activities determine the extent of damage and which assets or equipment can be salvaged.
- Communications are a vital part of disaster response and include communications to staff, suppliers, customers, regulators, shareholders, and authorities.
- Disaster recovery and business continuity plans need to take into account the possibility of long-term interruptions in public transportation and utilities.
- Restoration and recovery is primarily concerned with repairing facilities and equipment to permit the resumption of business operations in the primary work locations.
- Staff members, particularly those who are identified as response personnel, need to be trained on response and recovery procedures.
- The types of BCP and DRP testing are document review, walkthrough, simulation, parallel test, and cutover test.
- After BCP and DRP plans have been developed and tested, they need to be periodically examined and maintained so that they remain up to date and effective.

Key Terms

Business continuity planning (BCP) The activities required to ensure the continuation of critical business processes in an organization.

Business Impact Analysis (BIA) The task of identifying the business impact that results from the interruption of a specific business process.

Cluster A group of two or more servers that operate functionally as a single logical server and will continue operating as a single logical server in the event that one of the servers fails.

Criticality analysis The process of ranking business processes according to their criticality to the organization.

Cutover test A test of a disaster recovery or business continuity plan in which backup or recovery systems or processes are operated in place of normal business operations.

Data replication See *replication*.

Disaster Any event that disrupts the operations of a business in such a significant way that a considerable and coordinated effort is required to achieve a recovery.

Disaster recovery planning (DRP) The activities concerned with the assessment, salvage, repair, and restoration of damaged facilities and assets.

Document review A review of a business continuity or disaster recovery procedure in which a single individual reviews procedures.

Electric generator See *generator*.

Failover An event in a server cluster where production workload is transferred from one server to another.

Generator A backup power source that derives its power from a fossil-fuel-powered electric generator.

Geographic cluster A cluster whose members are dispersed over a wide geographic area.

IT Service continuity The process of ensuring the continuity of IT-provided services and systems.

Man-made disaster A disaster caused by people or organizations.

Maximum Tolerable Downtime (MTD) The period of time after which the organization would suffer considerable pain were the process unavailable.

Natural disaster A disaster caused by a natural event such as an earthquake or flood.

Parallel test A test of a disaster recovery or business continuity plan in which backup or recovery systems or processes are operated alongside normal business operations.

Recovery Capacity Objective (RCapO) The measure of processing capacity on a disaster recovery system.

Recovery Consistency Objective (RCO) The measure of the integrity and consistency of data on a disaster recovery system.

Recovery Point Objective (RPO) The maximum acceptable amount of data loss or work loss for a given process.

Recovery Time Objective (RTO) The maximum period of time that a business process or IT system will be unavailable during a disaster.

Replication An operation concerning the data on a storage system, where additions and changes to the data are transmitted to a counterpart storage system where the same additions and changes take place.

Risk analysis The process of identifying risks, their probability of occurrence, impact, and mitigating steps to reduce probability or impact.

Simulation A review of a disaster recovery or business continuity procedure that is performed in a pretend disaster scenario.

Statement of impact A document that describes the impact that an interrupted business process would have on an organization.

Tabletop exercise See *walkthrough*.

Threat analysis The process of identifying potential threats, their probability of occurrence, impact, and mitigating steps to reduce probability or impact.

Uninterruptible Power Supply (UPS) A short-term backup power source that derives its power from storage batteries.

Walkthrough A review of a business continuity or disaster recovery procedure in which a group of individuals review and discuss procedures.

Review Questions

1. The purpose of a Business Impact Analysis (BIA) is to determine:
   a. The impact of a disaster
   b. The extent of damage in a disaster
   c. Which business processes are the most critical
   d. Which processes depend on IT systems
2. During the early phases of a disaster recovery project, the project team needs to identify the disaster scenarios that can jeopardize the ongoing viability of the organization. The team should perform:
   a. A business impact analysis
   b. A threat analysis
   c. A walkthrough test
   d. A failover test
3. Maximum Tolerable Downtime (MTD) should be determined by:
   a. The project manager
   b. The risk manager
   c. Senior management
   d. The threat modeling tool
4. Recovery Time Objective (RTO) is defined as:
   a. The maximum length of time that a business process will be unavailable during a disaster
   b. The maximum amount of data loss during a disaster
   c. The point in time when a recovery is initiated after a disaster
   d. The maximum period of time that a business can tolerate downtime during a disaster
5. Recovery Point Objective (RPO) is defined as:
   a. The maximum length of time that a business process will be unavailable during a disaster
   b. The maximum amount of data loss during a disaster
   c. The point in time when a recovery is initiated after a disaster
   d. The maximum point in time that a business can tolerate downtime during a disaster
6. The purpose of a criticality analysis is to:
   a. Develop a rank-ordered list of the most critical threats
   b. Develop a rank-ordered list of the most critical business processes
   c. Develop a rank-ordered list of the most critical vulnerabilities
   d. Develop a rank-ordered list of the most critical staff

7. Because of limited resources, Company A cannot develop disaster recovery plans for all of its processes. What should Company A use to determine which processes require recovery plans?
   a. Those that are ranked highest in the criticality analysis
   b. Those with the lowest MTD values
   c. Those with the highest MTD values
   d. Those that are ranked lowest in the criticality analysis

8. Which should be protected first during a disaster:
   a. Critical business records
   b. Critical systems
   c. Backup media for critical systems
   d. Personnel
9. The purpose of UPS is:
   a. Filter electric power created by an electric generator
   b. Delivery of critical supplies during a disaster
   c. Protection of electric generators during a power failure
   d. Continuous electric power during a power failure
10. Over a period of several years, an organization has exceeded the capacity of its emergency electric generator. The organization should:
    a. Increase UPS capacity to make up the difference
    b. Purchase a larger generator that can handle the entire workload
    c. Purchase an additional generator so that the old and new generators together will generate enough power
    d. Decrease UPS capacity to make up the difference
11. An organization is experiencing a large number of spikes, surges, and noise on its incoming electric power. The organization should consider:
    a. An electric generator
    b. An uninterruptible power supply (UPS)
    c. A line conditioner
    d. A power distribution unit
12. An organization has just completed development of a disaster recovery plan. The first test of the plan that should be performed is:
    a. Parallel
    b. Simulation
    c. Walkthrough
    d. Cutover

13. A company has determined that its Recovery Time Objective (RTO) for a critical system is three minutes. In order to ensure the continuous availability of its critical systems, the company should consider:
    a. An active-passive geographic server cluster
    b. An active-active local server cluster
    c. An active-passive local server cluster
    d. An active-active geographic server cluster
14. A company has determined that its Recovery Time Objective (RTO) for critical systems is two hours. In order to facilitate a timely resumption of critical applications, the company should consider:
    a. Data replication to servers in a hot site
    b. Data replication to servers in a warm site
    c. Clustered servers
    d. Disk to disk backup
15. The risk associated with a cutover test is:
    a. A failure will result in a service interruption
    b. A failure will result in data loss
    c. A failure will result in data corruption
    d. Adverse publicity

Hands-On Projects

Project 4-1: Develop a Personal Disaster Plan

In this project you will develop a personal disaster preparedness plan.

1. Determine which types of natural disasters are the most common for the region in which you live.
2. Find out which government or private agencies and organizations have information on disasters for your area.
3. Develop a written plan for how you will prepare in advance for the most likely disaster(s) that may occur in your area.
4. Develop a written plan for how you will communicate with others during the most likely disaster(s) in your area. Identify who you will communicate with, and why.
5. Develop a written plan for what you will do after a disaster strikes.
6. Include in your written plans a process for teaching the plan to other family members, and how the plan will be periodically updated.

Project 4-2: Improve a Contingency Plan

In this project you will analyze an existing contingency planning document and make recommendations for improvement.

1. Go to the U.S. Department of Health & Human Services web site and download the Business Pandemic Influenza Planning Checklist at http://www.flu.gov/planning-preparedness/business/businesschecklist.pdf.

2. Imagine that you are responsible for emergency planning in your organization. Is this plan adequate? Can this plan be implemented in your organization?

3. Make any recommendations for how the plans in the publication can be implemented, as well as any changes that should be made.

Case Projects

Case Project 4-1: Set Recovery Objectives for a Web-Based E-Mail Application

As a consultant with the Ace Security Consulting Co., you have been hired to establish recovery objectives for a web-based e-mail application that is used by the Smith Chemical Company.

Smith Chemical does not have the analytical skills to make proper and reasonable determinations for Recovery Point Objective (RPO), Recovery Time Objective (RTO), Recovery Consistency Objective (RCO), and Recovery Capacity Objective (RCapO). Your objective is to establish reasonable recovery targets and justify them by comparing the value of the application against any additional costs required to achieve the targets.

Case Project 4-2: Evaluate NIST 800-34

As a consultant with the Ace Security Consulting Co., you have been asked to evaluate the use of NIST 800-34 as a framework and guide to contingency planning for a medium-sized business.

NIST 800-34 can be downloaded from http://csrc.nist.gov/publications/PubsSPs.html.

Answer the following questions:

1. Does NIST 800-34 adequately address the issue of protecting sensitive data during recovery operations?

2. Have any technology advances since the publication of this document made contingency considerations outdated?

chapter 5

Cryptography

Topics in This Chapter:

- Applications and Uses of Cryptography
- Encryption Methodologies
- Cryptanalysis
- Management of Cryptography
- Key Management

The $(ISC)^2$ *Common Body of Knowledge* (CBK) defines the key areas of knowledge for cryptography in this way:

The Cryptography domain addresses the principles, means, and methods of applying mathematical algorithms and data transformation to information to ensure its integrity, confidentiality and authenticity.

The candidate will be expected to know basic concepts within cryptography; public and private key algorithms in terms of their applications and uses; algorithm construction, key distribution and management, and methods of attack; the applications, construction and use of digital signatures to provide authenticity of electronic transactions, and non-repudiation of the parties involved; and the organization and management of the Public Key Infrastructure (PKIs) and digital certificates distribution and management.

Key areas of knowledge:

- *Understand the application and use of cryptography*
- *Understand the cryptographic life cycle (e.g., cryptographic limitations, algorithm/protocol governance)*
- *Understand encryption concepts*
- *Understand key management processes*
- *Understand digital signatures*
- *Understand non-repudiation*
- *Understand methods of cryptanalytic attacks*
- *Use cryptography in network security*
- *Use cryptography to maintain application security*
- *Understand Public Key Infrastructure (PKI)*
- *Understand certificate related issues*
- *Understand information hiding alternatives (e.g., steganography, watermarking)*

Applications and Uses of Cryptography

Cryptography is the science of hiding information in order to conceal it from unauthorized parties.

An early use of cryptography was employed in the first century B.C. to **encipher** secret messages during military conflicts. The so-called Caesar Cipher (depicted in Figure 5-1) consisted of letters in the message being shifted three characters to the right, so that the message:

ATTACK AT ONCE VIA NORTH BRIDGE

...would appear as:

DWWDFN DW RQFH YLD QRUWK EULGJH

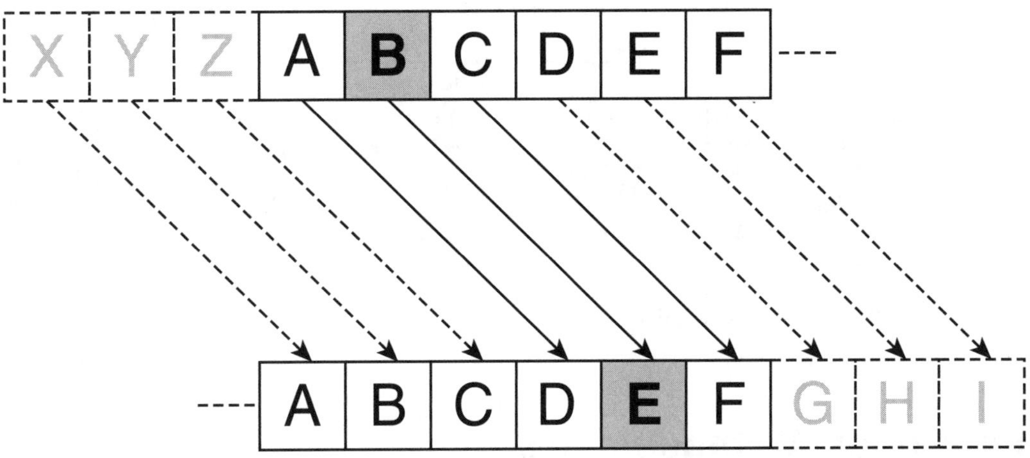

Figure 5-1 Caesar substitution cipher

The science of cryptography has steadily improved from ancient times to the present day with increasingly complex methods and mathematical models.

Encryption Terms and Operations

Cryptography has a language all its own that is explained in this section.

Plaintext **Plaintext** is an original message. Plaintext may literally *be* a message, or it may be a document, data file, image, database field, or any other type of digital information.

Ciphertext **Ciphertext** is a message that has been transformed by the process of encryption.

Encryption The process of transforming plaintext into ciphertext. Also known as *encipherment* (the terms *encrypt* and *encipher* have the same meaning). The process of encryption requires the use of a *key*.

An encrypted message can be safely transmitted to another party, even using means that may permit third parties to read the ciphertext—provided that no third party is able to obtain the encryption key.

Decryption The process of transforming ciphertext back into plaintext. When the recipient receives the ciphertext message, the recipient decrypts (or **deciphers**) the message, which yields the original plaintext.

Encryption Key Both the sender and the recipient must have an encryption key. This **key** is used to encrypt and decrypt the message. The key must be carefully guarded; if any third party is able to obtain the key, that third party can decrypt messages, and the third party can also create encrypted messages.

The operations used to this point are illustrated in Figure 5-2.

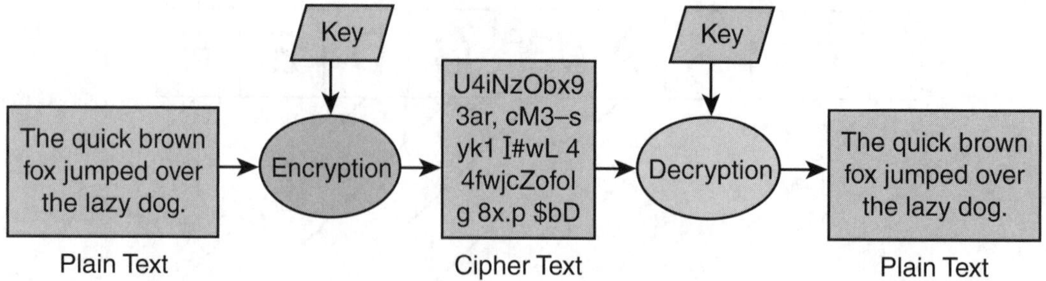

Figure 5-2 Typical encryption and decryption operations

Encryption Methodologies

There are several forms of encryption in use. The discussions in this section center around three concepts:

- *Methods of encryption.* These are the ways in which plaintext is transformed into ciphertext.
- *Types of encryption.* The two main types of encryption are stream ciphers and block ciphers.
- *Types of encryption keys.* The two types of keys are *symmetric* and *asymmetric.*

Methods of Encryption

There are several ways in which a plaintext message can be transformed into ciphertext. The methods range from simple to complex, with the more complex methods typically affording a higher degree of protection. The methods of encryption discussed here are:

- Substitution
- Transposition
- Monoalphabetic
- Polyalphabetic
- Running-key
- One time pads

These encryption methods are described in detail in this section.

Substitution A **substitution cipher** employs some scheme of character substitution. For instance, every instance of "A" in plaintext is changed to "r" in ciphertext, "B" is changed to "8," and so on, using a pattern or algorithm that is known to both the sender and recipient of a message.

The *Caesar Cipher*, used in the first century B.C., was an early substitution cipher, in which plaintext characters were shifted three characters to the right to yield ciphertext. *ROT13* is another simple substitution cipher in which English alphabet letters are shifted 13 to the right. The Caesar Cipher is illustrated in Figure 5-1.

Transposition A **transposition cipher**—also known as **permutation cipher**—is one in which the characters in a plaintext message are rearranged—or *transposed*—to form the ciphertext.

The characters in a plaintext message still appear in the ciphertext, but in different order. This makes a transposition cipher—as well as a substitution cipher—vulnerable to frequency analysis—a type of attack against a cryptosystem where the frequency of occurrence of the characters in ciphertext is examined.

An early transposition cipher is rectangular substitution. Using the example used previously:

ATTACK AT ONCE VIA NORTH BRIDGE

The encryption would first write the characters into a rectangle pattern such as:

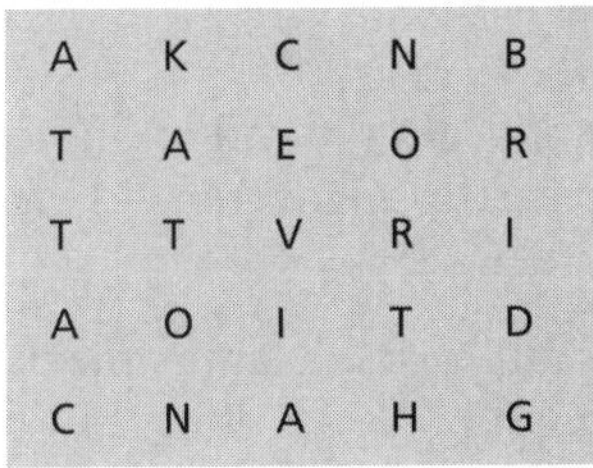

A	K	C	N	B
T	A	E	O	R
T	T	V	R	I
A	O	I	T	D
C	N	A	H	G

... and then read the characters out of the table by reading across, giving the following ciphertext:

AKCNBTAEORTTVRIAOITDCNAHG

The secret to effective transposition cipher is a more complex method of transposing characters than the simple example used here.

Monoalphabetic A **monoalphabetic cipher** is a type of substitution cipher where one alphabetic character is substituted for another. In the example of the Caesar Cipher, letters are shifted by three:

A	B	C	D	E	F	G	H	I	J	...	Z
D	E	F	G	H	I	J	K	L	M	...	C

The substitution can be more "random" instead of just a shift to the left or right. For example:

A	B	C	D	E	F	G	H	I	J	...	Z
W	E	R	T	B	N	P	Q	C	U	...	X

Using this key, the plaintext word CAGED would be encrypted as RWPBT.

Like a transposition cipher, a monoalphabetic cipher is subject to a frequency analysis attack.

Polyalphabetic The problem with a monoalphabetic cipher is the vulnerability to frequency analysis. A more advanced form of an alphabetic substitution cipher is the **polyalphabetic cipher**. This cipher uses two or more substitution alphabets to encipher plaintext. Here is an example.

Plaintext	A	B	C	D	E	F	G	H	I	...	Z
Alpha 1	W	E	R	T	B	N	P	Q	C	...	X
Alpha 2	R	B	I	K	Q	D	X	U	N	...	E
Alpha 3	V	B	D	R	H	W	A	X	I	...	U
Alpha 4	M	U	T	X	D	G	P	O	W	...	F
Alpha 5	Y	D	V	B	J	I	K	E	Z	...	O

Each letter of plaintext is substituted with the letter from its column in each successive row. In this example, the plaintext message CAGED becomes RRADB. Note that the letter R appears twice in the ciphertext, but we note there are no repeated letters in the plaintext. Frequency analysis will be nearly fruitless against this cipher.

Running Key Cipher A **running key cipher** is a practical application on how a substitution cipher is applied to typical messages that are usually many times longer than an encryption key.

Running key ciphers and other encryption algorithms utilize modular mathematics, where alphabetic characters are converted to numeric values, typically A = 0, B = 1, C = 2, ..., Z = 25. When the sum of these numeric values are greater than 26, we subtract 26 until the sum is less than or equal to 26—this is known as *modulo arithmetic.*

For example, if a message is encrypted with the key SECRET, the encryption is carried out by adding the values of the plaintext to the values of the running (repeating) key, yielding the ciphertext:

Plaintext	A	T	T	A	C	K	A	T	O	N	C	E	V	I	A	N
Key	S	E	C	R	E	T	S	E	C	R	E	T	S	E	C	R
Plaintext	0	19	19	0	2	10	0	19	14	13	2	4	21	8	0	13
Key	18	4	2	17	4	19	18	4	2	17	4	19	18	4	2	17
Sum	18	23	21	17	6	3	18	23	16	4	7	23	11	12	2	4
Ciphertext	S	X	V	R	G	D	S	X	Q	E	H	X	L	M	C	E

The ciphertext in this example is SXVRGDSXQEHXLMCE.

The process of decryption is the reverse: subtracting the values of the keys from the ciphertext, yielding the original plaintext. And in modulo arithmetic, where ciphertext–key < zero, we add 26 to the result.

One-Time Pads Also known as a **Vernam cipher, one-time pad** encryption operates like a running key cipher in terms of the process of adding the values of the ciphertext characters and the key characters using modulo arithmetic. The differences between a running key cipher and one-time pad are:

- The key is as long as the message
- The key is used only one time for that message only and then destroyed

Continuing the ATTACK AT ONCE VIA NORTH BRIDGE example, a random key is generated and is equal to XVGJERIOQWJPEKAFANIOPSNERJ. The encryption operation is:

Plaintext	A	T	T	A	C	K	A	T	O	N	C	E	V	I	A	N
Key	X	V	G	J	E	R	I	O	Q	W	J	P	E	K	A	F
Plaintext	0	19	19	0	2	10	0	19	14	13	2	4	21	8	0	13
Key	23	21	6	9	3	17	8	14	16	22	9	15	4	10	0	5
Sum	23	14	25	9	5	1	8	7	4	9	11	19	25	18	0	18
Ciphertext	X	O	Z	J	F	B	I	H	E	J	L	T	Z	U	A	U

A one-time pad is considered unbreakable by most means, but the administration of a one-time pad makes it impractical for use in information systems.

Types of Encryption

Information systems utilize cryptography in two principal settings: when storing data and when transmitting data. Two types of encryption have arisen from these two contexts: block ciphers and stream ciphers, respectively.

Block Ciphers A **block cipher** is used to encrypt and decrypt a block of data such as a message, document, or data file. A typical block size is 128 bits. Typical uses of block ciphers include:

- File encryption
- Web browser communications sessions (HTTPS)
- SSH (secure shell)
- VPN (virtual private networks)

Some of the common block cipher algorithms are:

- AES. This is the Advanced Encryption Standard that was established in 2000. AES uses the Rijndael cipher.
- DES, the Data Encryption Standard, in common use since 1976. With a key length of 56 bits, this algorithm is no longer considered sufficient for commercial use.
- 3DES. Known as "triple DES", 3DES is an extension of DES with an effective key length of 168 bits.
- CAST
- Blowfish
- Serpent

Block Cipher Modes of Operation Several modes of operation have been developed for block ciphers. These modes have to do with the way that plaintext blocks are brought into the cipher and encrypted. The modes are:

- Electronic codebook (ECB)
- Cipher-block chaining (CBC)

- Cipher feedback (CFB)
- Output feedback (OFB)
- Counter (CTR)

These modes are discussed in this section—but first it is necessary to discuss initialization vectors.

An **initialization vector** (IV) is a starting block of information that is required for several block cipher modes. The IV is used as a part of the input data needed to encrypt the first block in the plaintext message. In order for the encryption to be secure, the IV must be random and can never be reused.

A **pseudo-random number generator** (**PRNG**) is a mechanism that is frequently used to create an initialization vector. A PRNG uses an algorithm of some kind to create random numbers. The quality of the PRNG is related to how easy it is for an attacker to guess the random numbers that will be generated.

Electronic Codebook (ECB) The **electronic codebook** (ECB) mode is the simplest mode of block cipher operation. In ECB, each block is encrypted separately. The disadvantage of ECB is that each identical plaintext block encrypts into an identical ciphertext block, making it relatively easy to attack the cipher. ECB is shown in Figure 5-3.

Cipher-Block Chaining (CBC) **Cipher-block chaining** (CBC) uses the ciphertext output from each encrypted plaintext block in the encryption used for the next block. Specifically, the plaintext for block N is XOR'd with the ciphertext for block N-1. For the first block, since there is no previous block's ciphertext to work with, the plaintext is XOR'd with the initialization vector (IV). This is illustrated in Figure 5-4.

Cipher Feedback (CFB) **Cipher feedback** (**CFB**) is similar to cipher-block chaining, where the result of encrypting a block of plaintext is used to encrypt the next block. In CFB, the plaintext for block N is XOR'd with the ciphertext from block N-1. In the first block, the plaintext XOR'd with the encrypted IV. This is shown in Figure 5-5.

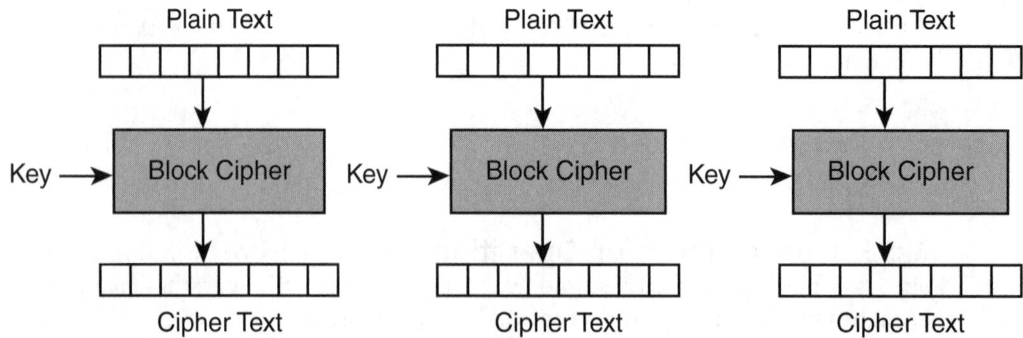

Figure 5-3 Electronic code book (ECB) mode block cipher

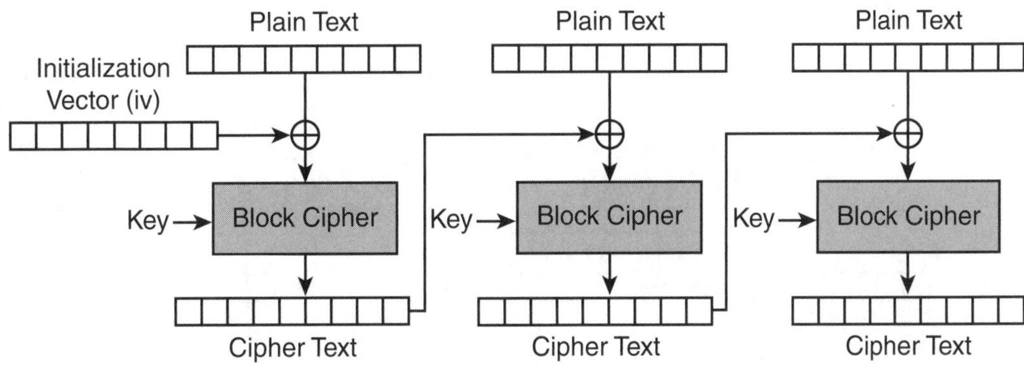

Figure 5-4 Cipher-block chaining (CBC) mode block cipher

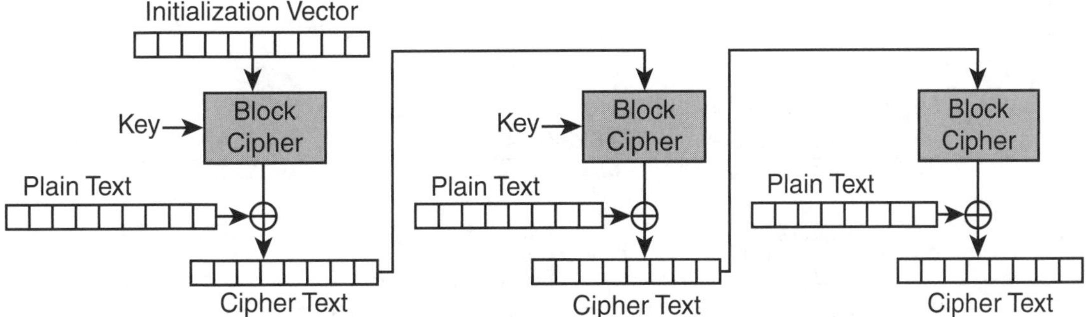

Figure 5-5 Cipher feedback (CFB) mode block cipher

Output Feedback (OFB) **Output feedback** (**OFB**) mode is similar to CBC and CFB, where the results of the previous plaintext block are used in the encryption of the next block. With OFB, plaintext is XOR'd with the encrypted material in the previous block to produce ciphertext. This is illustrated in Figure 5-6.

Counter (CTR) **Counter** (**CTR**) mode uses a "nonce" (a random number that is used once) that is concatenated with a counter or other simple function, which is encrypted by the block cipher, and the output XOR'd with the plaintext block to product the ciphertext block.

Figure 5-7 illustrates CTR encryption. In this case, the IV is a simple counter, but other non-repeating functions can also be used to create the IV.

Stream Ciphers As the name may suggest, a **stream cipher** is an encryption algorithm that operates on a continuous stream of information, such as a video or audio communications channel.

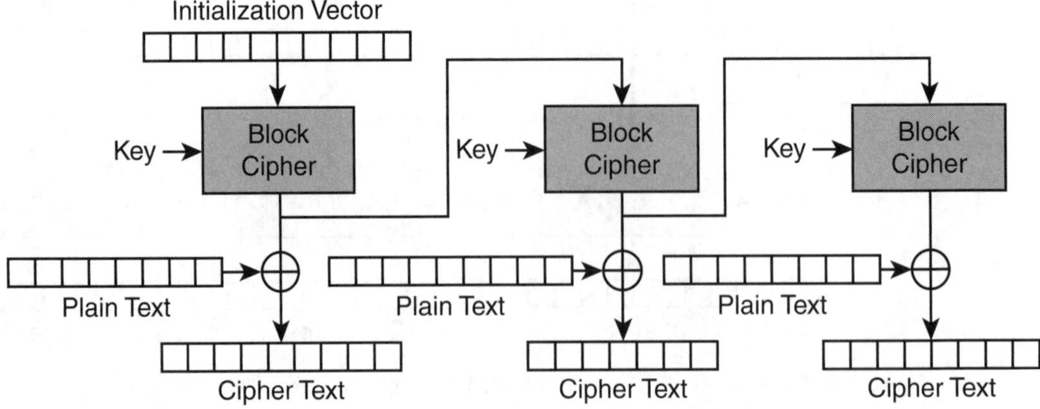

Figure 5-6 Output feedback (OFB) mode block cipher

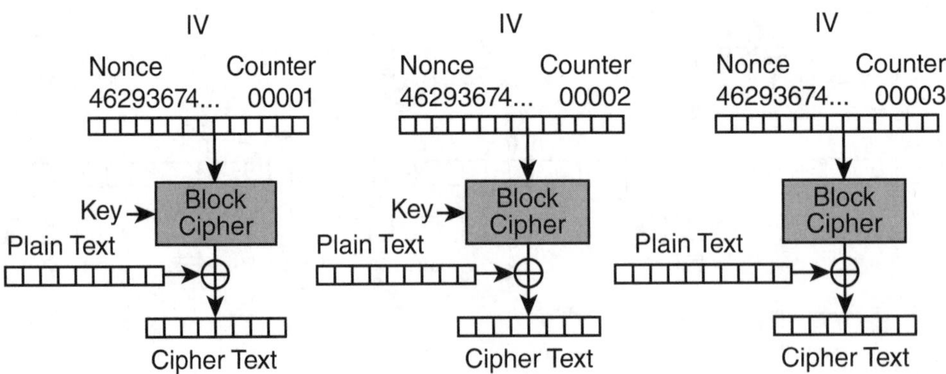

Figure 5-7 Counter (CTR) mode block cipher

A stream cipher is a substitution cipher that typically uses an exclusive-or (**XOR**) operation that can be performed very quickly by a computer.

An exclusive-or (XOR) is a binary operation. When the values are different, that is, 1 + 0 or 0 + 1, the result is 1. When the values are the same, that is, 0 + 0 or 1 + 1, the result is 0.

Here is an example of a stream cipher. Plaintext, the encryption key, and the ciphertext are all shown in binary so that the XOR operations can be easily seen.

Plaintext	1	1	0	1	0	0	1	1	0	1	0	0	1	1	0	0
Key	0	1	1	0	1	0	0	1	0	1	1	0	1	0	1	0
Ciphertext	1	0	1	1	1	0	1	0	0	0	1	0	0	1	1	0

To decrypt the ciphertext, we just XOR it with the same key to yield the plaintext:

Ciphertext	1	0	1	1	1	0	1	0	0	0	1	0	0	1	1	0
Key	0	1	1	0	1	0	0	1	0	1	1	0	1	0	1	0
Plaintext	1	1	0	1	0	0	1	1	0	1	0	0	1	1	0	0

The most common stream cipher algorithm in use is **RC4**. Other stream ciphers in use include A5/1, A5/2, FISH, Phelix1, ISAAC, MUGI, Panama, Phelix, Pike, Sapphire-II, SEAL, SOBER-128, and WAKE.

Types of Encryption Keys

Historically, the only type of encryption key that was available was the *shared secret*. Both parties had to have the encryption key in their possession in order to be able to encrypt and decrypt messages.

A relatively recent innovation in cryptography is *public key cryptography*, described later in this section.

Symmetric Keys **Symmetric cryptography** implies the use of a shared secret—that is, both parties must have possession of the same encryption key in order to be able to send encrypted messages to each other.

Both parties must robustly protect their symmetric encryption keys: if any third party is able to obtain a symmetric encryption key, that party will be able to decrypt any encrypted message exchanged between the original parties, and the third party will also be able to create new encrypted messages that the original parties may believe originated from the other party.

Some of the well-known encryption algorithms that use symmetric keys include:

- *DES (Data Encryption Standard)*. Developed in 1976 by IBM and designed as the U.S. NSA (National Security Agency) official cryptographic standard. DES uses a 56-bit key, considered short by today's standards. DES uses the **Digital Encryption Algorithm** (**DEA**).
- *3DES*. Known as triple-DES, this extension to the original DES algorithm effectively increases the key length to 168 bits.
- *AES (Advanced Encryption Standard)*. A replacement for the aging DES standard, designated in 2000. AES uses the **Rijndael** cipher.
- *Blowfish*.
- *IDEA (International Data Encryption Algorithm)*. A block cipher that is not in wide use because it is patented.
- *RC5*.

Asymmetric Key Cryptography The classic problem in cryptography is the exchange of keys between parties that have not communicated previously. Parties that have not communicated before do not possess a common shared secret. Establishing secured communications between two parties can be a challenge, since there is sometimes no convenient means available for securely exchanging encryption keys.

Enter **asymmetric cryptography**, which is more often known as **public key cryptography**. It is so-named because a user's public key can be disclosed to the entire world with no risk that any third party will be able to decrypt a message that is encrypted using this technique.

In public key cryptography, each user has two keys: a **public key** and a **private key**. These keys are mathematically related to each other. The advantage of public key cryptography is that a user's public key can be distributed to a wide audience, and yet there is no way for any third party to derive or calculate a user's private key when they know the value of that user's public key. A user must, however, protect the private key with the same rigor that would be used to protect a symmetric key.

If a sender encrypts a message with *only* the recipient's public key, the sender will not be able to decrypt it (nor will any other party, other than the recipient). If a sender wishes to be able to decrypt a message that he or she sends, the message must *also* be encrypted with the sender's public key!

Public key cryptography can best be illustrated through several use cases as follows:

- *Encrypt message to recipient.* An individual can publish his or her public encryption key that says, in effect, "send me a private (encrypted) message." Anyone can retrieve the recipient's public key, encrypt a message, and send it to the recipient. No one but the recipient will be able to decrypt the message, even if they have the recipient's public key. After receiving the message, the recipient decrypts the message with his or her private key.
- *Sign message.* A user who wishes to assert authenticity and integrity of a message can sign it with his or her private key, creating a digital signature. Any recipient can confirm the authenticity and integrity of the message by retrieving the sender's public key and verifying the digital signature.
- *Sign and encrypt message.* A user can perform both the encryption and the digital signature operations simultaneously. The user would encrypt a message using the public key(s) of the message recipient(s) and digitally sign the message using his or her own private key. Recipients would decrypt the message using their own respective private keys, and verify the digital signature of the message using the sender's public key.

These use cases are illustrated in Figure 5-8.

Some of the well-known asymmetric key encryption algorithms in use include:

- *RSA.* A key transport algorithm based upon factors of large prime numbers.
- *El Gamal.* Based upon discrete logarithms.
- *Elliptic Curve.* A new and stronger method for factoring prime numbers based upon elliptic curves.

Key Exchange Protocols One of the problems with symmetric cryptography is the matter of transmitting a shared secret (symmetric key) to another party. A symmetric key cannot be transmitted in the clear, or else an eavesdropper will be able to intercept the key and decrypt any subsequent communications encrypted with the key, as well as be able to forge communications encrypted with the key. If the two parties are communicating with each other for the first time and they have no other means for communicating, then getting an encryption key to another party can be difficult.

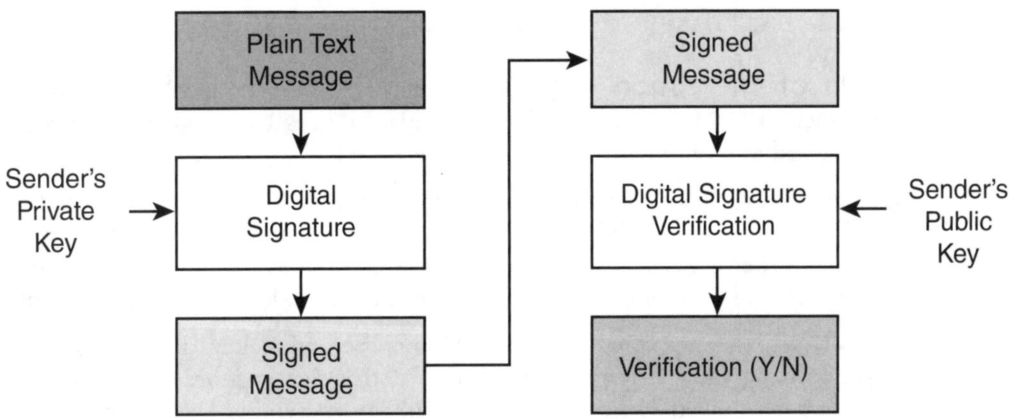

Figure 5-8 Uses of public key cryptography

Diffie-Hellman Key Exchange The **Diffie-Hellman (D-H) key exchange** protocol is a means for two parties with no prior knowledge of each other to securely establish a symmetric (shared secret) encryption key.

Diffie-Hellman key exchange works like this:

1. Jane and Tom agree to a large prime number p and a base integer g. The values p and g may be transmitted over the network in the clear.
2. Jane picks a secret integer a, then calculates g^a mod p and sends the result to Tom.
3. Tom picks a secret integer b, then calculates g^b mod p and sends the result to Jane.
4. Jane computes $k = (g^b \bmod p)^a \bmod p$.
5. Tom computes $k = (g^a \bmod p)^b \bmod p$.

The result k in steps 4 and 5 that Jane and Tom calculate are the same and can be used as a symmetric encryption key.

Here is a real example:

Jane and Tom agree to $p = 53$ and $g = 16$. Jane picks secret integer $a = 14$ and Tom picks secret integer $b = 11$.

Jane calculates $16^{14} \bmod 53 = 16$ and sends the result (16) to Tom.

Tom calculates $16^{11} \bmod 53 = 47$ and sends the result (47) to Jane.

Tom then calculates $16^{11} \bmod 53 = 47$.

Jane then calculates $47^{14} \bmod 53 = 47$.

The secret key that Jane and Tom have calculated is 47.

Typically, the value p will be a prime number of at least 300 digits, and the integers a and b will be at least 100 digits in length. With numbers of this size, it is computationally infeasible to break the D-H protocol even with all of mankind's computing power.

The *mod* function used above is the remainder after division. For example, 79 mod 14 = 9.

In other words, 9 is the remainder after the calculation of 79 divided by 14.

Length of Encryption Keys The value of an encryption algorithm is its ability to resist attack. The strength of an encryption algorithm is based on two factors: the quality of the algorithm itself, and the length of the encryption key used.

For example, TLS (known at the time as SSL) encryption in the mid-1990s used a key length of 56 bits, which was considered adequate at the time. More recently, however, improving computing power made attacks of 56-bit TLS quite feasible, and the new recommended minimum key length is 128 bits. Encryption keys of 256 and 512 bits are also available in TLS.

Why not just use super-long 512- or 1024-bit encryption keys in the first place? Longer encryption keys, while they result in extremely strong encryption, also require considerably more computer power. The end result is usually an encryption key length that provides reasonably secure encryption while avoiding a significant performance penalty that translates into sluggish performance and lower throughput.

Over time, as newer computer processors are made to be faster, longer encryption keys are used. Faster computer processors can more quickly encrypt and decrypt data, but faster processors can also be used to attack cryptosystems. Think of it as an arms race: encryption is the defensive weapon, and cryptanalysis (discussed later in this chapter) is the offensive weapon. Computer processors make both possible. Longer encryption keys and higher-quality encryption algorithms provide a balance of power.

There is no "magic" key length for all algorithms that is equally adequate. Remember that the algorithm itself plays a role in the strength of the encryption. If you need to select key lengths for encryption, you will need to consult with current practices for individual algorithms to determine adequate key sizes.

Protection of Encryption Keys The secrecy of encrypted communications relies upon the strength of the encryption algorithm and the protection of encryption keys.

A defense in depth strategy should always be used to protect encryption keys. A single means of protection should not be relied upon.

Protecting Symmetric Keys In symmetric cryptography, the encryption key must be protected from unauthorized access by any third party. In some instances, the encryption key is accessed via a software program and controlled by a password. Protection of the key will, in part, depend upon the strength of that password. In other instances, the encryption key is contained in a stored file. Permissions on the file, and on the directory that contains the file, should be limited so that only the owner of the encryption key can access the directory or the file. Any system containing symmetric keys should also be hardened and protected with other controls such as firewalls, intrusion prevention systems (IPSs), and file integrity monitoring systems (FIMs).

Protecting Public Cryptography Keys In public key cryptography, a user's public key needs less protection than a symmetric key. To this end, the public key can be published to a wide audience. However, while the user can publish his or her public key to the world, he or she must ensure that no one else is able to overwrite the key with an imposter. Thus, a user's public key will need to be verified, to ensure the authenticity of the claimed individual. Typically a public key is verified by an out-of-band communication such as a telephone call.

A user's private key requires the same level of protection as a symmetric key. A private key must be protected with a password and/or file and directory permissions, system hardening, and other means. To protect against loss, both the public and private keys should be backed up, and the backup media protected against theft or other loss.

Protecting Encryption Keys Used by Applications Encryption is frequently used by applications to encrypt and decrypt stored data. Whereas an end user can protect his or her encryption key with a password, protecting an encryption key that is used by an application is somewhat more difficult: if the application stores an encryption key's password, then the security of the encrypted data is really no stronger than just the simple password that can be found in the application.

Think about it. If an application can access an encryption key (whether a registry value, a flat file, a field in a database, or a variable in the application itself), then so can an intruder, right?

More complex means are needed to protect an encryption key used in an application, including:

- *Utilize separation of duties.* For instance, if encrypted data resides in a database, hide the encryption key in a file that the DBA cannot read. Further, permissions to the data should be set so that system administrators cannot read the data. The application itself should use a third account that neither DBAs nor system administrators can use.
- *Store encryption keys in hardware.* Key management appliances can be used to store and retrieve encryption keys.
- *Use a key-encrypting key.* The actual **key** used to encrypt and decrypt data should itself be encrypted by another key called the key-encrypting key.

A combination of these methods may also be used in order to provide the required level of protection.

Cryptanalysis—Attacks on Cryptosystems

Cryptanalysis is the study of deciphering an encrypted message without access to the encryption key. The need to decipher encrypted messages dates back to the ninth century, when Arabian mathematician Abu Yusuf Yaqub ibn Ishaq al-Sabbah Al-Kindi published a manuscript on techniques for deciphering messages.

There are several modern methods used in cryptanalysis, including:

- Frequency analysis
- Birthday attacks
- Ciphertext-only attack
- Chosen plaintext attack
- Chosen ciphertext attack
- Known plaintext attack
- Man in the middle attack
- Replay attack
- Rubber hose attack
- Social engineering

Frequency Analysis

Frequency analysis is the study of the frequency of occurrence of characters in a message ciphertext. If a message is encrypted using a substitution cipher, then the frequency of occurrence of the characters in the ciphertext can be used to discover the original plaintext.

Birthday Attacks

The *birthday paradox* states that in a group of twenty-three or more randomly chosen people, there is a 50 percent probability that two of the people share the same birthday. This paradox leads to the **birthday attack** on a **hashing** (message digest) algorithm, where the attacker attempts to find messages that result in the same hash value. When two messages are found to compute the same hash value, this is known as a **collision.**

Ciphertext-Only Attack

A **ciphertext-only attack** (COA) is a cryptanalysis where the attacker has only ciphertext to work with. A COA attack can be successful by using frequency analysis and other means to either deduce the encryption key or the plaintext itself.

A well-known ciphertext-only attack exploited weaknesses in the **Wired Equivalent Privacy (WEP)** protocol, the first encryption protocol used for WiFi networks.

Chosen Plaintext Attack

In a **chosen plaintext attack** (CPA), the attacker is able to choose known plaintext messages, get them encrypted, and obtain ciphertexts for those plaintexts.

Chosen Ciphertext Attack

An attacker in a **chosen ciphertext attack** (CCA) can choose ciphertext, have it decrypted, and obtain the plaintext. This is a trial-and-error attack that requires many decryption operations before the attacker can begin to deduce the key and/or the decryption algorithm.

Known Plaintext Attack

An attacker who possesses both plaintext and corresponding ciphertext messages can analyze both in order to obtain the encryption key. This will enable the attacker to be able to decrypt all encrypted messages. This type of attack is called the **known plaintext attack** (**KPA**).

Man in the Middle Attack

A **man in the middle attack** (**MITM**) is a cryptanalysis attack where the attacker is able to read, insert, and modify communications between two parties without those parties' knowledge or awareness. MITM can be effective against public key cryptography and Diffie-Hellman (D-H) key exchange.

An MITM attack can be used to conduct several other types of cryptanalysis including known plaintext attack(KPA), chosen ciphertext attack(CCA), ciphertext-only attack(COA), and frequency analysis.

Replay Attack

In a **replay attack**, the attacker intercepts and records network transmissions for the purpose of replaying or repeating the transmissions at a later time. An eavesdropper who records a **Telnet** (a point-to-point command line interface) or **FTP** (**File Transfer Protocol**, a TCP/IP protocol used to copy files from one system to another) login sequence can use the intercepted userid and password pair at a later time in an attempt to masquerade as the original party.

Rubber Hose Attack

This is an attack on any of the persons who operate the cryptosystem who may be coerced into providing encryption keys to an attacker. This attack is so-named only as an illustration; a social engineering attack could be just as effective. The term *rubber hose attack* is deliberately tongue-in-cheek, and highlights the fact that the human factor can be a significant and effective means for obtaining encryption keys through a real or imagined threat.

Social Engineering Attack

This attack technique is mentioned here to remind readers that the owner or custodian of a private key or symmetric key can be tricked into unknowingly revealing the key or its password to an adversary. All of the classic methods for social engineering attacks are fair game for an adversary who wishes to obtain encryption keys.

Application and Management of Cryptography

Cryptography is used in several ways to protect information from disclosure to unauthorized parties. Practically everywhere information is stored or transmitted, encryption can be used to provide protection against disclosure. In some instances, cryptography is used as an *additional* source of protection as part of a defense in depth information protection strategy. However, in some contexts, such as the transmission of information over a public network, cryptography is often the only means available for protecting information.

Uses for Cryptography

The settings where encryption is often used are:

- Files and directories
- Entire disks and volumes
- E-mail
- Web browsing
- Web services
- Remote network access

File Encryption Encryption is one form of access control that can be used to determine who is permitted to access files. When a file—even when it is present on a public file server—is encrypted, only individuals who possess the encryption key can access its contents. File encryption can also be used to protect the contents of a file when it is transmitted over a public network by e-mail or FTP.

Tools used to encrypt files and directories include:

- *EFS (Encrypting File System)*. This is the file and directory encryption capability that is built in to the NTFS file system on Windows 2000, XP, Windows Vista, 7, and 8. EFS protects files in place, protecting them from access by other users on the workstation. Both files and directories can be encrypted with EFS. When a directory is encrypted with EFS, new files and subdirectories created within the encrypted directory will be automatically encrypted.
- *PGP (Pretty Good Privacy)*. This popular tool can be used to encrypt files using one or more recipient public keys, or symmetric encryption using a shared secret. Unlike EFS, PGP does not encrypt files in place; instead, it is used to create a separate encrypted file that can be left in place or sent to another party who can decrypt it.
- *GPG (Gnu Privacy Guard)*. This public domain tool is compatible with most PGP functions.
- *WinZip*. This popular file archiving tool can also encrypt the contents of archives using AES.
- *Crypt*. This is a standard UNIX/Linux encryption tool that creates an encrypted copy of a file.

Disk Encryption An entire hard disk or volume (a logical subset of a hard disk) can be encrypted. Tools available for encrypting an entire volume include:

- *PGP (Pretty Good Privacy)*. Commercial versions of PGP include PGP Disk, a tool used to create an encrypted volume on a computer's hard drive.
- *TrueCrypt*. This is a public domain tool that can be used on Windows, Mac, and Linux systems to encrypt the entire hard drive or create an encrypted volume.
- *BitLocker*. This tool is built into premium versions of Microsoft Windows Vista, 7, and 8 and is used to create an encrypted disk volume that contains the operating system and user files.

- *SafeBoot*. A commercial disk encryption tool for Windows systems and PDA/smartphone platforms.

E-Mail Security Parties that communicate with each other via e-mail will sometimes wish to protect their messages with encryption. Some of the methods for protecting e-mail messages are:

- S/Mime
- PGP
- PEM
- MOSS

Secure/Multipurpose Internet Mail Extensions (S/MIME) **Secure/Multipurpose Internet Mail Extensions (S/MIME)** is a certificate-based e-mail encryption standard, used to encrypt and/or digitally sign e-mail messages. S/MIME has been incorporated into many popular e-mail programs such as Outlook, Thunderbird, and Lotus Notes.

PGP **PGP (Pretty Good Privacy)** and its public domain cousin, GPG (Gnu Privacy Guard) can be used to encrypt e-mail messages that are sent to other recipients.

PGP has a tool called *PGPKeys* that is used to manage the user's private and public keys, as well as the public keys of recipients. Commercial versions of PGP (as well as the public domain GPG) have integrations with popular e-mail programs such as Microsoft Outlook that make it easy for a recipient to encrypt e-mail messages without having to perform manual encryption.

PEM **Privacy-Enhanced Mail**, or **PEM**, is an older standard for e-mail encryption using public key cryptography. PEM is not widely used because it depends upon the existence of a hierarchical PKI with a single root. Such a PKI has never been globally implemented.

MOSS **MIME Object Security Services (MOSS)** is a standard protocol that provides confidentiality, authentication, and non-repudiation using message digests and public key encryption. MOSS has never been widely used.

Secure Point-to-Point Communications Encryption can be used to protect communications between any two systems—two servers, two workstations, or a workstation and a server, for instance. Some of the technologies available are:

- SSH
- IPsec
- SSL/TLS

SSH **Secure shell**, usually abbreviated as SSH, is a replacement for many of the first-generation tools that are now considered unsafe, specifically Telnet, FTP, and **rsh** ("remote shell", a network protocol used to establish a command line session on another system). Other protocols such as FTP can be encapsulated within SSH.

IPsec **IPsec** is an IP-based point-to-point communications protocol used to provide secure traffic between two endpoints. IPsec can run in one of two modes: transport mode or tunnel mode.

In transport mode, each packet's payload is encrypted. In tunnel mode, a tunnel is set up between the endpoints and the entire contents of each packet (headers plus payload) are encrypted.

Security associations (SAs) are necessary to facilitate the use of IPsec. A security association is a one-way trust relationship between two endpoints. In a one-way association, only one endpoint may initiate communications to the other endpoint. Two SAs are required if either endpoint is to be able to initiate communications.

IPsec runs in one of two modes: Authentication Header (AH), which provides authentication, integrity, and non-repudiation; and Encapsulating Security Payload (ESP), which provides encryption and limited authentication. A security association (SA) between two endpoints must specify whether IPsec will run in AH or ESP mode.

SSL and TLS **Secure Sockets Layer (SSL)** is a TCP encapsulation protocol used to provide secure communications. SSL has been superseded by **Transport Layer Security (TLS)**, although the term *SSL* is still in common use. In secured mode, web browsers communicate typically via TCP port 443. The URL in a secured session will always start with "https." The traffic between the web browser and the server will be encapsulated using the SSL or TLS protocol, using an encryption algorithm that is negotiated between the browser and the server at the start of the session. The strength of the encryption that is negotiated may be as low as a 56-bit key or as strong as a 512-bit key.

SSL/TLS are also discussed in Chapter 10, "Telecommunications and Network Security."

Web Browser and e-Commerce Security Web browsers are client programs that access web-based applications in an organization or across the Internet. Web browsers communicate with web servers using the HyperText Transfer Protocol (HTTP) in either a secured or nonsecured mode.

In nonsecured mode, the web browser communicates to the server, typically using TCP port 80. The URL in a nonsecured session will start with "http." In secured mode, the URL will start with "https."

It is perfectly possible (and commonplace) to have an "http" URL with an "https" POST method, which ensures that data typed into form fields are sent back to the server using SSL/TLS encryption. However, on such a form, the user will not see a "padlock" signifying a secure page, which will lead them to think that the sensitive data being requested on the form will not be encrypted (the opposite has also been observed: a login page is delivered encrypted to the user, but the userid and password sent back to the server is not). It is therefore more common for web sites to encrypt a page with sensitive form fields, forcing the padlock to appear and give the user the assurance that data is encrypted in transit.

Web Services Security Web services is the name for machine-to-machine communications that can take place within a distributed application or a client-server application. Web services are built upon the same HTTP/HTTPS protocols used by web browsers, but structured for noninteractive communications.

In e-commerce applications (that is, any web-based application in which sensitive information is displayed or exchanged such as banking, credit card, and personal information such as address, social security, and other identifying numbers), most or all data transmitted between the application and the user's browser will be encrypted. Further, session cookies will also be encrypted in order to make it more difficult for an attacker to hijack (take control of) a user's session.

The discussion of e-commerce security has a lot to do with application security. This entire topic is discussed in more detail in Chapter 3, "Software Development Security." A secure e-commerce application requires a lot more than just a secure application, however. Virtually every chapter in this book addresses one or more topics that are related to the protection of an e-commerce application and its supporting infrastructure.

Secure Hypertext Transfer Protocol (S-HTTP) **Secure Hypertext Transfer Protocol (S-HTTP)** is a connectionless protocol used to encrypt and authenticate data being sent from a server to a client. It utilizes public key cryptography for authentication and non-repudiation, symmetric encryption for payload protection, and message digests for message integrity.

The main distinction between S-HTTP and SSL is that SSL encrypts an entire session, whereas S-HTTP encrypts only single requests within a session.

S-HTTP and SSL are sometimes confused for one another. S-HTTP uses the URL *shttp:* whereas SSL uses *https:*. S-HTTP is no longer in common use.

Secure Electronic Transaction (SET) Developed jointly by MasterCard and Visa, **Secure Electronic Transaction** (**SET**) is designed for secure electronic commerce, utilizing X.509 digital certificates and symmetric encryption. SET has fallen out of favor and has been replaced by SSL/TLS.

Cookies: Used for Session and Identity Management The http and https protocols on their own do not provide session management. Http and https requests are essentially connectionless—from one click to the next, the http/https protocols offer no concept of a user's logical session. From one request to the next, a web server has no way to tell whether a subsequent request originating from an IP address is coming from the same workstation that sent a previous request. **Cookies** are typically used to identify a specific session ID when a web browser is communicating with a web application.

Cookies contain several elements, including:

- *Domain name*. This is the domain of origin for the cookie.
- *Name-value pair*. Thought of as a variable name and contents of the variable. This is often used to identify a userid or session ID during a user's logical session with a web application. Applications will frequently use an encrypted value, to protect against tampering and risks associated with such mischief as cookie theft. An example name-value pair is YLID=ANm6O0cniLMAALc7R9.6AAAniLMAr7E7R9. In this example, the variable name is YLID, and its value is ANm6O0cniLMAALc7R9.6AAAniLMAr 7E7R9. This value could be an encrypted or hashed session ID or userid.
- *Path*. An optional directory pathname value.
- *Expiration date*. The date when the cookie expires.
- *Secure flag*. Specifies whether the cookie should be sent over an ordinary (unencrypted) or secure (encrypted) channel.
- *HTTP only*. Specifies whether the cookie may be accessed by a client-side script (such as JavaScript), or only by the browser itself.

Each time a web application communicates with a browser, the application will request the browser's cookie. Values in the cookie will uniquely identify the individual browser and, hence, the user's session.

Virtual Private Networks A **virtual private network** (VPN) is a logical network connection between two points. All network traffic in a VPN connection is encapsulated in a "tunnel," and the traffic is usually (but not necessarily) encrypted, thereby protecting the contents of the traffic from disclosure to eavesdroppers.

VPNs can be used for secure remote access; when VPN technology is used, the remote access session is encrypted to protect it from eavesdroppers.

VPNs can be used to encrypt the traffic between two separate networks. This permits two networks to communicate with each other over the public Internet with no risk of disclosure through eavesdropping. A router in each network can be configured to encrypt all traffic destined for the other network.

Both of these methods are shown in Figure 5-9.

The two prevalent technologies used to encrypt VPNs are SSL and IPsec.

An IPsec VPN requires a client program, which adds a little administrative overhead, since this VPN program must be installed and maintained on all VPN users' workstations.

SSL encryption allows so-called clientless VPN connections that utilize SSL capabilities that are built in to virtually every workstation. This provides a VPN capability on a workstation without the need to install and maintain separate VPN client software.

Key Management

The protection of encrypted information is only as strong as its weakest link. Here, the protection factors are the strength of the encryption algorithm and **key management**, the activities related to the management of encryption keys.

The level of effort taken to protect an encryption key should correspond to the value of the information that is encrypted with the key. If an encryption key is compromised, then the ciphertext (if an intruder can find it) can also be compromised. It may be

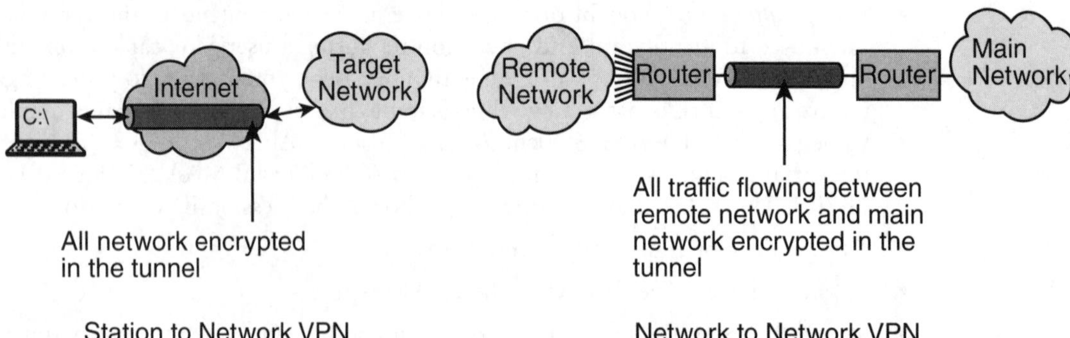

Figure 5-9 Virtual private networks

reasonable to assert the same level of protection for a key as one would for the original data in an unencrypted state.

The life cycle of encryption keys includes these activities:

- Key creation
- Key protection and custody
- Key rotation
- Key destruction
- Key escrow

Key Creation The creation of random encryption keys should be performed on a secure server, so that an intruder is not able to observe or re-create the key generation process or intercept generated encryption keys.

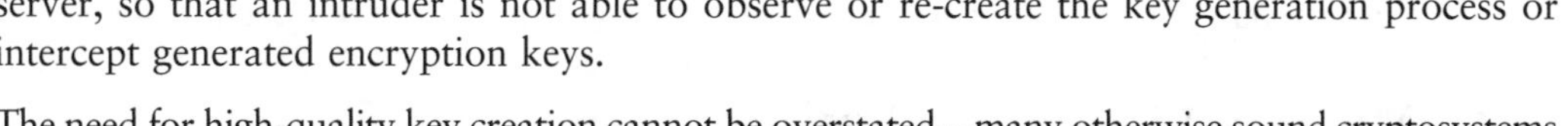

The need for high-quality key creation cannot be overstated—many otherwise sound cryptosystems have been compromised because of flaws in key creation. The issues involve two main themes:

- *Randomness*. An encryption key should be truly random. Like a good password, the quality of an encryption key is related to the extent to which its value is random. No one—including a cryptosystem's designer—should be able to know the value of any encryption key in a system.
- *Predictability*. In a system where encryption keys are created regularly and frequently (and, typically, automatically), the system's designers must take great care to ensure that the value of encryption keys cannot be predicted, based on any known conditions, including the values of many previous encryption keys.

Both of these topics are closely related. If a system's design is not sound, then an attacker may be able to determine the values of encryption keys that have not yet been created. This would permit an attacker to more easily decrypt ciphertext. The term **perfect forward secrecy** is used in this regard to describe whether past or future encryption keys can be predicted based on the value of any known encryption keys.

Key Protection and Custody Access to private keys and symmetric encryption keys must be tightly controlled. Confidentiality of encrypted information is only as good as the protection of encryption keys.

Organizations managing sensitive data may opt to employ *split custody* of encryption keys, where two or more persons are required to access an individual encryption key. Two or more people may have a portion of the key itself, or portions of the password used to access the key. This prevents any single individual from being able to access, alter, or destroy sensitive data that is protected with an encryption key.

Key Rotation Regulation or prudence necessitates the occasional rotation of encryption keys.

An organization that encrypts sensitive information should have formal procedures to be followed in the event that an encryption key is compromised.

Key Destruction When an encryption key is no longer needed, it should be destroyed securely. This means that the key must be destroyed in all locations where it was stored.

Further, effective key destruction requires that the key be *erased* (overwritten with patterns of data so that it cannot be recovered through data remanence), not merely deleted (in many operating systems a deleted data file can be easily recovered).

In some cases, key destruction is the only way to "delete" encrypted data. For instance, data that is encrypted by several different keys is written to a backup tape. When it is time for some of the data to be destroyed, the organization can destroy the encryption key, which effectively deletes the corresponding information from the backup tape.

Key Escrow A business arrangement can be established where a trusted third party will hold encryption keys in escrow. The typical purpose for key escrow is the greater certainty that data can be recovered, even in the event that the organization that encrypted the information experienced a disaster that destroyed its encryption keys, or upon the failure of the organization resulting in the potential loss or destruction of its information including encryption keys.

Message Digests and Hashing

A **message digest**, or hash, is the result of a cryptographic operation on a message or file. A cryptographic hashing algorithm will read the entire contents of a message or file and produce a fixed-length *digest*. A message digest is used to confirm that a message or file has not been altered.

A typical use of a message digest is the posting of a hash of a downloadable software program. A user who downloads the program can perform a hash of the program to confirm that the program is genuine and unaltered. This technique requires that the web site containing the stated hash value be well protected so that an intruder is not able to alter the program and the stated hash value.

Message digests are also used to verify whether the contents of an e-mail message have been tampered with while in transit from sender to recipient.

The principles of message digests are:

- It should not be possible to re-create the original message from the digest.
- It should be impossible (well, computationally *infeasible*) to create messages that will result in a given message digest.
- No two messages should result in the same message digest (although collisions are possible).
- A message digest should be the result of the *entire* message, not a portion of it.

Message digest algorithms include:

- *MD5*. A fast and robust message digest algorithm that is widely used, but now considered compromised. Organizations using MD5 are advised to use SHA-2.
- *SHA-1 (Secure Hash Algorithm)*. A robust message digest algorithm that has weakened somewhat. Developers considering using a hashing algorithm are advised to use SHA-2 instead.
- *SHA-2*. A family of hash functions (SHA-224, SHA-256, SHA-384, and SHA-512) published by the National Institute of Standards and Technology (NIST) in 2001. SHA-2 is still considered a strong message digest algorithm.

- *SHA-3*. A new message digest algorithm that became available in 2013.
- *Whirlpool*. A hash function developed in 2000 and adopted by ISO (International Organization for Standardization) and IEC (International Electrotechnical Commission).
- *HMAC (Hashed Message Authentication Code)*. An algorithm that utilizes a message digest (such as MD5, SHA-1, or SHA-2) together with a secret key.

A message digest does not authenticate (prove the origin of) the message or file. If a user needs to verify the authenticity and origin of a message or file, then digital signatures should be used instead of (or in addition to) hashing.

Digital Signatures

A **digital signature** is a method used to verify the authenticity and integrity of a message or document.

To create a digital signature, the creator or sender will "sign" a document using a program that employs a digital signature algorithm. The program will read the entire contents of the message or file, and combine it cryptographically with the private key of the person signing the document. This creates the "digital signature," which is a string of characters that may either be embedded in the document or be stored separately.

When the recipient receives the document and the digital signature, the recipient can verify the integrity of the digital signature. This requires access to the sender's public encryption key. The recipient uses a digital signature verification program, which examines the original document and the digital signature, and cryptographically compares this to the originator's public encryption key. If the verification is confirmed, the recipient knows that a) the document was really signed by the originator, and b) the document has not been altered since it was signed. Thus, the recipient has confidence that the document is authentic.

Use of a digital signature alone provides document integrity and origination only; a digital signature does not provide any confidentiality by protecting the document against viewing by any third party. Encryption should be used if the parties wish to prevent any third party from viewing a document or message.

Some of the algorithms used for digital signatures are:

- Digital Signature Algorithm (DSA)
- El Gamal
- Elliptic Curve DSA (ECDSA)

Digital Certificates

A digital certificate is an electronic document that contains an individual's public encryption key together with identifying information such as the person's name and contact information. The digital certificate includes a digital signature of the public key and identifying information. Typically the certificate is signed by a trusted certificate authority (CA), which will provide a level of confidence in the identifying information in the certificate.

The most common form of a digital certificate is **X.509**, an ITU (International Telecommunication Union) standard. The structure of an X.509v3 digital certificate is:

- Version (usually a "3" for X.509v3)
- Serial Number
- Algorithm ID (the encryption algorithm used)
- Issuer (the organization that signed the certificate)
- Validity
  - Not Before (date)
  - Not After (date)
- Subject (identifying information about the certificate user)
- Subject Public Key Info
  - Public Key Algorithm (the algorithm used)
  - Subject Public Key (the actual public key)
- Issuer Unique Identifier (optional)
- Subject Unique Identifier (optional)
- Extensions (optional)
- Certificate Signature Algorithm (the actual digital algorithm)
- Certificate Signature (the actual digital signature)

Non-Repudiation

The use of digital signatures and other factors such as strong authentication give rise to situations where it can become difficult for an individual to reasonably deny that he or she performed a transaction. This ability for a system to prove that an individual actually performed a transaction is known as **non-repudiation**. In other words, a user is unable to repudiate their performance of a transaction, because of the strength of the cryptographic tools and algorithms used to perform or support the transaction.

One possible "out" that such a subject might try to claim is that the password he or she uses to perform a transaction was compromised. But such a claim might be an admission of sloppy practices, which itself may tarnish the individual's reputation.

Public Key Infrastructure (PKI)

A **public key infrastructure** (PKI) is an online facility where parties' public keys can be easily retrieved. For instance, an e-mail system can store the public encryption keys for a community of recipients on a central server where e-mail programs can easily retrieve them, permitting encryption of messages for selected recipients.

A PKI can store other information in addition to public encryption keys, and serve multiple purposes in an identity management service. For instance, the PKI can also be used as an enterprise authentication server or **certificate authority** (CA). The LDAP (Lightweight

Directory Access Protocol) standard is the most widely used directory standard and a popular platform for PKIs. Microsoft Active Directory is a popular commercial PKI platform.

Encryption Alternatives

There are other means available for protecting information, primarily watermarking and steganography. These methods are described in this section.

Steganography

Steganography, which is also known as "stego," is the practice of hiding a message within another medium. For instance, a message can be hidden in an image file, where the inclusion of a message—typically interspersed throughout the image—is unlikely to be noticed by someone viewing the image. In steganography, a message can be hidden in an image, a sound file, a video clip, or other human-read medium where the inclusion of the message will produce slight variations that may not be noticeable. Messages can also be hidden in a file's slack space and other places where others may not look.

A classic example of text-based steganography is a written message that was sent to a condemned prisoner, Sir John, a Royalist during a civil war in England. The message to the prisoner appeared to be a rambling letter, but the third letter after each punctuation mark formed a secret message, which gave the prisoner a valuable clue that permitted him to escape through a hidden door in a prayer chapel that supposedly contained only one entrance and exit.

The message: *Worthy Sir John: Hope, alas, cannot, I fear, help you now. So bravely have you endured your fate, I regret there is nothing more to be done. I thought: friends would come to your rescue, find you in prison. And, what result? Only that you will soon, go to your untimely, deadly fate. Perhaps, in some better future, able, bright, undaunted men will meet, ever certain their cause was—just.*

The hidden message: *panel behind altar slides.*

In stego, a message may or may not be encrypted. If the method used to hide a message can be discovered, then the contents of the message will be compromised.

The act of communicating through the use of steganography can be thought of as one form of a *covert channel.*

Watermarking

Often considered the visible form of steganography, **watermarking** is the practice of inserting a mark, image, or message onto a file or data stream as a means of claiming or asserting ownership of the file. Often this is done as a means for protecting intellectual property.

Examples of watermarking include:

- Asserting a claim of ownership on an audio or video medium such as a song or movie.
- Visibly marking a sample image that is for sale.

An example of watermarking to protect an image from illegal copying is shown in Figure 5-10.

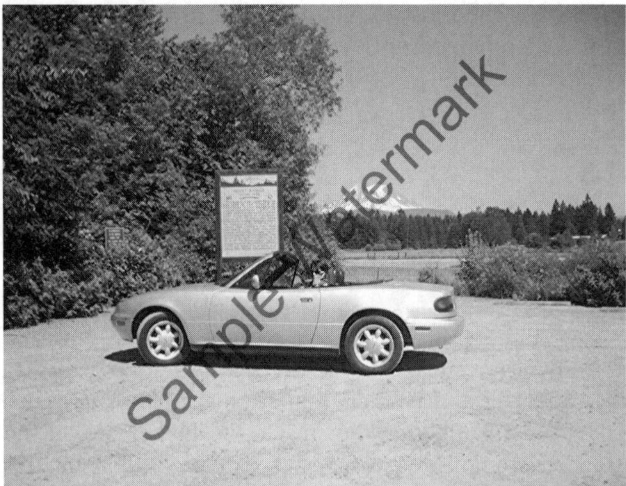

Figure 5-10 Example of watermarking

Photo by Rebecca Steele

Trusting Cryptography

The information security profession, and cryptography in particular, has passed into a new era where credible evidence has surfaced that reveals that several world governments have played a role in the deliberate weakening of cryptosystems to facilitate domestic and international espionage. Prior to these revelations, information security professionals could place their trust in national standards bodies, major encryption product vendors, and government organizations. This trust has been broken and will not be easily mended.

A significant challenge in both public and private sectors will be the establishment of new ways to measure the validity and integrity of cryptosystems. Or perhaps a new approach will involve novel uses of cryptography in order to make the compromise of a cryptosystem more difficult than before. The collective discussion on this topic will run its course over several years, resulting in the development of new validation platforms as well as improved application of cryptosystems.

Chapter Summary

- Cryptography is the science of hiding information in plain sight, usually through the use of algorithms-based upon mathematical operations.
- Encryption is the process of transforming original plaintext into unreadable ciphertext. Encryption typically involves the use of an encryption key, which is a block of text that is kept secret.
- The methods of encryption are substitution, transposition, monoalphabetic, polyalphabetic, running key, and one-time pads.
- The types of encryption are block ciphers and stream ciphers. Block ciphers are used to encrypt messages and files. Stream ciphers are used to encrypt continuous streams of data, such as video or audio.

- The modes of operation for a block cipher are electronic codebook (ECB), cipher-block chaining (CBC), cipher feedback (CFB), output feedback (OFB), and counter (CTR).
- An initialization vector (IV) is a randomly generated block of data that is required by several of the modes used by block ciphers.
- The two types of encryption keys are symmetric keys and asymmetric keys. Symmetric keys are also known as "shared secrets." Asymmetric keys cryptography is more commonly referred to as *public key cryptography*.
- Encryption keys must be protected from disclosure. The values of encryption keys must not enable the values of past or future encryption keys to be predicted.
- The Diffie-Hellman key exchange protocol is a method that two parties can use to develop an encryption key over an unsecure channel.

- Cryptanalysis is the process of attacking a cryptosystem in order to discover its method of operation. Some of the well-known methods used in cryptanalysis are frequency analysis, birthday attacks, ciphertext-only attack, chosen plaintext attack, chosen ciphertext attack, known plaintext attack, man in the middle attack, and replay attack.
- Cryptography is often used to encrypt files, directories, disk volumes, e-mail messages, and communications between persons and network in contexts such as web-based applications and remote access.
- Key management encompasses several procedures and safeguards used to create, manage, protect, use, and (eventually) destroy encryption keys.
- Hashing is the process of using a cryptographic algorithm to create a message digest of a file or message, used to ensure the integrity of a message.
- Non-repudiation is the concept of ensuring that a person cannot later deny having performed some action.
- A public key infrastructure (PKI) is a network-based service used to store digital certificates or public encryption keys of individuals in a community.
- Steganography is used to hide information within some other media, such as an image, audio file, video stream, or slack space in a file.
- Watermarking is a visible form of steganography that is used to "label" a document, image, or data.

Key Terms

Advanced Encryption Standard (AES) The encryption standard established in 2001 by the U.S. government. AES uses the Rijndael algorithm.

Asymmetric cryptography A class of cryptographic algorithms that utilize public-private encryption keys.

Block cipher An encryption algorithm that operates on fixed blocks of data.

Birthday attack A cryptanalysis attack against a message digest.

Certificate authority (CA) An entity that issues digital certificates.

Chosen ciphertext attack (CCA) A cryptanalysis attack where the attacker has chosen ciphertexts decrypted and obtains cleartext results.

Chosen plaintext attack (CPA) A cryptanalysis attack where the attacker is able to have chosen plaintexts encrypted and obtain the ciphertext results.

Cipher feedback (CFB) A block cipher mode where the result of encrypting a block of plaintext is used to encrypt the next block.

Cipher-block chaining (CBC) A block cipher mode where ciphertext output from each encrypted plaintext block is used in the encryption of the next block.

Ciphertext The result of applying an encryption algorithm to plaintext.

Ciphertext-only attack (COA) A cryptanalysis attack where the attacker has only ciphertext.

Collision An occurrence where two different messages are found to compute to the same hash value.

Cookie A mechanism used to store identifying information, such as a session ID, on a web client system.

Counter (CTR) A block cipher mode that uses a one-time random number and a sequential counter.

Cryptanalysis The process of attacking a cryptosystem in order to discover its method of operation and/or its encryption and decryption keys.

Cryptography The science of hiding information, usually through the use of algorithms based upon mathematical operations.

Data Encryption Standard (DES) The data encryption standard established in 1976 by the U.S. government. DES uses the Digital Encryption Algorithm (DEA).

Decipher Another word for *decrypt.*

Decryption The process of turning ciphertext back into original plaintext.

Diffie-Hellman (D-H) key exchange A secure mechanism for two parties with no prior knowledge of each other to jointly establish a shared symmetric encryption key.

Digital Encryption Algorithm (DEA) The data encryption algorithm chosen in 1976 as the new Digital Encryption Standard (DES).

Digital signature The result of cryptographic functions used to verify the integrity and authenticity of a message.

Electronic codebook (ECB) A block cipher mode wherein each plaintext block is encrypted separately.

Encipher Another word for *encrypt.*

Frequency analysis A cryptanalysis attack where the frequency of occurrence of the characters in ciphertext are examined.

FTP (File Transfer Protocol) A protocol used to transfer files from one system to another.

GPG (Gnu Privacy Guard) An open source software program that implements the PGP (Pretty Good Privacy) encryption standard.

Hashing See *message digest.*

HMAC (Hashed Message Authentication Code) A message digest (hashing) algorithm.

Initialization vector (IV) A random block of data that is used by some cryptographic functions.

IPsec A tunneling protocol used to protect communications between two systems.

Key A block of information that is used in an encryption algorithm.

Key management Processes and procedures used to create, protect, and destroy encryption keys.

Known plaintext attack (KPA) A cryptanalysis attack where the attacker has samples of plaintext and corresponding ciphertext messages.

Man in the middle attack (MITM) A cryptanalysis attack in which the attacker is able to read, insert, and modify messages passing between two parties without their knowledge.

MD5 A message digest (hashing) algorithm.

Message digest A fixed-length block of data that is the result of a hash function.

MIME Object Security Services (MOSS) A protocol that provides confidentiality, authentication, and non-repudiation.

Monoalphabetic cipher A cipher in which plaintext characters are substituted for ciphertext characters according to a single alphabetic table.

Non-repudiation The concept of ensuring that a person cannot later deny having performed some action.

One-time pad An encryption algorithm where the key is the same size as the message and is used only once.

Output feedback (OFB) A block cipher mode where the results of the previous plaintext block are used in the encryption of the next block.

Perfect forward secrecy The property of encryption keys, such that any past or future encryption keys can be predicted based on known values of one or more encryption keys.

Permutation cipher See *transposition cipher*.

Plaintext Data that is not encrypted.

Polyalphabetic cipher A cipher in which plaintext characters are substituted for ciphertext characters according to a multiple alphabet table.

Pretty Good Privacy (PGP) A popular computer program, as well as a published standard for encryption, that is used to encrypt and decrypt data.

Privacy Enhanced Mail (PEM) A standard for encrypting e-mail that depends upon a global PKI.

Private key An encryption key used in public key cryptography that is kept private by its owner.

Pseudo-random number generator (PRNG) An algorithm used to create random numbers for initialization vectors (IVs) and for other purposes.

Public key An encryption key used in public key cryptography that can be widely distributed to users.

Public key cryptography A class of cryptographic algorithms that utilize public-private encryption keys.

Public key infrastructure (PKI) A network-based service in which public encryption keys or certificates are stored and available for retrieval.

RC4 A common stream cipher.

Replay attack A cryptanalysis attack where the attacker records transmissions and replays them at a later time, usually to masquerade as one of the parties whose transmissions were recorded.

Rijndael The data encryption algorithm chosen in 2001 as the new Advanced Encryption Standard.

Rsh (remote shell) An unsecure protocol used to establish a command line session on another system over a network.

Running key cipher A cryptography technique used when plaintext is longer than the key.

Secure Electronic Transaction (SET) A protocol used to protect electronic transactions. SET is not widely used and has been replaced by SSL and TLS.

Secure/Multipurpose Internet Mail Extensions (S/MIME) A protocol used for protecting e-mail messages through encryption and digital signatures.

Secure shell (SSH) A TCP/IP layer 5 tunneling protocol used for secure remote management of systems. Supersedes rsh, rcp, rlogin, and Telnet.

Secure Sockets Layer (SSL) A TCP/IP layer 5 tunneling protocol used to protect network traffic through encryption. Superseded by Transport Layer Security. See also *Transport Layer Security*.

Security association A one-way trust relationship between two endpoints.

SHA-1 (Secure Hash Algorithm) A message digest (hashing) algorithm.

SHA-2 (Secure Hash Algorithm) A set of message digest (hashing) algorithms (SHA-224, SHA-256, SHA-384, SHA-512).

SHA-3 (Secure Hash Algorithm) A message digest (hashing) algorithm.

S-HTTP (Secure Hypertext Transfer Protocol) A connectionless protocol used to encrypt and authenticate data being sent from a server to a client.

Steganography The practice of hiding a message in another medium, such as an image or sound file.

Stream cipher An encryption algorithm that operates on a continuous stream of data, such as a video or audio feed.

Substitution cipher An encryption algorithm where characters are substituted for others.

Symmetric cryptography A method of cryptography where each party is in possession of the same encryption key.

Telnet A TCP/IP layer 5 protocol that is used to establish a raw TCP session over a network to a service on another computer.

Transport Layer Security (TLS) A TCP/IP layer 5 tunneling protocol that protects network traffic through encryption. Transport Layer Security supersedes Secure Sockets Layer (SSL).

Transposition cipher An encryption method where characters in plaintext are rearranged to form ciphertext.

Vernam cipher See *one-time pad*.

Virtual private network (VPN) An encrypted communications channel that is used for secure remote access or for protecting the traffic between two networks.

Watermarking The process of placing an image or mark in a file for identification purposes.

Wired Equivalent Privacy (WEP) A standard for encrypting packets on a WiFi wireless network. Superseded by WPA and WPA2.

X.509 The prevailing digital certificate standard. See also *digital certificate*.

XOR A logical operation on two operands, where the return value is TRUE only if one of the two operands (but not both) is TRUE.

Review Questions

1. A secret message has been encrypted with a key that is as long as the message itself. The key will be used for only this message. The type of encryption used here is:
   a. Running key cipher
   b. One-time cipher
   c. One-time pad
   d. Diffie-Hellman
2. The weakness of a monoalphabetic cipher is:
   a. It is vulnerable to frequency analysis
   b. It requires excessive computing resources
   c. The key is embedded in the ciphertext
   d. The key is too short
3. DES, AES, and CAST are examples of:
   a. SSL encryption algorithms
   b. Public key cryptography algorithms
   c. Stream cipher algorithms
   d. Block cipher algorithms
4. Advanced Encryption Standard uses the:
   a. Twofish cipher
   b. Reykjavík cipher
   c. Rijndael cipher
   d. Keccak cipher
5. The disadvantage of electronic codebook is:
   a. It is a manual encryption algorithm not suited for use in computers
   b. It is a patented encryption algorithm
   c. Each identical plaintext block encrypts into an identical ciphertext block
   d. It uses a 56-bit encryption key that is considered too short

6. RC4 is an example of a:
   a. Message digest
   b. Stream cipher
   c. Block cipher
   d. Key exchange
7. SHA-2 is an example of a:
   a. Message digest
   b. Stream cipher
   c. Block cipher
   d. Key exchange
8. Public key cryptography is so-named because:
   a. It is highly popular
   b. Its use is not restricted by patents
   c. It utilizes an open source encryption algorithm
   d. The key that is used to encrypt a message does not need to be kept a secret but can be made public
9. Two parties wish to exchange encrypted messages using symmetric key cryptography. The parties do not have an out-of-band method for exchanging keys. The parties should use:
   a. A stream cipher
   b. Message digests
   c. Public key cryptography
   d. Diffie-Hellman key exchange
10. Frequency analysis refers to:
    a. Analyzing the rate of occurrence of characters in ciphertext
    b. Eavesdropping on spread-spectrum radio frequency transmission in order to harvest encryption keys
    c. Analyzing the rate of occurrence of characters in plaintext
    d. Analysis of emanations in order to harvest encryption keys
11. An attacker is trying to crack an encryption scheme in order to discover secret information. The attacker is able to get his own plaintext messages encrypted by the same mechanism used to protect the secret information he is trying to obtain. This method of attack is known as:
    a. Chosen plaintext attack
    b. Chosen ciphertext attack
    c. Cryptanalysis
    d. Man in the middle

12. An attacker is trying to discover the contents of encrypted messages that he can easily intercept. The attacker attempts to break messages by intercepting and substituting his own messages in a communications stream between two parties. This type of attack is known as:
    a. Unknown plaintext
    b. Known ciphertext
    c. Man in the middle
    d. Replay
13. An administrator wants to have all traffic between two servers encrypted. The administrator should use:
    a. PGP
    b. IPsec in transport mode
    c. IPsec in tunnel mode
    d. SSL

14. Cookies are suited for session management:
    a. When the session or user ID is encrypted
    b. If the session is encrypted with SSL/TLS
    c. Only as a last resort
    d. Only on a protected LAN or VPN
15. VPNs can be used to protect network traffic:
    a. Between any nodes on two different networks
    b. Between a station and any node on a network
    c. Between two stations
    d. All of the above

Hands-On Projects

Project 5-1: EFS Encryption on a Multi-User Workstation

In this project you will encrypt files and directories using Microsoft Windows EFS (Encrypting File System).

Required for this project:

- Windows Vista, 7, or 8.
- Administrative access to the Windows operating system.
- Ability to create other user accounts.

1. Create some text files in a directory. Encrypt these files using EFS through one of the following methods:

- In Windows Explorer, (called File Explorer in Windows 8) right-click the file and select **Encrypt.**
- In Windows Explorer, right-click the file and select **Properties.** Then select **Advanced,** and then select **Encrypt contents to secure data.** Click **OK.** Then, choose "Encrypt the file and its parent folder (recommended)" or "Encrypt the file only", then click **OK** in the Encryption Warning dialog box. Then click **OK** again in the Properties dialog box one last time.

2. The file(s) you encrypted should be shown in green text instead of black text, signifying that the files are encrypted.
3. If needed, share the file(s) (or their parent directory) so that they may be viewed by other users.
4. Log out of Windows and log in as another user.
5. Using Windows Explorer, navigate to the directory containing the file(s) encrypted in step 1.
6. Attempt to read the text file(s) that were encrypted in step 1. What happens, and why?

Project 5-2: Encrypt Data with WinZip

In this project you will create archives containing encrypted files and make some observations about the archives.

Required for this project:

- Windows Vista, 7, or 8.
- Administrative access to the Windows operating system for purposes of installing software.

1. Obtain a copy of WinZip software, version 9 or newer.
2. Create a new directory on the desktop or another location.
3. Create some text files in the directory created in step 2.
4. Create a new ordinary Zip archive and place the files created in step 3 into the archive.
5. Create a second Zip archive. When placing files into the archive, choose AES encryption. You will be asked to supply a password. See Figure 5-11.
6. Place one or more additional files into the Zip archive, this time using a different password.
7. Close the Zip archives.
8. Open the Zip archive created in step 5. What do you observe?

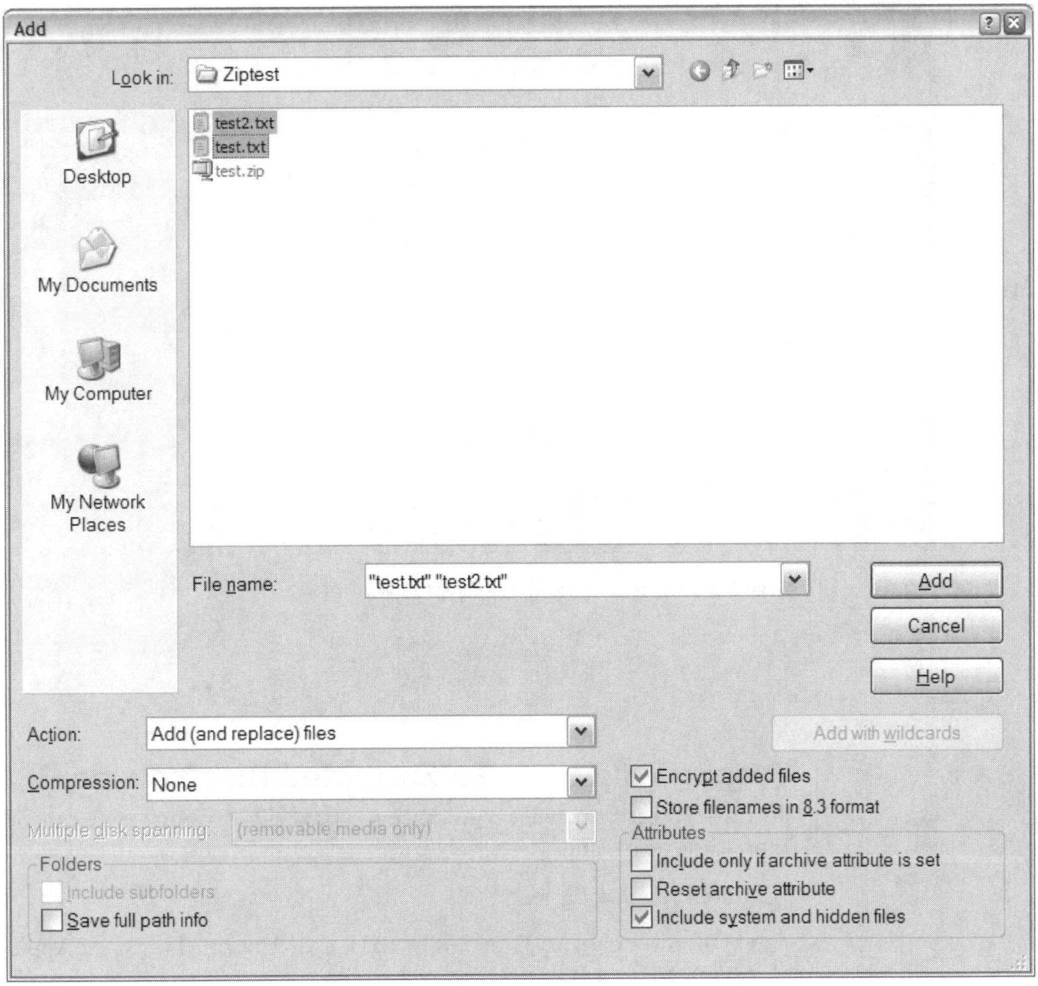

Figure 5-11 Creating a WinZip archive using AES encryption

Source: WinZip

9. Attempt to extract files from the Zip archive. What do you observe?
10. Open the Zip archive created in step 5 (see Figure 5-12) with Notepad or other program that shows plain text. What do you observe?

The encryption program 7Zip may be used instead of WinZip.

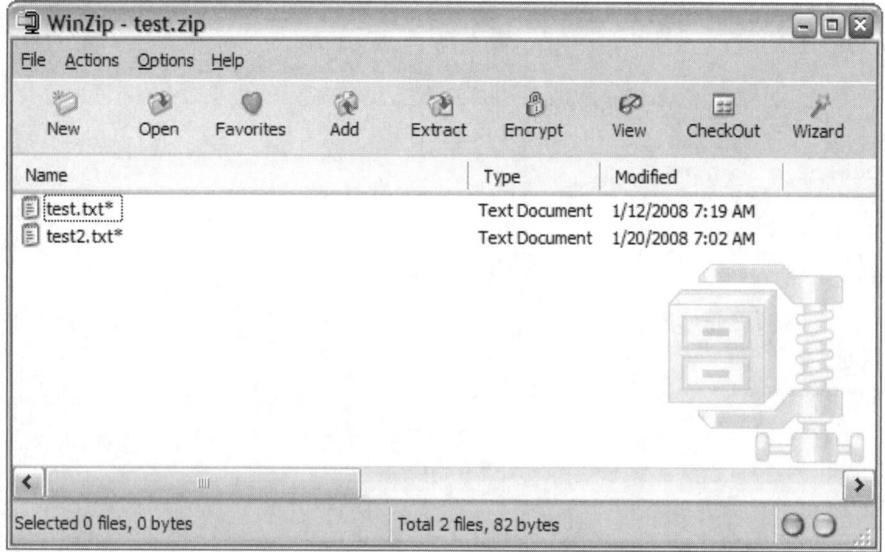

Figure 5-12 A WinZip archive contains files encrypted with AES

Source: WinZip

Project 5-3: Create an Encrypted Disk Volume

In this project you will create an encrypted disk volume that can be used to store directories and files.

Required for this project:

- Windows Vista, 7, or 8; OpenSUSE or Ubuntu Linux; or Apple Mac OS X.
- Administrative access to the operating system for purposes of installing software and administering disk volumes

1. Obtain a copy of TrueCrypt. You can obtain it from https://truecrypt.ch.
2. Install TrueCrypt on your system.
3. Create a small encrypted volume. See Figure 5-13.
4. Mount the encrypted volume.
5. Create some files and directories in the volume. What are your observations?
6. If your volume is small enough, give it to another person who has TrueCrypt and ask him or her to try to mount it (do not give the person your password). What are your observations?

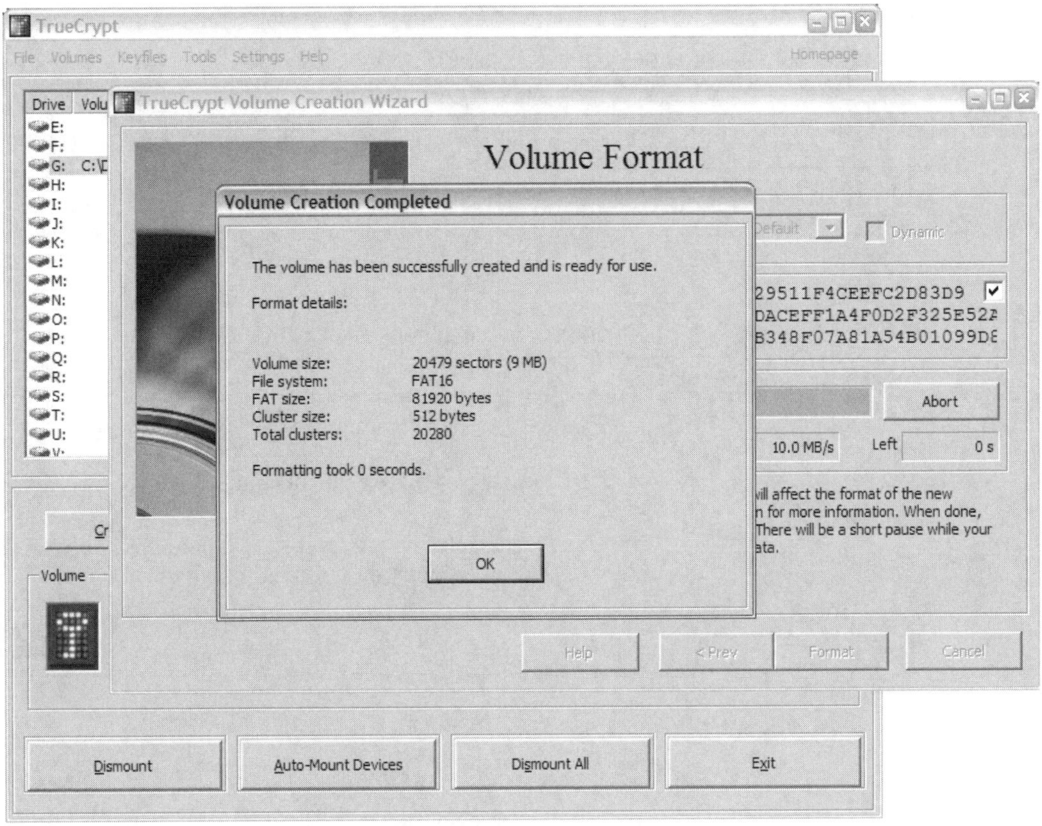

Figure 5-13 Creating a logical disk volume with TrueCrypt

Source: TrueCrypt

At the time of writing this book, TrueCrypt was undergoing an "identity crisis," during which time the historic sources of the software were no longer making fully functional versions of the software available for use. Research may be needed to obtain full working copies of the software for this project.

Project 5-4: Encrypt E-Mail Messages

In this project you will send and receive encrypted e-mail messages.

Required for this project:

- Windows Vista, 7, or 8; Apple Mac OS X
- Administrative access to the operating system for purposes of installing software

1. Obtain a copy of GnuPG (GPG), the freeware version of PGP. You can obtain it from http://www.gnupg.org/.

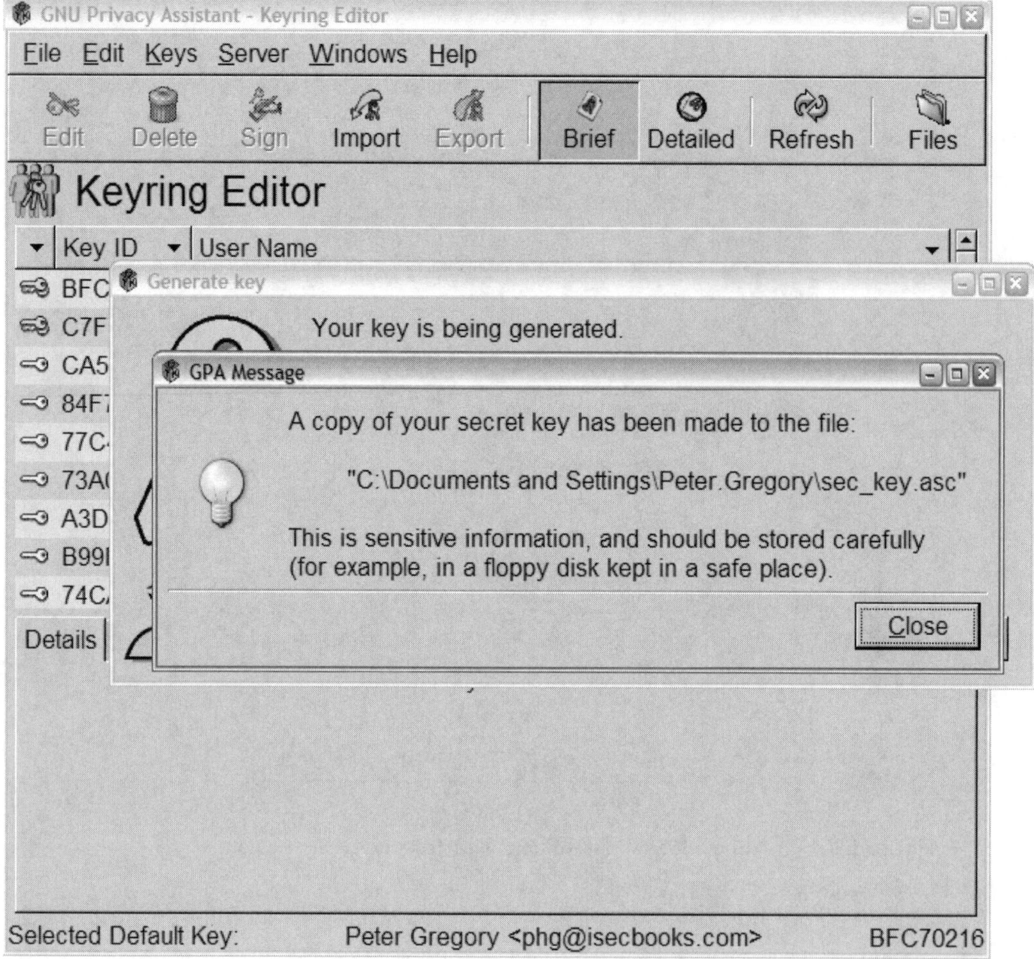

Figure 5-14 Creating a public-private key pair using GnuPG

Source: GnuPG

2. Install GnuPG on your system. Find another person who will do the same on another system, so that you can exchange messages.
3. Create a private-public key pair, per the instructions. See Figure 5-14.
4. Send your public key to another person. Have the other person send his or her public key to you.
5. Import the other person's public key using the **Keys>Import** command. See Figure 5-15.
6. Using your local e-mail program (Outlook, etc.) create an encrypted e-mail message. Alternately, encrypt a file using the other party's public key. Have the other person encrypt a file or message with your public key. Send the encrypted files/messages to each other.

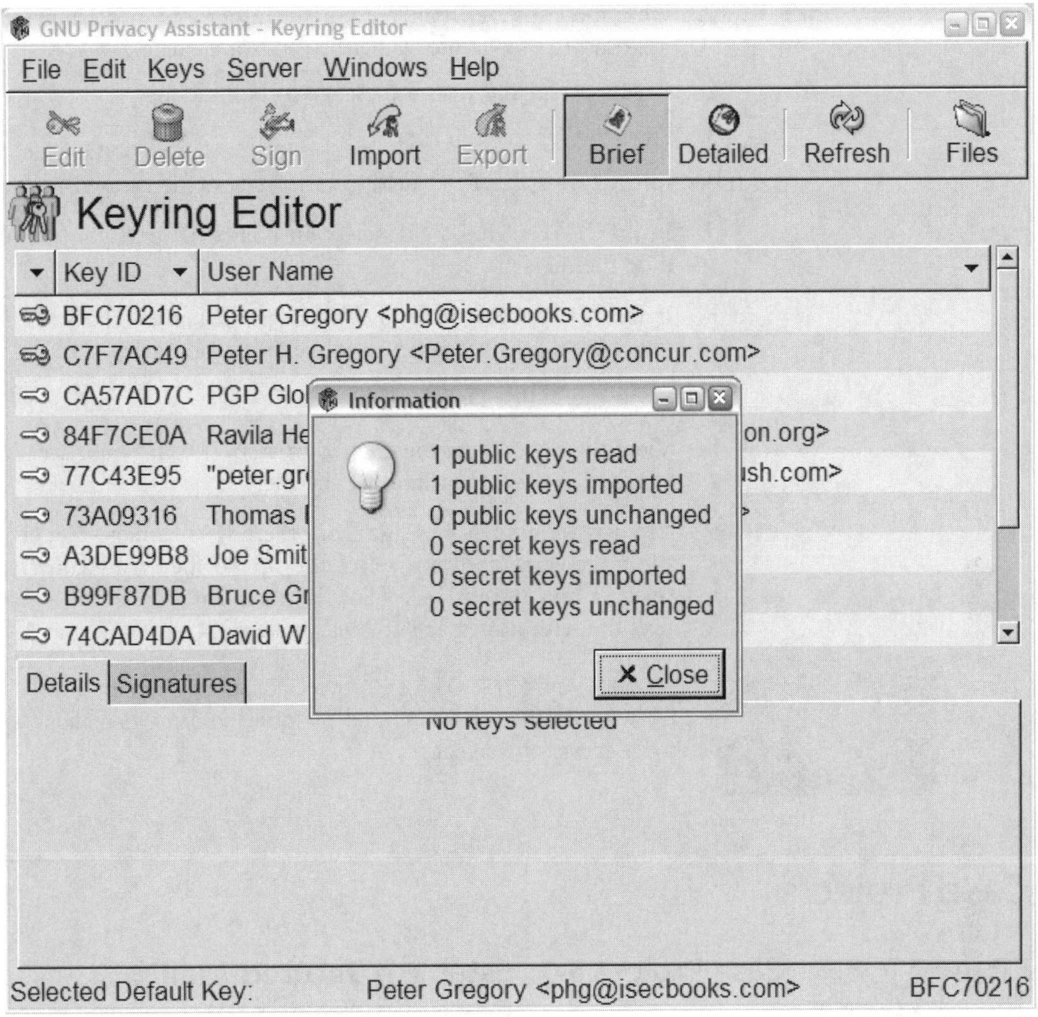

Figure 5-15 Importing a public key using GnuPG

Source: GnuPG

7. Open the message/file sent from the other person. What are your observations?

8. If available, have a third person encrypt a file with his or her public key and send it to you. Try to open the file. What are your observations?

Project 5-5: Steganography

In this project you will use steganography to hide messages in image files.

Required for this project:

- Windows Vista, 7, or 8

1. Obtain a copy of OpenStego, a steganography tool. You can obtain it from http://sourceforge.net/projects/openstego/.
2. Create a text file with a message to be hidden.
3. Start the OpenStego tool.
4. In the "Message File" field, select the text file created in step 2.
5. In the "Cover File" field, select an image file that you will use to hide the message.
6. In the "Output Stego File" field, select a file name—this will be a new image file that will visually resemble the original image selected in Step 5.
7. Click the "Hide Data" button.
8. View the new image file created in step 7. Can you discern any differences in the appearance of the file?
9. Extract the hidden message from the GIF file.image file; click the "Extract Data" button; select the image file created in step 7, and select a text output file. Click Extract Data. This will create a new text file with a message created in step 2.

Users with Apple Mac OS X can download iSteg from http://www.hanynet.com/isteg/index.html and perform the same operations as shown above for OpenStego.

Case Projects

Case Project 5-1: Establish Secured-Mail Communications

As a consultant with the Ace Security Consulting Co., you have been asked to design and implement secure e-mail for two hundred users at the Big City Insurance Company. Users at Big City use a Linux-based POP and SMTP-based e-mail server, and users use Mozilla Thunderbird, Microsoft Outlook, or Microsoft Outlook Express.

Among the solutions you can choose:

- GnuPG
- S/MIME with digital certificates obtained from Comodo (www.comodo.com) or CACert (www.cacert.org)
- PGP

Which of these solutions do you expect will be the easiest to implement? Which do you think will be the easiest to maintain? Which will result in the fewest support calls from users? What other factors will influence your decision?

Case Project 5-2: Make Encrypted Files Available to Employees in a Large Organization

As a consultant with the Ace Security Consulting Co., you have been asked to determine how encrypted documents containing sensitive information can be made available to several hundred office workers in the Very Good Software Company. The encrypted files can be downloaded from an internal web site at Very Good Software.

What considerations and methods can be used to ensure easy downloading and reading of the encrypted documents while minimizing the risk of compromise?

Case Project 5-3: Implement TrueCrypt Disk Encryption on User Workstations

As a consultant with the Ace Security Consulting Co., you have been asked to develop a plan to implement disk encryption using TrueCrypt on about fifty users' laptop workstations. You should assume the following:

- PC technicians will install and configure the software
- Users are not technical

The primary business objectives supporting the use of TrueCrypt are:

- Protection of business information in the event a laptop computer is lost or stolen
- Recoverability of business information if a user forgets his or her TrueCrypt password
- Low cost

Develop a plan for implementing TrueCrypt on the user workstations. What issues do you anticipate during and after implementation? What can be done to manage these issues?

chapter 6

Legal, Regulations, Investigations, and Compliance

Topics in This Chapter:

- Computer-Related Crime
- Categories of Law and Computer Crime Laws in the United States and Other Countries
- Security Incident Response
- Investigations
- Computer Forensics
- Professional Ethics

The $(ISC)^2$ *Common Body of Knowledge* (CBK) defines the key areas of knowledge for Legal, Regulations, Compliance, and Investigations in this way:

The Legal, Regulations, Compliance, and Investigations domain addresses ethical behavior and compliance with regulatory frameworks. It includes the investigative measures and techniques that can be used to determine if a crime has been committed, and methods to gather evidence (e.g., forensics). A computer crime is any illegal action where the data on a computer is accessed without permission. This includes unauthorized access or alteration of data, or unlawful use of computers and services. This domain also includes understanding the computer incident forensic response capability to identify the Advanced Persistent Threat (APT) that many organizations face today.

Key areas of knowledge:

- *Understand legal issues that pertain to information security internationally*
- *Understand professional ethics*
- *Understand and support investigations*
- *Understand forensic procedures*
- *Understand compliance requirements and procedures*
- *Ensure security in contractual agreements and procurement processes (e.g., cloud computing, outsourcing, vendor governance)*

Computers and Crime

Computers are increasingly involved in criminal activities of nearly every kind. The growth of computing and the Internet have given rise to new crimes and laws that did not exist before. This section explores the roles of computers in crimes, and the types of computer crimes.

The Role of Computers in Crime

Because individuals use computers to communicate, maintain records, and conduct business, quite often a computer is involved in the crime, whether it is the target of the crime, an instrument (or weapon) used to commit a crime, or it contains evidence related to the crime.

There are three ways in which computers are associated with crimes:

- *Target.* A computer or other system is the target of a crime. The following activities are examples of crimes where a computer—or the data stored in a computer—are the target of a crime:
  - *Equipment theft.* Computer or network hardware is stolen.
  - *Equipment vandalism.* Computer or other hardware is damaged or defaced.
  - *Data theft.* Data stored on a computer is stolen.
  - *Data vandalism.* Data (which can include software) stored on a computer is changed, damaged, or destroyed.
  - *Trespass.* A party logically enters a computer or other system without authorization.

- *Instrument.* A computer is used to commit a crime. Examples of computer-aided crimes include:
  - *Data theft and vandalism.* A criminal uses a computer as a tool to access another party's computer in order to change, damage, or destroy data stored there.
  - *Trespass.* A criminal uses a computer to trespass onto a computer or other type of system owned by another party.
  - *Harassment.* A criminal uses a computer to intentionally harass another person.
  - *Spam.* A criminal uses a computer to create, control, and/or monitor spam (unsolicited commercial e-mail).
  - *Child pornography.* A criminal may use a computer to create, distribute, control, or monitor child pornography or other illegal content.
  - *Libel and slander.* An individual uses a computer to libel or slander another individual.
  - ***Fraud.*** A criminal uses a computer as a tool to defraud another party.
  - *Eavesdrop.* A criminal may use a computer as a means to eavesdrop on communications between other parties.
  - *Espionage.* A criminal may use a computer as a means to commit **espionage**—obtaining secrets from an organization or government without its permission.

- *Support.* A computer is used *in support of* criminal activities. Examples of computers in support of crimes include:
  - *Recordkeeping.* A criminal may use a computer to track or support criminal activities.
  - *Conspiracy.* Two or more individuals may conspire to commit a crime, using computers as the means to communicate and plan the crime.
  - *Aid and abet.* A party may aid and abet criminals through the use of a computer, for instance, by providing information via e-mail or sending funds via e-mail or an online service.

The three major categories above are not exclusive. Often a computer-related crime will involve more than just one of the major categories above. For instance, computer trespass involves the use of a computer used as an instrument to trespass onto a victim's computer. Phishing involves all three: a computer is used as an instrument and for recordkeeping when targeting a victim's computer.

The increase in the involvement of computers in criminal activities has put a strain on law enforcement agencies and the private sector: an acute shortage of people with computer **forensics** skills has resulted in a large body of computer-related evidence being collected improperly or ignored altogether.

The Trend of Increased Threats in Computer Crimes

Computer crime has moved steadily from the realm of the lone hacker and **script kiddie** to sophisticated and resourceful criminal and nation-state-sponsored organizations. At the same time, the skills required to launch a devastating wide-scale attack have been replaced by

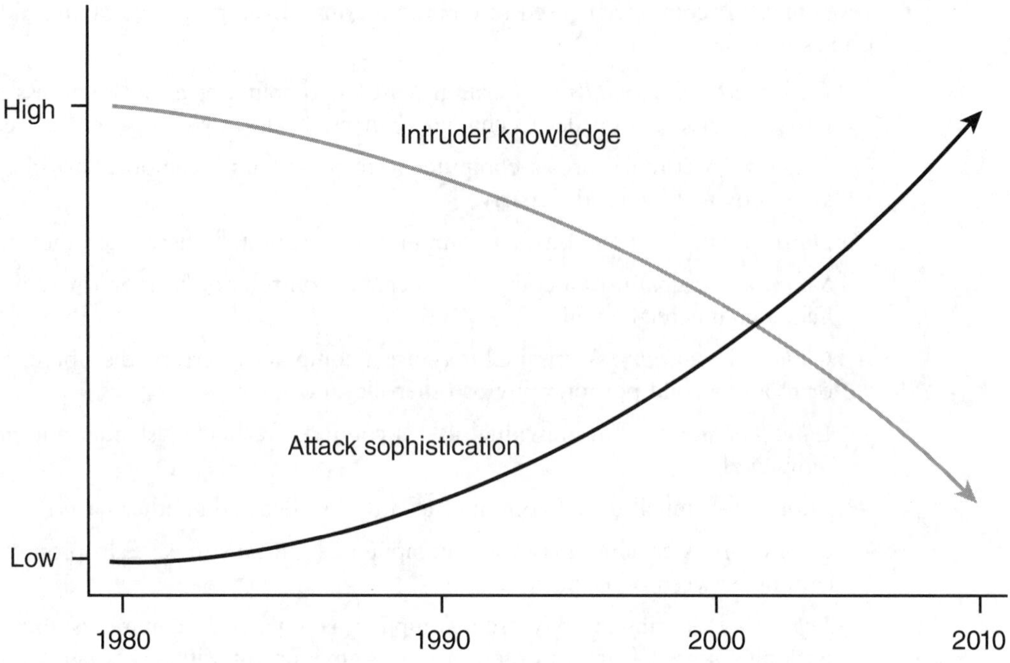

Figure 6-1 Increasingly sophisticated attacks require less knowledge

automatic processes that inexperienced individuals can easily deploy. Indeed, an entirely new economic ecosystem has been developed by individuals with strong technical expertise. This system is often available to individuals with little or no skill for a fee. The result creates a larger population of potential threats. For example, **botnets** are available for rent by the hour, vulnerabilities are bought and sold on the open market, and increasingly sophisticated malware that can evade detection continues to emerge with turn-key development kits. According to a U.S. Treasury report published in 2006, organized crime is making more money from cyber-related criminal activities than from the illegal drug trade. Figure 6-1 shows the inverse relationship between the knowledge required to launch attacks of growing sophistication.

Categories of Computer Crimes

There are several reasons why an individual or group will perpetrate a crime against a computer system. The major categories of computer-related crimes are:

- Espionage and cyber-warfare
- Terrorism
- Theft and fraud
- Commercial espionage
- Harassment
- Hacktivism
- Cybervandalism

Espionage and Cyber-warfare Military professionals added cyber-space to the traditional war-fighting domains of air, land, sea, and space. The decision sparked controversy while simultaneously acknowledging the growing role of cyber operations in modern war. Cyber-warfare involves activities carried out by military and government-sponsored intelligence agencies that are engaged in war-fighting activities against enemies of that nation-state. These operations involve the discovery, disruption, and dissolution of data resources owned or used by enemy forces. As a fifth war-fighting domain, the purpose of military operators is to achieve dominance in support of more traditional military strategies and tactics. While some military operations fall into the category of espionage, that category also incorporates actions carried out for the purpose of obtaining state secrets. Espionage also features a broader array of actors including those supporting a political, social, philosophical, or religious cause. Other individuals steal secrets for personal profit. In all cases, the actions are taken against a government.

Terrorism These attacks are perpetrated by terrorist organizations that are typically motivated by the desire to harm other countries' governments or citizens. Known as **cyberterrorism** and **information warfare**, these attacks are directed at a wide variety of targets, including:

- Government systems
- Military systems
- Public utilities
- Public health organizations
- Communications and media organizations
- Transportation systems
- Financial services organizations

The U.S. National Conference of State Legislatures (NCSL) defines **cyberterrorism** as: "*the use of information technology by terrorist groups and individuals to further their agenda. This can include use of information technology to organize and execute attacks against networks, computer systems and telecommunications infrastructures, or for exchanging information or making threats electronically. Examples are hacking into computer systems, introducing viruses to vulnerable networks, web site defacing, denial-of-service attacks, or terroristic threats made via electronic communication.*"

The U.S. Federal Bureau of Investigation (FBI) defines **cyberterrorism** as any "*premeditated, politically motivated attack against information, computer systems, computer programs, and data which results in violence against non-combatant targets by sub-national groups or clandestine agents.*"

Theft and Fraud Theft involves direct attacks specifically designed to illegally obtain funds or information. Fraud generally results in theft, but does so through illicitly obtaining information from individuals who have legitimate access to the targeted resources. Some of the most common targets are:

- *Direct access to funds.* Attackers conduct direct attacks on financial services organizations in an attempt to transfer funds to the attacker's account. One of the most famous attacks is the 1994 attack by Russian hacker Vladimir Levin, who reportedly accessed Citibank's cash management system using stolen credentials (and possibly insider help) to distribute over US$10 million between him and accomplices. Attackers occasionally choose other sources of value that can be exchanged for money. In 2014, Mt. Gox, the largest exchange of Bitcoins, filed for bankruptcy following a theft of 744,000 Bitcoins, or 6 percent of the world's supply. Bitcoins are not government-backed currency but can be used as a form of barter irrespective of currency prices, exchanges, or banks. Their popularity created exchanges like Mt. Gox where individuals could trade money for Bitcoins, and their growing value made the exchanges a tempting target.

- *Access to credit card and bank account information.* Attacks can target databases containing transactions or account numbers that can later be used in attempts to withdraw or transfer funds. The Target Corporation credit card heist in late 2013 is a watershed example of such an attack.
- ***Embezzlement.*** Insiders can conduct attacks on their own organizations' computers in order to embezzle funds for personal gain.
- ***Extortion/blackmail.*** Attackers can cripple an organization's activities in a variety of ways, with demands for payments in order to stop the attack.
- *Identity theft.* Attacks can be used to steal private information on private citizens with the intent to conduct **identity theft**, a crime that involves the illegal use of another person's identity.

Commercial Espionage This consists of attacks that target computer systems owned by private organizations. These attacks often focus on theft of information, most notably intellectual property such as patents, copyrighted works, and trademarked formulations, product specifications, and so on. Attacks on businesses are carried out for a variety of reasons, including:

- ***Competitive intelligence.*** Individuals want to discover secrets about an organization's products, services, financials, or other business secrets.
- *Financial gain.* See the earlier section on Theft and Fraud.
- ***Denial of service.*** Individuals may wish to harm or disable an organization's computer-based operations.

Businesses are often attractive targets for computer-based attacks for several reasons, including:

- Businesses will often not report the attack to law enforcement in order to avoid embarrassing, potentially damaging news reports that can negatively impact their valuation if the company issues publicly held stock or bonds.
- Businesses often lack the required expertise to carry out forensic investigations that can be used to collect damages from the attacker.
- Businesses often lack the required resources to properly address the incident.

In many jurisdictions, businesses are not required by law to report computer-related crimes; instead, businesses can often choose to keep the crime a private matter. Businesses are finding this more difficult, however, as many jurisdictions have passed laws that require the disclosure of security breaches involving the loss or exposure of citizens' personal information. This is discussed later in this chapter.

Harassment Online harassment against individuals is rising, most notably among teenagers. Schools actively participate in programs against cyber-bullying after a Florida case netted national headlines. Rebecca Sedwick was a twelve-year-old girl who committed suicide after being bullied online. State prosecutors dropped aggravated stalking charges against two other teenagers police officials linked to the case. The practice is similar to **cyberstalking**, which is the act of stalking or harassing an individual or group through the use of computers and/or networks. Cyberstalking activities may include bullying, defamation, libel, and slander. State legislatures are drafting new laws to keep pace with the growing number of incidents.

Hacktivism Hacktivism occurs against government and business concerns that are targeted by individuals with sociopolitical motivations. **Hacktivist** Jeremy Hammond received a ten-year prison sentence for maliciously destroying or stealing data from Strategic Forecasting, Inc. He justified his actions based on political reasons for opposing the company's business.

Cybervandalism **Cybervandalism** occurs when individuals and groups are motivated by feelings of anger, hostility, curiosity, or boredom. An attacker may have a grudge against an organization; often this will be a former employee who may possess much "insider" information that potentially makes such an attack easier to carry out.

Thrill seekers attack computers for entertainment. Often these attacks are performed by "script kiddies," persons of little skill who are able to obtain easy-to-use attack tools developed by others. These attacks often end in disaster, as attackers are compelled to tell their friends and associates about their latest conquests. Sooner or later an associate's loyalty will be swayed by a financial reward or knowledge that it is the "right thing" to turn in the attacker so that he or she will face justice.

Computer Crime Laws and Regulations

Criminal activities and enterprises seem to move into every new domain, institution, nook, and cranny that is developed. Like many technologies and inventions, computers and the Internet were invented for the benefit of business and society but have also become the means to commit crimes against others. As the rate and style of criminal activities increased, it soon became apparent that the set of laws and regulations in place were insufficient to address the often-abstract concepts of theft, vandalism, or trespass when they occur within computers and networks. In response, most countries have added new laws and regulations to specifically address crimes that involve the use of computers in one way or another.

Categories of U.S. Laws

The U.S. legal system consists of three categories of laws that cover all of the different types of circumstances that can bring parties to the courtroom to air their grievances. They are:

- *Criminal law*. This includes laws of public order against persons such as assault, arson, theft, burglary, deception, obstruction of justice, bribery, and perjury. Law enforcement agencies are responsible for enforcing criminal laws. Criminal laws in the United States are published in the **United States Code (U.S.C.)**.

- *Civil law*. This includes contract law, tort law, property law, employment law, and corporate law. Civil law is the branch of laws that generally involve two parties that have a grievance that needs to be settled. Law enforcement agencies generally have little to do with civil laws. Civil laws in the United States are published in the United States Code (U.S.C.).
- *Administrative law*. These laws form the framework for the operation of U.S. government agencies such as the Federal Trade Commission, the Department of Agriculture, and the Federal Communications Commission. Administrative law in the United States is published in the **U.S. Code of Federal Regulations**, commonly known as the **C.F.R.**

U.S. Computer Crime Laws

There are several categories of laws that protect networks, computers, and information stored on computers. These categories protect different types of activities and information used by individuals and businesses. They are:

- Intellectual property law
- Privacy law
- Computer crime law

U.S. Intellectual Property Law **Intellectual property** is the product of creation such as information, architecture, inventions, music, images, and design. **Intellectual property laws** in the United States protect the results of creative endeavors by individuals and organizations. The categories of intellectual property protected by these laws are:

- *Copyrights*. Copyrights, symbolized by "©," represent the creator's claim of exclusive rights on a wide variety of works including literary works, movies, dances, musical compositions, audio recordings, paintings and drawings, sculptures, photographs, radio and television broadcasts, software, and industrial designs.
- *Trademarks*. Trademarks, symbolized by "®," "TM," and "SM," represent a creator's claim on names, slogans, and logos that represent the creator's product or service. The creator of a product or service name, slogan, or logo must register it with the U.S. Patent and Trademark Office (USPTO). The creator of a work can affix a "TM" or "SM" on a product or service name, respectively, immediately upon first use. When the creator files and receives the trademark from the USPTO, the creator can affix the "®" mark on it.
- *Patents*. The intellectual property rights of inventors are protected by patents. Patents protect the designs of machinery, processes, and software. A patent protects a design or process from being copied by another person or company, but the main disadvantage of a patent is that the product or process is made public and is no longer secret.
- *Trade secrets*. Organizations can choose to not register their secrets as trademarks or patents but instead decide to keep their secrets closely guarded.

Noteworthy laws in the United States that protect intellectual property laws include:

- *Economic Espionage Act of 1996*. This law makes it a crime to steal trade secrets for commercial or economic purposes or for the benefit of a foreign power.

- *Digital Millennium Copyright Act (DMCA) of 1998*. DMCA is a copyright law that criminalizes any means that can be used to circumvent copy protection and other access controls for copyrighted works. DMCA also criminalizes the circumvention of an access control, even when there is no infringement of copyright itself. DMCA also defines and increases penalties for copyright infringement on the Internet.
- *No Electronic Theft (NET) Act*. This law defines criminal penalties when copyright violations are committed through the use of computers and networks.

U.S. Privacy Law Privacy has become a "lightning rod" issue in the United States and elsewhere in recent years. Personal information about virtually every citizen in industrialized countries is circulating among government and corporate information systems, most of it beyond the knowledge and control of most citizens. If this weren't alarming enough, news of security breaches numbering in the tens or hundreds of thousands surface every week. Stolen laptops, lost backup tapes, and hacking attacks are the majority of security breaches.

There is an added dimension to privacy that concerns many citizens: the misuse of sensitive or private information that further erodes citizens' civil rights and freedoms. For example, citizens fear that employers will discriminate against workers with health problems, now that a vast amount of health-related information is present on a relatively small number of health insurance company systems. In the absence of legal barriers, some corporations would consider screening employees based on health history if they were permitted to. In the United States this would be a violation of the right to privacy.

Several laws address privacy rights, including:

- *Fourth Amendment*. The basis for privacy rights in the United States, the fourth amendment to the Constitution states, "The right of the people to be secure in their persons, houses, papers, and effects, against unreasonable searches and seizures, shall not be violated, and no Warrants shall issue, but upon probable cause, supported by Oath or affirmation, and particularly describing the place to be searched, and the persons or things to be seized." In other words, law enforcement may only search the private residence of an individual when there is probable cause that a crime has occurred and when a search warrant has been signed by a judge. The fourth amendment has been extended into cyberspace in case law through specific laws, including some listed in this section.
- *Privacy Act of 1974*. Following privacy abuses perpetrated by the Nixon administration, this law forbids U.S. federal agencies from sending private information on citizens to other persons or agencies without those citizens' request or consent.
- *Electronic Communications Act of 1986*. This law provides protections for stored electronic communications.
- *Electronic Communications Privacy Act (ECPA) of 1986*. This law extended restrictions on telephone wiretaps to also include similar restrictions on wiretaps of electronic communications among computers. Requirements for obtaining warrants for wiretaps of electronic communications are defined in this law.
- *Computer Matching and Privacy Protection Act of 1988*. An amendment of the Privacy Act of 1974, this law put restrictions on the 1980s practice of computer matching of citizens' private information.

- *Communications Assistance for Law Enforcement Act (CALEA) of 1994*. This law requires telecommunications carriers to cooperate with law enforcement agencies' requests for wiretaps of subscribers' telephones. The law also requires the manufacturers of telecommunications equipment to provide the means for legal wiretaps. Wiretaps require a signed warrant.
- *Economic and Protection of Proprietary Information Act of 1996*. Addressing espionage, this law defines information and trade secrets as property, making theft of trade secrets and information a crime.
- *Health Insurance Portability and Accountability Act (HIPAA) of 1996*. This comprehensive law requires greater uniformity in health information data, which allows it to be more easily transmitted between health-related organizations (such as health care providers and insurance companies for claims purposes), but also protects health information from unauthorized disclosure. HIPAA's "Security Rule" imposes many requirements on the security of Electronic Patient Health Information (EPHI).
- *Children's Online Privacy Protection Act (COPPA) of 1998*. This law restricts online services' ability to collect information from children under the age of thirteen.
- *Identity Theft and Assumption Deterrence Act of 1998*. This law strengthened the law regarding fraud and related activity in connection with identification documents, authentication features, and information.
- *Gramm-Leach-Bliley Act (GLBA) of 1999*. The Financial Privacy Rule and the Safeguards Rule require financial services organizations to disclose privacy policies to customers and to provide adequate safeguards to protect customers' private information.
- *Provide Appropriate Tools Required to Intercept and Obstruct Terrorism (PATRIOT) Act of 2001*. The Patriot Act, as it is commonly known, expanded the authority of U.S. law enforcement agencies for the intention of fighting terrorism in the United States and abroad. The Patriot Act gave law enforcement agencies greater ability to search telephone and e-mail communications and medical, financial, and other records.
- *Health Information Technology for Economic and Clinical Health Act (HITECH) of 2009*. This law passed as part of the American Recovery and Reinvestment Act and provided $19.2 billion to increase the use of electronic health records by Medicaid and Medicare providers. This provision sought to shift the medical industry away from paper-based systems and into a national network of healthcare information exchanges.

U.S. Computer Crime Law Several laws have been passed in the United States that further define lawful and unlawful acts. With the widespread use of computers by government and private organizations, protection of computers and the information stored on them was ambiguous at times, and activities that were pretty clearly criminal in nature were sometimes difficult to prosecute. Notable U.S. cybercrime laws include:

- *Access Device Fraud, 1984*. This law codifies criminal activities related to the fraudulent use of "access devices," which generally is associated with the fraudulent use of credit and debit cards, ATMs, computer passwords and PINs, and cellular phones.
- *Computer Fraud and Abuse Act of 1984*. This law was the first to define "computer trespass" by making it illegal to knowingly access a computer without authorization for purposes of obtaining national secrets or information with an intent to defraud.

This was the first real anti-hacking law in the United States. Previously, it was difficult to prosecute hackers who accessed computers without authorization.

- *Computer Security Act of 1987*. This law improves the protection of private information when stored on U.S. federal information systems. This law also assigned to the National Institute of Standards and Technology (NIST) the task of developing standards for security practices for federal information systems.
- *National Information Infrastructure Protection Act of 1996*. This was an update to the Computer Fraud and Abuse Act, with newer language on the topic of fraud in connection with computers.
- *Sarbanes-Oxley Act of 2002*. Also known as the Public Company Accounting Reform and Investor Protection Act of 2002, or just SOx, this law requires U.S. public companies to implement a comprehensive control framework around their financial accounting, including supporting IT systems and infrastructure. This has resulted in a significant increase in security controls in most public companies.

- *Federal Information Security Management Act of 2002 (FISMA)*. This law extended the Computer Security Act of 1987 by requiring annual audits of federal information systems as well as those of affiliated parties (typically U.S. government contractors).
- *Controlling the Assault of Non-Solicited Pornography and Marketing (CAN-SPAM) Act of 2003*. This law made it illegal to send unsolicited commercial e-mail (UCE—but more often known as "spam") to individuals without their consent.
- *Identity Theft and Assumption Deterrence Act of 2003*. This act updated the law on "fraud related to activity in connection with identification documents, authentication features, and information" by making it illegal to possess of any "means of identification" used to "knowingly transfer, possess, or use without lawful authority."
- *State laws regarding information disclosure*. The majority of U.S. states have passed laws that require organizations to disclose security breaches that involve the unauthorized disclosure of personally sensitive information. The states have done so because the U.S. federal government has not yet passed such a law. These state laws require an organization to notify citizens in writing when their personally sensitive information has been compromised. Each state's laws vary somewhat, although many are modeled after the first such law, California's SB-1386.

Canadian Computer Crime Laws

Canada has passed laws defining many activities involving computers and networks as crimes, including:

- *Interception of Communications (Criminal Code of Canada, § 184)*. This law makes it illegal to intercept any private communication over any medium.
- *Unauthorized Use of Computer (Criminal Code of Canada, § 342.1)*. This law criminalizes unauthorized uses of computers.
- *Privacy Act, 1983*. This law placed restrictions on the Canadian government on the collection, storage, and use of private information.
- *Personal Information Protection and Electronic Documents Act (PIPEDA)*. This law restricts the collection, storage, and use of a citizen's private information by private companies in Canada.

European Computer Crime Laws

The European Union, as well as many of its member countries, has developed laws to protect computer systems and information. The basis of laws and cultural differences between Europe and the United States has resulted in laws that sometimes take a different approach to the protection of information.

- *Computer Misuse Act 1990 (CMA)*. This UK law defines unauthorized access to a computer as a crime, as well as the use of hacking tools against a computer, whether or not successful.
- *The Regulation of Investigatory Powers Act 2000*. This is a controversial UK law that permits wiretapping and surveillance and can in some circumstances force an individual to surrender an encryption key to government authorities.
- *Anti-terrorism, Crime and Security Act 2001*. This UK law was passed shortly after the September 11, 2001, attacks on the United States. The law gives the government additional powers regarding seizure and freezing of terrorist funds. It also allows for the deportation of suspected terrorists and others who are threats to national security. Other parts of the law make changes in airline security, hate crimes, police powers, bribery, weapons of mass destruction, and retention of data by telephone companies and Internet service providers.
- *Data Protection Act 1998 (DPA)*. This is a pivotal UK privacy law that governs the protection of personal data. The law defines eight principles of data protection, which are:
  1. Personal data shall be processed fairly and lawfully and, in particular, shall not be processed unless—
     (a) at least one of the conditions in Schedule 2 is met, and
     (b) in the case of sensitive personal data, at least one of the conditions in Schedule 3 is also met.
  2. Personal data shall be obtained only for one or more specified and lawful purposes, and shall not be further processed in any manner incompatible with that purpose or those purposes.
  3. Personal data shall be adequate, relevant and not excessive in relation to the purpose or purposes for which they are processed.
  4. Personal data shall be accurate and, where necessary, kept up to date.
  5. Personal data processed for any purpose or purposes shall not be kept for longer than is necessary for that purpose or those purposes.
  6. Personal data shall be processed in accordance with the rights of data subjects under this Act.
  7. Appropriate technical and organisational measures shall be taken against unauthorised or unlawful processing of personal data and against accidental loss or destruction of, or damage to, personal data.
  8. Personal data shall not be transferred to a country or territory outside the European Economic Area unless that country or territory ensures an adequate level of protection for the rights and freedoms of data subjects in relation to the processing of personal data.

- *Fraud Act 2006*. This UK law defines three categories of fraud—fraud by false representation, fraud by failing to disclose information, and fraud by abuse of position. This law makes identity theft and activities related to it unlawful, because identity theft is a form of fraud.
- *Police and Justice Act 2006*. A part of this law amended the Computer Misuse Act 1990 by criminalizing acts that have the intent to impair the operation of a computer.
- *Privacy and Electronic Communications Regulations 2003*. This is a UK law that makes it illegal to use equipment to make automated telephone calls that play recorded messages. This is similar to the U.S.-based "do not call" laws.
- *Convention for the Protection of Individuals with Regard to Automatic Processing of Personal Data*. This 1981 treaty signed by the Council of Europe was the first move towards protecting citizens' private data that was, at the time, being processed by computers. This treaty obligated the signatories to enact laws to protect private information.
- *Directive on the Protection of Personal Data*. This European Union law is also known by its number, *95/46/EC*. This is a wide-sweeping privacy law that applies to all of Europe and is used to protect the flow of information related to European citizens.

6

Computer Crime Laws in Other Countries

Practically every other country in the world has enacted one or more laws that define various computer activities as crimes. By far the most common activities classified as crimes are:

- *Unauthorized entry*. In many countries it is now a crime to access a computer when one is not authorized to do so.
- *Creation or distribution of malware*. Many countries now make it illegal to create, release, or distribute malware.

Managing Compliance

Organizations in many countries and in most industrial and government sectors are required to comply with laws and regulations that are related to the protection of information and information systems. In many cases, such as with financial institutions in the United States, organizations are subject to multiple sets of laws and regulations. This can prove to be quite challenging with regards to coordinating and tracking activities to ensure that they are compliant. In many cases, regulatory or statutory compliance mandates the type of information that must be recorded and stored along with a time frame for holding the information.

Organizations usually approach this issue by adopting or developing a framework of controls that can help to organize business and security controls into a logical arrangement. Control frameworks that are most often adopted include:

- ***COBIT (Control Objectives for Information and Related Technology)***. Developed by the Information Systems Audit and Control Association (ISACA) and the IT Governance Institute (ITGI) in 1996 and updated several times since, the COBIT framework consists of key control objectives and a life cycle of planning and internal audit.

- *COSO*. Originally developed in 1994, the COSO control framework was developed by the Committee of Sponsoring Organizations of the Treadway Commission, a private organization sponsored by the American Institute of Certified Public Accountants (AICPA), the American Accounting Association (AAA), Financial Executives International (FEI), the Institute of Internal Auditors (IIA), and the Institute of Management Accountants (IMA). The COSO controls framework was developed in response to new U.S. laws aimed at improving corporate financial reporting and eliminating fraud and corruption. COSO was updated in 2004 as a result of the Sarbanes-Oxley Act, which imposed further controls on corporate financial reporting as a result of the Enron scandal.
- *ISO 27002:2013*. Formally entitled the Code of Practice for Information Security Management, ISO 27002:2013 is a framework of controls covering the entire spectrum of security management.

Organizations generally use one of these frameworks as a starting point and then develop additional controls that reflect the results of risk analysis or specific laws and regulations.

The life cycle activities for these and other frameworks resemble the Plan-Do-Check-Act process lifecycle, also known as the Deming Cycle, as shown in Figure 6-2. The activities are described here:

- *Plan*. Establish policies, processes, procedures, architectures, and so on.
- *Do*. Implement and perform the processes and procedures.
- *Check*. Periodically verify the correct operation and implementation of processes and architectures through internal or external audit and control testing.
- *Act*. Make improvements to processes and architectures based upon the results of internal and external audits.

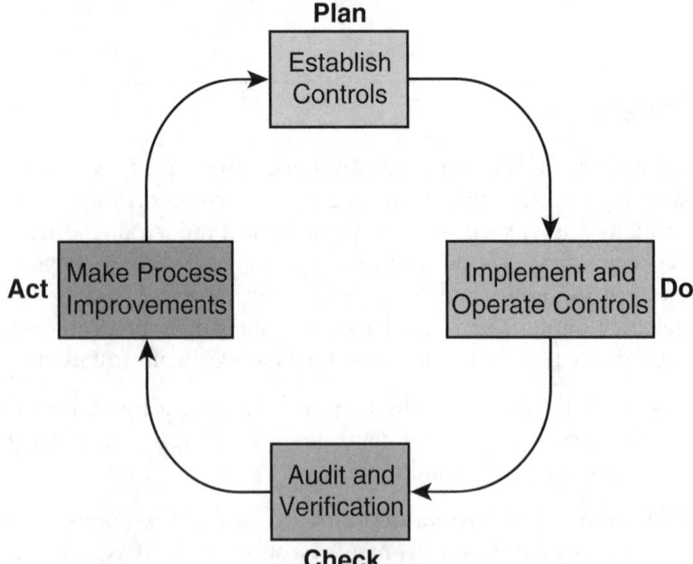

Figure 6-2 The process-based controls life cycle

Security Incident Response

Security incident response is the discipline of creating coordinated response plans in advance of an incident.

A **security incident** is defined as a violation of security policy. For example, if security policy states that users are forbidden from sharing computer passwords and it is learned that a user has shared a password with another person (deliberately or not), an **incident** has occurred. If the other person has used the employee's computer account, this would be a somewhat more significant incident, and it would be more significant still if it were discovered that this other person was an outsider who accessed company or personal information. As you can see from this example, an incident can vary in criticality, scope, and impact, as well as the actual response required.

The Security Incident Response Process

Security incident response should follow a structured model, so that staff and management will not overlook important steps as the incident plays out. The phases of security incident response are:

- Incident declaration
- Triage
- Investigation
- Analysis
- Containment
- Recovery
- Debriefing
- Continuous improvement

The activities triage, investigation, and analysis may occur in a continuum without distinct boundaries. As the following sections explain, triage is the search for evidence, investigation is the focus on the evidence, and analysis is the process of determining what happened.

Incident Declaration A security incident will be declared when trained individuals become aware that a policy violation has occurred. But the trouble is, incidents are often unrecognized in their early stages and instead thought to be non-security in nature.

Security incidents can be triggered by several events, including:

- *Apparent malfunctions or outages*. System malfunctions, slowness, or failures that are initially attributed to defects may actually be the actions of malware or an attacker. Only after an engineer has been dispatched to determine the cause of a problem does the organization realize that malicious activity is the problem's root cause.
- *Threat or vulnerability alerts*. The nature of a specific threat or vulnerability alert received from a product vendor or security organization may prompt the declaration of a security incident, if the threat is thought to be active or imminent.

- *News media*. On occasion, an organization learns about a security incident in its own environment through the news media.
- *Customer notification*. A user or customer may be experiencing difficulties that may be caused by a security policy violation.

Triage When a security incident has been declared, designated and trained staff members and management should initiate incident triage procedures. In the context of security incident management, the triage process involves the search for—and examination of—clues that will hopefully lead to a root cause and the ability to apply corrective measures.

The origins of the term *triage* are best described in Merriam Webster's definition: "*the sorting of and allocation of treatment to patients and especially battle and disaster victims according to a system of priorities designed to maximize the number of survivors*." In an emergency room setting, a triage nurse quickly sorts through patients according to the urgency of their need for care. Back in the context of security incident response, staff members searching for clues that will lead them closer to the cause of the incident will briefly examine each bit of information and, like a triage nurse, prioritize the clue as to its likelihood to be associated with the incident or not.

Incident handlers need to use some caution when searching for information. Because of the possibility that the systems that they are examining may literally be a crime scene, noninvasive techniques need to be used as much as possible, according to computer forensics practices, which are discussed later in this chapter. It is highly likely that a security incident will not be declared until the triage stage of what is thought to be a non-security-related incident. Often, only after staff members begin to understand why a particular incident is occurring will they come to the realization that they are not looking at an ordinary malfunction, but a security incident.

Investigation The triage and investigative phases can almost be thought of as one continuous activity. Both are concerned with the identification of evidence that will lead the response team closer to knowledge of the incident's root cause. Investigation is the closer study of information that is thought to be related to the cause of the incident. Where triage is the search for substantive information, investigation is the deeper study of the *right* information.

Analysis As the incident unfolds and triage leads to investigation, so investigation leads to analysis. Analysis is a deeper study of the information that is directly related to the incident. Analysis helps to answer one or more of the following questions about the incident:

- What happened?
- How did this happen?
- What is the scope of the incident?

Another important objective of analysis is the determination of the steps needed to begin containment and recovery operations.

Containment As the nature of the security incident becomes known, the response team must take steps to contain the incident—that is, to halt the incident and to prevent its spread.

If the incident is of the type where the unwanted activity is still ongoing, the team needs to figure out how to make it stop. If the unwanted activity has ceased, measures must be taken to prevent its recurrence.

Every incident is different. In some cases, containment may be performed in stages, sometimes early in the incident in the form of disconnecting a system from the network, and again later on in the form of stopping unwanted processes, for instance.

Sometimes containment will be the first active steps taken on a system where staff members are making actual changes to the way the system is behaving (for instance, halting unwanted programs). The response team may need to take its last forensic samples prior to commencing containment activities that may alter the "pristine" (pre-action) state of the system—this is also often the first moment when the attacker becomes aware that he or she has been discovered.

Recovery **Recovery** is the process of restoring a system to its pre-incident condition. Depending upon the nature of the incident, recovery may involve one or more of the following activities:

- Repairing or replacing hardware
- Reinstalling operating system or application software
- Reconfiguring operating system or application software
- Removing unwanted programs and data
- Restoring damaged or missing data from backup media

Like other phases in security incident management, containment and recovery have blurred lines—or one may be more dominant than the other, depending upon the type of incident. With some types of incidents, containment and recovery may be one and the same, while in others they are distinctly separate activities.

Work done during the investigative and analysis stages of the incident response may also include measures that need to take place to prevent the recurrence of this or a similar incident. Recovery operations may also include these additional measures, but sometimes these measures are not determined until the next stage of incident response, debriefing.

Debriefing The final step of security incident response is a **debriefing** of the response team and management. The purpose of the debriefing is to reflect on the incident itself and the organization's response to it, in order to learn from these activities. Some of the improvements that can be identified in the debriefing include:

- *Technical architecture*. An incident may have revealed weaknesses in some aspect of the technical architecture that, when improved, will reduce the probability or the impact of recurrence.
- *Technical controls*. An incident may have uncovered the absence or a defect in a technical control that would have minimized or prevented the incident.
- *Processes and procedures*. Sometimes an incident is caused not by a weakness in technology but a weakness in a business process or procedure. For example, an

incident caused by a disgruntled employee's actions may reveal that the process and procedures associated with terminating employee access had some holes.

- *Security incident response.* The response team may reflect on the handling of the incident and discover improvements that will make subsequent responses more effective.

Continuous Improvement No organization can hope to avoid repeating past mistakes unless it adopts a mindset of continuous improvement. In a security incident debriefing, it is not enough to just understand how an incident occurred. An organization needs to employ **root cause analysis** (RCA) to determine the true reason that the incident occurred in the first place, so that meaningful changes can be made to reduce the probability and/or likelihood of future incidents.

Assumption of Breach A new way of thinking about security incident prevention and response, called **assumption of breach**, is leading security professionals to think differently about security incidents. Prior to assumption of breach, the popular mindset among security professionals was to prevent security breaches from occurring. With assumption of breach, security professionals adopt the mindset that one or more breaches have already occurred in their organizations, whether those breaches have been discovered or not.

This author asserts that this is a more realistic philosophy than prior ways of thinking. Adversaries wield advanced tools and techniques and are often able to compromise networks with even advanced defenses. Assumption of breach also requires humility on the part of security managers and executives, who might otherwise believe that their networks are impenetrable.

Incident Management Preventive Measures

A mature security incident program should include a preventive component. If the impact or scope of an incident can be reduced or prevented altogether, then the effort expended in investigation and recovery will similarly be reduced.

Primarily, incident prevention consists of two components:

- *Creation of a vulnerability and threat awareness capability.* Many types of incidents can be minimized or avoided altogether if personnel are aware of an active threat or vulnerability. Such awareness is available from both internal and external sources, including:
  - *Security alerts from US-CERT, Secunia, SANS, anti-virus tool vendors, and suppliers.* These alerts include security advisories regarding vulnerabilities and threats that give organizations time to prepare for emerging threats.
  - *Company internal events, such as terminations.* Because many events are the results of actions carried out by current and former employees, awareness of terminations can give the organization an opportunity to take any measures necessary to thwart a former employee's attempt to inflict damage on the organization.
  - *Events detected by Intrusion Detection Systems (IDS) and Intrusion Prevention Systems (IPS).* IDS and IPS can detect an emerging threat that may be contained through the enactment of additional preventive measures.

- *Implementation of a defense in depth strategy to protect assets*. The results of risk assessments ought to indicate characteristics in an environment where defenses can be improved in order to reduce the probability, impact, or scope of a threat or vulnerability. The addition of detective, preventive, or deterrent controls will either make an incident less likely to happen or reduce the impact of a threat if it is realized.

Incident Response Training, Testing, and Maintenance

To effectively manage an incident, the staff members who will likely be involved in a security incident need to know how they are expected to respond when a real incident occurs. Incident response training can involve one or more of the following activities:

- *Procedure review*. Staff members can become acquainted with incident handling by reading the response procedures.
- *Formal training*. Staff members can attend formal training sessions that review response procedures and provide opportunities for group discussion and questions.
- *Incident walkthrough*. The security incident response team can perform a security incident walkthrough. Primarily this involves a step-by-step review of security incident procedures, discussing possible scenarios, responses, and issues at each step. A walkthrough is also considered a test of incident response procedures.
- *Incident simulation*. More involved than a walkthrough, a simulation is the acting out of the procedures by response personnel as though a real incident were playing out. A simulation provides more realism than a walkthrough and usually includes a facilitator who orchestrates the event by providing regular "updates" as the simulated event unfolds. A simulation is both an excellent way to test incident response procedures as well as a training opportunity by giving incident handlers some "experience" at performing incident procedures.

In order to maintain the ongoing effectiveness of the incident response team, training needs to be considered an ongoing, regularly scheduled activity. Changes in the makeup and management of teams, procedures, and technologies should necessitate a periodic review of incident response procedures to make sure that they will remain effective while these expected changes take place over time.

Incident Response Process Models

Organizations that want to develop their own security incident response capability can adopt the model described in this text or develop one of their own. There are also several incident response models available from well-respected security organizations including:

- *CERT Coordination Center (CERT/CC)*. Formed in 1988 after the Morris Worm Incident, CERT/CC has developed and published a wealth of information on the development of security incident response capabilities. www.cert.org/csirts/
- *Forum of Incident Response and Security Teams (FIRST)*. Founded in 1990, FIRST has several documents including the Best Practice Guide Library (BPGL) and CERT-in-a-Box. www.first.org
- *National Institute of Standards and Technology (NIST)* special publication 800-61, Computer Security Incident Handling Guide. www.nist.gov

Reporting Incidents to Management

An organization's security policy should include the requirement that its personnel report security incidents at once. Doing so will result in an appropriate response that can be started sooner, often resulting in less damage or disruption to the organization. Employees should be directed to not attempt to manage security events on their own, regardless of the circumstances.

Investigations

Some security professionals may be responsible for conducting or guiding security-related investigations. There is a distinction between security incidents that require a coordinated and well-orchestrated response from teams, and small isolated events that do not require a team effort.

There is not a well-recognized and distinct boundary between the types of events that require an incident team response and those that can be handled by an individual security professional. Criteria that separate the two capabilities that work for one organization may not work in another. Still, a general distinction is made in Table 6-1.

An investigator's work must have integrity in several key areas, including:

- *Evidence collection.* A simple case such as employee misconduct can result in the employee's dismissal, which may be followed by a wrongful-termination lawsuit. This is discussed in detail later in this chapter.
- *Consistent procedures.* Every security matter should be handled in a consistent manner, so that there is no hint of favoritism or bias.
- *Recordkeeping.* Every investigation should be documented in the event that it plays a part in a larger incident or investigation in the future.
- *Management review.* Management should review all incidents, so that they have visibility into events that provide a clearer view of overall risk in the organization.

Event Type	Investigation	Incident Response
Employee misconduct	Pornography, harassment	Sabotage, disclosure of sensitive information to outsider
Malware	Isolated to individual system or as a result of misuse	Malware infection that results in business disruption
Stolen asset	Stolen laptop	Information stolen by outsider where there is a threat or fear of disclosure
Violation of acceptable use policy	Misuse of company assets	Misuse of company assets that results in material impact to the organization

Table 6-1 Incident response versus and investigations: examples

Working with Law Enforcement Authorities

When an incident or issue has taken place, response procedures and policies should require the person(s) responsible for business or data security determine whether a crime has been committed. This is a simple and obvious task when a tangible asset such as a laptop computer has been stolen, but decidedly less clear when other types of events take place.

Many organizations often consider unauthorized entry into a computer system as a private matter and do not contact law enforcement authorities for several reasons, including:

- *Embarrassment.* Organizations wish to avoid the public humiliation and embarrassment of a computer crime, as it may lead many to conclude that the organization cannot properly manage or secure its systems.
- *Disruption of services.* Organizations fear that reporting computer-related crimes will cause disruptions in computer-provided services if law enforcement agencies will wish to confiscate affected computers as evidence.
- *Difficulty of prosecution.* Often when a computer-related crime takes place, law enforcement may make no effort to identify or prosecute the perpetrator, but if they do, prosecution is often difficult, particularly when it relies on computer-based forensic evidence.

With regards to security incidents that involve the unauthorized disclosure of personally sensitive information, many U.S. states, as well as other countries, now require organizations to report such disclosures to affected citizens and/or law enforcement authorities. Further, regulations in some industries require that organizations disclose security incidents. Often, organizations no longer have a choice but are required to report security incidents to involved citizens, law enforcement, or industry regulators.

It is recommended that information security professionals establish relationships with local and national law enforcement authorities in order to become acquainted with the procedures for reporting crimes as well as guidance for preventing them.

Forensic Techniques and Procedures

According to Merriam-Webster, the definition of **forensics** is "the application of scientific knowledge to legal problems, especially the scientific analysis of physical evidence as from a crime scene." In the context of computers and networks, forensics is the body of procedures used to examine a computer system and its contents for evidence that may be used in an anticipated legal action.

The primary activities in computer forensics are:

- Identify and gather evidence
- Preserve evidence
- Establish a chain of custody
- Present findings

The U.S. National Institute for Standards and Technology (NIST) has published several documents on computer forensics, including:

- Special Publication 800-72, Guidelines on PDA Forensics.
- Special Publication 800-86, Guide to Integrating Forensic Techniques into Incident Response.
- Special Publication 800-101, Guidelines on Cell Phone Forensics.
- Bulletin 11-01, Computer Forensics Guidance.

All of these documents are available at http://csrc.nist.gov/publications/PubsSPs.html.

Identifying and Gathering Evidence

Computers and other devices store a tremendous volume of information. As storage media continues to drop in price, the amount of storage capacity on newer systems is increasing at substantial rates. This provides a challenge to forensics professionals, who are sometimes overwhelmed by the sheer volume of data present on systems.

Generally, a computer forensics professional will be given some initial indications on the nature of an investigation. Some of the likely possibilities are:

- *E-mail.* The user may be suspected of sending inappropriate messages or leaking company secrets via e-mail.
- *Web access.* A user may be under suspicion of visiting specific web sites, or categories of web sites, that are deemed to be inappropriate.
- *Storing data.* A user may be suspected of storing information inappropriately, such as company secrets on a laptop computer in violation of policy against such a practice.
- *Inappropriate access.* An employee may be using a computer to inappropriately access other computers in the organization in violation of stated policies.

These leads provide a starting point for the forensic specialist. Rather than being given a "we think the employee is doing something wrong," suspected activities such as those listed above provide direction for a forensic investigation.

Prior to the start of a forensic investigation, the computer forensics professional must carefully consider independence and objectivity: does the forensics professional have any interest (or appearance of interest) in the outcome of the matter being investigated? If so, the forensics investigator should consult with management and consider recusing himself or herself from the matter.

Evidence Collection Techniques

The nature of a forensics investigation helps to define the approach taken by the investigator. Some of the activities that may be performed include:

- *Examination of surroundings.* The forensic specialist will usually wish to examine the undisturbed surroundings, where he or she may see and possibly want to also take any removable media, documents, notes, and so on. The investigator will probably want to take several photographs of the computer and its surroundings for later analysis.

- *Live system forensics*. The nature of the investigation may prompt the investigator to examine the running system. It may involve recording open applications and documents, running processes, and examining the memory space of running processes.
- *Physical examination*. The investigator may wish to carefully examine the computer's case and fasteners, and in some situations examine the interior of the system using fiber-optic technology, if there is suspicion that the computer's owner/operator may have implemented forensics countermeasures that could obliterate evidence (or the investigator) should the case be opened prematurely.
- *Examination of storage*. The examiner will almost certainly wish to examine the contents of the computer's storage. In most cases this is a hard drive but sometimes a computer's main storage is semiconductor-based, particularly in the case of mobile devices and very small laptop computers.

Examination of a computer's main storage usually necessitates the use of a tool used to make a forensic copy of the hard drive or other storage. Sometimes an investigator will make more than one copy, in cases where the investigator wishes to boot a computer with one copy (which will change the contents of the copied media) to see how it behaves.

As the investigator uses forensic tools to search through programs, files, and directories, the search will be focused on those parts of main storage that are associated with the activity that is under suspicion. For instance, if the user is suspected of visiting unauthorized web sites, the investigator will examine certain files that provide evidence of the specific pages on web sites that have been visited. Again, because the amount of data stored on a system's main storage can be so vast, the investigator needs to stay focused on specific areas.

Whole-disk encryption (also known as full disk encryption) is growing in popularity because of its ability to protect stored data. However, whole-disk encryption makes examination of a computer's main storage all but impossible, leaving live forensics as one of few viable options.

Preserving Evidence

When the forensic investigator identifies the evidence he or she is looking for, the investigator must take care to preserve it properly. Some aspects of evidence preservation are straightforward, such as copying hard drives, but others are more difficult, such as capturing the contents of memory on a running system or the main storage on a mobile device such as a smartphone.

The forensic investigator must follow several principles of evidence preservation, including:

- *Collection*. Digital evidence must be secured with measures designed to prevent malware, electrostatic discharge, or human tampering from altering the contents of the drive or system. Even shutting a system down and restarting it can be sufficient cause to dismiss digital evidence in court.
- *Recordkeeping*. The investigator must record every step taken during the forensic investigation, starting with the investigator's visit to the room where the computer is kept. The records themselves will become a part of the body of evidence.
- *Use of reliable tools*. The investigator must use tools that are known to be reliable and to produce consistent results. The investigator must also record the versions of tools that are used.

- *Evidence safekeeping*. All evidence that is gathered and created must be kept safe from tampering by others. Evidence should be kept in locked cabinets in a locked room except when the investigator is physically present and working on the case.
- *Work in isolation*. The examiner's workstation(s) that are used to examine the evidence should not be connected to any network. Doing so may give an opposing attorney or examiner the opportunity to put into question the integrity of the investigator's work by presenting the possibility that being connected to the Internet can introduce external forces, such as malware, that can alter the evidence.
- *Chain of custody*. Whenever evidence is created, moved, stored, or transferred to another custodian, thorough records must be kept and evidence safeguarded to ensure its integrity. This is discussed in more detail in the next section.

Chain of Custody

Chain of custody is *the document or paper trail showing the seizure, custody, control, transfer, analysis, and disposition of physical and electronic evidence*. As evidence is examined and created (in the case of the investigator's notes and records), it is vitally important that the investigator follows consistent procedures and records all activities in order to support the chain of custody.

If the chain of custody is broken, then it will be possible for a legal opponent to successfully challenge the integrity of the evidence by suggesting that it has been tampered. This could result in the evidence so painstakingly collected being entirely disregarded, which could affect the outcome of the legal proceeding. Techniques used for chain of custody include:

- Use of a separate computer for forensic purposes only, one that is never connected to the Internet where it could be exposed to malware that could alter the results of forensic analysis.
- Making digitally identical copies of files, media, and entire disk drives to ensure that the originals are not subject to possible contamination.
- Performing hashes or checksums of files, media, and entire disk drives to ensure that they are free from tampering.
- Use of tamper-evident envelopes for storage of paper records and electronic media.

Presentation of Findings

After completing the investigation of the computer or mobile device, the investigator will then write a formal report that states what evidence was found and its condition and characteristics. A good forensics report will contain only the facts and well-supported conclusions and will not include any speculation or statements regarding the motive of the person whose system is being examined.

Ethical Issues

The subject of ethics involves the behavior of professionals in a variety of business situations, particularly when challenged with choices that involve the potential for political favor, personal gain, escaping responsibility, or unfair advantage over others. In order to deter such activity, many organizations have developed a formal code of conduct statement that defines the types of activities that are permitted and that are discouraged. The Internet Activities Board (IAB) published an ethics statement entitled *Ethics and the Internet* in 1989, and $(ISC)^2$, the governing corporation for the CISSP certification, has developed its own **code of ethics**.

Professional Ethics

The Merriam-Webster dictionary defines **ethics** as "the discipline dealing with what is good and bad and with moral duty and obligation." It defines *professional ethics* as "the principles of conduct governing an individual or a group." From these two definitions, we understand that security professionals' behavior should reflect a high level of morality, integrity, and responsibility. The consistent appearance of good judgment should be the result of sound ethical behavior.

Security professionals are expected to lead by example. Security professionals should abide by security policies that they expect other employees to follow. In a real sense, security professionals are like law enforcement and should be held to an even higher standard than the rank and file.

6

Many professional organizations have published a code of ethical standards that members are required to uphold. $(ISC)^2$, the governing body of the CISSP certification, has a comprehensive code of ethics that all security professionals, CISSP or not, should adopt as their own.

Each CISSP certification holder is required to support the $(ISC)^2$ Code of Ethics, which appears in Appendix B.

Codes of Conduct

Many organizations publish a **code of conduct** in order to define specific activities that are either permitted or forbidden. A typical code of conduct will include the following topics:

- Obey all laws.
- Always dress and act professionally.
- Avoid conflicts of interest.
- Avoid outside employment.
- Engage in good public relations through community activities.
- Avoid activities with customers or suppliers that would raise suspicion of favoritism or activities that result in personal gain.
- Use organizational resources and funds for business purposes only.
- Always maintain accuracy in all books, records, and communications.
- Separate personal activities from business activities.
- Maintain privacy and confidentiality of all business-related information.

In most cultures these activities define an overall manner of professional integrity in line with moral and natural laws, as well as established laws and regulations that the organization is required to conform to.

RFC 1087: Ethics and the Internet

In 1989 the Internet Activities Board (IAB) developed a policy statement entitled *Ethics and the Internet*, regarding the proper use of Internet resources. The policy reads,

The Internet is a national facility whose utility is largely a consequence of its wide availability and accessibility. Irresponsible use of this critical resource poses an enormous threat to its continued availability to the technical community.

The U.S. Government sponsors of this system have a fiduciary responsibility to the public to allocate government resources wisely and effectively. Justification for the support of this system suffers when highly disruptive abuses occur. Access to and use of the Internet is a privilege and should be treated as such by all users of this system.

The IAB strongly endorses the view of the Division Advisory Panel of the National Science Foundation Division of Network, Communications Research and Infrastructure which, in paraphrase, characterized as unethical and unacceptable any activity which purposely:

(a) seeks to gain unauthorized access to the resources of the Internet,

(b) disrupts the intended use of the Internet,

(c) wastes resources (people, capacity, computer) through such actions,

(d) destroys the integrity of computer-based information,

and/or

(e) compromises the privacy of users.

The Internet exists in the general research milieu. Portions of it continue to be used to support research and experimentation on networking. Because experimentation on the Internet has the potential to affect all of its components and users, researchers have the responsibility to exercise great caution in the conduct of their work. Negligence in the conduct of Internet-wide experiments is both irresponsible and unacceptable.

The IAB plans to take whatever actions it can, in concert with Federal agencies and other interested parties, to identify and to set up technical and procedural mechanisms to make the Internet more resistant to disruption. Such security, however, may be extremely expensive and may be counterproductive if it inhibits the free flow of information which makes the Internet so valuable. In the final analysis, the health and well-being of the Internet is the responsibility of its users who must, uniformly, guard against abuses which disrupt the system and threaten its long-term viability. (Internet Engineering Task Force, http://www.rfc-editor.org/rfc/rfc1087.txt)

RFC 1087 was published prior to the passage of many of the laws that define many of the unacceptable uses as illegal. But, laws or not, we are obligated to protect the Internet and uphold its nearly universal utility to the countries and citizens of the world and to discourage and oppose all acts and persons who seek to bring ill favor or harm to it.

The $(ISC)^2$ Code of Ethics

A **code of ethics** is a formal written statement—a code of responsibility used in an organization to define permitted and forbidden activities. Places of employment and professional organizations often develop a code of ethics (sometimes called a code of conduct). $(ISC)^2$, the organization that manages the CISSP certification, has a code of conduct. The canons of the (ISC)^2 Code of Ethics read:

- Protect society, the commonwealth, and the infrastructure.
- Act honorably, honestly, justly, responsibly, and legally.
- Provide diligent and competent service to principals.
- Advance and protect the profession.

The entire (ISC)^2 Code of Ethics appears in Appendix B of this book.

All persons holding certifications from (ISC)^2 are required to uphold the (ISC)^2 Code of Ethics. Failure to do so can result in the loss of one's certification. But what does it mean to apply this code of ethics in the security profession? The meaning of each of the (ISC)^2 Code of Ethics canons is expanded here:

- *Protect society, the commonwealth, and the infrastructure.* We must uphold personal and corporate liberties and act to protect the ongoing viability of peoples, governments, and the means used to communicate with one another. We must help others to better understand how to protect themselves and their ability to communicate with others. More specifically, we are duty bound to help others better understand how to protect their computers and their networks.
- *Act honorably, honestly, justly, responsibly, and legally.* We are to contribute to the good name of our profession, information and business security. We are to always be truthful, but beyond that, to defend the truth. We cannot show favoritism, bias, or partiality. We must always uphold the law and encourage others to do so.
- *Provide diligent and competent service to principals.* We must value and perform excellent work for our employers. We should work with our heads to discover better ways to do our jobs and to contribute to the good of our employers.
- *Advance and protect the profession.* We must promote the arts and sciences of business and data security, doing so in ways that bring respect and favor to our profession. We need to encourage others to join our profession, mentoring and guiding them, ultimately making them new guides to lead still others into our vocation.

By upholding these canons we must bring honor to ourselves and our profession. In the eyes of others we must act like model citizens. After we retire, or die, we should each be remembered for our honor and service to others.

Guidance on Ethical Behavior

The following principles provide additional guidance on ethical behavior in the workplace.

- *Behave transparently.* Say what you mean and mean what you say.
- *Make decisions openly.* Give no impressions of a person who makes "back room deals."
- *Shun politics.* Do not give in to a pervasive political culture.
- *Show no favoritism or self-interest.* Treat everyone fairly. Do not give or accept favors or appear that you are doing so.
- *Respect the privacy and dignity of others.* Keep private matters private and continue to earn and keep the respect of others.

- *Keep your commitments*. Be a man or woman of your word.
- *Promote accountability and responsibility*. People must be responsible for their behavior and for the consequences of their decisions. Act in this regard and expect others to do the same.
- *Document your actions*. Keep a logbook of conversations, decisions, and actions, to aid the memory and to provide a record of matters considered.

Here are some examples of situations that an information security manager may face:

- Someone reports seeing another manager in the organization encouraging employees to make illegal copies of a registered ISO standards document.
- An executive is discovered to be viewing child pornography on business premises using business resources. When confronted, the executive makes threatening statements to his accuser about "career limiting decisions."
- An IT manager encourages the use of free versions of anti-virus and file compression programs, even though their terms of use prohibit commercial use.

In these types of situations, the information security manager considers his or her professional integrity, accountability on the part of the manager and his or her colleagues, and legal obligations.

Chapter Summary

- Computers play a variety of roles in computer crimes: they are the target of crimes, they are an instrument of crimes, and they support crimes.
- The categories of computer crimes are espionage and cyber-warfare, terrorism, theft and fraud, commercial espionage, harassment, hacktivism, and cybervandalism.
- The categories of U.S. law are criminal, civil, and administrative. Criminal laws address matters of public order; civil laws address grievances between parties; and administrative law governs the actions of federal agencies.
- The categories of U.S. law that protect information and computers are intellectual property laws, privacy laws, and computer crime laws.
- The types of intellectual property protections are copyrights, trademarks, and patents.
- Most countries have passed laws that protect the privacy of personally sensitive information. Many U.S. states have passed laws that require the disclosure of unauthorized disclosures of personally sensitive information, most notably California's SB-1386.
- Security incident response consists of several steps including incident declaration, triage, investigation, analysis, containment, recovery, and debriefing.
- Staff members should be trained in security incident response procedures so that they will act more effectively during a real incident.
- Forensic procedures should be followed when investigating a security incident, because of the possibility that the incident may become a part of a future legal action.

- The primary activities in a forensic investigation are: identify and gather evidence, preserve evidence, establish a chain of custody, and present findings.
- Strict procedures must be followed when performing a forensic examination, so that the original evidence is not altered and information identified and gathered is never altered or compromised.
- In a forensic examination, the chain of custody is the paper trail that shows the seizure, custody, control, transfer, analysis, and disposition of physical and electronic evidence.
- Many organizations will develop a *code of conduct* to define the activities that are acceptable and unacceptable.
- Security professionals should adhere to a strict code of professional conduct and ethics.
- The $(ISC)^2$ Code of Ethics defines the desired and undesired behavior that it expects of its CISSP and SSCP certification holders. The $(ISC)^2$ will consider stripping the certification from anyone who violates the code of conduct.
- The Internet Activities Board (IAB) published RFC 1087: Ethics and the Internet, a statement of ethics concerning the acceptable use of the Internet.
- Security professionals should always conduct themselves so as not to ever give even the appearance of violating an organization's security policy or the $(ISC)^2$ Code of Ethics.

Key Terms

Administrative law The branch of law in the United States that defines the rules and regulations that govern activities in executive departments and agencies in the U.S. government.

Assumption of breach The way of thinking about security breaches, that security breaches have already occurred, whether discovered or not.

Blackmail *See extortion.*

Botnet A collection of software robots (or "bots") under centralized control that run autonomously and automatically.

C.F.R. See *U.S. Code of Federal Regulations.*

Chain of custody The procedures and paper trails that track forensic evidence in a legal investigation.

Civil law The branch of law that deals with disputes between individuals and/or organizations.

COBIT (Control Objectives for Information and Related Technology) A controls framework for the management of information technology and security.

Code of conduct A policy statement published by an organization that defines permitted and forbidden activities.

Code of ethics A code-of-responsibility statement that is used in an organization to define specific permitted and forbidden activities.

Competitive intelligence Activities regarding the acquisition of information and secrets about a competing organization's products, services, financials, and other business activities.

Copyright The legal right to exclusive use that is given to the creator of an original work of writing, music, pictures, and films.

COSO (Committee of Sponsoring Organizations of the Treadway Commission) A controls framework for the management of information systems and corporate financial reporting.

Criminal law The branch of law that enforces public order against crimes such as assault, arson, theft, burglary, deception, obstruction of justice, bribery, and perjury.

Cyberstalking Acts of stalking or harassing an individual or group through the use of computers and/or networks.

Cyberterrorism Acts of violence against civilians and governments that are carried out in cyberspace.

Cybervandalism Vandalism that is carried out against information or information systems.

Debriefing A meeting or conference during which the details of an incident are discussed, in order to learn from the incident and the organization's response to it.

Denial-of-service An attack against a computer or network that is designed to incapacitate the target.

Embezzlement The act of dishonestly or illegally appropriating wealth from another party, often an employer or service provider.

Espionage The process of obtaining secret or confidential information without the permission of the holder of the information.

Ethics The discipline of dealing with a code of professional behavior.

Extortion The act of obtaining money or other valuables from a person or organization through coercion, intimidation, or threat.

Forensics The application of scientific knowledge to solve legal problems, especially the analysis of evidence from a crime scene.

Fraud An act of deception made for personal gain.

Hacktivist A person who attacks information systems for political or religious motives.

Identity theft A crime that involves the illegal use of some other person's identity.

Incident An unexpected event that results in an interruption of normal operations. See also *security incident.*

Information warfare The use of information or information systems in the pursuit of an advantage over an opponent.

Intellectual property (IP) A product of creation such as information, architecture, invention, music, image, or design.

Intellectual property law The branch of law that protects created works and includes such safeguards as copyrights, trademarks, service marks, and patents.

Patent A means of legal protection for exclusive rights to an invention or process.

Recovery The process of restoring a system to its pre-incident condition.

Root cause analysis (RCA) The technique of incident analysis whereby the true cause of an incident is identified.

Script kiddie An individual with relatively low skills who breaks into computer systems using tools written by others.

Security incident An event in which some aspect of an organization's security policy has been violated.

Security incident response The procedures followed in the event of a security incident.

Trade secret A formula, design, process, or method used by an organization to gain competitive advantage over others.

Trademark A means of legal protection for exclusive rights to a name or symbol.

United States Code (U.S.C.) The body of published criminal laws in the United States.

U.S. Code of Federal Regulations (C.F.R.) The code of administrative law in the United States.

Review Questions

6

1. The categories of U.S. laws are:
   a. Executive, judicial, and legislative
   b. Criminal, civil, and administrative
   c. Laws and regulations
   d. Criminal and civil
2. Where are U.S. laws published?
   a. Criminal and civil laws are published in the United States Code (U.S.C.), and administrative laws are published in the U.S. Code of Federal Regulations (C.F.R.)
   b. Criminal and civil laws are published in the U.S. Code of Federal Regulations (C.F.R.), and administrative laws are published in the United States Code (U.S.C.)
   c. Executive and judicial laws are published in the United States Code (U.S.C.), and legislative laws are published in the U.S. Code of Federal Regulations (C.F.R.)
   d. Regulations are published in the United States Code (U.S.C.), and laws are published in the U.S. Code of Federal Regulations (C.F.R.)
3. The most appropriate intellectual property protection for the design of a system is:
   a. Trade secret
   b. Copyright
   c. Trademark
   d. Patent
4. An organization has invented a new type of semiconductor for use in computers, and wishes to protect its intellectual property rights in a manner where no other company can know how the semiconductor was designed or constructed. The best course of action is:
   a. Obtain a patent for the design
   b. Obtain a trademark for the design
   c. Keep the design a trade secret
   d. Obtain a copyright for the design

5. The first U.S. law to define computer trespass is:
   a. Federal Information Security Management Act
   b. Sarbanes-Oxley Act
   c. Computer Fraud and Abuse Act
   d. Computer Misuse Act
6. The purpose of debriefing after a security incident includes all of the following EXCEPT:
   a. Discussion of changes in processes and procedures
   b. Discussion of changes in incident response
   c. Discussion of sanctions against contributing personnel
   d. Discussion of changes in technical controls
7. An organization has discovered that an employee has been harvesting credit card information from its databases and selling them to a criminal organization. The organization should:
   a. Update its privacy policy
   b. Quietly terminate the employee
   c. Install a key logger and continue to monitor the employee's actions
   d. Notify the owners of the compromised credit card numbers
8. A computer forensics expert has been asked to collect evidence from an individual's workstation. The collection techniques used by the computer forensics expert should include all of the following EXCEPT:
   a. Examination of the running system
   b. Physical examination
   c. Examination of surroundings
   d. Collection of fingerprints
9. What factor will motivate a computer forensics specialist to examine a running system instead of waiting to take an image of the system's hard drive?
   a. Full disk encryption
   b. BIOS boot password
   c. Data present in the paging file
   d. Live Internet connection
10. A computer forensics examiner is about to conduct a forensics examination of a computer's hard drive and anticipates that he will be cross-examined in a deposition. What should the examiner do to ensure that the image he takes of the computer's hard drive is an exact copy of the hard drive?
    a. Reconcile the numbers of files and directories on the original and copied image
    b. Perform SHA-1 and MD5 checksums of the original drive and the copied image
    c. Use a write blocker when making a copy of the original drive
    d. Make a copy of the hard drive and perform forensics on the original

11. The process of safekeeping and recordkeeping of computer forensics evidence is known as:
    a. Chain of custody
    b. Chain of evidence
    c. Burden of proof
    d. Best evidence rule
12. The statement that defines principles of behavior for Internet usage is:
    a. Computer Fraud and Abuse Act
    b. $(ISC)^2$ Code of Ethics
    c. RFC 1087: Ethics and the Internet
    d. Computer Misuse Act
13. The statements, "Protect society, the commonwealth, and the infrastructure," "Act honorably, honestly, justly, responsibly, and legally," "Provide diligent and competent service to principals," and "Advance and protect the profession" are contained in:
    a. Internet Activities Board (IAB) Guiding Principles
    b. $(ISC)^2$ Code of Ethics
    c. RFC 1087: Ethics and the Internet
    d. Computer Fraud and Abuse Act
14. A security manager in a government post needs to hire an outside consultant to perform risk analysis. A relative of the security manager is qualified to perform the work. The security manager should:
    a. Document why the relative is the best choice
    b. Consider alternative consultants instead
    c. Recuse himself from the decision-making process
    d. Hire the relative
15. The U.S. law that permits a law enforcement agency to conduct a search without a court order is:
    a. PATRIOT Act
    b. Communications Assistance for Law Enforcement Act
    c. Personal Information Protection and Electronic Documents Act
    d. Executive Order 13402

Hands-On Projects

Project 6-1: Compare Forensic Analysis Tools

In this project you will compare the features of some forensic analysis tools to be used in a small company's IT department.

Find one or more web sites that discuss and review forensic analysis tools that would be suitable for use in a smaller organization. The tools to be considered should possess ability to:

1. Copy the contents of a computer's hard drive.
2. Find and recover files that have been deleted on a computer's hard drive.
3. Determine a history of web sites that have been recently visited.
4. Search the computer's hard drive for files containing key words.
5. Compare the contents of files on a computer's hard drive.
6. Copy the contents of other storage devices such as USB drives.
7. Log the activities performed with the tool.

The company may want to consider one or more of the following tools that are available, including:

- AccessData FTK Imager
- AccessData Forensic Toolkit
- EnCase
- ProDiscover
- Safeback
- DFF

Project 6-2: Conduct a Security Incident Simulation

In this project you will create a procedure for a walkthrough of a security incident simulation.

Develop a plan for security incident simulation. The plan should include the following:

1. A description of possible scenarios that will be the subject of the walkthrough.
2. A list of participants by function (network engineer, helpdesk tech, IT manager, and so on).
3. A choreographed set of "events" or "issues" that will unfold throughout the incident (examples of these events will be incoming news of observations seen by various staff members or of incoming communications).
4. A log of discussions and responses by participants.
5. Time allocated to debrief and discuss what was learned in the simulation.

How many participants have you chosen to participate in the simulation? What possible scenarios are you considering? How much total time are you allocating for the simulation?

Project 6-3: Analysis of the Internet Code of Ethics

In this project you will download and analyze the Internet Code of Ethics.

Retrieve a copy of RFC 1087: Ethics and the Internet and answer the following questions:

- Is the document still relevant today? Explain why or why not.
- Is the document written in a form that can be understood by today's Internet users? Explain why or why not.
- If you were asked to update the document, what changes would you make?

Case Projects

Case Project 6-1: Development of Information Security Incident Response Plan

As a consultant with the Risk Analysis Consulting Co., you have been asked to develop the information security incident response plan for the Raising Dough Baking Company, a statewide business that employs over three hundred employees. Raising Dough collects online orders from homes and small businesses and delivers their products with a company-owned fleet of trucks.

The company does not currently have a security incident response plan. How will you approach the task of creating one? What information will you need to obtain from the company before you begin?

Will you develop a plan from scratch, or will you use a model or template?

Case Project 6-2: Protection of Intellectual Property

As a consultant with the Data Protection Consulting Co., you have been assigned to help a client determine how to protect its intellectual property. The client is a software company that has developed several types of intellectual property, including:

- Computer software that helps programmers test their own programs more easily.
- A new technique for analyzing software source code for defects.
- Brand names for programs that it offers for sale to customers.
- Business processes that it uses to process new orders more efficiently.

The client company does not know what kinds of safeguards should be used for each of these pieces of intellectual property. You need to determine whether the client should pursue a trademark, patent, or copyright for each. You also need to advise the client on the advantages and disadvantages of keeping one or more of these pieces a trade secret.

Case Project 6-3: Develop a Code of Conduct

As a consultant with the Risk Advisors Co., you have been asked to take a consulting assignment with a client, the Rancid Fish Sauce Company, which needs help with the development of its new code of conduct.

Rancid Fish Sauce had problems with employee misconduct in the past, which has led company management to commission the development of a code of conduct.

You need to develop an outline for the code of conduct. Describe how you will approach this assignment and where you will go for information.

Case Project 6-4: An Ethical Challenge

You are a security consultant with the Security Advisors Co. and have been asked to help investigate a recent security incident that took place at the law firm of Dewey, Cheatham, and Howe. In your assignment you have been assigned to work with the vice president of IT.

The security incident that you are investigating appears to be a case of an intruder who broke into a company computer to remove and destroy information on an upcoming legal case. A forensic examination revealed that the incident was actually an inside job that was perpetrated by one of the new programmers, who is a relative of the VP of IT.

When you wrote your findings and presented them to your client, the VP of IT asked you to change the findings in your report to show that the perpetrator could not be found. The VP has promised future work for your company and a good recommendation for your work if you comply.

What will you do next?

Topics in This Chapter:

- Applying Security Concepts to Computer and Business Operations
- Records Management Security Controls
- Backups
- Anti-Virus Software and Other Anti-Malware Controls
- Remote Access
- Administrative Management and Control of Information Security
- Resource Protection
- Incident Management
- High Availability Architectures
- Vulnerability Management
- Change Management and Configuration Management
- Operations Attacks and Countermeasures

The (ISC)² *Common Body of Knowledge* (CBK) defines the key areas of knowledge for Security operations in this way:

Security Operations domain is used to identify critical information and the execution of selected measures that eliminate or reduce adversary exploitation of critical information. It includes the definition of the controls over hardware, media, and the operators with access privileges to any of these resources. Auditing and monitoring are the mechanisms, tools, and facilities that permit the identification of security events and subsequent actions to identify the key elements and report the pertinent information to the appropriate individual, group, or process.

The candidate is expected to know the resources that must be protected, the privileges that must be restricted, the control mechanisms available, the potential for abuse of access, the appropriate controls, and the principles of good practice.

Key areas of knowledge:

- *Understand security operations concepts:*
  - *Need-to-know/least privilege*
  - *Separation of duties and responsibilities*
  - *Monitor special privileges (e.g., operators, administrators)*
  - *Job rotation*
  - *Marking, handling, storing, and destroying of sensitive information*
  - *Record retention*
- *Employ resource protection*
  - *Media management*
  - *Asset management (e.g., equipment life cycle, software licensing)*
- *Manage incident response*
  - *Detection*
  - *Response*
  - *Reporting*
  - *Recovery*
  - *Remediation and review (e.g., root cause analysis)*
- *Implement preventative measures against attacks (e.g., malicious code, zero-day exploit, denial of service)*
- *Implement and support patch and vulnerability management*
- *Understand change and configuration management concepts (e.g., versioning, baselining)*
- *Understand system resilience and fault tolerance requirements*

Most of this chapter contains information on how to put into operation the concepts discussed in much of this entire book.

Security Operations Concepts

Other chapters in this book define some of the basic concepts and tenets of control and good practice in information and business security. This section takes those concepts and describes how they are put into practice in an organization. The concepts discussed in this section are:

- Need-to-know
- Least privilege
- Separation of duties
- Job rotation
- Monitoring of special privileges
- Records management controls
- Backups
- Anti-malware
- Remote access

An organization intent on identifying and reducing risk will first undertake a risk assessment. Then, the organization will remediate risk through the enactment of controls and policies. As discussed in Chapter 1, "Information Security and Risk Management," the flow of control is Policy, Guidelines, Processes, Procedures, and Recordkeeping. This section describes many of the concepts that are used in the information security industry and often find themselves embodied in policy.

Need-to-Know

The concept of **need-to-know** states that individual personnel should have access to only the information that they require in order to perform his or her stated duties. Even if any specific individual has the necessary clearance to access specific information, access should still be granted *only* if the individual actually requires access to specific information in order to perform the duties.

Here is an example. Managers in the marketing department of a company have access to a directory on a file server that contains a wide variety of marketing documents, including some that pertain to future expansion plans for the company. Of the ten managers, two are responsible for working on future expansion plans. Under the principle of need-to-know, only these two managers should have access to the documents related to future expansion.

In this example, only the persons who need to have access to sensitive future expansion information would be granted that access.

The advantage of need-to-know-based access control is reduced risk. When fewer people have access to a given set of information, then the risk of unauthorized disclosure and compromise due to actions performed by employees is reduced proportionally. If the number of persons with access to a data set is reduced from ten to two, then the risk of disclosure through user access is statistically reduced by 80 percent.

Carried to its logical conclusion, applying the concept of need-to-know can impose much additional administrative overhead on the management of access rights on a system.

Organizations need to decide if, and where, to implement this level of access control. An organization going in this direction should first develop a policy statement that specifies where and under what circumstances need-to-know access controls will be implemented. Processes, procedures, and guidelines should specify *how* they will be implemented.

Least Privilege

The concept of **least privilege** states that users should have the fewest or lowest number of privileges required to accomplish their duties. In an environment where privileges are assigned to persons, those persons should be assigned the fewest, or lowest level, of privileges they require to accomplish their assigned duties.

For example, an organization purchases a financial management system that has many predefined roles and capabilities. When assigning individual users to the predefined roles, management should assign roles such that each user will have the fewest privileges possible while being able to perform their required duties.

The advantage of least privilege is the reduced risk. When users' unnecessary privileges are eliminated, then any risks associated with those prevented actions are reduced or removed.

The concepts of need-to-know and least privilege are very similar and mostly reflect different points of view. Where need-to-know is focused on access to specific information, least privilege is concerned with access levels.

Separation of Duties

The literal definition of **separation of duties** is to take a duty or task and separate it so that two or more persons must be present in order to complete it. In modern business, tasks that require separation of duties include:

- *Deployment of a nuclear weapon.* Two or more staff members are required to insert a key or type a password.
- *Opening a bank vault.* Two vault tellers each possess one half of the combination to the vault.
- *Issuing an arrest warrant.* Law enforcement documents a probable cause to arrest an individual, which is signed by a judge.

The objective of separation of duties is to ensure that no single individual can subvert a business process; separation of duties is accomplished through placing the completion of a task into the hands of two or more separate individuals. This requires that the two (or more) cooperate in order to perform the task. Employing separation of duties reduces the likelihood that an improper task will be performed:

- *Inappropriately.* When completion of a task requires two or more persons, chances are better that one of the participants will see any potential problem and call a halt to the task if there is some reason that the task should not be performed.
- *Fraudulently.* When completion of a task requires two or more persons, the risk of fraud against the organization is reduced. Where an employee working on his or her own may follow through on committing fraud or embezzlement against the employer, when two or more persons are involved the chances of them cooperating and carrying it out are reduced.

Examples of separation of duties in the realm of business and information security include:

- *Payments to third parties.* In an accounting department (and on the software application that is used to carry out its transactions), the process of making payments to third parties such as suppliers should be controlled by two or more individuals: one person should make a payment request, another should approve the request, and still another should print the check, and still another should sign the check. If there is any reason that the payment should not be made, there are four people who will have an opportunity to scrutinize the payment and ask questions about it.
- *Add a user account.* The creation of a user's computer account should not be done by a sole individual. Instead, the end-to-end process should consist of an HR (human resources or personnel department) person creating a record of a new worker in the organization; another person (perhaps the worker's manager) should request the creation of the user account for the worker, and a third person should create the user account.
- *Add an administrator account.* The creation of a computer or network account that includes administrative privileges should go through at least one additional layer of approval than an ordinary user account. This additional approval could be the approval of a senior manager or executive.

- *Change a firewall rule.* Any change in a firewall rule (which controls network access between networks) should be controlled by two or more persons. This can not only reduce mistakes but also decrease the chances that a network administrator will act inappropriately.
- *Create an encryption key.* The creation of an encryption key often requires two or more persons. The concept of **split custody** is a special case of separation of duties where two persons each possess one half of a password to an encryption key, which requires these two individuals' involvement in any activities related to the key.
- *Respond to a security alert.* A system that monitors computers and networks for performance and security purposes should send all of its security alerts to at least two individuals. This would reduce the likelihood that the single individual who monitors security alerts would carry out some inappropriate action that would create such an alert. A person working on his or her own could cover up the action or claim that it was a false alarm, but when two or more people receive such alerts, someone intent on performing an inappropriate action might be dissuaded from carrying it out.

An organization probably has many more activities that should be designed so that they require two or more individuals to carry them out.

Job Rotation

The practice of moving individual workers through a range of assignments over time is known as *job rotation*. This practice adds value to the organization by exposing employees to a wider variety of activities, providing additional opportunities for excellence and reducing monotony and boredom.

Job rotation also reduces risk by moving people out of specific tasks. An employee who is performing inappropriate or illegal actions would be less likely to do so if aware that he or she would be rotated out of that task and be caught, especially if these changes are made with little or no notice.

Monitoring of Special Privileges

In most environments, administrative-level privileges give the administrator the ability to perform many powerful functions. In some cases, these functions permit the administrator to directly alter business information instead of altering it through the software application that other personnel must use. Also, because administrators' capabilities are greater than most other users, a mistake can be far more costly, resulting in a partial or complete loss or corruption of data, or more subtle errors that may not be immediately obvious.

For this reason it is especially important for an organization to implement controls to monitor actions carried out by administrators. These controls need to record the activities of the following functions:

- *Network administrator.* Changes to routers, firewalls, intrusion detection systems, spam filters, switches, and VLANs.
- *System administrator.* Changes to OS configuration, performance, and security settings; installation of upgrades, software patches, device drivers; changes to user accounts and authentication rules.
- *Database administrator.* Changes to DBMS configuration and security settings, changes to application data, triggers, and stored procedures.
- *Application administrator.* Changes to application configuration, security settings, roles, user role changes, and application data.

The reasons for monitoring these functions include:

- *Accountability.* Administrators must be held accountable for their actions; they should have nothing to hide nor have any objection to the practice of logging their actions.
- *Audit logging.* Some laws and regulations require that the types of changes made by administrators be logged, to support the management integrity of a supporting environment.
- *Troubleshooting.* If an outage or other problem occurs, administrators can review recent actions, changes, and activities that could provide valuable clues during the troubleshooting effort.

Records Management Controls

Business records are the information that is produced in support of business operations. Business records will consist of many types of information, including:

- Management records
  - Policy documents
  - Memos
- Legal records
  - Contracts
- Personnel records
  - Applications
  - Performance reviews

- Operational records
  - Process and procedures
  - Transactions

Admittedly, I'm just scratching the surface with the above list. Organizations create an enormous amount of information in these categories, and then some. Most of the data that exists on information systems is never printed, so the vastness of this information may not be readily apparent, and the true extent will be known by few.

In the context of information security, several activities are vital for records management, including:

- ***Data classification.*** Establishing sensitivity levels and handling procedures.
- ***Access management.*** Choosing who may access information.
- ***Records retention.*** How long information must be kept.
- ***Backups.*** Making sure information is not lost due to a failure or malfunction.
- ***Data destruction.*** How information must be safely discarded when no longer needed.

Data Classification Organizations will have many different sets of information that will vary widely in their sensitivity. The different levels of sensitivity will call for different procedures for protecting, storing, transmitting, and discarding information.

While an information security department can prescribe safeguards on a case-by-case basis, it is far more effective to establish a schedule of three to five (or more) predefined levels of sensitivity, each with specific procedures for creation, storage, transmitting, destruction, and so forth. A typical schedule would be a chart of columns of sensitivity and rows of procedures.

Chapter 1, "Information Security and Risk Management," explores data classification in more detail.

Access Management Access management refers to the policies, procedures, and controls that determine how information is accessed and by whom. All business information should be housed in a location (physical or logical) that provides a level of access control that is commensurate with its sensitivity (as discussed in the previous section).

An organization that wishes to implement access controls must first develop an access control policy that consists of several components, including:

- *User account provisioning.* Policy needs to specify the person or group that provisions user accounts, as well as the process used to assign and remove computer accounts to users.
- *Privilege management.* Policy needs to define which persons may be given privileged (administrative) access, and how the request and approval process should work.
- *Password management.* Policy needs to define how passwords are stored (encrypted, hopefully!) as well as rules about assignment, complexity, expiration, and so on.
- *Review of access rights.* Policy needs to define how often user access rights will be reviewed and by whom, and the steps followed if exceptions are found.

- *Secure log on.* Policy needs to define whether (and how) a computer logon needs to be secured (hopefully by encryption so that eavesdroppers cannot harvest credentials).

The abovementioned policies then need to be operationalized, meaning that processes and procedures need to also be developed that describe step-by-step how the policies are to be carried out.

The policies and procedures described here need to be applied not only to computers and networks that contain business records, but also in the physical sense, since an organization also has paper records that must be protected. The sensitivity of paper records may also require formal access controls in the form of locked rooms, locking cabinets, safes, or vaults.

Chapter 2, "Access Controls," explores access management in considerably more detail.

Record Retention Organizations collect and maintain business records on paper and electronically. Organizations need to develop policies that specify how long different types of records must be retained. A typical way to implement this is to develop a high-level policy that states that business records must be kept for certain periods of time, according to a schedule that lists different types of records and their minimum and maximum retention periods.

The types of records that may be included in a records retention schedule are:

- Payroll records
- Personnel records
- Financial records
- Legal contracts
- E-mail
- Audit reports
- Audit logs from applications

The above-listed categories are very general; chances are an organization's retention schedule will be more granular. For instance, in a Human Resources department, employee files might be kept for one period of time, while resumes from applicants might be kept for a shorter interval.

Organizations establish records retention policies and schedules in order to manage risks including:

- *Risk of compromise of sensitive information.* The longer an organization keeps credit card transactions, for instance, the greater the impact if that set of data is compromised. Statistically speaking, if a company changes the retention of credit card transactions from eight years to two years, then it has reduced the impact of exposure by 75 percent.
- *Risk of loss of important information.* The flip side of the risk of compromise is the risk associated with situations where needed information is no longer available. Without clear direction on the minimum period of time that certain information needs to be retained, well-meaning employees might discard information too soon, which could deprive the organization of the value that the discarded information would otherwise have provided.
- *E-discovery.* If an organization keeps information longer than is really necessary, then a discovery or e-discovery process can take longer, increasing costs and potentially revealing additional information.

- *Regulation.* Various laws and regulations require that certain business records be kept for minimum—or maximum—periods of time.

Another important reason for establishing a retention policy is to reduce the cost of maintaining data for periods of time that exceed the true need. If a given set of paper records needs to be kept for only five years, for example, then the organization would be unnecessarily consuming resources such as floor space to keep those records for ten years.

The organization needs to ensure that its records retention schedule is in compliance with applicable laws or regulations.

Backups Information that is worth acquiring and maintaining on a system is generally worth retaining. Information processing and storage equipment can be prone to failure, resulting in the irretrievable loss of valuable information. For this reason (and others), it is important to make frequent backup copies of information in the event an accidental loss of any kind occurs. **Backup** is the process of copying important information from a computer or storage system to another device or system for recovery or archival purposes. The causes for information loss include:

- *Equipment malfunctions.* Data storage devices rely on electronic, optical, and/or mechanical technologies that are prone to breakdown, and they just wear out.
- *Software bugs.* Mistakes in coding and configuration can result in accidental changes in, or erasure of, information.
- *Human error.* A wide range of man-caused errors can result in damaged or destroyed information.
- *Disasters.* Fires, floods, hurricanes, and many other types of natural and man-made disasters can damage or destroy computer equipment and stored information.
- *Malicious damage.* A bad actor or malware may delete, encrypt, or otherwise damage information for several reasons, including ransom or disruption of services.

Data Restoration Backup copies of valuable information should be maintained in case any of these events occur. When data is lost or damaged, backup copies of the data can be copied from the backup media back into the system. This is called a **restore** operation.

It is recommended that a computer operations group periodically test the ability to restore data from backup media. This is really the only way to prove that good backups are being performed in the first place.

Protection of Backup Media Backup media that contain copies of business information need to be given the same level of physical and logical protection that the original data receives. This includes physical controls such as locked doors, surveillance cameras, and visitor logs. Accurate records also need to be kept on backup media so that personnel can restore business information: if a particular file or database needs to be recovered, operators must know which volumes contain the specific information. Records will indicate the location of each volume.

There exists a dichotomy regarding the protection and availability of backup media. On one hand, backup media should be kept in locked cabinets in or near the systems containing the original information so that data can be quickly restored when needed. But on the other hand, backup media should be located far away from the original data, to protect it against a disaster.

Offsite Storage of Backup Media

Copying important information to backup media is a necessary safeguard that protects the organization against losses due to equipment failures and human errors. However, since backup media is usually located close to the equipment that stores the original information, that backup media (as well as the original equipment) is at risk of destruction in the event of a disaster. For this reason, it is necessary to locate backup media far away from the original location.

This practice is known as **off-site storage**. Because of the sensitivity of business information on backup media, the backup media needs to be protected, during transit as well as during storage. Factors to consider when searching for a suitable offsite-storage facility include:

- *Distance from business location*. The offsite-storage facility should not be so close to the main business location that both become involved in a regional disaster such as a flood. However, it should not be located so far away that the time required to retrieve media would be unacceptably long.
- *Security of transportation*. The mode and security of transportation between the organization and the offsite-storage facility should be proportional to the value of the data in transit.
- *Security of storage center*. The facility should also have good records management controls so that it handles stored information properly.
- *Resilience against disasters*. The offsite-storage facility should have robust physical controls to ensure the safety of the facility and stored records from events such as earthquakes, fires, and floods.

Another common method of off-site storage is known as **e-vaulting**. Instead of copying data to backup media and transporting the media to another location, e-vaulting means data is copied over a network to a remote data storage facility.

The topic of off-site storage harkens back to the bigger topic of business continuity and disaster recovery planning. This topic is discussed in detail in Chapter 4.

Data Destruction

A **records retention** policy specifies how long business records need to be kept in an organization. When it's time to discard information, a data destruction policy should be in place to instruct employees how to properly discard the information.

The primary purpose of a data destruction policy is to ensure that discarded information is truly destroyed and not salvageable by either employees or outsiders. Information being discarded is of varying levels of sensitivity, according to a data classification or data sensitivity policy. Once information has reached the end of its need, its destruction needs to be carried out in a manner that is proportional to its sensitivity.

Examples of methods available to destroy information include:

- *Degaussing*. Applies to magnetic-based media such as hard drives and backup tapes. **Degaussing** is a process of erasing the data on magnetic media by exerting a strong magnetic field that effectively erases any stored data.

- *Shredding*. Applies to paper records as well as electronic media such as CD/DVD-ROM discs, floppy disks, backup tape, and hard drives.
- *Wiping*. Applies to files on magnetic-based media such as hard drives.

Often, evidence of data destruction needs to be produced to provide a record of the details of the destruction, including who performed it, when it was performed, and what methods or equipment or software erasure tools were used.

Anti-Malware

Every organization needs to assess the risk of exposure to and infection by malicious code (also known as malware) such as viruses, worms, Trojan horses, and spyware, and then respond to the risk by implementing anti-virus and anti-spyware controls. Anti-virus software is used to detect and remove malicious code including computer viruses. Similarly, anti-spyware detects and removes spyware.

Malware has the capacity to disrupt the operation of user workstations as well as servers, which could result in:

- Loss of business information
- Disclosure or compromise of business information
- Corruption of business information
- Disruption of business information processing
- Inability to access business information
- Loss of productivity

Applying Defense-In-Depth Malware Protection The problem of malware is so pervasive that nearly every organization that uses computers uses anti-virus software to protect them against the effects of malware. At the same time, changes in malware technology—namely, the proliferation of so-called **zero-day exploits**—have rendered traditional anti-virus programs all but ineffective in many cases. As a result, many organizations apply a defense in depth malware protection strategy that could include many of the following controls:

- Anti-malware software on user workstations
- Firewall software on user workstations
- Anti-malware software on e-mail servers
- Anti-malware software on file servers
- Anti-malware appliances
- Anti-malware web proxy servers
- Firewalls on network boundaries
- Next-generation firewalls
- Unified threat management (UTM) appliances
- Web application firewalls
- Intrusion prevention systems
- Network-based malware communication detection and prevention systems

- Application whitelisting systems
- Application sandboxing systems
- Spam filter appliances
- Spam filters in e-mail servers

Central Anti-Malware Management Anti-malware systems are usually controlled or managed through central consoles. An enterprise edition of workstation-based anti-virus usually includes console management that permits the following capabilities:

- Centralized configuration control
- Centralized control over workstation anti-malware activities such as immediate scans or updates, or workstation firewall configuration changes
- Centralized reporting of malware infections
- Centralized view of which systems have working anti-malware software

Virtually all of the other anti-malware systems listed above employ console-style management to support the following functions:

- Configuration
- Status of workstation and/or network-based agents or appliances
- Events and event reporting

Many larger organizations also employ a **Security Incident and Event Management (SIEM) system** for improved effectiveness in combating malware and other intrusions. A SIEM system typically acts as a central repository for logs and events sent from workstations, servers, and network devices. A SIEM collects, analyzes, correlates, and reports on suspected intrusions and incidents and can be used to alert appropriate personnel of these suspected events.

Remote Access

Remote access is the broad term that signifies the connectivity to a network or system from a location away from the network or system, usually from a location apart from the organization's premises. Such access usually requires the use of a public network—either a dial-up over voice or ISDN service, or (more often) a connection over the public Internet.

Remote access often provides a remote employee with connectivity to most or all internal network resources as though he were physically connected to the internal network. Because internal networks often employ private (non-routable) addresses, a tunneling technology will be used. Often, because of the sensitivity of business information being accessed, the connection will be encrypted to prevent disclosure of business information to anyone or anything that may be eavesdropping on the connection. The technology commonly used to satisfy these requirements is known as **Virtual Private Network**, or **VPN**. In fact, VPN is in such wide use for remote access that VPN is often the term used to describe remote access.

Risks and Remote Access While the technology behind VPN is fairly straightforward and commonplace, several risks associated with the management and operation of VPNs require sound processes and controls, including:

- *Remote client security*. Because a client workstation that connects to an organization's network via VPN is functionally a node on the enterprise network, several measures need to be taken to ensure that the remote workstation does not increase risk. Some of the measures include:

- *Anti-malware software*. Because the remote client workstation will be connected to the Internet without the protection of other organization anti-virus controls, it is especially important that anti-virus software on remote client workstations be active and functioning properly.
- *Secure configuration*. Remote workstations should have up-to-date security patches and other security configurations, so that they do not pose a threat to the enterprise network when connected to it.
- *Firewall software*. Because the remote client workstation will often be connected to the Internet without the protection of the corporate firewall, remote client workstations should have their own firewall software installed and operating. Firewall software will reduce the risk of network-borne attacks from penetrating and infecting remote client workstations.
- *Split tunneling*. Some VPN software can be configured to permit a "split tunnel," whereby all access to the organization's network passes through the VPN, while all other Internet access bypasses the VPN tunnel. The main disadvantage of a split tunnel is that the remote workstation is not protected by enterprise network safeguards such as firewalls and anti-malware. Organizations that need to rely on enterprise network safeguards to protect remote workstations should forbid split tunnels. Figure 7-1 illustrates split tunneling.
- *Bypassing VPN*. Endpoints should never be allowed to connect to the Internet unprotected. When in a remote location, VPN should be mandatory, so that internal security controls will protect remote devices.

• *Remote client policy*. The risks associated with remote client security compel many organizations to permit only their own managed client workstations to connect via

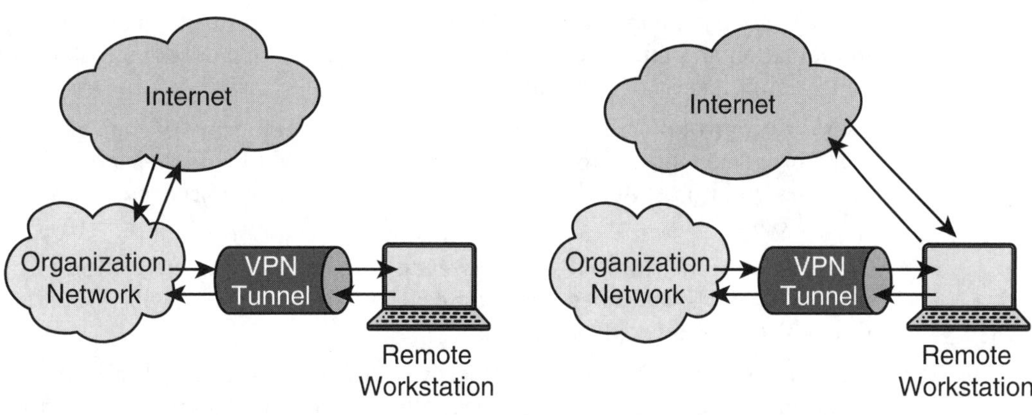

Figure 7-1 Remote access split tunneling

VPN to the organization's network. While this may seem an imposition, the alternatives are even more challenging:

- Managing firewall, anti-virus, and anti-spyware on non-company-owned systems will be exceedingly more difficult and labor intensive.
- Permitting non-company-owned systems to connect to the network via VPN and also store company documents causes the organization to give up a measure of control over its intellectual property and blurs the lines of control and ownership.

These factors often result in organizations permitting only their own systems to connect to the network via VPN, forbidding *non*-company-owned systems from connecting.

Administrative Management and Control

All of the activities that are related to the protection of assets must be controlled by company management in a formal manner that facilitates true management control and oversight.

A model that is gaining wide international acceptance for top-down security management is ISO 27001, which prescribes the establishment of an Information Security Management System (ISMS). The cornerstone to an effective security program is management oversight through the following activities:

- *Define the scope and boundaries of security management.* Management decides what portions of the business are subject to security policy and controls. All exclusions must be documented.
- *Establish and approve a security policy.* This is the top-level document that defines acceptable and unacceptable behaviors and characteristics in the organization.
- *Define the approach for risk assessment.* This is the process and procedures for identifying and documenting risks.
- *Identify, evaluate, and address risks.* When risks are identified, a consistent approach to evaluation and mitigation is needed. In a broad sense, addressing risk could mean mitigation, transfer, or acceptance of risk.
- *Establish control objectives and control activities.* The primary control objectives make broad statements about how security policy will be implemented. Control activities go into greater detail and specify how control objectives are to be carried out.
- *Establish a security training and awareness program.* All personnel need to be aware of risks, controls, and safeguards and develop good judgment, which is all established through security awareness training.
- *Allocate resources.* Once control objectives, risk assessments, and security awareness programs are established, management allocates resources so that these activities can be regularly carried out.
- *Perform internal audits.* Regular verification of proper performance of controls and adherence to policies must be performed.

- *Monitor and review the security program.* Key performance indicators must be established so that management can measure how security is performing in the organization over time. Events and issues are regularly reviewed by senior management.
- *Enact continual improvement.* Whenever deficiencies are identified, improvements must be identified and implemented, in order to gradually improve the risk position of the organization.

Types and Categories of Controls

Earlier in this section, I discussed the need to establish control objectives and control activities. Control activities are often called controls. A **control** is a designated process (or a part of a process) that is key to the objectives of an organization. There are three types of controls and six categories of controls.

The types of controls are:

- Technical
- Physical
- Administrative

The categories of controls are:

- Detective
- Deterrent
- Preventive
- Corrective
- Recovery
- Compensating

The typing and categorization of controls is used to better understand a control framework and how controls support policy and mitigate risk. The types and categories of controls are discussed in detail in Chapter 2, "Access Controls."

Employing Resource Protection

Business resources are used to support daily business operations, enabling the business to produce the goods and/or services that it delivers to its customers. These resources consist of:

- Facilities
- Hardware
- Software
- Documentation
- Records (covered in the earlier section, Records Management Controls)

Resource protection is the set of controls and activities enacted to protect these business resources.

Facilities

Facilities are the buildings and other structures that house the space where people work and the equipment that they use. Besides the structure itself, a facility has several systems that are integral to its operation, including:

- *Water and sewage.*
- *Electricity.* If sensitive equipment such as computers or networks is in use, then electricity needs to be conditioned and protected against spikes, brownouts, and complete failures with power conditioners, uninterruptible power supplies (UPSs), and electric generators.
- *Fire alarms and suppression.* This will consist of smoke, heat, and fire detectors, pull stations, fire extinguishers, sprinkler systems, alarms, and possibly communications to a fire department.
- *Environmental controls.* This includes heating, ventilation, and air conditioning (HVAC).
- *Communications.* Phone and data connections that support voice and data communications needs.
- *Security controls.* This will include locking doors and may also include fencing, gates, keycard systems, and video surveillance.

Each of these requires some schedule of maintenance and inspection—some by outside authorities. The management and protection of facilities is discussed in greater detail in Chapter 8, "Physical and Environmental Security."

Hardware

Hardware is the inclusive term to signify many types of computing and ancillary equipment that support information processing and storage. The types of hardware that protect—and also require protection—include:

- *Workstations.* Known also as end user workstations, PCs, or personal computers, workstations are located in offices and other workspaces. In many settings they must be protected from theft, restrained usually by locking cables or brackets.
- *Mobile devices.* These consist of smartphones, tablets, and other highly portable computers. Mobile devices are often the property of employees and not owned by the organization.
- *Servers.* These are the beefier computers that store and process information for the organization. They are usually located in special higher-security rooms equipped with special environmental controls to control heat and humidity. Servers need to be protected from theft but more importantly from unauthorized access, and this is usually accomplished through locking doors, keycard controls, and video surveillance.
- *Consoles.* Usually found in server rooms, consoles resemble workstations (and sometimes they *are* workstations). Like servers, they need to be protected from unauthorized access as well as theft.
- *Network devices.* These are the **routers, hubs, switches,** VPN servers, security appliances, intrusion detection systems, and other devices that permit and control the

flow of information within the organization, and between the organization and entities in the outside world. Like servers, they need to be protected from unauthorized access and are usually located in server rooms that have specially designed environmental and security controls. Network devices also protect the organization's information and systems in a variety of ways:

- *Firewalls* protect the network from unwanted traffic to and from the Internet and from other external organizations. Firewalls are configured with "rules" that specify exactly what types of traffic are permitted to enter (and leave) the organization's network, as well as which devices and systems the traffic is permitted to travel to and from.
- ***Routers*** connect different networks together and can also control network traffic, similar to a firewall's traffic-limiting capability.
- ***Switches*** transmit network traffic among different devices (which includes workstations, printers, and servers) in a network, as well as to and from routers in the case of traffic to and from other networks.
- *VPN* servers provide safe remote access for off-site employees who need to access resources within the network. VPN servers authenticate users and then encrypt all traffic to prevent any eavesdroppers from viewing company secrets.
- *Security appliances* perform a variety of tasks including filtering web site content (protecting employees from malware and also blocking access to non-business-related sites) and spam.

- *Wireless networks*. These let an employee roam around the office with a laptop and stay connected to network resources without having to find a cable to plug into. Wireless networks use radio waves, which can leak outside of the building, permitting people outside the physical perimeter to also eavesdrop on the company's network. Wireless networks can be protected with encryption using **WEP (Wired Equivalent Privacy)** or **WPA (WiFi Protected Access)**, which both employ secret keys and can also require a user to provide a userid and password. The WEP encryption protocol is no longer considered secure, and organizations are urged to use WPA2 instead.
- *Printers and copiers*. Printers are often connected directly to the corporate network, which allows employees to print to most any printer from anyplace. Because some printed information is sensitive, users are urged to pick up their printouts as soon as possible. Multifunction copiers are connected to the network, permitting users to print multiple copies of reports and also perform tasks like scanning, collating, and stapling.
- *Cabling*. Network cabling carries the communications throughout the organization's network and also between the organization and outside entities such as partners and suppliers and the global Internet. Physical and logical cabling diagrams should be maintained. Cabling needs to be protected from physical access to prevent tampering, damage, and eavesdropping through "vampire taps" and other techniques that can be used to try to listen to network communications. Vampire taps are discussed in Chapter 10, "Telecommunications and Network Security."

Software

Every organization that uses computers has **software** that it has acquired, and possibly software that it has developed internally. The Windows and UNIX operating systems are software, as are relational databases (like Oracle or Microsoft SQL Server), web servers (Apache, Web Logic, or Microsoft IIS), and business applications.

An organization needs to control and manage its software in many respects, including:

- *Inventory*. Organizations need to know where its software assets are installed and used. For complex systems, organizations need to track both the running instances of software as well as the components required to install and manage software.
- *Licensing*. Organizations need to track how many copies of software they have installed and are using; many software providers collect license fees based upon the number of computers that are running the software and also (sometimes) on the size of the computers (number of CPUs or amount of memory) that licensed software is running on.
- *Access control*. In order to remain in compliance with any licensing agreements (and to protect the intellectual property aspect of software from disclosure to unauthorized parties), access to software must be controlled. Often this is accomplished by using the same controls that are used to control access to data.
- *Source code*. For the software that the organization develops and maintains on its own, source code needs to be protected from unauthorized disclosure. There are a number of reasons for this, including:
  - *Intellectual property*. Source code may be an organization's intellectual property that it wishes to keep closely guarded.
  - *Security*. Sometimes the security of a program is compromised if someone is able to read its source code and discover how the software is used to protect information.
- *Source code control*. As part of its **software development life cycle (SDLC)**, an organization needs to keep strict controls over the software that it develops, integrates, and maintains. Source code control is used to control which developers are able to access what parts of software, and also keep track of changes and versions of software. The software development life cycle is discussed in detail in Chapter 3, "Software Development Security."
- *Vulnerability*. As part of situational awareness, organizations need to watch lists of known vulnerable software and know their exposure, based on what they have running.

Documentation

Processes, procedures, instructions, diagrams, charts, and tables are all **documentation** that describes how an organization is organized, how it was built, and how it is operated and maintained. Documentation is an organization's "owner's manual" and blueprints that its employees refer to in order to better understand how to do their tasks properly.

An organization's documentation must be properly managed in order to preserve the integrity of each document as well as "look-and-feel" consistency among documents that makes them more easily understood. Each document should have a "home" where its official "source" is kept. Ideally it will reside on a server that is regularly backed up, to preserve documents even when a disaster occurs.

Documentation must also be protected from disclosure to unauthorized parties. While most documentation needs to be protected from disclosure to outside parties, some documentation is sensitive enough that access to it must be restricted on a need-to-know basis.

Documentation is just one aspect of an organization's records. A more detailed discussion on the management of records is found earlier in this chapter in the Records Management Controls section.

Incident Management

Strictly speaking, an incident is an unexpected event that results in an interruption of normal operations. In ITIL (IT Infrastructure Library) terms, an incident is *an event which is not part of the standard operation of a service and which causes, or may cause, an interruption to, or a reduction in, the quality of that service.*

In the context of security, a **security incident** is an event in which some aspect of an organization's security policy has been violated. But another way to view a security incident is to describe it as an unauthorized access to, or accidental exposure of, a system or information, or an event that prevents legitimate access to a system or information.

A security incident nearly always has a human root cause. This is true if the security incident is the result of malware (which is written by humans) or a targeted break-in by an intruder. Regardless, the response to a security incident should be organized and systematic and generally consists of the following steps:

- Detection
- Incident declaration
- Triage
- Investigation
- Analysis
- Containment
- Recovery
- Debriefing

These steps should be documented in the form of written procedures, which should be reviewed from time to time to ensure their continued accuracy and relevance. Personnel who will be expected to respond in the event of a security incident should be trained, in order to better prepare them for response and remediation.

Security incident response is discussed in greater detail in Chapter 6, "Legal, Regulations, Investigations, and Compliance."

High-Availability Architectures

Information systems and applications are vital to organizations and their customers, so much so that in many cases extra steps need to be taken to ensure their continuous availability.

Well-organized computer operations departments can develop quite a good record of application uptime, but in order to keep systems running smoothly, periodic maintenance is required for the installation of patches, software updates, hardware upgrades, and so on. And unexpected failures do sometimes occur, seemingly at the most inopportune times. These predictable and unpredictable occurrences often drive an organization to develop a more resilient architecture than is achievable with standalone servers and other equipment. Options available include:

- Fault tolerance
- Clusters
- Failover
- Replication
- Virtualization

These aspects can give an application architecture the **resilience** it needs to achieve the high availability that the organization and its customers require. Usually, a resilient architecture seeks to avoid a **single point of failure**, a characteristic of an environment where a single component failure will cause an entire system or application to fail. Often, a component in a system that has no backup or alternative path is considered a single point of failure—even if it is unlikely that the component will actually fail. Figure 1-2 in Chapter 1, "Information Security and Risk Management," illustrates the concept of a single point of failure.

Fault Tolerance

Fault tolerance refers to the design of a device whereby its failure-prone components are duplicated, so that the failure of one component will not result in the failure of the entire device. Some examples of fault-tolerant devices include:

- *Multiple power supplies.* A server or device that has two or more removable power supplies may be considered fault tolerant, especially if a faulty power supply will not cause failure of the device and the faulty power supply can be replaced while the system continues to operate.
- *Multiple network interfaces.* Servers and network devices may have multiple network interfaces in the event that one of them fails. While the system or device may not permit the replacement of the network interface while the system is operating, it still could be considered fault tolerant if the system can continue operating with one less network interface until the next maintenance period.
- *Multiple processor units.* Some servers and network devices are designed to house multiple processor units, and may even permit a "hot replacement" of a faulty unit while the system continues to operate.
- ***RAID (Redundant Array of Independent Disks,** originally referred to as Redundant Array of Inexpensive Disks).* Servers and disk storage systems often use RAID-5, RAID-6, or RAID-10 architectures, which are the most common types of multiple-disk architecture in a storage system or server. RAID permits a storage system to continue operating—without data loss or interruption—in the event that a single disk drive in the system fails. RAID systems further usually permit the "hot replacement" of a faulty drive while the system continues to operate.

Fault tolerance can also refer to an architecture that utilizes redundant components that permit the whole system to continue operating should one of the systems or devices in the system fail. Figure 1-2 in Chapter 1, "Information Security and Risk Management," shows an architecture where most of its components have counterparts that permit the entire system to keep functioning even if one of the components fails.

Clusters

A cluster refers to a group of two or more servers that operate functionally as a single logical server and will continue operating in the event that one of the servers fails.

Clusters generally operate in one of two modes: active-active or active-passive. In **active-active** mode, both servers (or all three, four, or more if the cluster is that large) actively operate and service incoming requests. In **active-passive** mode, one (or more) servers actively services requests, and one (or more) server(s) remains in a standby state but is ready at a moment's notice to switch to active mode should one of the active servers in the cluster fail. In active-passive mode, servers change state automatically through a process called a failover.

Systems in a cluster need not be located near each other. Instead, they can be next to each other or halfway around the world from each other in what is called a **geographical cluster** or *geo-cluster*.

Failover

A **failover** is an event in a server cluster running in active-passive mode, where an active server has failed and a passive server is switching to active mode. This permits requests for service to be continuously serviced, with little or no interruption from the point of view of the systems requesting service.

A failover can be likened to a highway toll plaza, where one tollbooth will close but another one will immediately open, which permits the continuous servicing of cars paying tolls.

Replication

Replication is an operation concerning the data on a storage system, where additions and changes to the data are transmitted to a counterpart storage system where the same additions and changes take place. It is said that changes to the data on one storage system are *replicated* to a counterpart storage system.

Replication often takes place under the control of the operating system, database management system, or the hardware storage system. This means that an application will require little or no changes in order to establish replication, making replication far easier to implement.

Replication is usually set up in conjunction with clustering. Clustering will manage the states of each of its member servers, controlling whether each is in active or passive mode. Alongside, replication will make sure that the most up-to-date data is available across all storage systems, so that any server that becomes an active server in a cluster will have access to current data. This is illustrated in Figure 7-2. Server 1 is the active server in a cluster, and its data is replicated from its Storage System 1 to its counterpart, Storage System 2. If a failure occurs anywhere in Server 1 or Storage System 1, then Server 2 can become the new active server (through a failover), and Server 2 will have up-to-date data because of the replication that was taking place from Storage System 1 to Storage System 2.

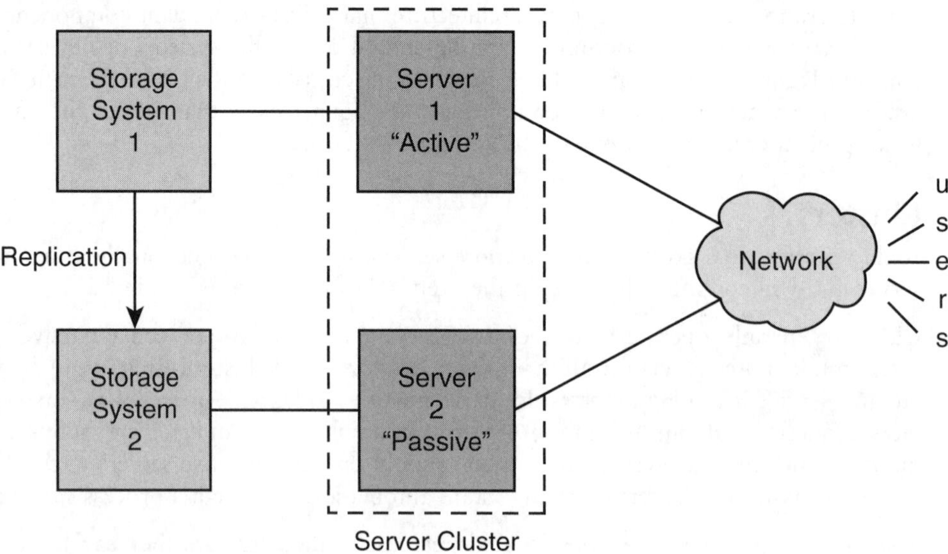

Figure 7-2 Clustering and replication working together to form a highly available architecture

High-availability architectures are usually implemented in conjunction with, and as a result of, a risk analysis and/or business impact assessment that is performed in a business continuity effort.

Virtualization

Virtualization software has begun to replace physical server clusters and failover servers. Using servers connected to a storage area network or other shared storage device, network administrators can create multiple servers on a single hardware platform. These servers can migrate from one physical server to another. This improves the utilization of each server's resources and reduces the total server footprint in the data center. This practice reduces costs by deploying fewer physical boxes. The ability to move virtual servers around provides new strategies for load-balancing, duplication, and failover recovery accompanied by an increase in network complexity.

Business Continuity Management

A **business continuity plan** is the result of a management activity where analysis is performed to better understand the risks associated with potential disaster scenarios and the steps that can be taken to reduce the impact of a disaster should one occur. A common outcome of a business continuity project is the implementation of a high-resilience architecture that will permit critical business functions to continue operating even when a disaster strikes. Highly resilient architectures are discussed in the previous section, High-Availability Architectures, in this chapter.

Business continuity planning and disaster recovery planning are discussed in much detail in Chapter 4, "Business Continuity and Disaster Recovery Planning."

Vulnerability Management

The process of identifying vulnerabilities in a system and then acting to mitigate those vulnerabilities is known as **vulnerability management.**

Vulnerabilities result when a software program contains a weakness that, if exploited, could lead to the malfunction of the system or, worse yet, unauthorized disclosure of information contained in the system.

Vulnerabilities can be discovered in one of two basic ways: through passive means or through active means. Passive means includes receiving alerts of vulnerabilities from sources such as the components manufacturer or independent sources such as US-CERT or Secunia. Active means includes performing vulnerability scanning and penetration tests.

Vulnerability Scanning

Vulnerability scanning is a technique used to identify security defects and vulnerabilities in network devices, systems, and/or applications. One or more automated tools are used to scan networks, systems, or applications with the objective of identifying security defects and vulnerabilities. These tools list the vulnerabilities found, and some tools may even provide information on techniques available for remediation of these defects.

Application Scanning

Application scanning is the process of performing security tests on an application (usually, but not always, a web-based application) in order to find vulnerabilities in the application code itself. Application scanning is like penetration testing in that a tool or technique is used to discover vulnerabilities in a system. But where application scanning and penetration testing differ is the target of the testing: penetration testing examines the operating system and other major components such as database server or web server, whereas application scanning concentrates its testing only on an application.

The tools used to perform penetration scanning and application scanning are usually different. While a single tool could perform both kinds of tests, generally these tools are written to do just one type of testing and not the other. The audience is usually different, too. The results of penetration tests will be of interest to system administrators who will make configuration changes or apply operating system security patches, whereas the results of application scans will be of interest to application developers who will make changes in the source code of the target application.

Application scanning tools most often are used to assess the security of web-based applications, to ensure that the application's developers have written the application to be robust enough to avoid any of the common pitfalls, including:

- Cross-site scripting
- Cross-site request forgery
- SQL injection
- Script injection
- Parameter tampering
- Buffer overflow

- Boundary checking
- Defective or unsecure session management
- Defective or unsecure logon
- Malicious file execution

Penetration Testing

Penetration testing is a technique used that mimics the actions of an attacker who examines a system, network, or application for exploitable defects. Penetration testing typically starts with vulnerability or application scanning, and is followed by manual testing with a variety of tools in search of vulnerabilities. A skilled "pen tester" could spend dozens or even hundreds of hours performing these manual tests in search of a difficult-to-find vulnerability that could lead to the discovery of a serious defect in a target system.

Source Code Reviews and Scanning

Source code reviews and **source code scanning** are two techniques used to identify defects in source code that could lead to exploitable vulnerabilities.

In a source code review, trained and qualified developers examine changes to application source code to ensure that there are no defects present among the changes. Source code reviews are oftentimes manual efforts and are typically limited to situations where source code for certain parts of applications are changed, such as authentication, access control, session management, and cryptography.

Source code scanning utilizes purpose-built tools used to scan application source code to identify security and quality defects. In some instances, source code scanning can be instantiated automatically in conjunction with source code check-in or periodic software builds.

Source code reviews and source code scans are important parts of the software development life cycle, which is discussed in detail in Chapter 3, "Software Development Security."

Threat Modeling

Threat modeling is the process of performing analysis on a system's design in order to discover potential threats against the system. Another way to think about threat modeling is an analysis of potential design flaws in a system that could be exploited by an adversary.

Threat modeling is an important activity in both the initial design as well as throughout the maintenance of software programs. This is a part of the software development life cycle, which is discussed in detail in Chapter 3, "Software Development Security."

Patch Management

Patch management is a process—usually assisted with one or more tools—to manage the installation of patches on target systems. Generally, a patch management tool will have the ability to scan systems (for instance, the servers or end user workstations) to determine the existence of operating system and software patches. Generally, the same tool has the ability to also remotely install selected patches on target systems.

Patch management tools are generally considered to be time-savers by making a labor-intensive task (installing patches on hundreds or thousands of systems) far more automated.

However, it is considered unwise to simply "spray and pray" by installing all possible patches on all systems, because the indiscriminate installation of patches can introduce subtle performance or stability problems, not to mention consuming resources (the "undo" information for each patch) and incurring more downtime. Rather, it is recommended that skilled analysts perform a risk analysis on each applicable patch and make an informed, risk-based decision on whether each available patch should be installed (and, if so, after how much testing). Many respected voices in the security industry (including the author of this book) urge organizations to *not* install patches by default but instead install each patch only as specifically needed.

Change Management

Change management is the name of a management process whereby each proposed change in an environment is formally planned and reviewed by peers and stakeholders prior to the change being made.

The object of change management is the improvement in stability and the reduction of unscheduled downtime in an environment. When stakeholders are given the time to review a proposed change, they have an opportunity to identify issues that could adversely impact the environment. For instance, a system administrator wishes to make changes to certain security settings on database servers. A database administrator, reviews the proposed change, identifies a problem that could result in a malfunction in the database. As a result, the system administrator takes another approach and proposes an alternative change that will not affect the database.

The steps in a simple change management process are:

1. *Prepare the change.* The proposed change should include: a) the procedure for making the change; b) the time the change will be made; c) how the change will be verified; d) how the change will be backed out if it fails; e) whether there will be downtime associated with the change; and f) test plans and results.
2. *Circulate and review the change.* The proposed change is circulated to a set of stakeholders and subject matter experts who will review the change.
3. *Discuss and agree to the change.* All of the stakeholders, usually in a formal meeting, will meet to discuss the proposed change. Concerned parties can ask questions of the person proposing the change. The team can agree to permit the change to be made or request that the change be altered and re-presented at a later time.
4. *Perform the change.* Those personnel who are designated to make the change do so according to the procedure in the proposed change. After verifying that the change is complete and correct, they can close the change. If the change encountered any problems, it can be reattempted or backed out.

The primary principle of change management is: only approved changes are made to an environment. No unapproved changes are made. This will help the organization recognize unapproved changes, which could be caused by mistakes, policy violations, or intruders.

In the event of an emergency, the organization can establish a procedure for making emergency changes (usually through an incident management process) and then review the emergency change at the next regular change management meeting.

Configuration Management

Configuration management is the process of recording configuration changes that are made in an environment. In all but the simplest environments, configuration management is enabled through the use of a configuration management tool that is used to record, manage, and capture changes automatically and store them in a **configuration management database (CMDB)**. Without such a tool, it can be exceedingly difficult to keep the configurations of supposedly identical systems in sync.

Configuration management is often used in conjunction with change management as the means of implementing and recording approved changes to systems. Configuration management tools that are able to detect changes in a system can also be used to detect changes that were not authorized through the change management process.

Operations Attacks and Countermeasures

An attack on security operations is primarily an attack on processes and controls. The targets of attacks may be personnel, records, or information systems. This section discusses some of these attacks and the countermeasures that reduce their probability of occurrence or their impact.

Social Engineering

Social engineering is a person-to-person attack where an individual is attempting to cause a staff member to do something improper, such as provide sensitive information to an untrusted third party or allow a stranger to enter a secure facility.

The primary countermeasure to social engineering is education and training, so that personnel are better prepared to recognize a social engineering attack and respond appropriately to it.

Social engineering is discussed in detail in Chapter 2, "Access Controls."

Sabotage

An insider or outsider may attack an organization's security operations by attempting to alter or destroy an information system that supports operations. Such an attack, for instance, may be an attempt to destroy records that provide evidence of unauthorized action, or the deliberate destruction of backup tapes. "Accidental errors" on the part of disgruntled employees can fall into this category as well.

Effective countermeasures include controls to protect systems and records from unauthorized access and alteration. These controls will typically consist of access controls (discussed in Chapter 2, "Access Controls."), cryptography (discussed in Chapter 5, "Cryptography"), and physical controls (discussed in Chapter 8, "Physical and Environmental Security").

Theft and Disappearance

Stealing equipment and media is a certain and effective attack on operations. Employees carry laptops, mobile devices, and portable media such as thumb drives everywhere, and thousands are lost and stolen every month in the United States alone. Equipment is stolen from work locations with alarming regularity. There have even been some equipment heists from commercial data centers.

Several countermeasures are needed to curb theft and disappearance, including:

- Awareness training and safeguards such as cable locks for laptop users
- Video surveillance
- Restricted access to areas containing valuable equipment and media

These and other physical controls are discussed in more detail in Chapter 8, "Physical and Environmental Security."

Extortion

An individual might threaten to cause harm to information or information systems and coerce an organization to make payments of money or services in order to avoid the threatened harm. Recent examples in the context of information technology include:

- Perpetrator threatens to implant victim's computer with porn and other illegal content unless the victim makes a payment.
- Perpetrator encrypts victim's data files and will decrypt it for a fee.
- Perpetrator threatens to launch a Distributed Denial of Service (DDoS) attack unless victim organization makes a payment. Similarly, perpetrator launches the attack and requires payments in order to stop the attack.

Extortion countermeasures consist of controls that would thwart or repel the threatened attacks and actions.

Bypass

An individual may attempt to **bypass** security operations controls in order to be able to access or alter information, or to access a facility without authorization. This is known as a **bypass attack**.

Effective countermeasures consist of:

- Tests of operations controls to ensure that they are effective and that they are operating properly
- Enact a *defense in depth* control environment, so that the failure of one control is compensated by the existence of one or more other controls

Bypass attacks are discussed in more detail in Chapter 2, "Access Controls."

Denial of Service

A denial-of service (DoS) attack is any type of attack that is designed to incapacitate its target, either through a sheer volume of stimulus (e.g., a flood of network traffic) or a specially crafted attack that causes the target's malfunction.

Generally, a denial-of-service attack is a technical attack that is launched over a network, but a denial-of-service attack can also be an attack on people. Examples include a high volume of incoming phone calls, or a false fire alarm that results in building evacuation.

For technical systems, countermeasures against a denial-of-service attack include security patches to eliminate vulnerabilities, and increased capacity or other means for absorbing or shunting a network flooding attack. For personnel, countermeasures should include emergency procedures and training, and controls to ensure the continued protection of critical assets even during emergencies.

Chapter Summary

- The concept of *need-to-know* states that individual personnel should have access to only the information that they require in order to perform their stated duties.
- The concept of *least privilege* states that users should have the fewest or lowest numbers of privileges required to accomplish their duties.
- The concept of *separation of duties* states that a high-value or high-risk task should be designed to require two or more individuals to complete them.
- The concept of *job rotation* moves individual workers through a range of assignments over time.
- The actions of individuals with special privileges should be monitored to detect potential problems as well as to deter individual wrongdoing.
- Controls must be established that will manage the creation and use of business records.
- *Data classification* is the practice of assigning security levels and handling procedures to documents and databases.
- *Access management* is used to control who and what can access specific business records.
- *Records retention* governs the minimum and maximum periods of time that specific business records must be retained.
- *Backups* ensure the survival of business records even if malfunctions, errors, or disasters destroy original records.
- Backup media must itself be protected, to guard against unauthorized disclosure of records and to protect it from damage or loss.
- Data *destruction* is the process of securely discarding data when it is no longer needed.
- Malware has the capacity to disrupt the operation of user workstations as well as servers, which could result in loss or compromise of business information and the inability to access or process business information.
- *Anti-virus, anti-spyware*, and other anti-malware controls such as firewalls, intrusion prevention systems, and application whitelisting are used to prevent malware from entering the organization and compromising systems or data. Often a *defense in depth* strategy is used to ensure that malware cannot complete its objective.

- *Remote access* equipment enables workers not on physical premises to access network-based resources such as file servers, applications, and internal web sites. Technology such as *VPN (virtual private networks)* encrypts remote access communications to prevent business information from compromise or disclosure.
- The activities that are related to the protection of assets must be controlled by company management, in a formal, top-down manner that facilitates true management control and oversight.
- Management should establish security policies, control objectives, a risk assessment methodology, a security awareness program, direct internal audits, and strive for continuous improvement.
- The *types of controls* are technical, physical, and administrative.
- The *categories of controls* are detective, deterrent, preventive, corrective, recovery, and compensating.
- *Resource protection* ensures that the buildings, equipment, and systems used to operate the business are protected from harm, damage, or loss.
- *Facilities* protective measures include electric power conditioning, storage, and generation equipment to ensure the continuous supply of clean power; fire detection and prevention equipment; environmental controls to control temperature and humidity, and security controls to restrict access to sensitive areas.

- Hardware assets that need protection include workstations, mobile devices, servers, consoles, network devices, wireless networks, printers and copiers, and communications cabling.
- Organizations must protect their software to ensure compliance with license agreements and to control access to source code.
- Access to documentation must be restricted, and documentation needs to be protected from damage or loss.
- A *security incident* is an event in which some aspect of an organization's security policy has been violated.
- A *security incident response plan* is a process or procedure that is followed when a security incident occurs. The plan will usually include these steps: incident declaration, triage, investigation, analysis, containment, recovery, and debriefing.
- A *high-availability architecture* is a system or application architecture that includes one or more of the following characteristics: fault tolerance, clusters, failover, or replication.
- *Fault-tolerant* devices typically are equipped with redundant components that can be changed while the device continues operating.
- A *cluster* is a group of servers that logically functions as a single server, which will continue operating even if one of the servers in the cluster fails or is shut down for maintenance or repairs.
- A *failover* is an event that occurs in a cluster where the role of an *active* server is transitioned to another server in the cluster.
- *Virtualization* enables a more flexible application of high-availability architectures without the need to purchase additional hardware.

- *Business continuity planning* is an activity that is concerned with the continuation of critical business operations during and after a disaster.
- *Vulnerability management* is a collection of activities all concerned with the identification and remediation of vulnerabilities in an environment.
- *Penetration testing* is a vulnerability management activity employing scanning tools and manual techniques to identify exploitable defects in a target system.
- *Security scanning* is a vulnerability management activity employing scanning tools to identify vulnerabilities in a target system.
- *Patch management* is a vulnerability management activity that is used to identify important software patches and the systems and devices where they should be installed.
- *Change management* is an operations process where all changes in an environment are analyzed in a peer-review process prior to implementation.
- *Configuration management* is an operations process where all changes to systems and components are recorded or controlled by a configuration management tool and recorded in a configuration management database (CMDB).

Key Terms

Access management The policies, procedures, and controls that determine how information is accessed and by whom.

Active-active An operating mode in a cluster where all of the servers in the cluster actively operate and process incoming requests.

Active-passive An operating mode in a cluster where one or more servers actively operate and process incoming requests and one or more servers remain in a standby mode.

Application scanning The task of identifying security vulnerabilities in a software application.

Backup The process of copying important information from a computer or storage system to another device for recovery or archival purposes.

Business continuity plan A contingency plan that governs the business response to a disaster in order to keep critical business functions operating.

Bypass attack An attack that attempts to bypass security controls to access or alter information.

Change management The management process where proposed changes in an environment are formally planned and reviewed prior to implementing them.

Configuration management database (CMDB) A database containing the configuration settings of a system or environment.

Data classification The process of assigning sensitivity levels to documents and data files in order to assure their safekeeping and proper handling.

Data destruction The process of discarding information that is no longer needed, in a manner that will render it irretrievable.

Degaussing The process of bulk-erasing magnetic-based storage media by imposing a strong magnetic field onto the media.

Documentation Processes, procedures, and even records, whether in paper or electronic form.

E-vaulting A method of data backup where data is transmitted over a network to a remote data storage facility. See also *backup*.

Facilities The buildings and other structures that house the space where people work and the equipment that they use.

Fault tolerance The design of a device or system where failure-prone components are duplicated, so that the failure of one component will not result in the failure of the entire device or system.

Geographical cluster A cluster whose members are dispersed over a wide geographic area.

Hardware Computers and ancillary equipment that support information processing and storage.

Hub A device used to connect multiple computers together to form a network. A hub sends all packets on the network to all nodes. See also *switch*.

Need-to-know The access control concept where individual personnel should have access to only the information that they require in order to perform their stated duties.

Off-site storage The storage of storage media or paper documents at an off-site storage facility, to protect against irrecoverable loss of information in the event of a disaster.

Patch management The process of managing the installation of patches on target systems.

Penetration testing An activity that consists of the use of vulnerability scanning tools and manual testing techniques to discover exploitable vulnerabilities on a target system.

Records retention The determination of the minimum and/or maximum period of time that specific business records must be retained.

Redundant Array of Independent Disks (RAID) A disk storage technology that allows for greater reliability and performance in a disk-based storage system.

Remote access Any means used to connect to a target network from a remote location.

Resilience A design characteristic of a system that assures its availability despite unplanned failures.

Resource protection Controls and procedures enacted to protect business resources including facilities, hardware, software, documentation, and records.

Restore The process of copying data from backup media to a system.

Router A network device that connects two or more networks together logically and can also control the flow of traffic between networks according to a set of rules known as an access control list (ACL).

Security Incident and Event Management (SIEM) System A system used to collect, correlate, and report on security incidents and events across a population of workstations, servers, and networks.

Separation of duties The work practice where high risk tasks are structured to be carried out by two or more persons.

Shredding The process of cutting paper, magnetic, or optical media into small pieces for the purpose of secure destruction.

Software Computer instructions that fulfill a stated purpose.

Source code scan The use of an automated tool to examine program source code to identify software defects and security vulnerabilities.

Source code review A review of a program's source code in order to ensure that recent changes were applied correctly and that the program contains no unwanted code.

Split custody A control safeguard in which an important secret (such as a password) is broken into two or more parts, each of which is kept by different individuals.

Switch A device used to connect multiple computers to form a network. A switch sends packets only to destination nodes. See also *hub*.

Threat modeling. See *threat risk modeling*.

Threat risk modeling A process where threats in an environment are identified and ranked, and mitigating controls introduced to counter the identified threats. Also known as *threat modeling*.

Virtualization The use of specialized software to facilitate the existence of two or more logically separate running operating systems (virtual machines) on a single physical system.

Vulnerability management The process of identifying vulnerabilities in a system and then acting to mitigate those vulnerabilities.

WiFi Protected Access (WPA) A wireless network encryption protocol.

Wiping The process of destroying data stored on magnetic media by overwriting the media several times.

Zero-day exploit Malware that evades detection by anti-malware systems through a variety of techniques, including polymorphism.

Review Questions

1. The concept of "need-to-know" states:
   a. Paths to data containing sensitive information should not be published
   b. Documents should be marked as "confidential" and distribution kept to a minimum
   c. Individual personnel should have access to only the information they require to perform their jobs
   d. Documents should be marked as "restricted" and distribution kept to a minimum
2. The process of periodically changing workers' assigned tasks is known as:
   a. Job rotation
   b. Cross-training
   c. Privilege rotation
   d. Separation of duties
3. The purpose of data classification is:
   a. To notify users that documents are subject to special handling procedures
   b. To notify users that they may be required to ask permission of a document's owner before sending it to another person
   c. To notify users that documents may be subject to restrictions when sending them via e-mail
   d. All of the above

4. Data retention standards specify:
   a. The minimum and maximum periods of time that specific types of data should be retained
   b. Procedures for retention of backup media
   c. Procedures for destruction of backup media
   d. Standards for archiving data that resides in databases

5. Data backups are performed:
   a. To protect critical data in the event of a disaster
   b. To protect critical data in the event of a hardware failure
   c. To protect critical data in the event of a disaster, hardware failure, or data corruption
   d. To protect critical data in the event of data corruption

6. Data destruction procedures:
   a. Ensure that expired backup media are destroyed
   b. Ensure that discarded paper documents are shredded
   c. Ensure complete and irrecoverable destruction of data
   d. Act as a safeguard in the event a user forgets to delete data

7. An organization is considering adding anti-virus software to its email- servers and file servers. This reflects:
   a. A defense in depth strategy
   b. The fact that anti-virus on workstations is unreliable
   c. The need to protect systems that lack anti-virus software
   d. The need to protect the organization from malicious code contained in spam

8. A device whose design employs duplication of failure-prone components so as to ensure the greatest possible availability is known as:
   a. Optimized
   b. Redundant
   c. Highly available
   d. Fault tolerant

9. A collection of four servers that act in coordination to give the appearance of a single logical server is known as a:
   a. Grid
   b. Virtual
   c. Fault tolerant
   d. Cluster

10. A systems engineer is managing a server cluster. A memory fault has occurred in one of the active servers; the cluster software has caused another server in the cluster to become active. The system engineer has witnessed a:
    a. Pairing
    b. Failover
    c. Load balance
    d. Synchronization
11. The recovery point objective (RPO) for a critical application is set to two hours for a 4TB database; the recovery time objective (RTO) is set to twenty-four hours. An IT architect needs to design a solution where a server in a remote data center can assume production duties within the RPO and RTO specifications. Which method for data transfer to the alternate data center should the IT architect use?
    a. Replication to a warm server
    b. Replication to a cold server
    c. Recovery from backup tape
    d. Recovery from an electronic vault
12. A security manager needs to find a professional services firm to identify exploitable vulnerabilities in a running web application. The security manager should find a professional services firm that can perform:
    a. Code reviews
    b. Penetration testing
    c. Threat modeling
    d. Ethical hacking
13. A security engineer is testing a web application for vulnerabilities and has inserted the following characters into a form field: "script OR name LIKE %user%;." The security engineer is performing:
    a. Buffer overflow
    b. Cross-site scripting
    c. SQL injection
    d. Script injection
14. The purpose of a change management process is to:
    a. Test the changes made to a system
    b. Record the changes made to a system
    c. Plan and review the changes made to a system
    d. Reduce unplanned downtime

15. The best approach for applying security patches is to:
    a. Apply only the security patches that are applicable
    b. Apply all available security patches as soon as possible
    c. Apply no security patches
    d. Apply all available security patches one at a time

Hands-On Projects

Project 7-1: Security Evaluation for Remote Access

In this project you will compare the security features of VPN remote access products.

Research and compare features from "thick client" VPN software from companies like Cisco and Juniper. Also research the "clientless" SSL VPN clients that are available.

What products can you find that are suitable for smaller organizations? You may wish to examine "all in one" network-based products that combine a router, firewall, and VPN server in a single appliance.

Some of the features to consider are:

- Thick client versus SSL clientless
- Authentication types supported (userid/password, token, smart card)
- Encryption options (IPsec, SSL, etc.)

Project 7-2: Centrally Managed Anti-Virus

In this project you will research workstation- and server-based anti-virus software that can be managed from a central management console.

Collect information from four or more companies that have enterprise-class anti-virus software for servers and workstations. Identify the features that these products have in common, and also identify any unique features.

Express your opinion on the following:

- What is the business value of the feature(s) that are in common among the different products?
- What is the business value of the unique features you found?
- What features are unnecessary? Why?

Project 7-3: Physical Security Survey

In this project you will perform a survey of the physical security at your school or workplace.

Identify vulnerabilities in the design and use of the following aspects of the facility:

- Use of locking doors at main entrances
- Access to sensitive areas
- Cabling, communications, or computing equipment readily accessible
- Video surveillance
- Personnel badges
- Loading area
- Fire suppression

Make a list of issues you found. Include a categorization of risk and a suggested remedy to reduce the risk.

Do not enter any "employee only" areas during this exercise unless you have obtained permission in advance or are escorted by authorized personnel.

Case Projects

Case Project 7-1: Data Replication Products Survey

As a consultant with the Risk Analysis Consulting Co., you have been asked to research data replication products for a manufacturing company, XYZ Plastics. XYZ Plastics has decided to build its backup application servers in a distant city. In its headquarters and in the other location, the servers run Solaris (operating system) and Oracle (database), and the database resides on an EMC SAN system. XYZ Plastics would like transactions on its headquarters servers to be transmitted over a wide-area connection to the SAN in the other city.

Find some reviews and information on data replication products. Some possible sources of information include:

- www.Searchstorage.techtarget.com
- www.Computerworld.com
- www.emc.com
- www.Oracle.com

Make a comparison of some of the replication products you have identified. Discuss the differences and similarities among the products and discuss their business value.

Case Project 7-2: Administrative Access Process

As a consultant with the Data Protection Consulting Co., you have been assigned to the Thick Slice Bread Co. You are to develop a process for assigning administrative access. Requirements for this process include:

- Subject (the person for whom administrative access is being requested) must hold a job description that is eligible for administrative access.

- Subject's manager must make the request.
- Request must specify the system(s) for which administrative access is being requested.
- VP of IT must approve all requests.
- VP of Security must approve all requests.
- Security token must be issued to the subject if he or she does not have one already.
- Subject must verify access within twenty-four hours of notification.

Note whether these requirements are sufficient for the development of the process. Identify any issues or ambiguities that need to be addressed.

Case Project 7-3: Quarterly Review of Access Rights

As a consultant with the Security Advisors Co., you have been asked to develop a process for a quarterly review of privileged access rights for a company with two thousand employees. Requirements for this process include:

- Access review for physical, network, VPN, system, database, and application must be performed.
- Access reviewers must have access to a list of employees terminated in the past ninety days, as well as a list of active employees.
- Access reviews must include the creation of evidence that the review was performed, so that auditors may confirm this activity later in the year.

Develop the procedure(s) needed to support this process.

Are there any additional requirements that should have been included?

Are there any ambiguities or issues?

chapter 8

Physical and Environmental Security

Topics in This Chapter:

- Site Access Controls Including Key Card Access Systems, Biometrics, Video Surveillance, Fences and Walls, Notices, and Exterior Lighting
- Secure Siting: Identifying and Avoiding Threats and Risks Associated with a Building Site
- Equipment Protection from Fire, Theft, and Damage
- Environmental Controls Including HVAC and Backup Power

The (ISC)^2 *Common Body of Knowledge* (CBK) defines the key areas of knowledge for physical and environmental security in this way:

The Physical (Environmental) Security domain addresses the threats, vulnerabilities, and countermeasures that can be utilized to physically protect an enterprise's resources and sensitive information. These resources include people, the facility in which they work, and the data, equipment, support systems, media, and supplies they utilize.

Physical security describes measures that are designed to deny access to unauthorized personnel (including attackers) from physically accessing a building, facility, resource, or stored information; and guidance on how to design structures to resist potentially hostile acts.

The candidate will be expected to know the elements involved in choosing a secure site, its design and configuration, and the methods for securing the facility against unauthorized access, theft of equipment and information, and the environmental and safety measures needed to protect people, the facility, and its resources.

Key areas of knowledge:

- *Understand site and facility design considerations*
- *Support the implementation and operation of perimeter security*
- *Support the implementation and operation of internal security*
- *Support the implementation and operation of facility security*
- *Support the protection and securing of equipment*
- *Understand personnel privacy and safety*

Physical security is concerned with the protection of business premises and assets through the use of physical controls that restrict and manage the movement of people and equipment. The main categories of physical security are:

- Access security
- Secure siting
- Equipment protection
- Environmental controls

Site Access Security

The purpose of a site's access security is the protection of the site and its occupants and assets from intruders. This is achieved through access control systems, detective and deterrent controls, and sound site selection.

Site Access Control Strategy

Other chapters in this book discuss the concept of **defense in depth** (particularly Chapter 2, "Access Controls"), which is the general technique of using layers of controls to protect valuable assets. Defense in depth is commonly used to protect information systems by protecting them with one or more layers of physical controls, in addition to logical controls discussed elsewhere in this book. The concept of defense in depth is illustrated in Figure 8-1.

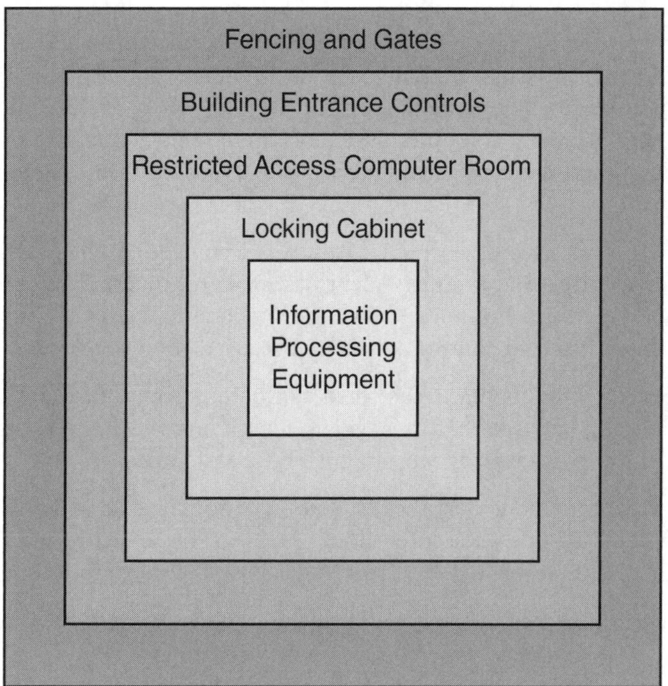

Figure 8-1 Defense in depth protects information resources and other assets

8

Site Access Controls

The purpose of site access controls is to restrict the movement of people, so that only authorized persons are permitted to enter the facility and specific work zones within the facility; and also to record the movements of those personnel.

The categories of controls are:

- Detective
- Deterrent
- Preventive
- Corrective
- Recovery
- Compensating

These categories of controls apply as much in physical space as in the logical space of computers. In fact, they are probably easier to understand in physical space, since physical controls aren't abstract like logical, computer-based access controls are.

For a detailed explanation on the meaning of these control categories, go read the section in Chapter 2, "Access Controls." Their names should be pretty intuitive, however, so even if you haven't read that section in Chapter 2 you'll probably be fine.

Key Cards Key cards are a form of preventive and detective control that is used to control which persons are permitted to enter a facility, as well as specific zones within a facility. A key card is one part of a larger system that includes **card readers** (devices used to read the contents of key cards) and electrically operated door latches that, when activated, unlock the door for a few seconds, and a central computer system that contains a database of all registered key cards and which doors they are permitted to enter. Figure 8-2 shows an entire key card system.

A **key card** is typically the same size as a credit card and is embedded with a RFID chip, smartcard chip, or magnetic stripe that uniquely identifies the cardholder. A key card is typically issued to each employee who is authorized to enter the facility. Figure 8-3 illustrates a typical key card reader that is used to control access to a secured room or system.

One weakness of a key card system is that a lost card can be used by a third party to enter the facility. For this reason it is advised that there be no identifying information on the card that would provide any clues to a passerby who might find a lost card.

Another weakness of a key card system is the tendency for some personnel to "tailgate" those who use their key cards to open a secured door. This can be remedied in one of several ways:

- Enforcing a "one card, one person" policy that includes consequences for breaking the policy
- RFID-equipped cards that can be detected as a person passes through (or near) a secured door, even if the person does not pass her card through the card reader
- Mantraps that enforce one-at-a-time entrance or exit of personnel
- Security guards who observe and intervene when necessary

Another control that mitigates the problem of a lost key card is the use of a PIN pad at some or all entrances. A **PIN pad** is a numeric keypad that is typically used in connection with an access control system. Someone who wishes to enter the facility must have not only

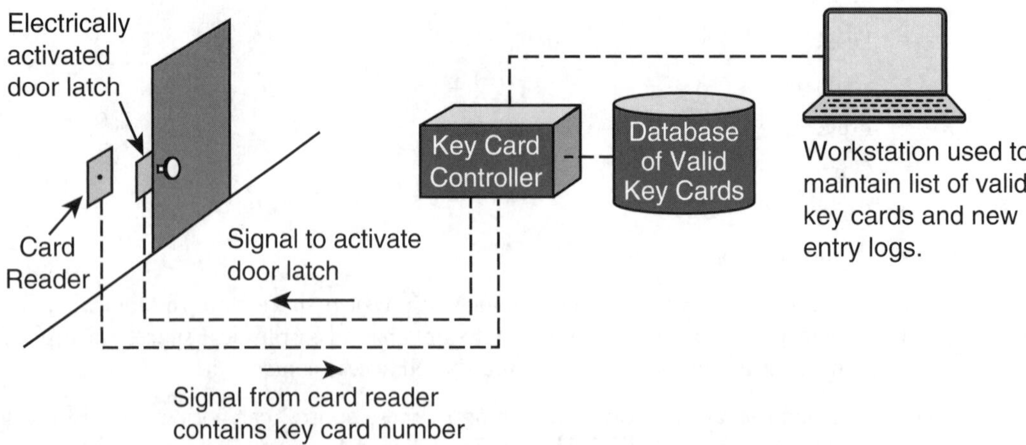

Figure 8-2 Key card system schematic

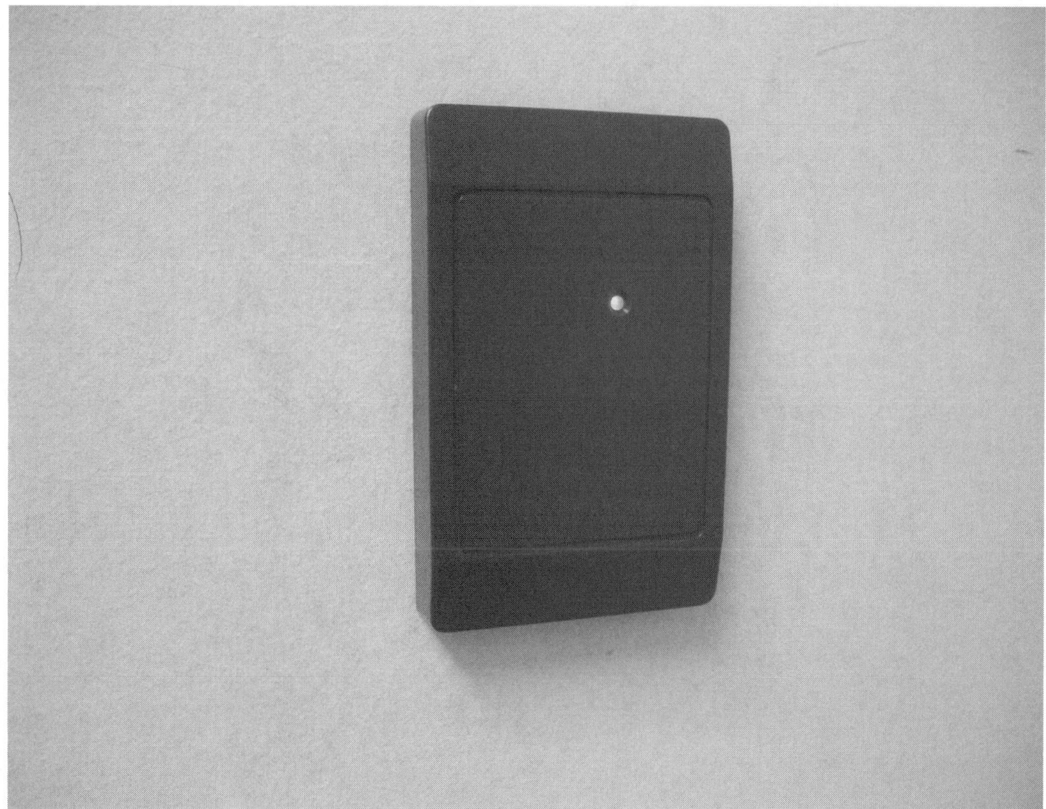

Figure 8-3 Key card reader used to control physical access

Photo by Rebecca Steele

the key card in their possession but must also know a PIN before the doorway will be activated. A combination card reader and PIN pad is shown in Figure 8-4.

Another weakness of key card systems is the ability to clone or copy key cards. Key cards using older RFID technology can be cloned through the use of a radio frequency device that is able to obtain the key card number through close proximity to the card. Magnetic stripe and smartcard key cards can also be copied; newer cryptographic techniques used in smartcard key cards can make this more difficult. As with the case of lost key cards, the use of a PIN pad can mitigate the risk of key card cloning.

The events that permit an employee with a key card to enter a protected entrance are described here.

First, a key card is issued to the employee as a part of a process that documents the request, approval, and issuance of the card.

Then, security personnel specify which doorways or zones the employee is permitted to enter.

1. Employee approaches a doorway and causes the card reader to read the key card. If the card reader has a PIN pad, then the employee keys the PIN at this time.

Figure 8-4 Card reader with PIN pad protects sensitive facilities

Photo by Rebecca Steele

2. Card reader sends a signal to the central key card controller, which looks up the key card number in its database and, further, determines if the key card is authorized at the particular doorway.
3. Central controller logs the attempted entrance, including the date and time, key card number, door number, and whether the entrance was permitted.
4. Central controller activates the doorway's electric latch if the key card is permitted at that doorway.
5. Employee pushes or pulls the door open to access the facility or room.

The controller that controls the system's card readers and door latches should be located in a locked cabinet or room and be accessible by selected security personnel who manage physical access control for all or part of the organization.

The controller will usually have a backup power supply, so that personnel can still enter the facility even during a building or circuit power failure. However, in the event of a malfunction of the key card system, usually an organization will issue hard keys to a limited number of highly trusted personnel who can enter the facility using hard keys.

Biometric Access Controls While key card-based controls are widely used for facility access controls, certain drawbacks—such as the ability for another person to use a lost card—persuade organizations to use a more effective control. PIN pads in combination with key cards, as discussed in the previous section, reduce risks somewhat, but PINs can sometimes be easily guessed or obtained through other means. An organization that wants a stronger control can consider biometric-based building access controls. Biometrics is a means for measuring a physiological characteristic of a person as a means for positively identifying him or her.

Biometric controls rely upon a measurement of a feature of someone's body as a means for establishing positive identification. This is an example of who a person is as an added layer of security to what a person has, in this case, the key card. The most common biometrics in use in facility access controls are:

- *Fingerprint*. A small fingerprint reader scans the fingerprint of someone who wishes to enter a facility or doorway within a facility. The reader sends the scanned fingerprint to a central access controller for comparison. A security panel that incorporates a fingerprint reader is illustrated in Figure 8-5.
- *Hand print*. Another popular biometric measurement is the geometry of a human hand.
- *Iris scan*. Human irises are as unique as fingerprints, and high-resolution digital imaging is able to capture a high-quality image from a comfortable distance from the subject. Iris scan-based biometric systems are available and growing in popularity. An image of the human iris is shown in Figure 8-6.

8

Figure 8-5 Fingerprint reader

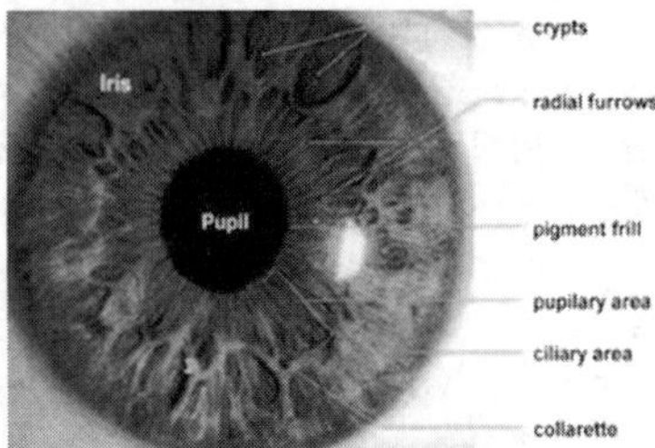

Figure 8-6 The human iris is a reliable and unique biometric subject

Image courtesy of John Daugman

Metal Keys Metal keys are used to unlock doors and other locks. Metal keys are discouraged for use as a primary access control for the following reasons:

- Keys are easily copied
- No record of who entered a room or facility is available
- Many key-operated locksets are vulnerable to a specially crafted key called a "bump key" that can be used to open a lock with no sign of forced entry

Metal keys do, however, make a suitable secondary control in limited situations, including:

- A backup method for entering a facility, in the event of the failure of the primary method, for example
- A locking cabinet located in a room protected by a key card or other recording access control

All metal keys should be issued according to a strict procedure that includes written records. When possible, each key should be serialized (stamped with a unique identifying mark or number), which enables identification of a specific key, should it be found. Employees who are issued metal keys should sign a form that describes their responsibility for safekeeping of the key.

Mantraps A **mantrap** is a set of interconnected double doors used to control the entrance or exit of personnel. The typical operation of a mantrap is:

1. Person approaches first door and issues access control (such as a key card, PIN pad, or biometric) to open it.
2. Person steps into the mantrap, and the first door closes.
3. When the first door has closed, person is able to open the second door and proceeds through it.

The "mantrap" area is usually small, just large enough to hold a few persons. A functional diagram of a mantrap appears in Figure 8-7.

Some mantraps are manually operated by a guard who is physically isolated from the mantrap itself.

Security Guards **Security guards** are trained personnel who perform a variety of duties in a facility. Some of these duties include:

- Checking employee identification
- Handling visitors

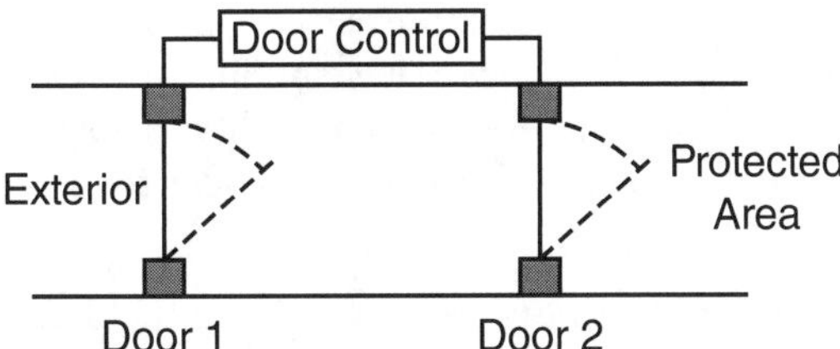

Figure 8-7 A mantrap permits only one door at a time to be opened, thus restricting movement of personnel

- Checking parcels and incoming/outgoing equipment
- Managing deliveries
- Apprehending suspicious persons
- Calling additional security personnel or law enforcement
- Assisting persons as needed

Most of these activities cannot be achieved with automated controls such as key card systems. There are several advantages to security guards, including:

- *Human judgment*. Through situational awareness, a guard can spot a suspicious activity that no automated system can handle.
- *Flexibility*. A guard can perform many other duties such as helping visitors and employees.
- *Roaming*. A guard can walk to another part of a facility to check on a suspicious activity or apprehend an intruder.

Guard Dogs A **guard dog** is a trained dog that is employed to guard against or detect unwanted or unexpected personnel or substances. Guard dogs are a physical control that can serve as detective, preventive, and deterrent controls. Guard dogs can accompany security personnel and assist in detecting and apprehending intruders, as well as detecting substances including explosives and illegal drugs.

Access Logs Access logs are a detective control, meaning they serve to record events such as the comings and goings of personnel. An **access log** is a record that contains building access attempts. The types of access logs that should be maintained at a work facility include:

- *Personnel entrance and exit*. This can usually be accomplished with a key card system or some other automated means.
- *Visitor log*. This allows the organization to track all visitors who have entered the facility. The log should contain identifying information and the nature of their visit.
- *Vehicles*. If the facility includes a gated parking facility, the entrances and exits of all vehicles should be recorded.
- *Packages*. All incoming and outgoing parcels should be logged, including their contents, origin or destination, and personnel associated with the parcel.
- *Equipment*. Personnel taking equipment into and out of the facility should be logged, including serial numbers where applicable.

Fences and Walls Fences and walls are an effective preventive and deterrent control that is designed to prevent unwanted persons from accessing specific areas such as the grounds of a building. They can also force visitors to approach a facility through a manned control point such as a guard station or entrance gate. Refer to Table 8-1 for various fence and wall heights and their effectiveness.

Fencing can be further protected with motion detection (thereby making the fencing both a preventive and a detective control) that will trigger alarms when someone may be attempting to climb over a fence. Video surveillance can also be used to observe fence lines and fenced areas.

Video Surveillance In most settings it is not economically feasible to place security guards at all vantage points at a facility. An effective addition to a smaller number of security guards is a video surveillance system that provides comprehensive visual coverage of a place of particular interest. A **video surveillance system** is a system consisting of one or more video cameras, together with viewing, storage, and playback features that are used to observe and/or record activities such as personnel movement. Typical locations for video cameras include:

- Building entrances and exits
- Lobby and reception areas
- Loading docks
- Refuse collection and disposal areas
- Stairwells
- Corridors
- Data center rooms

Camera Types Surveillance systems obtain their video images from video cameras that are placed in strategic locations at a facility. Surveillance systems can support several types of cameras, including:

- *Closed Circuit Television (CCTV) cameras*. The mainstay of surveillance systems, CCTV cameras send standard composite video (and, sometimes, audio) signals through CCTV cabling. CCTV is a technical standard for the transmission of video signals through a cable. A surveillance camera is shown in Figure 8-8, and surveillance monitors that view images from surveillance cameras are shown in Figure 8-9.
- *IP cameras*. Cameras can send their video signals through wired TCP/IP networks to an IP-enabled controller.

Height	Effectiveness
3–4 ft	Deters casual trespassers
6–7 ft	Too difficult to climb easily
8 ft plus 3 strands of barbed/razor wire	Deters all but the most determined trespassers

Table 8-1 Fence and wall heights to control intrusions

Figure 8-8 Video surveillance camera

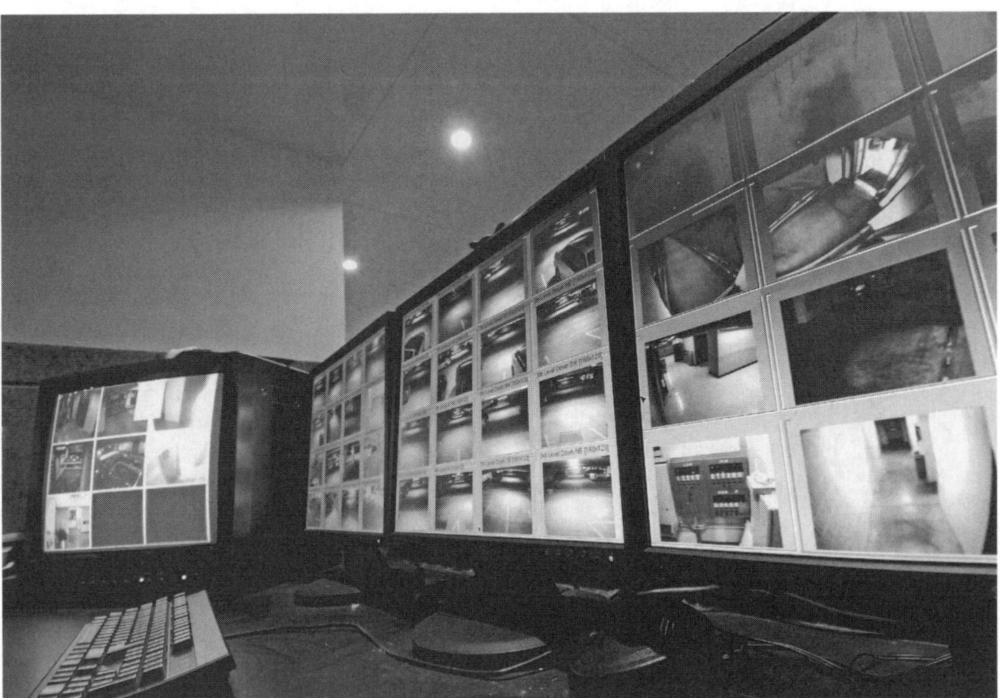

Figure 8-9 Video surveillance monitors

- *IP wireless cameras*. Cameras can transmit their video signals through WiFi, Bluetooth, or other wireless networks.
- *Night vision cameras*. Some video surveillance cameras are designed with night vision capability. This enables surveillance of an area even in complete darkness.
- *Fixed cameras*. Video cameras that are permanently aimed in one direction.
- *Pan/tilt/zoom cameras*. Video cameras that can be remotely controlled by an operator for a closer look at some activity or person of interest.
- *Hidden cameras*. Surveillance cameras can be placed secretly out of sight to record activities that might not take place if cameras were visible. Hidden surveillance cameras that are disguised as common objects like clocks, smoke detectors, books, radios, and other objects are available.

Recording Capabilities Video systems can provide real-time-only viewing, recording of video information, or both. The range of recording and viewing capabilities includes:

- *Real-time viewing only*. Events taking place will be viewable only when they are occurring.
- *Motion-activated recording*. Surveillance system can record video only when there is motion to record, such as a person walking or a vehicle driving through a camera's field of view.
- *Periodic still images*. A surveillance system can record still images from each camera every few seconds, whether something is going on or not.
- *Continuous video recording*. A surveillance system can continuously record video whether there is motion or not.

Surveillance systems can record data onto videotape, hard drive, or DVR/RW media. Systems can be configured to retain images for a day, a month, several months, or longer, depending upon the storage capacity of the system.

Intrusion, Motion, and Alarm Systems Intrusion- and motion-based alarm systems are a supplement or substitute for video surveillance systems. An **alarm system** is an apparatus that consists of a central controller called an alarm panel, plus several sensors of different kinds including:

- Door and window sensors that detect when the door or window is opened
- Motion sensors
- Thermal sensors
- Floor sensors that detect foot traffic
- Glass-break sensors that detect the sound of a broken window

Alarm systems also have some means for alerting building owners, occupants, or security staff that an intrusion has occurred. Typical alarm methods include:

- Audible siren or bell
- Strobe light to guide security personnel or law enforcement to the location of the intrusion
- Alert on an in-building monitoring center
- Alert via a backup phone line to a remote monitoring center

- Alert via a cellular call to a remote monitoring center
- Alert via broadband to a remote monitoring center
- An alarm system is configured and operated via the alarm panel. Typically the alarm is activated when employees vacate the premises by entering a security code or password. Then, when employees return, the alarm system is similarly deactivated by entering a security code or password and then the instructions for deactivating the alarm. This prevents an intruder from being able to deactivate an alarm system. The key issue with alarm codes is maintaining confidentiality of the code. This requires strong security and human resources policies, user training, and awareness.
- Organizations considering an alarm system should consider one where each employee who has responsibility for operating the alarm will get his or her own separate alarm code. This will enable the organization to track which persons activate and deactivate the alarm. Further, the alarm system should record the days and times that the alarm system is activated and deactivated. This will deter a dishonest employee with the alarm code from returning to the premises after hours to steal company property, since the alarm system will have recorded their employee's entries and exits.

Duress Alarms Often used in conjunction with an alarm or video surveillance system, the purpose of a duress alarm is to give personnel a means for discretely signaling others of some sort of an emergency situation. Duress alarms are common in banks and in stores selling high-value merchandise such as jewelry, as well as in the reception areas of many businesses. Duress alarms are often worn by elderly persons, who can use the device to summon assistance in case of an accident or other home emergency.

8

Visible Notices Physical security controls usually include deterrent controls that are designed to discourage would-be intruders from considering entering or damaging a facility or asset. These deterrent controls include visible notices such as:

- No Trespassing signs
- Surveillance notices
- Surveillance monitors

Laws or regulations in some areas require an employer to post visible notices if video surveillance is present at a facility. The visible notice shown in Figure 8-10 is an example of such a notice.

Exterior Lighting In addition to guiding safe passage for authorized personnel, lighting is a deterrent control that is designed to discourage intruders during nighttime hours. Lighting is intended to illuminate an intruder's actions so that others may see them and call appropriate authorities.

- Lighting should not betray the locations of other security controls such as surveillance cameras, motion detectors, or guard posts. The purpose of lighting is usually not to illuminate security controls.
- NIST (National Institute for Standards and Technology) standards require that critical areas be illuminated with at least two foot-candles of power at a height of eight feet. When lights on poles illuminate a facility, the poles should be spaced so that there are no dark areas between the lights; for example, if lights illuminate a diameter of fifty feet, then they should be placed no more than fifty feet apart.

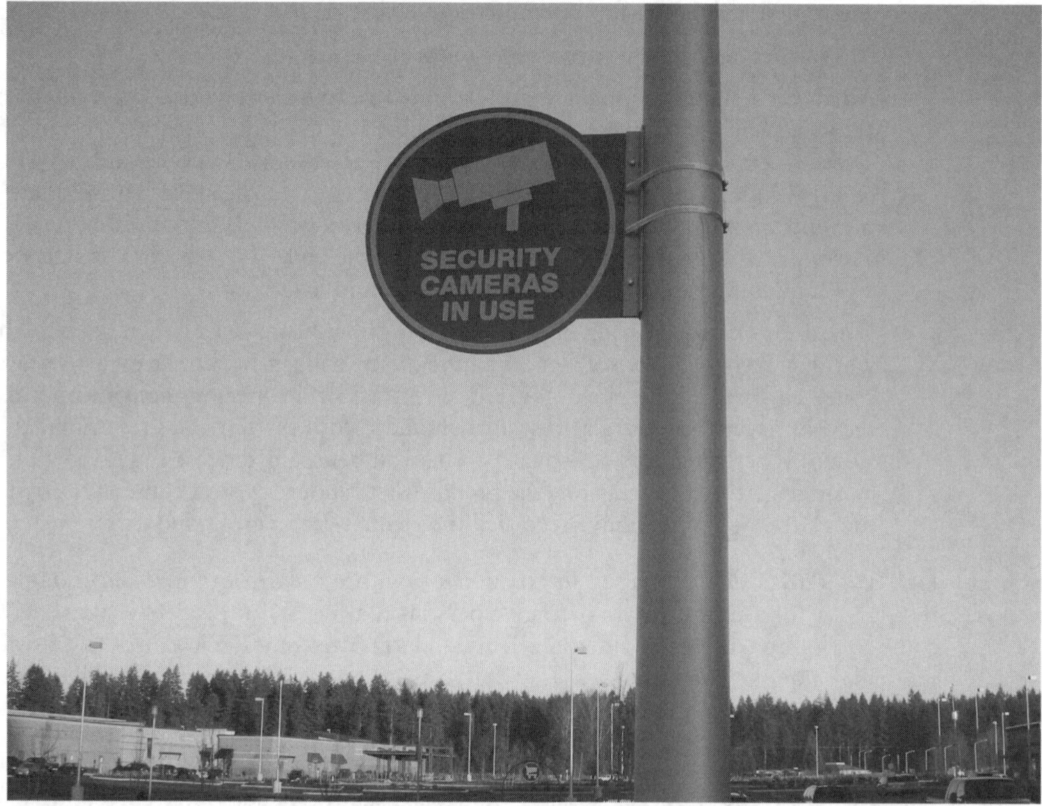

Figure 8-10 Visible notices inform intruders of physical security controls

Photo by Rebecca Steele

Other Physical Controls There are other physical controls that organizations may consider using that provide additional protection against intrusions.

- *Bollards*. These heavy upright posts restrict vehicle traffic while permitting pedestrians to walk between them. The primary purpose of bollards is to prevent vehicles-as-weapons from getting too close to buildings. Some bollards are retractable or removable, to allow access for maintenance vehicles, for instance. Figure 8-11 shows bollards that block vehicles from the entrance to an office building.
- *Crash gates*. A movable device that can be used to prevent the entry or exit of a vehicle. Crash gates are so-named because an attempt to drive a vehicle through one would result in a crash, as shown in Figure 8-12.

Security for Business Travelers

In addition to protecting personnel while they are at work locations, organizations have an obligation to protect their personnel when they are traveling as a part of their duties.

Figure 8-11 Bollards restrict vehicle traffic

Photo by Rebecca Steele

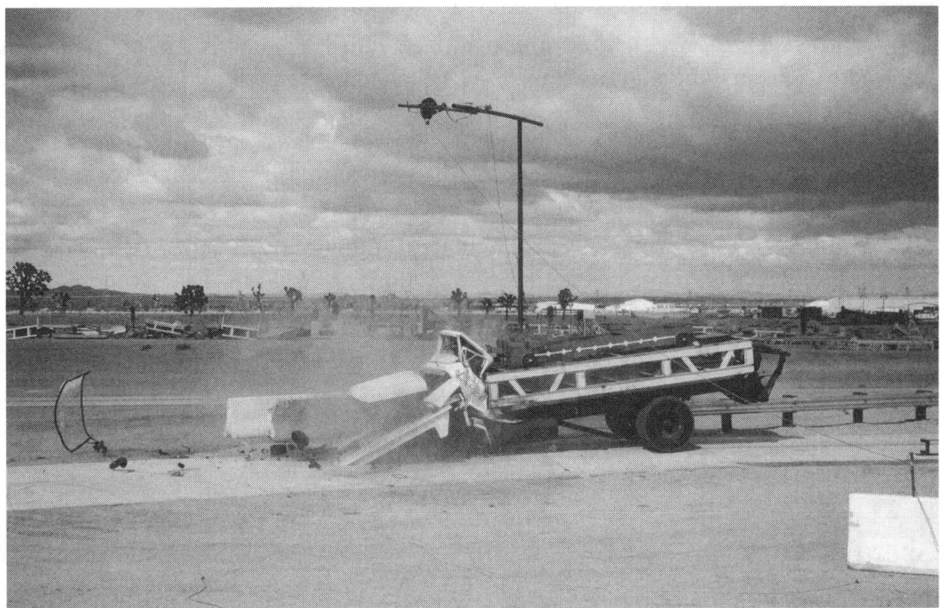

Figure 8-12 Crash gates prevent unwanted vehicles from entering (or leaving) a facility

Photo courtesy of Delta Scientific

Organizations will typically publish a travel policy that includes required and recommended measures that personnel take to improve their safety and security, including:

- *Access to emergency medical care*. Employers usually provide medical insurance or other means for employees to be able to seek urgently needed medical assistance while traveling.
- *Security of company property*. Organizations typically require their workers to keep laptop computers and other assets with them at all times. Workers should not pack computers in checked baggage, and they should not leave them unattended in hotel rooms or vehicles or leave them with hotel staff. Hard drive encryption processes also facilitate a more secure system. Mobile devices should be equipped with tracking and device wiping software to locate the device and/or destroy the data in the event of loss or break-in attempts.
- *Situational awareness*. Business travelers are often advised to be wary while in foreign places so that they do not become targets of crime.
- *Changes in travel itinerary*. Business travelers are often required to check in with their employers if they have made changes in their travel itinerary. This helps the organization know the whereabouts of its employees at all times.
- *Emergency communications*. Organizations often provide a means for travelers to be able to contact local or distant authorities in cases of emergency. Also, many organizations are acquiring means of being able to notify business travelers of local emergencies the travelers may not be aware of, including impending severe weather, nearby social unrest, or other situations that travelers may need to avoid.

Personnel Privacy

Organizations need to take appropriate measures to safeguard the privacy of their employees. Depending on the nature of the organization, this may include:

- *Concealment of personal information*. Generally, personal information such as home address, telephone numbers, and other personal details should not be available to other personnel or to visitors or customers. Employees may be required to conceal such information from the public; human resource and payroll departments often restrict visitors—including other employees—from visiting HR and payroll work areas to protect this information from being seen.
- *Concealment of full name*. In some organizations, it's unsafe for customers and others to know the full name of their personnel. Organizations in these situations will develop policies and other safeguards to meet this objective.

On a global scale, consensus on privacy is still being debated: privacy regulations in various nations are widely varied in their requirements and approach, resulting in compliance challenges for international organizations and Internet-based services.

Secure Siting

The concept of **secure siting** is, simply, locating a business at a site that is reasonably free from hazards that could interfere with or threaten its ongoing operation.

No location is free of all threats. And threats are not the only factor that is considered in business site selection. A business operation also needs a facility that is reasonably close to customers, suppliers, transportation, workers, and other necessary resources. But when threats are also considered and weighed in the decision-making process, company management can make an informed decision.

The presence of a threat does not automatically mean that a business should not locate its operation at a particular site. Some threats can be mitigated, reduced, or transferred. Some are simply accepted. For instance, locating an operation close to an airport or railroad may increase the threat from a transportation accident (plane crash or train derailment), but those threats might be considered to be highly improbable and the risk transferred in part by insurance. This topic of risk analysis and risk management is covered fully in Chapter 1, "Information Security and Risk Management."

An organization needs to take into consideration the threats associated with the site that is selected and incorporate those threats into its business continuity and disaster recovery planning. These topics are discussed in detail in Chapter 4, "Business Continuity and Disaster Recovery Planning."

Threats can directly or indirectly affect a business operation. For instance, a business can be safely located away from areas prone to flooding or landslides, but if the community's only transportation and/or communications are subject to these threats, then an event can disrupt business operations by severing transportation or communications that are required to continue business. For this reason the site selection process needs to consider the bigger picture and not end at the boundary of the premises.

Natural Threats

Several natural phenomena can occur that may disrupt business operations. These factors should be taken into account when making a site selection, so that management is aware of all of the factors related to the selection decision.

These natural threats include:

- *Floods*. Overflowing streams, rivers, and lakes may threaten a business directly or indirectly. A local hydrologist should be consulted in order to determine the risk of any particular location that may be near a body of water.
- *Landslides and avalanches*. These events can damage buildings, transportation, utilities, and communications.
- *Earthquakes*. A seismologist can be consulted to help determine the risk of a seismic event at or near the site.
- *Volcanoes*. These violent events can produce many effects, including falling rocks and ash, pyroclastic flows, landslides, and flooding, that damage buildings, transportation, utilities, and communications infrastructure. A pyroclastic flow that is racing down the side of an erupting volcano is shown in Figure 8-13.
- *Tsunamis, waves, and high tides*. These events can damage buildings and infrastructure such as transportation, utilities, and communications.
- *Severe weather*. Hurricanes, tornadoes, heavy rain, blizzards, ice storms, and windstorms can damage buildings and equipment as well as supporting infrastructure

Figure 8-13 Pyroclastic flow from a volcano

Source: U.S. Geological Survey/photo by Peter W. Lipman

such as transportation and public utilities. While most of these threats are regional in nature, knowledge of these threats may help the organization to choose the type of building it occupies.

Man-Made Threats

Several types of man-caused events can potentially disrupt business operations and should be considered in the site selection process.

- *Chemical spills*. A business located near a refinery, chemical factory, or business that uses hazardous substances could be disrupted by an event such as a spill, leak, or explosion.
- ***Biological hazards***. Also known as biohazards, consisting of medical waste, toxins, and infectious agents that could infect, injure, or kill humans or animals.
- *Transportation*. A business wants to be close enough to transportation corridors to be able to send and receive materials and facilitate workers and visitors. However, if a business is too close to an airport, railroad, or highway, then the hazards of accidents can pose a threat to nearby businesses.
- *Utilities*. Site selection needs to consider the proximity to overhead and buried power transmission lines, natural gas pipelines, LPG (liquefied petroleum gas) pipelines and storage facilities, gasoline pipelines, and so on, and consider the types of events that could require evacuation or could damage business premises.
- *Military base*. A business located near a military base might consider the hazard of being located near a location that may be high on an enemy state's list of targets.
- *Social unrest*. Being located near areas prone to demonstrations and other mass gatherings could prove to be disruptive at inopportune times. These areas include major downtown thoroughfares, public squares, schools, and universities.

- *Terrorism.* A terrorist attack can result in damage to property and equipment, as well as loss of human life. Being near a major transportation hub or in a prominent building are just a few of the potential risks associated with terrorist attacks, unlikely though they may be.

Other Siting Factors

In addition to natural and man-made threats, other security-related factors should influence site selection, including:

- *Building construction and materials.* The composition and quality of construction of a building has a direct bearing on the protection of its occupants and business equipment.
- *Building marking.* While many businesses are proud to erect a large sign that proclaims the presence of a business location, oftentimes doing so is like hoisting a giant target that says, "Hit me here." Sometimes it's enough to simply display the address without advertising the name of the organization that is located there.
- *Loading and unloading areas.* Areas where freight and deliveries take place require additional safeguards such as video surveillance, auto-closing doors, and double sets of doors so that a delivery agent cannot access the premises while loading or unloading goods.
- *Shared tenant facilities.* Many office buildings called shared-tenant facilities house two or more separate organizations. This makes physical access control far more complicated, since they cannot be erected at the whim of one of the tenants without affecting others. Further, the businesses that occupy shared tenant buildings typically do not own the building, which means that any changes to improve physical security must be approved by the facility's owner. Some controls, such as access to the building's main entrances, may be held in common by all of the businesses that occupy the building; this makes implementation of controls such as key card systems more complicated.

Equipment Protection

Business equipment needs to be protected from theft and damage, so that business operations that depend upon equipment can continue functioning. This section discusses the protection of business equipment located in a business facility. Topics covered here include theft protection, damage protection, fire prevention and response, and cabling security. The protection and security of communications cabling is also discussed.

Theft Protection

Business equipment must be protected from theft. While part of the risk can be transferred through insurance, in many cases stolen equipment cannot be *immediately* replaced, resulting in business disruption and fines or possible loss of revenue. However, if the stolen equipment also contains business information, then the loss and business disruption may be more significant and difficult to quantify, and the results could be more widespread and complex. For example, a stolen backup tape or laptop computer containing sensitive business or personal information could result in negative publicity, embarrassment, fines, and customer distrust.

Several measures can be taken to reduce the threat and probability of theft, including:

- *Protection of laptop computers.* Employees who are issued laptop computers need to understand their responsibilities and be held accountable for their actions. This will probably include:
  - Use of cable locks to prevent or discourage theft.
  - Use of defensive software such as firewalls, anti-virus, anti-spyware, location tracking, and self-destruct-if-stolen controls.
  - Use of two-factor authentication such as fingerprint or smart card.
  - Use of encryption to protect sensitive information from disclosure.
  - Training to make personnel aware that they must not leave laptop computers unattended or allow their use by unauthorized personnel.
- *Protection of servers and backup media.* Place servers in locked rooms that few personnel can access. Attach servers to racks or cabinets with locking fasteners. Clearly mark equipment with difficult-to-remove asset tags or labels. Place backup media in locking cabinets. Use a reliable off-site storage vendor that utilizes secure transportation and transfer. Use keycard systems to restrict personnel entry into computer and server rooms. Use video surveillance to record entry and exit from sensitive areas.
- *Protection of sensitive documents.* Place sensitive documents in locking, fire-resistant cabinets. Institute a "clean desk" policy that requires sensitive documents to be locked away when not in use. Discarded documents containing sensitive information should be shredded.
- *Protection of valuables.* Items such as currency, blank checks, precious metals, or gems should be placed in a safe.
- *Institute equipment check-in/check-out.* All equipment that enters or leaves a facility should be tracked. A log that is similar to a visitor sign-in/sign-out sheet should be instituted that records the worker's name, equipment description, and serial number. Laptop computers issued to employees can be exempted from this since they can be considered to be permanently checked out to an employee. Some organizations require that any laptop computer leaving the premises be logically scrubbed, to remove sensitive data in order to eliminate the risk of a security incident if the laptop computer is lost or stolen while out of the physical control of the organization.

Damage Protection

Business equipment needs to be protected from damage that can be caused by a variety of events such as fires, floods, earthquakes, and so on. Some of the safeguards that can be instituted include:

- *Earthquake bracing.* Shelves and racks used to store equipment and supplies (as well as running equipment) can be braced, to minimize the possibility that they will fall over in an earthquake or other event. Equipment can be fastened to racks and shelves so that it will not slide off and fall, resulting in damage and injury.

- *Water detection and drainage*. Ground floor rooms of buildings with business equipment and machinery should have water detectors connected to alarms, to alert personnel that water is present in the facility. This is especially true in computer rooms with raised floors where the incursion of water may not be noticed until it has begun to cause damage. Floor drains and/or sump pumps may also be needed to help channel water away from equipment to prevent damage.

There are probably other means for equipment protection available and perhaps even necessary in some circumstances and locales.

Fire Protection Fire prevention capabilities are required in virtually every locale in the world. Required systems in business locations include one or more of the following:

- Fire extinguishers
- Smoke detectors
- Automatic sprinkler systems
- Fire alarm systems

Fire Extinguishers **Fire extinguishers** are portable devices that an individual can use to extinguish small fires. There are five types of fire extinguishers that are used to extinguish different types of fires. In the United States, these types are:

- *Class A*. Ordinary combustibles: wood, paper, and so on.
- *Class B*. Flammable liquids and gases: gasoline, propane, and so on.
- *Class C*. Energized electrical equipment.
- *Class D*. Combustible metals: magnesium, and so on.
- *Class K*. Cooking oils.

Fire extinguishers come in single-type and combination-type models. A common type of combination fire extinguisher is Class ABC, which can be used to fight fires of those types.

England and Australia have similar standards for fire extinguisher types.

Smoke Detectors **Smoke detectors** are automatic devices that sense the presence of fire in its incipient stages, at the very beginning of combustion. Detectors are either equipped with annunciators or wired into a central fire alarm system. There are two types of smoke detectors:

- *Optical*. These types of detectors utilize an infrared LED and a photo detector, and they function by detecting minute changes in the refraction of light caused by smoke.
- *Ionization*. These detectors detect smoke before it is visible by measuring slight changes in current between electrodes in the vicinity of a small amount of radioactive Americium-241.

Smoke detectors are powered by small batteries, external electric current, or both. Smoke detectors in commercial buildings are usually powered by external electric current and do not rely solely on internal batteries.

Figure 8-14 Fire alarm manual pull station

Photo by Rebecca Steele

Fire Alarm Systems **Fire alarms** function by alerting personnel of smoke or fire in a facility. Alarms can also be wired to a fire department or centrally monitored public safety center in order to alert a fire department. Alarms can be triggered in several ways, including:

- ***Pull stations***. These are manually operated switches, activated by personnel who observe smoke or fire. A pull station is shown in Figure 8-14.
- *Smoke detectors*. Devices that detect smoke, described earlier in this section.
- *Sprinkler system flow detectors*. Devices built into sprinkler systems that detect the flow resulting from activation of one or more sprinkler heads.

Fire alarms typically have annunciators located throughout a building that audibly and visibly notify personnel of the fire in the building. A typical fire alarm is shown in Figure 8-15.

Automatic Sprinkler Systems **Sprinkler systems** are systems consisting of water supply pipes and sprinkler heads that are used to douse a fire with water, or a combination of water and fire extinguishing foam. There are several types of sprinkler systems, including:

- *Wet pipe systems*. The simplest and most common type of sprinkler system, wet pipe systems are filled with pressurized water, which is released when a sprinkler head's fusible link is melted by heat from a nearby fire.

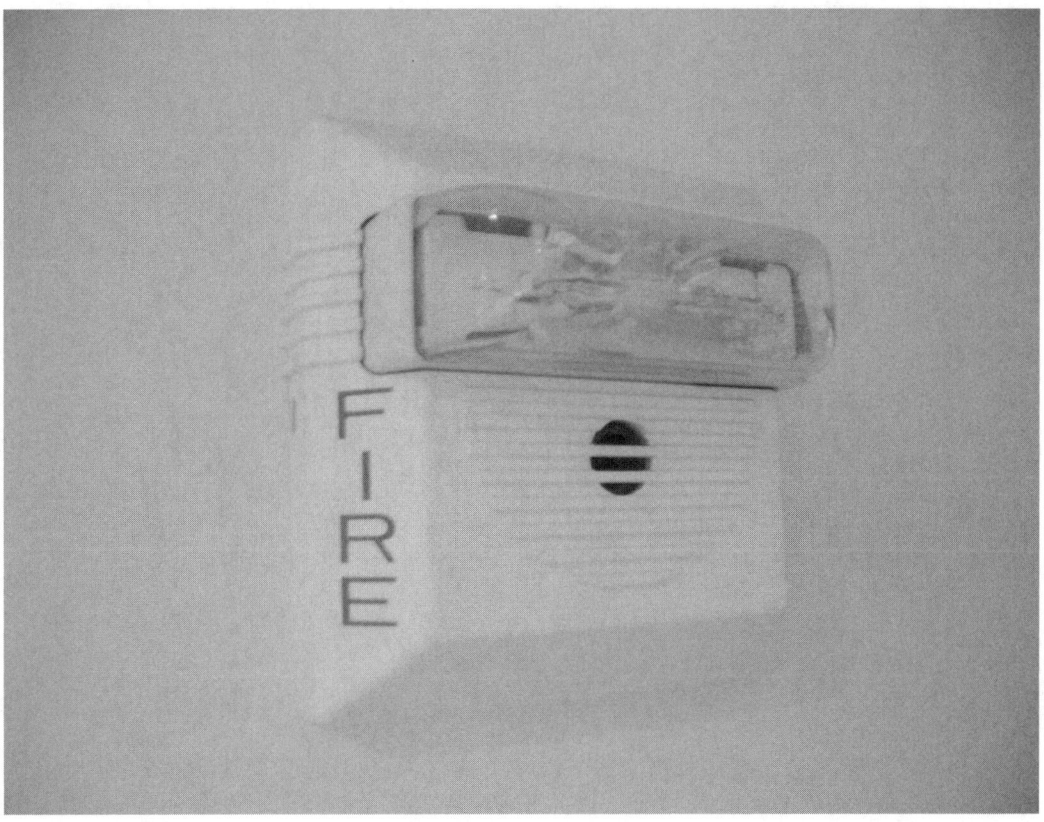

Figure 8-15 Fire alarm annunciator

Photo by Rebecca Steele

- *Dry pipe systems.* A more complex type of sprinkler system where water is not present in the pipes until the system is activated from a central valve.
- *Deluge systems.* A system where all sprinklers are open. When the system is activated, water is discharged from all sprinklers.
- *Pre-Action Systems.* A dry pipe that is converted to a wet pipe system when a smoke, fire, or heat alarm is activated. This type of system is often used in computing facilities, where the consequence of an accidental discharge is high.
- *Foam water sprinkler systems.* A variation of any of the water-based sprinkler systems where the liquid discharged is a combination of water and fire-retardant foam.

Figure 8-16 shows a close-up view of a fire sprinkler head.

Gaseous Fire Suppression An alternative to water- and foam-based fire suppression, **gaseous fire suppression** systems consist of inert gas in storage tanks, delivered via piping and nozzles. Gaseous fire suppression systems are used in areas with valuable electrical equipment such as computer systems. They work by displacing oxygen from the room(s) where the fire is located. In the heat-oxygen-fuel fire triangle, gaseous fire suppression works by removing oxygen from the fire by interfering with chemical combustion. Examples of substances used for gaseous fire suppression include FM-200 and Inergen.

Figure 8-16 Fire sprinkler head

Photo by Rebecca Steele

Gaseous fire suppression lowers the amount of oxygen in a facility; thus, these fire suppression systems have additional alarms and signage to alert personnel of the hazard. Still, a discharge is not directly lethal to humans.

Cabling Security

Voice and data communications cabling must be protected from accidental or deliberate damage and tapping that can result in eavesdropping or man in the middle attacks. Because organizations are connected to one another over private and common carrier networks, not all cabling is in the direct control of the organization, so there's only so much that an organization can do directly on its own.

Some of the threats and remedies for cabling risks are:

- *Exposure of organization's own cabling on its premises*. Place cabling in conduits or reroute away from exposed areas.
- *Exposure of common carrier's cabling to threats outside of business's control*. The common carrier must protect its cabling on behalf of its business customers. But there are remedies that businesses can take to mitigate possible threats, including:
  - Select a different common carrier that does a better job of protecting its cable plant.

- Utilize **diverse network routing**, a strategy of utilizing physically separate communications circuits so that damage or malfunction in one circuit will not result in a total loss of communications.
- Utilize encryption on common carrier networks to thwart eavesdropping.

Environmental Controls

Environmental controls are the various electric and mechanical systems that support the heating, cooling, humidity, and electric power needs for a facility. Environmental controls provide a comfortable environment for workers, as well as the heating, cooling, humidity, and energy required to support business equipment and information systems in the building.

Heating and Air Conditioning

Heating, ventilation, and air conditioning (HVAC) systems ensure a steady temperature within a range that is comfortable for workers and beneficial to business equipment and information systems.

Information systems can produce a great deal of heat that must be continuously removed with air conditioning systems. Overheating for even short periods can greatly reduce the life of systems, making them far more likely to fail.

Because computer systems have so little tolerance for HVAC failures, redundant HVAC systems are often used. HVACs are electromechanical systems that require periodic shutdown and maintenance, another reason why redundant systems are often used. It is important to note that a facility should be able to operate indefinitely when one of its HVAC systems is offline.

The cooling capacity of HVAC systems is rated in one of two ways:

- BTU/hour
- Tons

Engineers will calculate the required capacity of a building's HVAC system by measuring the building's size as well as obtaining an estimate of the amount of heat output from computer equipment.

Ventilation should be a concern. Building designers need to be aware of external conditions in areas where ventilation air is drawn into a building, in order to avoid the introduction of harmful gases into the building. Areas in a building that require contaminant-free air may need to utilize additional filtering as well as positive pressure flow so that opened doorways do not permit contaminated air to enter areas that require cleaner air.

HVAC systems also have controls for the regulation of humidity, which is described next.

Humidity The amount of water vapor in the air is a measure of the **humidity. Relative humidity** is the amount of water vapor in a sample of air compared to the maximum amount of water vapor the air can hold. Relative humidity is expressed as a percentage, from 1 percent to 100 percent.

The relative humidity in a facility with workers and computing equipment should range from 30 percent to 50 percent. Levels below 30 percent will result in discomfort and excessive thirst for staff, cause electronic equipment to become more brittle, and permit more static electricity.

Levels above 50 percent will permit dust mites to survive, and higher levels may result in condensation, where moisture causes corrosion. Moisture condensing on equipment will cause short circuits.

Air circulation systems also need to perform **filtering** so that air is free of dust, pollen, and other particulates that can clog air filters and cause other problems.

Traditionally, so-called HVAC systems have employed refrigeration to cool air as needed to control the temperature of computers and other equipment. Newer computing facilities use non-refrigeration techniques such as **ambient air** for cooling. In the absence of refrigerated air, the concepts of temperature, humidity, and freedom from particulates still apply.

Electric Power

Information processing equipment requires clean power, lots of it, and is intolerant of the wide variety of electric power problems that can occur. Electric power is similar to piped water in that events like leaks or sudden turn-ons and shut-offs will create changes in pressure and even shockwaves that will travel up and down the pipeline that affect other users. Some of the electric power anomalies include:

- *Blackout*. A total loss of power.
- *Brownout*. A prolonged reduction in voltage below the normal minimum specification.
- *Dropout*. A total loss of power for a very short period of time (milliseconds to a few seconds).
- *Inrush*. The instantaneous draw of current by a device when it is first switched on.
- *Noise*. Random bursts of small changes in voltage.
- *Sag*. A short drop in voltage.
- *Surge*. A prolonged increase in voltage.
- *Transient*. A brief oscillation in voltage.

Several different types of equipment are available to improve the quality of electric power.

The remainder of this section discusses these:

- Line conditioner
- Uninterruptible power supply
- Electric generator

Line Conditioner A **line conditioner** (sometimes called a power conditioner) is a device that filters or removes some of the undesirable anomalies in a power feed, "smoothing out" incoming power to make it cleaner for sensitive equipment. Line conditioners smooth out the smaller rises and dips in incoming voltage by using an isolation transformer that filters incoming electric power.

Line conditioners aren't usually seen as standalone devices but instead are found in UPS systems, discussed next.

Uninterruptible Power Supply (UPS) An **uninterruptible power supply** (UPS) is a device that produces a continuous supply of electric power. A UPS can be thought of as a line conditioner with a battery or bank of batteries connected to it, so that it functions both as a line conditioner but also as a temporary supply of electric power.

UPS systems do require maintenance on their batteries, which must be checked from time to time and replaced every few years. Also, it is common to load-test a UPS by shutting off the power feed to the UPS to confirm that it will actually support the equipment that it supplies power to.

The period of time that a UPS can serve as a source of electricity depends entirely upon the storage capacity of its batteries and on the electric load of the equipment it supplies power to. The shortest period of time commonly used ranges from a low of ten to fifteen minutes, which is enough time to either shut down the equipment or start an electric generator (discussed in the next section), to as long as several hours. Regardless, a UPS system is considered a short to medium time interval substitute for utility-supplied electric power.

Electric Generator An **electric generator** is a device that consists of an internal combustion engine (usually diesel-powered, but also natural gas or gasoline) that is connected to a generator—the engine-generator combination is simply called a generator. They vary greatly in size from a few hundred watts to megawatts.

A generator will usually be switched off and idle except when utility power fails, at which time the generator is started. It can take as long as a few minutes for a generator to be started and be ready to assume the full electric load. Because of this, a facility that utilizes vital computing equipment will have both a UPS system plus an electric generator. When utility power fails, the UPS system will supply a continuous supply of electricity to computer equipment. If utility power is not restored within a minute's time, the electric generator will be started, and within a few more minutes the generator will supply electricity to the facility. After utility power is restored, the generator will run a few minutes longer (to make sure utility power will remain) and then shut down.

A generator can be run almost continually for long periods of time during extended power outages. But at facilities such as Tier IV Internet data centers, two or more generators will be used, permitting on-site power generation for even several weeks if necessary, provided a sufficient fuel supply is available. An electric generator that provides electricity for a work site is shown in Figure 8-17.

Redundant Controls

Some facilities will have a demand for higher than the typical availability and reliability from their environmental control equipment. These facilities include:

- Larger buildings
- Buildings containing a large quantity of information systems
- Buildings containing business-critical information systems

Redundant control systems enable the facility to continue operating even if one of the components fails. All of the control systems can be duplicated, although the duplication may be expensive in some cases. A facility can have:

- Dual electric utility power feeds
- Redundant generators
- Redundant UPS systems
- Redundant HVAC systems

Figure 8-17 Electric generator produces electric power when utility power is unavailable

Photo by Rebecca Steele

A term often used to describe this redundancy is "N + 1." This means that if a building has a need for "N" control systems, then having N + 1 systems means there is some redundancy that will enable the facility to continue operating even if one of the control systems fails completely.

Chapter Summary

- A site access control strategy should consider a defense in depth approach.
- Key cards are a preferred method for personnel access control because they can be deactivated at any time and because all accesses are logged.
- A PIN pad in conjunction with a key card can provide a stronger access control for sensitive areas.
- Biometrics is a stronger access control method that utilizes some unique measurement of a person's body such as a fingerprint, hand print, or iris scan.
- Metal keys can also be used for personnel access control, but should only be used by the fewest possible number of personnel and only as an emergency means for accessing a building in the event the primary access system fails.

- A mantrap is an access control that consists of a set of two doors, one after the other, where only one door can be open at a time.
- Guards are trained personnel who protect a facility and manage the entry and exit of personnel and visitors. The advantage of guards is their judgment and versatility.
- Guard dogs improve site security through their ability to deter and apprehend intruders.
- Access logs are the records that show all successful and unsuccessful entrances by personnel and visitors.
- Fences and walls can be used to keep intruders away from a facility. A height of three to four feet keeps casual trespassers away, while a height of six to seven feet is too high to climb easily. A fence or wall that is at least eight feet in height and contains three strands of barbed wire or razor wire is sufficient to deter even the most determined intruders.
- Video surveillance is used to observe site perimeters, entrances and exits, and control points.
- Video signals from cameras can be viewed in real time and/or recorded for later use.
- Intrusion and motion alarm systems utilize sensors that detect entry through doors and windows and motion in a room or corridor and send an alarm signal if intrusion or motion is detected.
- Visible notices such as "No Trespassing" signs deter persons from entering a facility.
- Exterior lighting reduces the ability for an intruder to work under cover of darkness. Critical areas should be illuminated with at least two foot-candles of power at a height of eight feet.
- Bollards and crash gates restrict the movement of vehicles.
- Organizations need to take steps to protect their business travelers so that they have access to emergency medical facilities, take proper precaution when traveling to foreign countries, and can be reached in case of emergency.
- Organizations need to take precautions to ensure that private and sensitive information about personnel is protected from unauthorized access by other personnel as well as outsiders.
- A business should be located in an area that is reasonably free of hazards and threats.
- Natural threats include floods, landslides, avalanches, earthquakes, volcanoes, tsunamis, and severe weather.
- Man-made threats include chemical spills, biological hazards, transportation corridors, utilities, social unrest, and nearby military bases.
- Other siting issues include building construction techniques and materials, building marking, loading and unloading areas, and shared tenancy.
- Business equipment should be physically secured to prevent theft.
- Laptop computers should be issued with cable locks. Personnel should be trained on safe and unsafe use of laptop computers.
- Sensitive documents should be locked away and safely and securely discarded.
- Organizations should institute a "clean desk" policy so that personnel do not leave sensitive documents where others can find them.

- Records of equipment leaving and entering a facility should be maintained.
- Equipment should be protected from damage by water with water sensors, drains, and sump pumps. Racks and freestanding shelving should be braced to protect them from toppling over.
- Fire prevention equipment is a necessary part of disaster recovery. Organizations need to have smoke detectors, fire extinguishers, fire alarms, and fire suppression systems such as sprinklers and gaseous discharge systems. These are required by law in most locations.
- Cabling should be protected from unauthorized access. Because an organization cannot protect cabling that is a part of a common carrier's network, other means such as route diversity and encryption should be used to protect sensitive transmissions over common carrier networks.
- Heating, ventilation, and air conditioning (HVAC) systems control the temperature and humidity of air in buildings.
- Line conditioners remove the undesirable anomalies from incoming electric power such as spikes, surges, and noise.
- Uninterruptible power supplies (UPSs) provide a continuous supply of electric power, even when utility power has failed.
- On-site electric generators can produce electric power for extended periods of time in the event that utility power has failed for even as long as several days.
- Facilities that cannot tolerate downtime due to the failure of HVAC, UPS, or generators should consider redundant, or "N + 1," environmental controls.

Key Terms

Access log A record that contains building or computer access attempts.

Alarm system A system of sensors and a control unit that is designed to detect intrusions into a building or room and send an alarm signal if an intrusion is detected.

Biological hazard Any of several substances that pose a threat to humans and animals. Also known as a **biohazard**.

Bollard A heavy upright post used to restrict vehicle traffic.

Card reader A device used to read the contents of a key card.

Closed Circuit Television (CCTV) A standard for the transmission of video signals over a cable, often used in video surveillance systems. See also *IP camera*.

Crash gate A movable device that can be used to restrict the entry or exit of a vehicle.

Digital video recorder (DVR) A device used to store digital video surveillance data for later viewing.

Diverse network routing A network design strategy where two or more separate circuits to a given location will be located in different areas. If a mishap severs one of the circuits, communication will continue via the other circuit(s).

Electric generator See *generator*.

Filtering The process of removing particulates and other matter from the air in a building or processing center.

Fire alarm An alarm system that warns human occupants of the presence of a nearby fire.

Fire extinguisher A portable fire suppression device that sprays liquid or foam onto a fire.

Gaseous fire suppression An installed system of pipes and nozzles that sprays a fire-retardant gaseous substance into a room.

Generator A device consisting of an internal combustion engine and an electric generator.

Guard See *security guard*.

Guard dog A dog that is employed to guard against or detect unwanted or unexpected personnel.

Heating, ventilation, and air conditioning (HVAC) A system that is used to control the temperature and humidity in a building or a part of a building.

Humidity A measurement of the amount of water vapor in the air.

IP camera A video surveillance camera that sends its video signal over a TCP/IP data network.

Key card A credit card-sized plastic card with a magnetic stripe or embedded electronic circuit encoded with data that uniquely identifies the cardholder, and generally used to access restricted areas in a facility.

Line conditioner A device that filters or removes some of the undesirable anomalies in an incoming power feed.

Mantrap A set of interconnected double doors used to control the entrance or exit of personnel.

PIN pad A numeric keypad that is typically used in connection with an access control system.

Pull station A manually operated device that is used to trigger a building fire alarm.

Relative humidity The amount of water vapor in a sample of air compared to the maximum amount of water vapor that the air can hold.

Secure siting Locating a business at a site that is reasonably free from hazards.

Security guard A trained person who is responsible for protecting building assets and controlling access to the building.

Smoke detector A device that detects the presence of combustion-related smoke and contains or is connected to an audible warning alarm.

Sprinkler system An installed system of piping and nozzles used to spray water or foam onto a fire.

Uninterruptible Power Supply (UPS) A short-term backup power source that derives its power from storage batteries.

Video surveillance system A system that consists of monitors and/or recording equipment plus one or more video cameras, which together are used to observe and/or record activities such as personnel movement.

Review Questions

1. An organization has issued metal keys to its employees and has recently suffered some after hours employee thefts. The organization should consider acquiring:
   a. PIN pads
   b. Guards
   c. A key card entry system
   d. Mantraps
2. An organization that is setting up a key card entry control system should:
   a. Establish different zones and determine which personnel should be able to access each zone
   b. Establish one zone and assign all personnel to the zone
   c. Determine, for each employee, whether they should be able to access each controlled door
   d. Permit employees to access all general-entrance doors and issue metal keys to more sensitive areas
3. An organization needs to keep determined intruders away from its facility. The organization should install:
   a. Fencing that is six to seven feet high
   b. Fencing that is six to seven feet high with three strands of barbed wire
   c. Fencing that is six to seven feet high with three strands of razor wire
   d. Fencing at least eight feet high with three strands of razor wire
4. A video surveillance system that does not have the ability to record:
   a. Is adequate as a detective control
   b. Is adequate as a deterrent control
   c. Must be continuously attended and monitored by security personnel
   d. Is adequate as a preventive control
5. An organization that wishes to implement additional deterrent controls should consider:
   a. An intrusion alarm system
   b. A key card entry control system
   c. "No Trespassing" signs
   d. Fencing
6. A business is considering relocating to another city. The selection criteria for a new site should include:
   a. The proximity to possible social unrest events
   b. Proximity to man-made threats
   c. All of these
   d. Proximity to natural threats

7. In a facility with workers and computing equipment, the appropriate range for humidity should be:
   a. Between 30 percent and 50 percent
   b. Between 50 percent and 70 percent
   c. Between 20 percent and 40 percent
   d. Less than 20 percent
8. An organization has a computer facility that is powered by utility power and a generator. When utility power fails:
   a. Personnel will have to start the generator to restore power
   b. Power to computing equipment will dip slightly and then be restored
   c. Power to computing equipment will be down for one to two minutes, then restored
   d. Power to computing equipment will not be interrupted
9. An organization experiences many transients, surges, and dropouts in its utility power. In order to prevent damage to its computer equipment, the organization should install:
   a. A line conditioner
   b. An uninterruptible power supply (UPS)
   c. An electric generator
   d. A power distribution unit (PDU)
10. A commercial Internet hosting facility advertises that it has "N+2" HVAC systems. This means:
    a. One more HVAC unit than is needed to provide cooling to the entire facility
    b. Two more HVAC units than are needed to provide cooling to the entire facility
    c. Spare parts on-hand for two HVAC units
    d. Twice the HVAC capacity than is needed to provide cooling to the entire facility
11. The primary purpose for earthquake bracing is:
    a. Protection of human life
    b. Protection of computing equipment
    c. Protection of network infrastructure
    d. Protection from excessive lateral movement
12. The hazard from natural threats includes:
    a. Damage to supporting infrastructure
    b. Direct damage to facilities and equipment plus damage to supporting infrastructure
    c. Direct damage to facilities and equipment
    d. Damage to communications facilities

13. The NIST standard for outdoor lighting requires:
    a. At least two lumens of power to a height of eight feet
    b. Lights no more than fifty feet apart
    c. At least six foot-candles of power to a height of eight feet
    d. At least two foot-candles of power to a height of eight feet
14. Video surveillance is generally appropriate in all of the following areas except:
    a. Employee cubicles and offices
    b. Loading docks and storage areas
    c. Computer rooms and data closets
    d. Power control rooms
15. A corporation is considering leasing office space in a shared tenant building. The security manager has expressed a concern regarding building access control. The most likely cause of the concern is:
    a. Shared management of a building access management system
    b. Common access to corridors and stairwells
    c. Common access to video surveillance data
    d. Common access to workspaces

Hands-On Projects

Project 8-1: Site Review of Video Surveillance System

In this project, you will perform a survey of the video surveillance system at your school, place of work, or other business location.

In order to avoid drawing suspicion, you should first ask for permission to perform this survey beforehand. You should not enter any restricted areas unless you are escorted or have explicit permission.

1. Visit your school, place of work, or other business.
2. Observe grounds and building entrances and note any video cameras that may be present. If possible, determine whether each is a fixed camera or if it is the pan/tilt/zoom type.
3. Note the interior and exterior areas that appear to be lacking video surveillance.
4. Prepare a short written report with your findings and recommendations.

Project 8-2: Site Review of Building Access System

In this project you will perform a survey of the access management system at your school, place of work, or other business location.

In order to avoid drawing suspicion, you should first ask for permission to perform this survey beforehand. You should not enter any restricted areas unless you are escorted or have explicit permission.

1. Visit your school, place of work, or other business.
2. Observe building entrances and interior doors and note any key card readers or other controls that may be present.
3. Note any areas that appear to be lacking access controls.
4. Prepare a short written report with your findings and recommendations.

Project 8-3: Perform a Building Site Threat Analysis

In this project you will perform a threat analysis (also known as a site survey) at your school, place of work, or other business location.

In order to avoid drawing suspicion, you should first ask for permission to perform this survey beforehand. You should not enter any restricted areas unless you are escorted or have explicit permission.

1. Visit your school, place of work, or other business.
2. Observe the building grounds and surrounding areas, as far as a quarter mile from the building.
3. Note any hazards that could pose a threat to the premises.
4. Prepare a short written report with your findings and recommendations.

Project 8-4: Perform a Dumpster Diving Analysis

In this project you will perform a survey of one or more centralized waste collection receptacles ("Dumpsters") at your school, place of work, or other business location.

In order to avoid drawing suspicion, you should first ask for permission to perform this survey beforehand. You should not enter any restricted areas unless you are escorted or have explicit permission.

In some places of business, looking through waste materials may expose you to potentially hazardous materials that may cause injury, sickness, or death. You should seek the guidance of qualified and experienced personnel before putting yourself at risk.

1. Visit your school, place of work, or other business.
2. Locate one of the trash receptacles ("Dumpsters") on the premises. While paying careful attention to personal safety, observe whether you can see any discarded documents or other materials that could contain potentially sensitive business information.
3. Prepare a short written report with your findings and recommendations.

Case Projects

Case Project 8-1: Research Biometric Access Controls

As a consultant with the Risk Analysis Consulting Co., you have been asked to research biometric access controls for a chemical company, Colorful Plastics.

A number of security incidents in the past year has prompted Colorful Plastics to consider using biometrics for its building access control system. Using online research, identify several biometric access control products that could be used. Consider systems that are based on fingerprint, iris scan, and hand print.

Recommend two finalists that Colorful Plastics should consider testing on-site.

Case Project 8-2: Research Document Shredding Options

As a consultant with the Information Protection Consulting Co., you have been assigned to Smokey Fire Insurance Company. Three hundred employees in this company handle paper documents with sensitive information that must be shredded when discarded. Company management has considered three options:

- Personal shredders at each desk
- Shredders near each printer
- Secure shred bins near each printer (once a week, an on-site shredding service empties these bins and shreds documents in the presence of a security guard)

Using online research, find pricing for each of these options. Create a written report that includes recommendations, noting what factors besides cost were considered.

Case Project 8-3: Video Surveillance Upgrade

As a consultant with the Seeing Eye Security Advisors Co., you have been asked to develop a plan for upgrading the video surveillance system for your client, a small high-tech manufacturing company. Recent thefts of high-value materials have prompted the client to upgrade its video surveillance system in order to be able to identify and apprehend the person(s) who are stealing materials.

Today, your client's video system includes fixed cameras in the building's main lobby and in the computer room. The video surveillance controller can accept video signal inputs from a maximum of four cameras. No surveillance capability exists for any of the other building entrances, the grounds, the shipping and receiving area, or the high-value materials storage areas.

Using online research, identify candidate video surveillance systems with recording and real-time viewing capabilities that can take inputs from several cameras. Create a written report that includes candidate systems and your recommendations.

chapter 9

Security Architecture and Design

Topics in This Chapter:

- Security Models Including Biba, Bell-LaPadula, Access Matrix, Clark-Wilson, Multi-Level, Mandatory Access Control, and Discretionary Access Control
- Information Systems Evaluation Models Including Common Criteria, TCSEC, ITSEC
- Computer Hardware Architecture
- Computer Software: Operating Systems, Applications, and Tools
- Software and System Security Threats and Countermeasures
- Cloud Security Threats and Countermeasures

The $(ISC)^2$ *Common Body of Knowledge* (CBK) defines the key areas of knowledge for security architecture and design in this way:

The Security Architecture and Design domain contains the concepts, principles, structures, and standards used to design, implement, monitor, and secure, operating systems, equipment, networks, applications, and those controls used to enforce various levels of confidentiality, integrity, and availability.

Information security architecture and design covers the practice of applying a comprehensive and rigorous method for describing a current and/or future structure and behavior for an organization's security processes, information security systems, personnel and organizational sub-units, so that these practices and processes align with the organization's core goals and strategic direction.

The candidate is expected to understand security models in terms of confidentiality, integrity, data flow diagrams; Common Criteria (CC) protection profiles; technical platforms in terms of hardware, firmware, and software; and system security techniques in terms of preventative, detective, and corrective controls.

Key areas of knowledge:

- *Understand the fundamental concepts of security models (e.g., Confidentiality, Integrity, and Multi-level Models)*
- *Understand the components of information systems security evaluation models*
- *Understand security capabilities of computer systems (e.g., memory protection, virtualization, trust platform module)*
- *Understand the vulnerabilities of security architectures*
- *Understand software and system vulnerabilities and threats*
- *Understand countermeasure principles (e.g., defense in depth)*

The title of this chapter is "Security Architecture and Design," the name for Domain 6 of the CISSP Common Body of Knowledge (CBK). However, the subject matter in this chapter is a good deal bigger than that. This domain contains the loosely related topics of:

- Abstract security models
- Information system evaluation criteria
- Computer system architecture
- Software

Security Concepts

The protection of information systems and data boils down to three principle concepts: confidentiality, integrity, and availability.

- *Confidentiality*. This concept refers to the protection of systems and data so that only authorized subjects are permitted to access them. Depending on the context, there are several different types of controls to ensure confidentiality. Preventive controls include userids and passwords, firewalls, intrusion prevention systems, data leakage prevention systems, and encryption. Detective controls include access logs and video surveillance.

- *Integrity*. This concept refers to the protection of systems and data so that only authorized changes may be made to them. Preservation of integrity means that systems can be counted on to provide reliable information that will not be questioned.
- *Availability*. This concept refers to the resilience of systems so that they will be available when needed, even when considering scenarios such as hardware failure and disasters.

These concepts are the core of the information security mission and often known as the CIA Triad. Sometimes during discussions regarding the security controls and features used to protect systems and data, it is necessary to be reminded of what's at stake. It will always come down to confidentiality, integrity, availability, or a combination of these.

Security Models

In the context of this chapter, a *model* is a simplified representation used to explain a real-world system. In the natural sciences, models are used as a means for understanding some phenomenon in nature. In data security it's the other way around: models are used as the basis for the design of a security mechanism that can be used to protect secrets and systems.

Several security models are discussed in this section, roughly in the chronological order of their development. They are:

- Bell-LaPadula
- Biba
- Clark-Wilson
- Access matrix
- Multi-Level
- Mandatory access control (MAC)
- Discretionary access control (DAC)
- Role-based access control (RBAC)
- Rule-based access control
- Non-interference
- Information flow

When designing a new information system (or the access model for a new or existing system), a system developer may wish to use a security model in order to build or choose an access model that will fulfill the system's security access requirements. Similarly, an analyst or developer who is studying an existing security system might wish to compare the system to security models in order to better understand the system.

There are two important terms used in discussions of security models. They are:

- *Subjects*. These are usually people who use a system. In cases of system-to-system communication, a subject can also be another system, or a process running on another system.
- *Objects*. These are the systems, data, or other resources that someone wants to access.

Using these terms, typical statements about security models and access control assert that there are subjects who access objects.

Bell-LaPadula

Published in 1973, the **Bell-LaPadula** model is a *state machine* model that addresses the *confidentiality* of information. This **data confidentiality model** was developed to formalize and explain the DoD multilevel security policy.

In the Bell-LaPadula model, a subject can read all objects (typically, documents) at or below his or her level of security but cannot read any objects above his or her level of security. This is called *no read-up*, or *NRU*. This prevents a subject from learning secrets at a higher level than the subject's own. For example, a diplomat can read objects intended for common citizens but cannot read objects intended for the president.

In the model, a subject can write (create/modify) objects at or above his or her level of security but cannot write objects below his or her level. This is called *no write-down*, or *NWD*. This prevents a subject from accidentally leaking secrets at the subject's level into an object at a lower level. For example, a diplomat can write objects intended for the president but cannot write objects for common citizens, out of the concern that the diplomat may accidentally leak sensitive information to the common citizens.

Bell-LaPadula had one shortcoming that is addressed by the Biba model.

Biba

The **Biba** model was published in 1977, a few years after the Bell-LaPadula model, and after a lot of people in the security community had opportunities to discuss it and put it into practice. Biba is often considered the first formal integrity model because it prevents modifications to objects by unauthorized subjects. For that reason, Biba is called a **data integrity model**.

Biba addresses a shortcoming in the Bell-LaPadula model whereby a subject at a lower security level is able to overwrite and potentially destroy secret information at a higher level.

In the Biba model, a subject cannot read objects below his or her level. This is called *no read-down*, or *NRD*. For example, a diplomat can read documents written by the president but cannot read documents written by common citizens.

Further, a subject cannot write objects above his level. This is called *no write-up*, or *NWU*. For example, a diplomat can write procedures to be read by common citizens but cannot write procedures to be read by the president.

Neither the Bell-LaPadula nor the Biba are perfect security models; each has its shortcomings and advantages. Principles from each can be used to construct other security models and mechanisms.

Clark-Wilson

Clark-Wilson is a data integrity model that was published in 1987 as a rebuttal to the Bell-LaPadula and Biba models, which Clark and Wilson argued were more suited for confidentiality than integrity. The Clark-Wilson model consists of two principals—authenticated users and programs (called *transformation procedures*, or TPs)—which operate on two types of data items: *unconstrained data items* (UDIs) and *constrained data items* (CDIs). One type of TP, called an *integrity verification procedure* (IVP), is used to transform UDIs into CDIs.

In the model there are two sets of rules: *certification* (C) rules and *enforcement* (E) rules:

- C1—an IVP must ensure that CDIs are valid.
- C2—for a given CDI, a TP must transform the CDI from one valid state to another valid state.
- C3—*allowed relations* (or *triples* that consist of a user, a TP, and one or more CDIs) must include separation of duties.
- C4—TPs must create a transaction log that contains all transaction details.
- C5—TPs that accept a UDI as input may perform only valid transactions on the UDI (to convert it to a CDI) or reject the UDI.
- E1—the system must permit only the TPs certified to operate on a CDI to actually do so.
- E2—the system must maintain the associations between users, TPs, and CDIs. The system must prevent operations outside of registered associations.
- E3—every user must be authenticated before they may run each TP.
- E4—only a TP's certifier may modify its associations.

Access Matrix

An **access matrix** security model consists of a two-dimensional matrix that defines which subjects are permitted to access which objects. An example access matrix appears in Table 9-1.

9

Multilevel

The **multilevel** security model is one in which a system will have several levels of security and be used by persons of varying levels of security clearances, where the system will control access to objects according to the clearance level of subjects.

For example, a file server contains documents at three different levels of security: Confidential, Secret, and Top Secret. The users of the system are registered as having one of three levels of clearance: Confidential, Secret, or Top Secret. A user with Secret clearance can view documents at Confidential and Secret levels, but not Top Secret. A user with Confidential clearance can only view Confidential documents. A user with Top Secret clearance can view all documents (before application of "need to know"). This is illustrated in Table 9-2.

Subject	Directory: Contracts	Directory: Personnel	Process: Expense Reports
Warren	Read	Read	Submit
Wilson	None	None	Approve
Wyland	Read/Write	None	Submit
Yelte	Read/Write	None	None

Table 9-1 Sample access matrix

User Access Level	Authorized to View
Top Secret	Top Secret Secret Confidential
Secret	Secret Confidential
Confidential	Confidential

Table 9-2 Multilevel access

Mandatory Access Control (MAC)

Mandatory access control (MAC) describes a system (such as an operating system) that controls access to resources. When a subject (which could be a program, process, or thread) requests access to an object (which could be a file, device, stream, or port), the system examines the subject's identity and access rights together with the access permissions associated with the object. The system will permit or deny the requested access.

Discretionary Access Control (DAC)

In the **discretionary access control** (DAC) model, the owner of an object controls who and what may access it. DAC is so named because permission to access an object is made at its owner's discretion.

DAC is common in information systems where owners of files, directories, web pages, and other objects can set access permissions on their own, to control which users or groups of users may access their objects.

Role-Based Access Control (RBAC)

Role-based access control (RBAC) is usually used to simplify the task of managing user rights in a complex system that contains many objects and users.

Instead of managing the access rights of individual users, an RBAC system relies on the existence of roles, which contain collections of allowed accesses. Each subject is then assigned to one of the established roles, and each subject then inherits the rights defined by the role to which the user is assigned. It's easy to think of roles as access templates.

For example, a financial accounting application in a corporation will have hundreds or even thousands of access controls. The application will have several predefined roles such as *Accounts Payable Clerk*, *Accounts Payable Manager*, *Accounts Receivable Clerk*, *Accounts Receivable Manager*, *Corporate Controller*, and many others. Each role contains all of the access rights required by a person assigned to the role.

Rule-Based Access Control

Rule-based access control is used to manage aspects of access control aside from which subjects are permitted to access which objects. Examples of rule-based access control include:

- Time-of-day access restrictions
- Geographic access restrictions

Non-Interference

The **non-interference** model states, in fairly abstract terms, that low inputs and outputs will not be altered by any high inputs or outputs. In other words, a user with low clearance cannot gain any knowledge of any activities performed by high-clearance users. The term *noninterference* means that activities performed by a user with high clearance will not interfere with any activities performed by a user with low clearance, thus providing information about the activities of the high-level clearance user to the low-level user.

Information Flow

Information flow models are based upon the flow of information rather than upon access controls. Objects are assigned to a class or level of security, and the flow of these objects is controlled by a security policy that specifies where objects of various levels are permitted to flow.

Information Systems Evaluation Models

It is insufficient for an organization to build a system and simply assert that it is secure. An organization that is concerned about security is not likely to put much credibility in such an assertion. But how can an organization reliably test a system's security?

Several evaluation models and frameworks have been established for the purpose of objectively evaluating the security (that is, the effectiveness of its controls to ensure the confidentiality, integrity, and availability) of a system. The frameworks discussed in this section are:

- Common Criteria
- TCSEC
- TNI
- ITSEC
- SEI-CMMI
- SSE-CMM

The general processes of certification and accreditation are also discussed in this section.

Common Criteria

Common Criteria for Information Technology Security Evaluation is usually known as just the **Common Criteria** or *CC*. This is the formal name for the international standard, **ISO 15408**. The Common Criteria is a framework for the specification, implementation, and evaluation of a system against a given set of security requirements.

Common Criteria supersedes TCSEC and ITSEC.

A system called a **Target Of Evaluation** (**TOE**) is evaluated against one of seven **Evaluation Assurance Levels** (**EALs**), which are:

- EAL1: Functionally Tested.
- EAL2: Structurally Tested.

- EAL3: Methodically Tested and Checked.
- EAL4: Methodically Designed, Tested, and Reviewed.
- EAL5: Semiformally Designed and Tested.
- EAL6: Semiformally Verified Design and Tested.
- EAL7: Formally Verified Design and Tested.

Evaluation of a system to CC standards is both expensive and time-consuming. According to the U.S. General Accounting Office (GAO), evaluation at levels EAL2 through EAL4 can take as long as two years and cost as much as US$350,000. See Figure 9-1.

TCSEC

The **Trusted Computer Security Evaluation Criteria** (**TCSEC**) is the system evaluation criteria that address confidentiality of information. Developed by the U.S. Department of Defense in the 1980s, TCSEC is commonly known as the *Orange Book*, which is a part of the *Rainbow Series*.

TCSEC defines four main levels, plus sublevels of security protection:

- *A*—Verified protection
- *B*—Mandatory protection
- *B3*—Security domains
- *B2*—Structured protection
- *B1*—Labeled security
- *C*—Discretionary protection

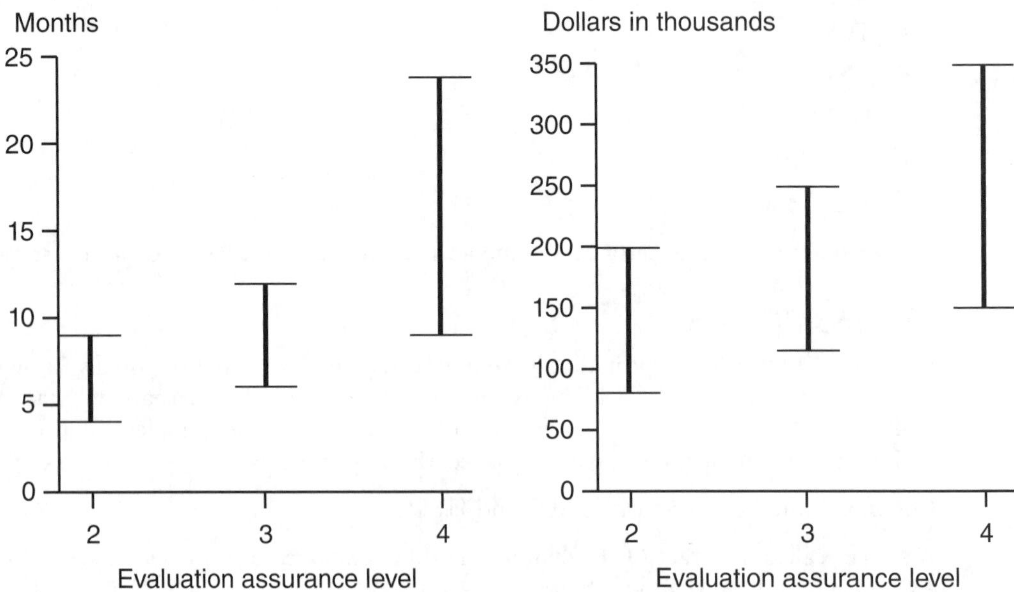

Figure 9-1 Evaluation of a system to various assurance levels of the Common Criteria requires considerable time and cost

Source: United States Government Accountability Office

- *C2*—Controlled access
- *C1*—Discretionary protection
- *D*—Minimal security

TCSEC has been superseded by the Common Criteria.

Trusted Network Interpretation (TNI)

The **Trusted Network Interpretation** (**TNI**) evaluation criteria is known as the *Red Book* in the Rainbow Series. TNI is used to evaluate confidentiality and integrity in trusted communications networks.

ITSEC

Information Technology Security Evaluation Criteria (**ITSEC**) is the European standard for the security evaluation of systems. Whereas TCSEC addresses only data confidentiality, ITSEC addresses confidentiality as well as integrity and availability.

ITSEC uses two sets of security levels (functionality and evaluation) that map to TCSEC's levels. See Table 9-3 for a side-by-side comparison of TCSEC and ITSEC levels.

ITSEC has also been superseded by the Common Criteria.

ITSEC Functionality Level	ITSEC Evaluation Level	TCSEC Level
NA	E0	D
F-C1	E1	C1
F-C2	E2	C2
F-B1	E3	B1
F-B2	E4	B2
F-B3	E5	B3
F-B3	E6	A1
F-IN	NA	TOEs with high integrity requirements
F-AV	NA	TOEs with high availability requirements
F-DI	NA	TOEs with high integrity requirements during data communication
F-DC	NA	TOEs with high confidentiality requirements during data communication
F-DX	NA	Networks with high confidentiality and integrity requirements

Table 9-3 Comparison of ITSEC and TCSEC security levels

SEI-CMMI

The Software Engineering Institute at Carnegie-Mellon University developed a model to objectively assess the maturity of an organization's systems engineering practices. The model is called the **Software Engineering Institute Capability Maturity Model Integration** (SEI-CMMI).

The objective of an organization's assessment is to arrive at a rating of maturity levels, which are:

- *Level 0—Incomplete*. Processes are incomplete and many activities are performed ad hoc if at all.
- *Level 1—Performed*. Processes are documented and performed.
- *Level 2—Managed*. Processes are managed and supported with skilled workers and tools.
- *Level 3—Defined*. Processes are defined according to a standard process framework model.
- *Level 4—Quantitatively Managed*. Processes are measured and managed according to the results of those measurements.
- *Level 5—Optimizing*. Processes are measured and changed over time in order to improve them.

SSE-CMM

The **Systems Security Engineering Capability Maturity Model** (SSE-CMM) is a process evaluation reference model that is focused on the requirements for implementing security in a system. Developed by the International Systems Security Engineering Association (ISSEA), SSE-CMM has five levels of performance, which are:

- Capability Level 1—Performed Informally
- Capability Level 2—Planned and Tracked
- Capability Level 3—Well Defined
- Capability Level 4—Quantitatively Controlled
- Capability Level 5—Continuously Improving

Certification and Accreditation

Certification and **accreditation**, sometimes called *C&A*, are the processes used to evaluate and approve a system for use. These activities are not generally seen in average businesses, but instead are found in government and military environments, and also in highly regulated industries such as pharmaceuticals and aeronautics.

C&A is a two-step process:

- Certification is the process of evaluation of a system's architecture, design, and controls, according to established evaluation criteria.
- Accreditation is the formal management decision to approve the use of a certified system.

Six standards for certification and accreditation are discussed in this section: FedRAMP, FISMA, DITSCAP, DIACAP, NIACAP, and DCID 6/3.

FedRAMP **Federal Risk and Authorization Management Program** (**FedRAMP**) is a U.S. government-wide program that defines a standardized approach to security assessments, authorization, and continuous monitoring for cloud-based service providers. FedRAMP was implemented in 2012 and made fully operational in 2013. FedRAMP marks the first major shift from compliance-based security to risk-based security and is aligned with NIST 800-137, "Information Security Continuous Monitoring (ISCM) for Federal Information Systems and Organizations."

FISMA **Federal Information Security Management Act** (**FISMA**) of 2002 is a law that requires all U.S. federal information systems to conform to security standards and processes used to evaluate them.

The compliance process required by FISMA includes the following steps:

- *Determine Scope*. In other words, define the components and boundaries of a system and the subsequent assessments that will take place.
- *Determine the Information Types*. It is necessary to know what kinds of information will be present in the system (whether stored in, transmitted through, or both). This includes performing a FIPS-199 categorization of information.
- *Document the System*. This includes the full collection of documents that describe the system including architecture, design, hardware and software components, connections, and procedures for building, operating, and maintaining.
- *Risk Assessment*. A comprehensive identification of threats, vulnerabilities, impact, and steps available to mitigate threats and vulnerabilities.
- *Implement Security Controls*. Once the architecture, types of information, and risks of a system are known, security controls can be established.
- *Certification*. This is the formal evaluation of the system to confirm that it has been built as intended.
- *Accreditation*. This is the formal decision to allow use of the system.
- *Continuous Monitoring*. Once the system has been placed into operation, it must be continuously monitored to ensure that it is performing adequately and correctly.

DITSCAP **Department of Defense Information Technology Security Certification and Accreditation Process** (**DITSCAP**) is the process used to certify and accredit information systems used by the U.S. military.

The four phases of the DITSCAP process are:

- System definition
- Verification
- Validation
- Re-Accreditation

In 2006 DITSCAP was superseded by DIACAP, which is discussed next.

DIACAP The **Department of Defense Information Assurance Certification and Accreditation Process (DIACAP)** is the successor to DITSCAP and is used to certify and accredit military information systems.

The steps in the DIACAP process are:

- Initiate and plan information assurance (IA) C&A
- Implement and validate information assurance (IA) controls
- Certify and accredit the system
- Maintain authorization to operate system and conduct reviews
- Decommission

NIACAP **National Information Assurance Certification and Accreditation Process (NIACAP)** is the process used to certify and accredit systems that handle U.S. national security information. It is modeled after the DITSCAP that is discussed earlier in this section.

The phases of a NIACAP certification and accreditation are:

- Definition
- Verification
- Validation
- Post accreditation

NIACAP is administered by the U.S. National Security Agency.

DCID 6/3 **Director of Central Intelligence Directive 6/3 (DCID 6/3)** is the process for protecting sensitive compartmented information within information systems at the U.S. Central Intelligence Agency (CIA). This directive defines security standards, classification levels, and the C&A process for certifying and accrediting information systems.

DCID 6/3's process for C&A includes these steps:

- Perform Certification Evaluation
- Perform Security Testing
- Identify Shortfalls
- Define Vulnerabilities
- Conduct Risk Analysis
  - Identify and Prioritize Risks
  - Identify additional Countermeasures
  - Make risk assessment recommendations
- Develop Certification Package
- Obtain interim approval to operate, if applicable
- Obtain Accreditation

Computer Hardware Architecture

This section describes the hardware architecture used in contemporary computer systems. While it may, at first, seem irrelevant to security, it is asserted that a security manager must fully understand how every facet of information systems works, including the underlying hardware. The security manager is explicitly responsible for the protection of information and information systems; a working knowledge of every facet and layer of the organization's information systems is necessary in order to be able to protect it.

Computers contain several components, including:

- Central processor
- Bus
- Main storage
- Secondary storage
- Communications
- Firmware

Other components and concepts related to computer architecture that are discussed in this section are Trusted Computing Base and Reference Monitor.

This section describes the architecture of individual computer systems. Discussions of architectures, such as clustering, are found in Chapter 7, "Security Operations."

9

Central Processor

The **central processing unit** (**CPU**) (Figure 9-2) is the portion of a computer where program instructions are executed. Historically, CPUs consisted of discrete components (transistors, resistors, capacitors, diodes, and so on) on circuit boards, but starting in the 1970s, CPUs were constructed from integrated circuits (ICs), and in that form they were often known as *microprocessors*.

Components CPUs have a number of components, including:

- *Arithmetic logic unit (ALU)*. This is where arithmetic and logic operations are performed.
- *Registers*. These are temporary storage locations that are used to store the results of intermediate calculations. A CPU can access data in its registers far more quickly than main memory.
- *Program counter*. A register that keeps track of which instruction in a program the CPU is currently working on.
- *Memory interface*. This is the circuitry that permits the CPU to access main memory.

Operations CPUs do a computer's work by performing the instructions in computer programs. They do this by performing a small number of basic operations, which are:

- *Fetch*. The CPU fetches (retrieves) an instruction from memory.
- *Decode*. The CPU breaks the instruction into its components: the *opcode* (or *operation code* —literally, the task that the CPU is expected to perform) and zero or more

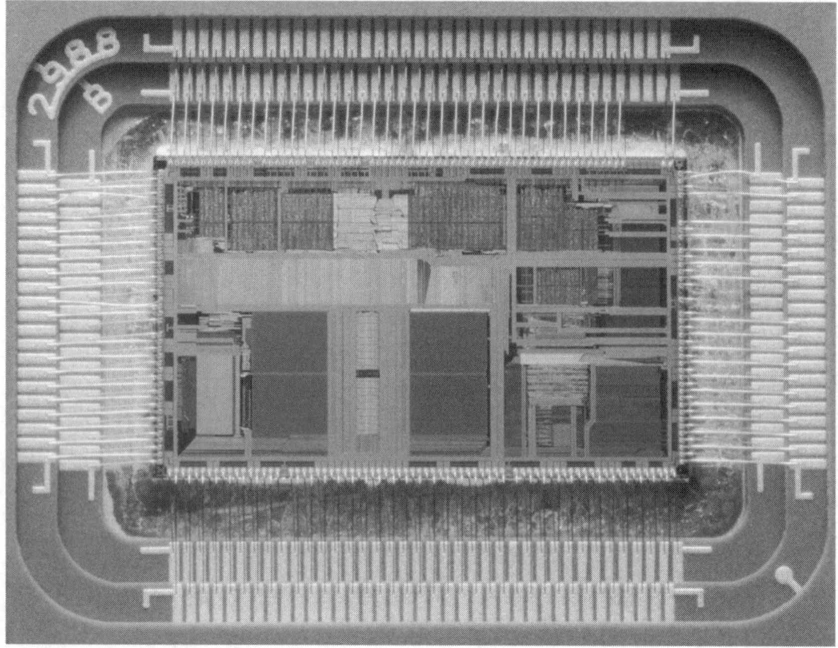

Figure 9-2 Typical CPU

Photo by Rebecca Steele

operands, or numeric values that are associated with the opcode (for example, if the CPU is to add two numbers together, the opcode will direct an addition, and two operands will be the two numbers to add together),.

- *Execute*. This is the actual operation as directed by the opcode.
- *Writeback*. The CPU writes the result of the opcode (for instance, the sum of the two numbers to add together) to some memory location or register.

Instruction Sets Each type of CPU has an *instruction set*—the set of instructions or opcodes that it can use to run a program. Some of the common instruction set models in use are:

- *CISC (Complex Instruction Set Computer)*. A microprocessor architecture in which each instruction can execute several operations in a single instruction cycle. Earlier microprocessors had larger instruction sets to more closely match the semantics of high-level languages. Examples include VAX, PDP-11, Motorola 68000, and Intel x86.
- *RISC (Reduced Instruction Set Computer)*. A newer microprocessor design where the CPU has a smaller (reduced) instruction set that permits it to be more efficient. Examples include SPARC, Dec Alpha, MIPS, and PowerPC.
- *Explicitly Parallel Instruction Computing (EPIC)*. A microprocessor that permits parallel execution in a single CPU. The prime example in use is the Intel Itanium.

Single-Core and Multi-Core Designs Microprocessor CPUs began as single-core designs; that is, the CPU die consisted of a single processor unit. Newer *dual-core* CPUs have two independent CPUs present on a single die. There are also quad-core and eight-core CPU designs.

Single- and Multi-Processor Computers While end user workstations generally have only one CPU (whether single- or dual-core, as discussed earlier), servers can have several, even dozens or hundreds, of CPUs. There are two main types of multiprocessor designs: symmetric and asymmetric.

- *Symmetric multiprocessing (SMP)*. This is a computer architecture where two or more CPUs are connected to the computer's main memory. An operating system that supports SMP can easily move tasks among CPUs in order to improve computing efficiency and throughput. Most multiprocessor systems use the SMP model.
- *Asymmetric multiprocessing (ASMP)*. This computer architecture employs an asymmetrical design that may be built on the theme of master- and slave-processors, processors of different types, or processors that are dedicated to specific tasks. ASMP has fallen out of favor, so much so that no current operating system supports ASMP.

CPU Security Features CPUs contain security features that offer protection of processes and information and improve the integrity of a running system. Some of these features are:

- *Protected mode*. This is a feature wherein the CPU itself prevents a process from being able to attempt to access the memory space assigned to another running process.
- *Executable space protection*. This refers to any of several mechanisms that prevent the execution of data. A running computer program consists of instructions (the program) and data (stored variables); executable space protection prevents the CPU from executing instructions that reside in data.

9

Bus

A computer's **bus** is a subsystem used to transfer data among the computer's internal components, including its CPU, storage, network, and peripherals. A bus can also be used to transfer data between computers.

A computer bus is really a high-speed network that facilitates communication among the computer's internal components. This communication may be token-based (like a token ring network), synchronous (like an ATM network), or interrupt-driven.

Contemporary computers often have more than one bus—one or more for communication with high-speed components such as main memory, as well as separate buses for disk I/O and peripherals.

One or more of a computer's buses usually contains connectors that permit the installation of additional components such as additional memory, storage, or peripheral devices.

A selection of internal bus architectures used over the past twenty years includes:

- *PCI (Peripheral Component Interconnect)*. Used by several brands in modern PCs. PCI connectors on a computer's motherboard are shown in Figure 9-3.

Figure 9-3 PCI bus connectors on a computer motherboard

Photo by Rebecca Steele

- *Microchannel*. Used by IBM in PS/2 systems as a replacement for the slower *ISA* bus.
- *SBus*. Used in SPARC-based computers, including those made by Sun Microsystems.
- *Unibus*. Used by Digital Equipment Corp. PDP-11 and VAX computers.

Some of the external bus architectures include:

- *SCSI (Small Computer System Interface)*. Used primarily for the connection of a computer to its disk storage. Within the SCSI framework are many standards including Fast-SCSI, Fast-Wide SCSI, Ultra-SCSI, Ultra2-SCSI, and Ultra640-SCSI.
- *SATA (Serial ATA)*. Used primarily for communications with disk storage.
- *PCI Express*. Used primarily for communications with storage devices and graphics processors.
- *IEEE 1394*. Also known as **FireWire**, this is a serial bus standard used to connect high-speed external devices such as video cameras.
- *PC card*. Formerly known as PCMCIA, this standard is used for the connection of peripheral devices for laptop computers.

- *Universal Serial Bus (USB).* This is a serial bus protocol used to connect computer peripherals such as keyboards, mice, storage devices, network adaptors, printers, scanners, and cameras.

The once-clear distinction between bus communications and network communication is blurring. With network traffic being carried over bus architectures such as USB and IEEE 1394, and bus-like traffic being carried over networks, both are forms of high-speed communications between computers.

Storage

A computer uses storage to store programs and data. There are two primary types of storage: main storage and secondary storage, which are discussed in this section. The concept of virtual memory is discussed as well.

Main Storage Also known as **primary storage** or **memory**, a computer's **main storage** is used to store instructions and data being actively worked on. In contemporary computers this is also known as the computer's **RAM** (*random access memory*—a reference to the way that main storage is used).

A computer's main storage is the fastest storage: the CPU can access data in main storage far more quickly than data in secondary storage.

The purposes for main storage include:

- *Operating system.* As the arbiter of access to memory and peripherals, active parts of the operating system program code, as well as a good deal of information that the OS keeps track of including:
  - Active processes
  - Memory usage
  - I/O buffers
- *Active processes.* Each active process will occupy a portion of main storage for storage of program code and active data in use.

In most contemporary computer architectures, main memory is volatile; this means that the contents of main memory will mostly vanish if power is removed from the computer. Secondary storage is used to store information that needs to be retained if the computer stops running or if power is removed.

Two primary technologies are in use for main storage, including:

- **Dynamic random access memory (DRAM)** is RAM that must be "refreshed" many times per second in order to retain the correct values stored. Some of the common packages of DRAM include SIPP (Single In-line Pin Package), SIMM (Single In-line Memory Module), DIMM (Dual In-line Memory Module), and SO-DIMM (Small outline DIMM).
- **Static random access memory (SRAM)** is RAM that needs no refresh as does DRAM. Because it draws more power and is less dense than DRAM, SRAM is usually not used for personal computer main storage, but it is sometimes found in devices such as modems and CD-ROM drives for buffer storage.

Secondary Storage **Secondary storage** is the much larger and much slower means of storage used by a computer. Secondary storage is often implemented with **hard disk drives** (HDD) and **solid state drives** (SSD). The reasons for secondary storage include:

- *Persistence*. Secondary storage is usually permanent; data stored in secondary storage will remain intact even if the computer is powered down or disconnected.
- *Capacity*. The available amount of storage in secondary storage is usually far greater than in main storage, by a factor of hundreds to tens of thousands.

Secondary storage is usually organized according to a structure through the use of partitions and file systems.

Partitions are a means used to divide an entire storage device into logical components that can be used for separate purposes.

A secondary storage device can also contain a **Master Boot Record** (**MBR**), which contains computer instructions that can be read into memory when a computer is powered up or restarted.

One or more of a storage device's partitions can contain a **file system**. Depending upon a few factors such as the type of hardware used and the capabilities of the operating system, a file system may include:

- Files
- Directories that include files
- A hierarchy of directories that include files and subdirectories, all of which can include files

Secondary storage can also be unstructured, or *raw*. UNIX operating systems use the term *raw* for secondary storage that is used to store raw characters or blocks of data, and the term *cooked* for secondary storage that contains one or more file systems that can be accessed by the operating system, its tools, and software applications.

Virtual Memory **Virtual memory** is a memory management technique whereby the operating system can permit a process's memory to become fragmented and even overflow onto secondary storage without the process being aware. Virtual memory permits inactive parts of a program's memory to occupy secondary storage, which provides memory that can be used by other processes.

Operating systems employ two methods for moving a process's memory between main storage and secondary storage: swapping and paging.

Swapping **Swapping** is a technique where the contents of main storage occupied by a process are written to a location in secondary storage (disk). This permits a scheme where a process that wants to run can be permitted to run, after the OS has swapped out another process.

Some operating systems are able to support a fixed number of running processes. When more processes are started, they are placed in a queue of waiting processes until one or more active processes either terminate or are swapped out. A system will experience *thrashing*, which is the severe performance degradation that occurs when too many active processes are causing excessive swapping.

Swapping was employed by early timesharing operating systems.

Paging **Paging** is another approach to the problem of limited resources, where there are more processes that want to occupy main memory than can be accommodated. Instead of swapping out an entire process's memory space, only the unused parts of memory (called "pages") are written to disk. Using this scheme, a process can be active and executing while unused parts of its memory space are not in main memory at all, but occupying disk space instead.

When an active process is running and it addresses a page of memory that is not presently occupying main memory, a **page fault** occurs. This causes the operating system to fetch the requested page from disk and place it in main memory for the process to use. In an active operating system, page faults can be occurring at a high rate (hundreds or even thousands per second) while the OS is moving requested pages in from secondary storage and moving idle pages from main memory to secondary storage.

In NT-based versions of Windows (Windows XP, Windows Vista, Windows 7, and Windows 8), all of the system's paging data is stored in a single file, pagefile.sys.

Communications Computer communications are generally performed by hardware modules that are connected to the computer's bus. Because computers almost universally are equipped with means for communications, there is a separate section on the subject.

These hardware modules are usually called *adaptors, communications adaptors, communications controllers, interface cards*, or **network interface cards** (NICs). A typical adaptor is shown in Figure 9-4. A network interface card is a computer hardware component that connects the computer's bus to a communication channel or network.

Generally, a computer's bus is many times faster than external communications. Because of this, the hardware module must be able to manage the differences in communications speed as well as the differences in the style of communications between the bus and the communications medium. This is accomplished with *communications buffers*—temporary storage of data being transmitted through the hardware module, as well as the necessary logic to communicate properly on the bus and on the communications medium.

Firmware

Firmware is the term used to describe software that is embedded in persistent memory chips in the computer. Firmware generally is used to store the initial computer instructions required to put the computer into operation after power is applied to it. Instructions in firmware permit the computer to begin running and load further software from secondary storage

Figure 9-4 Network interface card connects the bus to a communications medium

Photo by Rebecca Steele

(usually a hard drive, optical disc, floppy disk, or external storage device) to complete the loading and startup of the operating system.

Firmware is used to store the *BIOS* (Basic Input/Output System) in an Intel-based PC.

Several technologies are used to store firmware, including:

- **PROM (Programmable Read-Only Memory)**
- **EPROM (Erasable Programmable Read-Only Memory)**
- **EEPROM (Electrically Erasable Programmable Read-Only Memory)**
- **Flash memory**

All of these technologies utilize the capability to store data even after power is removed. The methods used to update the data stored vary by the technology in use.

Trusted Computing Base (TCB)

The DoD Orange Book defines the **trusted computing base** (TCB) as the hardware, firmware, operating system, and software that effectively supports security policy. The Orange Book itself defines the trusted computing base as "*the totality of protection mechanisms within it, including hardware, firmware, and software, the combination of which is responsible for enforcing a computer security policy.*"

Reference Monitor

A **reference monitor** is a hardware or software component in a system that mediates access to objects according to their security level or clearance. A reference monitor is an access control mechanism that is auditable: it creates a record of its activities that can be examined at a later time.

Virtualization

Virtualization refers to software technology used to emulate one or more *virtual machines* running on a single computer system. A **virtual machine** is a software program that emulates computer hardware, such that an operating system running in a virtual machine will have little or no awareness that it is running in a virtual machine instead of directly in the computer system's hardware.

A **hypervisor** is the software program that runs virtual machines. There are two types of hypervisors:

- *Type 1*, also known as native, or bare metal. A type 1 hypervisor runs directly on the computer system hardware.
- *Type 2*, or hosted. A type 2 hypervisor runs within an active operating system.

Type 1 and type 2 hypervisors are depicted in Figure 9-5.

Any of the operating systems running in virtual machines are known as **guests**. VMs are a guest of the hypervisor.

Security Hardware

Computer systems sometimes contain hardware that is used to improve the security of the entire system.

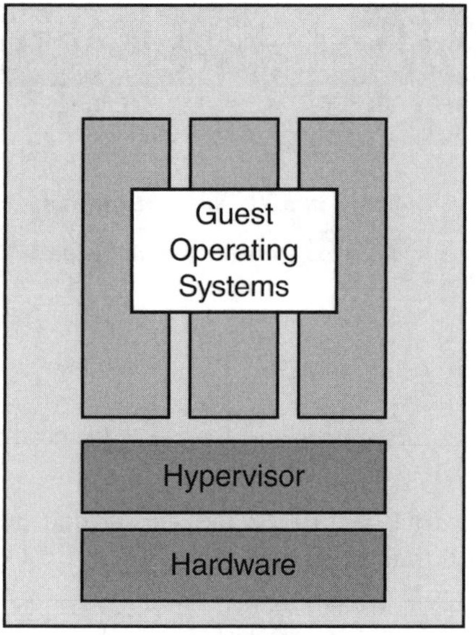

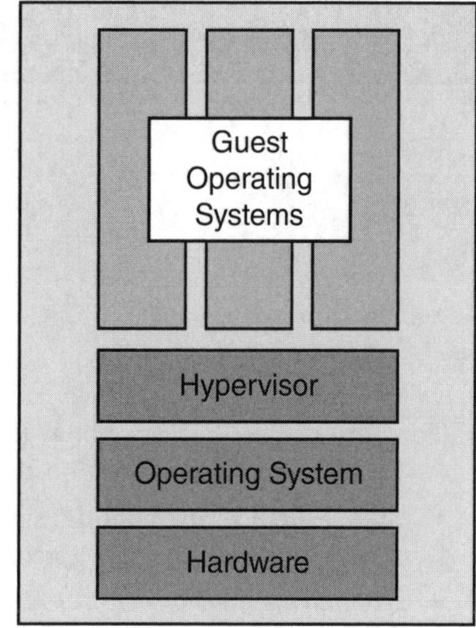

Figure 9-5 Type 1 and Type 2 hypervisors

Trusted Platform Module **Trusted Platform Module** (TPM) is the implementation of a secure cryptoprocessor, a separate microprocessor in the computer that stores and generates cryptographic keys and generates random numbers for use in cryptographic algorithms. TPM is used for a variety of cryptographic functions such as disk encryption and authentication.

Hardware Authentication Many systems, particularly end user desktop and laptop systems, have built-in user authentication hardware, including:

- *Fingerprint reader*. Provides biometric-based authentication that requires the user permits the scanning of his or her finger in order to permit use of the system.
- *Facial recognition camera*. A small built-in camera will view the user's face and compare it to a baseline image to decide whether the current user is the same as the registered user.
- *Smart card reader*. A built-in smart card reader will read a user's smart card (a memory card with memory and sometimes active devices) as a part of two-factor authentication.

Security Modes

Security modes of operation is the term used to designate the type of security in place on a MAC (*mandatory access controls*) based system containing classified information. This term is generally used only in the context of U.S. government and military systems. The modes are:

- ***Dedicated security mode***. This is a system with only one level of security. All users can access all data. All of the information on the system is at the same security level, and

Mode	Signed NDA	Proper Clearance	Formal Access Approved	Need-to-Know
Dedicated	All data	All data	All data	All data
System High	All data	All data	All data	Some data
Compartmented	All data	All data	Some data	Some data
Multilevel	All data	Some data	Some data	Some data

Table 9-4 Security modes of operation

all users must be at or above the same level of security and have a valid need-to-know for all of the information on the system.

- ***System high security mode.*** Similar to dedicated security mode, except that users may access *some* data on the system based upon their *need-to-know.*
- ***Compartmented security mode.*** Similar to system high security mode, except that users may access *some* data on the system based upon their need-to-know plus formal access approval.
- ***Multilevel security mode.*** Similar to *compartmented security mode*, except that users may access some data based upon their need-to-know, formal access approval, *and* proper clearance.

These modes are illustrated in Table 9-4.

Security Countermeasure Principles

Discussions about security architecture would be incomplete if they didn't include key principles. Professionals who design applications, systems, networks, data centers, and work centers rely on basic countermeasures that give the objects of their design added resilience against forces that would otherwise threaten their viability. Key countermeasures are discussed in this section.

Defense in Depth

Defense in depth is a method for protecting an asset with layers of defense. Reliance on a single layer or means for protecting an object puts that object at risk if that single defense should be compromised. Such compromise can be the result of several events, including:

- Software bug
- Hardware failure
- Mechanical failure
- Manufacturing defect
- Environmental events such as over-temperature
- Configuration error
- Man-made or natural disaster

- Sabotage
- Deliberate attack

An important shade of meaning in the term *defense in depth* includes the practice of using different types of controls to protect an object. For example, an organization might utilize two layers of firewalls to protect a system. Part of the principle of defense in depth would suggest that these two firewalls should not be identical but instead should be of different makes. Using two identical firewalls does not really accomplish true defense in depth, since a malfunction, vulnerability, or misconfiguration in one may exist in the other.

System Hardening

System hardening refers to a technique where system configuration is done in a way that makes the system as resilient as possible against compromise. Here, the term *system* may mean a computer operating system, network device, storage device, or software program (including database management system, application server, web server, etc.).

There are several common principles utilized within the practice of system hardening, including:

- Removal of unnecessary services, user accounts, and other components
- Change the name of administrator-level user accounts
- Change all default passwords
- Disable, close, or remove unnecessary network ports
- Configure access security to "deny all", and grant specific access only as necessary

The primary objective of system hardening is the removal or alteration of all possible avenues of attack, in order to make the prospects of successful compromise as low as possible. System hardening reduces a system's "attack surface," which is discussed in the next section.

Attack Surface

The term **attack surface** describes the complete set of components in a system that may be the object of compromise by an attacker. **Attack surface** is a qualitative term that is meant to invoke a mental image of a system's level of vulnerability.

The size of an environment's attack surface is related to the number of addressable addresses, features, functions, services, components, ports, APIs, and so on that are available to its users or neighboring systems. The larger and more complex a system, the larger its attack surface will likely be.

Security through Obfuscation

Security through obfuscation refers to the practice of changing common settings and values to nonstandard settings in an attempt to hide them from potential attackers. Examples of obfuscation include:

- *Nonstandard port numbers*. For example, the administrative web interface on a network device can be changed from port 443 to port 943.
- *Nonstandard accounts*. For example, the administrator account on a Unix system can be changed from "root" to "privacct."

- *Code obfuscation.* Here, the computer instructions or variables in an application may be scrambled in order to make reverse engineering a more daunting task. This can make important functions such as encryption and key management far more difficult for an attacker to figure out.

It is often said in the information security profession that security through obscurity is not real security at all. However, there are times when obfuscation is the only available choice, or (better yet) a part of a defense in depth strategy.

Single Use

The term **single use** refers to a practice of segregating functions in a complex, distributed environment so that each system in the environment is dedicated to performing a single task. For instance, in a three-tier environment with web servers, application servers, and database servers, these three functions should be segregated and run on separate systems.

The practice of single use can also be applied to environments where virtualization is used. Continuing the prior example, web servers, application servers, and database servers should reside on separate physical systems; each physical system may contain several virtual machines of a single type. One physical system may contain several virtual machines that are web servers, another physical system may contain several virtual machines that are the application servers, and yet another physical system may contain several virtual machines that are the database servers.

The reason for this type of arrangement in a virtualized environment is to provide a defense in depth architecture. If an attacker were able to compromise a web server, we would not want the attacker to be able to then attack the hypervisor and be able to reach an application server. Instead, putting different server types on different physical machines preserves the "air gapping" achieved in non-virtualized environments.

Homogeneous and Heterogeneous Environments

A **homogeneous environment** is one where the majority of its systems are all the same type. For instance, a large complex system with many servers that are all running Windows Server 2008 would be considered a homogeneous environment. An environment containing different types of systems would be considered a **heterogeneous environment**.

The advantage of a homogeneous environment is ease of management: with systems that are all of the same type, tools can be used to configure them all the same way, and with less effort. The primary disadvantage of a homogeneous environment is that a vulnerability in one of the systems is more likely to be present in all of the systems.

A practical use of heterogeneous environments is an environment with multiple layers of firewalls. A good heterogeneous approach would be to use firewalls from different manufacturers at each layer. This way, if one of the firewalls is found to be vulnerable to a new type of attack, it is likely that the other firewalls do not share the same vulnerability.

Software

Software is the overall term referring to sets of computer instructions that are built to fulfill some purpose. The two main types of software are **operating systems** and **applications**.

Operating Systems

An *operating system* is the software that facilitates the use of application programs and tools and controls access to the computer's hardware resources. Examples of desktop operating systems are AIX, Linux, Mac OS, Solaris, and Windows.

The primary components of an operating system are:

- ***Kernel.*** This is the "core" software that runs on the computer to allocate resources and control processes.
- ***Device drivers.*** These are programs that permit the operating system and other programs to communicate with hardware devices that are a part of the computer or connected to it.
- ***Tools.*** These are separate programs that are used to build and maintain a system. Tools are used to change system configurations, edit files, create directories, and install other programs.

The primary functions of an operating system are:

- *Process management.* Processes are programs that are running on the computer. The operating system's process management includes the means for starting processes, allocating resources to processes, and terminating processes.
- *Resource management.* The operating system provides access to resources such as primary storage, secondary storage, and devices such as displays and external storage devices.
- *Access management.* The operating system employs authentication as well as access controls to determine whether to grant access to a specific resource such as a file or a device.
- *Event management.* The operating system responds to common events and error conditions in a variety of ways including logging, starting or stopping processes, or communicating with internal processes or external entities.
- *Communications management.* The operating system facilitates communications via the resources and devices present in the computer for that purpose.

Operating systems employ security protection: preventing one process from interfering with other processes, and controlling access to resources. Two common protection models are:

- ***Privilege level.*** This is a scheme where the operating system implements levels of privilege. The Windows operating system implements this through the administrative-level privilege, user-level privilege, and guest privilege. UNIX implements this through root and non-root privilege levels.
- ***Protection ring.*** This is a scheme of concentric rings, starting with Ring 0 in the center that is the highest security that the kernel uses, plus one or more additional rings where device drivers and user programs run.

The operating system kernel enforces these protection models.

Subsystems

A computer's operating system provides the software framework to support the use of the computer. Depending upon the intended use of the computer, some *subsystems* may be required. *Subsystems* are software programs that perform functions that are required by applications and programs. Examples of subsystems include:

- ***Database management system (DBMS).*** A DBMS is a software component used to manage large organized collections of data, called *databases*. Example DBMS programs include Microsoft SQL Server, IBM DB2, Oracle, and Sybase. The types of database management systems are described in detail in Chapter 3, "Software Development Security."
- ***Web server.*** A *web server* is a software component used to accept and process incoming requests for information that are sent from end users running browsers or other applications via *web services*. A web server may fulfill incoming requests by returning static content that is stored on the computer, or pass the request to an application server program running on the same computer or on a different computer.
- *Authentication server*. This is a software component that is used to provide authentication services for other programs running on the same computer, or for other computers on the network.
- *E-mail server*. An *e-mail server* is used to transmit, receive, and store e-mail messages. An e-mail server may be used to relay messages to other servers, or it may be used to store e-mail messages to be read directly by end users.
- *File server*. A *file server* is a software component that is used to store and make available directories and files to users over a network. The Windows and UNIX/Linux operating systems have basic file server capabilities built in, and there are third-party software components available that provide advanced capabilities.
- *Directory services*. A *directory server* is a software component that provides reference services for other computers or users on the network. Examples of directory services includes:
  - Domain Name Service (DNS)
  - Network Information Service (NIS)
  - Active Directory (AD)
  - Lightweight Directory Access Protocol (LDAP)
- *Virtualization server*. A *virtualization server* is a software component that provides the ability for one or more instantiations of operating systems to run on a single hardware system. Virtualization is discussed in more detail earlier in this chapter.

Programs, Tools, and Applications

Applications, tools, and programs are the broad class of software that runs on computers under the control of an operating system.

- ***Program.*** A single set of instructions for a computer that usually resides in a single file. A program can refer either to an executable program that contains machine-readable instructions or to the source code that contains human-readable instructions. Examples of programs that would run on an end user's computer include:
  - *Firefox*. A web browser used to communicate with web servers
  - *Writer*. A program used to create human-readable documents or simple web pages

- *Photoshop*. A program used to manipulate digital images
- *Winamp*. A program used to listen to audio recordings or view video recordings or broadcasts

- *Tool*. A tool is also, strictly speaking, a program, but is used for some simpler purpose in support of applications, programs, and subsystems. Example tools include:
  - *Compilers*. Programs used to create machine-readable executable programs from human-readable source code
  - *Debuggers*. Programs used to test and debug the operation of a computer program
  - *Defragmenters*. Programs used to reorganize the files stored in a file system in order to make the file system more efficient
- *Application*. A collection of programs and tools that support a business function. Example applications include:
  - Financial management applications that support general ledger (GL), accounts payable (AP), accounts receivable (AR), and so on
  - Customer relationship management
  - Incident management applications
  - Enterprise resource planning (ERP)
  - Material requirements planning (MRP) and manufacturing resource planning (MRP II)

Applications often require the support of subsystems such as database management systems (DBMSs) to manage stored data, authentication servers, directory servers, and web servers to provide users with a user interface.

Software Security Threats

A *threat* is a potential and harmful action that—if realized—can cause some harm to its target. In the realm of computer architecture and security models, there are a number of threats including covert channels, side-channel attacks, state attacks, emanations, maintenance hooks and back doors, and privileged programs.

Other types of threats, such as malware, social engineering, and dictionary attacks, are discussed in several other chapters in this book.

Covert Channels

A **covert channel** is an unauthorized, hidden channel of communications that exists within a legitimate communications channel. Because many communication channels include some idle time (or space), it can be quite difficult to detect a covert channel.

There are two types of covert channels, *storage* and *timing*, explained below.

A *covert storage channel* involves a storage location used by a target system. The location may be a memory location, a disk sector, or a file. The unauthorized third party may be able to directly or indirectly read the storage location and gain some level of knowledge about the information stored there.

A *covert timing channel* uses observable timings seen in an information system to determine what is happening in the system.

Examples of covert channels include:

- *Use of unused fields.* Covert messages can be inserted into the padding or unused fields in network communications frames or packets, or in unused fields in stored or transmitted data streams.
- *Steganography.* This is the technique of hiding data within images, sounds, or video files.

Side-Channel Attacks

A **side-channel attack** is an attack on a system where a subject can observe the physical characteristics of a system in order to make inferences on its operation. Generally the term *side-channel attack* is used to describe an attack on a cryptosystem.

Some of the observations that can be used include *timing*, *power consumption*, and *emanations*, any of which may provide clues to a system's operation that may permit an attacker to compromise it.

Inference Attacks

An **inference attack** is an attack that is performed through the analysis of available data in order to illegitimately learn about targeted data that is not directly available. A simple example of an inference attack is the analysis of positions offered announcements that list the technologies in use in an organization; this can help an attacker better understand the technologies in use in an organization and possibly help an attacker avoid detection.

Aggregation Attack

An **aggregation attack** is a data mining technique where an attacker gathers and combines data elements in order to further the ability to illegitimately obtain sensitive data.

An example of an aggregation attack is the mining of public records about citizens in order to be able to compromise sensitive or valuable computer accounts. Obtaining dates of birth and mothers' maiden names can help an attacker gain illegitimate access to banking and other high-value user accounts.

Data aggregation also refers to the legal (or, in some cases, barely legal) activity of combining databases containing sensitive information that results in databases with even greater economic value. For instance, organizations providing background check data to paying customers can obtain information from various public domain and open source data sources that are, by themselves, practically harmless, but when combined may be quite valuable.

State Attacks (TOCTTOU)

A **time of check to time of use** (**tocttou**) bug is a defect in software or hardware that can result in a malfunction or security violation in a system. An example of a **race condition**, a **tocttou** bug is one where changes in a system occur between the *checking* of a condition and the *use* that results from the check.

Here is an example: Two users wish to open a file for exclusive use. The program that each user is running first checks to see if the file is in use; the program for each user reports that the file is not opened by anyone. Because of that, both users' programs open the file, expecting that they each have exclusive use of the file. Depending upon the use of the file, compromise occurs either because the attacker is able to view the contents of the file, or the attacker is able to disrupt normal operations related to the file.

Emanations

The term **emanations** refers to the phenomena where radio frequency (RF) electrical signals—called *compromising emanations (CE)*—are emitted from computing and network equipment. While this is most often associated with CRT (cathode ray tube) monitors and poorly terminated network wiring, emanations can also be emitted from circuits within computers and other devices themselves. Any time that data is processed by a system or transmitted through a network, electromagnetic radiation will tend to emanate from systems and network cabling, providing adversaries with opportunities to intercept or even alter it.

The U.S. Department of Defense conducted research into the field of emanations in a program that was code-named TEMPEST. The result has been a set of standards for shielding equipment, rooms, and entire buildings from compromising emanations.

Maintenance Hooks and Back Doors

During development, software programmers often place a **maintenance hook** or back door into the program they are working on in order to facilitate easier testing. These hooks and back doors are rarely documented, and sometimes programmers will forget to remove them, which results in a program in production or commercial use having vulnerabilities that can be exploited by the programmer or someone else who discovers them.

Occasionally, programmers deliberately place hooks and back doors into programs and leave them there intentionally, either to ease the support process or for malicious reasons, such as falsifying information or theft.

Privileged Programs

Developers and other persons may accidentally or intentionally place tools or utilities on a system that have privileged levels of operation. The purpose of these tools or utilities is to permit the tools' user to surreptitiously perform unauthorized functions on the system.

These privileged programs may be an acceptable artifact on a development or testing environment where the developer or tester needs quick, privileged-level access to programs or data in order to facilitate a rapid and efficient development or testing process. But if these programs are installed on the production environment, they may permit unauthorized and inappropriate access, allowing personnel to manipulate the system.

An additional security risk of privileged programs is discovery by an outsider who is seeking ways of gaining unauthorized entry to a system.

Supply Chain Attacks

A **supply chain attack** is one where an attacker attempts to compromise a system by compromising one of its externally developed components. For instance, a successful compromise of a company that produces the BIOS (basic input/output system—in other words, the firmware) for a computer system will enable an attacker to compromise those computer systems via a defect introduced into their firmware. Another way of compromising a target's supplier is to steal its secrets. An example follows.

The SecureID product produced by RSA was attacked in 2011; attackers obtained specific secrets that permitted them to compromise the SecureID product. The objective of this attack was thought to be certain U.S.-based defense contractors that used the SecureID product. Compromise of SecureID would permit attackers to access those defense contractors' networks as though they possessed SecureID tokens.

In a second example, an adversary is able to compromise the manufacturing process for merchant credit card payment terminals by inserting malicious code into the firmware of each terminal, creating the ability to steal sensitive credit card data. Later, after these terminals are used to accept customer payments, the credit card numbers and PINs are transmitted to the adversary.

In another example, there are allegations that the U.S. NSA intercepted shipments of computer networking equipment so that said equipment could be modified in a way to permit espionage. Similarly, there are allegations of influence or tampering with cryptographic algorithms to permit cryptanalysis of encrypted data.

Software Security Countermeasures

Countermeasures are actions that can be taken to reduce the potential of a threat by reducing its probability of occurrence or its impact. The countermeasures in this section are those that can be used to reduce the threats discussed in the previous section.

Sniffers and Other Analyzers

Sniffers are devices used to record communications on a network medium, such as Ethernet or WiFi. A sniffer can be used to analyze communications in order to study what communications are taking place. Other types of analyzers include bug detectors, which are devices used to detect covert wireless transmitters.

Source Code Reviews

A **source code review** is an activity where programs analyze a program's source code in order to ensure that recent changes were applied correctly and that the program contains no unwanted code, such as back doors or maintenance hooks. To be effective, source code reviews must be performed by skilled programmers who have not made recent changes to the program being reviewed; if a malicious programmer has placed illicit code in a program, he or she will deliberately overlook it in order to make sure that it is not detected and removed.

Source code reviews can be improved through the use of source code scanning tools that can examine application source code and identify many different types of defects, including those that may lead to a successful attack on the program.

Auditing Tools

Auditing tools include a wide range of tools that are used to examine a system in order to detected unwanted conditions. Examples of auditing tools are:

- *File system integrity checking*. These tools periodically examine the part of a system's file system (and perhaps its firmware and other characteristics) where the operating system and important programs reside and report any changes that occurred. These changes could be the result of normal maintenance, unauthorized changes, or an intruder. *Tripwire* is a well-known file system integrity tool.
- *Configuration checking*. These tools periodically examine the configuration of an operating system in order to detect any changes, configurations, and outdated versions of installed software that would be considered unsafe or unsecure.
- *Log analyzers*. These tools examine system and network logs to identify any suspicious activity that could be the result of an intrusion or an administrator performing unauthorized activities. *LogRhythm* is a well-known tool for this purpose.

Vulnerability Scanning Tools

Vulnerability scanning is a technique used to detect weaknesses in a system that could be exploited by an intruder. Vulnerability scanning tools work by sending a collection of specially formed packets over a network to a target system and then examining any responses returned from the target system.

Vulnerability scanning tools are designed to identify weaknesses in network components, server operating systems, and server subsystems such as web servers and database management systems.

A different class of network-based testing tools is used to detect vulnerabilities in web-based applications. These tools operate like intelligent web browsers and send a collection of specially formed messages to the application to look for signs of weaknesses that could be exploited by intruders and that could result in the compromise of sensitive data. Many noteworthy hacking incidents have occurred because of web application vulnerabilities.

Penetration Testing

Penetration testing is a technique that goes beyond what vulnerability scanning tools are designed to achieve. "Pen testing," as it is often called, includes the use of techniques and tools to manually identify and exploit weaknesses that automated vulnerability scanning tools are not able to identify. Pen testing is a labor-intensive activity carried out by highly skilled individuals who have a deep understanding of the internal operation of server hardware, operating systems, database management systems, and software applications.

Software Security Countermeasures and OWASP

Vulnerability scanning, penetration testing, source code reviews, and other means for identifying security-related software defects can be aligned with common vulnerabilities published by the Open Web Application Security Project (OWASP). Dedicated to the improvement of security of web applications, the OWASP organization publishes materials and conducts training events for web application software developers. OWASP can be found at http://www.owasp.org.

Cloud Computing Threats and Countermeasures

Cloud computing is generally regarded as the delivery of application, systems, or infrastructure services over a network. The main impetus for organizations' use of cloud computing services is the ability to utilize services from a service provider at lower cost than organizations could achieve on their own.

Typically, cloud-based services realize an economy of scale through the implementation of a single large system that is shared by many customers. Logical segregation in the cloud-based service gives each customer the perception that they are the service's only customer: each customer is, by design, unaware of any other customers' use of the service.

Cloud computing offers several advantages over an organization's implementing a system on its own:

- *Reduced costs.* Organizations using cloud computing services do not need to spend capital on IT equipment, nor make large purchases on systems, storage, or application software. Instead, organizations utilize **cloud services** through operational subscription costs.
- *Reduced need for specialized expertise.* Organizations using cloud computing services do not need to hire IT personnel to manage specialized systems and components.
- *Focus on core competencies.* Using cloud computing services may permit the organization to focus on its core business and not on its IT systems.

Threats against cloud computing environments include all of the usual threats against information systems. Cloud-based environments invite threat agents seeking to steal data or disrupt services related to multiple business customers. Put another way, cloud services attract more threats because they contain information and perform functions for many organizations in a single targeted environment.

Multitenancy and Logical Separation

Cloud-based services do, by their nature, provide those services to multiple organizations from a single infrastructure. For those services that include the storage or processing of data for its customers, the subject of logically separating data between customers is perhaps the defining characteristic. In addition to the repertoire of safeguards required to protect any information system, a cloud-based system also requires controls and safeguards to assure that the data and functions among its tenants remain absolutely separate.

In the same manner that safeguards are employed on a system in a defense in depth method, the safeguards to ensure logical separation should also follow a defense in depth methodology.

Data Sovereignty

A principal concern related to an organization storing data in a cloud-based service is its control over its data. **Data sovereignty** is the term that describes the data owner's legal control over its data, and the jurisdictional issue of electronic data stored in a particular country or state.

Since in most if not all cloud-based services, the infrastructure and other components are managed by the cloud services provider, arguably the customer lacks direct control over its data. After all, its data resides on systems or devices the organization does not own or physically control. To some degree, the organization has ceded direct control over its data to its cloud-based service provider. This is closely related to the matter of data jurisdiction, which is discussed next.

Data Jurisdiction

Another significant concern on the part of organizations utilizing cloud computing services is the notion of data jurisdiction. The heart of the problem is this: an organization, located in one legal jurisdiction, is the legal owner of data located on a cloud service provider's systems, which may physically be located in one or more separate legal jurisdictions. The applicability and reach of security and privacy laws gets rather complicated. Because cloud computing services have only recently become widely used, there are few well-tested legal precedents that help organizations and providers understand the full extent of legal jurisdiction in a number of situations including data and privacy compromise.

One well-known issue is the U.S. PATRIOT Act that gives federal law enforcement secret subpoena powers that include examination of data in cloud-based systems. Through a National Security Letter, law enforcement would compel a cloud-based service provider to turn over records and data and prevent the service provider from informing affected customers.

Controls and Audits

An organization using a cloud services provider may be responsible for implementing and monitoring security controls related to the security and integrity of data and processes. In many cases, the effectiveness of some controls may be difficult to establish since they are in the control of the cloud services provider. For reasons of security and/or the protection of intellectual property, a cloud services provider may be less than forthcoming on the details of certain key controls that the client organization is responsible for. Fortunately, there are remedies for this.

A cloud services organization can have objective audits of key controls performed by external, independent audit firms. Depending on the location and nature of services provided, these external audits can carry enough weight to be accepted by a client organization's internal or external auditors. Two well-known examples of these external audits are:

- *ISAE 3402 (International Standard on Assurance Engagements No. 3402)*. This is an international external auditing methodology governed by the International Auditing and Assurance Standards Board (IAASB), which is part of the International Federation of Accountants (IFAC).
- *SSAE-16 (Statement on Standards for Attestation Engagements No. 16)*. This is a U.S.-based external auditing methodology standard governed by the American Institute of Certified Public Accountants (AICPA). The SSAE 16 standard was built upon the ISAE 3402 framework.

In both SSAE 16 and ISAE 3402 audits, the cloud services provider selects the controls to be audited, and a qualified external audit firm performs audits of those controls according to well-established auditing procedures. The cloud services provider then makes the audit report available to its customers on request.

The key to successful use of SSAE 16 and ISAE 3402 audits is the selection of controls that represent the audit concerns of its customers.

The SSAE 16 and ISAE 3402 standards are so similar that an organization can have both reports for both audit standards produced as an outcome of a single external audit.

Chapter Summary

- The concepts of confidentiality, integrity, and availability are the three pillars of information security.
- Bell-LaPadula and Biba are state machine models that describe access to various levels of information for subjects at various levels of clearance.
- Clark-Wilson is a data integrity model that consists of principals that operate on data items.
- Common Criteria for Information Technology Security Evaluation is a framework for specifying, implementing, and evaluating a system against a set of security requirements. Common Criteria supersedes TCSEC and ITSEC, which are older security evaluation methodologies.
- The Capability Maturity Model Integration, or CMMI, is a model used to evaluate the maturity of systems engineering processes. The Systems Security Engineering Capability Maturity Model (SSE-CMM) is a model used to evaluate the maturity of security in an organization.
- Certification is the process of evaluating a system against a set of criteria. Accreditation is the process of formally approving the use of a system. These two terms are often used together and called *C&A*.
- FedRAMP is the U.S. government-wide program for assessing, authorizing, and monitoring cloud-based service providers.
- FISMA is the U.S. federal government mandated framework for certifying and accrediting information systems.
- The *DoD Information Assurance Certification and Accreditation Process*, or DIACAP, is used to certify and accredit military information systems. DIACAP supersedes DITSCAP (Department of Defense Information Technology Security Certification and Accreditation Process). The *National Information Assurance Certification and Accreditation Process* (NIACAP) is the process used to certify and accredit systems that handle national security information. DCID 6/3 is the process used to certify and accredit systems used by the U.S. Central Intelligence Agency (CIA).
- A computer's hardware consists of a CPU (central processing unit, which executes the instructions in *programs*), a bus, main storage, secondary storage, firmware, and communications capabilities.
- A CPU contains an arithmetic logic unit (ALU), registers, program counter, and memory interface. The CPU's basic functions are fetch (retrieve an instruction from memory), decode (parse an instruction), execute (perform the instruction), and writeback (write the results of the instruction to a register or memory location). A CPU chip may have a single core (CPU) or multiple cores (CPUs).
- Most computers with multiple CPUs have a symmetric multiprocessing (SMP) architecture in which all CPUs are connected to main memory. Some older computers employ an asymmetric multiprocessing (ASMP) architecture that employs master and slave CPUs or some other asymmetric scheme.
- A computer's bus is used to connect the computer's main components (CPU, main memory, secondary memory, peripherals) together. Many modern computers have more than one bus.

- A computer's main memory usually consists of electronic random access memory in the form of DRAM (dynamic random access memory) or, less often, SRAM (static random access memory). A computer's secondary storage usually consists of one or more hard disk drives, although some compact computers employ flash memory for secondary storage.
- Virtual memory is the means used to accommodate more active processes than can be directly supported by main memory. Swapping (archaic) and paging (contemporary) are used to shuttle process memory images back and forth between main storage and secondary storage.
- Firmware is software that is permanently (or semipermanently) stored on memory chips in a computer and usually used to store machine-readable instructions for bootstrapping the computer.
- Virtualization is the software technology that permits several computer operating systems to simultaneously run on a single hardware computer system.
- Trusted computing base (TCB) is a DoD *Orange Book* term used to describe the entire set of hardware, firmware, operating system, and programs that support a stated security policy.
- The *security modes of operation* are dedicated, system high, compartmented, and multilevel.
- *Defense in depth* is the practice of protecting an asset with a combination of security controls, such that if any one control fails, the others will still provide some protection.
- *System hardening* is the practice of reducing the number and type of exploitable components on a system, thereby reducing its *attack surface* and making it more difficult to attack. *Security through obfuscation* is a hardening technique where objects in a system are hidden in simple ways, such as changing the port numbers through which a service communicates over a network.
- *Single use* is a technique in overall systems architecture where each system in the environment performs a single task.
- An operating system (OS) is the software that facilitates the use of application programs and tools and controls access to the computer's hardware resources. The primary functions of an OS are process management, resource management, access management, event management, and communications management. The OS may use the *privilege level* model or the *protection ring* model to enforce security policy.
- A computer system may have one or more software subsystems installed including a database management server (DBMS), web server, authentication server, e-mail server, file server, directory server, and virtualization server.
- A *program* is a set of computer instructions used for some business purpose. A *tool* is a program usually used for some system maintenance purpose. An *application* is a collection of programs and tools that supports a high-level business activity, such as financial accounting or manufacturing resource planning.
- Threats to computing architectures include covert channels (unauthorized—and perhaps hidden—communications that occupy a legitimate communications channel); side-channel attacks (inference attacks that use observations of timing, power consumption, and emanations to discover facts about a system); state attacks (also known as race conditions);

emanations (usually RF radiation from devices such as CRT monitors and network cabling to eavesdrop on computer activity); supply chain attacks; and maintenance hooks, back doors, and privileged programs (to gain illicit access to information).

- Countermeasures to these threats include source code reviews (to discover unwanted or illicit program instructions); auditing tools (to detect unauthorized changes or unwanted events); and vulnerability scanning tools (to discover weaknesses in systems and software) and penetration testing.
- Cloud-based systems can provide economical and effective services for organizations as a viable alternative to building and managing the same capabilities in-house. Issues of data segregation and multitenancy, data jurisdiction, data sovereignty, and audits need to be addressed in order to give client organizations the assurances that services are performed properly.

Key Terms

Access matrix A security model that consists of a two-dimensional matrix of subjects and objects and the permissions for each subject's access to each object.

Accreditation The process of formally approving the use of a system.

Aggregation attack A data mining technique where data elements related to target subjects are combined in order to obtain even more target data.

Application A collection of programs and tools that fulfill a specific business purpose.

Arithmetic logic unit (ALU) The portion of a CPU where arithmetic and logic operations are performed.

Asymmetric multiprocessing (ASMP) A multi-CPU computer architecture consisting of master and slave CPUs or some other asymmetric arrangement.

Attack surface The complete set of components in a system that may be the object of compromise by an attacker.

Bell-LaPadula A security model that addresses the confidentiality of information.

Biba A security model that addresses data integrity.

Bus A hardware subsystem used to transfer data among a computer's internal components, including its CPU, storage, network, and peripherals.

Central processing unit (CPU) The portion of a computer where program instructions are executed.

Certification The process of evaluating a system against a specific criteria or specification.

Clark-Wilson A security model that addresses data integrity that is a rebuttal to the Bell-LaPadula and Biba models.

Cloud services Any of several varieties of IT services delivered to customers; services may include software applications, operating systems on demand, and data storage on demand.

Common Criteria The current framework for evaluating the security of a system.

Compartmented security mode One of the security modes of operation where users can access some data based upon their need-to-know and formal access approval.

Complex Instruction Set Computer (CISC) A microprocessor architecture in which each instruction can execute several operations in a single instruction cycle.

Covert channel An unauthorized channel of communications that exists within a legitimate communications channel.

Data confidentiality model A security model whose chief concern is the confidentiality of data.

Data integrity model A security model whose chief concern is data integrity.

Data sovereignty The legal issue regarding the jurisdiction of electronically stored information.

Database management system (DBMS) A set of software programs used to manage large organized collections of data called databases.

Dedicated security mode One of the security modes of operation where all users can access all data.

Department of Defense Information Assurance Certification and Accreditation Process (DIACAP) The process used to certify and accredit information systems used by the U.S. military.

Department of Defense Information Technology Security Certification and Accreditation Process (DITSCAP) The process used to certify and accredit information systems used by the U.S. military; superseded by DIACAP.

Device driver A program that permits the operating system and other programs to communicate with a specific hardware device or type of device.

Director of Central Intelligence Directive 6/3 (DCID 6/3) The process for protecting sensitive compartmented information within information systems at the U.S. Central Intelligence Agency (CIA).

Discretionary access control (DAC) An access control model where the owner of an object may grant access rights to subjects based upon the owner's discretion.

Dynamic random access memory (DRAM) A random access memory (RAM) technology used in computer main storage.

Electrically Erasable Programmable Read-Only Memory (EEPROM) A form of erasable semiconductor memory used to store firmware.

Erasable Programmable Read-Only Memory (EPROM) A form of erasable semiconductor memory used to store firmware.

Evaluation Assurance Level (EAL) The seven levels of evaluation in the Common Criteria.

Explicitly Parallel Instruction Computing (EPIC) A microprocessor design that permits parallel execution in a single CPU.

Federal Information Security Management Act (FISMA) A U.S. law that requires the evaluation of all systems used by the U.S. federal government.

FedRAMP The U.S. government-wide program for assessing, authorizing, and monitoring cloud-based service providers.

File system A logical collection of files that resides on a storage medium.

FireWire See *IEEE 1394*.

Firmware Computer instructions that are stored on a nonvolatile memory device such as a PROM or EPROM.

Flash memory A form of erasable semiconductor memory used to store firmware.

Guest An operating system that is installed on a virtual machine.

Hard disk drive (HDD) A hardware device, consisting of spinning platters coated with magnetic storage material and moving read-write heads, used to store data, used as secondary storage.

Homogeneous environment A community of systems that are alike.

Hook See *maintenance hook*.

Hypervisor A software program that creates and runs virtual machines.

IEEE 1394 An external bus architecture used to connect high-speed external devices such as video cameras.

Inference attack A technique using analysis of available data to gain knowledge about targeted data that is not directly available.

Information flow A security model that describes permitted and forbidden flows of information rather than access controls.

Information Technology Security Evaluation Criteria (ITSEC) The European framework for system security evaluation now superseded by the Common Criteria.

ISAE 3402 (International Standard on Assurance Engagements No. 3402) An international audit methodology used to provide audit assurance to clients of service organizations.

ISO 15408 See *Common Criteria*.

Kernel The part of an operating system that actively manages processes and access to resources.

Main storage The primary, but usually volatile, high-speed storage used by a computer.

Maintenance hook A feature in a program that permits easy maintenance or access to information that bypasses security controls.

Mandatory access control (MAC) An access control model where subjects are permitted to access objects based upon specific security policies.

Master boot record (MBR) A place on a mass storage device (such as a hard drive) that contains computer instructions that can be read into memory when a computer is powered up or restarted.

Memory See *main storage*.

Memory interface The portion of a CPU that facilitates access to the computer's main memory.

Microchannel An internal bus architecture used by IBM in PS/2 systems as a replacement for the slower ISA bus.

Multilevel A security model consisting of several clearance levels for subjects and objects.

Multilevel security mode One of the security modes of operation where users can access data based upon their need-to-know, formal access approval, and security clearance.

National Information Assurance Certification and Accreditation Process (NIACAP) The process used to certify and accredit systems that handle U.S. national security information.

Network interface card (NIC) A computer hardware component that connects the computer's bus to a communication channel or network.

Non-interference An abstract security model that states that subjects with low clearance levels cannot learn anything about information at higher clearance levels on account of activities performed by subjects at higher clearance levels.

Operating system The software that facilitates the use of application programs and tools, and controls access to the computer's hardware resources.

Page fault An event where a process attempts to access data in a memory location that has been moved to secondary storage.

Paging The memory management technique of moving inactive memory pages between main storage and secondary storage.

Partition A separate division of storage, usually on a hard disk drive.

PC card An external bus architecture used for the connection of compact peripheral devices to laptop computers.

PCI (Peripheral Component Interconnect) An internal bus architecture used in modern computers.

PCI Express An internal bus architecture used in modern computers

Primary storage See *main storage.*

Privilege level An operating system protection scheme where users are assigned levels of permissions that dictate the resources and data that they are permitted to access.

Program A set of computer instructions that usually resides in a file and is used to perform a specific task.

Program counter A CPU register that tracks the current instruction in a program.

Programmable Read-Only Memory (PROM) A form of semiconductor memory used to store firmware.

Protection ring A hierarchical operating system protection scheme used to protect resources based upon levels of privilege.

Race condition See *time of check to time of use (tocttou) bug.*

Random access memory (RAM) See *main storage.*

Reduced Instruction Set Computer (RISC) A newer microprocessor design where the CPU has a smaller (reduced) instruction set that permits it to be more efficient.

Reference monitor A hardware or software component in a system that mediates access to objects according to their security level or clearance.

Register A storage location within a CPU.

SBus An internal bus architecture used in SPARC-based computers including those made by Sun Microsystems.

Secondary storage The slower, but persistent, form of storage used by a computer.

Security modes of operation The security classifications for systems that determine the types of permissions necessary for users to access data.

Security through obfuscation The practice of changing common settings and values to non-standard settings in an attempt to hide them from potential attackers.

Serial ATA (SATA) An external bus architecture used primarily for communications with disk storage.

Side-channel attack An attack on a system where a subject can observe the physical characteristics of a system in order to make inferences on its internal operation.

Single use The practice of segregating functions in a complex, distributed environment so that each system in the environment is dedicated to performing a single task.

Small Computer System Interface (SCSI) An external bus architecture used to connect a computer to disk storage devices.

Sniffer A device or program used to record communications on a network.

Software Engineering Institute Capability Maturity Model Integration (SEI-CMMI) A framework for evaluating the maturity of an organization's systems engineering practices.

Solid-state drive (SSD) A hardware device, consisting of memory chips, used to store data, used as secondary storage.

Source code review A review of a program's source code in order to ensure that recent changes were applied correctly and that the program contains no unwanted code.

SSAE-16 (Statement on Standards for Attestation Engagements No. 16) A U.S.-based audit methodology used to provide audit assurance to clients of service organizations.

Static random access memory (SRAM) A random access memory (RAM) technology used in computer main memory.

Supply chain attack An attack on a system via one of its software or hardware suppliers, through the introduction of a defect that will permit compromise of the target system.

Swapping The memory management technique of moving an entire process's memory contents between main storage and secondary storage.

Symmetric multiprocessing (SMP) A computer architecture where two or more CPUs are connected to the computer's main memory in a symmetrical arrangement.

System high security mode One of the security modes of operation where all users can access some data based upon their need-to-know.

Systems Security Engineering Capability Maturity Model (SSE-CMM) A framework for evaluating the maturity of an organization's security implementation practices.

Target of evaluation (TOE) A system being evaluated with the Common Criteria.

Time of check to time of use (tocttou) bug A resource allocation vulnerability where a period of time elapses between the time when a resource's availability is confirmed and the resource is assigned or used.

Tools Separate programs that are included with an operating system that are used to change system configurations, edit files, create directories, and install other programs.

Trusted Computer Security Evaluation Criteria (TCSEC) The U.S. DoD framework for system security evaluation now superseded by the Common Criteria.

Trusted computing base (TCB) The hardware, firmware, operating system, and software that effectively support security policy.

Trusted Network Interpretation (TNI) The evaluation criteria for evaluating the confidentiality and integrity of communications networks.

Trusted Platform Module (TPM) A secure cryptoprocessor used to store cryptographic keys and perform some crypto functions.

Unibus An internal bus architecture used by Digital Equipment Corp. PDP-11 and VAX computers.

Universal Serial Bus (USB) A serial bus communications standard, used for the connection of peripheral devices to a computer including keyboards, mice, storage devices, and network adaptors.

Virtual machine A simulation of computer hardware, performed by software, for the purpose of housing one or more guest operating systems running on a single computer system. See also *Guest*.

Virtual memory A memory management technique whereby the operating system can permit a process's memory to become fragmented and even overflow onto secondary storage.

Virtualization The use of specialized software to facilitate the existence of two or more logically separate running operating systems (virtual machines) on a single physical system.

Web server A software component used to accept and process incoming requests for information sent from end users who are using web browsers.

Review Questions

1. The framework for evaluating a system against a set of security requirements that supersedes TCSEC and ITSEC is:
   a. The Orange Book
   b. The CMMI
   c. The Common Criteria
   d. COBIT
2. An organization has completed the certification of a new information system. The next step(s) is (are):
   a. Accreditation and business use
   b. Business use
   c. Coding, testing, and implementation
   d. Security testing and implementation
3. A computer's internal bus is used for:
   a. Enforcing process separation
   b. Communication with peripherals
   c. Communication between CPU and peripherals
   d. Communication between CPU, memory, and peripherals

4. The purpose for secondary memory is:
   a. Temporary storage
   b. Paging
   c. Permanent storage
   d. Virtual memory management
5. Most computers with multiple CPUs have what kind of architecture?
   a. Parallel
   b. Symmetric multiprocessing
   c. Asymmetric multiprocessing
   d. Linear
6. Code reviews are effective countermeasures for all of the following threats EXCEPT:
   a. Back doors
   b. Maintenance hooks
   c. Weak passwords
   d. Buffer overflow
7. All of the following are functions of an operating system EXCEPT:
   a. Database management
   b. Process management
   c. Resource management
   d. Access management
8. A security manager is developing security requirements for new end user workstations and wishes to have a secure cryptoprocessor in systems to support security. What should the security manager specify be present?
   a. Trusted Computing Base
   b. Reference monitor
   c. Trusted Module Platform
   d. Trusted Platform Module
9. Firmware is most often used for:
   a. Small electronics
   b. BIOS
   c. Storage of operating parameters
   d. Storage of initial computer instructions used at startup time

10. The purpose of a program counter is to:
    a. Keep track of which process the CPU is currently working on
    b. Keep track of which instruction in a program the CPU is currently working on
    c. Keep track of the number of active processes
    d. Keep track of the size of the active program
11. Another name for the Trusted Network Interpretation is:
    a. The Red Book
    b. The Orange Book
    c. SEI-CMMI
    d. SSE-CMM
12. A security manager needs to simplify how user permissions are managed. The security manager should consider using:
    a. Discretionary access control (DAC)
    b. Mandatory access control (MAC)
    c. Role-based access control (RBAC)
    d. Authentication, authorization, and accounting (AAA)
13. The security model with *no read-down* and *no write-up* is:
    a. Multilevel
    b. Clark-Wilson
    c. Bell-LaPadula
    d. Biba
14. A system that hides the activities of high-privilege users from low-privilege users employs the model known as:
    a. Non-interference
    b. Compartmented
    c. Access matrix
    d. Biba
15. SATA, SCSI, and USB are examples of:
    a. External bus architectures
    b. Internal bus architectures
    c. Peripheral command protocols
    d. Mass storage adaptors

Hands-On Projects

Project 9-1: Motherboard Specifications Review

In this project you will examine the specifications of selected PC motherboards and make a selection recommendation based upon the specifications and cost.

1. Using search tools, search for available motherboards from Abit, ASUS, AOpen, EPox, Intel, MSI, and XFX. Consider other suppliers if these are not readily available. Find specifications for currently available products.
2. Create a chart of the specifications that you feel are the most useful, but include at least eight specifications that you can compare among the different products. Include security features and price in your specifications.
3. From the specifications you have gathered and charted, select the top two motherboards from the entire list. Describe why these two are the most favored and be prepared to justify your decision to others.

Project 9-2: Examine Running Processes

In this project you will examine running processes on your system.

1. Download Process Explorer from technet.microsoft.com.
2. Run Process Explorer on your Windows system.
3. In the main view, click the **Process** column header until you see a hierarchical view of the running processes on your system. What does this view depict?
4. Click **View > Show Lower Pane**, then **View > Lower Pane View > Handles**. Then click on different processes in the upper pane. What does this view depict?
5. In the upper pane, right-click a selected process and click **Properties**. View the available data on the different tabs. What do they show?
6. (For advanced users) Click Find, then click Find Handle or DLL. In the search field, type procexp.exe. Click different entries in the result and notice what is happening in the main Process Explorer window. What is Process Explorer showing you?

On Linux systems, the System Monitor tool shows running processes. On Mac systems, Activity Monitor shows running processes.

Project 9-3: Simple Port Scanning

In this project you will perform simple port scanning to discover open ports on nearby network systems.

Port scanning may be considered a security violation in the work or school network. You must obtain permission from the network manager before downloading and using such a tool.

1. Download the NMAP tool from www.nmap.org.
2. Install the tool on your computer.
3. Start the NMAP tool and select **Ping scan.**
4. Select an IP address for a known system on the network and use NMAP to send pings to the device. Click Scan. NMAP will scan target systems.
5. On the NMAP tool, select Regular scan and then click Scan. NMAP will scan commonly used ports and display what open ports were found, as shown in the screen shot in Figure 9-6.

What open ports are shown? What is the function of these ports? Are there any security implications on account of these ports being open?

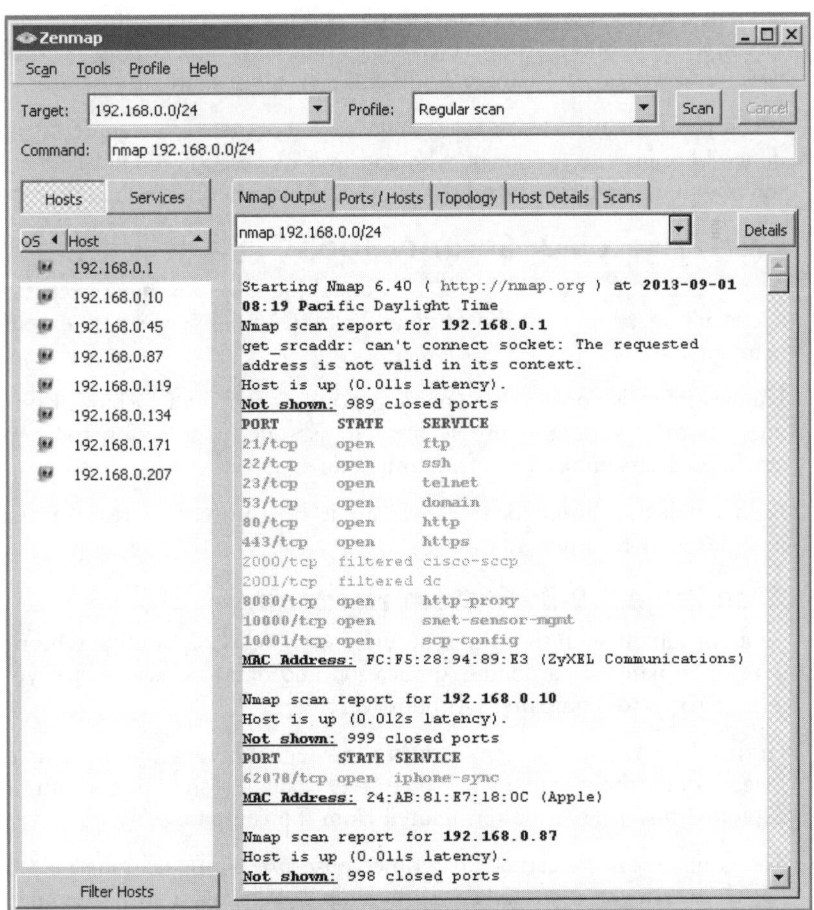

Figure 9-6 The NMAP tool is used to scan for open ports

Source: NMAP.org

Case Projects

Case Project 9-1: Develop a Role-Based Access Control Matrix

As a consultant with Best Security Consulting Co., you have been asked to develop a role-based access control matrix for the IT department in an insurance company, Overland Underwriting.

Overland Underwriting has provided a list of job titles and roles associated with access management. You are to develop an access matrix that specifies which job titles are permitted to perform which roles.

The job titles are: System Engineer I, System Engineer II, Network Administrator, System Engineering Manager, Security Administrator I, Security Administrator II, Security Manager, and IT Manager.

The roles are: Review end user account request, Approve end user account request, Create end user account, Audit end user accounts, Review end user file server access request, Approve end user file server access request, Perform end user file server access change, Audit end user file system permissions.

When you map job titles to roles, make sure that there is adequate "separation of duties." For instance, someone who approves requests should not be the same person who fulfills requests—and someone else altogether needs to audit requests.

Case Project 9-2: Security Tools

As a consultant with the Waterfall Consulting Co., you have been assigned to a consulting project at the Hughes Paint Company, a small manufacturing company.

Hughes Paint is considering enacting a policy that will forbid all but security analysts to possess and use security tools such as scanning tools, password crackers, disassemblers, sniffers, and code analyzers.

Is this policy a good idea? How can it be enforced? Create a report that includes your recommendations.

Case Project 9-3: System Hardening

As a consultant with the Alpha Security Advisors Co., you have been asked to develop a plan for hardening application and database servers for your client, a large software company, Grid Software.

Grid Software had a recent security incident where a former employee had logged onto the company's web server using a shared account and later exploited this after being terminated from the company.

The company is concerned that other unsecure configurations may exist that are waiting to be discovered and exploited. What system hardening steps do you recommend Grid Software take? Create a written report that includes your recommendations.

chapter 10

Telecommunications and Network Security

Topics in This Chapter:

- Wireline and Wireless Telecommunication Technologies
- Wired and Wireless Network Technologies
- Network Topologies and Cabling
- The OSI and TCP/IP Network Models
- TCP/IP Networks, Protocols, Addressing, Devices, Routing, Authentication, Access Control, Tunneling, and Services
- Network-Based Threats, Attacks, Vulnerabilities, and Countermeasures

The (ISC)² *Common Body of Knowledge* (CBK) defines the key areas of knowledge for telecommunications and network security in this way:

Telecommunications and Network Security domain encompasses the structures, techniques, transport protocols, and security measures used to provide integrity, availability, confidentiality and authentication for transmissions over private and public communications networks.

The candidate is expected to demonstrate an understanding of communications and network security as it relates to data communications in local area and wide area networks, remote access, internet/intranet/extranet configurations. Candidates should be knowledgable with network equipment such as switches, bridges and routers, as well as networking protocols (e.g., TCP/IP, IPsec), and VPNs.

Key areas of knowledge:

- *Establish secure network architecture and design (e.g., IP and non-IP protocols, segmentation)*
- *Securing network components*
- *Establish secure communication channels (e.g., VPN, TLS/SSL, VLAN)*
- *Understand network attacks (e.g., DDoS, spoofing)*

Because many threats are propagated over **networks** or attack networks, a thorough knowledge on the inner workings of networks is essential knowledge for any security professional.

Telecommunications Technologies

Telecommunications providers, also known as *common carriers* or *telcos*, have developed and constructed numerous regional and worldwide networks that are used to carry voice and data communications between individuals and businesses. There are many wired and wireless technologies in use that are described in this section.

Wired Telecom Technologies

Also known as **wireline**, these technologies are all based upon copper or fiber optic cabling that can span a few miles in local communities or thousands of miles in aboveground or ocean floor cabling.

DS-1 **Digital signal 1**, known as **DS-1** or **T-1**, is a multiplexed telecommunications protocol family developed by Bell Labs and is used in North America, Korea, and Japan.

The line rate of a DS-1 circuit is 1.544 Mbit/s. When used to carry voice traffic, a DS-1 carries 24 voice channels (each called a **DS-0**) at 64 kbit/s each. When used to carry data traffic, a DS-1 can be divided into 24 data channels at 64 kbit/s each, into a smaller number of faster channels, or a single data channel at 1.544 Mbit/s.

Other rates of this type of technology are available, as shown in Table 10-1.

European T-carrier protocols, such as E0 and **E1**, are similar to those used in North America, and shown in Table 10-2. The European protocols are used in most of the remainder of the world.

Name	Rate	Voice Channels
DS0	64 kbit/s	1
DS-1, aka T-1	1.544 Mbit/s	24
DS-2	6.312 Mbit/s	96
DS-3, aka T-3	44.736 Mbit/s	673
DS-4	274.176 Mbit/s	4,032
DS-5	400.352 Mbit/s	5,760

Table 10-1 North American T-carrier protocols

Name	Rate	Voice Channels
E0	64 kbit/s	1
E1	2.048 Mbit/s	32
E2	8.558 Mbit/s	128
E3	34.368 Mbit/s	512
E4	139.264 Mbit/s	2,048
E5	565.148 Mbit/s	8,192

Table 10-2 European T-carrier protocols

10

When higher data rates are required, SONET technology is often employed. SONET is discussed later in this section.

SONET **Synchronous optical networking** (SONET) is the prevalent standard in North America for transporting voice and data over optical fiber. SONET is a physical-layer technology that can be used to encapsulate network technologies such as ATM, MPLS, and TCP/IP. SONET is also used to encapsulate slower DS-1 type technologies.

The data rates available for SONET are shown in Table 10-3.

Higher SONET rates are in development including OC-3072, whose rate is 160 Gbit/s.

MPLS **Multiprotocol Label Switching** (MPLS) is a packet-switched technology that is used for both voice and data and can be used to carry IP, ATM, SONET, and Ethernet frames over **Wide Area Networks** (WANs). MPLS is ideal for carrying both voice and data because of its QoS (Quality of Service) capabilities that permit the network to transport voice and other streaming media at acceptable rates even during times of heavy data usage.

Telecommunications service providers have MPLS networks that subscriber companies connect their networks to, usually for wide-area transport of voice and IP traffic.

MPLS has been replacing Frame Relay and ATM as a preferred WAN protocol.

Name	Rate
OC-1	48.960 Mbit/s
OC-3	150.336 Mbit/s
OC-12	601.344 Mbit/s
OC-24	1,202.688 Mbit/s
OC-48	2,405.376 Mbit/s
OC-192	9,621.504 Mbit/s
OC-768	38,486.016 Mbit/s

Table 10-3 SONET data rates

DSL **Digital Subscriber Line (DSL)**, also known as **xDSL**, is a group of technologies used to deliver digital data services over telephone wires. DSL is primarily used by residents and small businesses that require higher-speed data services but cannot afford dedicated DS-2 or MPLS.

DSL uses the same pair of wires that are used for a telephone customer's voice service. Data is carried over the wires on a high frequency band, while analog telephones continue to use the lower voice frequency band. Small filters are used to block the high frequencies from the data signal from interfering with telephones that are connected to the same wires.

DSL service employs a modem-like device on the subscriber end and a **Digital Subscriber Line Access Multiplexer** (**DSLAM**) on the service provider's network.

Typical DSL topology is shown in Figure 10-1.

ATM **Asynchronous Transfer Mode** (**ATM**) is a packet-switching network protocol that uses a fixed-size packet called a *cell* to transport data. ATM is a data link-layer protocol that is transported on various physical-layer media, usually twisted-pair copper, fiber optics, or SONET. ATM's cell size is 53 bytes—48 bytes of data and 5 bytes of header.

ATM is connection-oriented; before data is transmitted between nodes, an end-to-end virtual circuit is established.

ATM was intended to replace Ethernet and TCP/IP in local area networks that required higher performance, but this was not realized, as organizations were more apt to adopt faster Ethernet technologies that were more familiar to them. However, ATM is used in wide area networks by larger organizations and service providers, but even there it is giving way to MPLS.

Other Wireline Technologies Other telecommunications technologies that are provided over wired networks include:

- *Data Over Cable Service Interface Specification (DOCSIS)*. This is the technology that facilitates Internet access over *hybrid fibre coaxial* (HFC) television networks through popular *cable modems*. Because a part of the HFC network is a shared medium, data between the service provider and the subscriber are encrypted. Service providers also employ MAC-layer security to prevent unauthorized parties from accessing the network.

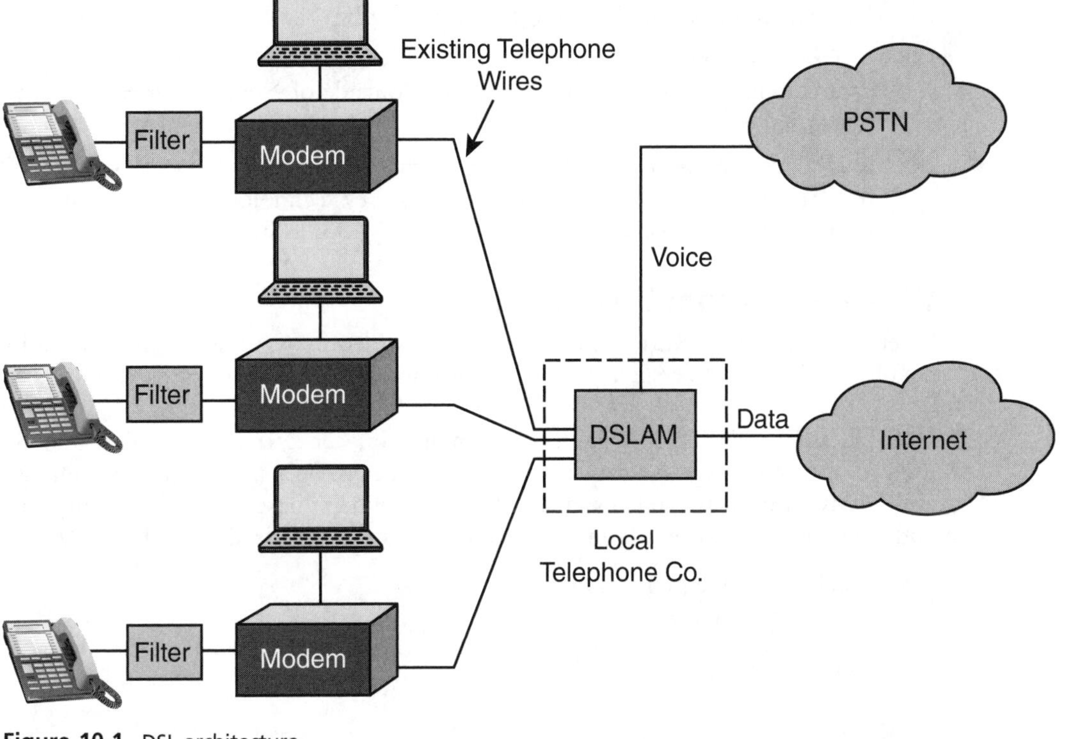

Figure 10-1 DSL architecture

- ***Public Switched Telephone Network (PSTN)***. This is the voice telephone network that has been in place for over a century. This is also known as *POTS* (plain old telephone service). PSTN is *circuit-switched*, which means that a telephone call uses a physical circuit for the duration of the call (this is not *exactly* true anymore—the core of a telco network converts PSTN calls from circuit-switched at the edge of the network to packet-switched at the core).
- ***Frame Relay***. Frame Relay is an early packet-switched telecommunications network technology that permitted business customers to transmit data between locations at a lower cost than dedicated DS-1 circuits. Frame Relay permitted the creation of Switched Virtual Circuits (SVCs) and Permanent Virtual Circuits (PVCs) that emulated the permanence of a dedicated DS-1 by providing the appearance of a dedicated circuit that actually employed the transmission of packets in a shared medium. Frame Relay is a data link-layer protocol that is built on DS-1 (and faster) network technology with special equipment that facilitated the creation of SVCs and PVCs. Frame Relay is considered a successor to the older and slower X.25 technology, but is now giving way to newer technologies such as DSL, MPLS, and VPN.
- ***Integrated Services Digital Network (ISDN)***. This is a digital service designed for voice, data, or both. Introduced in the late 1980s, ISDN was used to extend digital-based corporate phone networks to subscribers' residences and also for Internet connectivity.

The maximum throughput is 128 kbit/s, which was soon overcome by DSL and DOCSIS and has contributed to the decline of ISDN.

- *Synchronous Digital Hierarchy (SDH)*. This is the prevalent standard for voice and data communications over fiber networks outside of North America. It is the functional equivalent of SONET, which is used in North America.
- *X.25*. This is a packet-switched network that is transported over lease lines, ISDN, and regular phone lines. X.25 is considered a legacy technology, having been largely replaced by other technologies such as MPLS, DSL, ISDN, and frame relay.

Wireless Telecom Technologies

Several wireless data-centric technologies are provided by wireless telecommunications providers for business and personal use. Many technologies in use are discussed in this section.

CDMA2000 **CDMA2000 (code division multiple access)** is a mobile radio technology used to transmit voice and data between subscriber devices (usually cellular phone handsets and PCMCIA cellular modems) and network providers' base stations, for purposes of voice and data communications. Some of the data transport standards used by CDMA2000 are:

- 1xRTT, capable of 153 kbit/s
- EVDO, capable of 2.4 Mbit/s
- EVDV, capable of 3.1 Mbit/s

GPRS **General Packet Radio Service (GPRS)** is a data-centric mobile radio technology used in the **Global System for Mobile Communications (GSM)** network. GPRS devices include mobile handsets and PCMCIA-based modems for PCs. The maximum throughput for GPRS is 114 kbit/s. GPRS traffic is encrypted. The successor to GPRS is EDGE, discussed next.

EDGE **Enhanced Data rates for GSM Evolution (EDGE)** and **Enhanced GPRS (EGPRS)** are the successors to GPRS and provide bandwidths up to 1 Mbit/s.

LTE **Long Term Evolution (LTE)** is a high-speed wireless data communication technology that is based on GSM and UMTS technologies. LTE is capable of speeds up to 300 Mbit/s (downlink) and 75 Mbit/s (uplink). LTE is often marketed as 4G or 4G LTE.

UMTS **Universal Mobile Telecommunications System (UMTS)** is another data-centric mobile radio technology found in wireless handsets and PC card modems. UMTS is usually transported over W-CDMA networks and supports up to 14 Mbit/s throughput.

WiMAX **Worldwide Interoperability for Microwave Access (WiMAX)** is a data-centric radio technology for point-to-point and mobile access. Based on IEEE 802.16, WiMAX is a wireless competitor to DSL and cable modems but also competes with the strictly mobile data standards such as CDMA2000, GPRS, EDGE, LTE, and UMTS.

Throughput for WiMAX subscribers depends upon distance from the nearest base station. Rates can range from 2 to 12 Mbit/s, but could theoretically go as high as 70 Mbit/s. Rates for fixed stations can reach 1 Gbit/s. Like other wireless technologies, WiMAX is a shared medium, meaning that more simultaneous users means lower effective throughput.

Other Wireless Telecom Technologies Some other wireless data technologies include:

- *CDPD (Cellular Digital Packet Data)*. An early mobile data service that utilized bandwidth on the *AMPS* (Advanced Mobile Phone System—the original analog cellular technology used in North America that is no longer in use).
- *Packet radio*. A method of transmitting data over amateur radio bands. The *AX.25* standard defines the protocols used to transport data over amateur radio.

Network Technologies

Many network technologies for use within businesses and educational institutions have been developed in the past five decades, and some of these are still in use today. These technologies are used to facilitate communications between computers in building and campus environments.

There are many wired and wireless technologies in use that are discussed in this section.

Wired Network Technologies

This section describes several wired network technologies that are used in organizations to connect networks to each other.

Ethernet **Ethernet** is a family of frame-based technologies that is used to connect computers in a **Local Area Network (LAN)** (a computer network covering a small geographic area such as a residence, building, or group of buildings). Ethernet is a data link-layer standard that defines frames and error-correcting measures.

Ethernet Cable Types Ethernet runs over many types of cabling, including:

- *10BASE-T*. This is the commonly twisted-pair network cable that supports the **Category 3, 5, 5e, 6, or 7** ANSI standard. This cable has eight conductors, of which four are used. An 8-pin RJ45 connector is used to connect a cable to a device, as shown in Figure 10-2.
- *100BASE-TX*. The same twisted-pair network cable (Category 5 and 6) and connectors as 10BASE-T, and also uses just four of the eight conductors. This is designed for 100 Mbit/s network signals.
- *1000BASE-T*. The same twisted-pair network cable and connectors as 100BASE-TX, except that all eight conductors are used. This is designed to carry 1000 Mbit/s network signals.
- *10BASE2*. The old *thinnet* coaxial cabling with twist-lock BNC connectors—rarely used now.
- *10BASE5*. The original Ethernet cabling medium, this is the old *thicknet* coaxial cabling that is now rarely used. One interesting feature of 10BASE5 is the ability to install a vampire tap that allows the addition of a node to the network while existing nodes continue communicating.

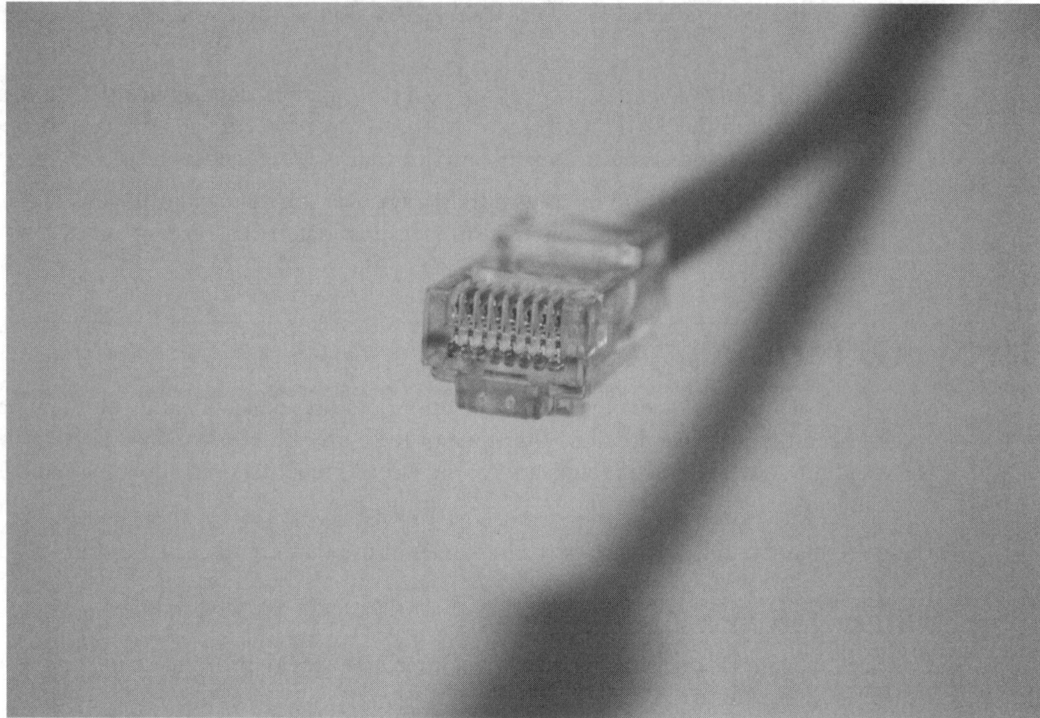

Figure 10-2 100BASE-TX cabling with RJ45 connector
Photo by Rebecca Steele

Ethernet Frame Layout Ethernet is a frame-based network protocol, meaning data is transported in blocks of characters (frames) instead of one at a time. An Ethernet frame consists of a header, payload, and checksum as follows:

- *Header*. The Ethernet header consists of 14 bytes that include:
  - Preamble. This consists of 7 octets of 10101010.
  - Start of frame. This consists of 1 octet of 10101011.
  - 6-byte destination MAC address.
  - 6-byte source MAC address.
  - 2-byte Ethernet frame type.
- *Payload*. This is the *data* in the Ethernet frame that is of variable length, from 46 to 1500, bytes.
- *Checksum*. This is a 4-byte CRC (cyclic redundancy check) that is used to verify the integrity of the entire frame. The CRC is calculated by the sending node and placed in the header; the destination node calculates the CRC and compares it to the value in the header; if they match, the packet arrived correctly; if they do not match, the packet is dropped.
- *Interframe gap*. After the frame is transmitted, the sending station pauses for 960 ns before sending the next frame.

Ethernet Error Detection Ethernet is a **Carrier Sense Multiple Access with Collision Detection (CSMA/CD)** network protocol. This means that any station that wants to transmit frames on the network first listens to see if any other station is transmitting. This is the *carrier sense* part of CSMA.

If a station that is transmitting detects that another station is also transmitting, a *collision* has occurred. The station stops transmitting, sends a *jam signal*, (a pattern of sixteen "1-0" bit combinations that essentially means, "Everybody stop transmitting!"), and then waits for a random length of time before transmitting again. The wait interval is known as a *backoff delay*; the length of the delay is calculated using the *truncated binary exponential backoff algorithm*, which is designed to help prevent Ethernet networks from crashing due to excessive traffic. This is the *collision detection* part of CSMA/CD.

In Full Duplex Ethernet (where transmits and receives occur on different wires), collision detection is not implemented because collisions cannot occur, since every node is connected to a switch, which segments the collision domain. In this case, Ethernet is really not a shared medium but a point-to-point medium.

Ethernet MAC Addressing On an Ethernet network, stations are uniquely identified by their **Media Access Control (MAC) address.** A MAC address is 6 bytes in length and is permanently assigned to a device, such that no two devices in the world have the same MAC address. The first three bytes of a MAC address are known as the **Organizationally Unique Identifier (OUI)**, which identifies the organization that manufactured the device. The last three bytes are assigned by the device's manufacturer and must be unique.

A MAC address is usually shown in hexadecimal format with colons or dashes separating the bytes. A typical MAC address is 00-14-4F-C1-05-4D. The first three bytes (00-14-4F) identify the device as being manufactured by Sun Microsystems.

Some manufacturers of computer equipment permit an administrator to change a device's MAC address; this is not the norm, however. MAC addresses can be spoofed, a logical attack performed by manipulating frame data instead of actually changing the physical nature of the hardware.

Ethernet Devices Several types of devices are used to connect computers to one another on a network. These devices are:

- *Hub*. An early type of network device, a hub is a device used to connect multiple computers together to form a network. A hub can be considered a *multiport repeater*, which is to say that every frame that is present on the network is transmitted to all computers on the network. Once the only way to create computer networks, hubs are still sometimes used in very small business or home networks.
- *Bridge*. A bridge is a device used to connect two or more separate networks, creating a larger aggregate network. A simple bridge is similar to a hub, where frames on the network are sent to all stations on all networks connected by the bridge. There are also smarter bridges that can learn the topology of the networks and only transmit frames on networks containing destination nodes.

- *Repeater*. A repeater is a device that is used to receive and retransmit the signal of a network connection, usually in a situation where a very long cable run is necessary to reach one or more distant computers in a network. Repeaters are seldom used, as there are other, more effective means for getting signals to distant computers, for instance, fiber optic cables that transmit signals over greater distances.
- *Switch*. A switch is a network device used to connect multiple computers to form a network. While the physical appearance is the same, a switch differs from a hub by sending packets only to a destination computer on a network, instead of to every computer as a hub does. A switch is able to do this by listening to network traffic and learning which system(s) are present on each physical connection. After learning which MAC (or IP) address(es) are present on each port, a switch can send packets to only the ports where destination computers are present. This technique improves the potential throughput of the entire network.
- *Router*. A router is a device that connects multiple networks together. In a larger organization with many networks, routers are used to connect the networks together so that systems on one network can communicate with systems on other networks. In any size organization, a router is used to connect one or more internal networks with one or more external networks such as the **Internet** (the global network of interconnected networks). Each interface on a router is connected to a different network, usually to a hub or switch that is connected to other computers. Routers exchange information with neighboring routers in order to know where to route packets.
- *Gateway*. A gateway is a device or system that translates various types of network communications together. Strictly speaking, a router is a type of gateway, but other types exist, including frame relay switches, ATM to IP switches, and so on.

Token Ring **Token ring** is a LAN technology developed by IBM. While initially successful, token ring gave way to Ethernet and its inexpensive cabling and easily used *RJ*-style connectors. Token ring cables had large, fragile connectors that resulted in a relatively low density of connectors in a device; an enterprise with many token ring devices would have to consume considerable rack space for token ring hubs, which were called *Multistation Access Units*, or MAUs.

A token ring network is a physical star. Each station on the network is connected to a *Multistation Access Unit* by a cable. The first token ring networks operated at a rate of 4 Mbit/s; later token ring networks operated at 16 Mbit/s.

A token ring network is a logical ring. Data transmission is facilitated by the use of a logical *token*; only the station in possession of the network's token may transmit data. The token is passed from station to station; when a station has nothing to transmit, it merely passes the token to the next station. When a station does have data to transmit, it is attached to the token and passed along. When the token (with its payload) reaches the destination station, the payload is removed, and the destination station then passes an empty token along. Algorithms in the MAU handle situations such as a lost token, the introduction of a new node on the network, and network rebooting.

USB Universal Serial Bus (USB) is a serial bus communications standard, used for the connection of peripheral devices to a computer. USB is the successor to RS-232 serial, IEEE 1284 parallel, as well as PC keyboard and mouse connection standards.

- USB 1.0/1.1—the first version (1996) with two speeds: 1.5 Mbits/s and 12 Mbits/s.
- USB 2.0—the current version (2000) with a higher speed of 480 Mbits/s, which makes USB highly suited for external hard drives.
- USB 3.0—the updated version (2008) with a higher speed of 4.8 Gbits/s.

USB permits *hot-plugging* of devices, which permits peripherals to be connected and disconnected while the computer and its operating system are running.

The types of devices that can be connected to a computer via USB include keyboards, mice, printers, scanners, mass storage devices (disk drives and memory devices), and network adaptors to connect to WiFi, Bluetooth, and Ethernet networks.

The USB standard includes the use of a five-port hub (one port that connects to the host computer and four open ports) that facilitates the connection of additional peripherals.

RS-232 RS-232, also known as *serial*, is an older serial communications technology that was widely used with computers from the 1960s through the 2000s, but is now being displaced by USB. RS-232 has been (and is still) used for many applications, including:

- Connecting terminals to central computers
- Connecting printers to computers
- Connecting modems to computers
- Connecting mice to computers
- Connecting miscellaneous peripherals to computers

10

The RS-232 standard accommodated many throughput speeds ranging from 110 bps to 115 kbps. Flow control has been implemented in several ways, including hardware signaling (through various additional connector pins) and software signaling (through the use of *XON* and *XOFF* (ASCII 0x11 and 0x13, respectively).

The computer end of an RS-232 connection is often called DCE (Data Circuit-terminating Equipment); the peripheral end is often called DTE (Data Terminal Equipment).

Other Wired Network Technologies

- *High-Speed Serial Interface (HSSI)*. A high-speed serial protocol often used to connect WAN devices such as routers together. HSSI's bandwidth is 52 Mbit/s, and its maximum cable length is 50".
- *Fiber Distributed Data Interface (FDDI)*. A token network technology transmitted over fiber optic cable, to a maximum distance of 200 km (124 miles). Largely displaced by Gigabit Ethernet and SONET.
- *Fibre Channel*. A gigabit network protocol usually used in storage area networks (SANs). There are three modes of fibre channel:
  - *FC-P2P*. Fibre Channel Point to point.
  - *FC-AL*. Fibre Channel Arbitrated Loop, similar to Token Ring.
  - *FC-SW*. Fibre Channel Switched Fabric, similar to an Ethernet switched network.

Network Cable Types While some of the types of network cabling are explicitly or implicitly mentioned earlier in this section, all of the common types are listed here.

- *Coaxial cable.* This type of cable consists of a single or dual inner conductor, a dielectric insulator, a metallic shield, and an outer plastic jacket. Once common in computer networks, it is now rarely found in commercial applications. Coaxial cable is still commonly used to transmit television broadcasting together with voice and data into a residence or business.
- *Twisted-pair cable.* This includes several types of copper conductor cable that utilizes the twisting of conductors in order to resist interference and improve throughput. Twisted-pair cabling may be shielded or unshielded, with the latter the more common type in use. Figure 10-3 shows twisted-pair cable with part of the outer jacket removed to reveal the four twisted pairs of conductors. Classes of twisted-pair cabling include:
  - *Category 3.* Consists of four twisted pairs in a single jacket. Suitable only for 10 Mbit/s Ethernet. Superseded by Category 5 and 5e.
  - *Category 5.* Consists of four twisted pairs in a single jacket. Maximum length is 100 meters. Suitable for 100 Mbit/s and can be used for Gigabit Ethernet.
  - *Category 5e.* Supersedes Category 5 and includes specifications for far end crosstalk. Maximum length is 100 meters.

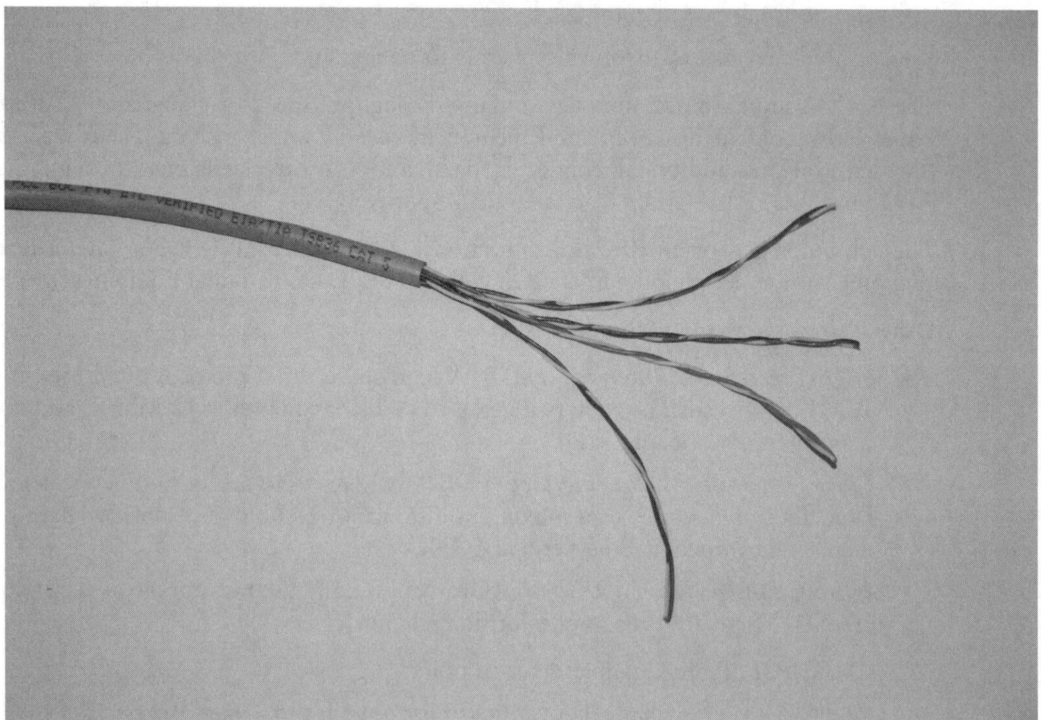

Figure 10-3 Twisted pair cabling

Photo by Rebecca Steele

Category 6. Backward compatible with Category 5 and 5e, but higher specifications for noise and crosstalk, making it more suitable for Gigabit Ethernet. Maximum cable length is 100 meters.

Category 7. Even more stringent than Category 6 cabling, Cat-7 is suitable for 10 Gbit/s networks. Maximum length is 100 meters.

- *Optical fiber*. This is a cable type used to carry signals in the form of light instead of electricity as is used in copper cabling. While more expensive, optical fiber can carry signals over greater distances and with far greater bandwidth than copper cable.

Network Topologies

The topology of a network refers to its physical as well as logical arrangement. The four principle physical network topologies are:

- *Bus*. In a bus network, all of the nodes in the network are connected to a single conductor. A break in the network conductor will cause some or the entire network to stop functioning. Early Ethernet networks consisting of thinnet coaxial cabling were bus networks.
- *Ring*. All of the nodes are connected to exactly two other nodes, forming a circular loop. Breaking any conductor will cause the network to stop functioning.
- *Star*. All nodes are connected to a central device. A break in a conductor will disconnect only one node, and the remaining nodes will continue functioning. Ethernet networks are physical stars, with computers connected to central hubs or switches. Token ring networks, while operating logically as a ring, are physically wired as a star.
- *Mesh*. Nodes connect to all other proximate nodes within their maximum range, creating multiple redundant paths through a system where each node relays information for its neighbors. Mesh networks are typically wireless, and they are deployed in places where physical wiring would be difficult, reliability is important, and nodes are physically close enough to each other to provide multiple paths.

Bus, ring, star, and mesh topologies are depicted in Figure 10-4.

Wireless Network Technologies

This section describes commonly used wireless network technologies that provide connectivity between computers and devices.

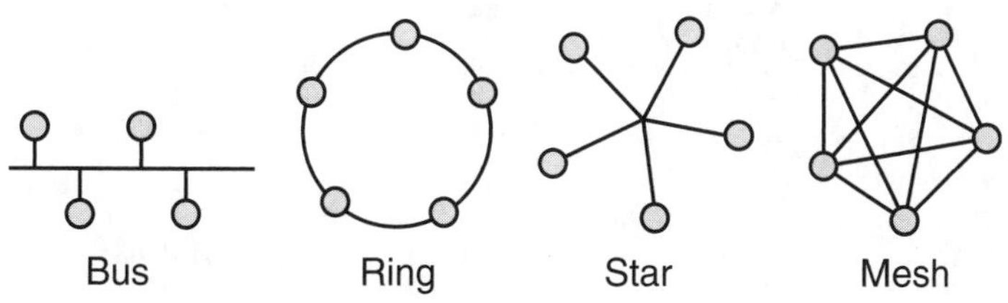

Figure 10-4 Network topologies

WiFi Known by several names, including ***Wireless LAN, WLAN***, and **IEEE 802.1a/b/g/n**, **WiFi** is the common name for a radio frequency-based data link-layer (OSI layer 2) network protocol used in computer networks. With bandwidths of up to 54 Mbit/s over a distance of 100 meters, WiFi is a practical alternative to wired Ethernet networks in businesses and residences. WiFi is also the basis for hundreds of thousands of public *hot spots* equipped with free or fee-based Internet connectivity in airports, hotels, resorts, coffee shops, and libraries, as well as municipal public access networks.

WiFi is not considered a low-power consumption protocol, so it is not well suited for mobile devices such as smartphones or headsets.

A WiFi network originates from an **access point**, a device that performs radio frequency communications and allows wireless devices to connect to it if they have the correct configuration and security credentials.

WiFi Standards Several technical standards for WiFi radio technology have been developed since its inception in 1997. These standards are shown in Table 10-4.

WiFi Security Several capabilities improve the security of a WiFi network, in order to make it resistant to eavesdropping, including:

- *No broadcast*. A WiFi access point (AP) can be configured so that it does not broadcast the network's SSID (service set identifier), making it slightly more difficult for a node to discover available WiFi networks.
- ***Service set identifier (SSID)***. A WiFi network's SSID can be changed to a value that is not easily guessed.
- *MAC Access Control*. A WiFi network access point can be configured so that only preauthorized nodes, based upon their MAC addresses, may connect.
- *Authentication*. Workstations that wish to join a WiFi network can be required to furnish a userid and password. Userid-password pairs can be stored in an access point, or the access point can refer to an authentication service such as RADIUS.
- *Encryption*. WiFi over-the-air communications can be encrypted by one of several means:
  - **Wired Equivalent Privacy (WEP)**, an encryption algorithm that has been compromised and can be broken within minutes.

Standard	Spectrum	Data Rate	Range	Released
802.11a	5 GHz	54 Mbit/s	120 m	1999
802.11b	2.4 GHz	11 Mbit/s	140 m	1999
802.11g	2.4 GHz	54 Mbit/s	140 m	2003
802.11n	2.4/5 GHz	248 Mbit/s	250 m	2009
802.11y	3.7 GHz	54 Mbit/s	5000 m	2008

Table 10-4 WiFi standards

- **WiFi Protected Access (WPA)**, a protocol standard that is a replacement for WEP. WPA is a subset of the IEEE 802.11i-2004 (WPA2) specification.
- **WPA2** is the full IEEE 802.11i-2004 specification, a superset of WPA. Both WPA and WPA2 can operate in a PSK (pre-shared key) mode, where the encryption key is stored in the WiFi access point.
- **WPA2 Enterprise** is the WPA2 protocol when an external authentication source, such as RADIUS, is used.

Bluetooth **Bluetooth** is a wireless **personal area network** (PAN) technology for relatively low-speed data communication over short distances.

Typical Bluetooth applications include wireless mobile phone headsets, computer mice and keyboards, wireless stereo headphones and speakers, and GPS receivers. Because Bluetooth uses radio spectrum, devices do not require line-of-sight to connect.

Bluetooth data rates range from 1 Mbit/s to 3 Mbit/s. Bluetooth's power consumption is very low, which makes it suitable for low-power devices. The maximum range for communications is 10 meters. Bluetooth Low Energy (BLE) is a newer feature in the Bluetooth standard that operates on very little power and over distances up to 100 meters.

Bluetooth devices can authenticate through a process called *pairing*, during which two devices can exchange a cryptographic secret key that the two devices can later use to securely identify themselves. Communications between paired devices can also be encrypted.

IrDA **Infrared Data Association** (IrDA) is the governing body that has developed a number of line-of-sight optical protocols known as IrDA. IrDA operates in the infrared light spectrum from 2.4 kbit /s to 16 Mbit /s. Once popular with laptop computers, PDAs, printers, and other devices, IrDA has been largely replaced by WiFi and Bluetooth, both of which require no line-of-sight for connectivity.

Wireless USB **Wireless USB** (WUSB) is a wireless protocol designed for wireless connectivity of various computer peripherals such as printers, digital cameras, hard disks, and other high-throughput devices. WUSB's bandwidth ranges from 110 Mbit/s at 10 meters to 480 Mbit/s at 3 meters and occupies the wireless spectrum from the 3.1 to 10.6 GHz frequency range.

Near Field Communication **Near Field Communication** (NFC) is an extremely short-range (10 cm , or ~4") network technology generally used by mobile phones for mobile payment and other applications. NFC's data rates are 106, 212, or 424 kbit/s.

NFC can operate in passive mode and active mode. In passive mode, one device is acting as a transponder, not unlike an RF-powered key card. In active mode, both devices are actively communicating to one another.

NFC's short range makes it ideal for use as a mobile wallet application where a mobile device such as a wallet card or cell phone can be used as a payment token for a merchant transaction or ticketing application.

Network Protocols

Network protocols are the standards by which network messages are constructed. The protocols themselves are complicated enough that layered models have been developed to describe them. The two most common models are the OSI network model and the TCP/IP network model. These two models are described in detail in this section.

The OSI Network Model

Prior to discussion about specific network protocols, it's first helpful to understand the **Open Systems Interconnect** (**OSI**) network model. OSI is a seven-layer model whose layers represent various abstractions of communication. Each layer provides services to the layer above it and receives services from the layer beneath. The common terminology for these layers is a *protocol stack*.

The layers in the OSI model are:

- Physical
- Data link
- Network
- Transport
- Session
- Presentation
- Application

These layers are shown in Figure 10-5. Some of the phrases that can help the reader remember the layers are:

- Please Do Not Take Sales People's Advice
- Please Do Not Throw Sausage Pizza Away
- Please Do Not Touch Steve's Pet Alligator
- People Desperately Need To See Pamela Anderson
- All People Seem To Need Data Processing (this one is backwards)

These layers are discussed in more detail below.

Physical

The **physical layer** of the OSI model is concerned with a network's physical media, whether electrical, optical, or radio frequency, as well as details such as voltages and frequencies. Several standards in use at the physical layer include RS-232, RS-422, T1-, E1, 10BASE-T, SONET, DSL, 802.11a physical, and Twinax.

Data is transmitted in *bits* or *frames* (depending on the standard used) at the physical layer.

The physical layer provides services to the data link layer.

Data Link

The **data link layer** of the OSI model is concerned with the transfer of data between nodes. The data link layer also manages error correction for any errors that take place at the physical layer.

In most physical media, bits in the physical layer are arranged into **frames**.

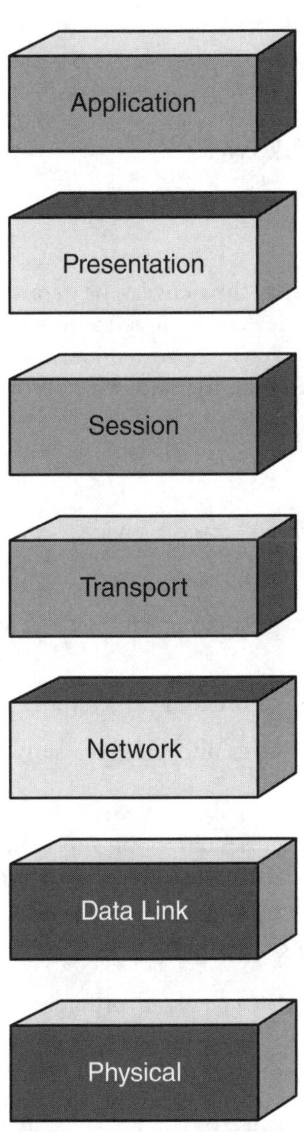

Figure 10-5 The seven layers of the OSI network model

Examples of standards found in the data link layer are 802.3 (Ethernet), 802.11a MAC, GPRS, AppleTalk, ATM, FDDI, Fibre Channel, Frame Relay, PPP, SLIP, Token Ring, and Wi-MAX.

The data link layer uses services provided by the physical layer and provides services to the network layer.

Network The **network layer** is used to transport variable-length data sequences between nodes. Where devices cannot handle frames or packets of certain lengths, the network layer manages fragmentation and reassembly. Communications at the network layer are point to point, and there is no notion of a *connection* or guarantee of delivery as to the order of delivery of data.

Examples of standards used in the network layer are IP, ICMP, ARP, and IPX.

Data is transmitted in *packets* or ***datagrams*** at the network layer.

The network layer uses services provided by the data link layer and provides services to the transport layer.

Transport The **transport layer** in the OSI model manages the delivery of data from node to node on a network, even when there are intermediate devices such as routers and a variety of physical media between the nodes. The transport layer manages *connections* that can guarantee the order of delivery of data packets, packet reassembly, and error recovery.

Examples of transport layer standards are UDP, TCP, IPsec, L2TP, and SPX.

Data is transmitted in *packets* at the transport layer.

The transport layer uses services provided by the network layer and provides services to the session layer.

Session The **session layer** manages connections between nodes, including session establishment, communication, and teardown.

Examples of standards found in the session layer include NetBIOS, TCP sessions, and SIP.

The session layer uses services provided by the transport layer and provides services to the presentation layer.

Presentation The **presentation layer** deals with the presentation or representation of data in a communications session. Activities that can occur at this layer include character set translation, compression, and encryption.

Examples of presentation-layer standards include SSL, TLS, MIME, and MPEG.

The presentation layer uses services provided by the session layer and provides services to the application layer.

Application The **application layer** is the topmost layer in the OSI network model. This layer is concerned with the delivery of data to and from applications.

Examples of application layer standards are DNS, NFS, NTP, DHCP, SMTP, HTTP, SNMP, SSH, Telnet, and WHOIS.

TCP/IP

The TCP/IP network protocol is built on a four-layer model that is conceptually similar to the seven-layer OSI model. The four layers in the TCP/IP model are:

- Link
- Internet
- Transport
- Application

These layers operate similarly to the seven-layer OSI model, which is to say that the layers are hierarchical and employ encapsulation. TCP/IP encapsulation is illustrated in Figure 10-6. The layers in the TCP/IP model are shown in Figure 10-7.

TCP/IP Link Layer The **link layer** is layer 1 in the TCP/IP model. The link layer is concerned with node-to-node delivery of bits or frames. Examples of link layer technologies include:

- WiFi
- Ethernet
- Token ring

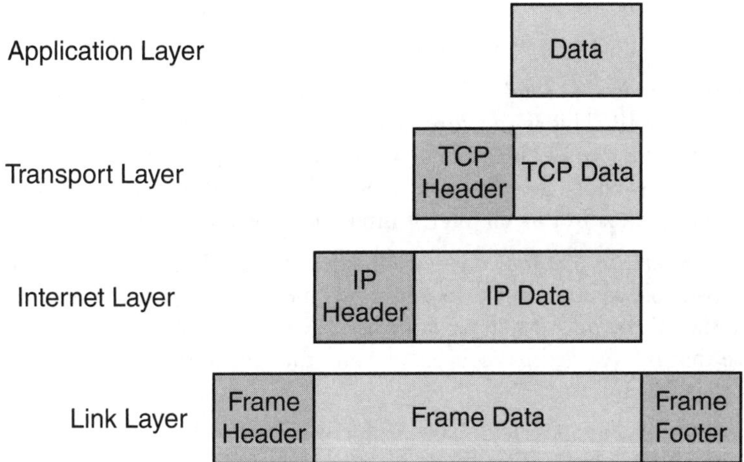

Figure 10-6 Encapsulation in the TCP/IP network model

Figure 10-7 Layers of the TCP/IP network model

- ATM
- Frame Relay
- PPP

Node addressing at this layer is accomplished through some type of MAC addressing. Ethernet MAC addressing is described in detail earlier in this chapter.

TCP/IP Internet Layer The **Internet layer** is layer 2 in the four-layer TCP/IP model. The Internet layer is the layer that is concerned with end-to-end packet delivery, whereas layer 1 is concerned with node-to-node delivery. End-to-end delivery means that a packet can originate at one node and pass through several intermediate nodes (usually routers) before arriving at the destination node.

Internet Layer Protocols Some of the protocols used at the Internet layer include:

- *Internet Protocol version 4 (IPv4).* The original Internet Protocol, IPv4 is usually referred to as simply IP. This is the core layer 2 protocol in the TCP/IP protocol suite on which most layer 3 protocols are built. IP uses a 32-bit addressing scheme that is expressed as the four octets, *xx.xx.xx.xx*. Network addressing is described in more detail in the section later in this chapter, "Internet layer addressing".
- *Internet Protocol version 6 (IPv6).* Generally expressed as IPv6, this newer version of the Internet Protocol was developed to address some of the shortcomings of IPv4, primarily the size of the address space and the lack of security. IPv6 uses a 128-bit address space that is expected to forever alleviate the current shortage of available addresses in the IPv4 Internet.
- *Address Resolution Protocol (ARP).* This protocol is used to translate a network IP address into a network MAC address. For instance, if a node wants to send a network packet to a local node at address 192.168.5.2, it will send an ARP request onto the network that asks, essentially, what station has IP address 192.168.5.2? If a node on the network has that address, it will answer and provide its MAC address in the response.
- *Reverse Address Resolution Protocol (RARP).* This protocol is used to translate a known MAC address into an IP address. RARP has been superseded by DHCP, which has a richer feature set than merely MAC to IP translation.
- *Internet Control Message Protocol (ICMP).* ICMP is a protocol used for error messages and utility functions such as **Ping** (a tool used to test connectivity to another node on a network) and **Traceroute** (a tool used to discover the node-by-node path to a destination node). When a node sends a message to another node that is temporarily unreachable, the router on the destination node's network will send a "destination host unreachable" error back to the requesting node. There are 255 different message types available in ICMP that are used for different purposes; for instance, Echo Request is message number 8 while Echo Reply is message number 0.
- *Internet Group Management Protocol (IGMP).* This protocol is used to manage multicast groups and is analogous to ICMP, which is used for unicast.
- *IP security (IPsec).* This is a suite of protocols used for securing IP communications with authentication and encryption. IPsec is typically used as a tunneling protocol, wherein messages at higher levels of the TCP/IP protocol (layers 4 and 5) are

encapsulated within encrypted IPsec packets. This use is typically found in remote access and site-to-site tunneling over the Internet.

Internet Layer Routing Protocols Routing protocols are used by network routers to determine how to send network packets to nodes on destination networks. Some network routing protocols exist in the Internet layer, including:

- RIP
- OSPF
- IS-IS
- BGP

Network routing protocols are described in more detail later in this chapter.

Internet Layer Addressing TCP/IP's Internet layer addressing is designed to uniquely identify nodes on networks including the global Internet. Network addresses in IPv4 are 32 bits in length and are expressed as a dot-decimal notation, xx.xx.xx.xx, where the range of each 'xx' is 0–255 decimal. A typical network address is 141.204.13.200.

The TCP/IP Internet layer addressing scheme has several characteristics, including:

- ***Subnets** and subnet masking*. While an IP address is 32 bits in length and expressed in the dot-decimal notation, an IP address is, for some purposes, actually divided into two parts: the network address and the node address. For instance, the first 24 bits of an IP address may be a network address (that is, the IP address of a *network* rather than a single station), and the remaining 8 bits is the station address. Nodes on the network need to know what part of the IP address is for the network; this is determined by the network's **subnet mask**. A typical subnet mask is 255.255.255.0, which in this case indicates that the first three decimal numbers (or the first 24 bits, every instance of a binary "1" in this example) of an IP address is the network identifier, and the last decimal number (or the last 8 bits) is a node address. When a node wants to send a packet to another node, it will mask the destination's address with the subnet mask to determine whether the destination node is on the same network or a different network; if the same network, the node will send the packet directly; if a different network, the node will send the packet to the network's gateway, which is usually a router.
- *Gateways*. Every network has a *gateway*, which is usually a router that is connected to the path leading to other networks. When a node wants to send a packet to another node, it must first determine whether the destination node is on the same network by masking the destination's IP address with the subnet mask. If the destination node is on a different network, the node sends the packet to the node at the gateway IP address; that node is usually a router that will consult its routing tables to determine how to forward the packet to its destination.
- *Address allocation*. Organizations that wish to communicate with other nodes on the Internet must obtain routable addresses from a Regional Internet Registry (RIR), usually an ISP (Internet Service Provider) provider. The RIR/ISP will assign a single address or a block of addresses (usually a subnet or a part of a subnet). The organization then assigns individual addresses to devices on its network.

- *Reserved address blocks*. Not all IP network addresses are available for general use. Some address blocks that are reserved include:
  - *10.0.0.0–10.255.255.255—private networks*. Organizations are encouraged to assign private network IP addresses to nodes in its internal networks and then utilize Network Address Translation (NAT) at its border routers to dynamically translate those private network addresses into one of its allocated addresses.
  - *127.0.0.1–127.255.255.254—loopback*. This is a special address that is used to signify a node's own address. In the vernacular, 127.0.0.1 is always "me" on a network.
  - *172.16.0.0–172.31.255.255—private networks*. Used for the same purpose as 10.0.0.0–10.255.255.255.
  - *192.0.2.0–192.0.2.255, 198.51.100.0–198.51.100.255, 203.0.113.0–203.0.113.255—example networks*. These ranges may be used for examples in documentation.
  - *192.168.0.0–192.168.255.255—private networks*. Used for the same purpose as 10.0.0.0–10.255.255.255.
  - *224.0.0.0–239.255.255.255—multicast*. Reserved for multicast traffic.

- *Network address translation (NAT)*. This is a scheme whereby an organization's border router (the router connecting its internal networks to its external networks—usually the Internet) will dynamically translate the address of packets crossing the network boundary from internal, private addresses to routable, public addresses. NAT was developed as one of the stopgap measures to forestall the impending shortage of allocated IP addresses by requiring that organizations assign private network addresses to nodes in their internal networks.
- *Classful networks*. Originally, the entire available IP address space was divided into two parts: the network number that consisted of the first 8 bits of an IP address, and the host address that consisted of the remaining 24 bits. This resulted in only 256 possible networks in the entire Internet, which was infeasible. The concept of *classful networks* was introduced, which results in a far greater number of smaller networks. The network classes that were developed are:
  - *Class A*. A *Class A* network consists of an 8-bit network address and a 24-bit host address. Thus, a Class A network could contain 16,777,214 nodes; 126 such networks were created for the very largest organizations.
  - *Class B*. A *Class B* network consists of a 16-bit network address and a 16-bit host address. Each network could contain 65,534 nodes; 16,382 of these networks were created.
  - *Class C*. A *Class C* network consists of a 24-bit network address and an 8-bit host address. Thus, a Class C network could contain 254 nodes; over 2 million such networks were created.

This scheme of classful networks would prove to be short-lived; this gave rise to Classless Inter-Domain Routing, discussed next.

- *Classless Inter-Domain Routing (CIDR)*. *Classless Inter-Domain Routing* did away with the rigid scheme of only Class A, B, and C networks and permitted the creation of any length subnet mask (called a *Variable Length Subnet Mask*, or *VLSM*), from 8 bits to 31 bits. This permitted ISPs to be able to allocate very small networks to customers that did not require more than a very few addresses. The introduction of CIDR led to a far more efficient allocation of available IP addresses on the Internet.

- *Addressing*. The Internet layer provides for different addressing types that will result in messages being sent to one or more destination nodes. These types are:
  - ***Unicast***. The most common type of addressing, where a packet is sent to a single IP address destination.
  - ***Broadcast***. A packet is sent to a network's *broadcast address*, which causes the packet to be sent to all nodes on a network. DHCP and ARP utilize broadcast.
  - ***Multicast***. A packet is sent to a group of receiving nodes. A packet is sent to a multicast address (in the range 224.0.0.0 to 239.255.255.255), and routers in the network track recipients and propagate packets to destinations as needed.
  - ***Anycast***. A packet is sent to only one of a group of nodes, whichever is closest or most available.

TCP/IP Transport Layer The **transport layer** is layer 3 in the four-layer TCP/IP model. The two protocols that are principally used in the transport layer are TCP and UCP; each is explained below.

TCP Transport Protocol **Transmission Control Protocol** (**TCP**) is a *connection-oriented* transport protocol used to carry messages within a *session* between two nodes. In TCP, two nodes can establish a persistent connection, over which messages can be sent back and forth.

Protocols in the application layer (layer 4) that use TCP include FTP, HTTP, and Telnet.

Characteristics of the TCP protocol are:

- *Connection*. A node that wishes to communicate to another via TCP will do so by establishing a connection. This is accomplished via a *three-way handshake* that consists of three messages that are sent between the two nodes to establish the connection:
  - The requesting station sends a SYN to the destination station
  - The destination station responds with a SYN-ACK
  - The requesting station responds with an ACK
  - At this point the connection is established. The two nodes may now send packets containing data to each other over this connection.
- ***Port number***. Packets in TCP have a *source port* number and a *destination port* number. This permits two stations to establish several unique connections that are distinguished by different port numbers. When a connection is established, the connection will first begin on a well-known port (for instance, FTP's port number is 21 and Telnet is 23), then the stations will agree to higher-numbered *ephemeral ports* over which their connection will take place.
- *Reliability*. By design, a packet sent over the TCP protocol is guaranteed to be delivered to its destination—provided the destination exists and is reachable. Packets that are lost are retransmitted, and duplicate packets are discarded.

- *Sequencing*. Packets sent over the TCP protocol are guaranteed to be delivered in the same order that they were sent. TCP packets include sequence numbers that permit device drivers within nodes to assure the correct order of delivery.
- *Flow control*. TCP by its design cannot send data faster than the receiving node can accept it. This is accomplished by the receiving station acknowledging the successful receipt of packets. Upon establishment of the connection, the two stations agree to the size of the *sliding window*, which is the number of in-transit packets that can exist at any given time.

UDP Transport Protocol The **User Datagram Protocol** (**UDP**) (sometimes coined the *unreliable datagram protocol*) is a connectionless protocol used to carry messages between nodes. UDP is very lightweight in comparison to TCP—it's a low-overhead protocol that is suitable for some types of connections. Some of the protocols that use UDP include DNS, VoIP, and TFTP.

The characteristics of the UDP protocol are:

- *Connectionless*. Unlike TCP, UDP has no sense of a connection or a session. When a station wants to send a packet over UDP to a destination, it just sends it.
- *Unreliable*. UDP does not guarantee that a packet will be delivered to a destination. If a UDP packet is lost because of some error or congestion on the network, the destination station will not receive it, and the sending station will be unaware of a lost UDP packet.
- *No sequencing*. There is no sequencing of packets. If several UDP packets are sent from one station to another, they *may* arrive in the correct order, but there is no guarantee of it.
- *No flow control*. If a sending station is able to send stream of UDP packets faster than the destination station can process them, then some packets may be lost.
- *Port number*. Like TCP, applications using UDP use reserved port numbers (for example, DNS uses port 53).

TCP/IP Application Layer The **application layer** is layer 4—the topmost layer—of the TCP/IP model. The protocols in the application layer provide application functions for application programs, some of which are used directly by computer users.

There is a multitude of protocols in the application layer of the TCP/IP stack. A few of them are described here:

- *Dynamic Host Configuration Protocol (DHCP)*. This protocol is used to configure basic network configuration settings for network nodes such as workstations. A workstation sends a broadcast query on the network, which is answered by a DHCP server that responds with parameters that the workstation uses to configure its network interface, including IP address, subnet mask, default gateway, and DNS servers.
- *Domain Name Service (DNS)*. This is the protocol that is used to translate domain names (such as www.cengage.com) to an IP address (such as 129.24.75.66). DNS servers throughout the Internet contain databases of domain names and their corresponding IP addresses.

- *File Transfer Protocol (FTP).* This protocol is used for batch and human-attended file transfers between computers.
- *Hypertext Transfer Protocol (HTTP).* This is the protocol used by web browsers and web servers to exchange HTML and XML content.
- *Lightweight Directory Access Protocol (LDAP).* This is a protocol used to authenticate users and provide directory services.
- *Network File Service (NFS).* This protocol is used to share file systems across a network.
- *Network Information Service (NIS).* This is the original directory service protocol developed by Sun Microsystems. NIS has been replaced by the more secure and versatile NIS+. NIS and NIS+ are used to centralize authentication and system configuration information for computers in a network.
- *Network Time Protocol (NTP).* This protocol provides high-precision time-of-day information so that participating computers' clocks will be more accurate. The clocks built in to computers are notoriously imprecise, which led to the development of this protocol.
- *Remote login (rlogin).* This protocol is used to log in to another computer over a network. This protocol is now considered unsafe, and has been superseded by the SSH protocol.
- *Remote Procedure Call (RPC).* This protocol provides the means for one computer requesting the execution of a subroutine or procedure on another computer.
- *Remote shell (rsh).* This protocol is used to execute commands on another computer. Now considered unsafe, rsh is superseded by the SSH protocol.
- *Session Initiation Protocol (SIP).* This is a signaling protocol used to establish voice or video communications sessions. SIP is often used to set up a VoIP telephone call.

- *Simple Mail Transport Protocol (SMTP).* This is the protocol that is used to transport e-mail among e-mail servers and across the Internet.
- *Simple Network Management Protocol (SNMP).* This is a network management protocol that is used to remotely monitor and manage network devices and systems.
- *Telnet.* This is a protocol used to establish a raw TCP session over a network to a service on another computer. It is possible to establish a session to virtually any service, such as DNS, SMTP, SNMP, or NFS, and then type commands in by hand and observe responses. Telnet is one of the first Internet standards.
- *Trivial File Transfer Protocol (TFTP).* This is a file transfer protocol that is a subset of FTP. TFTP has no authentication and is considered unsecure for most applications.
- *Voice over Internet Protocol (VoIP).* This protocol is used to transport voice traffic in Internet-based telephone calls.
- *Whois.* This protocol is used to query a whois server. Whois is usually used by Internet registrars that issue and manage Internet domain names and IP address space.

TCP/IP Routing Protocols

A routing protocol is a router-to-router communication protocol used by routers to help determine the most efficient network routes between two nodes on different networks.

In a routing protocol, routers communicate information about network destinations to neighboring routers. This sharing of routing information gives each router greater visibility of the greater network, which makes it more capable of making good routing decisions.

Prior to routing protocols, routers employed only static routes, in which each router was configured with information about neighboring networks. No dynamic route information was available. Today, routers in some environments are often configured with a limited number of static routes, usually for adjacent endpoints such as servers.

RIP One of the earliest routing protocols, the **Routing Information Protocol (RIP)** uses hop count as the primary routing metric. The fewer number of hops for a given destination, the more favored a destination will be, regardless of the actual link speeds involved. The maximum number of hops supported by RIP is 15, which seemed adequate when it was invented in the 1970s, but this limitation is one of several reasons why RIP has given way to more scalable and reliable protocols, such as OSPF and IS-IS.

RIP runs over the UDP protocol on port 520.

IGRP Cisco's proprietary **Interior Gateway Routing Protocol (IGRP)** was developed to overcome the limitations of RIP (mostly that its only routing metric was *hop count*). IGRP supports multiple metrics: bandwidth, delay, load, MTU, and reliability. IGRP's maximum hop count is 255. IGRP has been replaced by EIGRP, which is discussed later in this section.

IGRP does not use TCP or UDP but runs directly over IP.

EIGRP **Enhanced Interior Gateway Routing Protocol (EIGRP)** is a Cisco proprietary routing protocol that replaces IGRP through a number of improvements, including variable length subnet masks and improved algorithms.

OSPF The **Open Shortest Path First (OSPF)** routing protocol is a widely used routing protocol in large enterprise networks. Routers in an OSPF-routed network form peer relationships with neighbors called *adjacencies*.

An OSPF network is divided into *areas*; *area zero* is the backbone, or core, of an OSPF network. Other areas logically and physically connect to area zero. Route information is communicated from area zero routers to routers in other areas of the network.

OSPF can operate securely through the use of passwords in cleartext or hashed using MD5.

OSPF does not use TCP or UDP, but instead uses IP directly, using IP protocol 89.

IS-IS The **Intermediate System to Intermediate System (IS-IS)** routing protocol is primarily used by ISPs and other network service providers. It is based on *areas*, similar to OSPF, but does not rely on a central *area zero*.

IS-IS does not use TCP, UDP, or IP, but instead communicates at the data link layer. Routing information is established by neighboring routers that each build a table of routes based upon information accumulated through all of the network's adjacent router relationships.

BGP The **Border Gateway Protocol (BGP)** routing protocol is the protocol that is used for the Internet's main backbone routers. BGP peers (adjacent routers) are established through manual configuration. BGP routers build massive routing tables (with tens of thousands of entries) based upon the accumulation of peer relationships. The BGP protocol uses TCP port 179.

Remote Access/Tunneling Protocols

Several TCP/IP-based protocols have been developed that permit the *tunneling* of network traffic between computers, networks, and between a computer and a network. A **tunnel** provides packet encapsulation and can serve one of several purposes:

- *Protect communications*. A tunnel can utilize encryption, which will prevent an intermediate party from being able to eavesdrop on the communication.
- *Authenticate communications*. A tunnel can include authentication, in order to determine whether the party is permitted to communicate through the tunnel to the target network.
- *Hide a service provider network*. A service provider can provide a tunnel between the customer and the target network, thereby hiding its network from its customers.

Some examples of tunneling are shown in Figure 10-8.

VPN Virtual Privatep network (VPN) is a generic term that signifies any of the remote access tunneling protocols, including those discussed in this section. VPN does not refer to a specific protocol or technology but instead is a term that could mean *SSL, IPsec, L2TP*, or another protocol.

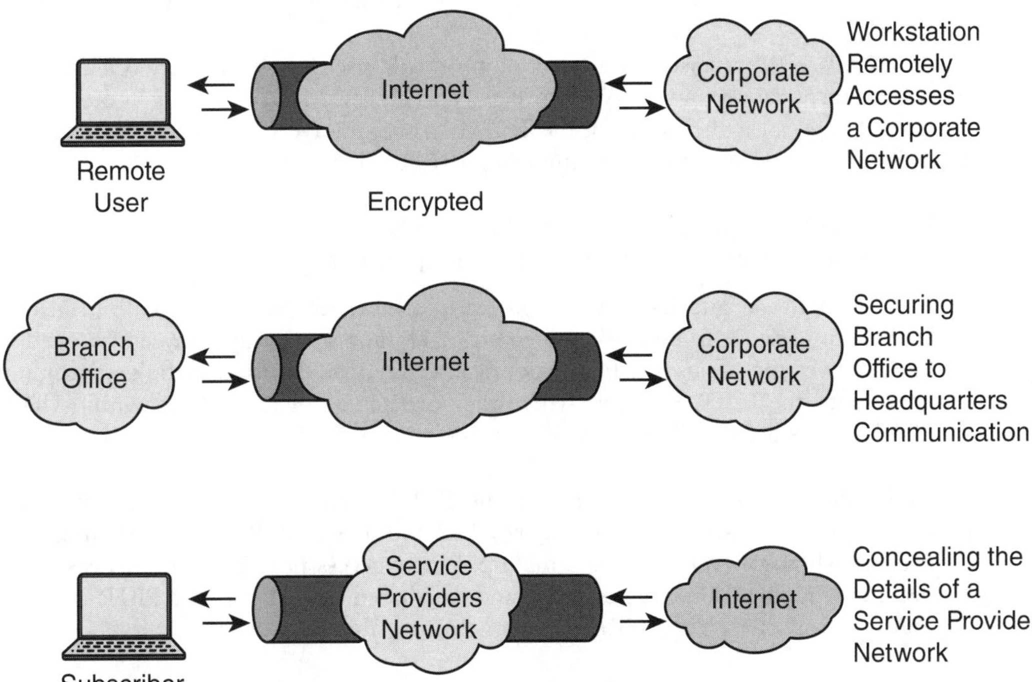

Figure 10-8 Examples of network tunneling

SSL/TLS **Secure Sockets Layer (SSL)** is a TCP/IP layer 4 encryption and tunneling protocol. An encrypted protocol that utilizes several encryption algorithms and key lengths, SSL is most often used to encrypt user application sessions such as:

- *HTTPS.* User HTTP sessions to web servers encrypted with SSL are known as **HTTPS.**
- *FTPS.* File transfer protocol (FTP) protected with SSL.
- *Remote access.* Some remote access software is designed to utilize the SSL software that is built in to client operating systems.

SSL is superseded by **Transport Layer Security (TLS)**, which is very similar to SSL.

SSH **Secure Shell (SSH)** is a TCP/IP layer 4 protocol that facilitates secure communications between systems. SSH began its life as a secure (encrypted) replacement for rsh (remote shell), rcp (remote copy), rlogin (remote login), and telnet, but it can also be used to tunnel other protocols, including:

- *File transfer.* The secure file transfer protocol, SFTP.
- *File backup and mirroring.* The *rsync* program uses SSH for file backup and mirroring.
- *Secure filesystem.* SSH permits the remote mounting of the SSH file system over a network.
- *VPN.* SSH can be used as the basis for a full-fledged VPN connection.
- *X11.* SSH can be used to protect X11 (X-Windows) connections between systems.

IPsec IPsec (IP security) is a suite of protocols used to secure network communications with authentication and encryption. It is typically used as a tunneling protocol to encapsulate messages at higher levels of the TCP/IP protocol (layers 3 and 4). IPsec is typically used in remote access and site-to-site tunneling over the Internet.

L2TP **Layer 2 Tunneling Protocol (L2TP)** is a TCP/IP protocol used to protect TCP/IP communications at higher levels through encapsulation.

L2TP emulates a data link layer protocol like Ethernet, but it is actually transported over UDP from network to network. When an L2TP tunnel is set up between two endpoints, the L2TP tunnel appears as a virtual network interface; packets for specific destination networks are sent to the L2TP *interface*, where they are actually encapsulated within UDP packets. L2TP tunnels are usually encrypted with IPsec.

PPTP **Point to Point Tunneling Protocol (PPTP)** is an early tunneling/encapsulation protocol that has been largely superseded by L2TP and IPsec. PPTP was implemented in early versions of Microsoft Windows as a dial-up remote access protocol that was easy to configure because it required only a password and no shared keys. Internally PPTP is a PPP session that is transported over a *GRE* (*General Routing Encapsulation*) tunnel.

PPP **Point to Point Protocol (PPP)** is a data link layer (TCP/IP layer 2) protocol that is commonly used for dial-up Internet access. Because it is a data link layer protocol, PPP can encapsulate not only TCP/IP but also NetBIOS, IPX (Novell), and AppleTalk.

SLIP **Serial Line Interface Protocol** (SLIP) is an early implementation for transporting TCP/IP over serial lines, fiber connections, and dial-up connections. SLIP has been largely superseded by PPP.

Network Authentication Protocols

There are several network-based protocols that are used for *authentication*, which is the verified identification of an individual who desires to access a resource.

There are two types of protocols used in network authentication: those that interact between a user and an access point or gateway, and those that occur between an access point or gateway and an authentication/authorization/accounting (*AAA*) server. Both types of protocols are often used in environments in which users are required to authenticate to a system or network.

RADIUS The **Remote Authentication Dial In User Service** (RADIUS) protocol is used to support the authentication of user access to networks and systems. The RADIUS server may store user credentials itself, or the RADIUS server may obtain them from an LDAP, Kerberos, Active Directory, or other authentication server.

Upon authentication, a RADIUS server will return information to the requesting client access device such as assigned IP address, permitted connection duration, and access restrictions. RADIUS also includes message types that are used for accounting—that is, the ability to measure a user's utilization of a network resource.

RADIUS messages travel between an access device and an *AAA* (authentication, authorization, and accounting) server. Figure 10-9 shows a typical access scenario, user access to the Internet via a wireless service provider.

Diameter Diameter is an AAA protocol that is the successor to the RADIUS protocol. Diameter is not an acronym, but a pun on the term RADIUS (a circle's diameter is twice its radius).

Like RADIUS, the Diameter protocol is found between a network access point or gateway and an AAA server such as LDAP or Active Directory.

TACACS Terminal Access Controller Access-Control System (TACACS) is a remote authentication protocol used to authenticate user access to a computer or network-based resource.

Like RADIUS, the TACACS protocol occurs between an access point or gateway and an AAA server such as LDAP.

TACACS has been largely replaced by two successors, TACACS+ and RADIUS.

802.1X IEEE 802.1X is a standard that is used for port-level network access control. A network that uses 802.1X requires all devices to authenticate to the network before the device will be able to communicate on the network. This is separate from any user authentication that may be required.

NAC **Network Access Control** (NAC) is an approach for network security that is meant to ensure that only systems meeting policy are permitted to connect to an organization's network. Note that NAC is not a protocol, but a general approach that may employ one or more proprietary or standard protocols.

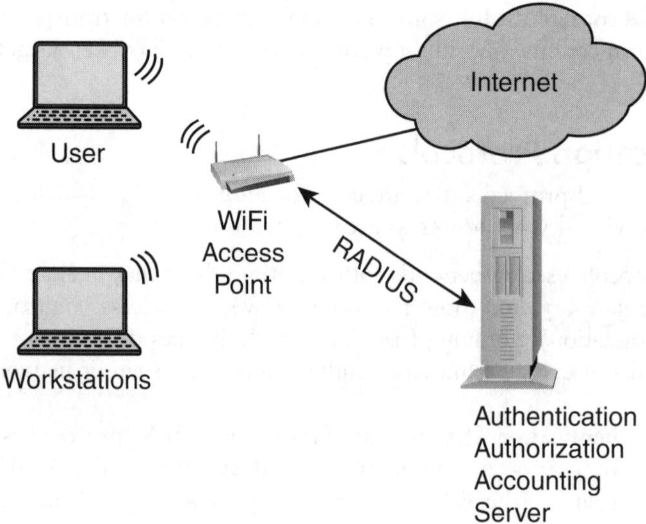

Figure 10-9 RADIUS support of a Wi-Fi access point

CHAP **Challenge-Handshake Authentication Protocol (CHAP)** is a protocol that is used to authenticate a user to a system or (usually) network resource. The CHAP protocol occurs between a user terminal or workstation and an access point or gateway.

CHAP works by using a *three-way handshake* as follows:

1. Gateway sends a challenge message to the user system
2. User system responds with a value that is a hash of the challenge plus a shared secret that both the user and the gateway know
3. Gateway compares user system's hashed value with its own; if they match, the connection is permitted; if they do not match, the connection is terminated

The PPP protocol uses CHAP to authenticate the PPP connection.

EAP The **Extensible Authentication Protocol (EAP)** is an authentication framework used to authenticate users in wired and wireless networks. EAP is used for authentication in WPA and WPA2 wireless network standards.

Several EAP protocols exist, including:

- *EAP-PSK*. This is a mutual authentication protocol using a Pre-Shared Key (PSK), usually to protect a network-based resource using a single password for all users.
- *EAP-IKEv2*. This is authentication based upon the Internet Key Exchange (IKE). protocol
- *EAP-AKA*. This is used for authentication in UMTS (Universal Mobile Telecommunications System), a mobile communications standard.
- *EAP-SIM*. Used for authentication in GSM (Global System for Mobile Communications), a global standard for mobility devices such as cell phones and wireless broadband modems.

- *LEAP*. This is the *Lightweight Extensible Authentication Protocol* that is a proprietary EAP protocol developed by Cisco Systems prior to the establishment of the 802.11i standard.

PEAP **Protected Extensible Authentication Protocol** (**PEAP**) (and sometimes known as *Protected EAP*) is a protocol used in wireless networks to authenticate users. PEAP uses an SSL/TLS tunnel to encrypt authentication information that is exchanged between the client and the authentication server or device.

There are two forms of PEAP:

- *PEAPv0*. This is the most common form, usually known as just PEAP. PEAPv0 uses CHAP for authentication.
- *PEAPv1*. This form, not in common use, supports authentication using token cards and directories.

PAP The **Password Authentication Protocol** (**PAP**) is a simple authentication protocol used by PPP to authenticate users. PAP is considered unsecure because user credentials are passed unencrypted.

Network-Based Threats, Attacks, and Vulnerabilities

By their nature, networks are *vulnerable* to *threats* and *attacks*. Large networks connect vast numbers of users together, and in many networks there is no overt control over the types of devices that users can connect to a network; hence, there is often little or no control over the nature of the traffic that a user can transmit over a network. These points are especially true of the global Internet, where hundreds of millions of computers are connected to millions of networks.

Sometimes the terms *threat, attack*, and *vulnerability* are interchanged or misused. They are defined in this section.

Threats

A *threat* is the expressed *potential* for the occurrence of a harmful event such as an attack. There are many types of threats, including:

- Malware in the wild that is spreading to vulnerable systems
- A disgruntled employee with the ability to do harm
- The high rate of stolen laptops

Attacks

Attacks are actions taken against a target resource with the intention of doing harm. There are many kinds of attacks that can take place over a network, including:

DoS A Denial-of-Service (DoS) attack is an attempt, on the part of the attacker, to incapacitate a target system or resource. The attack can take one of two forms:

- *High volume*. The attack may consist of a high volume of traffic that is designed to incapacitate the target by causing its resources to become exhausted.

- *Malfunction*. The attack may consist of one or more specially crafted messages that are designed to incapacitate the target by causing it to malfunction.

The intention of a DoS attack is to make the target resource unavailable for its intended use.

DDoS A Distributed Denial-of-Service (DDoS) attack is an attack that is designed to overwhelm a target with a vast amount of incoming traffic that originates from many sources. A DDoS attack may originate from dozens, hundreds, or thousands of systems.

A DDoS attack can originate from a *Botnet*, which is a collection of zombie computers that are remotely controlled by a botnet operator who uses software to control them. Figure 10-10 depicts a typical DDoS attack.

Teardrop A **teardrop** attack is one in which the attacker sends mangled packet fragments with overlapping and oversized payloads to a target system. Earlier versions of operating systems had bugs in the fragment reassembly code in their TCP/IP drivers that would cause the system to crash. This is a historic attack; most systems are no longer vulnerable to a teardrop attack.

Sequence Number A **sequence number attack** consists of an attacker who attempts to hijack or disrupt an existing TCP session by injecting packets that pretend to originate from one of the two computers in the session. The attack can be successful if the attacker correctly guesses the sequence numbers and the timing of packet injection; the target system may accept some or all of the spoofed packets instead of the legitimate ones.

Smurf A **smurf** attack consists of a large number of forged ICMP echo requests. The packets are sent to a target network's broadcast address, which causes all systems on the

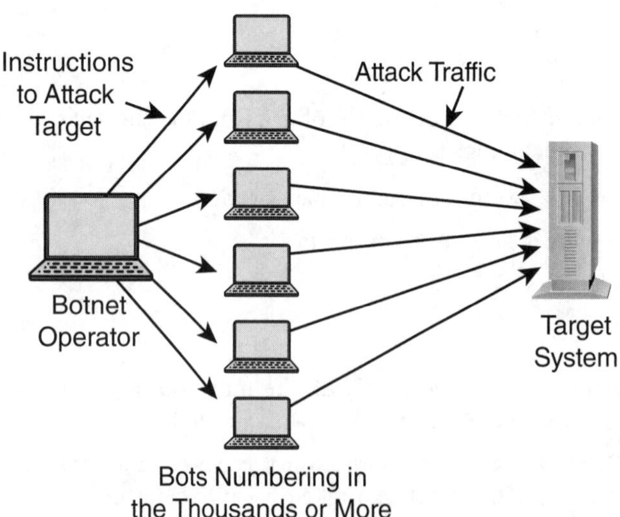

Figure 10-10 Distributed Denial of Service (DDoS) attack

network to respond. The packets are forged with the *from* address of the target system, resulting in a large number of ICMP echo reply messages from all of the systems on the network.

Ping of Death The **Ping of Death (PoD)** is an attack on a system where the attacker sends a ping packet of length 65,535 bytes to the target system. The TCP/IP protocol will fragment this packet as it travels through the network; it is then reassembled on the target system, causing a buffer overflow.

This is a historic attack; most systems have been fixed and are no longer vulnerable.

SYN Flood A **SYN flood** attack is a denial-of-service attack in which the attacker sends a large number of SYN packets to the target system. This attack is designed to overwhelm the resources of the target system until it is unable to respond to legitimate traffic.

A SYN packet is the first packet in a TCP connection *three-way handshake*. By sending a SYN packet to a system, it allocates resources in memory. When large numbers of SYN packets are sent to a system, the number of simultaneous TCP sessions will be exhausted, resulting in the system failing to respond to new, legitimate network messages.

Worms A worm is a type of *malware* that has the means for automatic self-replication. They spread by exploiting known vulnerabilities that permit the malicious program to infect new victims.

The most "successful" worms are able to spread quickly by virtue of efficient mechanisms used to locate and infect new hosts.

Worms usually inflict damage on account of the high volume of network traffic that they cause when large numbers of infected systems are searching for more victims.

Spam **Spam** is the common term for **unsolicited commercial e-mail** (UCE). Spam greatly adds to the volume of e-mail traffic on the Internet. Often, the volume of spam is so high that over 90 percent of all e-mail on the Internet is spam.

Spam's effect on networks is the degradation of performance through network and e-mail server congestion, as well as the machine cycles required to filter and remove spam messages.

Phishing Phishing is a type of spam where the contents of a message is designed to masquerade as a trustworthy organization, with the intention of defrauding recipients by tricking them into downloading and executing a malicious program or luring them to an authentic-looking website where they will enter secret information such as userids, passwords, bank account or credit card numbers, date of birth, social security numbers, and so on.

A phishing message can also ask its victim to simply reply to the e-mail, providing secret information in the reply message. Figure 10-11 shows a typical reply-requested phishing e-mail.

Vulnerabilities

Vulnerabilities are defined as weaknesses that make targets susceptible to attack, resulting in harm or compromise of sensitive information. Several types of network-oriented vulnerabilities are discussed in this section.

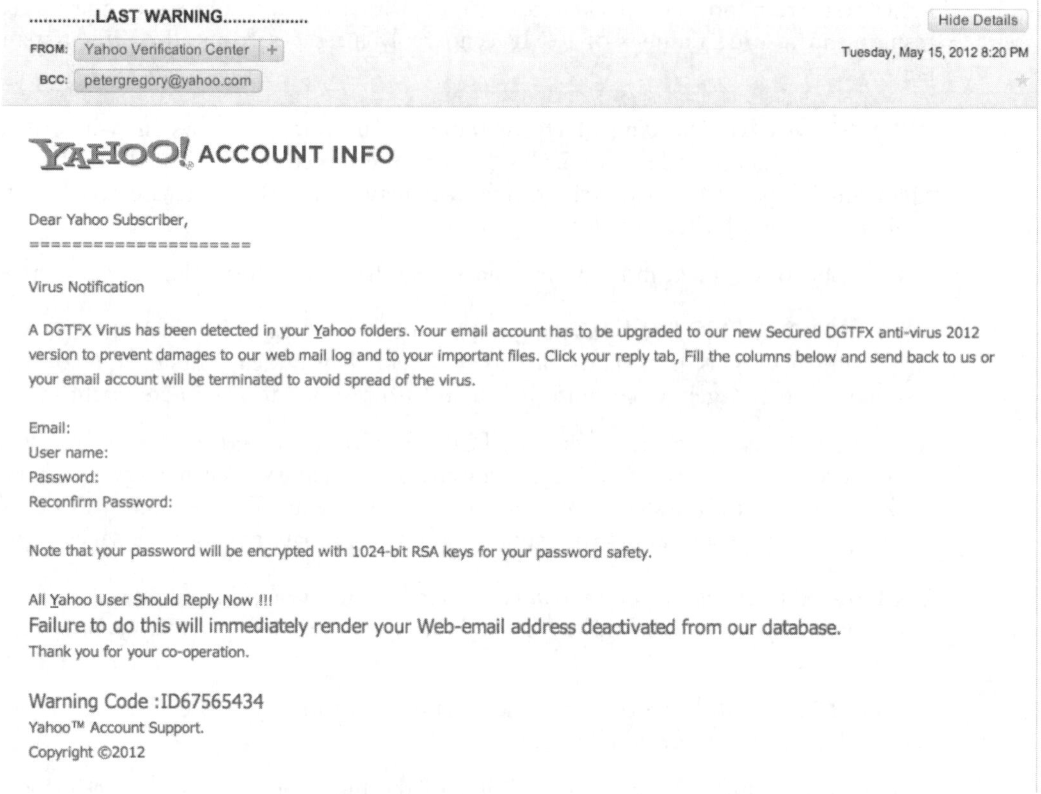

.............LAST WARNING.................

Hide Details

FROM: Yahoo Verification Center

Tuesday, May 15, 2012 8:20 PM

BCC: petergregory@yahoo.com

YAHOO! ACCOUNT INFO

Dear Yahoo Subscriber,
====================

Virus Notification

A DGTFX Virus has been detected in your Yahoo folders. Your email account has to be upgraded to our new Secured DGTFX anti-virus 2012 version to prevent damages to our web mail log and to your important files. Click your reply tab, Fill the columns below and send back to us or your email account will be terminated to avoid spread of the virus.

Email:
User name:
Password:
Reconfirm Password:

Note that your password will be encrypted with 1024-bit RSA keys for your password safety.

All Yahoo User Should Reply Now !!!
Failure to do this will immediately render your Web-email address deactivated from our database.
Thank you for your co-operation.

Warning Code :ID67565434
Yahoo™ Account Support.
Copyright ©2012

Figure 10-11 Typical phishing scam e-mail message

Source: Yahoo!

Unnecessary Open Ports An *open port* is a network-based listener that is associated with a program or service that runs on a system and that communicates via incoming network messages. An unnecessary open port is such a program or service that is not necessary for the system to carry out its functions.

Most vulnerabilities that are identified on systems are found within the software programs that accept messages through network ports. If a system has many such ports open, then the probability that the system as a whole contains serious vulnerabilities increases accordingly.

Unpatched Systems Security vulnerabilities in software programs and operating systems are found fairly regularly. Often, these vulnerabilities are known to hackers who create malicious code that is able to exploit these vulnerabilities, resulting in the compromise of the security of target systems.

The makers of software programs and operating systems usually respond quickly to news of vulnerabilities and create security patches, which are fixes to the programs so that the vulnerabilities are no longer present. But many systems do not have these patches installed, which makes them continually vulnerable and open to attacks.

Poor and Outdated Configurations The techniques used by hackers to break into systems are advancing regularly, resulting in systems that were once considered secure to become vulnerable to these new techniques. But frequently, systems are built that are not secure to begin with. Also, systems are sometimes moved from a low-threat area to a high-threat area, leaving them open to attack.

Default Passwords Operating systems and network devices such as routers often contain factory-installed default passwords for administrative accounts. If an organization does not change default passwords, attackers may be able to easily attack these systems because they can log in to them.

Exposed Cabling Any network cabling (other than what is usually found at a user's workstation) that is exposed can be targeted by an attacker. With the right tools and techniques, most cable types can be penetrated and network traffic intercepted and tampered with.

Network Countermeasures

Personnel at all layers of the technology stack, including network engineers, system engineers, database administrators, and application designers, all need to enact countermeasures to make their environments less susceptible to attack. Many of the common techniques for repelling network-borne attacks are discussed in this section.

Access Control Lists

The earliest, but still common, technique used to block unwanted traffic is the use of **access control lists** (ACLs) on network devices such as routers. While they may lack the fortitude to handle some of the more complex types of TCP/IP sessions that include the use of dynamically allocated ports, ACLs often represent a good first line of defense to block several types of unwanted traffic. If nothing else, this can relieve firewalls of many types of unwanted messages, improving overall throughput.

Firewalls

Invented in the 1980s, firewalls are devices placed at a network boundary that are designed to block unwanted incoming or outgoing traffic. A firewall works by examining each packet and consulting a list of *rules* to determine whether the packet should be permitted to pass through the firewall or be blocked. In a large organization, the list of rules in a firewall can become unwieldy, possibly resulting in unwanted traffic entering or leaving the network.

There have been three generations of firewalls, which are:

- *Packet filters*. The earliest firewalls made pass-or-drop decisions by examining the source and destination IP addresses and port numbers. They were unaware of TCP sessions and did not handle many of the advanced characteristics of TCP sessions that include the dynamic changes in port numbers that occur.
- *Stateful packet filters*. The second generation of firewalls overcame the problems in the first generation by being smarter about the techniques used by some TCP/IP protocols and how their use of dynamic port numbers confused early routers.

- *Application layer filters*. These are the newest types of firewalls that go one big step further by examining the payloads of network packets to determine whether they contain malicious patterns or content.

Several companies sell products called *next-generation firewalls*. These devices contain several features found in traditional packet filters and application firewalls, as well as features in other types of systems such as **intrusion detection systems** (IDS), all in a single unit known as a UTM (unified threat management) system.

Intrusion Detection Systems (IDS)

Intrusion detection systems (IDS) are programs or devices that are designed to observe network communications and generate alerts if any harmful or malicious traffic is detected.

There are two primary types of IDS, which are:

- *Network-based IDS (NIDS)*. A NIDS usually takes the form of a standalone appliance, or a blade in a modular network router or switch.
- *Host-based IDS (HIDS)*. An IDS program can be installed on a server. The HIDS will watch incoming network traffic and possibly other types of events on the system that indicate tampering.

The primary characteristic of an IDS is that it is passive. An IDS generates alert messages when unwanted traffic and other events occur, but does nothing else about them.

A common complaint about IDS systems is the number of *false positives*, or alerts that do not actually signify malicious traffic that warrants attention.

Intrusion Prevention Systems (IPS)

An **intrusion prevention system** (IPS) is a device or program that not only senses unwanted incoming traffic but also blocks that unwanted traffic. IPS is considered an evolution of passive IDSs that only generate alerts.

There are two primary types of IPS, which are:

- *Network-based IPS (NIPS)*. A network-based IPS can block individual packets, or even logically disconnect a suspected malicious device from the network. Like a NIDS, a NIPS can be a standalone appliance or a blade in a router or switch. A NIPS usually communicates with a router, firewall, or switch in order to cooperate in blocking traffic from offending IP addresses.
- *Host-based IPS (HIPS)*. A host-based IPS is a program on a server that can both detect as well as block unwanted events.

A potential risk of IPS systems is the possibility that traffic from legitimate systems may be blocked, resulting in disruption or downtime for applications or services.

Data Leakage Prevention Systems (DLP)

A **data leakage prevention** (DLP) system is a device that monitors networks, systems (or both) by detecting out-of-policy movement or storage of sensitive information. The purpose of a DLP system is the prevention of misuse of sensitive personal information such as credit card numbers or bank account numbers, or sensitive business information such as application source code. A DLP system can examine network traffic to detect the movement of sensitive information, or it can examine data stores to detect the presence of sensitive information.

Network Cabling Protection

All exposed network cabling should be moved, covered, or placed in conduits, so that it will not be subject to deliberate tampering or accidental damage. This topic is discussed in more detail in Chapter 8, "Physical and Environmental Security."

Anti-Virus Software

Anti-virus software that is installed on servers can detect worms and other malware and prevent them from installing themselves.

Private Addressing

While the primary purpose of private addressing was to conserve publicly routable IP addresses, a desirable side effect is the fact that systems with private IP addresses are more difficult to attack. Many home-based and small-business-based broadband routers rely only on private addressing to protect systems on home or small business networks.

Closure of Unnecessary Ports and Services

A highly effective method to reduce the probability of successful attack is to close all unnecessary and unused ports and services on systems and devices. Unused and unnecessary programs only increase the *attack surface* without providing any actual benefit—they are only a liability. Examining a system and eliminating everything that does not support the system's core purpose will reduce the likelihood that the system can be compromised.

Security Patches

All applicable security patches should be installed on servers and network devices as soon as it is practical to do so. In most cases, it is inadvisable to immediately install security patches, as doing so may impair legitimate functions. Instead it is recommended that patches are installed on less-critical systems first to ensure that the patches do not negatively affect their function. Then, when it's considered safe, security patches should be installed on production systems and devices.

Usually this process should take no less than thirty days, but there are times when patches are much more urgent, necessitating their installation within hours or days of release.

Unified Threat Management

Unified threat management (UTM) is a term used to describe a class of security devices and appliances that perform many functions in order to simplify the defenses in a network. A UTM system can contain one or more of the following:

- Firewall
- IDS
- IPS
- Anti-virus

- Anti-spam
- World Wide Web content filtering
- VPN remote access

A principle advantage of UTM is the consolidation of these important network-based security features in a single product.

Gateways

A gateway is a general term meaning a system or device that provides some intermediary or translating function in a network. Routers, firewalls, and e-mail servers are examples of gateways, but many more types exist.

In terms of security countermeasures, a gateway is a system or device that provides some protection against one or more threats. Examples of this type of use include:

- *E-mail gateway*. Rather than having e-mail from the Internet be delivered directly to an enterprise e-mail server, incoming e-mail can instead be delivered to an e-mail relay that resides in the DMZ. If a successful attack were launched against an e-mail server, such an attack on a DMZ e-mail relay could prove far less harmful than a successful attack on an internal e-mail server.
- *Multitiered application architecture*. Many web-based applications are designed so that web services, application services, and database services reside on different servers. By providing a multitiered application architecture (especially when firewalls are used in between the layers), the servers containing data are protected by a deep defense in depth.
- *World Wide Web content filter*. Because so many attacks are delivered via compromised web servers to end user systems via web browsers, employing web content filters reduces the risk that malicious code will reach an end user workstation. Organizations often use web content filters to block users from visiting unwanted sites that have no business purpose, on the presumption that doing so will reduce wasted time at work.

Chapter Summary

- Telecommunications networks include many types of wired and wireless network technologies. The wired technologies include DS-1 (T-1), SONET, Frame Relay, ATM, DSL, and MPLS. Wireless technologies include CDMA2000 (which includes 1xRTT and EVDO), GPRS, EDGE, LTE, UMTS, and WiMAX.
- Organizations build wired and wireless networks using a variety of technologies. The dominant wired technology is Ethernet, although ATM, Token Ring, and other technologies still have limited use. USB and RS-232 are used for limited and/or short-distance applications. Wireless technologies include WiFi and Bluetooth; IrDA, which is based on infrared light, is declining in use.
- Ethernet is a frame-based network standard in which nodes on a network transmit data in a *frame* that includes source and destination information, plus a *payload*. Ethernet has error correction capabilities that enable retransmission of frames when errors occur.

- Stations in an Ethernet network are addressed with a MAC (media access control) address that consists of six 8-bit octets. MAC addresses are unique in the world, to avoid the possibility that two devices with the same MAC address could ever be on the same network.
- Ethernet devices consist of hubs, bridges, switches, repeaters, routers, and gateways.
- Network cabling is typically one of three types: coaxial, twisted pair, or fiber optic. Fiber optic is the cable of choice for longer distances and the highest-speed connections, while twisted pair is prevalent in office environments.
- The four network topologies are bus, ring, star, and mesh. Ethernet networks are a physical star, but a logical bus.
- WiFi wireless networks can be made more secure by turning off SSID broadcast, changing to a non-default SSID, utilizing WPA or WPA2 encryption, and using user-based authentication and MAC-based access control. The WEP encryption standard has been compromised and is considered unsafe.
- Bluetooth and wireless USB are two other wireless technologies used to create personal area networks (PANs). Near field communication (NFC) is a short-range network technology.
- The OSI network model is a seven-layer model whose layers are physical, data link, network, transport, session, presentation, and application. The TCP/IP network model is a four-layer model consisting of link, Internet, transport, and application layers.
- The physical layer in the TCP/IP network model consists of the various cabling and wireless media such as twisted-pair cable, coaxial cable, fiber optic cable, WiFi, USB, and Bluetooth.
- The link layer in the TCP/IP network model includes various framing protocols such as Ethernet, Token Ring, ATM, Frame Relay, and PPP.
- The Internet layer in the TCP/IP network model contains the lowest-level protocols including IPv4, IPv6, ARP, RARP, ICMP, IGMP, and IPsec. Most TCP/IP routing protocols operate in the network layer and include RIP, OSPF, IS-IS, and BGP.
- Node addressing in the TCP/IP Internet layer in IPv4 uses 32-bit addresses expressed in a dotted decimal notation xx.xx.xx.xx. Networks are divided into subnets and are notated with a subnet mask that divides a node address into a network portion (the most significant bits) and a node portion (the least significant bits). The subnet mask indicates which bits belong to each portion. Standard subnet masks are established for Class A networks (which can contain 16,777,214 nodes), Class B networks (which can contain 65,534 nodes), and Class C networks (which can contain 255 nodes). Classless Inter-Domain Routing (CIDR) does away with Class A, Class B, and Class C networks and introduces flexible subnet masking for more efficient allocation of addresses in networks.
- IP addresses are allocated by Regional Internet Registries and Internet Providers. Blocks of reserved private addresses are used for organizations' internal nodes, and network address translation (NAT) is used to dynamically allocate addresses and ports for nodes with private addresses that communicate directly with nodes on the Internet.
- The transport layer in the TCP/IP network model includes the two primary transport protocols: TCP and UDP. The TCP protocol is connection-oriented and guarantees

delivery of packets, flow control, and order of delivery, whereas the UDP protocol is connectionless and does not guarantee packet delivery or flow control.

- The application layer in the TCP/IP network model includes the protocols that communicate directly with computer applications and tools. Some of the protocols found in the application layer include DHCP, DNS, FTP, HTTP, LDAP, NTP, RPC, SIP, SMTP, SNMP, Telnet, TFTP, and VoIP.
- Tunneling protocols are used to encapsulate TCP/IP packets. The reasons for tunneling include confidentiality (the payload in tunneling protocols can be encrypted) and authentication. Common tunneling protocols in use include SSL, SSH, IPsec, L2TP, PPTP, and PPP. These protocols support the creation of Virtual Privatevp networks (VPNs) that are often used to facilitate remote access to a private network.
- Authentication protocols are used to authenticate users who wish to use network or computing resources. Common authentication protocols in use include RADIUS, Diameter, CHAP, EAP, and PEAP. NAC is used to ensure that only systems meeting organization policy may connect to the network. The older protocols TACACS and PAP are not often used.
- Common network-based attacks include Denial of Service (DoS), Distributed Denial of Service (DDoS), teardrop, sequence number, smurf, ping of death, SYN flood, worms, spam, and phishing.
- Common network-based vulnerabilities include unneeded open ports, unpatched systems and devices, misconfigured systems and devices, default passwords, and exposed cabling.
- Effective countermeasures against attacks and vulnerabilities include access control lists (ACLs), firewalls, intrusion detection systems (IDS), intrusion prevention systems (IPS), data leakage prevention (DLP) systems, private addressing, closing unnecessary ports and services, installing security patches, and using gateways. UTM devices that perform many defensive functions are gaining use.

Key Terms

10BASE Any of a group of twisted-pair or coaxial network cabling types used to carry network traffic up to 10 Mbit/s. Types include 10BASE-T, 10BASE2, and 10BASE5.

100BASE Any of a group of twisted-pair network cabling types used to carry network traffic up to 100 Mbit/s, including 100BASE-TX.

1000BASE-T A twisted-pair network cabling type used to carry network traffic up to 1 Gbit/s.

802.1a/b/g/n See *IEEE 802.1a/b/g/n.*

802.1X See *IEEE 802.1X.*

Access control list (ACL) A method for filtering network packets on a router.

Access point A device used to connect multiple computers together to form a wireless network.

Address Resolution Protocol (ARP) A TCP/IP protocol that is used to translate a network IP address into a network MAC address.

Anycast A type of IP network communications where a packet is sent to only one of a group of available nodes.

Application layer Layer 7 of the OSI network model (and layer 4 of the TCP/IP network model), which provides communications to end user processes and programs.

Asynchronous Transfer Mode (ATM) A packet-switching network protocol that uses a fixed-size packet called a cell to transport data.

Attack An action taken against a target resource with the intention of doing harm.

Bluetooth A wireless network technology for low-speed and low-power data communication over short distances.

Border Gateway Protocol (BGP) A TCP/IP routing protocol primarily used by the Internet's backbone routers.

Broadcast A type of network communication where packets are sent to all nodes in a network.

Carrier Sense Multiple Access with Collision Detection (CSMA/CD) A data link layer protocol type where nodes verify the absence of traffic on the network before transmitting data. Nodes are able to detect collisions and back off before retransmitting.

Category 3/5/5e/6/7 Standards for twisted-pair network cabling that support bandwidths from 10 Mbit/s to 10 Gbit/s.

CDMA2000 A mobile radio technology used to transmit voice and data between subscriber devices and base stations for voice and data communication.

Challenge-Handshake Authentication Protocol (CHAP) A network-based authentication protocol used to authenticate a user to a system or network resource. CHAP is used to authenticate a PPP connection.

Checksum A method used to ensure the integrity of a packet or frame.

Coaxial cable A type of cable that consists of a single or dual inner conductor, a dielectric insulator, a metallic shield, and an outer plastic jacket.

Data leakage prevention A system used to detect and block unauthorized data transmissions on a network.

Data link layer Layer 2 of the OSI network model, which consists of protocols for transmitting frames over a network medium.

Data Over Cable Service Interface Specification (DOCSIS) The standard for delivery of Internet connectivity over television broadcast cable networks.

Datagram A self-contained set of data carrying information allowing it to be routed from a source to a destination node.

Digital Subscriber Line (DSL) A group of telecommunications technologies used to deliver digital data services (such as Internet connectivity) over telephone wires.

Digital Subscriber Line Access Multiplexer (DSLAM) A multiplexer node on a DSL service provider network that connects individual DSL subscribers to data networks such as the Internet.

Domain Name Service (DNS) A TCP/IP layer 4 protocol used to translate (via lookup) host and domain names into IP addresses.

DS-0 A single 64 kbit/s voice or data channel on a DS-1 circuit.

DS-1 The base North American telecommunications carrier protocol used to carry up to twenty-four 64 kbit/s voice or data channels.

Dynamic Host Configuration Protocol (DHCP) A TCP/IP layer 4 protocol used to assign IP addresses and other configuration settings to nodes on a network.

E1 The base European telecommunications carrier protocol used to carry up to thirty-two 64 kbit/s voice or data channels. See also *DS-1*.

Enhanced Data rates for GSM Evolution (EDGE) A wireless telecommunications standard that is a successor to GPRS that provides bandwidth up to 1 Mbit/s.

Enhanced GPRS (EGPRS) A wireless telecommunications standard that is a successor to GPRS that provides bandwidth up to 1 Mbit/s.

Enhanced Interior Gateway Routing Protocol (EIGRP) A Cisco proprietary routing protocol that is an enhancement of its earlier IGRP protocol. See also *Interior Gateway Routing Protocol (IGRP)*.

Ethernet A family of frame-based wired network technologies used to connect computers in a local area network (LAN).

Extensible Authentication Protocol (EAP) An authentication framework of protocols used to authenticate users to system or network resources. Several variants exist, including EAP-PSK, EAP-IKEv2, EAP-AKA, and EAP-SIM.

Fiber Distributed Data Interface (FDDI) A token network technology transmitted over fiber optic cable.

Fibre Channel A gigabit network protocol usually used in storage area networks (SANs) and transported over fiber optic or copper cable.

File Transfer Protocol (FTP) A TCP/IP layer 4 protocol used to transfer files between computers.

Frame A data packet at the data link layer in a network.

Frame Relay An early packet-switched telecommunications network technology used to connect together entities for data communications.

FTPS File transfer protocol (FTP) protected with SSL.

Gateway A device or system on a network that translates various types of network communications.

General Packet Radio Service (GPRS) The data-centric mobile radio technology used in the GSM (Global System for Mobile Communications) network.

Global System for Mobile Communications (GSM) One of the prevalent standards for wireless mobile voice and data telecommunications.

Header The portion of a network frame or packet that includes information such as the source address, destination address, and type of message.

High-Speed Serial Interface (HSSI) A high-speed serial communications protocol, usually used to connect nearby WAN devices together.

Host-based intrusion detection system (HIDS) An Intrusion Detection System (IDS) that is a part of a host computer. See also *Intrusion Detection System*.

Host-based intrusion prevention system (HIPS) An Intrusion Prevention System (IPS) that is a part of a host computer. See also *Intrusion Prevention System.*

Hypertext Transfer Protocol (HTTP) A TCP/IP layer 4 protocol used to transmit HTML and XML content from World Wide Web servers to client browsers.

Hypertext Transfer Protocol Secure (HTTPS) A TCP/IP layer 4 protocol used to transmit HTML and XML content from World Wide Web servers to client browsers that is protected with SSL/TLS encryption.

IEEE 802.1a/b/g/n A family of wireless network standards. See also *WiFi.*

IEEE 802.1X A network-based device authentication protocol that is based on EAP.

Infrared Data Association (IrDA) The governing body that has developed a number of line-of-sight optical protocols known as *IrDA*. Largely superseded by Bluetooth.

Integrated Services Digital Network (ISDN) A digital voice and data telecommunications service over copper wires.

Interframe gap A pause between transmitted frames on an Ethernet network.

Interior Gateway Routing Protocol (IGRP) A Cisco proprietary TCP/IP routing protocol that utilizes bandwidth, delay, load, MTU, and reliability metrics for determining the best path between endpoints.

Intermediate System to Intermediate System (IS-IS) A TCP/IP routing protocol used by ISPs and other network service providers.

Internet The global network of interconnected TCP/IP networks.

Internet Control Message Protocol (ICMP) A TCP/IP protocol used primarily for error messages and utility functions such as Ping and Traceroute.

Internet Group Management Protocol (IGMP) A TCP/IP protocol used to manage multicast groups. Analogous to ICMP.

Internet layer Another name for layer 3 of the OSI network model.

Intrusion detection system (IDS) A program or device that generates alerts when unwanted network traffic is detected. See also *intrusion prevention system.*

Intrusion prevention system (IPS) A program or device that blocks unwanted traffic when it is detected. See also *intrusion detection system.*

IPsec (IP security) A suite of protocols for securing IP communications with authentication and encryption.

IPv4 (Internet Protocol version 4) The original Internet Protocol (IP) that is layer 3 in the TCP/IP network model.

IPv6 (Internet Protocol version 6) The extended Internet Protocol, layer 3 in the TCP/IP network model that included extended addressing and security features.

Layer 2 Tunneling Protocol (L2TP) A TCP/IP layer 2 tunneling protocol used to encapsulate network traffic.

Lightweight Directory Access Protocol (LDAP) A TCP/IP layer 4 protocol used to query and modify directory services. LDAP is often used for authentication.

Link layer Layer 1 in the TCP/IP network model.

Local area network (LAN) A computer network covering a small geographic area such as a residence, building, or group of buildings.

Long Term Evolution (LTE) A high-speed wireless data communications technology that is based on GSM and UMTS technologies.

Media Access Control (MAC) address A notation for uniquely identifying nodes on a network, usually expressed as six octets.

Metropolitan area network (MAN) A computer network covering a geographic area the size of a city or region.

Multicast A method for efficiently transmitting network packets to groups of destination nodes. See also *unicast.*

Multiprotocol Label Switching (MPLS) A packet-switched telecommunications network technology used to transport voice and data.

Near Field Communication (NFC) A short-range (10cm) network technology generally used by mobile phones and other handheld devices for mobile payment and other applications.

Network A computer network covering any size geographic area from a few inches to international. See also *LAN*, *MAN*, *PAN*, and *WAN.*

Network Access Control (NAC) An approach to network security by employing a means of controlling which devices are permitted to connect to a network.

Network-based intrusion detection system (NIDS) An intrusion detection system (IDS) that is connected to a network. See also *intrusion detection system.*

Network-based intrusion prevention system (NIPS) An intrusion prevention system (IPS) that is connected to a network. See also *intrusion prevention system.*

Network File Service (NFS) A TCP/IP layer 4 protocol that is used to share file systems over a network.

Network Information Service (NIS) A TCP/IP layer 4 protocol that is used to centralize authentication and system configuration information for computers on a network.

Network layer Layer 3 of the OSI network model, which consists of low-level protocols used to transport data from computer to computer.

Network Time Protocol (NTP) A TCP/IP layer 4 protocol that is used to synchronize the time clocks on computers.

Open Shortest Path First (OSPF) A TCP/IP routing protocol used in large enterprise networks.

Open Systems Interconnect (OSI) The seven-layer network model whose layers are: Physical, Data link, Network, Transport, Session, Presentation, and Application.

Optical fiber A cable type used to carry high-speed communications signals in the form of light over a glass-like fiber.

Organizationally Unique Identifier (OUI) The first three octets of a MAC address that is assigned to an equipment manufacturer, in order to guarantee uniqueness of MAC addresses.

Packet filter A router with an access control list (ACL) or an early generation firewall. See also *access control list*, *firewall.*

Password Authentication Protocol (PAP) An authentication protocol used by PPP to authenticate users. PAP is unsafe because login credentials are not encrypted.

Payload The data that is contained in a network packet or frame.

Personal area network (PAN) A computer network that spans a distance close to one person.

Physical layer Layer 1 of the OSI and TCP/IP network models, which consists of a network's physical medium.

Ping A tool used to send an ICMP Echo Request to a specific node on a network.

Ping of Death (PoD) An attack where an attacker sends PING packets of length 65,535 bytes to the target system in hopes that the target system will crash.

Point to Point Protocol (PPP) A TCP/IP layer 2 protocol that is usually used for dial-up Internet access.

Point to Point Tunneling Protocol (PPTP) An early TCP/IP tunneling protocol that has been largely replaced by L2TP and IPsec.

Port number A numbering scheme in which messages of various types are distinguished.

Presentation layer Layer 6 of the OSI network model, which provides various methods for presenting data, for instance in different character sets or encryption algorithms.

Protected Extensible Authentication Protocol (Protected EAP or PEAP) A wireless network protocol used to authenticate users.

Public Switched Telephone Network (PSTN) The well-known public telephone network. Also known as *POTS* (plain old telephone service).

Remote Authentication Dial In User Service (RADIUS) An authentication protocol used to authenticate a user, control access rights through authorization, and provide accounting (usage) information for billing.

Remote login (rlogin) A TCP/IP layer 4 network protocol that is used to log in to another computer over a network.

Remote Procedure Call (RPC) A TCP/IP layer 4 protocol used to permit a computer to execute a subroutine or procedure on another computer.

Remote shell (rsh) A TCP/IP layer 4 protocol used to execute commands on other computers on a network.

Repeater A network device used to receive and retransmit a network signal, usually to extend the physical length of a network connection.

Reverse Address Resolution Protocol (RARP) A TCP/IP protocol that is used to translate a known MAC address into an IP address. Superseded by DHCP.

Ring A network topology where each node is connected to exactly two other nodes in a circular pathway.

Routing Information Protocol (RIP) An early TCP/IP routing protocol that uses hop count as the primary metric for determining the lowest cost of a route between endpoints.

RS-232 A serial communications technology used to connect computers to low-speed peripherals such as mice, printers, modems, and terminals. Superseded by USB.

Secure Shell (SSH) A TCP/IP layer 4 tunneling protocol used for secure remote management of systems. Supersedes Rsh, Rcp, Rlogin, and Telnet.

Secure Sockets Layer (SSL) A TCP/IP layer 4 tunneling protocol used to protect network traffic through encryption. Superseded by Transport Layer Security (TLS). See also *Transport Layer Security.*

Sequence number attack An attack in which an attacker injects packets with guessed sequence numbers that pretend to originate from one of the two computers in the session.

Serial Line Interface Protocol (SLIP) An early implementation for transporting TCP/IP over serial connections.

Service set identifier (SSID) A name that is used to identify a specific WiFi wireless network.

Session Initiation Protocol (SIP) A TCP/IP layer 4 protocol that is used to establish and tear down voice and video communications sessions.

Session layer Layer 5 of the OSI network model, which controls connections between computers.

Simple Mail Transport Protocol (SMTP) A TCP/IP layer 4 protocol used to transmit e-mail messages from one e-mail server to another.

Simple Network Management Protocol (SNMP) A TCP/IP layer 4 protocol used to remotely monitor and manage network devices and systems over a network.

Smurf An attack that consists of a large number of forged ICMP echo requests, which are sent to a network's broadcast address with a forged *source* address. Systems that receive the attack packets send large numbers of *reply* packets to the target.

Spam Unwanted e-mail that usually contains unsolicited commercial advertisements, pornography, or attempts to lure recipients into opening malicious attachments or visiting malicious web sites.

Star A network topology where all nodes are connected to a central device such as a hub or switch.

Subnet A range of network addresses in a network.

Subnet mask A numeric value, expressed in the same manner as an IP address, that is used to determine the network and host portions of an IP address.

SYN flood A denial-of-service (DoS) attack where the attacker sends large numbers of TCP SYN packets to the target system, hoping to overwhelm it and exhaust its resources.

Synchronous Digital Hierarchy (SDH) The prevalent standard for voice and data communications over fiber networks outside of North America. See also *SONET.*

Synchronous Optical Networking (SONET) The standard in North America for transporting voice and data over optical fiber.

T-1. See *DS-1.*

Teardrop An attack in which an attacker sends mangled packet fragments with overlapping and oversized payloads to a target system in an attempt to crash the target system.

Telnet A TCP/IP layer 4 protocol that is used to establish a raw TCP session over a network to a service on another computer.

Token ring A network technology consisting of a logical ring and the passing of a logical "token" from node to node over the network. Only a node in possession of a token may transmit data.

Traceroute A tool used to determine the network path to a specific destination.

Transmission Control Protocol (TCP) A connection-oriented TCP/IP transport protocol used to carry messages within a session between two nodes. TCP guarantees delivery, order of delivery, and flow control.

Transport layer Layer 4 of the OSI model and layer 3 in the TCP/IP network model, which provides reliable data transfer.

Transport Layer Security (TLS) A TCP/IP layer 4 tunneling protocol that protects network traffic through encryption. Transport Layer Security supersedes Secure Sockets Layer (SSL).

Trivial File Transfer Protocol (TFTP) A TCP/IP layer 4 protocol used to transfer files over a network.

Tunnel Any of several network protocols that use packet encapsulation to deliver packets to an endpoint.

Twisted-pair cable A type of cable that utilizes pairs of twisted copper conductors.

Unicast A type of network communication where packets are sent to a single node. See also *multicast*.

Unified threat management (UTM) A security device or appliance that performs many security functions such as firewall, IDS, IPS, anti-virus, anti-spam, or web content filtering.

Universal Mobile Telecommunications System (UMTS) A wireless telecommunications protocol for data communications.

Unsolicited commercial e-mail (UCE) See *spam*.

User Datagram Protocol (UDP) A connectionless TCP/IP transport protocol used to carry messages within a session between two nodes. UDP does not guarantee delivery, order of delivery, or flow control.

Voice over Internet Protocol (VoIP) A TCP/IP layer 4 protocol used to transport voice traffic over a network.

Whois A TCP/IP layer 4 protocol that is used to query a whois server, usually to determine the owner of a domain name or IP address.

Wide area network (WAN) A computer network covering large geographic areas spanning metropolitan, regional, national, or international.

WiFi A family of wireless data link standards for connecting computers together to form networks.

WiFi Protected Access (WPA and WPA2) Protocol standards that replace the Wired Equivalent Privacy (WEP) protocol.

Wireless USB (WUSB) A wireless protocol designed for wireless connectivity of various computer peripherals such as printers, digital cameras, hard disks, and other high-throughput devices.

Wireline Any of the telecommunications services that is transported over copper or optical fiber.

Worldwide Interoperability for Microwave Access (WiMAX) A wireless telecommunications standard for fixed-base and mobile voice and data communications.

WPA2 Enterprise The WPA2 protocol when an external authentication source, such as RADIUS, is used.

X11 The GUI-based window system that is used in UNIX and Linux operating systems.

X.25 A packet-switched telecommunications network.

xDSL See *Digital Subscriber Line (DSL)*.

Review Questions

1. The capacity of a DS-1 circuit is:
   a. 24 voice channels of 64 kbit/s each
   b. 32 voice channels of 64 kbit/s each
   c. 24 voice channels of 48 kbit/s each
   d. 16 data channels of 64 kbit/s each
2. Which of the following statements is true about MPLS:
   a. MPLS can be used to transport voice and data, and its traffic should be protected with encryption.
   b. MPLS can be used to transport voice and data, and its traffic does not need to be protected with encryption.
   c. MPLS is used for data only, and its traffic should be protected with encryption.
   d. MPLS is used for voice only, and its traffic should be protected with encryption.
3. A network architect is designing a remote access solution for mobile workers with laptop computers and will use GPRS technology for over-the-air communications. Because workers access sensitive information, what protection is required to protect GPRS traffic?
   a. GPRS's over-the-air encryption is sufficient and no VPN is needed.
   b. GPRS's over-the-air encryption has been compromised and a VPN is needed.
   c. GPRS has no over-the-air encryption and a VPN is needed.
   d. GPRS is not suitable for Internet communications and should not be used.
4. A security manager is concerned about the security of its WEP-encrypted WiFi network. How can security be improved to prevent eavesdroppers from viewing sensitive business information?
   a. Require VPN for all users using the WiFi network
   b. Require SSL VPN for all users using the WiFi network
   c. Upgrade authentication to EAP
   d. Upgrade authentication to PEAP
5. What protection is needed for a banking organization's internal 802.3 network?
   a. WEP
   b. WPA
   c. WPA-2
   d. None

6. A security engineer is using a sniffer to determine the source of apparently hostile traffic on an organization's internal routed network. When the engineer examines individual frames, he sees that the source MAC address for the hostile packets matches the MAC address for the router on the local network. What is the best explanation for this?
   a. The packets are encapsulated in a tunneling protocol such as PPTP.
   b. The packets have a spoofed originating MAC address in order to make identification of the hostile node more difficult.
   c. Frames carrying IP traffic originating on another network will have a MAC address for the local network's router.
   d. The packets are IPX protocol, not IP.
7. What steps should be taken to lock down a WiFi network?
   a. No SSID broadcast, non-default SSID, MAC access control, and WEP encryption
   b. No SSID broadcast, non-default SSID, MAC access control, and WPA-PSK encryption
   c. SSID broadcast, non-default SSID, MAC access control, and WPA-PSK encryption
   d. SSID broadcast, non-default SSID, MAC access control, WEP encryption, and RADIUS authentication
8. The layers in the OSI model are:
   a. Physical, Data link, Network/Internet, Transport, Session, Application
   b. Physical, Data link, Network, Transport, Socket, Presentation, Application
   c. Physical, Data link, Network/Internet, Transport, Application
   d. Physical, Data link, Network, Transport, Session, Presentation, Application
9. GPRS, ATM, FDDI, and SLIP are examples of:
   a. Data link layer protocols
   b. Physical layer protocols
   c. Network layer protocols
   d. Encryption protocols
10. A packet filter firewall is blocking ICMP protocols. This means that:
    a. Pings cannot pass through the firewall
    b. Pings and Traceroute cannot pass through the firewall
    c. Traceroute cannot pass through the firewall
    d. IS-IS cannot pass through the firewall

11. A requesting station sends a TCP SYN to a destination station. The destination station responds with a SYN-ACK. The requesting station responds with an ACK. What has occurred?
    a. An attacker was launching a SYN attack that has failed.
    b. A user is running Traceroute.
    c. A TCP connection was established.
    d. A TCP connection was torn down.
12. The purpose of the DHCP protocol is:
    a. Assign IP address and subnet mask to a station
    b. Assign default gateway address to a station
    c. All of these
    d. Assign DNS and WINS server addresses to a station
13. The rlogin protocol should no longer be used because:
    a. SSH is more efficient
    b. Its password encryption has been compromised
    c. It cannot be routed on an IPv6 network
    d. Credentials are passed in the clear
14. PPP is a poor choice for an Internet-based remote access protocol because:
    a. It does not utilize header compression
    b. PPP traffic is not encrypted
    c. PPP credentials are not encrypted
    d. It is not routable over IPv6 networks
15. The best countermeasure for a SYN attack is:
    a. Block SYN packets on border routers
    b. Block SYN packets at the firewall
    c. Increase the number of open SYN requests on the firewall
    d. Increase the number of open SYN requests on servers

Hands-On Projects

Project 10-1: Classful Subnet Mask Calculator

In this project you will calculate and observe subnet masks required for Class A, B, and C networks.

Visit the web site www.subnet-calculator.com.

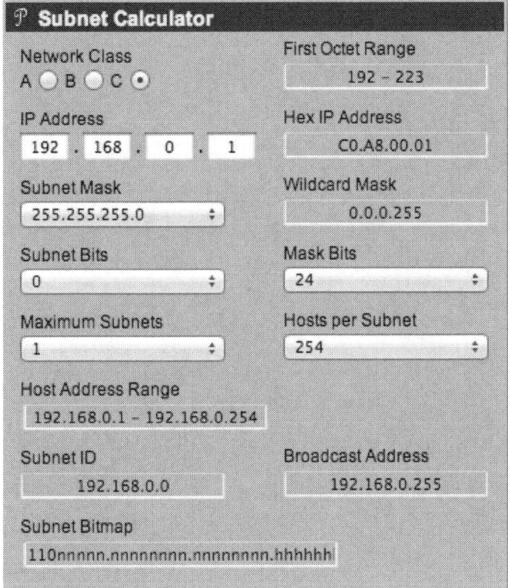

Figure 10-12 Classful subnet calculator

Source: http://www.subnet-calculator.com

1. Click C under **Network Class.** Observe the default values shown for the IP address 192.168.0.1 with subnet mask 255.255.255.0. Refer to Figure 10-12.
2. How many subnet bits are there? How many mask bits are there? How many subnets are available? How many hosts can be on each subnet?
3. Change the subnet mask to 255.255.255.224. Now how many subnet mask bits are there? How many mask bits? How many subnets are available, and how many hosts can be on each subnet?
4. Change the subnet mask to 255.255.255.252. How many subnets are available? How many hosts can be on each subnet? Why is the total number of hosts available on all subnets fewer than the number of hosts when the subnet mask is 255.255.255.0?
5. Keep your web browser open if you will be doing Project 10-2.

Project 10-2: Classless Subnet Mask Calculator

In this project you will calculate and observe subnet masks required for networks with Classless Inter-Domain Routing (CIDR).

1. Visit the web site www.subnet-calculator.com.
2. Click the **CIDR** link.
3. In the **IP Address field,** enter the IP address 10.0.0.1.

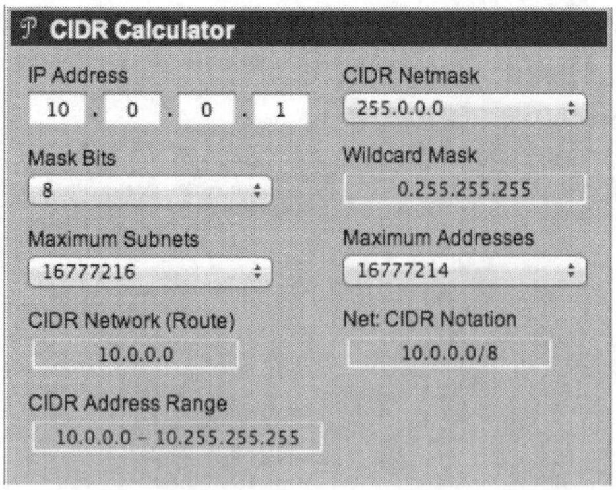

Figure 10-13 CIDR subnet calculator

Source: http://www.subnet-calculator.com

4. Select CIDR Netmask 255.0.0.0. Refer to Figure 10-13.
5. Observe the values shown. How many mask bits are there? How does this relate to the CIDR Notation? What is the range of IP addresses?
6. Change the IP address to 192.168.0.0 and the CIDR Netmask to 255.255.254.0. What is the range of available IP addresses? Why is this called a "supernet"?

Project 10-3: Network Sniffer

Required for this project:

- Windows Vista, 7, or 8; Apple Mac OSX; Linux
- Administrative access to the operating system for purposes of installing software

In this project you will capture network traffic with a sniffer.

In order to avoid any potential problems, you should first ask for permission to perform this project. You should not run a sniffer on a network unless you have explicit permission.

1. Download WireShark from www.wireshark.com.
2. Install WireShark using procedures available on the WireShark web site.
3. Start WireShark.
4. Ensure that WireShark is going to capture packets on the correct interface. Select **Capture** > **Options**, and see what interface is selected. Select the proper interface from the list. Make sure **Capture all in promiscuous mode** and **Update list of packets in real time** are selected. Refer to Figure 10-14.

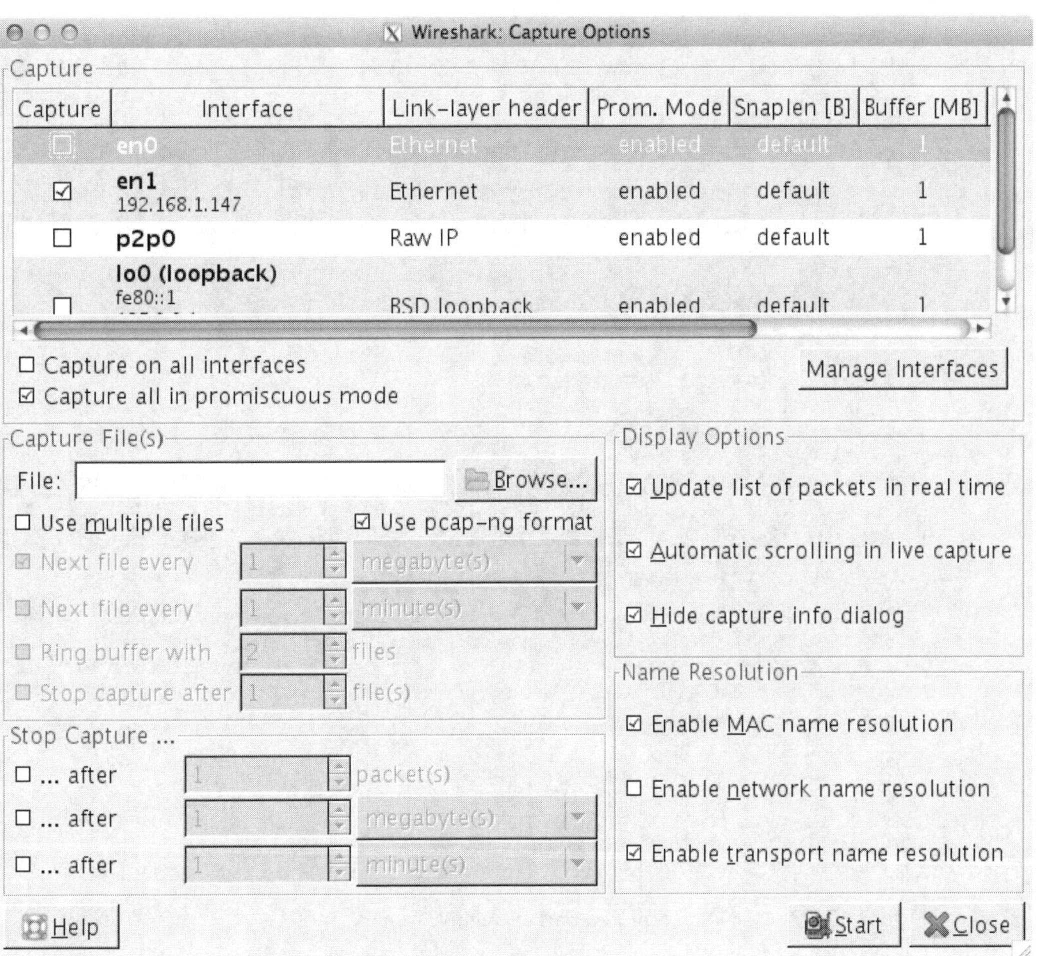

Figure 10-14 Selecting packet capture options in Wireshark

Source: WireShark Foundation

5. Begin capturing web traffic for your own workstation. Click Start.
6. After some packets have been captured, click **Capture** > **Stop**.
7. Click on a packet in WireShark's upper window, as shown in Figure 10-15. What does WireShark show you about the packet in the lower window? Examine the detail in each section (for example: Frame, Ethernet II, Internet Protocol, Transmission Control Protocol, Hypertext Transfer Protocol). What can you learn about the packet(s) that you are examining?

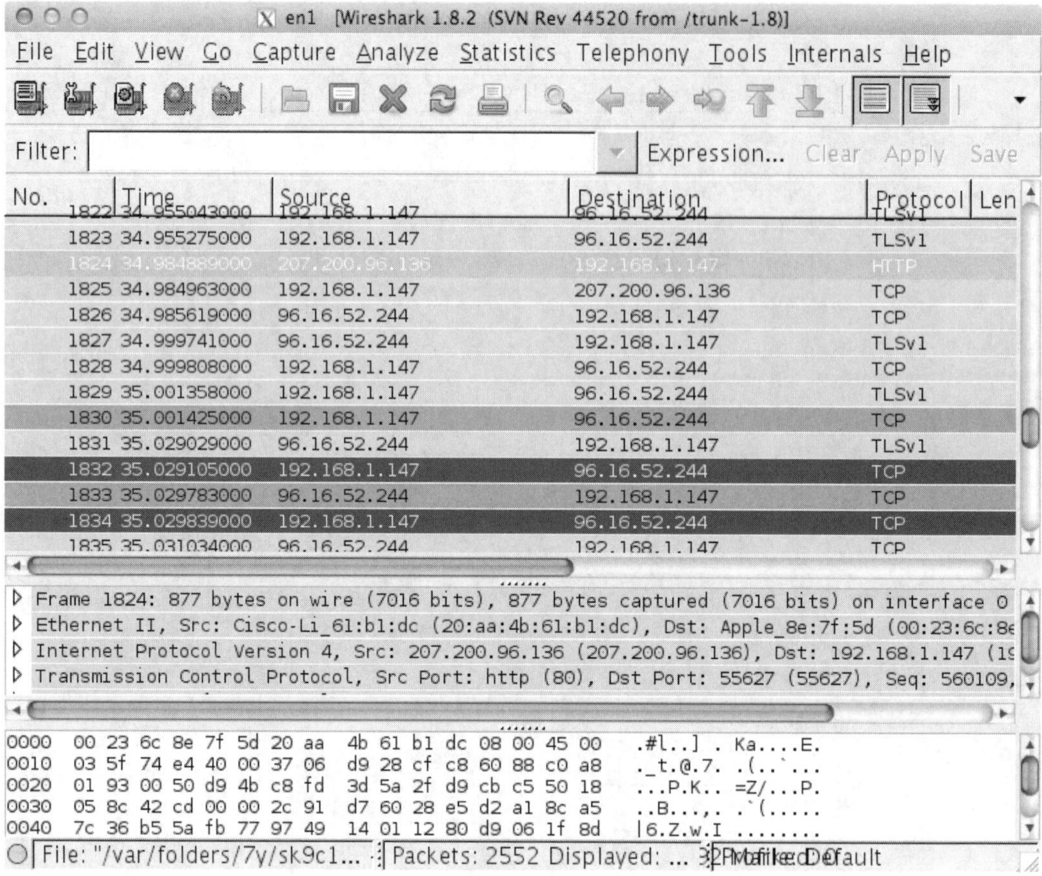

Figure 10-15 Examining captured packets with Wireshark

Source: WireShark Foundation

Project 10-4: Port Scanner

Required for this project:

- Windows Vista, 7, or 8
- Administrative access to the operating system for purposes of installing software

In this project you will perform simple port scanning to discover open ports on nearby network systems.

Note: Port scanning may be considered a security violation in a work or school network. You must obtain permission from the network manager before downloading and using such a tool.

1. Download the NMAP tool from www.nmap.org.
2. Install and start the tool. Refer to Figure 10-16.

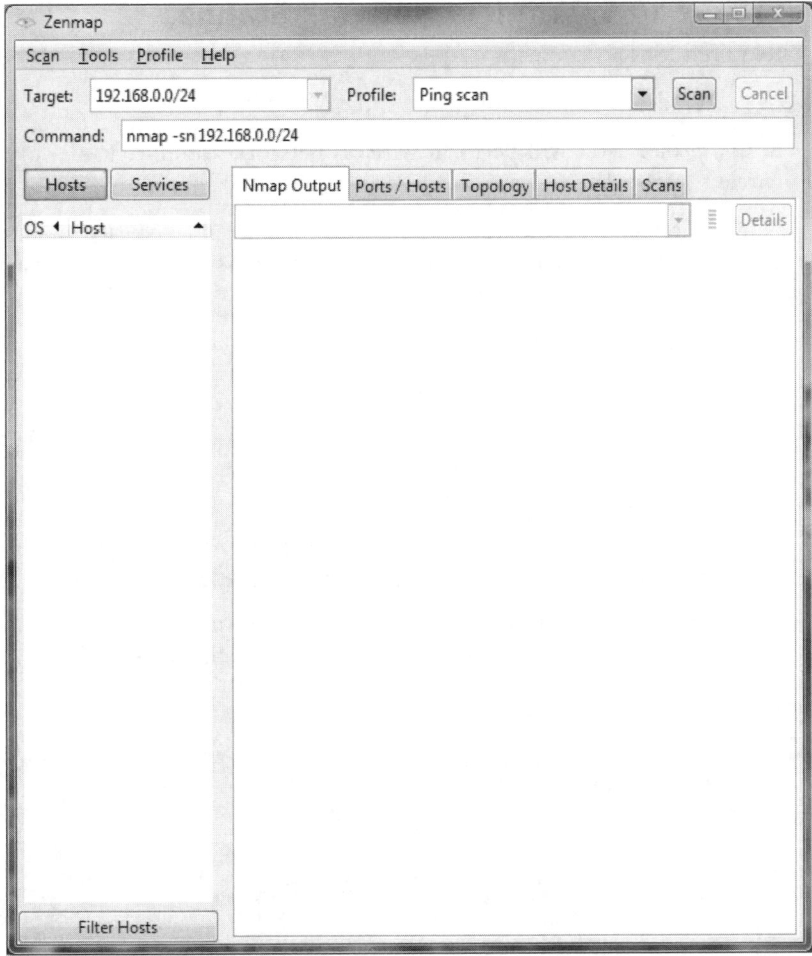

Figure 10-16 Scanning for network vulnerabilities with NMAP

Source: NMAP.org

3. Input a range of IP addresses to scan in the **Target** field. Select the type of scan you wish to run (the **Profile**), then click the **Scan** button.

4. NMAP will then scan the network and identify active hosts and security information about each. Results are seen in the Nmap Output tab.

5. What did NMAP tell you about the network you scanned? Did it find any vulnerable computers?

If NMAP identified any vulnerabilities in any of the systems that it scanned, you should notify respective system owner(s) as soon as possible.

Note: The SuperScan tool from Foundstone may also be used for this project. SuperScan is available for Windows computers and may be found at www.foundstone.com.

Project 10-5: Wireless Network Scanner

Required for this project:

- Windows Vista, 7, or 8, or Apple Mac OSX

In this project you will perform wireless network scanning to discover nearby wireless networks.

Note: Wireless network scanning may be considered a security violation in the work or school network. You must obtain permission from the network manager before downloading and using such a tool.

1. Download the Vistumbler tool from www.vistumbler.net.
2. Install the Vistumbler tool.
3. Start the tool and click the **Scan APs** button. If there are WiFi access points nearby, Vistumbler should soon discover them and list them on the screen. Refer to Figure 10-17.
4. In the left-hand pane, click the + next to **Encryption**. Click the + next to **None**. Are any access points are indicated?
5. In the left-hand pane, click the + next to **Authentication**. Click the + next to **Open**. How many access points are indicated?

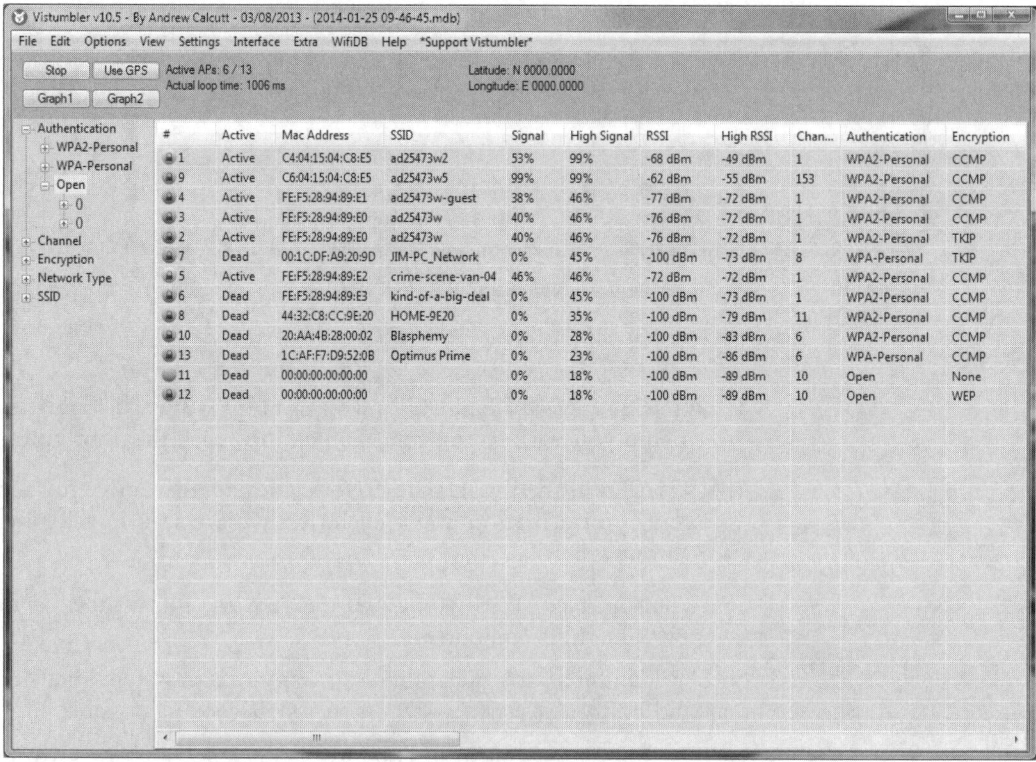

Figure 10-17 Scanning for wireless networks with Vistumbler

Source: Vistumbler

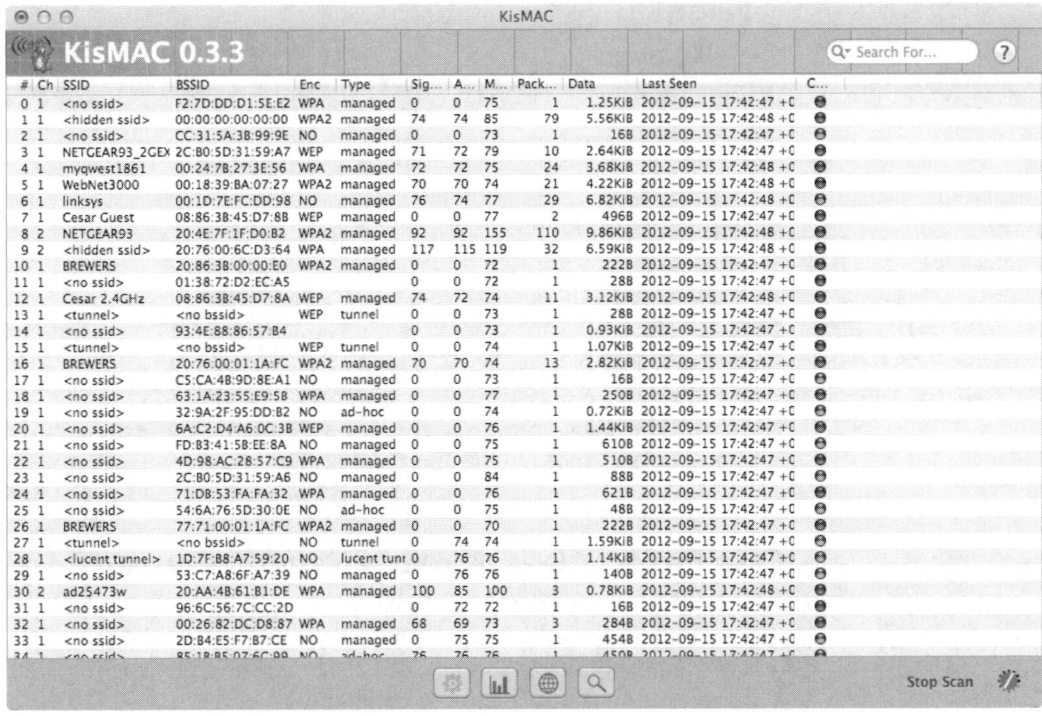

Figure 10-18 Scanning for wireless networks with KisMAC

Source: KisMAC

6. What have you learned about nearby access points?
7. Are you able to discern the owners of any access points based upon their SSID?

Even if you find open (unencrypted) access points, you should not attempt to connect to one without obtaining written permission from its owner. Doing so is a crime in many jurisdictions.

Note: The Netstumbler tool is similar to Vistumbler and may be substituted.

Note: If you are using a computer running Mac OS, the KisMAC tool is similar to Vistumbler. See Figure 10-18.

Case Projects

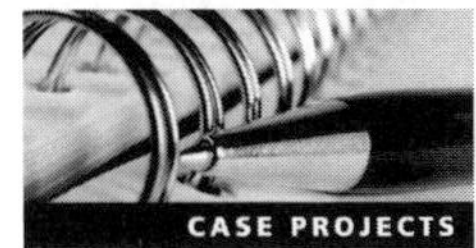

Case Project 10-1: Network Address Allocation

As a network engineer in the Have-A-Java Roasting Company, you need to develop a plan to re-IP address the entire network.

The network consists of the following systems on the local network:

2 DNS servers

2 routers

1 firewall

1 VPN server

E-mail server

External web server

Internal file server

300 user workstations

6 printers

Your ISP has requested that you return the two Class C network addresses that it assigned to your company ten years ago. They will allocate to you six externally routable IP addresses for any external-facing systems.

How will you allocate the six IP addresses among the externally facing systems and devices that require Internet access?

How will user workstations be able to access web servers on the Internet?

Case Project 10-2: Wireless Network Survey

As a consultant with the Sleuth Security Consulting Co., you have been asked to perform a wireless access point survey at the Good Software Company offices. Good Software is concerned that there may be rogue (unauthorized) WiFi access points in use in their company.

What tools will you use to look for rogue access points? Will you use a WiFi sniffer such as Netstumbler? What are the pros and cons of using this tool? Will you perform any LAN searches for rogue access points?

Case Project 10-3: Network Evaluation

As a consulting network engineer for the Excellent Network Consulting Co., you have been requested to perform an evaluation of the data network at the Zoom Trucking Company, which has just moved into an eighty-year-old office building.

Zoom Trucking's network engineer has not been able to get the network functioning on the network cable that was in the building when Zoom Trucking moved in. Part of the network uses coaxial thinnet cabling, and part of it uses Cat-3 network cabling. Less than half of the user workstations connected via Cat-3 cabling are working, and none of the workstations connected to coaxial cable are working because none of the user workstations have the right connectors.

Some specifics about Zoom Trucking:

Employees with workstations: 75

Servers: 8 servers located in a server room

Building size: 2 floors, 100” 200’× ’

Construction: wood frame and masonry exterior

Your job is to create a list of recommendations to Zoom Trucking: what steps should it take to get its data network working as soon as possible?

Appendix A

The Ten Domains of CISSP Security

Topics in This Chapter:

- An Introduction to the CISSP Certification
- The Ten Domains of CISSP Security

The **International Information Systems Security Certification Consortium**, or **(ISC)^2** (pronounced "I-S-C-squared"), is the governing body and owner of the CISSP certification. **CISSP**, or **Certified Information Systems Security Professional**, is one of the highest-rated professional certifications for information and business security. This is how (ISC)^2 defines a CISSP:

> *The Certified Information Systems Security Professional (CISSP) is an information assurance professional who has demonstrated a globally recognized level of competence provided by a common body of knowledge that defines the architecture, design, management and controls that assure the security of business environments.*

The reputation is due to several factors, including:

- *Longevity*. The CISSP certification was introduced in 1994, many years before information security was "cool." Computer, network, and physical security were well established in government and military establishments, and the Internet was just getting air under its wings.
- *Industry acceptance*. The CISSP certification is the first security credential accredited by the ANSI/ISO/IEC 17024:2003 standard in the field of information security. The U.S. DoD Directive 8570.1 requires its information security workers to obtain an ANSI-accredited commercial certification, such as CISSP.
- *Wide recognition*. CISSP is probably the most recognized security certification in all of the information technology profession. Having CISSP in one's title means that this is a security professional at the top of the security profession.
- *High standards*. The CISSP certification is considered the top-most certification in the information- and business-protection profession. It is difficult to earn the certification: the qualifying exam consists of six hours of mind-numbing multiple-choice questions that can trip up even the most senior professionals. The certification also requires that the candidate have five years of verifiable security experience, and a background free of association with hackers and convictions related to crimes of dishonesty.
- *Remains current and relevant*. (ISC)^2 actively offers educational opportunities for CISSP certification holders so that they can stay sharp and informed on the latest technologies, threats, and methods. The CISSP exam is continually updated to reflect the latest developments in security technology and techniques. New exam questions are written by experienced CISSPs in exam-writing workshops that occur several times each year.

The entire body of knowledge that comprises the CISSP certification is arranged in a living document called the **Common Body of Knowledge (CBK)**. It has often been said that the CBK is overly broad, yet shallow, "a mile wide and an inch deep." I'm not sure that I agree with this metaphor. It is true that the CBK contains a great many topics, and that the scope of knowledge that a CISSP candidate is expected to know is constantly expanding in breadth and depth. But the knowledge and experience required to earn the CISSP certification and be an effective security professional requires that your knowledge of security be a lot more than an inch deep.

This and every other book on the (ISC)^2 CISSP Common Body of Knowledge (CBK) should be considered a guide on the concepts that the reader should know, rather than a discrete list of topics and no more. The purpose of the CBK is to outline the technologies, practices, and laws that are related to the protection of an organization's information-related assets.

The ten domains in the CISSP CBK are:

- Domain 1: Access Control
- Domain 2: Telecommunications and Network Security
- Domain 3: Information Security Governance & Risk Management
- Domain 4: Software Development Security
- Domain 5: Cryptography
- Domain 6: Security Architecture & Design
- Domain 7: Security Operations
- Domain 8: Business Continuity & Disaster Recovery Planning
- Domain 9: Legal, Regulations, Investigations and Compliance
- Domain 10: Physical (Environmental) Security

Each of these domains is described briefly in the remainder of this appendix, and more fully in individual chapters in this book.

Changes in the CBK

(ISC)^2 changes the structure and contents of the CBK from time to time, as the state of the art of security technology and management continue to mature and change. Because publications are not immediately updated, you may even see inconsistencies between various (ISC)^2 publications. In the most recent major restructuring of the CBK in 2012, (ISC)^2 reordered and renamed some of the domains, and changed the wording in all of them. Further changes to the CBK are likely in the future.

(ISC)^2 does not require CISSP candidates to know the names of the CBK domains or which specific security topics are contained in each part of the CBK.

The Common Body of Knowledge

The (ISC)^2 *Common Body of Knowledge* contains ten domains, which are the major categories of business and data security. Activities in the ten domains work together to protect the confidentiality, integrity, and availability (CIA) of business information, information systems, and other important business assets.

The information in this section is a summary of the information published by (ISC)^2 in the Candidate Information Bulletin, a guide for aspiring CISSP candidates who wish to earn the CISSP certification.

Domain 1: Access Control

Access controls are used to control user access to computer systems, stored data, networks, and workspaces. A variety of techniques and technologies are used to manage access in organizations; in larger organizations, there tends to be a greater use of automation to manage user access.

Access controls are found in many layers of technology including network, remote access, operating system, database, and application. At each layer, access controls may be administered by different teams using different tools.

Access controls are the means through which legitimate users gain access to a system or workspace, and are also frequently the target of many forms of attack by intruders. Security professionals must understand attack methods as well as techniques to ensure that access controls are not vulnerable to these attacks.

Domain 2: Telecommunications and Network Security

This domain requires the security professional to fully understand computer networking and the telecommunications technologies that facilitate short- and long-distance networking. Because most security-related threats, vulnerabilities, and attacks are network-related, this requires intimate knowledge of the workings of network protocols, network devices, network-based services, and the way that devices communicate with each other using networks.

Almost without exception, to protect an organization requires the protection of its networks. A security professional must understand how secure networks are designed, built, and verified to achieve a desired security platform.

Domain 3: Information Security Governance & Risk Management

Security governance and risk management are the management-level activities that lead to the discovery and treatment of risks, the creation of security policy, and align with and support key business objectives. Security governance ensures that management is aware of and controls resources that protect an organization's assets and personnel. Risk management utilizes analysis methodologies that identify and quantify risks and propose risk treatments to reduce risks to acceptable levels.

Security managers must understand and utilize the concepts of defense in depth, avoidance of single paths of failure, and the pillars of security that are confidentiality, integrity, and availability. They must establish security requirements to ensure that systems and processes support security policy, awareness programs so that personnel are aware of security policies and procedures, and sound hiring practices to ensure that new staff are vetted and have verified professional backgrounds.

Security management is responsible for creating security standards, security architectures, document classification and handling guidelines, and ensuring that suppliers are properly vetted and will not introduce unwanted risks to the business. They must uphold the $(ISC)^2$ code of ethics and other codes of ethics in situations where good judgment is necessary.

Domain 4: Software Development Security

Software is used to store and manage information in support of key business processes and information systems. While the majority of line-of-business applications* are acquired in the form of common off-the-shelf (COTS) or software-as-a-service (SaaS), many enterprises still perform software development in the form of customizations, integrations, applets, agents, and tools.

---

*Common enterprise applications include Enterprise Resource Planning (ERP), Customer Relationship Management (CRM), Materials Resource Planning (MRP), and Manufacturing Resource Planning (MRP II).

Programmers, software developers, and software engineers need to know the principles of security in application design and coding.

Software applications and tools need to have a sound design that includes any required application-level access and authorization management that cannot be circumvented. The database management systems and data warehouses that support applications and tools must be properly configured and administered in order to reduce or eliminate security vulnerabilities that could otherwise threaten the confidentiality, integrity, and availability of data and systems.

Discipline is required in the software development life cycle (SDLC) to ensure that software applications and tools are properly developed to meet the needs of the business and not contain flaws that could result in malfunctions or security issues.

Beyond the SDLC, an organization must have sound practices such as change management, configuration management, and vulnerability management, to ensure that software vulnerabilities cannot be introduced into an application environment.

Domain 5: Cryptography

Cryptography is the science of hiding information that is in plain sight. A form of access control, cryptography is an effective means to prevent unauthorized parties from accessing or modifying sensitive or critical data that is protected by encryption.

Numerous encryption technologies are used to protect information. Data can be encrypted as it is transmitted from place to place, so that any eavesdroppers who are able to intercept the transmission will be unable to decipher the information. Data can also be encrypted when it is stored on a system, so that people who do (and don't) have access to the system but should not have access to the data are likewise unable to read it.

Hashing is a companion technology that can be used to verify the integrity and the source of a message or file. Hashing is the technology that is used to create digital signatures in e-mail messages. Hashing is also used as "one-way encryption" to protect information such as passwords.

The handling and protection of encryption keys is known as *key management.*

Public key infrastructures (PKIs) are used as certification authorities (CAs) to store public encryption keys and digital certificates that can be used to verify messages and services.

Domain 6: Security Architecture & Design

Security architecture and design is concerned with the abstract security models that are used both to better understand existing security structures as well as to assist in the design of new ones. Like any model, security models simplify protection concepts so that architects and designers can ascertain whether assets can be properly secured.

In addition to abstract models, security professionals are also expected to be intimately familiar with the inner workings of computer hardware and software. Like the other disciplines of security, the security professional can only protect something that he or she fully understands.

The security professional must understand threats and weaknesses such as covert channels, state attacks, and emanations, as well as countermeasures to counteract them.

Domain 7: Security Operations

Security operations are the day-to-day activities that provide continuous protection to an organization's information, information systems, and other assets. Many activities fall under the category of operations security, including security monitoring, vulnerability management, change management, configuration management, and information handling procedures.

Many key security concepts are operational in nature, including need-to-know, least privilege, separation of duties, and job rotation.

In the $(ISC)^2$ CBK, operations security also encompasses operational support of highly available systems, fault tolerance, virtualization, and mitigation of security-related cyber attacks.

Domain 8: Business Continuity & Disaster Recovery Planning

Business continuity planning (BCP) and disaster recovery planning (DRP) are two closely related activities that are concerned with the survival of the organization in the face of man-made and natural disasters.

The ability for an organization to survive a disaster requires the development of contingency plans that are developed prior to a disaster and activated when a disaster occurs. These plans are periodically tested to ensure that they will successfully support critical business processes in a disaster, ensuring continuity of critical business operations.

In order to allocate resources properly, a Business Impact Analysis (BIA) is performed that identifies which business processes are most critical; it is for these processes that most contingency plans are developed. This analysis includes information gathered as part of the organization's overall risk management process, which is crucial to the establishment of an effective strategy.

Business continuity and disaster recovery planning also involve the identification of measures that can be taken to reduce the impact of a disaster or prevent its effect altogether.

BCP and DRP are a part of the CBK because these activities help to assure the availability of business information and information systems, even in extreme circumstances such as man-made and natural disasters.

Domain 9: Legal, Regulations, Investigations and Compliance

For decades, information and business security was introduced primarily as a means of incident avoidance, but in recent years, security has been codified in numerous international, national, and local jurisdictions and in many industries such as banking, health care, and energy. Many security standards have been developed, some of which carry the weight of law. Unfortunately, as a result, many organizations are shifting their security efforts from risk management to compliance management.

Security management is responsible for the development of incident handling procedures that must also comply with applicable regulations and also ensure the preservation of evidence for potential prosecution. Management must undertake efforts such as internal audit and testing to ensure continued compliance with policy and regulations.

Domain 10: Physical (Environmental) Security

Physical and environmental security in the $(ISC)^2$ CBK includes the means for protecting assets from physical harm, which embodies the use of several types of physical controls to prevent unauthorized personnel from accessing valuable assets. These controls include surveillance, entry controls, guards, and perimeter controls such as security fencing and lighting.

This domain also includes the development and management of a proper environment for information systems that includes suitable power management systems that may consist of uninterruptible power supplies, power conditioners, electric generators, and power distribution units. Information systems also require proper heating, cooling, and humidification controls, fire detection and suppression systems, and controls to avoid problems associated with water leaks and the presence of other unwanted substances.

This domain also includes techniques for choosing proper facilities for housing staff, information systems, and other assets, by identifying and understanding site- and location-related risks.

Key Terms

Certified Information Systems Security Professional (CISSP) The highly esteemed data and business security certification that is the topic of this book.

Common Body of Knowledge (CBK) The entire collection of concepts, methodologies, and practices that a candidate for CISSP certification is required to understand.

International Information Systems Security Certification Consortium [$(ISC)^2$] The organization that created and manages the CISSP and other security certifications.

Appendix B

The (ISC)^2 Code of Ethics

Topics in This Chapter:

- The (ISC)^2 Code of Ethics*
- The Ethical Challenge Many Security Professionals Must Confront

The $(ISC)^2$ Code of Ethics

The Pursuit of Integrity, Honor, and Trust in Information Security

All information systems security professionals who are certified by $(ISC)^2$ recognize that such certification is a privilege that must be both earned and maintained. In support of this principle, all $(ISC)^2$ members are required to commit to fully support this Code of Ethics (the "Code"). $(ISC)^2$ members who intentionally or knowingly violate any provision of the Code will be subject to action by a peer review panel, which may result in the revocation of certification. $(ISC)^2$ members are obligated to follow the ethics complaint procedure upon observing any action by an $(ISC)^2$ member that breach[es] the Code. Failure to do so may be considered a breach of the Code pursuant to Canon IV.

There are only four mandatory canons in the code. By necessity, such high-level guidance is not intended to be a substitute for the ethical judgment of the professional.

Code of Ethics Preamble:

- The safety and welfare of society, duty to our principals, and to each other, requires that we adhere, and be seen to adhere, to the highest ethical standards of behavior.
- Therefore, strict adherence to this Code is a condition of certification.

Code of Ethics Canons:

- Protect society, the common good, necessary public trust and confidence, and the infrastructure.
- Act honorably, honestly, justly, responsibly, and legally.
- Provide diligent and competent service to principals.
- Advance and protect the profession.

The following additional guidance is given regarding pursuit of these goals.

Objectives for Guidance

The committee is mindful of its responsibility to:

- Give guidance for resolving good-versus-good and bad-versus-bad dilemmas.
- To encourage right behavior such as:
  - Research
  - Teaching
  - Identifying, mentoring, and sponsoring candidates for the profession
  - Valuing the certificate
- To discourage such behavior as:
  - Raising unnecessary alarm, fear, uncertainty, or doubt
  - Giving unwarranted comfort or reassurance
  - Consenting to bad practice

- Attaching weak systems to the public network
- Professional association with non-professionals
- Professional recognition of or association with amateurs
- Associating or appearing to associate with criminals or criminal behavior

These objectives are provided for information only; the professional is not required or expected to agree with them. In resolving the choices that confront him or her, the professional should keep in mind that the following guidance is advisory only. Compliance with the guidance is neither necessary nor sufficient for ethical conduct.

Compliance with the preamble and canons is mandatory. Conflicts between the canons should be resolved in the order of the canons. The canons are not equal, and conflicts between them are not intended to create ethical binds.

Protect Society, the Commonwealth, and the Infrastructure

- Promote and preserve public trust and confidence in information and systems.
- Promote the understanding and acceptance of prudent information security measures.
- Preserve and strengthen the integrity of the public infrastructure.
- Discourage unsafe practice.

Act Honorably, Honestly, Justly, Responsibly, and Legally

- Tell the truth; make all stakeholders aware of your actions on a timely basis.
- Observe all contracts and agreements, express or implied.
- Treat all members fairly. In resolving conflicts, consider public safety and duties to principals, individuals, and the profession, in that order.
- Give prudent advice; avoid raising unnecessary alarm or giving unwarranted comfort. Take care to be truthful, objective, cautious, and within your competence.
- When resolving differing laws in different jurisdictions, give preference to the laws of the jurisdiction in which you render your service.

Provide Diligent and Competent Service to Principals

- Preserve the value of their systems, applications, and information.
- Respect their trust and the privileges that they grant you.
- Avoid conflicts of interest or the appearance thereof.
- Render only those services for which you are fully competent and qualified.

Advance and Protect the Profession

- Sponsor for professional advancement those best qualified. All other things equal, prefer those who are certified and who adhere to these canons. Avoid professional association with those whose practices or reputation might diminish the profession.

- Take care not to injure the reputation of other professionals through malice or indifference.
- Maintain your competence; keep your skills and knowledge current. Give generously of your time and knowledge in training others.

An Ethical Challenge

Security professionals holding the CISSP certification are required to comply with the $(ISC)^2$ Code of Ethics at all times. Security professionals need to be self-aware and understand how their conduct may appear to others. Thus, it is important to avoid even the appearance of impropriety.

Security professionals also need to be keenly aware of the evil side of the profession, and the actors that operate in that realm. In order to protect information assets, security professionals need to be familiar with and face those adversaries without being tempted to join them.

Topics in This Chapter:

- Requirements for Earning the CISSP Certification
- About CISSP Computer-Based Testing (CBT)
- Suggested Study Methods
- Maintaining the CISSP Certification

All persons who desire to earn the CISSP certification are required to complete several tasks:

- Accumulate five years of direct, full-time professional work experience in two or more of the ten domains of the CBK (listed in Appendix A)
- Register for the exam
- Pass the exam
- Complete the endorsement process

All certification candidates are urged to obtain a current copy of the Candidate Information Bulletin from (ISC)^2. This can be found at https://www.isc2.org, then click on Certification, then CISSP.

Computer-Based Testing

Before 2012, all CISSP candidates took paper-based exams. Today, computer-based testing is employed in the United States, Canada, and other places. The rest of the world still utilizes paper-based testing.

Computer-based testing is conducted at Pearson Vue centers in the United States, Canada, and other places.

To register for a computer-based test, go to the registration site at http://www.pearsonvue.com/isc2/. You will need to create a user account and then sign in. Then, locate a test center where you wish to take the exam. Military personnel may be able to select an on-base exam location. Next, you will select the preferred language for the exam. Then you will be asked to select the date and time when you will take the exam. Choose wisely, as additional fees are assessed for making changes to the exam schedule.

When you arrive at the testing center, you will need to check in. It's suggested that you show up early for your testing appointment, so that you can start your exam on time.

You will be given a copy of testing rules and given a key to a storage locker where you will place all of your personal belongings—literally, everything in your pockets.

Testing candidates will be subjected to several security controls, including these:

- Test takers will be asked to present two forms of identification, one of which must be a government-issued photo identification.
- Test takers may be photographed.
- Hand vein scan recorded.
- Candidate's signature will be recorded.
- Candidate required to sign a non-disclosure agreement (NDA).
- Belongings, including wallet, purse, smartphone, wristwatch, and other items, must be placed in a locker.
- No study materials or reference books are permitted.
- Test takers may be asked to show that their pockets are empty of all items.
- Test takers will be monitored in person and/or with video surveillance while they take their certification exam.

- Test takers are permitted to take food and restroom breaks, under the control of test proctors.

You will take the actual exam on a computer with a monitor, keyboard, and mouse. You'll need to carefully follow all on-screen instructions.

At any time during the exam, you may raise your hand, and the exam proctor will assist you.

In most cases, test results are made available immediately after testing is completed. In some cases, however, exam results will be sent to candidates later.

Paper-Based Testing

Paper-based testing begins at the same time for all exam candidates. Typically the exam center will open at 8:00am. At 8:30am, the exam proctor will read exam instructions aloud to all exam candidates. Any candidates who arrive after this time are not permitted to take the exam.

The proctor will pass out test booklets, answer sheets, and pencils. The exam will start at 9:00am. Candidates are permitted to bring snacks into the exam room and are typically permitted to eat their snacks during the exam in the back of the exam room. The length of the exam is six hours.

Candidates are not permitted to have reference materials or smartphones with them when they take the exam.

Establishing a Study Plan

Whether you are a part of a formal class or study group, or if you are studying for the CISSP certification exam on your own, you need to understand your learning style. Learning methods include:

- Instructor-led higher education course
- Volunteer-led self-study group
- One-week "boot camp"
- Self-directed self-study

In general, we tend to retain material learned over time. Because of the breadth of subject matter in the CISSP *Common Body of Knowledge*, a typical study program for experienced IT professionals is three to six months. Various factors may increase or decrease this period of time, such as family and other outside obligations, the demands of employment, and the quality of rest.

This writer suggests this framework for a self-study plan:

- Read the contents of this book in its entirety over a few weeks.
- Take a practice CISSP exam, such as the practice exam available through this book.
- As you answer questions, make a note of how confident you are in your answer. For example, a 1 would indicate complete confidence; 2 a bit unsure; and 3 is "You mean that is really on the test?" Confidence plays a significant role in your ability to successfully obtain any certification. For any question that you did not answer with complete confidence, review the material.

- Note stronger and weaker areas from the practice exam results.
- Read additional materials and undertake other learning for weaker areas.
- Take a practice CISSP exam one or more additional times and note improvements in knowledge.
- Skim the contents of this book in its entirety.

Final Exam Preparations

In the four to seven days prior to the exam, it is suggested that the intensity of self-study be diminished. It is important to be well rested and get good sleep in the days prior to the exam, because the exam itself will place high demands on the candidate.

If the location of the exam center is unfamiliar, it is suggested that the candidate take whatever measures are necessary to ensure he or she will be able to travel to the exam site and arrive on time or, ideally, earlier than required. The further the candidate is traveling, the more complicated this may become, as this could include not only a driving route and parking, but also (or instead) public transportation, air travel, hotel accommodations, and more. Also consider the day of the week that the exam is scheduled—paper-based exams are often on a Saturday, when public transportation may be scaled back, and special events such as sporting events may make travel and parking more time-consuming or expensive. But all-important is preparation so that the candidate can travel to the exam center on time, free of anxiety and stress.

It is equally important to dress in loose-fitting, comfortable clothes, be well hydrated, and bring all snacks that will be required. Hunger, thirst, indigestion, and other distractions are unwelcome during the CISSP exam.

Completing the Endorsement Process

After passing the CISSP exam, there is one last obstacle: the endorsement process. Here, candidates are required to fully document their five (or more) years of direct professional security experience.

Each item of security experience must be verified in writing by an $(ISC)^2$ certified professional, referred to as the *endorser* in this situation. It is important that the endorser know the candidate well enough to endorse specific portions of the candidate's work experience, since the endorser is risking his or her own professional reputation and good standing with $(ISC)^2$.

Candidates need to be sure to report security experience accurately. $(ISC)^2$ audits a portion of certification candidates to ensure they reported their experience accurately.

Maintaining the CISSP Certification

Candidates who earn their CISSP certification are going to be lifelong learners if they desire to retain their certification. $(ISC)^2$ places three principal requirements on professionals who wish to retain their certification:

- Pay an annual maintenance fee
- Obtain and submit Continuing Professional Education credits (CPEs)
- Abide by the $(ISC)^2$ Code of Ethics

The CPE requirement warrants some explanation. CISSP certificate holders are required to obtain 120 CPEs every three years, with a minimum of 40 CPEs each year.

Certificate holders are required to report their CPEs on the $(ISC)^2$ website. Several details about the CPE events are required, and certificate holders are required to obtain and keep evidence of their CPEs; $(ISC)^2$ routinely audits some users' CPEs, so it is important to keep good records and report CPEs accurately.

Glossary

10BASE any of a group of twisted pair or coaxial network cabling types used to carry network traffic up to 10Mbit/s. Types include 10BASE-T, 10BASE2, and 10BASE5.

100BASE any of a group of twisted pair network cabling types used to carry network traffic up to 100Mbit/s, including 100BASE-TX.

1000BASET a twisted pair network cabling type used to carry network traffic up to 1Gbit/s.

802.1a/b/g/n see *IEEE 802.1a/b/g/n*.

802.1X see *IEEE 802.1X*.

Access Control List (ACL) a method for filtering network packets on a router.

Access controls any means used to control which subjects are permitted to access objects.

Access log a record that contains building or computer access attempts.

Access management the policies, procedures, and controls that determine how information is accessed and by whom.

Access Matrix a security model that consists of a two-dimensional matrix of subjects, objects, and the permissions for each subject's access to each object.

Access point a device used to connect multiple computers together to form a wireless network.

Access rights recertification the process of reviewing users' access rights to determine if each user still requires specific access rights.

Accreditation the process of formally approving the use of a system.

Accumulation of privileges the process of gaining more access privileges over a long period of time, most often by personnel who transfer from role to role in an organization.

Active Directory a Microsoft implementation of LDAP.

Active-Active an operating mode in a cluster where all of the servers in the cluster actively operate and process incoming requests.

Active-Passive an operating mode in a cluster where one or more servers actively operate and process incoming requests and one or more servers remain in a standby mode.

Address Resolution Protocol (ARP) a TCP/IP protocol that is used to translate a network IP address into a network MAC address.

Administrative controls the policies, procedures, and standards put in place in an organization to govern the actions of people and information systems.

Administrative law the branch of law in the U.S. that defines the rules and regulations that govern activities in executive departments and agencies in the U.S. government.

Advanced Encryption Standard (AES) the encryption standard established in 2001 by the U.S. government. AES uses the Rijndael algorithm.

Adware cookies, web beacons, and other means used to track individual Internet users and build behavior profiles for them.

Agent small, standalone programs that perform some task for a larger application environment.

Aggregation attack a data mining technique where data elements related to target subjects are combined in order to obtain even more target data.

Alarm system a system of sensors and a control unit that is designed to detect intrusions into a building or room and send an alarm signal if an intrusion is detected.

Annual loss expectancy (ALE) the yearly estimate of loss of an asset, calculated as: ALE = ARO × SLE.

Annualized rate of occurrence (ARO) the probability that a loss will occur in a year's time.

Anti-rootkit software that uses techniques to find hidden processes, hidden registry entries, unexpected kernel hooks, and hidden files in order to find rootkits that may be present on a system.

Anti-spyware software that is designed to detect and remove spyware.

Anti-virus software software that is used to detect and remove viruses and other malicious code from a system.

Anycast a type of IP network communications where a packet is sent to only one of a group of available nodes.

Applet a small program that runs within the context of another program.

Application a collection of programs and tools that fulfill a specific business purpose.

Application firewall a firewall that examines the contents of incoming messages in order to detect and block attempted attacks on an application.

Application layer layer 7 of the OSI network model (and layer 5 of the TCP/IP network model) that provides communications to end user processes and programs.

Application scanning the task of identifying security vulnerabilities in a software application.

Application vulnerability scanning a means of testing an application to identify any vulnerabilities.

Application whitelisting a means of controlling what software programs are permitted to run on a system, thereby preventing the execution of malware and unauthorized software.

Arithmetic Logic Unit (ALU) the portion of a CPU where arithmetic and logic operations are performed.

Asset an object of value to the organization. An asset may be a physical object such as a computer or it can be information.

Assumption of breach the way of thinking about security breaches, that security breaches have already occurred, whether discovered or not.

Asymmetric cryptography a class of cryptographic algorithms that utilize public-private encryption keys.

Asymmetric multiprocessing (ASMP) a multi-CPU computer architecture consisting of master and slave CPUs or some other asymmetric arrangement.

Asynchronous Transfer Mode (ATM) a packet switching network protocol that uses a fixed-size packet called a cell to transport data.

Attack an action taken against a target resource with the intention of doing harm.

Attack surface the complete set of components in a system that may be the object of compromise by an attacker.

Audit log the record of events that occur in an application environment.

Audit log analysis an activity used to detect unwanted events that are recorded in an audit log.

Authentication the act of proving one's identity to an information system by providing two or more pieces of information, such as a userid and a password, in order to gain access to information and functions.

Authorization the process of permitting a user to perform some specific function or access some specific data.

Availability the concept that asserts that information systems can be accessed and used when needed.

Back door a feature in a program that allows access that bypasses security.

Background verification the process of verifying an employment candidate's employment, education, criminal, and credit history.

Backup the process of copying important information from a computer or storage system to another device for recovery or archival purposes.

Bell LaPadula a security model that addresses the confidentiality of information.

Biba a security model that addresses data integrity.

Biological hazard any of several substances that pose a threat to humans and animals. Also known as **biohazard.**

Biometrics a means for measuring a physiological characteristic of a person as a means for positively identifying him or her.

Birthday attack a cryptanalysis attack against a message digest.

Blackmail see *Extortion*.

Block cipher an encryption algorithm that operates on fixed blocks of data.

Bluetooth a wireless network technology for low-speed and low-power data communication over short distances.

Bollard a heavy upright post used to restrict vehicle traffic.

Border Gateway Protocol (BGP) a TCP/IP routing protocol primarily used by the Internet's backbone routers.

Bot malicious software that allows someone to remotely control someone else's computer for illicit purposes.

Botnet a collection of software robots (or "bots") under centralized control that run autonomously and automatically.

Broadcast a type of network communications where packets are sent to all nodes in a network.

Buffer overflow an attack on a system by means of providing excessive amounts of data in an input field.

Bus a hardware subsystem used to transfer data among a computer's internal components including its CPU, storage, network, and peripherals.

Business continuity plan a contingency plan that governs the business response to a disaster in order to keep critical business functions operating.

Business Continuity Planning (BCP) the activities required to ensure the continuation of critical business processes in an organization.

Business Impact Analysis (BIA) the task of identifying the business impact that results from the interruption of a specific business process.

Bypass an attack that attempts to bypass security controls to access or alter information.

Card reader a device used to read the contents of a key card.

Carrier Sense Multiple Access with Collision Detection (CSMA/CD) a data link layer protocol type where notes verify the absence of traffic on the network before transmitting data. Nodes are able to detect collisions and back off before retransmitting.

Category 3/5/5e/6/7 standards for twisted-pair network cabling that support bandwidths from 10Mbit/s to 10Gbit/sec.

CDMA2000 a mobile radio technology used to transmit voice and data between subscriber devices and base stations for voice and data communication.

Central processing unit (CPU) the portion of a computer where program instructions are executed.

Certificate Authority (CA) an entity that issues digital certificates.

Certification the process of evaluating a system against a specific criteria or specification.

Certified Information Systems Security Professional (CISSP) the highly esteemed data and business security certification that is the topic of this book.

C.F.R. see *U.S. Code of Federal Regulations.*

Chain of custody the procedures and paper trail that tracks forensic evidence in a legal investigation.

Challenge-Handshake Authentication Protocol (CHAP) a network based authentication protocol used to authenticate a user to a system or network resource. CHAP is used to authenticate a PPP connection.

Change management the management process where proposed changes in an environment are formally planned and reviewed prior to implementing them.

Checksum a method used to ensure the integrity of a packet or frame.

Chosen ciphertext attack (CCA) a cryptanalysis attack where the attacker has chosen ciphertexts decrypted and obtain cleartext results.

Chosen plaintext attack (CPA) a cryptanalysis attack where the attacker is able to have chosen plaintexts encrypted and obtain the ciphertext results.

CIA Confidentiality, Integrity, and Availability.

Cipher feedback (CFB) a block cipher mode where the result of encrypting a block of plaintext is used to encrypt the next block.

Cipher-block chaining (CBC) a block cipher mode where ciphertext output from each encrypted plaintext block is used in the encryption of the next block.

Ciphertext the result of applying an encryption algorithm to plaintext.

Ciphertext-only attack (COA) a cryptanalysis attack where the attacker has only ciphertext.

Civil law the branch of laws that deal with disputes between individuals and/or organizations.

Clark-Wilson a security model that addresses data integrity that is a rebuttal to the Bell LaPadula and Biba models.

Class the defining characteristics of an object.

Classification see *Data Classification.*

Client-server application an application in which user interface logic resides on a client system and data storage and retrieval logic resides on a server.

Closed Circuit Television (CCTV) a standard for the transmission of video signals over a cable, often used in video surveillance systems. See also *IP camera.*

Cloud services any of several varieties of IT services delivered to customers; services may include software applications, operating systems on demand, and data storage on demand.

Cluster a group of two or more servers that operate functionally as a single logical server, and will continue operating as a single logical server in the event that one of the servers fails.

Coaxial cable a type of cable that consists of a single or dual inner conductor, a dielectric insulator, a metallic shield, and an outer plastic jacket.

Code of conduct a policy statement published by an organization that defines permitted and forbidden activities.

Code of ethics a code of responsibility statement that is used in an organization to define specific permitted and forbidden activities.

Collision an occurrence where two different messages are found to compute to the same hash value.

Common Body of Knowledge (CBK) the entire collection of concepts, methodologies, and practices that a candidate for CISSP certification is required to understand.

Common Criteria the current framework for evaluating the security of a system.

Compartmented security mode one of the security modes of operation where users can access some data based upon their need to know and formal access approval.

Compensating control a control that compensates for the absence or ineffectiveness of another control.

Competitive intelligence activities regarding the acquisition of information and secrets about a competing organization's products, services, financials, and other business activities.

Complex Instruction Set Computer (CISC) a microprocessor architecture in which each instruction can execute several operations in a single instruction cycle.

compartmented security mode one of the security modes of operation where users can access some data based upon their need-to-know and formal access approval.

Compromising Emanations (CE) emanations of electromagnetic radiation (EMR) that disclose sensitive information.

Confidentiality the concept of information and functions being protected from unauthorized access and disclosure.

Configuration management the process of recording configuration changes that are made in an environment.

Configuration management database (CMDB) a database containing all of the changes made to a system or environment.

Control an activity, process, or apparatus that ensures the confidentiality, integrity, or availability of an asset.

Control flow a computer language methodology where instructions are followed sequentially until a "goto" type statement is encountered, in which case the control is transferred to the location specified by the goto statement.

Control Objectives for Information and related Technology (COBIT) a controls framework for the management of information technology and security.

Cookie a mechanism used to store identifying information, such as a session ID, on a web client system.

Copyright the legal right to exclusive use that is given to the creator of an original work of writing, music, pictures, and films.

Corrective control an activity that occurs after a security event has occurred in order to prevent its reoccurrence.

Counter (CTR) a block cipher mode that uses a one-time random number and a sequential counter.

Countermeasure a control or means to reduce the impact of a threat or the probability of its occurrence.

Covert channel an unauthorized channel of communications that exists within a legitimate communications channel.

COSO (Committee of Sponsoring Organizations of the Treadway Commission) a controls framework for the management of information systems and corporate financial reporting.

Crash gate a movable device that can be used to restrict the entry or exit of a vehicle.

Criminal law the branch of law that enforces public order against crimes such as assault, arson, theft, burglary, deception, obstruction of justice, bribery, and perjury.

Criticality Analysis the process of ranking business processes according to their criticality to the organization.

Crossover Error Rate (CER) the point where False Reject Rate and False Accept Rate are equal.

Cross-site request forgery (XSRF) an attack where malicious HTML is inserted into a Web page or e-mail that, when clicked, causes an action to occur on an unrelated site where the user may have an active session.

Cross-site scripting (XSS) an attack where an attacker can inject a malicious script into HTML content in order to steal session cookies and other sensitive information.

Cryptanalysis the process of attacking a cryptosystem in order to discover its method of operation and/or its encryption and decryption keys.

Cryptography the science of hiding information, usually through the use of algorithms based upon mathematical operations.

Cutover test a test of a disaster recovery or business continuity plan in which backup or recovery systems or processes are operated in place of normal business operations.

Cybervandalism vandalism that is carried out against information or information systems.

Cyberstalking acts of stalking or harassing an individual or group through the use of computers and/or networks.

Cyberterrorism acts of violence against civilians and governments that are carried out in cyberspace.

Data classification the process of assigning sensitivity levels to documents and data files in order to assure their safekeeping and proper handling.

Data confidentiality model a security model whose chief concern is the confidentiality of data.

Data destruction the process of discarding information that is no longer needed, in a manner that will render it irretrievable.

Data integrity model a security model whose chief concern is data integrity.

Data link layer layer 2 of the OSI network model that consists of protocols for transmitting frames over a network medium.

Data loss prevention a system used to detect and block unauthorized data transmissions on a network.

Data Over Cable Service Interface Specification (DOCSIS) the standard for delivery of Internet connectivity over television broadcast cable networks.

Data remanence the unintentional data that remains on a storage device or medium.

Data replication see *replication.*

Data sovereignty the legal issue regarding the jurisdiction of electronically stored information.

Data warehouse a database management system that is designed and built to store archival data for decision support and research purposes.

Database an ordered collection of data that exists for a common purpose.

Database management system (DBMS) a system used to manage one or more databases.

Datagram a self-contained set of data carrying information allowing it to be routed from a source to a destination node.

Debriefing a meeting or conference during which the details of an incident are discussed, in order to learn from the incident and the organization's response to it.

Decipher another word for decrypt.

Decryption the process of turning ciphertext back into original plaintext.

Dedicated security mode one of the security modes of operation where all users can access all data.

Defense in depth a strategy for protecting assets that relies upon several layers of protection. If one layer fails, other layers will still provide some protection.

Degaussing the process of bulk-erasing magnetic-based storage media by imposing a strong magnetic field onto the media.

Demilitarized zone (DMZ) a means of protecting application servers and the remainder of an enterprise network by placing them on a separate firewalled network.

Denial of service (DoS) attack an attack against a computer or network that is designed to incapacitate the target.

Department of Defense Information Assurance Certification and Accreditation Process (DIACAP) the process used to certify and accredit information systems used by the U.S. military.

Department of Defense Information Technology Security Certification and Accreditation Process (DITSCAP) the process used to certify and accredit information systems used by the U.S. military; superseded by DIACAP.

Destruction the process of discarding information in a way that renders it non-retrievable.

Detective control a control that is used to detect specific types of activity.

Deterrent control a control used to deter unwanted activity.

Device driver a program that permits the operating system and other programs to communicate with a specific hardware device or type of device.

Diameter an authentication, authorization, and accounting protocol that is a replacement for RADIUS.

Diffie-Hellman (D-H) key exchange a secure mechanism for two parties with no prior knowledge of each other to jointly establish a shared symmetric encryption key.

Digital certificate an electronic document that utilizes a digital signature and an identity, used to reliably identify a person or system.

Digital Encryption Algorithm (DEA) the data encryption algorithm chosen in 1976 as the new Digital Encryption Standard (DES).

Digital Encryption Standard (DES) the data encryption standard established in 1976 by the U.S. government.

DES uses the Digital Encryption Algorithm (DEA) algorithm.

Digital signature the result of cryptographic functions used to verify the integrity and authenticity of a message.

Digital Subscriber Line (DSL) a group of telecommunications technologies used to deliver digital data services (such as Internet connectivity) over telephone wires.

Digital Subscriber Line Access Multiplexer (DSLAM) a multiplexer node on a DSL service provider network that connects individual DSL subscribers to data networks such as the Internet.

Digital video recorder (DVR) a device used to store video surveillance data for later viewing.

Director of Central intelligence Directive 6/3 (DCID 6/3) the process for protecting sensitive compartmented information within information systems at the U.S. Central Intelligence Agency (CIA).

Disaster any event that that disrupts the operations of a business in such a significant way that a considerable and coordinated effort is required to achieve a recovery.

Disaster Recovery Planning (DRP) the activities concerned with the assessment, salvage, repair, and restoration of damaged facilities and assets.

Discretionary access control (DAC) an access control model where the owner of an object may grant access rights to subjects based upon the owner's discretion.

Distributed application an application in which its components reside on many systems.

Distributed database a database that is logically or physically distributed among several systems.

Distributed Denial of Service (DDoS) a Denial of Service attack that originates from many systems. See also *Denial of Service.*

Diverse network routing a network design strategy where two or more separate circuits to a given location will be located in different areas. If a mishap severs one of the circuits, communication will continue via the other circuit(s).

Document review a review of a business continuity or disaster recovery procedure in which a single individual reviews procedures.

Documentation processes, procedures, and even records, whether in paper or electronic form.

Domain Name Service (DNS) a TCP/IP layer 4 protocol used to translate (via lookup) host and domain names into IP addresses.

DS-0 a single 64kbit/s voice or data channel on a DS-1 circuit.

DS-1 the base North American telecommunications carrier protocol used to carry up to 24 64 kbit/s voice or data channels.

Dumpster diving an attack where an attacker rummages through refuse bins ("dumpsters") in an attempt to discover sensitive discarded information.

Dynamic Host Configuration Protocol (DHCP) a TCP/IP layer 4 protocol used to assign IP addresses and other configuration settings to nodes on a network.

Dynamic Random Access Memory (DRAM) a random access memory (RAM) technology used in computer main storage.

E1 the base European telecommunications carrier protocol used to carry up to 32 64 kbit/s voice or data channels. See also *DS-1*.

Eavesdropping an attack where an attacker attempts to intercept communications.

EEPROM (Electrically Erasable Programmable Read Only Memory) a form of erasable semiconductor memory used to store firmware.

Electric generator see *Generator*.

Electronic codebook (ECB) a block cipher mode wherein each plaintext block is encrypted separately.

Elevation of privileges an attack where an attacker is able to perform some manipulation in order to raise his privileges, enabling him to perform unauthorized functions.

Emanations typically RF emissions from a computer or conductor that permits eavesdroppers to eavesdrop on computer activity.

Embezzlement the act of dishonestly or illegally appropriating wealth from another party, often an employer or service provider.

Employee handbook a formal document that defines terms and conditions of employment.

Employment agreement a legal agreement that specifies terms and conditions of employment for an individual employee.

Encapsulation a design attribute that permits the hiding of internal details about an object in an OO system.

Encipher another word for encrypt.

Encryption a means of transforming plaintext info ciphertext to make it unreadable except by parties who possess a key.

Enhanced Data rates for GSM Evolution (EDGE) a wireless telecommunications standard that is a successor to GPRS that provides bandwidth up to 1 Mbit/s.

Enhanced GPRS (EGPRS) a wireless telecommunications standard that is a successor to GPRS that provides bandwidth up to 1 Mbit/s.

Enhanced Interior Gateway Routing Protocol (EIGRP) a Cisco proprietary routing protocol that is an enhancement of its earlier IGRP protocol. See also *IGRP*.

EPROM (Erasable Programmable Read Only Memory) a form of erasable semiconductor memory used to store firmware.

Espionage the process of obtaining secret or confidential information without the permission of the holder of the information.

Ethernet a family of frame-based wired network technologies used to connect computers in a local area network (LAN).

Ethics the discipline of dealing with a code of professional behavior.

E-vaulting a method of data backup, where data is transmitted over a network to a remote data storage facility. See also *backup*.

Evaluation Assurance Level (EAL) the seven levels of evaluation in the Common Criteria.

Executable space protection an operating system or CPU feature that prevents programs from executing code in the stack or heap.

Expert system a software system that accumulates knowledge on a particular subject and is able to predict outcomes based upon historical knowledge.

Explicitly Parallel Instruction Computing (EPIC) a microprocessor design that permits parallel execution in a single CPU.

Exposure factor (EF) the proportion of an asset's value that is likely to be lost through the realization of a particular threat.

Extensible Authentication Protocol (EAP) an authentication framework of protocols used to authenticate users to system or network resources. Several variants exist, including EAP-PSK, EAP-IKEv2, EAP-AKA, and EAP-SIM.

Extortion the act of obtaining money or other valuables from a person or organization through coercion, intimidation, or threat.

Facilities the buildings and other structures that house the space where people work and the equipment that they use.

Fail closed the characteristic of a security control–upon failure, it will deny all access.

Fail open the characteristic of a security control–upon failure, it will permit all access.

Fail safe see *Fail closed*.

Fail soft the process of shutting down non-essential components on a system, thereby freeing up resources so that critical components can continue operating.

Failover an event in a server cluster where production workload is transferred from one server to another.

False Accept Rate (FAR) how often a biometric system accepts an invalid user.

False Reject Rate (FRR) how often a biometric system rejects valid users.

Fault tolerance the design of a device or system where failure-prone components are duplicated, so that the failure of one component will not result in the failure of the entire device or system.

Federal Information Security Management Act (FISMA) a U.S. law that requires the evaluation of all systems used by the U.S. federal government.

FedRAMP the U.S. government-wide program for assessing, authorizing, and monitoring cloud based service providers.

Fiber Distributed Data Interface (FDDI) a token network technology transmitted over fiber optic cable.

Fibre Channel a gigabit network protocol usually used in storage area networks (SANs), and transported over fiber optic or copper cable.

File system a logical collection of files that resides on a storage medium.

File Transfer Protocol (FTP) a TCP/IP layer 4 protocol used to transfer files between computers.

Filtering the process of removing particulates and other matter from the air in a building or processing center.

Fire alarm an alarm system that warns human occupants of the presence of a nearby fire.

Fire extinguisher a portable fire suppression device that sprays liquid or foam onto a fire.

Firewall a hardware device or software program that controls the passage of traffic at a network boundary according to a predefined set of rules.

FireWire see *IEEE1394*.

Firmware computer instructions that are stored on a non-volatile memory device such as a PROM or EPROM.

Flash memory a form of erasable semiconductor memory used to store firmware.

Forensics the application of scientific knowledge to solve legal problems, especially the analysis of evidence from a crime scene.

Frame a data packet at the data link layer in a network.

Frame Relay an early packet switched telecommunications network technology used to connect together entities for data communications.

Fraud an act of deception made for personal gain.

Frequency analysis a cryptanalysis attack where the frequency of occurrence of the characters in ciphertext are examined.

FTP (File Transfer Protocol) a protocol used to transfer files from one system to another.

FTPS File Transfer Protocol (FTP) protected with SSL.

Gaseous fire suppression an installed system of pipes and nozzles that sprays a fire-retardant gaseous substance into a room.

Gateway a device or system on a network that translates various types of network communications.

General Packet Radio Service (GPRS) the data-centric mobile radio technology used in GSM (Global System for Mobile Communications) network.

Generator a device consisting of an internal combustion engine and an electric generator.

Geographic cluster a cluster whose members are dispersed over a wide geographic area.

Global System for Mobile Communications (GSM) one of the prevalent standards for wireless mobile voice and data telecommunications.

Governance the entire scope of activities related to the management of policies, procedures, and standards.

GPG (Gnu Privacy Guard) an open source software program that implements the PGP (Pretty Good Privacy) encryption standard.

Guard see *Security guard.*

Guard dog a dog that is employed to guard against or detect unwanted or unexpected personnel.

Guest an operating system that is installed on a virtual machine.

Guideline information that describes how a policy may be implemented.

Hacktivist a person who attacks information systems for political or religious motives.

Hard disk drive (HDD) a hardware device, consisting of spinning platters coated with magnetic storage material and moving read-write heads, used to store data, used as Secondary Storage.

Hardening the process of configuring a system to make it more robust and resistant to attack.

Hardware computers and ancillary equipment that support information processing and storage.

Hash a computational transformation that receives a variable sized data input and returns a unique fixed-length string. Hashing is considered irreversible–it is not possible to obtain an original plaintext from a known hash.

Header the portion of a network frame or packet that includes information such as the source address, destination address, and type of message.

Heap overflow an attack that attempts to corrupt a program's heap (the dynamically allocated memory space created by a program for storage of variables).

Heating, ventilation, and air conditioning (HVAC) a system that is used to control the temperature and humidity in a building or a part of a building.

Hierarchical database a database model that is built on a tree structure.

High Speed Serial Interface (HSSI) a high speed serial communications protocol, usually used to connect nearby WAN devices together.

HMAC (Hashed Message Authentication Code) a message digest (hashing) algorithm.

Homogeneous environment a community of systems that are alike. See also *Monoculture.*

Hook see *Maintenance hook.*

Host based Intrusion Detection System (HIDS) an Intrusion Detection System (IDS) that is a part of a host computer. See also *Intrusion Detection System.*

Host based Intrusion Prevention System (HIPS) an Intrusion Prevention System (IDS) that is a part of a host computer. See also *Intrusion Prevention System.*

Hosts file a file on a workstation or server that associates host names and IP addresses.

Hub a device used to connect multiple computers together to form a network. A hub sends all packets on the network to all nodes. See also *Switch.*

Humidity a measurement of the amount of water vapor in the air.

Hypertext Transfer Protocol (HTTP) a TCP/IP layer 4 protocol used to transmit HTML and XML content from World Wide Web servers to client browsers.

Hypertext Transfer Protocol Secure (HTTPS) a TCP/IP layer 4 protocol used to transmit HTML and XML content from World Wide Web servers to client browsers that is protected with SSL/TLS encryption.

Hypervisor a software program that creates and runs virtual machines.

Identification the act of claiming identity to an information system.

Identity theft a crime that involves the illegal use of some other person's identity.

IEEE 802.1a/b/g/n a family of wireless network standards. See also *Wi-Fi.*

IEEE 802.1X a network based device authentication protocol that is based on EAP.

IEEE1394 an external bus architecture used to connect high speed external devices such as video cameras.

Incident an unexpected event that results in an interruption of normal operations. See also *Security incident.*

Inference attack a technique using analysis of available data to gain knowledge about targeted data that is not directly available.

Information flow a security model that describes permitted and forbidden flows of information rather than access controls.

Information Technology Security Evaluation Criteria (ITSEC) the European framework for system security evaluation now superseded by the Common Criteria.

Information warfare the use of information or information systems in the pursuit of an advantage over an opponent.

International Information Systems Security Certification Consortium (ISC)² the organization that created and manages the CISSP and other security certifications.

Infrared Data Association (IrDA) the governing body that has developed a number of line-of-sight optical protocols known as IrDA. Largely superseded by Bluetooth.

Inheritance the characteristics of a subclass that inherits attributes from its parent class.

Initialization vector (IV) a random block of data that is used by some cryptographic functions.

Injection attack an attack on a system where some scripting or procedural language is inserted into a data stream with the intention that the scripting will be performed.

Input attack any attack on a system where specially coded data is provided in an input field with the intention of causing a malfunction or failure of the system.

Insource the practice of using internal staff to perform a business function.

Integrated Services Digital Network (ISDN) a digital voice and data telecommunications service over copper wires.

Integrity the concept of asserting that information may be changed only by authorized persons and means.

Intellectual property (IP) a product of creation such as information, architecture, invention, music, image, and design.

Intellectual property agreement a legal agreement between an employee and an organization that defines ownership of intellectual property (IP) that the employee may develop during employment.

Intellectual property law the branch of law that protects created works and includes such safeguards as copyrights, trademarks, service marks, and patents.

Interframe gap a pause between transmitted frame on an Ethernet network.

Interior Gateway Routing Protocol (IGRP) a Cisco proprietary TCP/IP routing protocol that utilizes bandwidth, delay, load, MTU, and reliability metrics for determining the best path between endpoints.

Intermediate system to intermediate system (IS-IS) a TCP/IP routing protocol used by ISPs and other network service providers.

Internal audit the activity of self evaluation of controls and policies to measure their effectiveness.

Internet the global network of interconnected TCP/IP networks.

Internet Control Message Protocol (ICMP) a TCP/IP protocol used primarily for error messages and utility functions such as PING and TRACEROUTE.

Internet Group Management Protocol (IGMP) a TCP/IP protocol used to manage multicast groups. Analogous to ICMP.

Internet layer layer 3 of the OSI and TCP/IP network models.

Intrusion Detection System (IDS) a program or device that generates alerts when unwanted network traffic is detected. See also *Intrusion Prevention System.*

Intrusion Prevention System (IPS) a program or device that blocks unwanted traffic when it is detected. See also *Intrusion Detection System.*

IP Camera a video surveillance camera that sends its video signal over a TCP/IP data network.

IPsec a tunneling protocol used to protect communications between two systems.

IPsec (IP security) a suite of protocols for securing IP communications with authentication and encryption.

IPv4 (Internet Protocol version 4) the original Internet Protocol (IP) that is layer 3 in the TCP/IP network model.

IPv6 (Internet Protocol version 6) the extended Internet Protocol, layer 3 in the TCP/IP network model that included extended addressing and security features.

ISAE3402 (International Standard on Assurance Engagements No. 3402) an international audit methodology used to provide audit assurance to clients of service organizations.

ISO 15408 see *Common Criteria.*

ISO17799:2005 an international standard that defines a framework of controls for information security management.

IT service continuity the process of ensuring the continuity of IT-provided services and systems.

Job description a formal document that defines a particular job title, responsibilities, duties, and required experience.

Job rotation the practice of rotating personnel through a variety of roles in order to reduce the risk of unauthorized activities.

Jump-to-register a type of buffer overflow attack where a function's return pointer is overwritten, in order to alter the behavior of a program.

Kerberos an authentication service that utilizes a centralized authentication server.

Kernel the part of an operating system that actively manages processes and access to resources.

Key a block of information that is used in an encryption algorithm.

Key card a credit card-sized plastic card with a magnetic stripe or embedded electronic circuit encoded with data that uniquely identifies the cardholder, and generally used to access restricted areas in a facility.

Key logger a hardware or software component that records keystrokes on a computer.

Key management processes and procedures used to create, protect, and destroy encryption keys.

Knowledge based system a system that is used to make predictions or decisions based upon input data.

Known plaintext attack (KPA) a cryptanalysis attack where the attacker has samples of plaintext and corresponding ciphertext messages.

Labeling the process of affixing a sensitivity identifiers to a document or data file.

Layer 2 Tunneling Protocol (L2TP) a TCP/IP layer 2 tunneling protocol used to encapsulate network traffic.

Least privilege the access control principle that states that an individual should have only the accesses required to perform their official duties.

Lightweight Directory Access Protocol (LDAP) a TCP/IP layer 4 protocol used to query and modify directory services. LDAP is often used for authentication.

Line conditioner a device that filters or removes some of the undesirable anomalies in an incoming power feed.

Link layer layer 1 in the TCP/IP network model.

Local Area Network (LAN) a computer network covering a small geographic area such as a residence, building, or group of buildings.

Logic bomb computer code placed in a system that is intended to perform some harmful event when certain conditions are met–usually a specific day or time in the future.

Logical controls see *Technical controls.*

Long Term Evolution (LTE) a high-speed wireless data communications technology that is based on GSM and UMTS technologies.

Main storage the primary, but usually volatile, high-speed storage used by a computer.

Maintenance hook a feature in a program that permits easy maintenance or access to information that bypasses security controls.

Malicious code computer instructions that are intended to disrupt or control a target system.

Malware see *Malicious code.*

Man in the middle attack (MITM) a cryptanalysis attack in which the attacker is able to read, insert, and modify messages passing between two parties' without their knowledge.

Mandatory access control (MAC) an access control model where subjects are permitted to access objects based upon specific security policies.

Man-made disaster a disaster caused by people or organizations.

Mantrap a set of interconnected double doors used to control the entrance or exit of personnel.

Marking see *Labeling.*

Master boot record (MBR) a place on a mass storage device (such as a hard drive) that contains computer instructions that can be read into memory when a computer is powered up or restarted.

Maximum Tolerable Downtime (MTD) the period of time after which the organization would suffer considerable pain were the process unavailable for that period of time.

MD5 a message digest (hashing) algorithm.

Media Access Control (MAC) address a notation for uniquely identifying nodes on a network, usually expressed as six octets.

Media Access Control (MAC) layer a sublayer of the data link layer that provides channel access on a network.

Memory see *Main storage.*

Memory interface the portion of a CPU that facilitates access to the computer's main memory.

Message digest a fixed length block of data that is the result of a hash function. See also *Hash.*

Method a function or calculation that an object is capable of performing.

Metropolitan Area Network (MAN) a computer network covering a geographic area the size of a city or region.

Microchannel an internal bus architecture used by IBM in PS/2 systems as a replacement for the slower ISA bus.

MIME Object Security Services (MOSS) a protocol that provides confidentiality, authentication, and non-repudiation

Mobile code computer code that is downloaded or transferred from one system for execution on another system.

Monoalphabetic cipher a cipher in which plaintext characters are substituted for ciphertext characters according to a single alphabetic table.

Monoculture a community of information systems that run identical firmware or software.

Multicast a method for efficiently transmitting network packets to groups of destination nodes. See also *Unicast.*

Multi-Level a security model consisting of several clearance levels for subjects and objects.

Multilevel security mode one of the security modes of operation where users can access data based upon their need to know, formal access approval, and security clearance.

Multiprotocol Label Switching (MPLS) a packet switched telecommunications network technology used to transport voice and data.

National Information Assurance Certification and Accreditation Process (NIACAP) the process used to certify and accredit systems that handle U.S. national security information.

Natural disaster a disaster caused by a natural event such as an earthquake or flood.

Near Field Communication (NFC) a short-range (10cm) network technology generally used by mobile phones and other hand-held devices for mobile payment and other applications.

Need-to-know the access control concept where individual personnel should have access to only the information that they require in order to perform their stated duties.

Network a computer network covering any size geographic area from a few inches to International. See also *PAN*, *LAN*, *MAN*, and *WAN.*

Network Access Control (NAC) an approach to network security by employing a means of controlling which devices are permitted to connect to a network.

Network-based Intrusion Detection System (NIDS) an Intrusion Detection System (IDS) that is connected to a network. See also *Intrusion Detection System.*

Network-based Intrusion Prevention System (NIPS) an Intrusion Prevention System (IDS) that is connected to a network. See also *Intrusion Prevention System.*

Network database a database model based upon the hierarchical model, but with the ability for records to be related to other records in the database.

Network File Service (NFS) a TCP/IP layer 4 protocol that is used to share file systems over a network.

Network Information Service (NIS) a TCP/IP layer 4 protocol that is used to centralize authentication and system configuration information for computers on a network.

Network interface card (NIC) a computer hardware component that connects the computer's bus to a communication channel or network.

Network layer layer 3 of the OSI network model that consists of low level protocols used to transport data from computer to computer.

Network-stack attack an attack against network components of a target system.

Network Time Protocol (NTP) a TCP/IP layer 4 protocol that is used to synchronize the time clocks on computers.

Neural network a software system that simulates the human reasoning process and is able to make predictions and decisions based on prior results.

Non-compete agreement a legal agreement that stipulates terms and conditions regarding whether the employee may accept employment with a competing organization in the future.

Non-disclosure agreement (NDA) a legal agreement that requires one or both parties to maintain confidentiality.

Non-interference an abstract security model that states that subjects with low clearance levels cannot learn anything about information at higher clearance levels on account of activities performed by subjects at higher clearance levels.

Non-repudiation the concept of ensuring that a person cannot later deny having performed some action.

NOP sled a type of stack overflow attack where the attacker floods the stack with NOP (no-operation) instructions in an attempt to take control of the program.

NoSQL any of several database models that use non-tabular means for organizing data.

Obfuscation see *Security through obfuscation.*

Object an instance of an OO class.

Object orientation (OO) a methodology for organizing information and software programs that supports objects, methods, and object reuse.

Object oriented database (OODB) a database that is organized and stored as objects.

Object oriented programming (OOP) a programming language methodology that consists of code contained in reusable objects.

Object reuse an attack on a system where one user or program is able to read residual information belonging to some other process, as a means for exploiting the other process through a weakness that can be discovered in the residual data.

Offer letter a formal letter from an organization to an employment candidate that offers employment under a basic set of terms.

Offshoring the use of internal or external staff in another country.

Off-site storage the storage of storage media or paper documents at an off-site storage facility, to prevent against irrecoverable loss of information in the event of a disaster.

One-time pad an encryption algorithm where the key is the same size as the message and is used only once.

One-way hash see *Message digest.*

Onshoring the use of internal or external staff within a country.

Open Database Connectivity (ODBC) a TCP/IP based client-server communications protocol used to facilitate database transactions over a network.

Open Shortest Path First (OSPF) a TCP/IP routing protocol used in large enterprise networks.

Open Systems Interconnect (OSI) the seven layer network model whose layers are: Physical, Data link, Network, Transport, Session, Presentation, and Application.

Operating system the software that facilitates the use of application programs and tools, and controls access to the computer's hardware resources.

Optical fiber a cable type used to carry high-speed communications signals in the form of light over a glass-like fiber.

Organizationally Unique Identifier (OUI) the first three octets of a MAC address that is assigned to an equipment manufacturer, in order to guarantee uniqueness of MAC addresses.

Output feedback (OFB) a block cipher mode where the results of the previous plaintext block are used in the encryption of the next block.

Outsourcing a business arrangement where an organization contracts out a business process, which was previously performed internally, to another organization.

Packet filter a router with an Access Control List (ACL) or an early generation firewall. See also *Access Control List, Firewall.*

Page fault an event where a process attempts to access data in a memory location that has been moved to secondary storage.

Paging the memory management technique of moving inactive memory pages between main storage and secondary storage.

Parallel test a test of a disaster recovery or business continuity plan in which backup or recovery systems or processes are operated alongside normal business operations.

Partition a separate division of storage, usually on a hard disk drive.

Password a secret word or phrase entered by a user to authenticate to a system.

Password Authentication Protocol (PAP) an authentication protocol used by PPP to authenticate users. PAP is unsafe because login credentials are not encrypted.

Password cracking an attack where the attacker uses tools to methodically guess passwords in order to gain access to a system.

Password guessing an attack where the attacker guesses likely passwords in an attempt to gain access to a system.

Patch management the process of managing the installation of patches on target systems.

Patent a means of legal protection for exclusive rights to an invention or process.

Payload the data that is contained in a network packet or frame.

PC card an external bus architecture used for the connection of compact peripheral devices to laptop computers.

PCI (Peripheral Component Interconnect) an internal bus architecture used in modern computers.

PCI Express an internal bus architecture used in modern computers.

Penetration testing an activity used to identify and exploit vulnerabilities on a target system, subsystem, or application.

Perfect forward secrecy the property of encryption keys, such that any past or future encryption keys can be predicted, based on known values of one or more encryption keys.

Permutation cipher see *Transposition cipher.*

Personal Area Network (PAN) a computer network that spans a distance close to one person.

Personal Identification Number (PIN) a numeric password. See also *Password.*

Personally identifiable information (PII) items associated with an individual such as name, passport number, driver's license number, and social insurance number.

Pharming an attack where the attacker poisons DNS or hosts information to redirect communications intended for a legitimate system instead to an imposter system, as a means for harvesting sensitive information.

Phishing fraudulent e-mail messages that attempt to lure an unsuspecting user to provide private information via a fraudulent web site (usually) or in an e-mail reply (less often).

Physical controls mechanisms that control or monitor physical access and environmental systems.

Physical layer layer 1 of the OSI and TCP/IP network models that consists of a network's physical medium.

PIN pad a numeric keypad that is typically used in connection with an access control system.

PING a tool used to send an ICMP Echo Request to a specific node on a network.

Ping of Death (PoD) an attack where an attacker sends PING packets of length 65,535 bytes to the target system in hopes that the target system will crash.

Plaintext data that is not encrypted.

Point to Point Protocol (PPP) a TCP/IP layer 2 protocol that is usually used for dial-up Internet access.

Point to Point Tunneling Protocol (PPTP) an early TCP/IP tunneling protocol that has been largely replaced by L2TP and IPsec.

Policy an official statement that establishes plans, boundaries, and constraints on the behavior of information systems and employees.

Polyalphabetic cipher a cipher in which plaintext characters are substituted for ciphertext characters according to a multiple alphabet table.

Polymorphism the ability for an object to respond to a call differently, depending upon the object's type.

Port number a numbering scheme in which messages of various types are distinguished.

Presentation layer layer 6 of the OSI network model that provides various methods for presenting data, for instance in different character sets or encryption algorithms.

Pretexting an act of deception intended to persuade a targeted individual into providing information under false pretenses.

Pretty Good Privacy (PGP) a popular computer program that is used to encrypt and decrypt data.

Preventive control a control that blocks unauthorized or undesired activity.

Primary storage see *Main storage.*

Privacy the protection of sensitive information associated with individuals.

Privacy Enhanced Mail (PEM) a standard for encrypting e-mail that depends upon a global PKI.

Private key an encryption key used in public key cryptography that is kept private by its owner.

Privilege escalation an attack in which the attacker attempts to cause a system malfunction that will result in the attacker gaining additional system privileges.

Privilege level an operating system protection scheme where users are assigned levels of permissions that dictates the resources and data that they are permitted to access.

Procedure step-by-step instructions for performing a task.

Program a set of computer instructions that usually resides in a file and is used to perform a specific task.

Program counter a CPU register that tracks the current instruction in a program.

PROM (Programmable Read Only Memory) a form of semiconductor memory used to store firmware.

Protected Extensible Authentication Protocol (Protected EAP or PEAP) a wireless network protocol used to authenticate users.

Protection ring a hierarchical operating system protection scheme used to protect resources based upon levels of privilege.

Pseudo Random Number Generator (PRNG) an algorithm used to create random numbers for Initialization Vectors (IVs) and for other purposes.

Public key an encryption key used in public key cryptography that can be widely distributed to users.

Public key cryptography a class of cryptographic algorithms that utilize public-private encryption keys.

Public Key Infrastructure (PKI) a network based service in which public encryption keys or certificates are stored and available for retrieval.

Public Switched Telephone Network (PSTN) the well known public telephone network. Also known as POTS (plain old telephone service).

Pull station a manually operated device that is used to trigger a building fire alarm.

Race condition see *Time of check to time of use (tocttou) bug.*

Random Access Memory (RAM) see *Main storage.*

RC4 a common stream cipher.

Records retention the determination of the minimum and/or maximum period of time that specific business records must be retained.

Recovery the process of restoring a system to its pre-incident condition.

Recovery Capacity Objective (RCapO) the measure of processing capacity on a disaster recovery system.

Recovery Consistency Objective (RCO) the measure of the integrity and consistency of data on a disaster recovery system.

Recovery control a control that is used to restore conditions to normal.

Recovery Point Objective (RPO) the maximum acceptable amount of data loss or work loss for a given process.

Recovery Time Objective (RTO) the maximum period of time that a business process or IT system will be unavailable during a disaster.

Reduced Instruction Set Computer (RISC) a newer microprocessor design where the CPU has a smaller (reduced) instruction set which permits it to be more efficient.

Reduced sign-on a type of authentication where users have a limited set of userids and passwords that are used to access systems and applications.

Redundant Array of Independent Discs (RAID) a disc storage technology that allows for greater reliability and performance in a disc-based storage system.

Reference monitor a hardware or software component in a system that mediates access to objects according to their security level or clearance.

Register a storage location within a CPU.

Relational database a database model based upon tables of data and the relationships between them.

Relative humidity the amount of water vapor in a sample of air compared to the maximum amount of water vapor that the air can hold.

Remote access any means used to connect to a target network from a remote location.

Remote Access Trojan (RAT) a type of malware that permits an attacker to remotely control a victim system.

Remote Authentication Dial In User Service (RADIUS) an authentication protocol used to authenticate a user, control access rights through authorization, and provide accounting (usage) information for billing.

Remote login (Rlogin) a TCP/IP layer 4 network protocol that is used to log in to another computer over a network.

Remote Procedure Call (RPC) a TCP/IP layer 4 protocol used to permit a computer to execute a subroutine or procedure on another computer.

Remote Shell (Rsh) a TCP/IP layer 4 protocol used to execute commands on other computers on a network.

Repeater a network device used to receive and re-transmit a network signal, usually to extend the physical length of a network connection.

Replay attack a cryptanalysis attack where the attacker records transmissions and replays them at a later time, usually to masquerade as one of the parties whose transmissions were recorded.

Replication an operation concerning the data on a storage system, where additions and changes to the data are transmitted to a counterpart storage system where the same additions and changes take place.

Requirements statements of necessary characteristics of an information system.

Residual risk the risk that remains after countermeasures are applied.

Resilience a design characteristic of a system that assures its availability despite unplanned failures.

Resource protection controls and procedures enacted to protect business resources including facilities, hardware, software, documentation, and records.

Restore the process of copying data from backup media to a system.

Reverse Address Resolution Protocol (RARP) a TCP/IP protocol that is used to translate a known MAC address into an IP address. Superseded by DHCP.

RFC request for Comments; the formalized documents that describe the Internet's technical and procedural standards.

Rijndael the data encryption algorithm chosen in 2001 as the new Advanced Encryption Standard.

Ring a network topology where each node is connected to exactly two other nodes in a circular pathway.

Risk acceptance a form of risk treatment where an identified risk is accepted as-is.

Risk analysis the process of identifying risks, their probability of occurrence, impact, and mitigating steps to reduce probability or impact.

Risk assessment the process of examining a system or process to identify potential risks.

Risk avoidance a form of risk treatment where the activity associated with an identified risk is discontinued, thereby avoiding the risk.

Risk management the strategic activities related to the identification of risks through risk assessment and the subsequent treatment of identified risks.

Risk mitigation see *Risk reduction*.

Risk reduction a form of risk treatment where an identified risk is reduced through countermeasures.

Risk transfer a form of risk treatment where an identified risk is transferred to another party, typically through an insurance policy.

Role-based access control (RBAC) an access control method where access permissions are granted to roles, and users are assigned to those roles.

Root cause analysis (RCA) the technique of incident analysis whereby the true cause of an incident is identified.

Rootkit malicious code that is designed to avoid detection by hiding itself by some means.

Router a network device that connects two or more networks together logically, and can also control the flow of traffic between networks according to a set of rules known as an Access Control List (ACL).

Routing Information Protocol (RIP) an early TCP/IP routing protocol that uses hop count as the primary metric for determining the lowest cost of a route between endpoints.

RS-232 a serial communications technology used to connect computers to low speed peripherals such as mice, printers, modems, and terminals. Superseded by USB.

rsh (remote shell) an unsecure protocol used to establish a command line session on another system over a network.

Running key cipher a cryptography technique used when plaintext is longer than the key.

SATA (Serial ATA) an external bus architecture used primarily for communications with disk storage.

SBus an internal bus architecture used in SPARC based computers including those made by Sun Microsystems.

Script Injection an attack on a system where script language accompanies input data in an attempt to execute the script on the target system.

Script kiddie an individual with relatively low skills who breaks into computer systems using tools written by others.

SCSI (Small Computer Systems Interface) an external bus architecture used to connect a computer to disk storage devices.

Secondary storage the slower, but persistent, form of storage used by a computer.

Secure / Multipurpose Internet Mail Extensions (S/MIME) a protocol used for protecting e-mail message through encryption and digital signatures.

Secure Electronic Transaction (SET) a protocol used to protect electronic transactions. SET is not widely used, and has been replaced by SSL and TLS.

Secure Shell (SSH) a TCP/IP layer 4 tunneling protocol used for secure remote management of systems. Supersedes Rsh, Rcp, Rlogin, and Telnet.

Secure siting locating a business at a site that is reasonably free from hazards.

Secure Sockets Layer (SSL) a TCP/IP layer 4 tunneling protocol used to protect network traffic through encryption. Superseded by Transport Layer Security. See also *Transport Layer Security*.

Security Association a one-way trust relationship between two endpoints.

Security awareness training a formal education program that teaches security principles and expected behavior to employees.

Security guard a trained person who is responsible for protecting building assets and controlling access to the building.

Security incident an event in which some aspect of an organization's security policy has been violated.

Security Incident and Event Management (SIEM) system a system used to collect, correlate, and report on security incidents and events across a population of workstations, servers, and networks.

Security incident response the procedures followed in the event of a security incident.

Security management activities related to the development and implementation of security policies and controls.

Security modes of operation the security classifications for systems that determine the types of permissions necessary for users to access data.

Security policy a branch of organizational policy that defines security-related controls and behaviors.

Security through obfuscation the practice of changing common settings and values to non-standard settings in an attempt to hide them from potential attackers. Also known as *Security Through Obscurity*.

Segregation of duties see *Separation of duties*.

SEI CMMI (Software Engineering Institute Capability Maturity Model Integration) a framework for evaluating the maturity of an organization's systems engineering practices.

Sensitivity level a category of information sensitivity in an information classification scheme.

Separation of duties the work practice where high risk tasks are structured to be carried out by two or more persons.

Sequence number attack an attack in which an attacker injects packets with guessed sequence numbers that pretend to originate from one of the two computers in the session.

Serial Line Interface Protocol (SLIP) an early implementation for transporting TCP/IP over serial connections.

Service Level Agreement (SLA) formal statements that specify levels of service provided by a service organization.

Service set identifier (SSID) a name that is used to identify a specific Wi-Fi wireless network.

Session Initiation Protocol (SIP) a TCP/IP layer 4 protocol that is used to establish and tear down voice and video communications sessions.

Session layer layer 5 of the OSI network model that controls connections between computers.

SHA-1 (Secure Hash Algorithm) a message digest (hashing) algorithm.

SHA-2 (Secure Hash Algorithm) a set of message digest (hashing) algorithms (SHA-224, SHA-256, SHA-384, SHA-512).

SHA-3 (Secure Hash Algorithm) a message digest (hashing) algorithm.

Shredding the process of cutting paper, magnetic, or optical media into small pieces for the purpose of secure destruction.

S-HTTP (Secure Hyper-Text Transfer Protocol) a connectionless protocol used to encrypt and authenticate data being sent from a server to a client.

Side-channel attack an attack on a system where a subject can observe the physical characteristics of a system in order to make inferences on its internal operation.

Simple Mail Transport Protocol (SMTP) a TCP/IP layer 4 protocol used to transmit e-mail messages from one e-mail server to another.

Simple Network Management Protocol (SNMP) a TCP/IP layer 4 protocol used to remotely monitor and manage network devices and systems over a network.

Simulation a review of a disaster recovery or business continuity procedure that is performed in a pretend disaster scenario.

Single Loss Expectancy (SLE) the cost of a single loss through the realization of a particular threat. This is a result of the calculation, SLE = asset value x exposure factor (EF).

Single point of failure a component in a system that lacks a redundant or backup counterpart; the failure of the component will cause the failure of the entire system.

Single Sign-On an access control method where users can authenticate once and be able to access other systems and applications without being required to re-authenticate to each one.

Single use the practice of segregating functions in a complex, distributed environment so that each system in the environment is dedicated to performing a single task.

Smart card a credit-card sized memory device used for authentication.

Smoke detector a device that detects the presence of combustion-related smoke and contains or is connected to an audible warning alarm.

Smurf an attack that consists of a large number of forged ICMP echo requests, which are sent to a network's broadcast address with a forged "source" address. Systems that receive the attack packets send large numbers of "reply" packets to the target.

Sniffer a device or program used to record communications on a network.

Sniffing the act of eavesdropping on a network by capturing traffic.

Social engineering an attack on an organization where the attacker is attempting to gain secrets from staff members, usually for gaining unauthorized access to the organization's systems.

Software computer instructions that fulfill a stated purpose.

Software development life cycle (SDLC) the overall process used to design, create, and maintain software over its lifetime.

Solid-state drive (SSD) a hardware device, consisting of memory chips, used to store data, used as Secondary Storage.

Source code review a review of a program's source code in order to ensure that recent changes were applied correctly and that the program contains no unwanted code.

Spam unwanted e-mail that usually contains unsolicited commercial advertisements, pornography, or attempts to lure recipients into opening malicious attachments or visiting malicious web sites.

Spear phishing a specially targeted phishing attack. See also *Phishing.*

Split custody a control safeguard in which an important secret (such as a password) is broken into two or more parts, each of which is kept by different individuals.

Spoofing an attack where the attacker forges the origin of a message as an attempt to disrupt or control a system.

Sprinkler system an installed system of piping and nozzles used to spray water or foam onto a fire.

Spyware usually unwanted and sometimes malicious software that is used to harvest Internet usage information from a user's workstation.

SQL injection an attack where SQL statements are injected into an input stream in the hopes that the SQL commands will be executed by the application's database server.

SQL*Net a TCP/IP based client-server communications protocol used to facilitate database transactions over a network.

SSAE16 (Statement on Standards for Attestation Engagements No. 16) a U.S. based audit methodology used to provide audit assurance to clients of service organizations.

Standard a statement that specifies the brand, model, protocol, technology, or configuration of a system.

Star a network topology where all nodes are connected to a central device such as a hub or switch.

Statement of impact a document that describes the impact that an interrupted business process would have on an organization.

Static random access memory (SRAM) a random access memory (RAM) technology used in computer main memory.

Steganography the practice of hiding a message in another medium.

Stream cipher an encryption algorithm that operates on a continuous stream of data, such as a video or audio feed.

Strong authentication a means of authenticating to a system using a means strong than userid and password, such as a hardware token, smart card, or biometric. Also known as two-factor authentication.

Structured language a hierarchical computer language methodology that consists of main programs and called subroutines or functions.

Subnet a range of a network addresses in a network.

Subnet mask a numeric value, expressed in the same manner as an IP address that is used to determine the network and host portions of an IP address.

Substitution cipher an encryption algorithm where characters are substituted for others.

Supply chain attack an attack on a system via one of its software or hardware suppliers, through the introduction of a defect that will permit compromise of the target system.

Swapping the memory management technique of moving an entire process's memory contents between main storage and secondary storage.

Switch a network device used to connect multiple computers to form a network. A switch sends packets only to destination nodes. See also *Hub.*

Symmetric cryptography a method of cryptography where each party is in possession of an encryption key.

Symmetric multiprocessing (SMP) a computer architecture where two or more CPUs are connected to the computer's main memory in a symmetrical arrangement.

SYN flood a denial of service (DoS) attack where the attacker sends large numbers of TCP SYN packets to the target system, hoping to overwhelm it and exhaust its resources.

Synchronous Digital Hierarchy (SDH) the prevalent standard for voice and data communications over fiber networks outside of North America. See also *SONET.*

Synchronous optical networking (SONET) the standard in North America for transporting voice and data over optical fiber.

System high security mode one of the security modes of operation where all users can access some data based upon their need to know.

Systems Security Engineering Capability Maturity Model (SSE CMM) a framework for evaluating the maturity of an organization's security implementation practices.

T1 see *DS-1*.

Tabletop exercise see *Walkthrough*.

Target of evaluation (TOE) a system being evaluated with the Common Criteria.

Teardrop an attack in which an attacker sends mangled packet fragments with overlapping and oversized payloads to a target system in an attempt to crash the target system.

Technical controls programs and mechanisms that control user access system behavior.

Telnet a TCP/IP layer 4 protocol that is used to establish a raw TCP session over a network to a service on another computer.

TEMPEST U.S. DoD research in the fields of unwanted emanations and the resulting standards for shielding equipment.

Terminal Access Controller Access-Control System (TACACS) a remote authentication protocol used to authenticate user access to a computer or network based resource. Superseded by TACACS+ and RADIUS.

Termination the cessation of employment for an employee.

Thin client a client application that relies on other (usually central) computers to perform most functions.

Threat a potential activity that would, if it occurred, exploit a vulnerability in a system.

Threat analysis the process of identifying potential threats, their probability of occurrence, impact, and mitigating steps to reduce probability or impact.

Threat modeling see *Threat risk modeling*.

Threat risk modeling a process where threats in an environment are identified and ranked, and mitigating controls introduced to counter the identified threats. Also known as threat modeling.

Three tier application an application that consists of three logically separate layers, usually a user interface front end, business logic middle tier, and database management third tier.

Time bomb see *Logic bomb*.

Time of check to time of use (tocttou) bug a resource allocation vulnerability where a period of time elapses between the time when a resource's availability is confirmed and the resource is assigned or used.

Token a hardware device used for authentication.

Token Ring a network technology consisting of a logical ring and the passing of a logical 'token' from node to node over the network. Only a node in possession of a token may transmit data.

Tools separate programs that are included with an Operating System that are used to change system configurations, edit files, create directories, and install other programs.

Traceroute a tool used to determine the network path to a specific destination.

Trade secret a formula, design, process, or method used by an organization to gain competitive advantage over others.

Trademark a means of legal protection for exclusive rights to a name or symbol.

Transaction an event where data is updated within a database.

Transmission Control Protocol (TCP) a connection-oriented TCP/IP transport protocol used to carry messages within a session between two nodes. TCP guarantees delivery, order of delivery, and flow control.

Transport layer layer 4 of the OSI model and layer 3 in the TCP/IP network models that provides reliable data transfer.

Transport Layer Security (TLS) a TCP/IP layer 4 tunneling protocol that protects network traffic through encryption. Transport Layer Security supersedes Secure Sockets Layer (SSL).

Transposition cipher an encryption method where characters in plaintext are rearranged to form ciphertext.

Trap door see *Back door*.

Trivial File Transfer Protocol (TFTP) a TCP/IP layer 4 protocol used to transfer files over a network.

Trojan horse malicious computer code that claims to perform some benign function while actually performing some additional, malicious function.

Trusted Computer Security Evaluation Criteria (TCSEC) the U.S. DoD framework for system security evaluation now superseded by the Common Criteria.

Trusted Computing Base (TCB) the hardware, firmware, operating system, and software that effectively supports security policy.

Trusted Network Interpretation (TNI) the evaluation criteria for evaluating the confidentiality and integrity of communications networks.

Trusted Platform Module (TPM) a secure cryptoprocessor used to store cryptographic keys and perform some crypto functions.

Tunnel any of several network protocols that use packet encapsulation to deliver packets to an endpoint.

Twisted pair a type of cable that utilizes pairs of twisted copper conductors.

Two tier application an application that consists of two logically separate layers, usually a user interface and business logic front end and a data management back end.

Two-factor authentication see *Strong authentication.*

Unibus an internal bus architecture used by Digital Equipment Corp. PDP-11 and VAX computers.

Unicast a type of network communications where packets are sent to a single node. See also *Multicast.*

Unified Threat Management (UTM) a security device or appliance that performs many security functions such as firewall, IDS, IPS, anti-virus, anti-spam, or Web content filtering.

Uninterruptible Power Supply (UPS) a short-term backup power source that derives its power from storage batteries.

United States Code (U.S.C.) the body of published criminal laws in the United States.

Universal Mobile Telecommunications System (UMTS) a wireless telecommunications protocol for data communications.

Universal Serial Bus (USB) a serial bus communications standard, used for the connection of peripheral devices to a computer including keyboards, mice, storage device, and network adaptors.

Unsolicited Commercial E-mail (UCE) see *Spam.*

U.S. Code of Federal Regulations (C.F.R.) the code of administrative law in the United States.

USB Key a device, plugged into a computer's USB port, usually containing a digital certificate and used for strong authentication.

User Datagram Protocol (UDP) a connectionless TCP/IP transport protocol used to carry messages within a session between two nodes. UDP does not guarantee delivery, order of delivery, or flow control.

Vernam cipher see *One-time pad.*

Video surveillance system a system that consists of monitors and/or recording equipment plus one or more video cameras, which together are used to observe and/or record activities such as personnel movement.

View a virtual table in a relational database.

Virtual machine a simulation of computer hardware, performed by software, for the purpose of housing one or more guest operating systems running on a single computer system.

Virtual memory a memory management technique whereby the operating system can permit a process's memory to become fragment and even overflow onto secondary storage.

Virtual Private Network (VPN) an encrypted communications channel that is used for secure remote access or for protecting the traffic between two networks.

Virtualization the use of specialized software to facilitate the existence of two or more logically separate running operating systems (virtual machines) on a single physical system.

Virus malicious code that attaches to a file, document, or master boot record (MBR).

Voice over Internet Protocol (VoIP) a TCP/IP layer 4 protocol used to transport voice traffic over a network.

Vulnerability a weakness in a system that may permit the realization of a threat.

Vulnerability management the process of identifying vulnerabilities in a system and then acting to mitigate those vulnerabilities.

Vulnerability Scanning an activity where tools are used to identify vulnerabilities on a target system or application.

Walkthrough a review of a business continuity or disaster recovery procedure in which a group of individuals review and discuss procedures.

Watering Hole Attack an attack where a website is implanted with malicious code, which is used to infect the computers used by visitors to the site.

Watermarking the process of placing in image or mark in a file for identification purposes.

Web application an application that utilizes a Web browser as the client software.

Web server a software component used to accept and process incoming requests for information sent from end users who are using Web browsers.

Whaling a specially targeted phishing attack that targets executives in an organization.

Whois a TCP/IP layer 4 protocol that is used to query a whois server, usually to determine the owner of a domain name or IP address.

Wide Area Network (WAN) a computer network covering large geographic areas spanning metropolitan, regional, national, or international.

Wi-Fi a family of wireless data link standards for connecting computers together to form networks.

Wi-Fi Protected Access (WPA and WPA2) protocol standards that replace the Wired Equivalent Privacy (WEP) protocol.

Wi-Fi Protected Access (WPA) a wireless network encryption protocol.

Wiping the process of destroying data stored on magnetic media by overwriting the media several times.

Wired Equivalent Privacy (WEP) a standard for encrypting packets on a Wi-Fi wireless network. Superseded by WPA and WPA2.

Wireless USB (WUSB) a wireless protocol designed for wireless connectivity of various computer peripherals such as printers, digital cameras, hard disks, and other high-throughput devices.

Wireline any of the telecommunications services that is transported over copper or optical fiber.

Worldwide Interoperability for Microwave Access (WiMAX) a wireless telecommunications standard for fixed-base and mobile voice and data communications.

Worm malicious code that has the ability to self-propagate and spread rapidly from system to system.

WPA2 Enterprise the WPA2 protocol when an external authentication source, such as RADIUS, is used.

X.25 a packet-switched telecommunications network.

x.509 the prevailing digital certificate standard. See also *Digital certificate.*

X11 the GUI based window system that is used in UNIX and Linux operating systems.

xDSL see *Digital Subscriber Line (DSL).*

XOR a logical operation on two operands, where the return value is TRUE only if one of the two operands (but not both) is TRUE.

Zero-day exploit malware that evades detection by anti-malware systems through a variety of techniques, including polymorphism.

Index

Page references in **bold** denote pages on which terms are defined.

C

D

E

F

G

H

I

Q

R

T

U

V

X

Z